The Complete Works of Rosa Luxemburg

The Complete Works of Rosa Luxemburg

VOLUME III, POLITICAL WRITINGS 1:
ON REVOLUTION—1897–1905

Edited by Peter Hudis, Axel Fair-Schulz, and William A. Pelz

Translated by George Shriver, Alicja Mann, and Henry Holland

VERSO
London • New York

ROSA
LUXEMBURG
STIFTUNG

Verso would like to express its gratitude to Rosa Luxemburg Stiftung
for help in publishing this book

ROSA
LUXEMBURG
STIFTUNG

The publisher also gratefully acknowledges the assistance of
Dietz Verlag, publisher of Rosa Luxemburg's *Gesammelte Werke*,
the German source of all English translations herein

First published by Verso 2019
Translation © George Shriver, Alicja Mann, and Henry Holland 2018

1 3 5 7 9 10 8 6 4 2

Verso
U.K.: 6 Meard Street, London W1F 0EG
U.S.: 20 Jay Street, Suite 1010, Brooklyn, NY 11201
versobooks.com

Verso is the imprint of New Left Books

ISBN-13: 978-1-78663-533-4
ISBN-13: 978-1-78663-536-5 (U.S. EBK)
ISBN-13: 978-1-78663-535-8 (U.K. EBK)

British Library Cataloguing in Publication Data
A catalogue record for this book is available from the British Library

Library of Congress Cataloging-in-Publication Data
A catalog record for this book is available from the Library of Congress

Typeset in Minion Pro by MJ&N Gavan, Truro, Cornwall
Printed in the U.S. by Maple Press

Dedicated to the memory of William A. Pelz (1951–2017)
Scholar, teacher, activist, and friend of all who
sought to build a truly new society

Contents

Acknowledgments

This volume would not have been possible without the tireless efforts of numerous scholars who have done monumental work over the past several decades in bringing Luxemburg's manuscripts, unsigned articles, and other previously unknown or inaccessible writings to light, such as Annelies Laschitza, Eckhard Müller, Holger Pollit, and the late Feliks Tych and Narihiko Ito.

It would also not have been possible without Evelin Wittich of the Rosa Luxemburg Foundation, who assisted us at each step of this enormous and difficult project of issuing the *Complete Works*, as well as Jörn Schuetrumpf of Dietz Verlag, who advised us on the selection of the materials in this volume. Holger Politt provided us with the originals of the Polish-language articles as well as editorial assistance. We benefited greatly from the research of Eric Blanc as well as discussions on the Polish workers' movement with Krystian Szadkowski and Wiktor Marzec. Ottokar Luban provided invaluable advice and suggestions on the project as a whole. Special thanks to Rory Castle for his review of the manuscript and research assistance, Laura Fair-Schulz for devoting many hours to proofreading and editing, and Paul Le Blanc, Sebastian Budgen, and Jacob Stevens for their help on numerous aspects of the project.

Most of all, we wish to thank the Rosa Luxemburg Foundation in Berlin, which covered the cost of many of the translations, as well as the numerous individuals who made this volume possible through their contributions to the Toledo Fund, which also helped cover translation costs. And special thanks to our translators—George Shriver, Alicja Mann, and Henry Holland—who overcame many obstacles in performing a labor of love in bringing Luxemburg's voice to us anew.

Sadly, our colleague and friend William A. Pelz, who coedited this volume and coauthored its introduction, passed away in December 2017, before this book went to press. His tireless work as scholar, teacher, and friend to so many who sought to build a new society based on the principles embodied in the work of Rosa Luxemburg will be sorely missed. We dedicate this volume to his memory.

Editorial Foreword

This volume brings together Rosa Luxemburg's writings on the central theme of her life and work—*revolution*. It is the first of three volumes of the *Complete Works* devoted to this subject, containing her writings from 1897 to the end of 1905. Volumes IV and V of the *Complete Works* will consist of the rest of her writings "On Revolution," from the years 1906 to 1919.*

In organizing her political writings around specific themes, we by no means imply that Luxemburg's concern for revolution is restricted to the writings in the three volumes devoted to this subject. All of her work—from her economic theory to political writings on spontaneity, organization, nationalism, and democracy—has the concept of revolution at its core. The materials in this volume represent writings that *directly* address the question of revolution, most of all her discussions of the 1905 Russian Revolution—one of the most outstanding revolutionary upheavals of modern times.

The German-language articles and speeches in this volume are translated from volumes 1.2, 2, and 6 of her *Gesammelte Werke*; the Polish-language documents are translated from the original newspapers and journals in which they first appeared.

We have greatly benefited from consulting the editorial apparatus and footnotes provided by the editors of the *Gesammelte Werke*, as well as Holger Pollitt's footnotes and introduction to the German-language collection of some of Luxemburg's Polish writings in *Arbeiterrevolution 1905/06: Polnische Texte* (Berlin: Dietz Verlag, 2015). The editors of this volume have supplied the footnotes (as well as the Name Glossary), with the assistance of the work done by many others who came before us.

---

* Volumes I and II of the *Complete Works* consisted of her writings on economics and were published in 2013 and 2015, respectively. A third volume of economic writings, largely consisting of manuscripts that have only recently come to light, will be issued within the next several years.

Introduction

I. WHY A *COMPLETE WORKS OF ROSA LUXEMBURG*? WHY NOW?

The *Complete Works of Rosa Luxemburg* is a project almost a century overdue. That the world would be well served by a comprehensive series gathering together all of Luxemburg's thought-provoking writings has been widely accepted for the better part of a century. V. I. Lenin, sometimes critic and political rival of Luxemburg, wrote in *Pravda* a few years after her assassination of his frustration with German Communists whom he demanded should, at once, publish "her *complete* works."[*] Although this has yet to fully be realized even in the German language, English access is much further behind, since most of Luxemburg's work remains untranslated.

Luxemburg's life and work speaks to us in new ways today, since she raised vital questions about what it means to be human in subjecting to critique both capitalism as well as the revolutionary tendencies that claimed to represent its alternative. Few Marxists of her generation produced works that more thoughtfully pose the question of *what happens after the revolution*, as especially seen in her searing critique of Lenin and Trotsky's suppression of democracy in her 1918 manuscript *The Russian Revolution*. While recognizing and acknowledging the significance of the Bolshevik achievements during and after the October Revolution and their exceedingly difficult and adversarial circumstances, Luxemburg nevertheless became increasingly concerned about the authoritarian trajectory of the new Soviet state. Luxemburg may not have fully answered the overriding question that haunts us today—what is a viable alternative that avoids the disappointing, and in some cases even disastrous, outcomes of the various socialist and communist revolutions (and the efforts to achieve them) of the twentieth century? But her distinctive political and personal perspective can greatly aid the effort of socialists, feminists, anti-racist activists, and others to do so.[†]

The major barrier to appreciating Luxemburg's political and theoretical contributions is the fact that the vast bulk of her writings have never appeared in English. Indeed, much of her work has not even appeared in German or been accessible to the public for many decades. A five-volume edition of her Collected Works was published by Dietz Verlag several decades ago (the *Gesammelte Werke*), but at least 75 percent of its content has never been translated into

---

[*] V. I. Lenin, *Collected Works*, Vol. 33 (Moscow: Progress Publishers, 1973), p. 210.

[†] For a more systematic discussion of the complexities of the relationship between Lenin and Luxemburg, see Paul Le Blanc, "Luxemburg and Lenin Through Each Other's Eyes," in *Unfinished Leninism* (New York: Barnes and Noble, 2014), pp. 129–38. See also Ottokar Luban, "Rosa Luxemburg's Criticism of Lenin's Ultra Centralist Party Concept and of the Bolshevik Revolution," in *Critique: Journal of Socialist Theory*, 4 (3), August 2012, pp. 345–65.

English. Moreover, over 80 percent of her vast correspondence (also published by Dietz Verlag in six volumes) has never appeared in English. The problem extends further than this, since the *Gesammelte Werke* is itself incomplete as until recently it largely consisted of published pieces signed by Luxemburg. However, she wrote dozens of articles and essays under pseudonyms or anonymously—few of which appeared in the original *Gesammelte Werke*.

To correct this omission, renowned Luxemburg scholar and biographer Annelies Laschitza along with Eckhard Müller has spent the last two decades identifying and collecting her previously unpublished German-language writings. In 2014, Dietz Verlag published a 900-page collection of newly discovered articles and essays covering 1893 to 1906 as a supplementary volume of the *Gesammelte Werke.* Two additional half volumes totaling 1,300 pages—covering the years 1907 to 1919—appeared in 2017.† Almost none of the material in these volumes—over 2,000 pages—is known to the English-speaking world.

The problem of obtaining the full scope of Luxemburg's writings extends yet further. Although Luxemburg fled Poland for Switzerland in 1889 and subsequently lived in Germany for the rest of her life, she remained actively involved in the Polish revolutionary movement—especially helping to found and lead a revolutionary organization in Russian-occupied Poland, the Social Democracy of the Kingdom of Poland (SDKP), after 1900 under the name the Social Democracy of the Kingdom of Poland and Lithuania (SDKPiL). She was the intellectual nerve center of this organization and wrote regularly for such Polish-language publications as *Czerwony Sztandar* (Red Flag) and *Z Pola Walki* (On the Battlefield). Her writings in Polish total more than 3,000 pages—yet few of these appear in her *Gesammelte Werke* and almost none have ever found their way into English. These writings are now being collected and published by Holger Politt, who is continuing the pioneering work of the great scholar of the Polish labor movement Feliks Tych, who began work on this many decades ago.‡ The lack of access to Luxemburg's Polish writings has left important lacunae in the effort to understand her overall contribution, especially in the English-speaking world, where even fewer of her Polish writings are available in translation than those originally composed in German.

The need to fill this gap explains the impetus for issuing the *Complete Works of Rosa Luxemburg* in English. It will include everything she ever wrote—essays, articles, books, pamphlets, lecture and lecture notes, manuscripts, and letters—

---

* See Rosa Luxemburg, *Gesammelte Werke, Band 6: 1893 bis 1906*, edited by Annelies Laschitza and Eckhard Müller (Berlin: Dietz Verlag, 2014).

† See Rosa Luxemburg, *Gesammelte Werke*, Baende 7.1, 7.2, 1907 bis 1919, edited by Annelies Laschitza and Eckhard Müller (Berlin: Dietz Verlag, 2017).

‡ Politt has edited a German translation of some of these writings in *Rosa Luxemburg, Arbeiterrevolution 1905/06: Polnische Texte* (Berlin: Dietz Verlag, 2015). He is currently working on a German translation of many of her other Polish writings, which will appear as a supplementary Vol. 8 to the *Gesammelte Werke*.

newly translated from the languages in which they were composed (mainly from German and Polish, but also from Russian and Yiddish).* It will consist of seventeen volumes, of about 600 pages each. It is divided into three rubrics—the first containing her economic writing (three volumes), the second her political writings (nine volumes), and the third her complete correspondence (five volumes). Since her overall contribution cannot be grasped without engaging her work as an economic theorist, we chose to *begin* the series with her economic works. Admittedly, separating her oeuvres into economic and political writings is somewhat artificial. As she indicates in her correspondence, her overall approach to economic theory, which is that expanded capital accumulation is made possible through the continued destruction of non-capitalist social formations and the appropriation of markets and resources in the developing world, was largely stimulated by a *political* problematic, the expansion of European imperialism into Asia and Africa at the end of the nineteenth century. And many of her political writings—such as *Reform or Revolution*—contain brilliant analyses of the economic law of motion of capitalism and its proclivity for cyclical crises. Yet, given the amount of time, care, and attention that Luxemburg gave to developing her major economic works, it makes sense to begin the *Complete Works* with the works that contain her most detailed and analytically specific delineation of Marxian economics. Volume 1 (published in 2013) contains *The Industrial Development of Poland*, the first full English-language translation of *The Introduction to Political Economy*, and seven manuscripts of lectures and research notes on precapitalist society, the non-Western world, and economic history, composed while she taught at the German Social Democratic Party School in Berlin from 1907–1914.† Volume 2 (published in 2015),‡ contains a new (and much improved) translation of *The Accumulation of Capital*, the *Anti-Critique*, and the chapters on Volumes 2 and 3 of *Capital* that she wrote for Franz Mehring's biography of Karl Marx (she is very rarely acknowledged as the author of the latter).§ A third volume of economic writings, largely consisting of manuscripts that only recently came to light, will be issued within the next several years.

This volume is the first of nine thematically arranged volumes of Political

---

* This work would not be possible without the aid and assistance of the Rosa Luxemburg Foundation in Berlin as well as Dietz Verlag. It would also not be possible without the support of many individuals who have contributed financially to the fund established to help defray the cost of translations, The Toledo Fund (although the Luxemburg Foundation is providing some support for translation costs, they cannot cover all of it). Those who wish to contribute to the fund can do so via: toledo.nationbuilder.com/complete_works_rosa_luxemburg.

† See *The Complete Works of Rosa Luxemburg, Volume I: Economic Writings 1*, edited by Peter Hudis (London and New York: Verso Books, 2013).

‡ See *The Complete Works of Rosa Luxemburg, Volume II: Economic Writings 2*, edited by Peter Hudis and Paul Le Blanc (London and New York: Verso Books, 2015).

§ Mehring, a close colleague and friend of Luxemburg, asked her to write the chapters on Volumes 2 and 3 of *Capital* because of his lack of facility in economics. The English editions of his *Karl Marx* do not mention that Luxemburg wrote the chapters.

Writings. The first theme (covering three volumes) is "On Revolution." It will present all of Luxemburg's writings on the 1905 Russian Revolution, the 1917 Russian Revolution, and the 1918–19 German Revolution. This volume (the third in the series, and the first in this rubric) contains her writings on revolution from 1897 to 1905; Volume IV (the second volume of her writings on revolution) will cover 1906 to 1914; and Volume V (the third volume in this rubric) will cover 1915 to 1919. Why begin her Political Writings with the theme "On Revolution"? Simply because there is little question that her distinctive concept of revolutionary emancipation is the red thread that defines her originality and contemporary relevance as a theoretician. Revolution, for Luxemburg, was not merely a tool to secure political power and implement social control. It instead represented a process by which working and oppressed peoples shape their destiny and regain their stature as self-determining subjects. All of her work— be it on spontaneity, organization, nationalism, or economics—was integral to a distinctive concept of revolution that is worth reconsidering today.

The writings in this volume—almost all of which appear in English for the first time—provide a special vantage point for discerning her concept of revolution, since most of them consists of journalistic articles and reports on the ongoing 1905 Russian Revolution. It will be clear from the outset that this volume has a very different character than the first two in this series, which centered on a series of highly complex and dense theoretical analyses of the nature of capitalism as a *global* system and its incessant drive for self-expansion. Here, we instead have short articles and reports (most of them penned for the socialist press of the time) in which Luxemburg focuses on *local* developments, in reporting on strikes, demonstrations, political debates, and the response to them by the authoritarian tsarist regime on a daily basis. To be sure, Luxemburg viewed these local events in a global context (after all, the revolution was sparked by the Russo-Japanese War, which concerned the effort to carve up China by the various imperialist powers). Nevertheless, the content of these articles is not theoretical as much as descriptive. This does not in any way detract from their importance, however, for here we see Luxemburg in the laboratory of revolution—listening as intently as she can to events on the ground, reporting them to her readers, and trying to draw them into a deeper understanding of what revolutionary transformation actually involves. The empirical content of the material in this volume is therefore of utmost importance in comprehending the theoretical generalizations she will later develop as a result of her observations of (and by the beginning of 1906, her participation in) the revolution. Indeed, it is hard to think of a major Marxist theoretician who wrote so much and so directly about the character of a revolution unfolding before their eyes.

A second theme of the Political Writings (in two volumes) will be devoted to "On Spontaneity and Organization." It will present her numerous debates with such figures as Bernstein, Kautsky, and Lenin on organizational matters, as well as disputes on this subject within the Polish Marxist movement. A third theme (in three volumes) will be "On Nationalism and the National Question." And the fourth theme (in one volume) will be miscellaneous journalism and writings on cultural questions.

II. THE IMPACT OF LUXEMBURG'S WRITINGS OF 1905 IN DEVELOPING THE THEORY OF THE MASS STRIKE

Among others, Franz Mehring argued that Rosa Luxemburg possessed the best brain since Marx.[*] No one would question her brilliance—even those who may think this praise exaggerated. In this collection of writings, we are privileged to see that brain at work.[†] As one reads through her articles, it becomes increasingly clear that she is rethinking classical Marxist theory in light of the mass struggles taking place. Famously, this will result in Luxemburg's development of her theory of the mass strike. Throughout 1905, her articles appeared almost daily in the German Socialist press, most frequently in *Vorwärts*, the important central party journal appearing in Berlin. She realized that the way to overcome the tired debate about parliamentarianism versus radical adventurism would be solved, in practice, by the masses themselves. That is, neither by passive working-class voters casting ballots for representatives within a bourgeois system, nor by a self-anointed radical elite acting in the name of the proletariat. Divergent as these well-worn approaches may be, they share in common two essential pre-suppositions: that the common people are docile in nature and need to be saved. Luxemburg rejected this dogmatic and inherently elitist view of the masses and instead saw the common people as the real movers of human progress. In her view, the common people were a class in motion with a complex, dialectical interaction with political parties and trade unions.

Holger Politt, an expert on Luxemburg's engagement with the Revolution of 1905 in Imperial Russia, notes how deeply those developments impacted her very being, both intellectually and emotionally. "Without the hope of this revolution, the political life of Rosa Luxemburg would have unfolded differently, for when this revolution finally broke out it was preceded by long and well-justified anticipation."[‡] Luxemburg's most powerful means of engaging the revolutionary events of 1905 was, as many observers have noted, with her pen. While she was involved in actively building a revolutionary organization,

---

[*] See Mark L. Thomas, "Review of the Letters of Rosa Luxemburg," *Socialist Review*, March 2011.

[†] See Peter Hudis, "The Multi-dimensionality of Rosa Luxemburg: Perspectives, Challenges, and Ramifications of issuing *The Complete Works of Rosa Luxemburg*," paper presented to the conference Red Biography: Communist Life Histories in Global Perspective, Bloomington, Indiana, February 2017.

[‡] Holger Politt, *Rosa Luxemburg, Arbeiterrevolution 1905/1906: Polnische Texte*, (Berlin: Dietz Verlag, 2015), p. 9.

challenging the autocratic tsarist regime long before the cataclysmic events of 1905, her primary role was that of an exceedingly empathetic observer and (after early 1906) a direct participant. Thus, Ian D. Thatcher's observation that "the 1905 Revolution may have had more of an influence on [Leon] Trotsky than Trotsky had on the revolution" is doubly correct for Luxemburg.*

Luxemburg finished her essay *The Revolution in Russia*, published February 8, 1905, with the memorable and enthusiastic proclamation: "In Russia, as well as in the whole world, the cause of freedom and social progress now lies with the class-conscious proletariat. It is in very good hands." This statement, which is deceptively straightforward, deserves a closer examination as it contains several far more complex arguments that need to be unpacked. Luxemburg's words invite us to think about a variety of key issues, such as the evolving role of Russia, the intrinsic connection between social transformation and a socialist understanding of freedom, as well as what exactly is meant with a "class-conscious proletariat" in Marxist terms. These issues go to the very heart of Luxemburg's Marxism and her treatment of the relationship between socialism, democracy, and the touchy issue of the so-called dictatorship of the proletariat. Arguably, Luxemburg's analyses of the Revolution of 1905 in Russia functioned as a catalyst for her evolving conception of socialist democracy, in her own Eastern and Central European contexts. In addition, the events of 1905 had an impact on her analysis of which specific social forces, most of all the working class, could bring about democratic transformation and which organizational forms might be most effective in the process. A brief glimpse at the most important events of 1905 will give us the background to Luxemburg's political insights.

The name "Revolution of 1905" is shorthand for the interrelated developments that unfolded between the end of 1904 and the summer of 1907. While January 22, 1905, now known as "Bloody Sunday," is the date cited as the beginning of the Revolution, it was in fact the massive strike waves of December 1904 in St. Petersburg that set events into motion. Starting with the workers at the Putilov Plant and quickly igniting over 150,000 strikers in 382 factories, labor unrest fueled Georgi Gapon's famous procession of workers to the Winter Palace.† January 22, 1905 went down in history as "Bloody Sunday," as the tsarist troops that guarded the Winter Palace opened fire on the workers, resulting in the deaths of hundreds.

The revolutionary events shook the very foundations of the Russian Empire. They can be seen either as the last best chance for meaningful reform and modernization of the tsarist system or as the dress rehearsal for its revolutionary

---

* Ian D. Thatcher, "Leon Trotsky and 1905," in *The Russian Revolution of 1905: Centenary Perspectives*, edited by Jonathan D. Smele and Anthony Heywood (London and New York: Routledge, 2005), p. 236.

† Harrison E. Salisbury, *Black Night, White Snow: Russia's Revolutions 1905–1917* (Boston: Da Capo Press, 1981), p. 117.

overthrow. Ultimately, the Revolution was defeated. Tsar Nicholas II remained on the Russian throne while being forced to accept some concessions, such as the drafting of a constitution and the creation of a parliament, the State Duma. For most revolutionaries and their sympathizers, these measures were seen as largely cosmetic and merely provided cover for the autocratic tsarist system to continue as before. While the tsarist regime succeeded in stabilizing itself in the short run, it would not outlive World War I, finally collapsing in 1917.

Complex developments, such as the Revolution of 1905, cannot be reduced to any single cause. Out of the myriad of proposed causes, most historians usually identify four main factors that brought the tsarist system to the breaking point around 1905. Ever-wider layers of the Russian intelligentsia rejected tsarist authoritarianism, with colleges and universities becoming centers of opposition. At the same time, ethnic minorities rejected the tsarist policy of "Russification," associated with a myriad of official and unofficial forms of discrimination. Thirdly, peasants, freed from serfdom only a few decades earlier, found it difficult to survive on the small pieces of land that they were then able to own. The mass starvation of peasants created a deep-seated agrarian crisis, which the Imperial system could neither contain nor dissolve effectively. Finally, the small but rapidly expanding industrial working class in tsarist Russia realized that the tsarist system did little to protect their interests. While the government enacted some labor laws to curtail extreme forms of exploitation (such as outlawing child labor before the age of twelve, as well as prohibiting child labor for those under fifteen on holidays and Sundays), industrial workers in the Russian Empire had ample reason to resent their conditions. Employers subjected their workers to a host of cruel and arbitrary forms of discipline even for small infractions, paid them the lowest wages in Europe, and outlawed any attempts to form independent unions or engage in strike action.[*]

The revolution of 1905 had an especially strong impact on the so-called Kingdom of Poland, which represented the westernmost extension of the Russian Empire. Within a historically very short time period, an uproarious socioeconomic and cultural transformation unfolded and led, among other things, to the formation of an increasingly muscular industrial proletariat there. This new social class became increasingly class conscious and engaged in strike actions that involved tens of thousands of workers, such as in the famous

---

[*]   For a good overview on the Revolution of 1905, see Sidney Harcave, *The Russian Revolution*, (London; Collier Books, 1970); Abraham Ascher, *The Revolution of 1905*, Volumes 1 and 2: (Stanford University Press, 1988 and 1994); Ascher, *The Revolution of 1905: A Short History*, (Stanford University Press, 2004). In addition: *The Russian Revolution of 1905: Centenary Perspectives*, (London and New York: Routledge, 2005); *The Russian Revolution of 1905 in Transcultural Perspective: Identities, Peripheries, and the Flow of Ideas*, (Bloomington, Indiana: Slavica Publishers, 2013), as well as Volume 1 of J. P. Nettl's two-volume biography of Rosa Luxemburg, (London; Oxford University Press, 1966).

Łódź strike of May 1892. For nine days, the city and its factories were under the control of the strikers, which ended only when the Russian military moved in and killed over 100 workers.* The Polish territories of the Russian Empire were doubly oppressed. On the one hand, there was the lack of political freedom that characterized the empire as a whole, and on the other hand, there was the ethnic suppression of the Poles. Russian Poland only grew in importance to the tsarist state, in terms of both geopolitics and economics. Rapid industrialization changed the balance and composition of the social classes there.

Stemming from the experiences and traditions of the nineteenth century, the landed nobility saw itself as the main custodian of any desire for freedom and independence of the Polish people. This nobility, being primarily composed of the lower and middle ranks, still attached itself to the old dream of an independent Kingdom of Poland while being increasingly perplexed by growing working-class militancy. The industrial working class became more and more unwilling to accept the leadership of the Polish nobility and began to develop its own agenda. This required the creation of working-class political organizations, but by the 1890s this was impossible due to oppression within the Russian Empire. Thus, from that point Polish working-class parties could only be established abroad. In the fall of 1892, the Polish Socialist Party (PPS) was created by Polish exiles outside of Paris. This party pursued the goal of an independent Polish republic. While calling for solidarity with Russian Socialists, the PPS argued for an independent Polish path to democracy and socialism, given that Russia itself had fallen so far behind the level of socioeconomic development in the Polish realm.

Another attempt to unify the socialist circles of Polish emigrés abroad took place in July 1893 in Zurich, Switzerland. The first attempt resulted in the Social Democratic Party of the Kingdom of Poland (SDKP) led by Luxemburg and her close colleague (and lover) Leo Jogiches. Though never a mass organization, it provided an important vehicle for transmitting Social Democratic ideas to oppressed subjects of the Russian Empire. Although the group ceased to have much of an active existence after 1896, the effort to form a viable Social Democratic party in Russian-occupied Poland continued and led (in 1900) to the formation of its successor organization, Social Democratic Party of the Kingdom of Poland and Lithuania (SDKPiL). It openly rejected the legacy of Polish nationalism and saw any possible national uprisings as failed and out-dated. Instead, the SDKPiL advocated for close collaboration with German Social Democrats, as well as Russian Socialists.† In fact, it did not see itself as the custodian of any project of Polish national independence but instead as part

---

*   Politt, *Rosa Luxemburg, Arbeiterrevolution 1905/1906: Polnische Texte*, pp. 9–10.
†   This was not in itself unique to the SDKPiL, however; the PPS largely held to the same view up to 1906, and the PPS-Left (which split from the former in that year) upheld it throughout its existence.

and parcel of the Russian working-class movement. Luxemburg, together with Jogiches, became its chief envoy to the German SPD.

Her stern opposition to Polish nationalism, however logical it may have seemed on paper, was very problematic. That it placed Luxemburg in direct contradiction to both Marx and Engels who supported national self-determination is worth noting. Of greater importance was that it led Luxemburg to enter into virulent disputes with numerous other revolutionary tendencies on this issue, from the Bolsheviks and PPS-Left to numerous groupings within the Second International (ironically, rightists who opposed her in the SPD on other issues tended to share her opposition to Polish self-determination). Most important of all, her stubborn refusal to permit demands for national self-determination for Poland and other nationalities in Eastern Europe led to intense conflicts within the SDKPiL, leading to the expulsion of its members at numerous points (most famously in 1906, when the party split over the issue). Luxemburg and Jogiches maintained centralized control over the SDKPiL throughout these disputes, leaving little room for dissenters on the national question. In this there is some irony: the woman hailed as the great critic of Lenin's centralism actually behaved in a centralized manner as well. As the availability of Luxemburg's Polish-language writings becomes available through this series, there will be many opportunities to explore her contributions to as well as contradictions on these and related issues anew.*

III. THE REVOLUTION OF 1905 AND THE TRANSFORMATION OF THE ROLE OF RUSSIA IN MARXIST ANALYSIS

Carl Schorske notes, in his now classic study *German Social Democracy 1905–1917*, that "the year 1905 was a turning point in European history ... Almost overnight the ideological significance of Russia for Europe was transformed. The bastion of nineteenth-century reaction became the vanguard of twentieth-century revolution."† Schorske is certainly correct when he observes how the revolutionary events in tsarist Russia infused Marxist hopes for revolution with unprecedented energy, not only in Russia itself but also in Imperial Germany. As class antagonisms heightened, labor unrest intensified and advanced beyond largely economic issues toward openly political demands, such as the expansion of suffrage in the various German states.

The number of strikes greatly increased in 1905–1906. In 1905 alone, Germany witnessed 507,964 workers on strike, which is more than throughout the entire 1890s. Sixty-six percent of union members were mobilized in various

---

* Eric Blanc, "The Rosa Luxemburg Myth: A Critique of Luxemburg's Politics in Poland (1893–1919) *Historical Materialism* Online (2018). Accessed at: booksandjournals.brillonline.com.

† Carl E. Schorske, *German Social Democracy, 1905–1917: The Development of the Great Schism*, (Cambridge, Mass: Harvard University Press, 1983), p. 8.

wage struggles, within a context of significant increases in the cost of living. German capitalists had watched the growing strength and confidence of the German labor movement with hostility for some time. Several of them combined their resources and coordinated actions in employers' associations, with the Central League of German Industrialists as one of the most powerful players. The capitalist offensive tried out several different techniques of economic warfare, including massive lockouts of workers, in order to degrade and eventually break the financial reserves of unions. Yet, while rank-and-file union members and low-level organizers confirmed their gut-feeling that capitalism was ultimately irreconcilable with their interests as workers, union leaders actually strengthened their institutional and habitual conservatism, instinctively hesitating to engage in open conflict with the employers' associations. Schorske did not overstate, by concluding that "these developments had a profound impact on German Social Democracy. With the Russian Revolution, the issue of revolution versus reform acquired a new concreteness."[*]

This new concreteness convinced Luxemburg that the Russian Revolution had changed the objective situation and the existing balance of power in favor of revolutionaries within the Marxist camp. For several decades, the so-called Revisionists, around Eduard Bernstein, had undermined the traditional Marxist prediction that capitalism will not be able to resolve its endemic contradictions in the long run. Luxemburg, who had spent much of her time and energy opposing Bernstein and his allies, fought side by side with the leading party intellectual Karl Kautsky and his Marxist center party establishment against the Revisionists. Yet, the Russian developments convinced her to move beyond merely defending Marxism against the Revisionist attacks.

Already at the end of 1904, Luxemburg wrote to her friend Henriette Roland-Holst:

> I am amazed and marvel at the certainty with which some of our radical friends maintain that it is only necessary to lead the erring sheep—the party—back to the homely stall of "firmness of principle" … in this purely negative activity we are not making any steps forward. And for a revolutionary movement not to go forward means—to fall back. The only means of fighting opportunism in a radical way is to keep going forward oneself, to develop tactics further, to intensify the revolutionary aspects of the movement. Generally speaking, opportunism is a swamp plant that grows in swamps, spreading quickly and luxuriously in the stagnant waters of the movement; when the current flows swiftly and strongly it dies away by itself. It is precisely here in Germany that there is an urgent, burning need for the movement to go forward! And only the smallest number of us are aware of that. Some get bogged down in petty squabbles with the opportunists, and others, indeed, believe

---

[*]   Ibid.

that the automatic, mechanical growth of our members (in elections and in our organizations) in and of itself means "moving forward.""

Luxemburg argues, in essence, that the routine of bourgeois parliamentarianism is sterile, draining intellectual and emotional resources of revolutionaries. Equally draining would be the polemic and intellectual rebuttals of Revisionism. Incidentally, Kautsky expressed similar sentiments in his appendix to Luxemburg's letter to Henriette Roland-Holst, from July 3, 1905:

> In regard to Russia I am also entirely of Rosa's opinion. Things are going forward magnificently and I feel thoroughly refreshed by that. The Bernstein business made me old and tired before my time. The Russian Revolution has made me ten years younger. I have never worked so lightly and easily as now. *Vive la Révolution!*[†]

In one of her many articles on the Russian Revolution in 1905, Luxemburg elaborated on what the revolutionary developments meant to her:

> The capitalist world and with it the international class struggle seem to have emerged from the stagnation, from the long phase of parliamentary skirmishing, and seem inclined to enter a period of elemental mass battles again. But this time it is not the Gallic rooster which, a Marx expected, is announcing the next dawn of revolution in Europe with a harsh and raucous crowing. In fact it is precisely in France that the quagmires of the parliamentary era have manifested themselves to the most dangerous degree ... The starting point of the next wave of revolution has shifted from West to East.[‡]

Luxemburg saw this shift very enthusiastically, yet, she was also aware of some of the complexities of the Russian context. Given her own Polish-Russian origins and familiarity with not only the socioeconomic but also the cultural context, she lamented that so many outside observers, whether friendly or hostile to Russian events, lacked any real understanding of the situation. She had little patience for armchair Marxists, who claimed that overcoming tsarist autocracy should have been carried out largely under the leadership of bourgeois liberals:

> Above all, however, it would be totally wrong for the Social Democracy of Western Europe to see in the Russian upheaval merely a historical imitation of what has long since "come into existence" in Germany and France ... in opposition to Hegel it

---

[*]   Letter to Henrietta Roland-Holst, December 17, 1904, in *The Letters of Rosa Luxemburg*, edited by Georg Adler, Peter Hudis, and Annelies Laschitza (London and New York: Verso Books, 2011), p. 183.

[†]   Letter to Henrietta Roland-Holst, July 3, 1905, in *The Letters of Rosa Luxemburg*, p. 187.

[‡]   See this volume, p. 51, below.

can be said with much greater justification that in history *nothing* repeats itself. The Russian Revolution, *formally,* is attempting to achieve for Russia what the February [1848] revolution in France and the March [1848] revolution in Germany and Austria did for Western and Central Europe half a century ago. Nevertheless [the Russian upheaval] *precisely* because it is a seriously belated struggle of the European revolution is of an entirely special type unto itself.*

The unique features of the Russian Revolution consisted, for Luxemburg, in the failure of bourgeois liberalism, "and this is because the *bourgeoisie* in Russia *as a class* is not, to say it again, is *not* the vehicle of liberalism, but of reactionary conservatism or, even worse, of completely reactionary passivity."† Hence, only the fledgling Russian proletariat, in an alliance with other oppressed groups such as the peasantry, could orchestrate tsarist Russia's transformation into a bourgeois democracy, which then would provide the groundwork for the ultimate victory of socialism.

And at the very last moment, when over and over again people refused to believe in the independent revolutionary politics of the Social Democratic working class … in which proletarian politics must be subordinated and most urgently mashed together with all the others [so that there will be] a 'broader range of viewpoints' … January 22 made the word into flesh and revealed to the whole world the Russian working class as a politically independent force.‡

IV. SOCIAL TRANSFORMATION AND SOCIALIST DEMOCRACY

Luxemburg's political project focused on the defense and expansion of human freedoms. In doing so, she rejected the authoritarianism of the right—always a timely concern and blisteringly so today. But Luxemburg also rejected those on the left, who thought they could build any kind of socialist alternative without the utmost respect for civil liberties and democracy. In addition, Luxemburg understood only too well that the representative democracies of Western capitalist societies were perpetually undermined by the obscene socioeconomic and cultural inequalities in those societies. Her alternative, to the obvious structural limitations in the theory and practice of bourgeois liberalism, was never the elimination of democracy but instead its radical enlargement and expansion.

To her, genuine socialism could never be built on the foundations of one-party dictatorships, no matter how well meaning their leaders might be. Authentic socialism required the augmentation of political democracy with economic democracy, for the mutual enrichment of both. Any socialism worthy

---

*   See this volume, p. 53, below.
†   See this volume, p. 54, below.
‡   See this volume, p. 58, below.

of its name must be based on the transformation of electoral and representative democracy into participatory democracy. Thus, socialism thus could never be imposed from above. Only a grassroots socialism—originating from below—could defang both the destructive and self-destructive elements of humanity, on the one hand, and unleash human creativity, and its potential for justice, peace, and self-fulfillment, on the other.

Therefore, Luxemburg spoke out repeatedly on the need for the greatest freedom and democracy:

> Without general elections, without unrestricted freedom of press and assembly, without a free struggle of opinion, life dies out in every public institution, becomes a mere semblance of life, in which only the bureaucracy remains, as the active element. Public life gradually falls asleep, a few dozen party leaders of inexhaustible energy and boundless experience direct and rule. Such conditions must inevitably cause a brutalization of public life, attempted assassinations, shootings of hostages, etc.*

Moreover, she argued that "Freedom is always and exclusively freedom for the one who thinks differently," and "The more that social democracy develops, grows, and becomes stronger, the more the enlightened masses of workers will take their own destinies, the leadership of their movement, and the determination of its direction into their own hands."[†]

That Luxemburg had high hopes for the proletariat indicates to us her conviction that the proletariat could become conscious of itself as a class. That is to say, that the proletariat could make the leap from a class in itself to becoming a class for itself. She understood, of course, that working-class consciousness was often uneven. Thus, she had to think about what organizational forms might best aid this process. The Revolution of 1905 put her in a closer relationship with Lenin, which developed into life-long respect and a friendship built upon brutal honesty. Lenin and Luxemburg, personally acquainted since 1901, exchanged sharp polemics in 1904. Lenin accused Luxemburg of conceptualizing working-class political activities in terms of naive "spontaneity," while Luxemburg criticized Lenin's "hierarchical elitism." Despite those bitter exchanges, Luxemburg and Lenin came to find common ground in 1905.

Both rejected the idea that the 1905 Revolution was destined to repeat the course of the 1848 Revolutions, in which the role of a relatively weak working class was to push the "leading force," the liberal bourgeoisie, to the left. They shared the view of the workers as the leading force in a revolution that could not immediately create socialism, but could create the preconditions for it through the achievement of bourgeois democracy. The working class had not only proved

---

* See *The Russian Revolution*, in *The Rosa Luxemburg Reader*, edited by Peter Hudis and Kevin B. Anderson (New York: Monthly Review Books, 2004), p. 307.
† Ibid., p. 305.

its militancy and political independence in Russia, for it also utilized the tactic of the mass strike in new and creative ways. Luxemburg encouraged efforts to generalize the mass strike for *Western* Europe, insisting that it was no mere "Russian phenomenon" but of practical importance for the workers' movements in the "advanced" West. This is no small matter, since the issue of which social force or forces constitute the "leading role" in revolutionary transformation gets to the heart of her concept of revolution, which centered on workers' subjectivity.

Despite agreeing on the leading role of the proletariat, neither one could accept the others' position on national self-determination. Still, they united in their enthusiastic support of the revolution and their mutual disdain for Marxists such as Bernstein, Plekhanov, and the increasingly cautious and conservative SPD and Menshevik leadership (or rather lack thereof) in both Germany and Russia. During this time of personal friendship between Lenin and Luxemburg, serious disagreements remained regarding (a) what it would take to build revolutionary organizations that were both effective and democratic, (b) the relationship between socialism and democracy, (c) the complicated issue of internationalism vs. nationalism, and finally (d) the problem of imperialism as a distinct stage within capitalist development.

They concurred in their ways of conceptualizing what it would actually take to prepare for a revolution. Both essentially agreed that genuine working-class revolutions must be carried out by the workers themselves, as opposed to a conspiratorial elite. They further agreed that given how unevenly working-class consciousness evolved, those workers with an already more developed sense of class consciousness would need to take the lead. This would apply to Marxist intellectuals as well; they should intervene in the class struggle directly, by educating, agitating, and training less-developed workers. Both Lenin and Luxemburg acknowledged the necessity of forming a proletarian vanguard. This vanguard, however, was to remain open, transparent, and would need to include more and more members of the working class. To what degree either leader was successful in their bid for open, democratic parties is a debate that has reduced many a forest to wasteland as authors have written mountains of essays and articles attacking, or defending, "Leninism" or "Luxemburgism."

Still, already in her *Reform and Revolution*, Luxemburg challenged the increasingly widespread practice within German Social Democracy of fostering a permanent party and union bureaucracy. She also opposed the compartmentalization of intellectual activities, where only certain party intellectuals, like Bernstein and Kautsky, would focus on theoretical issues, while the rank-and-file members were to remain rather passive. To Luxemburg, every class-conscious worker needed to develop a systematic understanding of Marxist theory—in order to be actively involved in debates and the decision-making process.

After the permanent split, in 1912, of the Bolsheviks from the Mensheviks, Luxemburg became increasingly critical of Lenin's push for what she considered an overly centralist and authoritarian party of professional revolutionaries. To her, this undermined working-class unity. Of course, World War I changed everything. Luxemburg would ultimately help establish the Communist Party of Germany (KPD) as an alternative to the old SPD, which, in her eyes, was utterly compromised by its support of the imperialist war effort. For her, the new KPD was to be a broad-based party involved in parliamentary as well as extra-parliamentary work and firmly committed to never take power without the clear majority of the working class on its side. She welcomed the Russian Revolutions of 1917, including the Bolshevik efforts, while warning of their increasing dogmatism and authoritarianism.

Not only was Luxemburg aware of the utter bankruptcy of the conservative and hierarchical strains of thought and action, but she also foresaw that the reformist Liberal and Social Democratic movements would ultimately meet dead ends and exhaust themselves. And, of course, she was a prescient leftist critic of the peculiar bureaucratic dictatorship that would eventually evolve in the Stalinist and post-Stalinist Soviet Union and its satellite states. In fact, her critique of the evolving one-party state in Russia made her arguably the most outspoken advocate of civil liberties and personal freedom on the left. In this, Luxemburg anticipates and illuminates our current predicament: how the endemic structural and moral imbalances of capitalism will not be resolved by the system and pose an increasing threat to the very survival of our species. Today, while the crises mount, large segments of the current "left" seem to have lost faith in their own solutions and remedies. Thus, creatively reconnecting with Rosa Luxemburg's critiques has the potential to be an important catalyst in rebuilding and expanding a successful democratic and revolutionary left today and in the future.

William A. Pelz
Axel Fair-Schulz

Abbreviations

AAN, Archiw Akt Novykh—Archive of Modern [Historical] Documents

ADAV, Allgemeiner Deutscher Arbeiterverein—General Union of German Workers

Bund, General Jewish Workers' Union of Lithuania, Poland, and Russia

FVdG, Freier Verband der deutschen Gewerkschaften—Free Association of German Trade Unions

IAA, Internationale Arbeiter-Assoziation—the International Workingmen's Association, or First International

ISB, International Socialist Bureau

KPD, Kommunistische Partei Deutschlands—Communist Party of Germany

LSDP, Lietuvos Socialdemokratų Partija—Social Democratic Party of Lithuania

PPS, Polska Partia Socjalistyczna—Polish Socialist Party

PPS-L, Polska Partia Socjalistyczna-Lewica—Polish Socialist Party-Left

PPS-ZP, Polska Partia Socjalistyczna Zaboru Pruskiego—Polish Socialist Party in Prussia

PPSD, Polska Partia Socjalno-Demokratyczna Galicji i Śląska—Polish Social Democratic Party of Galicia and Silesia

RGASPI, Russkii Gosudarstvennyi Arkiv Sotsialno-Politcheskoi Istorii—Russian State Archive for Social and Political History

RSDRP, Rossiyskaya Sotsial-Demokraticheskaya Rabochaya Partiya—Russian Social Democratic Labor Party

SDAP, Sozialdemokratische Arbeiterpartei—Social Democratic Workers' Party

SDKP, Socjaldemokracja Królestwa Polskiego—Social Democracy of the Kingdom of Poland

SDKPiL, Socjaldemokracja Królestwa Polskiego i Litwy—Social Democracy of the Kingdom of Poland and Lithuania

SPD, Sozialdemokratische Partei Deutschlands—Social Democratic Party of Germany

SR, Sotsialisty Revolyutsionery—Socialist Revolutionary Party

USPD, Unabhängige Sozialdemokratische Partei Deutschlands—Independent Social Democratic Party of Germany

ZRP, Związek Robotników Polskich—Union of Polish Workers

ZZSP, Związek Zagraniczny Socjalistów Polskich—Union of Polish Socialists Abroad

Social Democratic Movement in the Lithuanian Provinces of Russia

(Arrests—Strikes—History—Unions— May Day—Party Newspaper)*

From *Vilnius* word is again being sent about *arrests*. The police have not been able to rest since the mysterious death of the police-spy informer *Raphal*, who in mid-April was found mortally wounded in the chest. [In response,] they are lashing out blindly at the Lithuanian Social Democrats, taking workers into custody without any reason, as well as individuals from the so-called intelligentsia.

But the movement is calmly marching along its way—not shaken by the blows from the police. Again, a series of strikes is to be noted. On May 12 [1897], the *shoemakers* struck at the Kahl work site, and on May 14 so did the shoemakers at Malewski's—with success in both cases. On May 20, eighty *bricklayers* stopped work that were employed in the construction of a building. The strike's aim, as in both of the earlier cases, was to win a wage increase, which was accomplished. On June 9, the *tanners* at the Meki Company went on strike. This time the cause was the arbitrary firing of a worker. In order to drive out of the employers' hearts the desire to exercise control over workers whom they do not like, all the colleagues of the fired worker laid down their tools. At the end of June, the employer turned to the police—which is the common practice in Russia. The chief of the gendarmerie, [Nikita Vasilyevich] Vasilyev, did the most that he could, making use of his *bons et mauvais offices*†—but in vain. The workers wanted to make use of the movement, once it was underway, to also win a wage hike. The tanners at the Ryfkin Company‡ joined the strikers in July, and two weeks ago, a general strike of the tanners (500 workers in Vilnius) was in preparation.

To give the readers a better orientation, we will comment that the above information relates only to the Social Democrats agitating in the *Polish* language among the *Christian* [Catholic] workers of Lithuania. That is to say, in

---

* This article first appeared anonymously in the SPD newspaper *Sächsische Arbeiter-Zeitung* (Workers Paper of Saxony), No. 222, September 25, 1897. The main title in German is "Sozialdemokratische Bewegung in den litauischen Gouvernments Russlands." It is translated (by George Shriver) from Luxemburg's *Gesammelte Werke* (Collected Works), Vol. 6 (Berlin: Dietz Verlag, 2014), pp. 111–13. Unless indicated otherwise, italics are by Luxemburg. We have used the current spelling "Vilnius" for the main city in Lithuania, which in Luxemburg's time was called "Vilna." In German, it was previously called "Wilna" and in Polish "Wilno," but the official Russian name was "Vilna" at the time this article was written.

　† Luxemburg uses this French phrase meaning "his good offices, and those not so good."
　‡ Leo Jogiches had been involved in organizing a strike at Ryfkin several years earlier.

Lithuania, among the *Jewish* workers a Social Democratic movement has existed for more than ten years, and it is led almost exclusively by *Russian* intellectuals, whose language is either Russian or Yiddish.[*] Quite independently of that, at the beginning of the 1890s there arose a socialist movement among the Polish [Catholic] workers, who had been neglected up until then. (The urban population is [mostly] either Jewish or Polish. Only the rural population still speaks true Lithuanian.) This young Polish-Lithuanian movement was initially trapped in the system of small closed-off political study circles, which were very widespread in Russia at that time[†] and in which all the emphasis was placed on training well-educated conscious socialists, but the actual mass movements involved in trade union and political struggles were left out of sight. Given the isolation of the local groups from the actual class struggle and the very highly developed phenomenon of political spouting-off [*Kannegiesserei[‡]*] in barroom style—for a time the entire organization strayed in the direction of *nationalism*. But soon a fresh wind was blowing in Lithuania as well. Because of the sterility of the small-circle propaganda work, the socialists were pushed onto a new road: they began to turn directly to the masses and urged them to engage in daily struggle for their immediate interests, above all the fight for a union and to organize, and in this process the need for a concrete political program arose, based on their immediate needs. On the other hand, the great Petersburg strike[§] definitively refuted the nationalist talk about Russia being absolutely and hopelessly rigid, and thus the Lithuanian organization came over to the Social Democratic program[¶] and to the struggle for political liberties throughout the Russian empire while the national utopians continued to wander about in the rumpus room of small-circle propaganda, in the dead end of small study circles.

With the transition to mass agitation, the Lithuanian party developed its activity in notable fashion. The greatest attention and energy were directed toward *union work*, and the most important branches of industry have already

---

[*]   Although the Social Democratic Party of Lithuania (Lietuvos Socialdemokratų Partija, or LSDP) was not formed until 1896 (a year before Luxemburg wrote this article), Jewish, Polish, and ethnic Lithuanians had been active in promoting Marxist ideas in the area for a number of years previously. Most of the Jewish activists viewed themselves as *Russian* Marxists, whereas many Polish and ethnic Lithuanians identified with the national aspirations of their respective communities. Leo Jogiches, Luxemburg's close colleague, was one of the leaders of the LSDP.

[†]   This is a reference to what became known as the "circle spirit" that predominated among activists in the Russian Empire prior to the emergence of large-scale political parties focused on public agitation. For some of the debates within the Russian movement over the need to break out of such self-enclosed study circles, see V. I. Lenin, "To the Party Membership," *Collected Works*, Vol. 7 (Moscow: Progress Publishers, 1963), pp. 140–4.

[‡]   *Kannegiesserei* is literally spoutings, outpourings, or effusions from a beer mug.

[§]   This refers to the strike that began in June 1896, and which involved 30,000 textile workers.

[¶]   The LSDP was founded as an underground Marxist party at a congress in Vilnius in 1896. The party was virtually wiped out by 1900 due to arrests and severe repression, which led some of its founding members (such as Felix Dzierżyński) to join Luxemburg's Social Democracy of the Kingdom of Poland and Lithuania (SKDPiL).

been organized in exemplary fashion. The influence of the party has been extended also to women workers—to washerwomen and seamstresses. And this happened in spite of the enormous difficulties created by the overwhelmingly handicraft character of those industries, with the nature of the work being scattered and dispersed. Among the major positive accomplishments of Polish Social Democracy in Lithuania is the introduction of *the eight-hour day* on Saturday in the railroad yards of Vilnius. A decree to this effect, applying to all state employees in the Russian empire, had been made known immediately after the Petersburg* strike, but it remained a dead letter in Lithuania at first. In January 1897, Social Democracy decided to make it a living reality. For this purpose, the workers at the railroad yards simply began going home every Saturday in a systematic way after working eight hours. The authorities did not sit back quietly and let this happen. Police and gendarmes were on hand of course, and they *locked the workers in at their various work areas* in order to forcibly compel them to continue working. Those who were locked in simply sat down quietly and would not lift a finger to do any work. This was repeated every Saturday. In order to encourage the fighting workers, the party distributed leaflets, in response to which the authorities also circulated their own leaflets. The outcome was—*a brilliant victory for Social Democracy*,[†] and the police, having been proved impotent, were left with nothing else to do but to resort to arrests.

During the *last two years*, the party led a countless number of strikes, and they affected almost all branches of industry and significant workplaces. This year's *May Day* was celebrated by a *work stoppage*—for the first time in Lithuania!—by a section of the shoemakers, carpenters, metal workers, garment workers, and brickyard workers. The police made searches at the residences of the striking workers and forcibly compelled them to go to work. But they were so slow and clumsy about getting dressed, etc., that it was not until 6 p.m. that they showed up in full numbers at the brickyards, where they were of course sent back home immediately by the infuriated employers. The party had also scheduled a May Day gathering that evening, where appropriate speeches were made and the *political* aims of the struggle were very heavily emphasized.

Since the end of March, the Polish Social Democrats in Lithuania have been putting out their own hectographed party newspaper, *The Echo of the Workers' Life*. The newspaper is edited with skill and passion and even features effective

---

* Known as St. Petersburg at the time, the city is almost always referred to as Petersburg by Luxemburg in these writings.

† At the time Luxemburg was writing this piece and all others in this volume, "Social Democracy" referred to the orthodox Marxism of the Second International, which proclaimed the need for the revolutionary transformation of society—even though many associated with Social Democracy were committed more to social reform than revolution. For Luxemburg, however, "Social Democracy" meant a commitment to what she considered to be genuine Marxism. Her nomenclature was to change only after the Second International capitulated to national chauvinism at the outbreak of World War I in 1914.

satirical graphics. The fifth issue has just now appeared—and so in the short time of its existence Social Democracy has accomplished a great deal. Recently, the government agencies in Lithuania were very sharply affected by the mysterious death of the hated police-spy informer *Raphal*; they obviously feel that perhaps it is better for them not to tread too closely on the toes of the workers' movement.

For the moment, the arrests [mentioned above] and the tanning-yard workers' strike are in the foreground of party life. Further news about both will be forthcoming.

Polish nationalism has already lost all signs of influence in the workers' movement,* and therefore the nationalists have to restrict themselves, instead of reporting facts about the movement, to merely reporting about some fictional dialogue between the workers and the gendarmes and such fabrications, which they are also successful in having published—owing to the ignorance that prevails about Russian conditions—in even such an honorable workers' newspaper as the *Wiener Arbeiter-Zeitung* (Vienna Workers' Paper).†

---

*   In fact, at the time of the writing of this article groups such as the Polish Socialist Party (PPS), which supported national independence for Poland, had significantly larger and more extensive roots in the working class than Luxemburg's Social Democracy of the Kingdom of Poland (SDKP)—not to be confused with the SDKPiL, founded in 1900.

†   The *Wiener Arbeiter-Zeitung* was founded in 1889 as the main newspaper of the Austrian Social Democrats. Victor Adler was its first editor, from 1889 to 1894.

A Workers Newspaper in Russia[*]

The first issue has just come out of a weekly newspaper for workers [in Russian] entitled *Znamya* (Banner),[†] which is [legally authorized] *under the Moscow censorship*. As is evident from the lead article, the editors stand unreservedly on the ground of the modern workers' movement and have set themselves the task of broadening class consciousness among the Russian proletariat.

The editors, after criticizing earlier socialist tendencies—the Narodniks [Populists] and the Narodnovoltsty[‡]—from the standpoint of Russia's modern economic development, conclude their "statement of beliefs" with the following: "We firmly believe in the possibility of actively influencing the elemental life process and of intervening in it, not with the aim or intention of turning the wheel of history backward. No, our goals are different and are fully realizable. The development of the self-activity, solidarity, and understanding of the foregoing, and of consciousness within the working class of its own interests—these are the requirements of the present phase of development."

The first issue of the paper is rather skillfully put together. It deals with the question of the relation of the individual to the life of society, as well as with the social views of John Ruskin, and also militarism and the disarmament manifesto, etc.[§] The bibliographical section of the newspaper refers to Antonio Labriola's materialist conception of history[¶] and Sidney Webb's history of labor in England during the last sixty years.[**] (Both of these works have just appeared in Russian translation.)

---

* The German title of this piece is "Ein Arbeiterblatt in Russland." It first appeared in *Leipziger Volkszeitung* (Workers Paper of Leipzig), No. 15, January 19, 1899. It is translated (by George Shriver) from Luxemburg's *Gesammelte Werke*, Vol. 6, pp. 253–4. The letter "L" was placed at the beginning of this item, implying "Brief Note by L." In a letter to Jogiches of January 14, 1899, Luxemburg reported that she had received "a new, popularized Marxist newspaper" from a Russian émigré, a woman named Shirman, "which will appear legally in Russia, apparently not under the aegis of the clique of Plekh[anov]-Struve etc." (at the time Luxemburg and Jogiches were not on good terms with Plekhanov, then the leading figure of Russian Marxism). She said that the impression the newspaper made on her caused her to feel "sympathetic" toward it, but it also seemed "a bit unfinished." She also said she would no longer sign her "Brief Notices" with "RL." See Luxemburg's *Gesammelte Briefe* (Collected Letters), Vol. 1 (Berlin: Dietz Verlag, 1989), p. 252.

† This should not be confused with a much later Russian literary journal under the same name, which began publication in 1931.

‡ This refers to supporters of the People's Will organization (Narodnaya Volya), which advocated revolutionary violence as part of sparking a socialist revolution based on the Russian peasantry.

§ This manifesto was issued at an international conference on questions of the maintenance of peace that was called by the Russian government and held in St. Petersburg on August 12, 1898. The conference was aimed at tamping down rivalries between various European powers and Russia, which felt itself in an increasingly vulnerable position.

¶ Labriola's *Essays on the Materialist Theory of History* (New York: Cosimo, 2005) was first published in Italian as *Del materialismo storico* (Rome: Loescher, 1899).

** This is a reference to Webb's pamphlet *Labor in the Longest Reign (1837–97)* (London: Fabian Society, 1897).

As a curiosity, it should be noted that in Russia at this same time there has appeared a particular newspaper [supposedly] for working people under the *official patronage* and with the lofty blessings of her gracious majesty the Empress.* This publication is entitled *Trudovaya Pomoshch* [Labor Aid].[†] This official newspaper writes, among other things, that because of the conditions of hunger among the needy at present,

> One cannot remain indifferent to the realities of the frightful impoverishment of the population. The danger threatening them keeps growing, because of new and acute calamities that have broken over our heads in this country. During the last eight years Russia has been visited four times by bad harvests. When there arises before our eyes the threatening and frightful *question of the systematic decline of our nation and people*, when the specter of suffering menaces everything that humanity holds dear, then one must gather all one's strength, all resources, to declare war against the approaching evil.

The official newspaper designates the appropriate means of struggle as follows: "The organization of labor," and it goes without saying that this must be "within legal limits."

In a word this is "the social monarchy in its tsarist form." It is blossoming splendidly, and as a further piece of evidence we will present next time—a detailed list of the latest arrests of socialist "troublemakers" and "rabble-rousers" in Russia.

---

* By the term "Empress," Luxemburg is probably referring to the Dowager Empress Maria Fyodorovna, the widow of Tsar Alexander II (and mother of Nicholas II). She was well known for her activity in charity work, unlike Empress Alexandra Fyodorovna, wife of Nicholas II.

† This so-called philanthropic journal was published from 1897 to 1918.

A New Tsarist Circular[*]

Count [Mikhail Nikolayevich] Muraviev, Russian Minister for Foreign Affairs, has addressed the following *Circular to Representatives of Foreign Powers in Petersburg*, December 30 [January 11]:[†]

When my Noble Lord instructed me last August to disseminate the proposal to those governments who have representatives in Petersburg for a conference aimed at finding effective means with which to secure the blessings of a true and lasting peace for all peoples in the world—and primarily to limit the continuing increase in present-day armaments—it seemed that next to nothing could block these plans from soon being realized, given their thoroughly humane character. The accommodating responses with which the foreign powers greeted this step of the Imperial Government have strengthened this initial assumption. The Imperial Cabinet highly appreciates the sympathetic manner in which the majority of governments has responded and finds great satisfaction in the validations of friendship that have been made, and are still making their way, to the Cabinet from all circles of society around the globe.

Despite public opinion flowing strongly and unanimously toward the idea of general peace, various parties have visibly tarred the political horizon with quite a different brush. Several powers have recently made new steps in rearmament, putting increasing efforts into their armed forces. Given this uncertain situation,

---

[*] Although this article, "Ein neues zaristisches Rundschreiben," was unsigned, Luxemburg was its author. It first appeared in *Leipziger Volkszeitung*, No. 20 and 25, January 25, 1899. It is translated (by Henry Holland) from Luxemburg's *Gesammelte Werke*, Vol. 6, pp. 255–60. The piece is closely connected to her article "Russia in the Year 1898" of January 18 and 20, 1899 (see *Gesammelte Werke*, Vol. 1 [Berlin: Dietz Verlag, 2007], pp. 318–25), in which she wrote: "It says a lot about tsarism's transformed international role in the years since the Holy Alliance, that while Russia is a participating guest at a West European *Anti-Anarchist Conference* on the River Tiber [on November 24, 1898 in Rome], it itself invites European governments to a *Disarmament Comedy* in Petersburg." Explaining her reasons for submitting her piece to *Leipziger Volkszeitung*, she wrote to Leo Jogiches on December 31, 1898: "I don't feel so at home in *Die Neue Zeit* as I am in the *Leipziger Volkszeitung*, where I can write what and how much I want, lashing out if the situation demands it, as is apparently necessary in polemics" (see Luxemburg's, *Gesammelte Briefe*, Vol. 1, p. 242). Bruno Schönlank had asked her to write about Russia in December 1898 as part of continuing her polemic against Eduard Bernstein. Other leading figures in the German movement also commented on the tsar's disarmament manifesto, such as Franz Mehring in "Thunder Clouds" (*Die Neue Zeit*, Vol. 16. 1897/1898, Vol. 2, pp. 737ff.) and Karl Kautsky in "Democratic and Reactionary Disarmament," (ibid., p. 740) and "A Russian Diplomatic Trick" (in *Vorwärts*, No. 202, August 30, 1898). Luxemburg's article characteristically focuses on broader issues of the international dangers and entanglements that result from imperialism, expansionist politics and *Weltpolitik*.

[†] At the time Luxemburg was writing, Russia still used the Julian calendar, which was thirteen days behind the Gregorian calendar (which was used in much of the rest of Europe). Russia adopted the latter (widely known as the "new style") in 1918, after the 1917 Revolution. The old style is the first date given, the new style the second.

one is tempted to *pose the question as to whether the foreign powers wish to judge the current moment as an apt one for commencing international discussions about the ideas raised in the August 12 circular.* Hoping, nonetheless, that the disquieting elements currently influencing political circles will soon make way for more peaceful circumstances better suited to aiding the success of the proposed conference, the Imperial Government considers that it is possible to now move toward a provisional exchange of ideas between the national powers, with the aim of finding without delay the means with which the palpable increase in naval and in land armaments can be limited. The answer to this question is *manifestly becoming more and more urgent,* considering the extent to which rearmament is advancing. Most of all, we should chart a path toward preempting conflicts fought out with arms by using the peaceful means that international diplomacy has at its disposal.

Should the powers consider the hour at hand favorable for gathering a conference on this basis, it would certainly be useful if the various participating cabinets could agree on its working program. We may summarize *the questions* that *international talks* would deal with in the context of this conference in the following broad outline: 1) A treaty for a specific time period agreeing not to increase the current strength of both land and sea forces or the budget for war and connected categories; furthermore, a provisional inquiry into ways in which it would even be possible to achieve a decrease in the effective strengths of such forces and their budget in the future. 2) A ban on the use of any *new firearms and explosives or stronger gunpowder types* than are currently used in armies and navies; this agreement would also cover rifles and canons. 3) Limits on the use of currently available explosives that have devastating effects during land wars; and a *ban* on firing *ammunition or any explosives* from aerial balloons and using any comparable vehicle to launch such weapons. 4) A *ban* on naval wars using *submarines or other diving torpedo boats* or any other comparable destructive technology, and a commitment not to build any more *warships with naval rams* in the future. 5) Applying the resolutions of the 1864 *Geneva Convention* to *naval wars,* based on the supplementary article of 1868.* 6) The granting of *neutral status* to *lifeboats* charged with saving persons ship-

---

*   The Geneva Convention of August 22, 1864, entitled "Concerning the Amelioration of the Condition of the Wounded in Armies in the Field," originated from the humanitarian work of Henry Dunant, a Swiss businessman who witnessed the bloody Battle of Solferino on June 24, 1859, during the Second Italian War of Independence. Shocked by the carnage, in which 23,000 were killed or wounded in a single day, he organized the civilian populace to care for the injured and published a book about his experiences, *Un Souvenir de Solferino* (A Memory of Solferino) in 1862. It included proposals for establishing voluntary aid agencies that could treat the wounded and sick in wars. This helped lead to the Geneva Convention of 1864, signed by twelve states (Baden, Belgium, Denmark, France, Hesse, Italy, the Netherlands, Portugal, Prussia, Switzerland, Spain and Württemberg). It formulated ten articles for aiding wounded soldiers and protecting aid agencies engaged in their treatment, and also adopted a flag with a red cross on a white background as a symbol of protection—the forerunner of the Red Cross, which was formed a year later. The Geneva Convention was the first international treaty stipulating rules of warfare. In the years that followed, additional countries acceded to the Convention, such as Norway and Sweden in December 1864,

wrecked during or after a naval battle, on the same basis as the preceding point. 7) The revision of the position developed during the Brussels Conference in 1874, which remains unratified to this day, concerning *spoils of war.*[*] 8) The fundamental acceptance of the beneficial service of negotiations and the use of non-obligatory *arbitration committees* in appropriate cases with the goal of avoiding armed confrontations between different peoples. 9) An agreement on how the above methods should be applied, and the construction of a uniform process for their application.

Of course *all questions concerning political relationships between states and regarding the order of things as regulated through these contracts* will *definitely be excluded as a subject of conference discussion*; as shall general questions that do not directly pertain to the program as adopted by the participating cabinets.

The press has already communicated the circular's principle proposals. It suffices to conclude that in Mr. Muraviev's second circular, the character of a *carefully calculated espousal* to benefit tsarist interests asserts itself much more gaudily and blatantly than in the first act of this international peace comedy.

This newest circular goes to great efforts to explicitly explain that in case this picnic of the diplomats really does take place, it will amount to no more than an academic discussion—or to use a fine colonial German expression for it, nothing but a "palaver." It is clear from the start that the only result will be sweet-sounding phrases and Platonic pronouncements, while in the empires of the military powers steel will clash on steel just as it always has—i.e., eternally increasing armaments are here to stay.

At best, the nine "practical proposals" of the tsarist "program" are nothing more than palliatives that do nothing to touch the essence and *continuance* of anti-cultural *militarism*. And even that is based on the fantastical and unfounded supposition that these academic proposals will be turned into reality.

The wish is to "humanize" war rather than to make it impossible, to turn the *mass murder factory companies* of the large states into an *industrial cartel* with specific rules and limits on production, in order to limit unbridled competition.

Hence, the whole thing amounts to no more than a fantastical performance. The Petersburg *Government Herald* has published the following official pronouncement: it is clear from the December 30 [January 11] circular that the

---

Great Britain in 1865, Austria in 1866, Russia in 1867, and the U.S. in 1882. In 1868, a proposal was made to extend the convention's application to cover naval war. Although fifteen states signed this additional article, no country ratified it and the proposal failed to be adopted due to lack of support.

[*] The Brussels Conference took place between July 27 and August 27, 1874, with representatives from fifteen European states, with the aim of adopting an international treaty concerning the laws and the methods of war. Russian Tsar Alexander II initiated this process. However, the motions adopted by the conference as formulated in the "Declaration Concerning the Laws and Methods of Warfare" never achieved the status of a binding international law treaty, because they, too, were not ratified. They nevertheless formed the basis for the Hague Peace Conference in 1899 and the Hague Convention, which was adopted in 1907.

government does not have *the least intention* of creating a *finalized program* for the conference to work on. Instead, the government is operating on the premise that conference members will be responsible for clarifying all aspects of the problem. It is leading them to believe that they only need to propose generalized and provisional questions for the parties to consider when the time has come to contemplate the collective development of a detailed conference program. As regards technical questions, these must of course be worked out with the assistance of *specialists*—which means that the most thorough inquiries only would be admissible, in order to keep pace with the disproportionate increase in *armaments*. By easing the way to a solution to these entangled questions, they will have contributed to producing an agreement between the powers, and, as a result, to the realization of the tsar's benevolent aims.

It is with unmistakable irony that [German] War Minister [Heinrich] Von Goßler justifies the restructuring of the German armed forces by referring una-shamedly to the tsarist peace pronouncement.* When you see how one military state after the other, large or small, from Washington to Stockholm, from the Golden Horn to London, zealously works to increase its army and naval capac-ity—when you see how tsarism, posing for a moment with its olive branch, draws together all its violent forces to arm itself for the decisive battle for hegemony in Asia against proud Albion—then this second Russian circular appears as a flip-pant mockery of the whole of politics of peace.

Even just the glimmer of an apparition that the planned conference's current agenda could resolve anything at all—albeit Platonically, and with ambiguous diplomatic reservations—serves as a welcome opportunity for the war minis-ters of participating states to take the stage with new demands that burden the world's peoples. Did we not just hear Herr [Carl Ferdinand Freiherr von] von Stumm[-Halberg] argue during the latest debates about military restructuring that Germany must move to increase the greatest possible size of its armed forces as rapidly as possible, so as to cover its back before negotiating a maximum level of arms as part of some fictive treaty? Such a development would enable the aforesaid gentleman to safeguard his political gains.

We are in no doubt that Nicholas II's solemn pronouncement is first of all a Russian diplomatic ruse, not lacking in skill, designed to protect Russia from an all-too-premature first strike. And it is intended to secure for Russia the elbow room needed to prepare its own far-reaching political plans for world

---

* Baron Max Freiherr von Thielmann, Secretary of State for the Imperial Treasury, introduced proposals to parliament for restructuring the German armed forces on December 12, 1898, and defended them in relation to the draft of the Imperial Budget for 1899. He proposed to increase the number of noncommissioned officers and soldiers in small military units by a total of 26,576, to retain the two-year period of military service until 1904, and to increase the size of the artillery and the cavalry corp. See the stenographic reports of the Reichstag debates in *Verhandlungen des Reichstags. X. Legislaturperiode. I. Session 1898/1900*, Vol. 1 (Berlin: Julius Sittenfeld, 1899), p. 19. For the speech of Heinrich von Goßler, Prussian war minister, see p. 186.

domination in the financial, transport and military spheres without being bothered by war and cries for war in Europe. In this light, the new circular almost leaves us with the impression *that the whole of international diplomacy commissioned this document from Little Father Tsar.* It seems like an actor's trick aimed at pulling the wool over the eyes of the over-the-top faction, which, with its peppy promises and pompous rulers' statements, leaves itself in a readily bribable position. It is a trick so that the actor can continue to fish sedately in troubled waters.

Today, in our age of *political costume dramas*, where a swanky performance trumps everything, you'll understand what's really going on in such glossy announcements. Bonaparte's phrase—"If you scratch the surface of a Russian you'll find a Tatar underneath"*—is valid for the totally Pharisaical two-faced character of this "affirmation" of international peace. The hegemons, wrapped in their philosopher's cloak of love-thy-neighbor and the-brotherhood-of-man, are wearing steel armor under their deceptive costumes. Behind the peace conference's rose lurks a glittering sword.

At this peak of historical development, in which big-money capitalism and militarism depend on each other like siblings, bourgeois republics, whether constitutional or absolute monarchies, are nothing more than meaningless company signs for the organization of the sectors of industry, trade, and agribusiness that make up capital. Moreover, capital is forced not only to restrain the unleashed production forces of the bourgeois economic sphere, but also to hold back the irresistible, aspiring and class-conscious proletariat. This is what makes this peace comedy appear as a necessary result of our advanced political technology.

Down with this terrible and ever-increasing burden of the armed forces that inflict pain right down to the bones on working people through military service and tax obligations! Down with hollow declamations of disarmament! Down with accumulating and accelerating international conflicts and entanglements that are born out of imperialism and its expansionist *Weltpolitik*,† which threaten the cultured world with horrible, head-on collisions. Down with those sleeping pills manufactured from the resolutions of debating clubs that commit to nothing!

That is how the rulers think they are able to lull that "big fool," the people, to sleep and deceive them about the brute facts of their misery and oppression. They think they can blind the working class with rhetorical fireworks, so that

---

* This phrase ("Grattez le Russe, et vous verrez un Tartare") has long been attributed to Napolean Bonaparte, but its use may well precede him. It was made famous by Marquis de Custine, who traveled to Russia in 1839 and wrote a highly critical study of its social structure and political system in his book *Le Russie en 1839* (Russia in 1839) (Brussels: Wouters & Co., 1843).

† *Weltpolitik* was the foreign policy pursued by Germany from 1891, which emphasized the need for colonial expansion, the assertion of German power on a global level, and increased competition with other European imperialist powers. It is often contrasted with Realpolitik, the earlier effort of Bismarck to emphasize a balance of power between competing capitalist states.

they can go on tyrannizing and exploiting them in the future. The possessors of power who calibrate their means of control miscalculate when it comes to assessing their acting abilities. The class-conscious proletariat will not swim into their net any longer; they will recognize this new pronouncement for what it is in essence. It is a bad comedy, deserving of one only critique—a *boo from the stage!*

Russian Women Workers in Battle[*]

Whoever needs convincing that women are just as capable as men of experiencing both citizenship in its highest sense and the noblest of civic virtues would do well to study the history of the liberation struggles that have shaken Russia since the abolition of serfdom. There is not a single newspaper here that doesn't name in lines of gold specific women who lived and suffered as heroes, with the courage of lions and a martyr's enthusiastic readiness to sacrifice —all for the cause of freedom and the liberation of the people. In all revolutionary phases, Russian women stood at the frontline of the conflicts and were shining examples of their work in the most responsible and dangerous of positions. During the years of peaceful dissemination of propaganda for the ideas of socialism, women and young girls wandered from village to village, and from factory to factory, to spread the gospel of a free and happy human race. During the period of bloody terrorist struggle against the henchmen of absolutism and the cruelty of the system, they submitted to the demands of the hardest revolutionary duties, including those that were much harder than sacrificing their own life would have been. When those years came in which the movement appeared to be extinguished, they studied and taught in quiet service to their ideals. Now however, that the revolutionary struggle catches fire anew—sometimes here, or sometimes there, in flames shooting up from smoldering coals—we find Russian women again among the freedom fighters' rank and file.

This movement in recent years is testimony to a tremendous and decisive transition that has taken place in Russia. A modern proletariat is gradually growing up that carries within itself all the lamentation and enslavement with which capitalism burdens the shoulders of the have-nots, and all the suffering and bondage with which tsarist absolutism blesses its subjects. Socialist thought is now recruiting more and more supporters and individuals from within the proletariat. This means that in Russia today it is not only the "intelligentsia"—the students of the well-educated—who are pressing for freedom. The proletariat, waking up to its own class consciousness, stands alongside the "intelligentsia" and announces a fight to the death against oppressive tsardom, in its effort to break the double yoke of absolutism and capitalism.

---

* This article, "Russische Arbeiterinnen im Kampfe," is not signed but was written by Luxemburg. She discussed writing it in a letter of March 1902 to Clara Zetkin, editor of *Die Gleichheit*, the paper of the SPD's women section. Luxemburg was unsure whether it would meet Zetkin's expectations, and excuses the length and the "emotionality" of the article (see Luxemburg's *Gesammelte Briefe*, Vol. 1, p. 632). It was published in *Die Gleichheit*, Year 12, No. 9 and 23, April 23, 1902. *Gleichheit* (Equality) was a bimonthly that began publication in Stuttgart in 1891; it bore the subhead *Zeitschrift für die Interessen der Arbeiterinnen* (Journal Published in the Interests of Working Women). It is translated (by Henry Holland) from Luxemburg's *Gesammelte Werke*, Vol. 6, pp. 388–91.

When we look back at earlier moments of the revolutionary movement, we encounter individual women workers who were freedom fighters alongside those of the intelligentsia—students, doctors, teachers, writers, etc. Yet now the number of female proletarians who want to construct "heaven here on earth" for themselves and their class is growing day by day. A profound and exhilarating desire for education shows itself in the ranks of the women workers as the socialist idea of emancipation is awakened. The revolutionary movement relates to these women as a bearer of culture, in the broadest sense of that word. Not only does it enlighten them socially and politically, not only does it steel their character by enjoining in them the principles of solidarity and self-sacrifice, but it also teaches them the most basic skills of reading, writing, arithmetic, etc. Those who take an interest in the people's education will encounter grateful and eager female students at the courses on Sundays and weekday evenings, and in conversations [with them and at] their reading groups. The living conditions of the female Russian proletarian sensitize her to the truths of socialist salvation. The number of women workers belonging to secret organizations and willing to make sacrifices for them through person-to-person agitation, such as disseminating texts and collecting money, is rising. More striking than ever is the participation of female workers' participation in economic conflicts and in the movement's political manifestations. And what a price they have to pay for participating! If a German factory is quite often a penitentiary, then a Russian factory is almost always hell. If in Germany the factory is the pious nursery, where the crude deeds of a police officer's nightstick are the ready reward for free speech, then in Russia it is a prison with the gallows standing beside it and Siberia always waiting.

Last year's May Day celebrations showed that Russian women workers also count among those who understand the slogan, "Workers of all the world, unite!" In almost all large industrial centers where workers carried out May Day celebrations—sometimes together with "intellectuals"—women workers also took part, in larger or smaller measures. They celebrated this festival even though they knew they would be punished with lockouts and wage penalties for doing so. They celebrated and demonstrated in the streets, even though they knew well that orders had been given to use the lash and guns upon them.

Furthermore, we have received two interesting reports about Russian women workers taking part in May Day actions for political freedom and the reform of working conditions. Both of these give us an idea of the difficulties and the dangers under which our Russian sisters united their voices with those of the exploited of all nations on May 1. They also take us into the worlds of thought and sensibility of Russian women revolutionary workers.

Iskra [Spark]* published the following letter from a woman worker in

_____

* *Iskra*, founded in 1900, was the official publication of the Russian Social Democratic

Petersburg, who as member of a secret organization had contributed to preparing the May Day celebration in recent years. She had orchestrated impressive demonstrations, and was battered down by police and the military in a barbaric fashion:

Do not take this letter as a sign of timidity. I have been treated with extreme brutality and cannot see a way forward … You have already heard that there has been a revolt here and that V. is no longer with us. I haven't seen him since the twenty-ninth, when he said that workers at his workplace would probably not work on May 1. When I heard that fights had broken out in the Siborskaya district, I downed tools and ran there, but it was impossible to reach the bridge—it was the workers themselves who weren't letting the women through. I waited for V. at his apartment but he did not come back. I asked after him at the barracks, but no one knew where he was, as was also the case when I asked at the Okhrana*… He was either dead or fatally wounded … Some said that they had seen him at the very front of the crowd, that he had cried, "Long live the revolution!"—and that he then fell to the ground. The police did not withdraw until all workers were gone, carting away those who could not get up by themselves.

You cannot understand how excruciating it was, both for me personally and for all of us, not to be able to get through to the fighting workers. We all wanted to get to the Nevsky† or into the middle of town. It is simply horrible to die like a dog in a corner where no one can see you. It is probably the fate of workers to die in isolation—truly, we will not even be granted a bearable death. And the really embarrassing thing is that they've been coming to call on us all winter, and have quarreled on our behalf, and now, of all times, nobody was there; they had gone away.‡ V. always said that we have to make our own decisions, and that is the most terrible thing—not dying! It seems to me that if one of you had been there then everything would have been different, and V. would still be alive. And this very moment when V. and others were making the passage to death, others were having a cozy time of it; perhaps A.'s wife came to visit him … I know that's not your fault, it's just sheer coincidence, but it is still painful, isn't it? …

I want to tell you something else. Although many of us have been arrested and some may no longer be alive, we will remain stalwart. It makes no difference that

---

Labor Party. We use the Russian initials, RSDRP, for the name of the party—Rossiyskaya Sotsial-Demokraticheskaya Rabochaya Partiya. *Iskra* was initially edited by Lenin and published in Leipzig, and then in Geneva and London. By 1903 it had fallen under the control of the Menshevik faction of the RSDRP.

* The Okhrana was the secret police of the tsarist government. Its official title was "Petersburg Department for Protecting the Public Security and Order."

† The Nevsky Prospect, Petersburg's main thoroughfare.

‡ [Footnote by Luxemburg] This statement relates to the disputes between the Russian Social Democrats and other revolutionaries from the intelligentsia. In contrast, the May Day demonstration in Petersburg was marked by the almost exclusive participation of proletarians, who appeared in tightly knit groups on the Nevsky.

people have gone back to work again, because we have reached a point in time where a mere walkout will no longer satisfy anyone. Now everyone aspires for more. People want to go out into the streets ... B. (a worker, who remained unharmed) thought it a shame that no one had a flag to march under. Next time we'll have a flag ready and pistols, too—stones and knives are not much use against bayonets ...

At the Russian Navy's Obukhov Steelworks in the village of Alexandrov near Petersburg, several hundred workers, including women workers, celebrated on May 1. In the cannon factory, for example, only twelve workers were on duty, instead of the usual 180. Plans were made to avenge this "sacrilege" by sacking sixty to seventy of the "rabble-rousers." Whereupon the workers demonstrated solidarity by demanding not only the reappointment of those affected by this disciplinary action, but also the eight-hour day, the repeal of punitive measures and the sacking of the Deputy Director. The management of the steelworks then called the police and gendarmerie to force these insubordinates into submission. They were met on arrival with the workers' cries of "We must have freedom!" and "We're fighting for political freedom and the eight-hour day!" Workers then threw stones to repel the attacks of the armed forces. Ten were left dead and several dozen wounded. The court case against the "ringleaders" opens in Petersburg at the start of October. These include two women workers, Yakovleva and Burchevskaya, who played an outstanding role during the clashes. The indictment reads: "The women workers Yakovleva and Burchevskaya tore up the road surface and carried rocks in their skirts to the fighting workers, during which Yakovleva cried, 'We stand beside our brothers!' According to one witness, the aforementioned women worker also took part in 'certain secret gatherings.'"

These events are signs of an awakening sense of class consciousness among Russian women proletarians. Others throng to join the creators of such events, which is a testament to the maturing knowledge and the crystal-clear willpower of our sisters, their feelings of solidarity, and their readiness for sacrifice. The Russian woman proletarian has become enlisted as a regular member of the fighting international proletariat. And when the Russian revolutionary movement has achieved its immediate goal of toppling absolutism, which will leave the road free for the toughest battle against capitalism, when the morning of political freedom dawns for those millions who are still tamed today by our Little Father's* lash, then Russian women and Russian women workers will deserve a good deal of credit for the spoils of victory.

---

* An ironic reference to Tsar Nicholas II, often used by Luxemburg in her writings.

The Russian Terrorist Trial[*]

The trial of the Russian terrorists [Grigori Andreyevich] *Gershuni and his comrades* has only now reached its end, after attracting so much attention in Germany and elsewhere. Various rumors about the trial did the rounds through the press. First, we heard that the leader of the sentenced group, Gershuni, had begged on his knees for mercy. We then heard that the man responsible for the assassination attempt on Count [Ivan Mikhailovich] Obolensky, [Thomas] Kachura, had made strongly incriminating statements about his comrades.[†] These were refuted, and finally the execution of three of the accused was reported as having already taken place. It now turns out that those who were supposedly put to death, as the *Berliner Tageblatt* felt its business to report, actually had their sentences commuted to "life imprisonment." Before the Russian government is able to patch its lies together for its official report, we can draw closer conclusions for ourselves by using the unabridged official text of the court indictment, which [Pyotr] Struve's own journal *Osvobozhdenie* [Liberation] has published.

The court case, chaired by Judge von Osten-Sacken, was held at the Petersburg Regional War Court this year from March 2 onward. Five people were accused: a pharmacist, *Hirsh Gershuni* (erroneously cast in the German press as a doctor and staff captain from Lithuania);[‡] *Aron Weizenfeld* from Zhytomyr (Volhynia); *Michael Melnikov*; the artillery lieutenant *Eugen Grigoryev*; and *Miss Ludmilla Remyannikova*.[§] The state prosecutor accused these five individuals of participating in three terrorist attacks carried out in 1902 and 1903. The killing of [Dmitry] *Sipyagin*, the Minister of the Interior, by a student, [Stepan] *Balmashov*, on April 15, 1902, is well publicized, as is the attempted shooting of Governor *Obolensky* by a worker, *Kachura*, in Kharkiv in August of that year. Finally, in May 1903, [Nicholas] *Bogdanovich*, the Governor of Ufa, was shot dead by two unknown

---

[*] This article, "Der russische Terroristen-Prozeß," was not signed. However, it is clear from Luxemburg's letter to Kurt Eisner on April 27, 1904 that she is the author (see *Gesammelte Briefe*, Vol. 2, p. 56). It was published in *Vorwärts* (Berlin), the SPD's central party newspaper, No. 91, April 10, 1904. It is translated (by Henry Holland) from Luxemburg's *Gesammelte Werke*, Vol. 6, pp. 494–8.

[†] After helping to form the Socialist Revolutionary Party in 1901, Gershuni founded the Socialist Revolutionary Combat Organization in 1902 with the aim of assassinating tsarist officials. In that year, he planned the assassination of Dimitry Sipyagin, Minister of the Interior, and Nicholas Bogdanovich, Governor of Ufa. His effort to assassinate Obolensky was a failure. In 1908 (following Gershuni's death), the Combat Organization was disbanded. For more on Gershuni, see Viktor Mikhailovich Chernov, *Grigori Gershuni: Zayn lebn un tetikayt* (His Life and Activities) (New York: Institute of Jewish Education, 1934) and Gershuni's memoir, *Iz nedavniago proshlago* (From the Recent Past) (St. Petersburg, 1907).

[‡] Gershuni's birthname was Gersh Isakov-Itskov Gershuni; of Jewish origin, he later Russified it to Grigori Andreyevich Gershuni.

[§] All of these individuals were members of the Socialist Revolutionary Party's Combat Organization.

persons in a municipal park. In addition, the accused were also charged with preparing to assassinate [Konstantin] Pobedonostsev in April and May 1902.

Before we proceed, we should note that the indictment creates a profoundly embarrassing impression. It is principally based on a *betrayal* committed by two members of the terrorist group—*Lieutenant Grigoryev* and *Kachura*, the worker. The former was the first in the group to be arrested, on February 21, 1903, and the conditions of his arrest were rather favorable—the only evidence they had against him was some Socialist Revolutionary Party* literature found in his possession, since he had in fact not participated in any terrorist attack. Despite this, he immediately began to provide the most thorough and meticulous information about his comrades, named all of his contacts and described in full detail meetings and conversations, and also singled out his comrades in the photographs that the gendarmes laid before him. In short, he betrayed absolutely everything that he knew, clearly hoping that in sacrificing his comrades he could buy himself clemency from the gendarmes† and the court. He received the best possible support in this from his wife, [Zoe] Yurkovskaya, whose brother— i.e., the prisoner's brother-in-law—had, just to top it all off, denounced the remorseful sinner to the gendarmes. (Incidentally, Yurkovskaya and her brother have not been charged as part of this trial.) This couple's confessions have proven disastrous for Melnikov, Remyannikova, and especially Gershuni. Melnikov had already been arrested prior to Grigoryev, on February 8, 1903, but under a false name, so that the police couldn't determine his identity. It was only through Grigoryev's statements that the authorities gained insight into the whole range of his activities. However, Remyannikova and Gershuni were arrested as a direct result of Grigoryev's statements, on February 25 and on May 26, 1903, respectively.

Kachura, a cabinet-maker by trade, functioned as the second witness for the prosecution at the trial and received a death sentence on November 8, 1902 for his attack on Count Obolensky. He was pardoned "by decree of Count Obolensky," who commuted his punishment to forced labor. During both his detention period and when in front of the court, Kachura acted with great self-assurance, writing a farewell letter to his comrades—in which he laid out his views on terrorism and his personal motivation for attacking Obolensky. This made a big impression in revolutionary circles at the time, even among those who judged his personal confession to be politically immature. "I joined the terrorist organization," wrote Kachura, "because I am convinced that it will be

---

*   The Socialist Revolutionary Party (SR), formed in 1901–1902, represented the interests of the peasantry and aimed at overthrowing tsarism and establishing a democratic republic. Terrorist attacks were one medium they used to further their political struggle. At the time of the 1917 Revolution they were the largest socialist group in Russia and were split into left-wing and right-wing factions. The Left-SR officially became an independent organization by the time of the October 1917 Revolution.

†   A member of the armed forces responsible for internal security.

successful in altering the government's habit of fighting us with a lash and its bare fists. I am convinced that it will be successful in opening up new spaces that will be used by the workers' and peasants' movements. No sacrifice is too large for such a purpose, and if it is necessary to offer my life for such a holy cause, then I count myself lucky to be permitted to do so." Evidently, the man who wrote these words was soon after so pulverized by tsarist thugs in a dark dungeon that he was prepared to submit a remorseful confession in July of last year—if, that is, you choose to believe what's in the indictment. He now came out with everything he knew, incriminating his comrades Gershuni and *Weizenfeld* in the process. The latter, who until that point had succeeded in avoiding the attention of the police, was arrested immediately afterwards in Dnipropetrovsk, leaving the reins of the case firmly in the gendarmes' hands.

It is of course a commonplace that traitors like Lieutenant Grigoryev and cowards like poor little Kachura have always existed and will continue to exist in all revolutionary struggles. But this is particularly so when it comes to the terrorist struggle in Russia, which places the greatest demands on the strength of souls and the capacity for self-sacrifice of its participants.

Yet this court case, based as it is on mindless betrayals, leaves us with the indubitable impression that *terrorist activities in Russia are imbued with a major internal weakness.* When you attempt to form an overall and detailed picture of the activities of the terrorist organizations, you are forced to conclude that really only one man, gifted with extraordinary charisma, really mattered—and that was Gershuni. He surrounded himself with what was essentially a revolutionary illusion, as opposed to a serious movement and organization. In the indictment, all five of the accused were charged with belonging to the much-talked-about "Boyevaya Organizatsiya" or "Combat Organization." But, by the prosecution's very own documents, it is clear that the fact that Grigoryev, Kachura, and Weizenfeld "belonged" to this "Combat Organization" only means that they communicated regularly with Gershuni—and with him alone—who sometimes turned up in Petersburg, sometimes in Kiev, and sometimes in Kharkiv. Yet aside from that, they didn't have the faintest clue as to the composition, function, or methods of this mysterious "organization." Perhaps this whole "organization" did not consist of much more than Gershuni himself. The material weakness of these undertakings is evident in the fact that Gershuni could commission a man like Lieutenant Grigoryev—utterly lacking in moral backbone—to assassinate Pobedonostsev, Chief Procurator of the Holy Synod;* and, indeed, in the fact that Grigoryev could be directly pressured into doing so. The same Grigoryev who, after all his mindless betrayals, fell on his knees in court and begged for the tsar's mercy. Just as with Grigoryev, Gershuni utilized all the influence of his

---

* Under the reforms of governing the church made by Peter I, the position of Patriarch of the Synod was abolished and a church layman headed the institution instead.

obviously fascinating personality to induce Kachura into carrying out the attack on Obolensky. Yet, in both cases, the heroism evaporated as soon as Gershuni's personal influence was removed from the equation. This corresponds with the rumor that Gershuni *dictated Kachura's moving farewell letter directly into his quill* before the assassination attempt—and then immediately copied the finished product. Gershuni used precisely the same tactics with Grigoryev, forcing him, come what may, into penning a political declaration with terrorist sentiments before he carried out the planned assassination attempt on Pobedonostsev.

Overall, the trial of Gershuni and his comrades leaves us with a distinct impression of *the extent to which the terrorist movement in Russia has lost the ground beneath its feet, and is hanging, disconnected, in the air.* It can hardly be doubted that the first assassinations by [Michael] Karpovich and Balmashov in 1901 and 1902 were anything more than spontaneous and isolated acts of bitterness and of self-defense. The first eruptions that harnessed oppositional and revolutionary energy in Russian society occurred by themselves, like the shot fired by Vera Zasulich at [Fyodor] Trepov in 1878;* these were simple reactions, necessitated by nature, against the inhumane and unbearable bestial acts that various servants of absolutism were committing. Society was not expecting them, yet they worked immediately like a liberating act of standing on our own two feet and of salvation from the coarse atmosphere of slavishly holding our tongues and tolerating all the impertinences of an animalistic and animalizing regime.

We also believe that such spontaneous actions of self-defense will be entirely understood by all civilized humans who have as much as half a clue about Russian absolutism's atrocities—that is, all people who don't see the world from the perspective of a member of the Prussian government, for whom only ruling-class persons are sacred and only *their* dignity is inviolable. Our Privy Councilors know only too well how to hound the African Hereros† and the "pig-tailed Chinese," calling for "revenge campaigns" for the death of every German colonial adventurer to be "atoned" by not one but by *thousands of foreign lives.* They understand their screams for revenge as being for "German honor," as soon as someone in Honolulu or Patagonia dares as much as look at the Germans disapprovingly. They simply do not understand that the Russian people—whose

---

* On January 24, 1878, Zasulich, then a member of the People's Will organization, attempted to assassinate Colonel Fyodor Trepov, Governor of St. Petersburg. He was widely hated for helping to suppress the Polish uprisings of 1830 and 1863 and for his extreme brutality. Trepov survived the attempt, and Zasulich was later found not guilty at her trial. It marked a turning point in the development of the revolutionary movement in the Russian Empire.

† The Hereros are an African people living in what was then known by Europeans as South West Africa; today it is Namibia. German colonists began entering their territory in 1892 and a genocidal conflict began almost at once. German reprisals against Herero resistance were brutal, resulting in the near genocidal destruction of their society. It is estimated that of the 100,000 Herero people living at the time of contact, the German army may have killed 85,000.

well-being and human dignity is trampled upon daily by their government in the most horrific way—will vent their spleen from time to time, in isolated, violent acts.

We, on the other hand, entirely *grasp* these incidents. It is however quite a different matter how such terrorist acts should be *judged* in terms of a method of political struggle. And we must say that the rise of terrorism in Russia is always *a sign of the revolutionary movement's weakness*, even if this sounds paradoxical. The need to vent stored-up bitterness and torment against individual support-ers of absolutism only occurs during those moments when no serious mass movement is expressing itself in a normal manner. It acts as a safety valve for revolutionary energy and oppositional spirit. The use of terrorist tactics actually arose from the disappointments caused by the failed attempts to bring a peasant mass movement to life in the 1870s.

Viewed from still another perspective, the terrorist struggle conveys the proof of its internal weakness as a political undertaking. To reiterate—Russian terrorism's plan is to intimidate absolutism through fear of an invisible and secretive revolutionary power to force it to grant concessions, or even to abdicate. Yet it is highly naive to believe that any government would capitulate to an invisible enemy that does no more than lead a half-mystical existence. It will only capitulate to a visible, tangible, and real power that can justifiably strike awe and respect into it. And such a power can only be a fully class-conscious *people's movement*, which enters the stage as an expression of historical necessities ripened over time. In contrast, as so strikingly demonstrated by the Gershuni trial, a tiny circle of people suffices for a terrorist movement. We have here individuals who operate totally disengaged from the country's social development and its social movements. Absolutism can divine its weakness only too easily.

Yet the same trial also clearly shows how much Russia's social sphere has developed and how much circumstances have changed. Today, not only have all of the terrorist's bygone theoretical preconceptions and articles of faith been ceaselessly washed away by Marxist critiques—so has their old talk of the [imagined] historical mission of the rural peasant commune [obschchina], and the significance of the peasantry as the future bearer of socialist revolt. Today, there is also a serious, growing mass movement of the industrial proletariat in Russia that naturally absorbs the country's revolutionary energy and unites its hopes around itself. And, in this movement, systematic terror has no chance of catching hold, as there is no suitable atmosphere in which any serious ter-rorist movement—even one that would function only as fatal experiment for a number of years—could establish itself.

The working classes' daily political struggle will only be severely damaged and endangered by terrorists, as terror would nonetheless succeed in sucking power away from the workers' movement and stoking false illusions. Even from its own point of view, terror cannot draw fresh energy from the workers' movement in

Russia today. Quite the contrary. When influenced by the atmosphere of the workers' movements, terror naturally loses its inner bearings, its inner sense of self-belief, and its appeal to new recruits.

Individual terrorist acts will continue to occur in Russia, and will probably continue to occur for as long as tsarist absolutism exists, because—and we allow ourselves to say this to Messieurs [Bernhard von] Bülow, [Karl Heinrich von] Schönstedt, and [Oswald von] Richthofen, as they hunt down scroungers, conspirators, and anarchists—absolutism in Russia produces spontaneous terror, in a manner identical to how the bourgeoisie's class hegemony in Western Europe produces anarchy. Yet just as Social Democracy is here the only real bulwark against the mad joke of anarchy, so has the Russian workers' movement—that has grown in the spirit of Marxism—shown itself to be the safest method against the illusions of terrorism. The period of systematic terror in Russia is over, and it is precisely this that is made evident by the profoundly tragic trial of Gershuni and his comrades.

Amid the Storm[*]

May Day will be celebrated this year under special circumstances, amid the tumult of war.[†] This year, the character of the May Day demonstrations will naturally be marked by the struggle for world peace. But not only that. Rather, this time of war requires more than a pacifist and proletarian demonstration; it must also promote an understanding that universal peace can be attained only in connection with our fight for the *final goal* of socialism.

If the Russo-Japanese War has shown anything, it is the vanity with which some socialist "lovers of humanity" speculate about being able to create world peace on the basis of preserving a balance of power between the Dual Alliance and the Triple Alliance.[‡] These eulogists for the two major military alliances cannot express enough their absolute satisfaction with the "lasting peace" that has been maintained in the center of Europe for thirty years.[§] The existence of this system of competing alliances allows them to predict "a coming peace" and "all of humanity at peace" as the most natural thing in the world. The thunder of cannons coming from Port Arthur, which has made the stock exchanges of Europe shudder convulsively, is a powerful reminder for these socialist ideologue-apologists for capitalist society that in their fantasizing about a European peace they have forgotten one factor—modern-day colonial policy, which has left the stage of local European conflicts far behind, because it has extended itself to the other side of enormous oceans.[¶] The Russo-Japanese War ought to have finally made it clear by now to the last unbeliever that the fateful question of war and peace in Europe cannot any longer be decided within the "four walls" that contain the European concert of powers. Rather, this question must be resolved "out there" in the gigantic maelstrom, the whirlpool of world politics and colonial policy.[**]

For Social Democracy, what the actual significance of this current war

---

[*] This article first appeared in French, in the newspaper of the Socialist Party of France (led by Jules Guesde), *Le Socialiste*, No. 81, May 1–8, 1904. Its title in French was "Dans la Tempête." It was signed by Luxemburg on behalf of the SDKPiL. It is translated (by George Shriver) from the German version in Luxemburg's *Gesammelte Werke*, Vol. 6, pp. 499–500.

[†] The reference is to the Russo-Japanese war, which began in January 1904 and ended by a peace settlement in September 1905, negotiated at Portsmouth, New Hampshire, under the auspices of President Theodore Roosevelt. Since the U.S. also had its eyes on China, it had an interest in limiting both Japan and Russia in their competing drive into Manchuria, Korea, and northeast China.

[‡] The Dual Alliance consisted of the German and Austro-Hungarian empires; the Triple Alliance consisted of the French, Russian, and British empires.

[§] That is, since the Franco-Prussian War of 1870–1871.

[¶] Many of the views of which Luxemburg is critical were expressed at the 1900 Paris Conference of the Second International, where some of the delegates refrained from taking a firm stand against European colonialism.

[**] That is, the competition for colonial possessions and "spheres of influence."

amounts to—aside from its short-term effects contributing toward the collapse of Russian absolutism—is what I have just stated above. This war directs the gaze of the proletariat in an international direction, toward the great political and economic interconnections that exist in this world, and it exerts strong pressure within our ranks against any kind of national egoism or narrow-minded pettiness of perspective, against the kind of thinking that always arises in periods of political *tranquility*.

The war rips apart all the veils of illusion with which the capitalist world surrounds us—this world of economic, political, and social fetishism.

The war destroys all illusory suggestions about peaceful social development, about the omnipotence and unchallengeable nature of bourgeois legality, about national sectionalism or regionalism, about the stability of political conditions, about "responsible" leadership in politics and the so-called conscientiousness of "trusted" statesmen or parties, about the power that supposedly exists in European parliaments, which are supposedly capable of shaking up and straightening out this world of strife, [about] parliamentarism as the presumed center of social existence.

War unleashes—simultaneously with the reactionary forces of the capitalist world—the forces of social revolution that are fermenting in the depths of society.*

Today, on this May Day, we will celebrate to the acrid smell of gunpowder while world events unfold at full tilt.

---

*   This statement is a prescient anticipation of the way in which the Russo-Japanese War led to the revolution that erupted in Russia eight months after the publication of this article.

Political Breakthrough*

Finally, after a very long period of seeming immobility, there has come a time of political breakthrough in the tsarist empire. Symptoms are multiplying every day that absolutism is living through a final crisis—before its demise. One such symptom, to be precise, was a congress of representatives of the Russian zemstvos† held in Petersburg, which drew up [the equivalent of] a draft of a constitution for Russia and submitted it to the tsar's minister.‡

This event seems to be of first-rate importance, and therefore the Chief Executive Committee of our organization has expressed its opinion about it in a proclamation that we reprint below.

The significance of this event lies mainly in that it is a *symptom* of an internal "loosening of the harnesses" within the tsarist government. Now that absolutism, which never tolerated the slightest sign of life, thought, or protest up until this point, is crushing with fist and bayonet any attempt tending toward political

---

   * This article is translated (by George Shriver and Alicja Mann) from the Polish original as it appeared in the December 1904 issue of *Czerwony Sztandar*, No. 22, pp. 1–2. The Polish title is "Przełom polityczny." It serves as an introduction to the Proclamation by the Chief Executive Committee of the SDKPiL, "Onward to Storm the Autocracy!" ("Do szturmu na samowładztwo!"). The latter is in the same issue of *Czerwony Sztandar* (pp. 2–3) and immediately follows this article, below. Luxemburg frequently refers to "our country" (*nasz kraj*), by which she means Poland, and to "the state" (*państwo*), by which she means the tsarist empire as a whole.

   † The zemstvos were a rural administrative body in tsarist Russia. Tsar Alexander II established them after the abolition of serfdom in 1861. They were in charge of such local matters as roads, elementary schools, medical facilities, etc. Liberals among the landowning aristocracy generally dominated the zemstvos over time. The Zemstvo Congress that Luxemburg mentions took place November 19–22, 1904 (November 6–9, old style). This congress was originally supposed to be held in Moscow, but was then relocated to Petersburg after the government promised it would permit it. The government did not keep its promise, but nevertheless the Congress was able to meet in private homes under police surveillance and was able to draft a proposal, which was submitted to the government. That proposal called for civil liberties and, above all, for an "independent elective institution" in which "representatives of the people would take their proper part in the exercise of legislative power." A minority of those attending the Congress stated that they would be satisfied with "representatives of the people" merely taking part in "the making of laws" rather than "in the exercise of legislative power." The proposal submitted to the tsarist government was known as the "Eleven Theses of the First Zemstvo Congress, November 1904." See Sidney Harcave, *The Russian Revolution of 1905* (London: Macmillan, 1964), pp. 55–7 and 279–81. The quotes are from Harcave's translation of the majority and minority positions at the Zemstvo Congress. Neither side at the Congress used the terms "parliament" or "constitution," but contented themselves with referring to "an independent elective institution." At the beginning of December 1904, in the name of the SDKPiL, Jogiches addressed a letter to the Party Council of the RSDRP in which he called on that body to take the initiative in view of the emerging political situation to bring about agreement for joint action among the various Social Democratic organizations in the tsarist empire. See *Archiwum ruchu robotniczego* (Archive of the Workers Movement), Vol. 5 (Warsaw: Książka i Wiedza, 1977), pp. 118ff.

   ‡ This refers to Russian Interior Minister Pyotr Danilovich Svyatopolk-Mirsky.

freedom—now that this blood-spattered absolutism has allowed the Russian liberals to deliberate for three whole days about various drafts of a constitution—it means that unprecedented fear must be prevailing in the camp of the knout.* The tsarist government, then, is following in the footsteps of every despotic government in the final throes of its criminal existence. Evidently it has ceased to believe in the power of the knout to ensure "order" in society. In order to avoid a popular revolution, it has allowed itself to turn onto a new road—to try out some pretended concessions. But history has shown that this is a slippery slope down which tsarism is sure to plunge to the bottom.

Now, the tsarist government is undoubtedly thinking only about deceiving public opinion with the *false appearance* that it is contemplating some sort of reforms, some sort of freedom of the press, something resembling a constitution. This is already an initial victory for the revolutionary movement. The knout has therefore lost faith in its own omnipotence and has begun to play the comedy of liberalism.

The whole task now is to turn this comedy into a tragedy for knout-ocratic tsarism of the lash. And this is precisely the task that falls to the *conscious working class of Russia and Poland.*

The situation that we find ourselves in is as important as any before. The proletariat ought to understand the full significance of this moment and the tasks that stand before it.

Above all, no illusions! Absolutism is waiting only for the first convenient moment, the first turn of events in the war [with Japan] most favorable to itself, so that it can later take off the mask of liberalism and return, as of old, to reaction and to unbridled barbarism and oppression.

On the other hand, these Russian liberals have now come forward—with the kind permission of the tsar and the [interior] minister—with the demand for a constitution, but they are waiting only for the first, most miserable concession to reconcile themselves with the tsarist government. If only there were some scrap of reform, some pretended loosening of the noose of censorship which is strangling the press, if there were the poorest, most meager little constitution (under which the whole mass of the people would be left outside its doors, while the noble lords and the wealthy bourgeoisie would figure as the "representatives of the people")—that would be entirely satisfactory for these liberals. But if tsarism, in case of a turn of events more favorable to itself, were to crack the whip again and bellow at the zemstvo gentlemen like Ivan the Terrible did in the past to his boyars, "*Poshli von, psy smerdyashchiye!*"†—then the zemstvo gentlemen would

---

*   Knout—a whip used in imperial Russia, made of rawhide and often with metal hooks attached, which could cause serious injury or death. In her writings of this period Luxemburg constantly referred to the tsarist regime as "the rule of the knout."

†   "Away with all of you, you stinking dogs!" The boyars were Russian noblemen that Ivan the Terrible worked to bring completely under his control.

run into their little mouse holes and would have no desire any more for any constitutional projects.*

Nothing surprising in that these Russian liberals represent only the dissatisfied nobility and the circles of the intelligentsia and educated people close to them—lawyers, doctors, etc. But these do not constitute at all a revolutionary class, for which the overthrow of tsarism and [the winning of] political freedom are like bread and life, as they are for the workers. The only thing that links these liberals with the workers is dislike of the rule of the bureaucrats. In essence, they represent a class that lives off the exploitation of the proletariat, a class that wants a constitution so that it can rule, together with the bourgeoisie, with more civilized forms of domination—over the working people.

Thus, for the working class, political freedom will not come from these liberal wooers of the tsar from the zemstvo nobility—not for the Russian or for the Polish workers. The present period of hesitation by the government will end either with a quick return to the old rule of the fist or to some kind of reconciliation between the tsar's throne and the nobility and bourgeoisie—with the complete exclusion of the mass of the people. As long ago as 1864, the International Working Men's Association proclaimed the motto: "*The emancipation of the working class must be the task of the working class itself.*"†

For us, this saying applies not only to emancipation from the hell of the capitalist system but also from the hell of absolutist government. The political freedom that the working class will gain with the downfall of absolutism does not depend on concessions from the autocracy or on the goodwill of the Russian liberals, but only on the degree of consciousness and organization—that is, on the *strength* of the working class itself.

From this there logically follows an obligation for the conscious Polish and Russian workers to intensify the struggle with all their might, an obligation to set the broadest masses into motion, to put forward our demands as loudly as possible.

In particular, our political agitation should be placed on a new foundation. Up until now the character of our agitation has been to aim generally for the overthrow of tsarism and for political liberties. Now it can and must be directed toward the immediate, tangible, and explicit slogan—*convocation of a Constituent Assembly*—on the basis of universal and equal suffrage, with the secret ballot, for the entire adult population of the state. Since the government is allowing representatives of the Russian zemstvo nobility to make proposals for a constitution, the working class must demonstrate that it does not accept these representatives and their proposals as theirs. We demand that our own voice be

---

* In her text, Luxemburg gave the Polish transliteration of this Russian language exclamation attributed to the sixteenth-century Muscovite Tsar Ivan IV ("the Terrible").

† See Marx's "Inaugural Address of the Working Men's International Association," in *Marx-Engels Collected Works*, Vol. 20 (New York: International Publishers, 1985), p. 13.

heard and that the will of the entire mass of the population should determine our fate.

From now on, we should not keep silent about that demand, not for a moment. It should become popular, a slogan used every day by all the people, the reply to every manifestation or action of the government—to every mobilization, recruitment campaign, act of police brutality, or reactionary government decree. Crowds at demonstrations, on the streets, should hear that demand force its way into town halls, public gatherings, and conferences. Our goal should be to thoroughly instill this demand in the mass of the people to such an extent that they live with the constant expectation of its fulfillment. To evoke this high level of revolutionary tension, directed with full force toward a single point, a tension that will not allow people to fall back into the dreary routine of "peaceful" everyday life—that is the task for Social Democracy today throughout the state* and in our country.†

The very essence of our political tasks must acquire new meaning as the next step. So far, a general demand has been sufficient in our agitation—*for democratic liberties*. Russian Social Democracy has also been satisfied until recently with this political demand in very general form, and therefore our movement [in Poland], which by the nature of things is only a part of the worker's movement in the whole state, had to conform [to the rest of the movement] in the formulation of our demands.

The revolutionary quality of a party does not depend on having slogans that are as extreme as possible in a program on paper. Only harebrained people, having written down in a narrow circle of party members the most radical demands [borrowed from] all the programs of foreign parties, would in all seriousness point with pride at what great revolutionary people they are. Really serious parties do not place so much importance on particularizing slogans that do not have real meaning for the movement. Up to now, the political program was important mainly for *agitational* purposes, but now *immediate action* has become the program, the object of practical realization. Accordingly, the focus needs to be placed on this with full emphasis—*the overthrow of absolutism and [establishment of] a democratic republic, which will ensure self-government for our country*. This will secure us against national oppression and give us the full possibility of free cultural development. That is today's political slogan, jointly for the Russian and the Polish working classes, and this is the ground on which our agitation for the convening of a Constituent Assembly must be based.

Our tasks, then, are clear. The Polish proletariat should understand that to fail to take advantage of the present situation in order to speed up the final victory over despotism—that would provide public proof that it has not reached

---

*   That is, the whole tsarist empire.
†   That is, Poland.

political maturity. History has at last prepared for us a moment of political breakthrough in the destinies of absolutism. But to convert this moment of breakthrough into a victory for the workers' cause can only be done by the working class itself through its own tireless struggle.

Proclamation of the SDKPiL Chief Executive Committee of December 1904: Onward to Storm the Autocracy[*]

Workers! A moment has come that has extraordinary importance for working people. For a long time, the class-conscious workers in Poland and in all of the Russian empire have been pressing for the removal of the heavy yoke of tsarist despotism and for winning political liberties and freedoms of the kind that already exist in the whole civilized world. Those freedoms are as necessary to us as the bread we eat and the air we breathe; they are necessary for us for an open fight against exploitation by capital, for improving our poverty-stricken lives, for winning rights for the benefit of workers, for the speedy elimination of all exploitation and oppression.

And now, at last, the hour has struck when it depends on you, workers, in a conscious struggle, a united struggle of the proletariat of Poland and Russia, for the winning of those longed-for freedoms.

The tsarist government, that monstrosity that for centuries has suffocated and sucked the living juices from millions of people, today is tottering on its foundations. The war with Japan has laid bare the inner rottenness of this monstrosity and has ignited revolutionary struggle among the wide masses of working people in Russia. Under the impact of absolutism's defeats in this war, under the pressure of universal dissatisfaction, even a section of the bourgeois classes, the party of the so-called Russian liberals, have begun to move. In recent days, an unusual event has taken place. In Petersburg, with the permission of the government, a congress was held—a hundred representatives of the Russian "zemstvos," that is, [the liberals among] the Russian landowning nobility. That congress elaborated a series of political demands and humbly submitted it to the tsarist government as a draft of a future constitution for Russia.

Workers! This congress of Russian liberals and their proposals are only a maneuver of the tsarist government with the aim of putting the revolutionary struggle to sleep for a while. Tsarism feels that it is disgraced and spat upon in the eyes of the whole world because of its bankruptcy in the war with Japan. It sees that the people of the entire empire are seething in ferment. And that is why it is permitting the liberal nobles to amuse themselves with a draft of a constitution in order to arouse illusory hopes that it will grant some sort of reforms, which will stop the struggle for a while. It allowed the Russian nobles to discuss

---

    * This proclamation was also printed by the SDKPiL as a leaflet in an extra-large print run of 9,000 and distributed in industrial centers, such as Warsaw, Łódź, and Częstochowa in December 1904. It was signed by the Chief Executive Committee of the SDKPiL. It is translated (by George Shriver and Alicja Mann) from *Czerwony Sztandar*, No. 22, December 1904, pp. 3–4.

and debate in Petersburg for three days about freedom of speech and the press, freedom of association and assembly. And, at the same time, it was ordering its thugs to murder the workers who were demonstrating for those very same freedoms in Petersburg and in Kharkiv and in Warsaw and in Białystok.

Workers! It is necessary to show the government of Nicholas the Last that no one among the conscious people is fooled by this liberal comedy of the knout, nor will they be deterred or delayed from the final reckoning with despotism.

A congress of a hundred little liberal nobles is not representative of us [the Polish people] or of the Russian people. It is representative of the property-owning classes, who today are living off the blood and sweat of the mass of workers. And tomorrow, after the overthrow of tsarism, they will hasten to garner all those rights and freedom for themselves and to disinherit the working people from those rights and freedoms.

Therefore, workers, we must reply to the congress and the projects of the Russian liberals with a thunderous cry: Don't you dare try to speak in the name of the millions of the working masses! The working people of Russia and Poland must speak for themselves! The demands for future political freedoms can only be worked out by an assembly elected by the broadest masses of people both in Russia itself and in all the countries and territories subject to the rule of the tsar, by all adult citizens of the empire. Only in that case will we have guarantees that the broad mass of working people will benefit from the future freedoms, and not a handful of bourgeois and noble parasites.

A Constituent Assembly elected on the basis of universal and equal suffrage, with the secret ballot, by all the people of the tsarist empire—that is our demand. Workers, that is our slogan, it is our reply to the congress of the Russian liberals.

Comrades! While, in Russia, even the cowardly liberals from the zemstvo nobility are daring at least to whimper [about political freedoms], what has our Polish society been doing? What part has it taken in even this miserable movement of Russian liberals? Where has there been the slightest push toward lifting the yoke of despotism? Where has there been any mention of self-government for our country? For protecting freedom of religion and national identity?

Workers! While Russian society is at last in ferment and the tsarist regime is shaking, in our country among the bourgeois classes there is the silence of the grave. Our [Polish] bourgeoisie and nobility are openly supporting the tsarist knout. Our intelligentsia has always mouthed high-flown platitudes about defending the people, the platitudes of patriotism. But when the hour strikes for fighting for rights and freedoms for our society, our cowardly intelligentsia keeps silent and hides in their little mouse holes.

Therefore, the task of overthrowing tsarism has fallen upon us, the workers, the conscious Polish proletariat, together with the Russian proletariat, to guarantee the participation of Polish society in the future political freedoms of the Russian state.

Comrades! Let us show that the Polish workers understand their tasks and the importance of the present historical moment.

Such maneuvers by the tsarist regime as the congress of Russian liberals and their projects are the first sign of the regime's approaching end.

While tsarism, in order to preserve its brigand-like existence from a revolution of the people, has begun trying to woo the liberal landowning nobility, we are issuing a powerful call for freedom of the people, by the people, for the people!

May the entire conscious proletariat go forward, as one man, into battle.

May the call for a Constituent Assembly elected by the whole people, to assure political freedom in the whole empire—let it become the never-to-be-silenced cry of millions of working people. Let it from now on be the main slogan of our meetings, our demonstrations.

May the echo of this call thunder through our whole country, just as it must thunder through the whole of Russia as barbaric tsarism sinks into ruins! Away with the autocracy!

Long live political liberty and the Constituent Assembly! Long Live Social Democracy!

The Russian Year[*]

New year—new life! Many an individual on the threshold of a newly beginning year, reflecting on his or her life up until then, may resolve to become a different person. The classes that rule Germany, and the world, however, have no time for such reflections or resolutions. Nothing can therefore be further from the thoughts of a newly rising class and a new way of social thinking than to waste its good time with preaching morality to bourgeois society. In the new year, it [bourgeois society] will remain what it was in the old year. Time places no limits on bourgeois society's spiritual and moral degeneration. And if a just and fair historian therefore will have to say about this bygone year that for official Germany it was a year of extreme disgrace, he will not be able to add the hope that somehow the coming year will remove the blot of that disgrace.

The year in Russia has taken its leave but the course being followed by Russia has not ended. The outstanding aspects that left the imprint of a Russian year on 1904 may express themselves in the coming year less prominently—but the system will remain as long as Russia remains what it is.

Thus, the Russo-Japanese War and the revolutionary movement in Russia are, properly speaking, for Germany, events of its own internal politics. It is to the great credit of this year not only that it has made a symbolic group out of a small element in the prisoner's dock, with which the workers of all countries have shown their fraternal solidarity, but also it has revealed the natural foundation on which this fraternization firmly rests.[†]

Ever since the time when the revolutionary bourgeoisie celebrated the Greeks,[‡] and later, when the young revolutionary journalist Karl Marx with breathless excitement described the Polish and Hungarian freedom struggle and recognized it as full of meaning for the future of all of Europe[§]—never since then has there been impressed so clearly on the consciousness of all politically thinking people how great is the significance of the major world-historical international connections, what significance they have for the future of each individual nation.

---

[*] This article first appeared anonymously in the main SPD newspaper, *Vorwärts*, No. 1, January 1, 1905. The title in German is "Das russische Jahr." Luxemburg's authorship is indicated by the Rosa Luxemburg Bibliography of Feliks Tych, which lists this as No. 308. See "Bibliografia pierwodruków Róży Luksemburg," in *Z Pola Walki*, 1962, Vol. 19, No. 3, pp. 161–226. The article is translated (by George Shriver) from the text in Luxemburg's *Gesammelte Werke*, Vol. 6, pp. 501–5.

[†] This is a reminder for readers of the International Socialist Congress, which was held in Amsterdam from August 14–20, 1904, and which among other things declared its sympathy with the fighting proletariat of Russia.

[‡] That is, in the fight of the Greeks against Turkish domination in the early nineteenth century.

[§] See especially Marx's "On the Polish Question: Speeches in Brussels on February 22, 1848, on the Occasion of the Second Anniversary of the Cracow Insurrection," in *Marx-Engels Collected Works*, Vol. 6 (New York: International Publishers, 1976), pp. 544–9.

> They're being slain on *Poland*'s plains—*France*'s children!
> Torn from their hinges in *Warsaw* are the gates of *Paris*!*

That is how a German poet cried out to the world at that time! It is true in the same sense that on the battlefields of Manchuria and in the streets of Petersburg it is not only Russian and Japanese but world destinies, including the destinies of Germany, that are being decided.

If the backward looking observer directs his view toward narrow national conditions only, a brightly colored play of the most memorable figures passes before his eyes. The bloody nightmare of Southwest Africa,† the distressful state of the German empire's financial system and the vain attempts to improve it,‡ the wild tumult in the House of Lords against the right to vote in the Reichstag elections,§ [Wilhelm von] Mirbach and the foul corruption in high circles.¶ And, as a counterpoint to all that, arbitrariness and violence against Poles and proletarians in legislative and administrative spheres, class justice, which truly is blind to the failings of more highly placed gentlemen but is vigilantly Argus-eyed when it comes to the slightest infractions by the little people. Soldiers who shoot at people who are running away are rewarded, but others who manfully defend the lives and honor of women against brutal attacks by drunken superiors are sent to jail for endless years.

But the eye sweeps away out into the world from the unbearably muggy premises of one's own little house to see how the weather vanes are rattling in the Far East. The tyrant's power has its limits! Anyone who in a moment of hopelessness had reason to doubt the truth of these promising words can now straighten up [and lift the head high].

---

*   These lines are from Franz Grillparzer's poem "Warsaw" (emphasis added by Luxemburg). See Grillparzer's *Sämtliche Werke* (Complete Works), Vol. 1 (Munich: Carl Hanser, 1960), pp. 200ff.

†   This refers to the brutal military campaign by German colonial troops against the Herero people in Southwest Africa, who rebelled in January of 1904 against the draconian colonial policies being pursued by Germany. The Herero rebellion was joined by the Khoikoi (termed by Europeans as "Hottentots" at the time) in October of 1904.

‡   In the trial of July 1, 1904 against the directors of a Berlin mortgage bank, it was established that by means of false assertions Baron von Mirbach, Lord High Steward to the Empress, had withdrawn from the Empress's account 350,000 marks for the building of churches, but only 25,000 had been spent. In this way, he was supporting the bank by maintaining unspent reserves. In addition, he demanded in a circular letter to his subordinates in the administration that funds be collected for church building among government officials, and he promised to award orders and titles in exchange for monetary contributions. On September 1, 1904, von Mirbach was dismissed from service as the administrator of the private purse of the Empress.

§   The reference is to the debates in the Prussian House of Lords on May 11 and 13, 1904, about a memorandum from the conservative political leaders Count Mirbach and Baron Otto Karl Gottlieb von Manteufel. In that memorandum, they called for a change in the law governing elections to the Reichstag, and also demanded exceptional laws against Social Democracy. Their demands were rejected by Chancellor Bernhard von Bülow.

¶   Von Mirbach, a German diplomat, served in various positions overseas, including in Russia before and after the 1905 Revolution.

And those fools who had believed that by shaking their fat fist they could put a stop to the powerful upsurge of an entire period of human development now become aware with surprise and horror when they see in the fate of tsarist despotism a distorted reflection of their own mirror image—and all the while, the Prussian minister of war* has the mindless gall, carried away with the mania for big numbers, [to call for more military spending] in order to justify a proposal in the German Reichstag [to make Germany] the biggest militarized state in the world, [at a time when tsarist Russia,] thanks to its inner rottenness, is displaying total and complete military incapacity. And while the same minister of war dares to proclaim that servile obedience is the guiding principle for the preservation of the state, this very same principle is experiencing defeats of the most painful kind in the waters of the Yellow Sea and the battlefields of East Asia.

What is in the works, and in obvious preparation, over there in East Asia is certainly not a victory of socialism, not even an actual total victory of democracy. However, on the field where we are accustomed to waging our battles, the field of *ideas*, the great events being played out on the world arena this past year have become our allies. Facts have demonstrated that logic is on our side. We who call ourselves revolutionaries have never conceived of that word in the narrow sense that one tends to use to designate "marching with pitchforks on the landlord's castle." It is not we who have called for violence; rather, we have tried to teach the ruling classes and have warned them all along that the means they resort to first and last in their politics, brutal violence, is powerless against great movements based on ideas. Physical conflict, which places men chest-to-chest against each other, and brings to the fore all the base aspects of their animal nature in the lower-lying recesses [of their psyches]—for us that has never been the ideal means for deciding great conflicts of interest. In all revolutionary struggles, since France won its liberty [in 1789 and after], for which the proletariat bears the least part of the responsibility, not one-tenth of the amount of human blood has been spilled which is now reeking on the altars of tsarist autocracy and capitalist "business interests." Is the battle for Manchuria more important than the fight for the freedom of the peoples of the world?

But this furious war being waged between two nations in Asia has taught lessons to a third party. The weapons being directed against each other by the oppressor classes of these two nations are basically being aimed against those ruling classes themselves. In the political and social revolution, there stand opposed to these two competing neighbors a third, who will overcome both of them. The ruling classes of the Earth are going to extremes, ready in the event of war to march against each other armed to the teeth—but in the German Reichstag we must grant to the Chancellor the honor of having spoken at least one truth: that the real winner in any future war will be *Social Democracy*.

---

*   A reference to Karl von Einem.

In the blind alley of such contradictions, bourgeois society has ended up in a position beyond all saving. While its ability to reason must tell it that nothing can be gained by employing brute force against the international workers' movement, its crude yet unreasoning instinct for self-preservation forces it again and again to show its fist to the masses who are pressing ahead with calm certainty and confidence of victory. This further tells us that every long drawn-out armed conflict between two capitalist powers, while it may bring victory *outwardly* to one of the two, in fact must necessarily bring defeat to both *inwardly*, since each power feels itself compelled to pursue a policy which bears within itself the possibility of conflict of that very nature. Thus, they come to know the poison from which they will die and yet they cannot turn away from it.

The year 1904 produced no lasting great decisions, nor has it left behind a worthwhile political legacy for its successors. Germany has not succeeded in making any internal progress—all pending questions of military, trade, finance, and colonial policy have had to be postponed—nor has the last blow been struck in the arena of the war and the Russian constitutional movement. Thus, the output for this past year seems small to those who evaluate a past stretch of time only on the basis of smoothly completed facts. We, however, who are accustomed to learning from the passage of our comrade, History, have gained rich spiritual lessons. The past year has not been "Father Christmas" with a bagful of gifts, but it has been a good schoolmaster. It granted no wish, but it did awaken many hopes, lifted many spirits, and newly revived much confidence.

The small-town hopes and fears of those who see one year's time as nothing more than a piece of their own petty human existence do not disturb us or frighten us. Neither utopian illusions nor considerations of Realpolitik will divert Social Democracy from the path on which it has been marching forward up until now. At year's end, we have experienced the additional pleasure of seeing the Prussian section of our party united in a gathering making a pronouncement against reaction.* And this event of lasting significance easily consoles us for all the petty and repulsive attributes of the day. In the world of passing phenomena the grand, disciplined, Social Democratic workers' movement will remain permanently as long as and until its function has been fulfilled with no leftover residue. Neither scorn and contempt nor cruel persecution nor inner chafing as a result of external pressure—none of these have been able to have any substantial inhibiting effect on the Social Democratic movement. Full of strength, it strides energetically over the threshold of the new year toward a future which will be its to possess in full.

---

*   This refers to the First Party Congress of the SPD of Prussia, held on December 28–31, 1904, in Berlin. It passed a resolution demanding universal, direct, and equal suffrage by secret ballot for all citizens over the age of twenty.

The Uprising of the Petersburg Proletariat[*]

At the moment when we were preparing to send this issue of *Czerwony Sztandar* to the printer, from Petersburg there came news that struck the whole world like a thunderclap. In the capital of the tsar amazing things were happening. One hundred thousand workers walked off their jobs and headed toward the tsar's palace, with the immediate aim of winning political freedom. At their head [were] striking workers from the armaments plants and shipyards, along with typesetters. Already the general strike had embraced 94,000 Petersburg workers, according to the official news, i.e., that of the government, but according to private sources the number was closer to 140,000. On Saturday, January 21, *not a single publication containing news dispatches was appearing any longer in Petersburg*, with the exception of one German-language newspaper and one small government publication, *Pravitelstvenny Vestnik* [The Government Herald].[†]

The beginning of this enormous movement[‡] had its origin, as has been usual in revolutionary epochs of history, in a minor incident. In Petersburg in February 1904 there was established a legal workers' association, approved by the minister of internal affairs, which set itself purely economic goals aimed at improving the daily lives of the workers.

At the head of this organization[§] stood a certain Russian Orthodox priest, [Georgi] Gapon, who had earnestly dedicated himself to the workers' cause. Recently at a giant metalworking plant, the Putilov Works, which employs more than 12,000 workers, four workers who belong to the above-named organization had suddenly been fired. The colleagues of the fired men demanded that the management of the company rehire them and responded to [the management's] stubborn refusal with a *general strike*. At the same time, the strikers formulated a whole series of demands, consisting of twelve points at the top of which was the eight-hour workday; [next came] commissions, which would include workers'

---

[*] This article is translated (by George Shriver and Alicja Mann) from the January 1905 issue of *Czerwony Sztandar* (Red Flag), No. 23, pp. 1–2. The title in Polish is "Powstanie petersburskiego proletariatu."

[†] The name of this official Russian publication when translated into Polish was *Goniec Rządowy*.

[‡] This organization was called the Assembly of Russian Factory and Plant Workers of St. Petersburg (in Russian, Sobranie Russkikh Fabrichno-Zavodskikh Rabochikh Sankt-Peterburga). It had about 9,000 members and a following of perhaps 100,000—more than half of the factory workers in the city.

[§] By the end of 1904, the Assembly had about 8,000 members. Gapon and his collaborators in this Assembly, influenced by some socialist workers who joined the organization, initiated the mass demonstration in St. Petersburg on Sunday, January 22, 1905. Although the aim was merely to petition the tsar, this event went down in history as "Bloody Sunday" when the tsar's troops and police fired on the workers, killing about 2,000 of them.

representatives, for resolving labor disputes at the factories and standardizing wages, with a one-rouble minimum hourly wage for workmen and seventy kopecks for women workers; elimination of unpaid overtime, or else double pay for such work; and also, improvement of health conditions at the factory.

The strike, together with varied demands, spread like wildfire from the Putilov Works to other factories. By the 17 and 18 of this month [January], 174 factories were idle in Petersburg.

At the same time, the strike went from being a [purely] economic strike to a political one, and it grew from being just a local conflict to being an epoch-making event. There began daily open mass meetings of the strikers, at which uniformed police did not dare show up. There began discussions about the general situation for workers and about what their needs were. And thus, in a natural way, there came to the surface, there and then, what were the [actual] political interests of the working class in Russia [that included, above all,] the overthrow of the *autocracy*. In this way, the strikers arrived at their own political demands, as follows:

(1) Equality of all before the law,
(2) Inviolability of the person,
(3) Freedom of conscience and of belief [i.e., religion],
(4) Immediate release of all those imprisoned for "political" offenses,
(5) Freedom of the press,
(6) Convocation of a [Constituent] Assembly, consisting of representatives elected by the people, which would have the right to immediately end the [Russo-Japanese] war.

Further on, there came economic demands, above all, the eight-hour workday.

The above list of demands was signed, as of January 21, by 70,000 workers.

The striking workers decided to march with this list of demands to the tsar's palace, at the same time delivering to him the following document:*

We, workers and residents of the city of St. Petersburg ... have come to Thee, Sire, to seek justice and protection. We have become beggars; we are oppressed and burdened by labor beyond our strength; we are humiliated; we are regarded, not as

---

*   At this point Luxemburg presents in Polish translation lengthy excerpts from the text of the petition that the workers attempted to deliver to the Winter Palace. These excerpts take up about half a column of her article of roughly three columns in the January 1905 issue of *Czerwony Sztandar*. For these excerpts, we have used the wording from a full English translation of the Gapon petition, which is included below, after this article. This English version comes from Sidney Harcave, *The Russian Revolution of 1905*, pp. 285–9. Aside from the version in Harcave's book, another version with more old-fashioned English wording is in the public domain as an Appendix to Gapon's autobiography, *The Story of My Life* (London: Chapman and Hall, 1905). In this part of Luxemburg's Polish text to German readers, a German translation of Gapon's petition, from the Vienna Social Democratic newspaper *Arbeiter-Zeitung* of January 22, 1905, was used.

human beings, but as slaves who must endure their bitter fate in silence. We ... are being so stifled by despotism and arbitrary rule that we cannot breathe. Sire, we have no more strength! Our endurance is at an end. We have reached that awful moment when death is preferable to the continuation of intolerable suffering.

Therefore, we stopped work and told our employers that we would not resume work until they complied with our demands. We asked for little. We desire only that which is indispensable to life, without which there is nothing but slavish labor and endless agony ... All of this seemed illegal to our employers ...

Sire, there are many thousands of us here; we have the appearance of human beings but, in fact, neither we nor the rest of the Russian people enjoy a single human right ... We have been enslaved, with the help and cooperation of Thy officials. Any one of us who dares to speak up in defense of the interests of the working class and the people is jailed or exiled ... The entire people—workers and peasants—are at the mercy of [arbitrary rule by] the bureaucratic administration ... Government by bureaucracy has devastated the country, has involved it in a horrible war, and is leading it further and further into ruin ... We, the workers and the people, have no voice at all in determining how the huge sums extracted from us are spent ... The people have no opportunity of expressing their desires and demands.

[All this is not] in accordance with God's law. [It is] not possible for us to live under such [lawlessness]. [It is] better to die—for all of us, the toiling people of all Russia, to die ... [Let the] capitalists (the exploiters of the working class) and the bureaucrats (who rob the government and plunder the Russian people) live and enjoy themselves ...*

Do not deny Thy people help ... Tear down the wall between Thyself and Thy people and let them rule together with Thee ... We do not speak from insolence, but from a realization of the need to find a way out of the unbearable situation in which we find ourselves ... Popular representation is essential. The people must help themselves and govern themselves. It is only they who know their true needs. Do not refuse their help; accept it; and immediately order the summoning of representatives of the Russian land from all classes and all strata, including representatives of the workers ...

This is our chief request ... Order these measures and take Thine oath to carry them out. Thou wilt thus make Russia ... happy ... *And if Thou dost not so order ..., we will die here ... We have only two roads—one leading to freedom and happiness, the other to the grave ... Let our lives be a sacrifice for suffering Russia. We offer this sacrifice, not grudgingly, but gladly.*†

---

*   In the passage above Luxemburg's Polish version alters somewhat the original text of Gapon's petition.

†   Luxemburg, in her Polish version, shortened this last passage somewhat, as indicated by the elliptical dots.

With this proclamation and list of demands, more than 100,000 Petersburg workers went to see the tsar, declaring that their petition could only be placed in his hands in person and asking that, for this purpose, the tsar should come to Petersburg from Peterhof, where he usually resided.

The tsar and his gang of ministers were overcome with fear in the face of this gigantic movement of the proletariat. The prospect of such a demonstration in front of the Winter Palace led to the already huge military garrison in Petersburg being reinforced by an entire division of soldiers from Narva, and according to foreign newspaper reports, the tsar promised to send three more cavalry regiments from Peterhof to the capital; in addition, artillery units with grapeshot were sent to Vasilyevsky Island, a working-class district of Petersburg. Also, military patrols were assigned to certain factories, to the State Bank, and to [various] government buildings.

In the light of such provocative moves on the part of the tsar's gangsters, who had decided that the despotic power of the state had to be preserved at all costs, and, on the other hand, in view of the determination with which the proletariat was stepping forward, it seemed certain that there would be a violent clash between the tsarist government's cutthroats and the mass of demonstrators. The autocracy that, in the opinion of the whole world, has suffered shameful defeats in the Far East [in the war against Japan], now showed its heroism by soaking the pavements of Petersburg with the blood of the proletariat—which is only fighting for freedom.

Even more detailed information about how this movement developed among the Petersburg workers will become known in days to come, and we will fill in or add to the information we have already received. But, in general outline, the tremendous significance of these events is already obvious to everyone. The colossal mass of striking workers in Petersburg, of course, is not yet fully informed or conscious about the political situation. The leading role of Father Gapon, and some wording in the workers' petition to the tsar, show that the workers must still be freed from illusions and false hopes.

Nevertheless, in spite of that—or rather, because of it—the revolutionary importance of this movement, as well as the importance of Social Democracy in Russia, is making itself felt in a most salient fashion. The demands that were formulated by these workers led by a priest went far beyond those put forward earlier by the zemstvo liberals, and in their main points they essentially restate the minimum program of Social Democracy.[*]

---

[*]   See Luxemburg's essay "Nacjonalizm a socjaldemokracja rosyjska i polska: 1. Socjalpatriotyczna robinsonada" (Nationalism and Social Democracy, Russian and Polish: 1. The Social Patriotic Robinson-Crusoe Cavalcade), in *Przegląd Socjaldemokratyczny* (Social Democratic Review, theoretical magazine of the SDKPiL), No. 10, October 1903, pp. 366–83, in which she wrote: "The entire minimum program of today's Social Democracy in all countries is nothing more than the political formulation of the most far-reaching and most pressing tendencies toward progress in the capitalist era."

Thus, the demand for political freedom, as presented by Social Democracy, has grown to be so much a part of the thinking of the Petersburg proletariat that even this half-conscious, spontaneous movement of the mass of workers is flowing with flood force down the riverbed of Social Democracy and taking on revolutionary form. Those masses of workers heading toward the Winter Palace were like ominous stormy petrels of a people's revolution. The Great French Revolution started the same way, with "hopes" and "pleas" addressed to the ruling monarch. In a similar way, the March 1848 revolution in Germany started. The Petersburg proletariat has stepped forward massively onto the political arena, and the subsequent course of this confrontation between the working people and the absolutist government is subject to the iron logic of the laws of history that will inevitably lead sooner or later to a people's revolution—and that will bury absolutism forever.

According to the latest reports from foreign newspapers, the Petersburg movement found an immediate echo in other parts of the empire. In Liepāja,* in Moscow, in the Caucasus, mass strikes have broken out. In Baku,† in the Caucasus, a strike had already begun on December 26 [1904], which quickly became a *general strike*. To judge by the latest reports, this strike became outstandingly *political* in character. The telegraph dispatches report that in Baku things have already reached the point of a bloody clash between the workers and the tsarist soldiers, with twenty workers being killed and many wounded. Absolutism, writhing like a monstrous serpent in its death throes, is murdering its subjects with the most wonderful impartiality, whether they be Russian, Polish, Armenian, or other.‡

---

*   Known at the time as Libau, a town in what is now Latvia.

†   In Baku, in December 1904, after an eighteen-day general strike in which as many as 50,000 workers took part, a collective bargaining agreement was concluded for the first time in the history of tsarist Russia, according to which the nine-hour day was established for most workers in the oil industry, and under certain conditions, a workday of eight hours was agreed to.

‡   In her 1906 *Mass Strike, Party, and Unions*, Luxemburg described the tie between Baku and Petersburg this way: "But the Petersburg rising of January 22 was only the climactic moment of a mass strike which the proletariat of the tsarist capital had begun earlier in January 1905. That January mass strike [in Petersburg] was without doubt carried through under the immediate influence of the gigantic general strike which in December 1904 broke out in the Caucasus, and for a long time had all of Russia holding its breath in suspense. The events of December [1904] in Baku were in turn only the last and powerful offshoot of those tremendous mass strikes that, like a powerful earthquake, had shaken the whole of south Russia [in 1902–1903] and whose prologue was the mass strike in Batum in the Caucasus in March 1902." She goes on to give a detailed account of that series of strikes in 1902–1903. See *The Complete Works of Rosa Luxemburg, Vol. IV: Political Writings 2* (forthcoming).

ADDENDUM: *PETITION OF WORKERS AND RESIDENTS OF SAINT
PETERSBURG FOR SUBMISSION TO NICHOLAS II ON JANUARY 9, 1905.*

We, workers and residents of the city of St. Petersburg, of various ranks and
stations, our wives, children, and helpless old parents, have come to Thee, Sire,
to seek justice and protection. We have become beggars; we are oppressed and
burdened by labor beyond our strength; we are humiliated; we are regarded, not
as human beings, but as slaves who must endure their bitter fate in silence. We
have endured it, and we are being pushed further and further into the depths
of poverty, injustice, and ignorance; we are being so stifled by despotism and
arbitrary rule that we cannot breathe. Sire, we have no more strength! Our
endurance is at an end. We have reached that awful moment when death is preferable to the continuation of intolerable suffering.

Therefore, we stopped work and told our employers that we would not
resume work until they complied with our demands. We asked for little. We
desire only that which is indispensable to life, without which there is nothing but
slavish labor and endless agony. Our first request was that our employers discuss
our needs with us, but this they refused to do; they denied that we have a right
to speak about our needs, on the grounds that the law does not recognize such
a right. They also treated as illegal our other requests—to reduce the working
day to eight hours, to establish wage rates in consultation with us and with our
consent, to investigate our grievances against lower administrative personnel of
the factories, to increase the daily wages for unskilled working men and women
to one rouble, to abolish overtime, to administer medical aid carefully and
politely, to construct workshops in which it would be possible to work without
danger of death from miserable drafts, rain, and snow.

All of this seemed illegal to our employers; each of our requests was treated
as if it were a crime, and our desire to improve our situation was considered an
act of insolence and insult.

Sire, there are many thousands of us here; we have the appearance of human
beings but, in fact, neither we nor the rest of the Russian people enjoy a single
human right—not even the right to speak, think, assemble, discuss our needs, or
take steps to improve our situation.

We have been enslaved, with the help and cooperation of Thy officials.
Any one of us who dares to speak up in defense of the interests of the working
class and the people is jailed or exiled; it is as if it were a crime to have a good
heart or a sympathetic soul. Even to feel for one who is beaten, deprived of his
rights, or tortured is a grave crime. The entire people—workers and peasants
—are at the mercy of the bureaucratic administration, which consists of men
who rob the government and the people, men who not only ignore, but also

---

* For the original of this document, see Akademiya Nauk, SSSR, Institut Istorii, *Nachalo
Pervoi Russkoi Revolyutsii* (Beginning of the First Russian Revolution), (Moscow: Akademiya
Nauk, Institut Istorii, 1955), pp. 28–31.

scorn, the interests of the people. Government by bureaucracy has devastated the country, has involved it in a horrible war, and is leading it further and further into ruin. We, the workers and the people, have no voice at all in determining how the huge sums extracted from us are spent; we are denied the means of participating in the levying of taxes or deciding how they are to be spent. The people have no opportunity of expressing their desires and demands. The workers are denied the opportunity to form unions for the defense of their interests.

Sire! Is this in accordance with God's laws, by the grace of which Thou reignest? And is it not possible for us to live under such laws? Is it better to die— for all of us, the toiling people of all Russia, to die, allowing the capitalists (the exploiters of the working class) and the bureaucrats (who rob the government and plunder the Russian people) to live and enjoy themselves? This is the choice we face, Sire, and this is why we have come to the walls of Thy palace. Here we seek our last chance of salvation. Do not deny Thy people help; lead them out of the depths of injustice, poverty, and ignorance; give them the chance to direct their own fate and rid themselves of the unbearable bureaucratic yoke. Tear down the wall between Thyself and Thy people and let them rule together with Thee. Hast Thou not been placed on the throne for the happiness of the people, and has not this happiness been denied to us by the bureaucrats, leaving us only unhappiness and humiliation? Examine our requests dispassionately and carefully; they are not evil in design, but are meant to help both us and Thee. We do not speak from insolence, but from a realization of the need to find a way out of the unbearable situation in which we find ourselves. Russia is too great, its needs too varied and profuse, to be governed by bureaucrats alone. Popular representation is essential. The people must help themselves and govern themselves. It is only they who know their true needs. Do not refuse their help; accept it; and immediately order the summoning of representatives of the Russian land from all classes and all strata, including representatives of the workers. Capitalists, workers, bureaucrats, priests, doctors, and teachers—let them all, whoever they may be, choose their own representatives. Let all have a free and equal vote; and toward this end, order the election of a Constituent Assembly on the basis of universal, secret, and equal suffrage.

This is our chief request; in it and on it all else is based; this is the chief and only means of healing our painful wounds; without it, our wounds will fester and bring us to our death.

But one measure alone cannot heal our wounds. Additional ones are indispensable. Directly and frankly as to a father, Sire, we tell Thee, in the name of all of the laboring class of Russia, what they are.

Indispensable are:

(1) The immediate release and return of all those who have suffered for their political and religious convictions, for strikes, and for peasant disorder.

(2) Universal and compulsory popular [primary] education at the expense of the state.

(3) Responsibility of the ministers to the people and the guarantee of legality in administration.

(4) Equality of all, without exception, before the law.

(5) Separation of church and state.

(6) Measures to eliminate the poverty of the people.

(7) Abolition of indirect taxes and their replacement by direct, progressive income tax.

(8) Abolition of redemption dues, [establishment of] cheap credit, and gradual transfer of land to the people.

(9) Placement of orders for the Navy in Russia, not abroad.

(10) Termination of the war in accord with popular demand.

(11) Measures to eliminate the tyranny of capital over labor.

(12) Abolition of the system of factory inspectors.

(13) Establishment in the factories and mills of permanent committees elected by the workers, which, together with the administration, will examine all claims of individual workers; no worker to be discharged except by decision of this committee.

(14) Freedom to establish consumers' and producers' [cooperatives] and trade unions—as of now.

(15) The eight-hour working day and regulation of overtime.

(16) Freedom of labor to struggle against capital—as of now.

(17) Wage regulation—as of now.

(18) Participation of working-class representatives in the preparation of a bill for government insurance of workers—as of now.

These, Sire, are our chief needs, concerning which we have come to Thee. The liberation of our motherland from slavery and poverty is possible only through the satisfaction of these needs; only thus can she flourish; only thus will it be possible for workers to organize in protection of their interests against high-handed exploitation by the capitalists and the plundering and oppressive governmental bureaucrats. Order these measures and take Thine oath to carry them out. Thou wilt thus make Russia both happy and famous, and Thy name will be engraved in our hearts and in those of our posterity forever. And if Thou dost not so order and dost not respond to our pleas, we will die here in this square before Thy palace. We have nowhere else to go and no purpose in going. We have only two roads—one leading to freedom and happiness, the other to the grave ... Let our lives be a sacrifice for suffering Russia. We offer this sacrifice, not grudgingly, but gladly.

—Georgi Gapon, priest
Ivan Vasimov, worker

After the First Act[*]

A week ago, we wrote about the revolution in Petersburg. Today it is the revolution in almost all of the Russian empire. In Moscow, Riga, and Vilnius, in Liepāja and Jelgava,[†] in Yekaterinoslav and Kiev, in Warsaw and Łódź, the proletarians have responded to the massacre in Petersburg with mass strikes—in Warsaw it was a general strike, in the literal meaning of the term—and they have energetically demonstrated their political class solidarity with the proletariat on the Nevá. And with the masses that have gone into action, something else is also growing—the "thoroughness" of commitment ("*die Gründlichkeit*,"[‡] to speak in the language of Marx) of those same masses, whose action it is.

In Petersburg, the uprising of the proletariat was spontaneous and the signal given for it was by a purely accidental leader [Father Gapon], even if the goals, the program, and thereby the *political character* of the uprising, as has been described in very precise news reports, were directly dictated by the intervention of *Social Democratic* workers. In the rest of the tsarist empire, and particularly in Poland, the initiative and the leadership of the movement from the very start was in the hands of the Social Democrats. Obviously [we are speaking] even here not in the sense that the Social Democrats of their own free will conjured up a mass strike out of nowhere merely at their own discretion. They had to adjust themselves everywhere to the pressure from the workers, who in reaction to the very first news and even rumors about the events in Petersburg became greatly aroused and instinctively seized on the idea of solidarity action. But it was the Social Democrats who immediately gave the necessary expression to the stormy outbreaks of the masses, provided political slogans, and gave the movement a clear direction.

Thus, the Russian Revolution, when viewed *as an entirety*, has already taken on the clearly defined character of a political rebellion by the whole working class—and that was on the very next day after the bloodbath of January 22. Because it is precisely this echo produced by the Petersburg events immediately in the other industrial cities and regions of Russia that is the best proof that in Petersburg itself we are not talking about an isolated, blind revolt of desperation by a particular section of the working class, as has frequently and bloodily occurred in the case of the Russian peasantry from time to time for many

---

[*] This article was first published in *Neue Zeit*, 1904–1905, Vol. 1, pp. 610–14, under the title, "Nach dem ersten Akt." It is translated (by George Shriver) from the text in Luxemburg's *Gesammelte Werke*, Vol. 1, Part 2, pp. 485–90.

[†] Then known as Mitau, in Latvia.

[‡] In addition to "thoroughness," the German word Gründlichkeit can also be translated as "profundity" or "solidity" (that is, "a solidly grounded quality; groundedness"). Luxemburg's wording was as follows: *Und mit der Masse, die in Aktion tritt, wächst, um mit Marx zu reden, auch "die Gründlichkeit" der Masse, deren Aktion sie ist.*

years. No, it was an expression of the same ferment and the same aspirations for something better that are vitally alive among the industrial workers in the whole empire. Open and conscious solidarity action of this kind, and indeed it was *political* solidarity action by the workers in the various cities and regions of Russia—no such thing has happened before during the existence of the tsarist regime. Even May Day, the idea of which has had a powerful impact in Russia, was never able to summon forth a comparably cohesive and composite mass outpouring.

Only the immediate struggle could bring them so suddenly together into action and show for the first time that the working class in the tsarist empire is no longer merely an abstract concept or a mechanical aggregation of separate groups of proletarians with similar interests and parallel aspirations, but rather is an organic whole fully capable of action, a *political class* with a common will and a class consciousness held in common. Since the battles of this past week in the tsarist empire there no longer exist scattered workers here and there, in the north, in the south, in the west, Latvian, Jewish, Polish workers, with each group acting by itself, rattling separately the chains of enslavement that they all suffer in common. Today a tight-knit proletarian phalanx is standing against the tsarist system, and by its terrible sacrifices and struggle has shown that it has understood how to reject the ancient slogan *divide et impera** —the reigning wisdom of every form of despotism. And by the blood that it has shed, which has a more powerful effect than any paper "instructions" issued by secret party conventicles, this proletariat has been forged together into *a single* revolutionary class.

Therein lies the enduring value of the last week of January, which has been epoch-making in the history of the international proletariat and its struggle for emancipation. The proletariat of Russia has stepped onto the political stage as an independent force for the first time. In the massacre of January 22, it had its baptism in blood, just as the Paris proletarians did in the slaughter of June 1848, and the proletariat of the Russian empire is now an active member of the international family of workers in struggle.

This tremendous fact does not exist for the bourgeois literati, who limit themselves to pumping out information about what they fear might be the martyrdom of Maxim Gorky, pumping it out as quickly as they can in the age-old, moss-covered common coin "for purposes of promotion."† But this was only to be expected. If one wanted to have a look in its purest form at the grotesque leaping about of today's bourgeois "intelligentsia" in the face of the historic

---

* Divide and conquer.
† Because of his participation in the struggle of the revolutionary proletariat, Maxim Gorky had already been subjected to repression by the tsarist authorities. After the workers' demonstration in St. Petersburg on January 22, 1905, he was arrested, but on February 27 he was released on bail.

drama on the Nevá, just for the fun of it, one need only take in one's hands Mr. [Maximilian] Harden's *Zukunft* [The Future], which shimmers in all the colors of "modern" decadence. This publication tries to keep in step with [Dmitri Fyodorovich] Trepov's telegraph agencies.* *Zukunft* reports that black is white, that the present political situation in Russia "meets the needs of the Russian masses," that the "poor" Petersburg workers, who are [supposedly] pious and innocent little lambs loyal to the tsar, are being "taken for a ride" by demagogues. Thus, Harden clears the name of the Petersburg proletariat before the eyes of the world, and explains that the death of 2,000 proletarians demanding freedom was actually mere child's play compared to the Decembrist revolt of eighty years ago.† Harden explains that "*even* officers of the guard" had already proclaimed the republic way back then. The standard thick skulls of the bourgeoisie were never designed, even in their heyday, to comprehend the historical grandeur of proletarian class struggle. At the very least in the period of the decline of the bourgeoisie some dwarf-sized thick skulls may be destined to do that.

But even for international Social Democracy, the uprising of the Russian proletariat is a new phenomenon, which needs to be assimilated mentally from the outset. We are all incorrigible metaphysicians, no matter how dialectically we imagine ourselves to think. In our immediate, everyday states of consciousness, we cling to the notion that things are unchangeable. And although we are the party of social progress, even for us, every healthy element of progress which has taken place unobserved now suddenly appears before us as a surprise— although it is an accomplished fact—so that at first we have to inwardly adjust our thinking patterns to this new reality.

In the imagination of quite a few Social Democrats in Western Europe, the Russian proletarian still lives in the form of the "muzhik," the Russian peasant of olden times, with long flaxen hair, feet wrapped in strips of cloth, and an expression of stupidity on his face, someone who only yesterday arrived from the countryside, a stranger and a mere visitor to the cultural world of the modern city. By no means have our people noticed the extent to which capitalism has raised the cultural and mental level of the Russian proletarian, as has also been done by the work of enlightenment and explanation carried on by the Social Democrats of the Russian empire, work performed beneath the leaden ceiling of the absolutist system of repression. We fail to notice that yesterday's muzhik has been transformed into today's intelligent worker with a thirst for

---

    * Dmitiri Trepov was the general in charge of the tsar's police forces in 1905, a hardline advocate of repressive action. He is not to be confused with Colonel Fyodor Trepov, the object of Vera Zasulich's assassination attempt in 1878. See the article below, pp. 64–8, "The Problem of the 'Hundred Peoples,'" for more about Maximilian Harden, pen name of a sensationalist entrepreneur in the newspaper business.

    † The Decembrists were a group of revolutionaries from the Russian nobility, who organized on December 14, 1825 (old style) a military uprising against tsarist absolutism and the continued reign of feudalism. The uprising was suppressed the very same day by troops loyal to the tsar.

knowledge—the big-city proletarians who are idealistic, ready for battle, and jealous of their honor. And when one recalls that the propaganda and agitation of the Social Democrats in Russia has been going on for only about fifteen years, that the first attempt at a mass union campaign in Petersburg dates from the year 1896*—then it must be admitted that in Russia the pace of this underground miner's work of social progress has been positively *"rip-roaring"* [*"rasendes"*].

All the sluggish mists and slow-brewing vapors of stagnation have suddenly been dispersed and blown away by the proletarian thunderstorm. And where yesterday the enigmatic fortress of rigid, centuries-old immobility seemed to loom like a menacing phantom over everything, there stands before us today a land thoroughly churned up and left quivering by storms of the most modern kind, a land from which the light of a mighty bonfire shines out upon the entire bourgeois world.

The Petersburg events have given us a fundamental lesson in revolutionary optimism. Forcing its way over and through a thousand obstacles and all the bulwarks set up by medievalism, lacking all the modern conditions of life politically and socially, the iron law of capitalist development has been carried through victoriously in the form of the birth, growth, and coming to consciousness of the working class. And in the volcanic outburst of this revolution it is first revealed to us how thoroughly and quickly the young mole has been working in the ground. How merrily it has worked, right under the feet of Western European bourgeois society! If one wished to use election statistics or figures about union membership or the number of existing voters' associations in order to measure the degree of political correctness or the latent revolutionary energy of the working class, that would mean trying to encompass Mont Blanc with a tailor's tape marked off in centimeters. In the so-called normal times of everyday life under capitalism, by no means do we know how powerfully our ideas have already taken root, how strong the proletariat is, and how inwardly fragile the superstructure of the ruling society already is. And all the vacillations and errors of opportunism in the last analysis result from such an incorrect estimation of the strength of the socialist movement, a subjective illusion about its *weakness*.

Therefore, the dull and vapid, shallow and empty petty-mindedness which only understands how to grasp at the copper pennies of immediate tangible results will bemoan the "misfired revolution," the "straw fire" of the Petersburg uprising, which supposedly produced no results, because, formally speaking, absolutism is still in the saddle; it still exists. No Constituent Assembly has yet been called, and the masses, which are still on strike today, will probably return

---

* In the summer of 1896 about 30,000 textile workers went on strike in St. Petersburg under the leadership of the (Marxist) League of Struggle for the Emancipation of the Working Class. They demanded a shorter workday and payment for the days of work lost during the holidays celebrating the coronation of Tsar Nicholas II. To prevent the strike from expanding into a general strike, the workers' demands were partly granted, and after three weeks the strike ended.

to business as usual tomorrow. Actually, the events of the past week have ripped a gigantic tear through the "everyday" existence of Russian society. Tsarism is no longer the same, nor is the working class, and it is no longer the same society that will emerge from the revolutionary whirlpool. Inwardly, tsarism already feels the fatal stab wound it has received, and its further existence, however brief or prolonged, can only consist of its death agony. For the first time, it has come face to face with a class from among the people that is destined to destroy it. This class has shown the world, above all, that tsarism can no longer continue to exist by virtue of the passivity of this social stratum but can only exist *against* the positive will of this stratum, a will that is now politically decisive. For the first time, the working class *as a whole* has engaged in a struggle for the political leadership of society against absolutism, and has assumed that leadership unto itself. Even the ultimate weapon of brute force, with which absolutism today has barely managed to hold on, has become shaky and unreliable precisely because this ultimate weapon has already been used. The military is certainly quite severely demoralized and politically shaken by the civil conflict—something that decades of underground agitation in the barracks had not been able to accomplish. The tsarist regime hardly dares to risk one more military test of strength with its own people.

And now the true task of Social Democracy is *beginning*—to keep the revolutionary situation going *in permanence.*[*] This task arises automatically as a counter to the inclination toward political shortsightedness, the inclination to see failure and the end of struggle exactly where the revolution is in fact just beginning. [The task is] to take steps to counteract any pessimistic downheartedness among the worker masses, for that is what reaction is gambling on; to make clear to the proletariat the inner meaning and the tremendous successes of the first attack; to dispel the hangover that the masses have been accustomed to experiencing in *bourgeois* revolutions when the goals of the revolution were not immediately and obviously achieved, and the *liberal* heroes in Russia will undoubtedly declare as early as tomorrow that those goals are unattainable—such is the fertile field of work that opens up for Social Democracy in the coming period. Neither in Russia nor anywhere else in the world has Social Democracy been able to artificially create historic moments or situations, even though youthful "mole-heroes" might perhaps imagine that they could. However, what it can and must do is make the best use of any such situation so that its historical meaning and consequences can help bring the proletariat to class consciousness and thus lead it on toward more advanced stages of struggle.

At the present moment in Russia, the most important necessity that presents itself is to stand with the masses after the first battle, explaining, encouraging,

---

[*]   This is one of the first uses of the term "permanent revolution" by any commentator on or participant in the 1905 Revolution.

and inspiring. And we will not leave *these* tasks to the Gapons—who characteristically flame like meteors across the sky of the revolution and then burn out forever. Nor will we leave them to the liberals, who after any timid attempt shrink back within themselves and clap themselves shut like pocketknives. Nor will we leave these tasks to various types of revolutionary adventurers, who are always ready to disappear just at the time when a large-scale assault is necessary. Only Social Democracy can fulfill this function in Russia, and it must be present at every particular moment of the struggle because it has a final goal that reaches over and beyond all the particular moments, and therefore it does not regard any immediate success or failure as the end of the world. In short, only Social Democracy can do this, because for it the working class is not the means to an end—political liberty—but political liberty is a means to the end of the emancipation of the working class.

The Revolution in Russia [January 22, 1905]*

Soon I'll be rattling my way toward the heights,
Soon I'll be back, gigantic, again!†

The capitalist world and with it the international class struggle seem finally to
have emerged from stagnation, from the long phase of parliamentary skirmish-
ing, and seem inclined to enter a period of elemental mass battles again. But this
time it is not the Gallic rooster that, as Marx expected, is announcing the next
dawn of revolution in Europe with a harsh and raucous crowing. In fact, it is
precisely in France that the quagmires of the parliamentary era have manifested
themselves to the most dangerous degree, and for the time being France seems
to have handed over its international leadership of the class struggle.

The starting point for the next wave of revolution has shifted from west to
east. In Germany and in Russia two mighty social struggles, two mass upsurges
of the proletariat, have now broken out almost simultaneously. All at once they
have again brought to the surface the elemental forces that are at work in the
depths of modern society, dispersing all the illusions about a peaceful and "law-
abiding" course of development, illusions that had grown up luxuriantly during
the period of international calm and now like salt spray are being scattered to the
winds in all directions. Who was it that "willed" the general strike in the Ruhr
region? Who was it that "summoned it forth"?

In this case, more than anywhere, it was everything within the working class
that is either fully or partly class conscious and organized—the religious unions,
the so-called "free unions," and Social Democracy. But at the same time, all of
these sought with great effort to *hinder* rather than encourage the uprising. If
it had been only a large strike, a far-reaching struggle over wages, of the kind

---

* This article, "Die Revolution in Rußland," appeared shortly after January 22, 1905 (January
9, old style), the "Bloody Sunday" in St. Petersburg, where tsarist forces massacred some 2,000
workers—men, women, and children. The article was first published in *Neue Zeit*, 1904–1905, No.
1, pp. 572–7. It is translated (by George Shriver) from the text in Luxemburg's *Gesammelte Werke*,
Vol. 1, Part 2, pp. 477–84. Italicized words and phrases are by the author. Luxemburg wrote a large
number of articles (in both German and Polish) in 1905 with the title "The Revolution in Russia."
For her coverage of the Russian revolution, Luxemburg introduced the *Rubrik* (standard heading
for a section of a newspaper), "Die Revolution in Rußland." Each time this standard heading occurs,
we have added in square brackets the date of the issue of the newspaper in which it appeared, to
distinguish the many different articles of this same heading. The date is given according to the
Western calendar, not the one in use in Russia at the time, which was thirteen days earlier than the
current one.

† These lines—*Bald richt' ich mich rasselnd in die Höh/Bald kehr' ich riesiger wieder!*—are
from Ferdinand Freiligrath's poem "Word of Farewell" ("Abschiedswort"). Marx printed the poem
on the front page of the final issue of *Neue Rheinische Zeitung*, May 19, 1849. By quoting these lines,
Luxemburg indicates her view that, despite all the differences, the revolutionary era of 1848–1849
was being revived in the events of January 1905 in Russia.

that break out from time to time, then perhaps it could have been slowed down, postponed, and caused to crumble. However, because the movement in the Ruhr region in its entire character—as shown by the multiplicity of the main grievances, which in their totality had exhausted the very being of the mineworker proletariat, and as shown by the indefiniteness of the final, direct causes of the strike—is not a partial fight against one or another partial manifestation, but at bottom a revolt of wage slaves against *the rule of capital* as such in its most naked form, it therefore broke out with elemental force, the way a lightning storm suddenly condenses out of the atmosphere. The conscious and organized part of the proletariat had only one choice—to place itself at the forefront of the storm wave or be flung aside by it. And the general strike in the Ruhr region is therefore a classical example,* full of instructive lessons, which Social Democracy as a party will have to assimilate as a whole, in the proletarian uprisings that will sooner or later break out, an example that lays bare the utter ridiculousness of the literary disputes over whether we can "make" a social revolution or whether such "outdated, uncivilized" methods of struggle should be thrown on the scrap heap and whether we should strive more diligently to elect larger numbers of people to parliament.

At this very moment, the same historical lesson in a different form is being presented to us in *Petersburg.*† Great revolutionary events have a certain peculiarity. No matter how much they can be foreseen and expected in broad outline, nevertheless, once they are present in all their complexity, in their specific shape and concrete form, they always confront us with a riddle like that of the sphinx, a lesson the sphinx wants us to grasp, absorb, and learn in every fiber of our being.

It is also completely clear that no justice can be done to the present Russian Revolution by such phrases as the "crashing and banging of ice floes," "the endless steppes," "weary souls weeping mutely," and the same kind of crashing and banging of literary clichés in the spirit of the bourgeois journalists, who derive all their knowledge about Russia from the latest theater production of Maxim Gorky's *Lower Depths* or from a couple of novels by [Leo] Tolstoy, and

---

*   On January 7, 1905, the mineworkers at the Bruchstrasse pit in Langendreer stopped work in protest of the lengthening of the workday and the planned closure of some mines. By January 16, about 100,000 workers from other pits had joined them. Under the pressure of these mineworkers, the leaders of the so-called free trade unions, the Catholic unions, and the Hirsch-Duncker Mineworkers Federation, were finally forced to proclaim the strike officially on January 17. After that, 215,000 more workers joined the struggle for an eight-hour work shift, for higher wages, for mine safety, and for setting aside all regulations against political activity. On February 9 the strike was broken off without any gains being made. This was done against the will of the mineworkers by the strike leadership, in which reformists and heads of bourgeois union federations predominated.

†   A reference to the demonstration of January 22, 1905 (January 9, old style) of 140,000 workers in St. Petersburg to the Winter Palace, asking that the tsar take steps to improve their conditions of life. The demonstrators, with women and children among them, were met with salvos of gunfire by order of the tsar. This bloodletting unleashed a wave of urban protest strikes and rural peasant disturbances throughout the Russian empire.

who simultaneously, with well-meaning ignorance of the same sort, slide over and disregard the social problems of both hemispheres.

Obviously, on the other hand, it would also be far too meager a tribute to pay to political wisdom and the lessons of history if we were to draw the first and most important conclusion about the Petersburg revolution in company with *l'Humanité* of Jean Jaurès, who wants to make an assertion—which for Russian absolutism is truly "devastating" and for the world proletariat so "inspiring"— that after the Petersburg bloodbath, the last Romanov has become unfit to be received in the salons of bourgeois diplomacy and that no "constitutional monarch" or "republican head of state" should consider the tsar any longer worthy of an *alliance*.*

Above all, however, it would be totally wrong for the Social Democracy of Western Europe to see in the Russian upheaval merely a historical imitation of what has long since "come into existence" in Germany and France—especially if it expressed this view with a tasteless shaking of the head like [Joseph] Ben Akiba.† In opposition to Hegel we can, with much greater justification, say that in history *nothing* repeats itself.‡ The Russian Revolution, *formally*, is attempting to achieve for Russia what the February [1848] Revolution in France and the March [1848] revolutions in Germany and Austria did for Western and Central Europe half a century ago. Nevertheless [the Russian upheaval]—*precisely* because it is a seriously belated straggler of the European revolution—is of an entirely special type unto itself.

Russia stepped onto the revolutionary world stage as the politically most backward country. From the standpoint of the development of the *bourgeoisie* as a class, it cannot withstand any comparison with the Germany of the pre–March [1848] era. However, precisely for this reason, despite all external appearances and contrary to the generally accepted opinion, the Russian Revolution of today has the most pronounced working-class character of any modern revolution up to now.

---

* In the mid-1890s, France made an alliance with tsarist Russia, directed against the German and Austro-Hungarian empires.

† Ben Akiba is considered one the founders of rabbinic Judaism. One of his reported sayings was, "He who esteems himself highly on account of his knowledge is like a corpse lying on the wayside: the traveler turns his head away in disgust, and walks quickly by." For Luxemburg's apparent confusion about Ben Akiba, given this rather derogatory comment about him, see Naomi Shepherd, *A Price Below Rubies: Jewish Women as Rebels and Radicals* (London: Weidenfeld & Nicolson, 1993), p. 114.

‡ Marx made the famous statement in his *Eighteenth Brumaire of Louis Bonaparte* that "Hegel remarks somewhere that all facts and personages of great importance in world history occur, as it were, twice. He forgot to add: the first time as tragedy, the second time as farce." Marx was referring to Hegel's *Philosophy of History*, which states, "In all periods of the world a political revolution is sanctioned in men's opinion, when it repeats itself. Thus, Napoleon was twice defeated, and the Bourbons twice expelled. By repetition that which at first appeared merely a matter of chance and contingency, becomes a real and ratified existence." See G.W.F. Hegel, *Philosophy of History*, translated by J. Sibree (New York: Dover, 1956), p. 313.

To be sure, the immediate goals of the uprising in Russia today do not go beyond a bourgeois-democratic constitution, and although the crisis can perhaps last, and most probably will last, for years, with rapid ebbs and flows taking place—the end result may possibly be nothing more than some miserable constitutional arrangement. And yet, the revolution, which is probably doomed historically to give birth to such a misbegotten bourgeois changeling [*Wechselbalg*], is as purely proletarian as any revolution up until now.

Above all, what is entirely lacking in Russia are the social classes that played the biggest role, in fact the leading role, in all previous modern revolutions because economically and politically they formed an intermediate layer between the bourgeoisie and the proletariat and served as a revolutionary link connecting both of them, thus determining the radical and democratic character of the bourgeois class struggle, through which the proletariat was won over to serve as a fighting force [*Heerbann*] for the bourgeoisie, and thus provided the necessary material mechanism for those previous revolutions. We are referring to the petty bourgeoisie. This was undoubtedly the living cement that held together the most varied social strata in the European revolutions, functioning to create and propagate the necessary fiction of a united folk ("the people") in the class struggles whose historical *content* actually boiled down to movements favoring the bourgeoisie. The same petty bourgeoisie was also the political, spiritual, and intellectual *educator* of the proletariat, and it was precisely in that February Revolution [of 1848] in which the Parisian proletariat for the first time entered into the revolutionary process with class consciousness, making a conscious distinction between itself and the bourgeoisie—it was in that February Revolution that the influence of the petty bourgeoisie became most strongly evident.

In Russia, no petty bourgeoisie in the modern European sense has existed at all. To be sure there is a small-town bourgeois element, but it is precisely here that we find the stronghold of the greatest political reaction and spiritual barbarism.

Certainly, a roughly analogous role to that of the Western European petty bourgeoisie is played in Russia by a widespread social stratum—the *intelligentsia*, those belonging to the so-called liberal professions. It is this stratum that has devoted itself for the past many years to the political education of the working people. However, this intelligentsia in itself is not, as previously was the case in Germany and France, the ideological representative of definite classes, that is, of the liberal bourgeoisie and the democratically minded petty bourgeoisie. And this is because the *bourgeoisie* in Russia *as a class* is not, to say it again, *not* the vehicle of liberalism, but of reactionary conservatism or, even worse, of a completely reactionary passivity. Liberalism, for its part, in the social witch's cauldron that is Russia, has not grown up out of a forward-looking modern bourgeois tendency among the industrial capitalists but rather out of the free-trade-minded *agrarian nobility*, which has been driven into opposition by the obligations forced upon [agricultural] capital by the state.

The work of enlightenment, training, and organization of the mass of the proletariat, which in all other countries had been attended to by the bourgeois classes, parties, and ideologists in the prerevolutionary eras—this work in Russia, from the beginning, was and remained the exclusive task of the intelligentsia— not the ideologically pro-capitalist, but the revolutionary *socialist* intelligentsia, the declassed intellectuals who themselves actually functioned as the ideological representatives of *the working class*. The sum total of class consciousness, political maturity, and idealism which was given expression in the mass revolt of the Petersburg proletariat, and which has become a historical reality, must be credited to the account of the untiring, decades-long labor, the "old mole's work," of socialist agitation, or to state it more precisely, to the agitators of the Russian Social Democratic party.*

And this sum total, when one looks more closely, is *enormous*. It is true, of course, that the first forward step by the mass of the Petersburg working class brought to the surface various peculiar odds and ends—illusions of trust in the tsar, and unknown accidental leaders left over from yesterday. As in all tremendous outbreaks of revolution, the glowing lava at first heaves up over the rim of the crater all sorts of slag or gross sediment from the depths. However, even in the case of these accidental and momentary features, these rudiments of an outdated world outlook—they were quickly stripped away in the fire of the revolutionary situation, and soon there came clearly to the fore a powerful, healthy, and well-developed nucleus of purely proletarian class consciousness along with a straightforward and unpretentious but heroic idealism *free of* all posing and posturing, and *free of* the theatrical gestures found at the "grand moments" in bourgeois history.

This is a typical and clearly defined feature of all class movements of the modern enlightened proletariat. In this connection, it is well known to anyone at all familiar with Russian conditions that once again, in contrast to the example of the proletariat in Western Europe, in the Russian *provinces* which are now following in the wake of the revolutionary wave, the proletariat in the south of Russia, in the western part of Russia, and in the Caucasus is even more clearly and definitely class conscious and better organized than the proletariat of the tsarist capital.

Certainly, this mass uprising of the Petersburg working class was an undoubted surprise for Russian Social Democracy itself, aside from the fact that the outward *leadership* of this colossal political revolt was obviously not in the hands of Social Democracy. People will therefore be inclined to say the

---

* The RSDRP, the Russian Social Democratic Party, was formed only seven years prior to the outbreak of the 1905 Revolution, in 1898. The first Social Democratic empire-wide party formed in the Russia Empire was the General Jewish Labor Bund, in 1897.

following: "Events have grown up over their heads." If by this is meant the basic idea that the elemental outpouring of this movement in its *scope* and *rapidity* has gone beyond the expectations of the agitators and also beyond the available forces and means of guiding and leading the movement, then this phrase would certainly apply to the present moment in Russia—the idea being that the Russian Social Democrats are "in over their heads" because of the overwhelming rush of events. Indeed, woe to that Social Democratic party which has *not* prepared and is not capable in a similar historical situation of summoning up its strength and stepping out onto the social stage—only *in that sense* have events "grown up over their heads." If the situation were truly beyond their capabilities that would indicate that Russian Social Democracy had failed to understand how to bring into motion a truly revolutionary *mass movement*. Revolutions are not summoned forth in a planned manner, thoroughly organized and well led. Such revolutions exist only in the blossoming imaginations of policemen with souls of the [Robert von] Puttkammer type, the standard type of Russian or Prussian public prosecutor.

But if the phrase "it has outgrown them; it's up over their heads" is to be understood in the sense that the *direction*, the *strength*, and the *phenomenon* of the proletarian revolution itself was a surprise for the political leaders of Russia's Social Democracy, that in the stormy course of events they had placed *their goals* far beyond what could be expected, then the fact is that the Social Democrats are precisely the *only* factor that counts in public life in the tsarist empire today, and for them the Petersburg events have *not at all* "grown up over their heads"; mentally they are fully masters of the situation.

A bolt from the blue—that's what the sudden mass political rebellion of the Petersburg proletariat was, not only for the mindless cretins in the gang of thieves who rule over the tsarist system, and not only for the rough crowds of thickheaded and narrow-minded industrial-moneybag folk who take the place of a bourgeoisie in Russia. It was no less so for the Russian liberals, the gentlemen who feasted *ad majoram libertatis gloriam,* who at banquets in Kiev and Odessa responded to the "intruding" working-class speakers with boos and shouts of "Get out of here!" And it was also [a bolt from the blue] for Messrs. [Pyotr] Struve & Co., who on the *very eve* of the Petersburg revolution still regarded revolutionary action by the Russian proletariat as an "abstract category" and who believed with the greatest certainty that only the liberal whining and meowing of "highly respected persons" could bring down absolutism like the walls of Jericho.

And lastly, it was not for that loose-jointed and agile stratum of revolutionaries from among the intelligentsia who wavered and swung back and forth at every moment like flexible reeds in the wind, now believing only in the saving action of the bomb and the revolver, engraved with fear-instilling verbiage; now in the

---

*   Latin for "To the greater glory of liberty."

blind revolt of the peasants and nothing else; now refusing to believe in anything anymore, but instead, howling to the heavens, mortally aggrieved; constantly shifting like quicksand, from terrorism to liberalism and back again; and the only thing they could not place a firm belief in was the independent class action of the proletariat.

And only for the rigid dogmatists of Russian Social Democracy, Plekhanov, [Pavel] Axelrod, Zasulich, and their followers—that uningratiating, single-minded company, who enjoyed the same respectful dislike in certain circles of the Socialist International as did the French "Guesdistes"*—for them, with their completely calm and rock-hard certainty, such as only a scientific, firmly founded world outlook could provide, the coming of January 22 in St. Petersburg was not a surprise. For decades they had *predicted* this, and through their class-conscious propaganda and education they *paved the way* for it and *brought it about*.

It was precisely Marx's "dogma" which enabled Russian Social Democracy to find its way in the bizarre "uniqueness" of social relations in Russia, to predict with near-mathematical certainty the broad outlines of capitalist development in Russia as early as twenty years ago, to anticipate its revolutionary consequences, and with planned activity to help make those a reality.

It was the "dogma" of Marx which enabled the Social Democrats in Russia to clearly distinguish the working class in the tsarist empire as a political class and as the only future vehicle, first for the political emancipation of Russia from absolutism, and then for its own emancipation from the rule of capital.

This same "dogma" of Marx allowed the Russian Social Democrats to defend unflinchingly against everyone and everything the independent class aims and class policies of the Russian proletariat. They deduced the *physical existence* of the working class in Russia by reading between the lines in the dry language of official industrial statistics, and were the first to describe the Russian factories. Thus, nearly every mathematically verified proletarian had to be fought over, so to speak, in the heat of polemics.

And when the always vacillating Russian intellectual was again plagued by concerns—namely, that Russian capitalism would not develop "broadly," but only "deeply," that is, that industry with its ready-made advanced technology borrowed from abroad would employ *too few* workers, so that perhaps the Russian working class would be too weak numerically to accomplish its histori-cal tasks.

And then the *cultural* existence of the Russian proletariat was revealed for "polite society" for the first time by memorable publications reporting the appearance of workers at public reading rooms, exactly like [reports of] the existence of new savage tribes in the primeval forests of the Americas.

---

*   Followers of the French Workers' Party of Jules Guesde. Luxemburg is referring to the criticisms launched against Guesde by reformist socialists over his adherence to Marxist orthodoxy. Hence her ironic comment about the "rigid dogmatists."

And then, despite the proven existence of the working class, despite the great strikes, confidence was placed exclusively in the political effectiveness of student terror.

And only the day before yesterday, despite Russia's enormous socialist movement, people in other countries believed, in truly doctrinaire fashion, primarily and essentially in the *liberal* movement in the tsarist empire.

And only yesterday, in light of the Russo-Japanese War, all hopes were actually placed, once again, not on the class action of the Russian proletariat but on action by the *Japanese.**

And at the very last moment, over and over again people refused to believe in the independent revolutionary politics of the Social Democratic working class, and only at the minimum in a mixture of all "revolutionary" and "oppositional" parties in Russia, a political *vol-au-vent*, a puff pastry filled with a stew, in which proletarian politics must be subordinated and most urgently mashed together with all the others into "a broader range of viewpoints" because of "the great urgency of the moment."

January 22 made the word into flesh and revealed to the whole world the Russian working class as a politically independent revolutionary force. It is the spirit of *Marx* that struck the first great blow in the streets of Petersburg and it is [that spirit] which, with the necessity of a law of nature, over time, in the short term or long, will win victory.

---

* The Russo-Japanese War marked the first time that a non-Western nation-state had inflicted a crushing defeat on an imperialist power.

Revolution in Petersburg!*

In Petersburg, a revolution has broken out, which the tsarist regime is trying to drown in rivers of workers' blood and kill with the silence of the press. In the capital city, the butchers of tsarism carried out a pitiless slaughter of the unarmed people. And, all the while, the press in our country and in the tsarist empire, muzzled by the censors, was forced to remain silent about these most important and dramatic historical events that will be recorded for centuries in the history of Russia and in fact in the history of the world. All the while, the press had to be satisfied with the bald-faced lies of the official communiqués. But the revolution cannot be killed by silence. And the streams of workers' blood that were shed in Petersburg will ultimately come pouring down on the house of the Romanovs. Not for nothing do the revolutionary people in Russia, with a premonition of a major historical drama soon to come, now refer to Nicholas the Second as—*Nicholas the Last*! The tsarist government did not hesitate to slaughter even women and children, who were innocently playing on the public plazas of the capital. With its own hand this government is digging a grave even for a constitutional monarchy of the Romanovs and preparing the way for a republic in Russia!

The revolution broke out totally spontaneously and unexpectedly. It was preceded by a *general strike* of the Petersburg workers, so that Petersburg was without lights at night, it had no daily papers coming out, and its factories and workshops stood empty. The revolution was started by a section of the workers who were loyal to the tsar and who wanted to combine loyalty to him with freedom! They wanted to march to the tsar's palace led by the priest Gapon, who had composed a petition that combined an appeal from loyal subjects with a plea for a little bit of freedom. But, before long, the government found itself in a very great hurry to free its loyal subjects from their naive illusions. Today, those very same workers are shouting, "Down with the tsar!" And that same Father Gapon is leading crowds in struggle against the tsar.

Because the censorship is not allowing any further news reports, thus blocking information to the general public, we are reprinting the most important dispatches from the foreign press. But even those reports are incomplete, since the government is not allowing any private correspondence, while the official Russian telegraph agency† is totally at the service of the government. As for the

---

* This article, "Rewoluja w petersburskiego," first appeared in Polish in *Z Pola Walki* of January 25, 1905. It is translated by George Shriver and Alicja Mann.

† This was formed in December 1902 as the Commercial Telegraph Agency (TTA, Torgovo-Telegrafnoe Agentstvo) under the Ministry of Finance, with the *Torgovo-Promyshlennaya Gazeta* being the main supplier of journalists. In February 1904, the agency changed its name to the St. Petersburg Telegraph Agency (SPTA). During the Soviet period, it was rebranded as TASS (Tyelyegrafnoye agyentstvo Sovyetskovo Soyuza).

activities of the revolutionary-minded masses of Social Democratic workers, and of any party committee, those can only be guessed at slightly from reports of red banners waving at barricades or of leaflets and underground writings being circulated in the capital city.*

---

*   Following Luxemburg's observations above about the tsarist regime's "Bloody Sunday" massacre in St. Petersburg on January 22, 1905 are a number of news dispatches in the order in which they appeared in the foreign press, which she presents in Polish translation from the semi-official Russian agency, Petersburg Telegraph Agency (PTA). This takes up more than a page of the Polish-language publication *Z Pola Walki* (From the Field of Battle), No. 1, a supplement to *Czerwony Sztandar* (Red Flag), the monthly organ of the SDKPiL. In addition to the dispatches from the PTA, which give a nearly hour-by-hour account of the events of "Bloody Sunday," she also cites various news items from different countries—a kind of press roundup taking up approximately two and a half more pages of the January 25, 1905 issue of *Z Pola Walki*—including reports from England, Austria (and Bohemia, part of the Austrian empire), Germany, and France.

The Revolution in Russia [February 8, 1905]*

The first mass revolutionary uprising of the Russian proletariat against absolutism on January 22 in Petersburg has been "victoriously" put down; that is,
drowned in the blood of thousands of unarmed workers, in the blood of slaughtered men, women, and children of the people. It is quite possible that for the
moment—at least in Petersburg—a break in the revolutionary movement has set
in, a pause to rest and recover. But the storm wave has flooded down from the
north, from Petersburg, across the entire giant empire and has taken over, one
after the other, all the larger industrial cities of Russia.

Anyone who expected the victory of the revolution *at a single blow*, anyone
who now, after the "victory" of the blood-and-iron policy in Petersburg, might
be inclined, depending on their partisan standpoint, either to give in to pessimistic despondency or to prematurely celebrate the "restoration of order"—such
people would only reveal thereby that the history of revolutions, whose inner
laws operate with iron necessity, is a history that remains for them a closed book
sealed with seven seals.

An eternity passed—at least when measured against revolutionary impatience and the torments suffered by the Russian people—before it happened
that beneath the centuries-old sheet of ice, the absolutist rule that covered the
country, the fire of revolution was fanned into a bright flame. The revolution will
certainly last for quite a long period of many struggles with alternating victories
and defeats for the people, costing numberless casualties, before the bloodthirsty
beast of absolutism, still dreadful even in its death agony, will finally be laid low.
We must gird ourselves for a revolutionary epoch in Russia lasting not days or
months but years, as with the Great French Revolution.

And indeed, all friends of civilization and freedom—which is to say, those
of the international working-class movement—can celebrate even now with all
their heart. In Russia, *as of now*, the cause of freedom has won, and the camp
of international reaction, as of January 22, with the events on the streets of
Petersburg, has already suffered a bloody defeat, the equivalent of the battle of
Jena.† *On that day [on January 22], the Russian proletariat as a class strode onto
the political stage for the first time.* There finally appeared on the battlefield the
force that alone is called upon by history to hurl the tsarist system onto the
rubbish heap, and is capable of doing it, and to raise the banner of civilization in
the land of Russia, as in every land.

---

*   In the German, this article was entitled "Die Revolution in Rußland." It was first published
in *Die Gleichheit*, No. 3, February 8, 1905, p. 13. It is translated (by George Shriver) from the text
in Luxemburg's *Gesammelte Werke*, Vol. 1, Part 2, pp. 491–3. Italicized words and phrases are by
the author.

†   Jena is where Napoleon's forces crushed the army of the Prussian monarchy in 1806. At
the time of the event, Hegel was writing the concluding chapters of his *Phenomenology of Spirit*.

The running battle against Russian autocracy has been going on for nearly a hundred years. In 1825, there was a revolt in Petersburg led by youthful members of the upper aristocracy, army officers who attempted to shake off the chains of despotism. Tombstone monuments to this failed rebellion, which was suppressed with brutal force, can still be found today in the snowfields of Siberia, where dozens of the noblest martyrs were laid to their eternal rest. Conspiratorial societies and anti-tsarist plots were revived in the 1850s, and again "order" and the knout soon prevailed over multitudes of desperate fighters. In the 1870s, a strong party of the revolutionary intelligentsia* oriented toward the masses of the peasantry and developed a systematic campaign of terrorist attempts on the life of the tsar. They wanted to overthrow the political system by this means. It soon became evident, however, that the mass of the peasants at that time constituted a completely disunited and unreliable element on which to base revolutionary movements. In addition, it turned out that the physical removal of individual tsars was quite an ineffective method if one wanted to get rid of the system of tsarist rule as a whole.

After the decline and fall of the terrorist movement in Russia in the 1880s there descended upon Russian society for a while—and this was also true for the friends of freedom in Western Europe—a profound despondency. The ice sheet of absolutism seemed unbreakable and social conditions in Russia seemed hopeless. And yet there came into existence at precisely that time in Russia the very movement whose outcome was to be—the events of January 22 in Petersburg—the Social Democratic movement.

It was quite a desperate idea for the tsarist government, after its severe defeat in the Crimean War [1855–56], from the 1860s on, to try and transplant Western European capitalism into Russia. For financial and military purposes, however, bankrupt absolutism needed to have within its territory railroads and the telegraph, iron and coal, machines, raw cotton, and textile manufacture. It imported capitalism using every means of plundering the people and a reckless policy of high protective tariffs. It lovingly nurtured a capitalist class, and with it capitalist exploitation, and thereby gave rise to the proletariat and its outraged rebellion against exploitation and oppression. Without knowing it, with its own hands, tsarism was digging its grave.

The role for which the peasantry had proved unsuitable in Russia became the historical task of the urban industrial working class. *This class became the vehicle of the freedom movement, the revolutionary movement.* The unremitting subterranean work of education and enlightenment by the Russian Marxists of the Social Democratic movement over a period of twenty years brought to fruition what a century of the most heroic and courageous revolts by the intelligentsia

---

*   A reference to the Populist movement.

had been unable to accomplish—to shake the age-old fortress of despotism to its foundations.

Now *all* the oppositional and revolutionary forces of Russian society can set to work—the elemental peasant rebellion, lacking clarity of purpose; the liberal dissatisfaction of the progressive landed nobility; the yearning for freedom among the educated intelligentsia, the professors, lawyers, and literati. All of them, relying on the revolutionary mass movement of the urban proletariat, can now help lead a huge army of fighters, the people as a whole, against tsarism.

But the *power* and the *future* of the revolutionary movement lies solely and alone with the class-conscious proletariat of Russia, because it alone has the understanding and is willing to sacrifice proletarian lives by the thousands on the battlefield of freedom. And no matter that the leadership of the uprising at the first moment fell into the hands of accidental figures, or that the movement might seem from the outside to be driven by all sorts of illusions, in fact it is the product of the enormous amount of work of political explanation that has been spread about by Social Democratic agitators among the ranks of the working class in Russia, by women and men who were not prominently visible.

In Russia, as everywhere in the world, the cause of freedom and of social progress now lies with the class-conscious proletariat. And it is in good hands!

The Problem of the "Hundred Peoples"*

Over the giant empire ruled by the Russian knout, the last refuge of the "divine right" of absolutism, there has finally arisen the blood-red dawn of freedom—or at least of bourgeois liberties. The emancipation of the international working class from the yoke of capitalism must necessarily be preceded by the emancipation of this latest modern-capitalist country from the iron swaddling clothes of medievalism. And, of course, at this point there is something that could not fail to happen. In reactionary circles in Russia, and internationally as well, an old familiar refrain has been struck up again—that the people are "not mature enough" for the liberties of a "civilized" bourgeois world. We know this methodology, and the wording is familiar. The same old tired game that has been played successfully many times before was bound to be repeated. The ruling classes have so long believed in the "immaturity" of the masses, their "unripeness" [for democracy], that with all good intentions they have delayed in granting them their rights for about as long as the masses have been yearning for those rights. [The rulers believe] there is something still lacking in the political insight and humane sensibility of the masses, even after the people have taken firm hold of the rights that were so stubbornly denied them for so long. For the ruling classes, it seems, the people pass the test of political "maturity" only when, to apply [Ferdinand] Lassalle's formula, the rulers get a fist in the eye or a knee on the chest.

Now, unless things go differently, the working people in Russia will without fail do both things. Surely the last remnant of their political "immaturity" has been thoroughly done away with, since that "immaturity" consisted in the naive hope that political freedom could be gained peacefully, that a peaceful working out of disagreements with the knout was possible.

Meanwhile, however, the barroom-style effusions of the bourgeoisie about the "unreadiness" of the common people for democracy are in many respects quite an interesting phenomenon in and of themselves. There is nothing more amusing than when a [Maximilian] Harden expresses his concern about freedom in Russia, and industriously copies out from his *Brockhaus Encyclopedia* information about all the Balts [i.e., Lithuanians], Poles, Finns, Jews, Latvians, Swedes, Armenians, Cheremiss, Estonians, Bashkirs, Kirgiz, Lapps, Kalmyks, and Buryats in the Russian empire, so as to reach the conclusion that this "land of a hundred peoples," with its big-city proletariat, whose "first entry into political life reeks of the barroom brawl" and the soles of whose feet are itching "to

* This article first appeared in *Die Neue Zeit*, Vol. 1, 1904–1905, pp. 643–6. The journal apparently did not give the date when Luxemburg completed or submitted this article, but judging by the contents and the historical context it was sometime in February 1905. It is translated (by George Shriver) from Luxemburg's *Gesammelte Werke*, Vol. 1, Part 2, pp. 494–9.

start looting," and with its peasants who can neither read nor write, will never be mature enough for a parliamentary system.

It is actually quite noteworthy that from the heights of bourgeois decadence, or rather from its depths, every literary rascal who lacks any bright or redeeming qualities feels called upon to hand down judgments like some final authority beyond appeal about the "ripeness" or "unripeness" [for democracy] of entire peoples. Ultimately, however, even the Kirgiz, Lapps, and Kalmyks, when their own skins are at stake, would know how to give the same kind of answer as a Kalash* woman when she was asked whether she liked her meat roasted or boiled. She coolly responded that above all she would like to be educated to learn how not to be devoured in any way.

The best bit of comedy, however, is the conceited image the bourgeoisie has of itself. God only knows what political "maturity" is required for partaking in the profound mysteries of bourgeois parliamentarism. How in the world is an ordinary Russian or Polish factory worker supposed to swing himself up to those dizzying heights? Every ordinary stockjobber and every Prussian landowner from East of the Elbe, whose worldly knowledge is limited to working a pitchfork in a cow's stall—it's as though every one of them was created with the capability of forming good judgments about the domestic and foreign policies of the state. But when it comes to a wage-working proletarian, or a simple peasant who "can neither read nor write"?

If such braggadocio† has ever been able to make an original impression and find an original form of belief, it was, at the most, during that first whirl of bourgeois democracy, while it still swelled pregnant with the glorious fruit of parliamentarism. But now, after around fifty years of parliamentary practice in capitalist countries—after the whole world has already seen through the great mystery of Sais‡ and has convinced itself that there's nothing at all behind the curtain superior to the normal mental abilities of an utterly ordinary mortal— today, the issue of the political maturity of the Russian people vis-à-vis the bourgeois constitution has left a very particular aftertaste, of fine, unintended irony and of self-satire. Often enough has the practice of German, French or Italian parliamentarism proven to the point of excess that it is exactly these

---

* A reference to the Karachay, a Turkish people living in the Caucasus region of southern Russia and northern Georgia. From the 1830s to the 1860s they carried out an active armed resistance to being incorporated into the Russian Empire.

† In the original Luxemburg uses "Renommisterie," a rather arcane word.

‡ According to Herodotus (c. 484–c. 425 BC), Sais is where the grave of Osiris is located, and on an adjacent lake "they enact by night the story of the god's sufferings, a rite which the Egyptians call the Mysteries." See Herodotus, *The Histories*, Book 2, Chapter 171, in *Herodotus*, trans. A. D. Godley (Cambridge: Harvard University Press, 1920). She is using this mythical reference to satirize the bourgeoisie's mystification of parliamentary democracy. In doing so, she will have been aware of the massive popularization of interest in mysticism, in part precipitated by the reception of Mozart's *The Magic Flute*, in which Osiris appears as a character in a number of scenes.

same classes and parties—which diligently shrug their shoulders with regret about the "immaturity" of the people—that have worked out how to simplify, for "the people," this delicate and entangled problem to the utmost degree: through all the lovely international practices of haggling for votes, and of the parliamentary cow trade. It is aimed at systematically turning "the people" into an undiscriminating and obedient voting animal. It can be hoped and can with certainty even be assumed that, in the liberated Russia of the future, a center, a national-liberal party, a class of large landowners will establish itself, to take in the poor, inarticulate "people" and to guide them with a strong hand through the dangers of parliamentary life—at least at first, until Social Democracy will relieve this class of its profitable efforts, and chase it to the devil.

Indeed, with regard to the political "ripeness" of the modern bourgeoisie, nothing betrays it so well as when it claims to predict that Russia's freedom will founder precisely on the question of the numerous different nationalities. The many Kirgiz, Bashkirs, Lapps, etc., for the most part pursue their isolated and passive existence on the periphery of the imperial territory—and, as in every modern state containing various ethnic groups or remnants, these unfortunate nationalities and subnationalities do not have any more voice in the political and social life of the country than, say, the Basques in France or the Wends in Germany.*

After all, how could twenty different nationalities, for example, elect a single parliament? How could they arrive at agreement on any unified policy? How decide on having particular laws in common and implementing them? Impossible, an insoluble problem, chaos! And that is why nothing can come of bourgeois freedom in Russia for the foreseeable future. But what is being said here behind all the verbiage? That this problem, which no parliament, no constitution, no bourgeois legal system could solve, can be eliminated in only one way, solely and exclusively—by that wonderful institution called "rule by the tsar."

It is obvious that together, all these hundred different peoples cannot make laws to be carried out in common, but the problem is readily solved when the laws are inscribed on their hundred backs by the old, reliable knout! Never would they be able to find a common language in a parliament, but living together works out as smoothly as the hum of a spinning wheel when all hundred nations have their languages taken from them, their religious faiths outlawed, and their native customs trampled underfoot.

In a word, if the "hundred peoples" were given a modern, constitutional way of life, they would in a matter of days be pulling each other's hair out, while on the other hand, at the crack of absolutism's whip, which is the only saving grace,

* The term Wends originally refers to Western Slavs living in German-controlled areas. Today's Wends are an ethnic minority living in eastern Germany.

suddenly all dangerous disputes are resolved into one harmonious round dance of reconciliation, accompanied by that old familiar song

> Dance, you Poles,
> And dance, you Krauts—
> All to the tune
> Of the same old knout*

Here again is a costly admission by the bourgeoisie that all important social and historical problems, all the *real* problems of policy and statecraft that go beyond the very crude political matters of feeding from the government trough or the equally crude art of robbing the people by forcible parliamentary means— is the admission that it does not understand any way of solving these problems other than to give up on the highly touted method of parliamentarism, to take all the headaches that world history has piled up for it and simply place them trustingly in the hands of the gendarmes. For the social question—exceptional laws; for the national question—the absolutist whip. That's how it's done in Germany, so that's how it is for Russia, they think.

The fact is that the events of the present day [in Russia] have already given a clear lesson on the only way in which the national question in its modern form will be solved and can be solved. The current revolutionary rising of the proletariat in common is at the same time the first act in the process of fraternization among the peoples of the tsarist empire. All the cunning tricks and devices of absolutism, all its arts of inciting nationalities against one another, have borne no fruit. Kishinev† has not worked. The systematic brutalizing of the Poles has not helped. The persecution of Uniates and Catholics has failed. The workers, regardless of their differing languages and religions, have become as one in the struggle against tsarism. They all felt that in Petersburg [on "Bloody Sunday"] murder was committed against the flesh of their flesh and the blood of their blood, and must be avenged. And thereby they have simultaneously fought in the best way for their proletarian class interests and the national interests of their respective peoples.

The bourgeois-nationalist movements have demonstrated their impotence vis-à-vis tsarist absolutism. The Polish rebellions in their day,‡ despite the terrible sacrifices, not only failed to shake the tsarist system in Russia but also were unable to defend the miserable constitutional liberties and autonomy of Congress Poland.

---

*   *Tanzt, o Polen—tanzt, o Deutsche, Alle nach der selben Peitsche!* The lines were written by the German revolutionary poet Georg Herwegh (1817–1875). See *Herweghs Werke in einem Band* (Herwegh's Works in One Volume) (Berlin-Weimar: Aufbau Verlag, 1967), p. 156.

†   A town in Bessarabia where a series of pogroms against the Jews occurred in April 1903.

‡   That is, the uprisings of 1830–1831 and 1863.

The Finns lived for nearly a century in their remote northern corner behind the "Chinese wall" of their historical, social, linguistic, and political isolation, and they did not concern themselves in the slightest with the rest of the empire or the revolutionary struggles inside it,* in the delusion that no storms brewing in the steppe lands of Russia could reach them or affect their autonomy, which had been "sworn and attested as their right."

Thus, both lands shared the same fate, despite their opposite behavior. Poland, regardless of its tempestuous struggles, and Finland, regardless of its proud and aloof display of loyalty to the double-headed eagle,† one after the other lost the remnants of their particularistic liberties. Their constitutional autonomy was sucked from them by the despotism rooted in the Russian heartland. The history of the martyrdom of *all* nationalities under the Russian yoke has demonstrated one truth—there cannot be autonomous freedoms in any part of the state territory as long as the ax has not struck at the root of despotism, including in Petersburg itself. But this task, to say it again, has fallen to the proletariat as a *class task* bequeathed to it by history—that is, to the working classes of all the nationalities in the tsarist empire acting in unity.

And so, it is true today in Russia as it already was in Austria that the class-conscious proletariat is the only force that represents not merely bourgeois liberties but also peaceful relations among the nationalities. It is an open secret nowadays that Austria is heading for destruction, not because of its multiplicity of nationalities but because of a *vis major*,‡ as the beer-bench politicians like to console themselves out of sheer laziness, because of the crazy administrative and constitutional system which puts the ruling power in the hands of classes and parties whose lifework it is to stir up the nationalities against one another, meanwhile excluding from rule the only class and party with substantial political influence, which in this case is truly capable of "holding the country together" because it works toward reconciling the nationalities and bringing them together—the Social Democratic working class.

In Russia too, it is not true that the bourgeois revolution will run aground and smash to pieces on the national problem, but rather the opposite; the national problem will develop on a healthier basis as a result of bourgeois freedoms, which are the product of the revolutionary class action of the proletariat.

---

* Since the beginning of the nineteenth century, Finland belonged to Russia as an autonomous grand duchy with its own Senate and Assembly (upper and lower houses of parliament). Toward the end of the nineteenth century, the tsarist rulers increasingly sought to deprive Finland of its autonomy and to subordinate it completely to the central government.

† A double-headed eagle was the symbol of Russia's Romanov dynasty.

‡ An insuperable force; a power greater than itself.

General Strike[*]

A general strike has taken over almost our entire country, from factory workers and artisans down to grade school children. This is a fact without precedent, unheard of in our history, because this is not an ordinary strike, but a revolutionary strike in the full sense of the term "revolutionary"—about this there is no doubt, and this is being emphasized sufficiently, even by our reactionary newspapers. But more should be said—*This is an uprising of the people—not an armed uprising, but one taking the form of a strike.*[†]

The significance of this historical fact can perhaps not be fully comprehended in all its ramifications. But one of its characteristic features is already remarkably evident. What has more significance than anything else, already striking everyone in the eye, is one very important feature. And that is that this movement arose completely spontaneously. Of course, no socialist organization could behave indifferently in the face of this movement. Every such organization tried, and necessarily had to try, to stand at the head of the movement and to provide it with definite political and organizational forms. And it was the obligation of every socialist organization to try and impart to this movement the greatest possible, most clearly expressed political awareness. That a general strike would break out in Warsaw—our organization already knew that the week before, because immediately after January 22, when the news came of the outbreak of a revolutionary strike in Petersburg, the idea of a general strike spread like an epidemic among the workers of Warsaw. And the same thing happened in Łódź. Thus, it became obvious that the movement would erupt on its own, with spontaneous natural force. And our organization, like any other, necessarily had to take up the idea of a general strike, to promote it, and to prepare for the outbreak of such a strike. Our organization did everything it could, everything appropriate and fitting for it to do, in order to provide planning for the coming eruption and to give it a natural political expression. But one point should be stated emphatically—this *movement grew beyond the strength and powers of all organizations*; its stormy and turbulent current overflowed all organizational banks and poured out across almost the entire country.

But in itself the fact that a spontaneous impulse was at work became a matter of great historical significance. To take away this hallmark would mean to assert that this was not an uprising of the whole people but merely some sort of conspiracy. Just as the uprising of the Petersburg workers on January 22 caused such a colossal sensation in all of Europe and in all of Russia, and attained such

---

   [*]   This article, whose title in Polish is "Strejk powszechny," is translated (by George Shriver and Alicja Mann) from *Z Pola Walki*, February 9, 1905, pp. 1–2, supplement to *Czerwony Sztandar*, No. 4, February–March 1905. *Czerwony Sztandar* was the monthly organ of the SDKPiL.
   [†]   Rosa Luxemburg's emphasis.

great political importance despite the fact that it was an outbreak that caught everyone by surprise, the fact that it was a movement not organized from above by any conspiracy or any "revolutionary" committee—in the same way the strike-rebellion in our country provided the first evidence that an uprising of the people was underway. And that is an exceptional, outstanding phenomenon in the history of our country and turns over a completely new page.

Every great popular revolution has begun in the same way, spontaneously and suddenly. And only political charlatans can assert that the outbreak of this movement was indebted to any committee or any party. Only political speculators, for their own purposes, could seek to reduce this movement to the level of a mere conspiracy, to turn it into a party-inspired movement, and thus to deny its great historical importance.

But the most important aspect of this movement, aside from its spontaneous character, is the *fact* of its *solidarity with the workers of Petersburg*. It is a response to January 22, the same natural response that we see in all of working-class Russia.

This fact was not just theoretical but tangible proof that in Russia, with our country as no exception, a single *working class* had risen up, without regard to national or historical differences. A working-class uprising in another part of the empire was enough to cause an outbreak immediately among the Polish proletariat. This is not only the result of the objective development of a bourgeois society, but also of the fact that the Polish people themselves had now set a boundary between the old Poland of national uprisings fighting for separation from Russia and the new bourgeois Poland, which created common interests between the Polish and Russian proletariat. This has now become an outstanding feature, such an obvious one that every party, beginning with the supporters of Stanczyk* and ending with the National Democrats,† acknowledged this immediately and repeated the now universal chorus that this was not a "Polish" movement but an all-Russian movement.

Without a doubt, neither our organization nor any other was, nor could be, in a position to fully take control and direct such a movement of the people. Anywhere that we might have been able to do this, we would have found ourselves unexpectedly confronted not with a bourgeois revolution but a socialist one. For above these crowds of people, who had avoided falling into the organizational hands of any party, there had arisen the spirit of Social Democracy, the spirit of solidarity and of common interests between the Polish and Russian proletariat.

---

* A conservative nationalist group in Galicia led by members of the nobility.

† The Polish National Democratic Party was founded by Roman Dmowski in 1897. It sought Poland's independence from Russia by peaceful means, but upheld a right-wing, xenophobic perspective that sought to "purify" areas of Poland (such as Galicia) by expelling its national minorities.

Before the outbreak of this general strike, our party distributed the following leaflets in Warsaw. On January 22 and 23, 9,000 copies of a proclamation by the party's Executive Committee on the subject of the anniversary of the execution of fighters belonging to the organization "Proletariat";* also, 8,000 copies of a proclamation by the Warsaw committee on the same subject; on January 25 and 26, a proclamation by the Executive Committee entitled, "General Strike and Revolution in Petersburg" (8,500 copies); on Saturday, January 28, 1,000 copies of an appeal by the Social Democratic Youth Circle entitled "To Our Colleagues," and 1,000 copies of *Z Pola Walki* (with details about January 22 in Petersburg); on Sunday, January 29, 14,000 copies of an appeal entitled "Forward to the General Strike," and on the next day the same number of proclamations by the Warsaw committee talking about the goals of the strike (printed inside our country).

All together about 43,000 leaflets were distributed, along with the supplement to our newspaper. Due to lack of space we will quote only a few paragraphs from some of these proclamations—"General Strike and Revolution in Petersburg," in which our organization as early as January 25 called for a general strike in Warsaw, while recounting the events and the significance of January 22:

Whatever happens in the coming days, the revolution cannot be stopped. The working people throughout Russia are undeniably following in the footsteps of our brothers and sisters in Petersburg. It is only to be expected that *general strikes* like the one in Petersburg will break out in other cities and that the working people will hasten to do battle for freedom. Workers! Do not be the last to take up the struggle, because the working people in all of Russia must confront and fight against the government of the tsar!

It depends on a solidarity struggle of the working people in Russia and Poland to make a reality of political freedom for all the people. Just as Social Democracy is demanding this all over Russia, so, too, working people must demand that Russia be transformed into a democratic republic, in which the working class will have the greatest freedom possible and every country within Russia, and that of course includes our country, will have its own self-government, that is to say, autonomy.†

* This refers to the Second Proletariat Party of Poland, which existed from 1888 to 1893. It was crushed owing to repression by the tsarist authorities. Luxemburg had joined the organization while still a teenager. The original Proletariat Party existed from 1882 to 1886.

† The proclamation of the Chief Executive Committee of the SDKPiL of January 25, 1905 was also reprinted in issue No. 24 of *Czerwony Sztandar*, No. 24, February–March 1905. The question of autonomy that was addressed in the proclamation was at the time not conclusively worked out within the SDKPiL. Only in 1908–1909 did Luxemburg present her views on this issue in detail in *The National Question and Autonomy*. See Rosa Luxemburg, *Nationalitätenfrage und Autonomie*, edited by Holger Politt (Berlin: Dietz Verlag, 2012). By 1908 she saw the Kingdom of Poland as being in a position to make use of territorial self-government, i.e., autonomy (which could include having certain legislative powers). In 1905, on the other hand, she spoke of autonomy only in terms

The appeal entitled "Forward to the General Strike" explained the significance of the strikes that had broken out in various parts of the Russian empire as follows:

> Go on strike, and together with the working class of the entire empire demand the following: The eight-hour day, introduced equally for all workers; a substantial wage increase, in accordance with your demands and needs and with local conditions; political freedom, which would ensure the working-class freedom of speech, of the press, of assembly and association, and the right to organize strikes, as well as participation in legislative elections. Demand that neither the tsar nor his bureaucrats should make the laws, but a Constituent Assembly, that is, a parliament elected by all the people of the empire on the basis of universal, equal, and direct suffrage and the secret ballot, so that every worker would have the right to elect representatives to a parliament and that parliament would be an expression of the will of the people in the entire empire. In order that the demands of the working class become a reality, demand the convocation of a Constituent Assembly, elected by all the people of the state, which would lay the basis for a new and better political system in the state, and which would declare a people's republic and autonomy for all the countries within the state.[*]
>
> Workers![†] The general strike quickly spread to all of Warsaw. It is a grand manifestation against the present governmental order—against the autocracy and against the present social system—really, against capitalism. Without thinking for a moment that we can overthrow that, we nevertheless fight for what is possible under existing conditions; thus we demand political freedom, that makes possible the free unfolding of our fight for our final goal, socialism; we demand the improvement of our economic conditions, even if this is only to a minor extent. We demand therefore a democratic republic.
>
> Thus, we need free and independent teaching. We need a type of knowledge that is pure and noble, not contaminated by any tendencies alien to it; we need an educational system truly capable of speaking to our minds and hearts, above all *in our own language*, and therefore only a free and democratic social system can assure us of all this ...[‡]

---

of a general principle. The changes in this conception had much to do with the sharp rejection of the idea of a federative republic made by Luxemburg and Jogiches by those opposing her position in the Polish Socialist Party (PPS) and later the PPS-Lewica (the PPS-Left).

[*]   After explaining the significance of the general strike that the Warsaw workers were calling for, the proclamation of the Warsaw committee presented the economic and political demands in more detail than had the SDKPiL Executive.

[†]   The proclamation of the SDKPiL's Warsaw committee of January 29, 1905 was also reprinted in *Czerwony Sztandar*, No. 24, February–March 1905.

[‡]   This was printed in the proclamation of the SDKPiL's Social Democratic Youth Circle, calling on the students to come out in joint action with the workers.

In this great work, turbulent but at the same time creative, we Polish people must eventually secure *full freedom of national-cultural development for ourselves.* A democratic republic in all of Russia would guarantee this for us—and one of its manifestations would be *autonomy for the Polish lands.* On the broad basis of democratic liberties, the need that is nearest and dearest to us will immediately be realized free and independent learning.˙

The Bund and the PPS also issued proclamations calling for the strike. The latter organization came out with demands that were *only economic.* Evidently this party, which is "also socialist," has more confidence in the economy's power of attraction than in its own politics, and it was afraid to bring up its own demand for an independent Polish state. It saw right away that the strike movement was not a "purely Polish" one, as the pure nationalists would say, but that it was a movement in common among the proletarians of the whole tsarist empire, and it did not know how to attach itself to that movement.

As it turns out, moreover, it was not until later, when the general strike was already coming to an end—that is, *not until Monday, January 30, that the "political declaration" of this peculiar party [the PPS] was distributed*—which had been signed with the date, January 28. That did not prevent these gentlemen from shouting in *Naprzód*† that the Warsaw workers with their general strike, which broke out on Friday, January 27, were supporting the "political declaration" of the PPS. In the same way the PPS could now issue a "political declaration" to the people of the United States and then claim that in electing [Theodore] Roosevelt as president [in 1904], they were supporting the PPS "declaration." It is true that the PPS on Saturday [January 28] at young people's rallies spoke about a "Polish Sejm"‡ but the "political declaration" addressed to the workers—and we repeat this undeniable fact with emphasis—did not show up until Monday.

And, in addition, in this wonderful "declaration" there disappeared any reference to the usual "independent, democratic Polish republic." Instead there remained only a demand for the use of the Polish language in all institutions and the removal of foreigners from government bodies in our country. In short, our demands for autonomy—but without any mention of autonomy.

And, in order to show that this whole hodgepodge§ was ready to eat, the "declaration" also included a demand for our own Constituent Assembly, but

---

* The Youth Circle's proclamation, entitled "To Our Colleagues," was also reprinted in *Czerwony Sztandar,* No. 24, p. 9ff. Immediately preceding the passages that Luxemburg quotes here, she wrote: "After many years of political inactivity we must again go into battle. We ought not to close ourselves off in our own narrow academic interests." For more about the question of education in the Kingdom of Poland, see Luxemburg's *Nationalitätenfrage und Autonomie,* pp. 223–40.

† The newspaper of the PPS published in Kraków.

‡ That is, a parliament.

§ *Groch z kapustą*—literally, pea soup with cabbage.

what that applies to remains unknown—whether for an independent Poland or a republic within the Russian state. Truly, a political "party" would have to be like this one in order not to say *clearly*, at this decisive moment in history, what it is aiming for. In other words, it would have to be a nationalist party trying to attach itself, at all costs, to the workers' movement.

The Revolution in Russia
[February 9 and 10, 1905]*

PART I

The development of revolutionary events in the tsarist empire, with the shifting of the proletarian uprising from Petersburg to the provinces of Russia and to the Lithuanian and Polish regions, has already removed all doubt about the fact that at present in the land of the knout we are dealing with, not a spontaneous, blind revolt of downtrodden slaves, but with a genuine political movement of the class-conscious urban workers, who are sticking together in the closest possible way, in an entirely unified manner, and who have come out onto the battlefield in response to the sudden signal from Petersburg. Here the Social Democrats are already standing at the head of the uprising.

And this is in keeping with the natural role of a revolutionary party at the outbreak of an open *political mass struggle*.

To win the leading position *in the country where the revolution is going on*, to skillfully make use of the first wins and losses in order to give guidance to the stream while in midstream oneself—that is the task of Social Democracy in revolutionary epochs. Not the *beginning* but the *conclusion* is what matters, and to directly affect the outcome of the revolutionary upsurge—that is the only goal that a political party can reasonably set for itself if it does not want to give in to fantastic illusions, overestimating itself, or to an indolent type of pessimism.

The extent to which this task of the party is successful, however, the extent to which the party *rises to the occasion*—that depends in the greatest degree on how widely Social Democracy has known how to make its influence felt among the masses in the *prerevolutionary* period, the extent to which it was already successful in putting together a solid central core [*Keimtruppe*] of politically well-trained worker activists with clear goals, how large the sum total of all its educational and organizational work has been. The events of the present in the Russian empire can only be evaluated and understood in the light of the previous paths taken by the workers' movement, only from the perspective of the entire fifteen- to twenty-year history of Social Democracy [in the tsarist empire].

If the question is asked, "What part did Social Democracy have in the current revolutionary upsurge?" we must firmly state, first of all, that for a long time and right down to the most recent period no one at all except Social Democracy, no other element in Russia proper, was concerned about the working class, about its cultural and material advancement, or about its political education.

---

* This article, "Die Revolution in Rußland," first appeared in two parts in the SPD's central party newspaper, *Vorwärts*: Part I on February 9, 1905, Part II on February 10. It is translated (by George Shriver) from Luxemburg's *Gesammelte Werke*, Vol. 1, Part 2, pp. 500–8.

The industrial and commercial bourgeoisie, in actuality, never bestirred itself as a class to attain even a lukewarm liberalism; and in the case of the liberals of the agrarian nobility, each stewed in his own juice, off in his own corner, and thus politically the liberals constantly moved along a virtuous straight and narrow path "between fear and hope." As political educators of the industrial proletariat they simply do not come into view. To the extent that the radical and democratic intelligentsia, however, concerned themselves about the Russian people, and they did concern themselves especially in the 1860s and 1870s, they directed their activity as well as their sympathy exclusively toward the people of the countryside, the peasantry. These Russian liberals and democrats sought to exert a cultural influence as village doctors, village teachers, statisticians in the rural bodies of "local self-government" (the zemstvos), and even as rural squires.* The peasants and Mother Earth—for the intelligentsia, those were the leverage points for lifting Russia up, and that remained true well into the 1890s. The urban industrial proletariat, on the other hand, along with modern capitalism, they regarded as something essentially alien to the Russian people, as a destructive element, as a wounded or injured part of the body politic, harmful to the well-being of the people. Even in the first half of the 1890s the spiritual leader of "oppositional Russia," the late [Nikolai] Mikhailovsky, at one time a brilliant writer, was then waging an all-out campaign against the Marxist teachings about the social significance of the industrial proletariat, and in the process he presented the evidence at hand, for example, the commercial popular songs [*Gassenhauer*] and such things [that had won favor in the cities], showing that the factory proletariat were contributing to the moral and intellectual degradation of the Russian "people."

But even *socialist* trends of thought in Russia moved along the same lines until the 1890s. The terrorist organization People's Will (Narodnaya Volya), based itself preeminently on the fiction of communal ownership of the land by the peasants and the supposed socialist mission of this "peasant commune," and this outlook still had its hold in revolutionary circles up until the end of the 1880s[†] and kept their minds trapped in the limited field of vision of the old Narodnik outlook, which had an aversion to the urban proletariat. And all this remained true [into the 1890s], even though the *political high point* of the movement that based itself on the idea of terrorism as a tactic had been reached in 1881 with the assassination of Tsar Alexander II.

Under such circumstances, the task was to get the urban modern proletariat in Russia to fight for their own social and historical rights as citizens, and to point out to them their own social and economic significance, that within them

---

*   That is, owners of country estates.

†   Marx and Engels had emphasized the importance of the communal ownership of the land by Russia's peasants as a possible basis for a socialist revolution in the 1882 preface to the Russian edition of the *Communist Manifesto*, but Luxemburg almost never references this in her writings.

there lay the slumbering kernel of a future revolutionary force, illustrating "the special connection between their status as wage workers and the political emancipation of Russia from tsarism."* The heated theoretical struggle in written form against the Narodnik anti-capitalist theories, this fight over the reality of the *existence* of capitalism in Russia, the fight over the right to even recognize its existence [in Russia], and the fight over the role of the modern proletariat in Russian society took up almost the *entire decade*.

Only toward the beginning of the 1890s, the pro-terrorist trends and pro-Narodnik prejudices among the Russian intelligentsia were finally overcome so extensively and Marx's teachings became so firmly implanted in people's minds that it became possible to begin Social Democratic practical work.†

But then, as the difficulties of practical work began, certain agonizing missteps also cropped up. To start with, this practical work more-or-less naturally took the form of clandestine propaganda in small, closed workers' circles. The Russian wage-worker proletarian, who was still quite raw, first of all had to be enlightened in a general sense, to be given the most fundamental elements of an education, before he would be capable of absorbing Social Democratic ideas. Thus, of necessity, propaganda work, with the emphasis on basic education, became transformed into an extremely slow-moving effort that made tortuous progress. Circles of five, ten, or twenty workers took years of time from the best of the combined forces of the Social Democratic intelligentsia. For a certain period of time in Russia, thanks to the conscientiousness and zeal with which this form of propaganda was pursued, with things always being carried to extreme lengths, even to the point of absurdity, an inevitable element of pedantry became mixed in with the educational work. The Social Democratic movement soon became aware that in these workers' circles socialism had been twisted almost into a caricature of Marx's teachings about class struggle. The workers in these circles were not becoming class-conscious, fighting proletarian activists, but rather something like learned rabbis of socialist doctrine, classic specimens of the well-trained "enlightened worker" who did not enter into the movement together with the masses as a whole. The opposite was true; they had been uprooted from their native soil and had become estranged from the masses.

"Grimly thorough"—that is how the first phase of Social Democratic propaganda work was evaluated and subjected to fierce self-criticism. It was judged and found wanting, and thrown out.

---

* Luxemburg does not indicate the source of this quotation.

† Plekhanov had formed the putatively "Marxist" "Emancipation of Labor" group as far back as 1884, but it largely consisted of an organization of exiles. Marxist ideas only began to seriously inform the development of Social Democratic organizations in Russia in the 1890s. The first Social Democratic Organizations in the empire were actually formed by members of such national groupings as Poles, Lithuanians, and Jews.

In place of this isolated "homework" assigned in workers' circles studying socialism, a new slogan was raised—*mass agitation*, direct engagement in the class struggle. But under absolutist rule mass agitation and mass struggle in the absence of any rights or any permitted forms of political activity, without any possibility of approaching the masses [legally], with no freedom of assembly or freedom of association (including the right to form labor unions), this slogan seemed to be a call for "squaring the circle," a crazy notion. It can be shown precisely from this example taken from the Russian experience that the material development of society is much more powerful and sensible than all sorts of "general laws" which have been instilled into the minds of many Western European Social Democrats, who regard them with holy reverence and with fixed expressions of awe on their stiff, yellow-parchment faces.

Mass struggle and mass agitation under absolutism proved to be possible after all; the problem of squaring the circle was first solved *in Poland*, where as early as 1890 the first Social Democratic organization made its appearance.* Obviously that first Social Democratic organization felt its way more-or-less empirically in relation to the economic struggle and was able to learn how to arouse a lively mass movement. The example of Poland was followed in Russia, and soon for the Social Democratic unions "the sky was hung full of violins."† By means of fresh and energetic agitation, based on immediate material needs, the masses were readily brought into motion, and after a long series of small and large strikes the agitation reached a peak with the enormous strike [of 40,000 textile workers] in Petersburg in 1896. This mass outpouring was exclusively led by the Social Democrats,‡ and seemed to crown their efforts, giving a brilliant testimony of success to the second phase of Social Democratic work.

The only thing was, the movement again ran into a snag. What happened in particular this time was that the Russian Social Democratic cart, as it rushed forward, came to a dangerous turn in the road of a different kind. In Poland, the first purely "economic" phase of agitation was overcome as early as 1893, and it morphed into an outspokenly *political* Social Democratic movement, but in Russia both political issues and the idea of socialism were nearly swamped; they nearly disappeared in the heat of mass agitation, and what remained, hardly noticed in many cases, was the development of a flat and uninspired trade unionism with a narrowly conceived fight for higher wages as the ideal, with the

---

*   This is a reference to the Second Proletariat Party, founded in 1888, in which Luxemburg was a member. It was preceded by the First Proletariat Party, founded in 1882. That Luxemburg refers to the latter as the first Marxist or Social Democratic organization is due to the fact that the former was still largely under the influence of Populist ideas.

†   "*Und bald hing der Himmel voller Geigen*," i.e., everything was going wonderfully well.

‡   The group that led the strike was the St. Petersburg League of Struggle for the Emancipation of the Working Class.

emphasis on negotiations with the factory authorities instead of the fight against the capitalist system of wage slavery in general.*

And just as, earlier, the individual worker in a study circle was led to Marx by way of an academic course which quite often took a small detour through [Charles] Darwin and the roundworms and flatworms of Professor [Karl] Vogt,[†] similarly now the workers as a whole were supposed to be led to the class struggle, like a large classroom full of pupils being instructed with the help of visual aids—they would be instructed by the gendarmes, and by being beaten by the police during strikes, and would be forced to reach a lucid conclusion on their own—to the view that the elimination of absolutism was an unavoidable necessity. In this way the groundwork was also laid to a certain extent for the tsarist regime's Zubatóv experiment.[‡]

The creatures involved at the head of these officially permitted workers' organizations gave the workers the same kind of advice that the German imperial chancellor Count [Bernhard von] Bülow recently gave in the Reichstag to the striking mine workers in the Ruhr region.[§]

For the third time, the Russian Social Democrats subjected their own methods of agitation to merciless criticism, and a brusque turn toward *clearly political* mass agitation marked the end of the 1890s. The ground was now so well prepared, the working class showed itself to be so responsive, that the idea of political struggle blazed out like lightning. With the beginning of 1901 a new phase opened—*mass political demonstrations*—linked up with unrest at the academic institutions. Street demonstrations swept from city to city like a thunderstorm, clearing the air and making it possible to breath. From Petersburg in the north they swept southward from city to city, and likewise from the west,

---

* It was this "economist" tendency that Lenin took sharp issue with in his famous pamphlet of 1903, *What Is to Be Done?*

† Karl Vogt was a German naturalist and zoologist; Darwin discussed him in *The Descent of Man*. An associate of Louis Agassiz, Vogt rejected Darwin's account of human origins in favor of a polygenist theory of evolution that claimed whites are a separate species from black Africans. Active in left-wing politics during the 1848 revolutions, he sharply attacked Marx, who responded with his 1860 polemic *Herr Vogt*. Vogt's racism and anti-Semitism notwithstanding, his avowal of atheism and materialism made him widely read in left-wing circles. In 1851, he established a single taxonomy for flatworms and nemerteans, which he called Platyelmia.

‡ On the initiative of the chief of the tsarist gendarmerie Sergei Zubatóv from 1901 to 1903, the regime made an attempt to divert workers from revolutionary struggle by allowing them to join legal workers' organizations that were controlled by the police and emphasized religious and "patriotic" values and loyalty to the government, as well as nonpolitical social and cultural activities. Radical workers, however, found ways to bring these official organizations into strikes and protest actions, especially in the south of Russia, and by the end of 1903 the government discontinued them—only to allow a similar organization to start up in early 1904, Father Georgi Gapon's "Assembly of St. Petersburg Plant and Factory Workers."

§ Luxemburg does not quote what Bülow said in the Reichstag, since it was probably quite familiar to the readers of *Vorwärts* in early February 1905, but given his conservative and chauvinist politics one can easily imagine his advice to the striking mine workers in the Ruhr region.

from Warsaw, eastward all the way to Tomsk and Tobolsk in faraway Siberia. And again the newly awakened revolutionary forces exploded into a mass strike—this time a *political mass strike* in the south of Russia, in Rostov-on-Don in [November] 1902.* In Rostov, day after day, 10,000–20,000 workers held assemblies under the open sky, surrounded by soldiers, where "newly baked, fresh out of the oven" Social Democratic orators improvised burning speeches, where tens of thousands erupted in response to the calls made by SD orators and [thus] gave a foretaste of the downfall of absolutism.

But already, for the fourth time, there arose a danger that the movement would again run into a dead end. In particular, it is characteristic of a healthy mass movement that if it does not want to slip backward, it must invariably keep striding forward, keep developing, onward and upward. And now the Russian workers' movement was rising rapidly and intensively. After the first cycle of political street demonstrations there immediately arose before the Russian Social Democrats the frightening question: "What next?" One cannot simply keep demonstrating indefinitely. A demonstration is merely one moment, an overture, a question mark. The answer hovered on the tip of the Social Democrats' tongues—but it was not easily spoken.

At that point, the war [with Japan] intervened.

With the war, the solution to the problem unfolded of its own accord. There was a word which in ordinary times, in an atmosphere of calm, a time of gray, plodding, day-to-day activity, would have a rather hollow ring to it, would smack of braggadocio [*Renommisterei*]. But with the beginning of the war it became a timely slogan, which awakened all vital spirits with the spark of life. It had the liveliest echo in the heart of the working class.

The Social Democrats of the entire empire agitated in harmonious unison with the events of the war. Providing suitable accompaniment to the thunder of cannons in Manchuria, they agitated for the idea of revolution, for open street fighting, for the proletariat to rise against tsarism. All articles in the Social Democratic papers, all the hundreds of thousands of Social Democratic leaflets—whether in Russian, Polish, Yiddish, Latvian, or other—and all gatherings concluded with a single idea: *Proletarian uprising against tsarism.* The agitating was done with bated breath, a certain anxious beating of the heart, a feeling of tightness in one's chest. Because there is nothing simpler than a revolution once it has happened, but nothing more devilishly difficult than one that is still to "be made." A thousand voices called for the revolution—and the revolution came.

It came as always "unexpectedly"—even though people had been preparing for it for roughly two decades. It came inaudibly, overnight, like a rising

---

*   In Luxemburg's original there was a typographical error, giving "1903" instead of the correct "1902."

flood—with all kinds of floating logs and junk picked up along the way and being carried high on the swollen, angrily swirling waters.

Whoever believes that the flotsam and jetsam rushing by was directing the course of the flood may believe that Father Gapon was the originator and leader of the revolution in Russia.

PART II

It is enough, then, to know the history of the Social Democratic movement in Russia to be clear in advance that today's revolution, no matter what form or outer expression it took to begin with, was not something shot out of a pistol, but rather grew up historically out of the Social Democratic movement, and that it constitutes a normal stage, a natural nodal point in the course of development of Social Democratic work, a point at which, once again, quantity is transformed into quality—a new *form* of struggle—an action that is reproduced in more intensified form on a higher rung of the ladder; it reproduced the Social Democratic–led mass rebellions of Petersburg 1896 and Rostov 1902.

If one reviews the history of the fifteen-plus years of Social Democratic practical activity in the Russian empire, then it does not appear as a series of zigzags, as it might have seemed *subjectively* at the time to Social Democrats active in the work there; it appears as an entirely logical course of development in which each higher stage arose out of the preceding one and would not have been conceivable without it. How bitterly the beginning phase of closed-circle propaganda work was criticized later by the Social Democrats themselves, but undoubtedly that labor of Sisyphus, which seemed so unpromising, produced a priceless reserve of enlightened individuals among the proletariat who later became sturdy load-bearers and solid points of support for the mass agitation based on the social interests of the working class. Likewise, the intensive economic agitation which shook up and stirred such wide layers among the workers, bringing the idea of class struggle to them on such a broad scale—precisely because of that, the later explicit and sharply accented *political* agitation found fertile soil. And so, it was possible to unleash the series of gigantic street demonstrations.

And all these phases of development taken together in their ever-increasing intensity and ever-expanding scope have created precisely the sum total of political enlightenment, capacity for action, and strenuous revolutionary exertion that led to the events of January 22 and the weeks since then. Without a doubt, it is solely as a result of the direct work of *Social Democracy* that such a strong feeling developed of everyone belonging together to the working class, of common class belonging for all proletarians in the tsarist empire, in spite of the promotion of every kind of national and ethnic hostility by the absolutist regime, so that the Petersburg uprising became a signal for a common universal uprising in all parts of the empire, a universal uprising of all the workers, not just in Russia proper but even more so in Poland and Lithuania, an uprising whose aims were held in common and whose demands were raised in common.

Of course, it does not follow that the Russian way should be *the officially authorized way*, that the historical path of the Social Democratic movement in Russia, described above, should be proclaimed as the best and only good and true way. Perhaps an even shorter and better way can be found or will make itself evident—especially now, after the fact. But social history remains an eternal primer and serves as an illustrative model which is given only once—but once it has been given, it follows, especially for Social Democracy, that the task is to learn to understand the paths of development taken so far in their actual specific inner logic, to learn and understand how things happened in each country and are still happening.

Obviously, military events and the crushing oppressiveness of absolutism, which had become unbearable, played a big and decisive role [in starting the revolution in Russia]. The only thing is that *the very fact* that the present war could bring about such an outbreak, *the very fact* that the oppressive quality of absolutism *subjectively* for the great mass of the industrial proletariat had become totally unbearable—while *objectively* this oppression had essentially always been the same as it was then—it is precisely here that the preliminary work of Social Democracy makes itself felt.

The Crimean War [1855–56] was no less devastating for official Russia, but in its day, it resulted only in the farce of the "liberal reforms" of the 1860s.[*] And this farce marked the exhaustion of Russian *liberalism*, displaying the equivalent of the total political force the Russian liberals were capable of exerting at that time, by themselves alone. The Russo-Turkish War,[†] which in terms of barbarically tossing tens of thousands of proletarian and peasant lives around— that was nothing by comparison with the present war.[‡] The Russo-Turkish War in its day caused great unrest in Russian society, but that only hastened the "comeuppance" suffered by the People's Will terrorist organization, and as the result of its blazing but brief and sterile existence, that experience revealed how little the *revolutionary intelligentsia*, which based itself on the liberal and democratic circles of "polite society," was capable of accomplishing. The party of systematic political terrorism was in its day a product of disillusion about the incapacity for organization and action of the *peasant masses* of Russia. And thus that particular social class of the tsarist empire demonstrated its historical inertness.

---

[*]   Russia's defeat in the Crimean War impelled the regime of Tsar Alexander II to embark on a series of reforms, the most important of which was the abolition of serfdom in 1861.

[†]   The first Russo-Turkish war, from 1877 to 1878, consisted of an effort by Russia to strip the Ottoman Empire of its possessions in the Balkans and the Caucasus region. Russia and the Ottomans each had some 200,000 soldiers facing each other during the conflict.

[‡]   More than a million soldiers were mobilized on each side in the Russo-Japanese War.

So then, the *present* war was able to stamp its foot and produce a revolutionary mass movement out of the earth, which immediately shook the foundations of the entire fortress of absolutism. It was precisely this present war that lent so much power to the nearly two-decades-long propaganda effort. And it shook the vast empire because it found a readily prepared and enlightened modern working class that is in a position for the first time in the history of Russia to demonstrate by revolutionary *action* the logical revolutionary consequences of this war.

It is upon the foundations of the Social Democratic workers' movement that the liberal stirrings and the democratic aspirations of the intelligentsia and of the progressive agrarian nobility first got an injection of blood and vitality, taking on some significance and acquiring some vigor. Then the proletarian revolution came precisely at the right moment—just as its predecessor of the time, the liberal zemstvo activity and the series of banquets held by the democratic intelligentsia in Russia, were threatening to shatter to pieces upon their own powerlessness, just when it was conceivable that a "deathly calm" was about to set in. Reaction would immediately be aware of that with the sure sense of smell of the ruling classes and which would encourage the rulers to put their foot down more firmly than ever. The muscular arm of the proletarian masses with one good shove set the cart rolling again, and in fact it gave the cart such a vigorous push that it cannot and will not come to rest before absolutism lies crushed beneath its wheels.

It is also true that in the tsarist empire, Social Democracy is not of the type that reaps where others have sown. It is true rather that Social Democracy deserves the credit for the sowing of revolutionary ideas and the giant work of cultivation of the proletarian soil. But the harvest also goes to all the elements in bourgeois society that represent progress, all the elements in world capitalist society—and not the least of these is *international Social Democracy*.

The Revolution in Russia
[February 11–16, 1905]*

PART I

The epoch-making events in Petersburg have not only stirred the ranks of the enlightened German working class most profoundly and aroused their burning indignation against the murderous regime of the knout, along with the warmest fraternal sympathy for the heroic fighters of the Russian proletariat. The events have also brought up a series of *questions* about the nature, significance, origin, and prospects of the Russian revolutionary movement—and it's only too justi-fied that those questions be asked. Above all for us to be clear about the inner *meaning*, the political, historical *content* of the movement—that is our first task.

The elder [Wilhelm] Liebknecht said in his reminiscences about Karl Marx that politics was for him, above all else, *ein Studium*.† And, in this respect, Marx should be a model for us all. As Social Democrats we certainly are and must always be *learners*, people who are studying at the school of that great school-mistress, *history*. In particular, for us as a revolutionary party, every revolution that we experience is a treasure trove of historical and political lessons, which broaden out our mental horizons and ought to make us more ripe and ready for our final goals, for the tasks that we ourselves must carry out. Thus the attitude of German Social Democracy toward the events in Russia must also differ from that of the bourgeois parties not only in the fact that we cheer where they foam at the mouth, if they are reactionaries, or waver back and forth between joy and despair if they are anxiety-ridden liberals, but also in the fact that we totally grasp and absorb the inner meaning of the events where they uncomprehend-ingly perceive only the externals, the clash of material forces, the oppression and the rebellion.

The most important question, which naturally must be of the greatest inter-est to us as Social Democrats, as the party of *conscious* intervention into the life processes of society, is the following:

Was the Petersburg revolution a blind, elemental outburst of the people's anger or were elements of conscious leadership and planned action also at play?

---

* This article, "Die Revolution in Rußland," first appeared as a three-part series in the SPD newspaper *Sächsische Arbeiter-Zeitung*), No. 35, 36, and 39 on February 11, 12, and 16, 1905. It is translated (by George Shriver) from the text in Luxemburg's *Gesammelte Werke*, Vol. 1, Part 2, pp. 509–18.

† That is, something to be systematically studied. See Wilhelm Liebknecht, "Karl Marx zum Gedaechtnis. Ein Lebensriss und Erinnerungen" (To the Memory of Karl Marx: A Sketch of His Life and Some Recollections), *Erinnerungen an Marx und Engels* (Recollections about Marx and Engels) (Berlin: Dietz Verlag, 1965), p. 77.

And, if the latter is true, what factors, which classes and parties, had the decisive role, and, in particular, what was the role of the Social Democrats in this movement?

At first glance, one might be satisfied to regard the Petersburg uprising as a totally planless, blind revolt, which on the one hand, under the immediate impact of developments in the [Russo-Japanese] war broke out quite unexpectedly for everyone, and on the other hand, to the extent that leadership and conscious influence come under consideration, those were in the hands of elements who in any case have no connection with Social Democracy. It is definitely a fact that at the head of the Petersburg uprising stood a legal workers' association that was established under the supervision of the gendarmerie, founded and tolerated for the purpose of "stealing Social Democracy's thunder." And, on top of everything, the whole uprising [of January 22] was led by a man who is a strange mixture of Biblical prophet and "demagogue," and for the German public is vividly reminiscent of the mystics depicted by Tolstoy.

Nevertheless, a judgment that tended to base itself solely on *these* external indicators would be totally wrong. In order to understand revolutionary moments in history correctly, one must approach them with the right measuring rod. Before all else one must approach them with a correct scale by which to measure them, and that ought not to be taken from peaceful times, from the petty workaday world of everyday life, and in particular not from everyday life in *parliamentary* countries. A real revolution, a great outpouring of the masses, is *never* and can *never become* an artificial product of conscious planning, leadership, and propaganda. One can work toward a revolution, in which case one seeks to make its objective necessity clear to particular classes in society who will act as the load-bearers of that revolution. One can foresee the general *direction* that the revolution must necessarily take, in which case one may explain as accurately as possible to the revolutionary social classes what their tasks are and what the social conditions are at that given historical moment. One can seek to speed up the moment of outbreak of the revolution, in which case, through skillful and ardent agitation one makes use of the revolutionary aspects of the situation in order to spur the popular classes to take political action.

However, once it has broken out, *particularly in its first phase*, a revolution still cannot be guided as though by command. Never can one set a definite time, a particular hour, for the elemental outbreak of great masses—as though for a theatrical performance—and even less can one lead the masses storming onto the streets like a company of well-drilled soldiers on a parade ground. The image of a revolution being "led" in this way is essentially unhistorical in its very basis, because it assumes the outbreak of the revolutionary storm all at one moment, in which the entire mass of people involved, down to the very last one, is regarded as politically enlightened and conscious of the goal, completely well organized and strictly subordinate to directions from a particular leadership body. The fact is that explosions of class struggle never wait until "all the preparatory work" has been done according to a schematic outline handed down from above, and which has been nicely run through down to the last shoelace. The piled-up grievances, the mass of instinctive, half-unclear feelings of class antagonism, are commonly much more pervasive among the people than the agitators themselves realize. And the revolution itself is the irreplaceable school that first gets rid of the remaining lack of clarity among the masses, eliminates it in the stormy process of struggle, and that which perhaps only yesterday was an *instinct*, an obscure urge or inclination among the masses, is forged in the fire of events into political consciousness.

Therefore, we see, as in *all* revolutions, that at the first moment the revolution brings with it all kinds of surprises, that it is accompanied by all sorts of quite accidental influences and accidental leaders, who have appeared at the last minute and who even rise to the top, so that to the uncritical eye they seem to be bearing the load of the revolution when in reality they are only being borne along with it. Undoubtedly, the Petersburg priest Gapon also belongs to this classical category of accidental leaders who believe they are doing the pushing when they are merely being pushed; also belonging to this category is the entire "Petersburg Workers Assembly" founded with the blessing of the absolutist regime. And it would be unpardonably superficial and shortsighted if one wished to judge the character of the whole Petersburg uprising by the fact that at its head, to begin with, there strode a clergyman with a cross and a portrait of the tsar. Such incidental influences, even if they might fall on fertile ground at the first moment among the backward-leaning mass of the people, will be *overcome* and *stripped away* in the stormy course and furious haste of revolutionary events. The masses, who went out onto the streets still believing in the tsar and still perhaps half-religious, by today have already been cured of all such illusions as quickly and thoroughly as they could never have been cured by years and even decades of socialist propaganda.

Among these same masses, however, whose mixed-up ideas are being stripped away, along with certain remnants of a backward world view—as we have said, in revolutionary epochs this can be the work of a few weeks or even *days*—among these masses accidental leaders and influences will be shoved aside and the leadership will more and more pass naturally into the hands of that solid core within the revolutionary mass which from the beginning saw clearly what the goals and tasks of the movement really were, that is, into the hands of the Social Democrats. Social Democracy consequently is the only force that deserves its predominance. It is not overcome by the situation precisely *because* it never shared in or nourished the terribly distorted illusions [that were so widespread], and furthermore, *because* it sees farther ahead, and after the first setbacks it continues to encourage the masses, who are usually dismayed and disheartened, becoming the force which fills them with courage and hope, with confidence in ultimate success and the iron *necessity* of the revolution's victory.

PART II

If one looks beyond the outer forms of appearance, in particular the first moments of the revolution in Petersburg, then it clearly presents itself as a *modern class uprising of explicitly proletarian character.*

To begin with, there is the circumstance that the Petersburg workers made their procession of supplication to the tsar with a *petition* asking for political liberties in the hope of obtaining something from his imagined goodness and understanding. On closer inspection, this petition is not at all what it was generally assumed to be under the first impression. What is decisive is not the question of the *form* the workers gave to their demands; the key question is: What were those demands? And, in this regard, the list of political reforms that the Petersburg workers carried with them in their massive procession to petition the tsar was an unambiguous expression of their political maturity and class consciousness, because this list was nothing other than a compilation of the fundamental articles of a *democratic constitution.* It was the same political program as that of Russian Social Democracy with the exception that it did not call for a republic.*

These demands for democratic liberties were, however, presented to the Petersburg workers either by the priest Gapon or by others in the "Workers' Assembly," which was tolerated by the gendarmerie and had the precise task of keeping all "politics" away from the workers, and yet these demands contained the very leitmotif of Social Democratic political agitation. And even if authentic reports by eyewitnesses had not become available, telling about the last stormy days before January 22, when at the gatherings of Gapon's "Assembly" the Social Democratic workers kept taking the floor and in presenting their ideas and proposals consistently understood how to carry their listeners with them, and thus were transformed into the actual leaders of the movement—even if these reports had not become available, the demands put forward by the Petersburg proletariat in and of themselves would be sufficient to lead us to the following conclusion—this is a product of Social Democratic educational work, which is and can only be the result of decades-long agitation, even if this outwardly might seem the work of a few days.

But it is not only the *wording* of the Petersburg demands, whose plain decisiveness and radical tone went way beyond the weak-kneed petitions of the *liberal* congresses, banquets, and "consultations," which for the most part were

---

* Translations of both the RSDRP program and Father Gapon's petition can be found in Sidney Harcave, *The Russian Revolution of 1905*, pp. 265–8 and 285–9.

ambiguous on certain points. The whole *character* of the Petersburg workers' demands as well as their *motivation*, reveals an explicitly proletarian thrust. Let us not forget that among the measures to be implemented *at once* was the demand for an eight-hour day. That stood in the forefront, and thereby the *social* side of the movement was given expression quite unambiguously, along with the *class basis* of the program for democratic liberties. Indeed, in the petition to the tsar itself, in the wording that served as an introduction to the list of demands, the strongest note that rings out is opposition to *exploitation*; the necessity for political reforms was explicitly based on *the conditions the workers faced as a class*, and in keeping with the whole sense and meaning of the petition the necessity for having political and legal freedom for the workers' movement was to enable them to wage a battle against exploitation by the dominant force of capital.

Here lies an extraordinarily clear basis for judging the whole movement in Russia. In Western Europe generally, people are too much inclined, unfortunately, to see the present-day revolution in Russia, on the basis of historical clichés, as a purely *bourgeois* revolution, going by their notion of what that is, even though this revolution in Russia was set into motion by the working class as a result of a special combination of circumstances. The idea that the proletariat at the present time in Russia is, so to speak, merely a historical proxy acting on behalf of the bourgeoisie is totally mistaken. Such a simplistic mechanical changing of places by classes and parties in the historical process—as though in a quadrille*—does not exist in any way. And, as a result of the very circumstance that in Russia today it is the working class, and one that is class conscious to the highest degree—the fact that this working class has systematically been educated by Social Democracy for many years—that such a class is fighting for "bourgeois" freedom lends the character of this freedom and the fight for it such a quality and affects this fight in such a way as to give it quite a unique physiognomy. Things are no longer as they were at one time in France, in Germany, or elsewhere in the more developed capitalist countries, [where there was] a battle for legal and political guarantees that would allow the unhindered economic development of capitalism and the political rule of the bourgeoisie. [It is no longer that], but instead it is a battle for political and legal guarantees that would allow an unimpeded class struggle by the proletariat against the economic and political domination of the bourgeoisie.

Obviously, from the formal point of view, the final outcome of the present revolutionary events in Russia is not likely to be that the working class takes the reins of power. Here, too, in all likelihood, the bourgeoisie will stand at the helm of the state and impose its political domination. But this very situation in Russia will be at an incomparably higher stage than for example in Germany

---

* A quadrille is a square dance performed by four couples.

after the March Revolution [of 1848]. It will conceal within itself from the very beginning a deep-going division, a cleavage [*Zwiespalt*], a contradiction that will decisively determine the further political development of Russia. But, even more than that, this contradiction will determine the course of events of the revolutionary period, and we presently stand only *at the beginning*. Events can take a course that will be very complicated, or convoluted, but also very important for Social Democracy.

In view of the great power of class consciousness and organization that the revolution has revealed in the entire empire since January 22 and the fact that, since the first bloodbath in Petersburg, the whole movement has without a doubt fallen into the hands of the Social Democrats—in Petersburg as well as in the provinces, in Russian-occupied Poland and Lithuania, and in the Caucasus—the further course of the revolution, which must be reckoned in years, not weeks, cannot possibly take the same path as, for example, the "mad year" [1848] in Germany. The working class, and therefore Social Democracy also, will be called upon in the most varied ways to intervene and take a hand in events, to seek much more than was ever possible before, and to carry through the immediate class demands of the proletariat to a much greater extent than was the case in any previous bourgeois revolution, because this is a *class rebellion of a modern proletariat, enlightened to the highest degree.*

PART III

In order to correctly grasp the further course of the movement, as well as its connection with its starting point, the Petersburg revolt, it is likewise necessary to have accurate knowledge about the first outbreak of the revolution, not according to its accidental and transitory appearances but according to its inner meaning and content.

Even in the first period of the revolution in the tsarist empire, which we have just been living through, the working class has already conquered and secured for itself a place in society as the *leading* class to a degree not seen before in a bourgeois revolution, and this was not the case in any previous revolution. Obviously, the modern revolutions in France, Germany, and other Western European countries were also accomplished by the laboring classes. Their blood flowed in the streets of Paris, Berlin, Vienna, etc., and their sons fell on the barricades. It was *their* sacrifice that was the price of victory for modern society over medieval feudalism. But, in these cases, the laboring classes were merely the auxiliary troops, the instruments of the *bourgeois* revolution. The spirit, direction, and leadership were determined by the bourgeoisie and its class interests were the historically driving force behind the revolutionary upsurge.

At present in Russia, things have a completely different look. Certainly, in the tsarist empire too, there are, and have been for a long time, bourgeois oppositional tendencies and groupings. In Russia itself, *liberalism* existed, and in the western part of the empire there was a national opposition, which in Poland twice led powerful uprisings—one in 1830–1831 and the other in 1863. However, it is precisely the history of recent times in the fight against tsarism that has revealed the total impotence of both these movements.

Russian liberalism, which was "bourgeois" more in the sense of not being proletarian, has long since been and has remained up to the present, not the expression of bourgeois capitalist development, but much more an expression of the agrarian nobility, which as a *grain-exporting* class was interested in *free trade* and was opposed to the extreme protective tariff policy of absolutism, which made life hard for them because it made imported agricultural machinery more expensive, and it was harder for them to win a market in foreign countries. Thus, they were hemmed in and trapped at every turn by the economic policy of the bureaucracy. On the other hand, the oppositional urban bourgeois intelligentsia, which was infuriated by the Asiatic suppression of free scientific research and inquiry, by the lack of freedom of the press, and the suppression of all intellectual life in general, and angry about the material deprivation and impoverishment of broad sections of the popular masses—all this caused it [the urban intelligentsia] to go into extreme opposition against the ruling regime. Finally, added to all this, there were various special interest groups and social strata, or partial interest groups, among the bourgeoisie: both urban and rural bodies of local "self-government,"* which were paralyzed completely, their freedom of movement being negated by the crude interference of the court camarilla. Out of all these elements there came into being, in the most recent period, a liberal ferment, in which since the war [with Japan] a sense of injured "patriotism" was mixed in and which was able to give a fairly imposing appearance at least outwardly for a time.

But how little this liberal ferment contained within itself any serious or powerful class interests on the part of bourgeois elements, how little the absolutist regime regarded it as dangerous in and of itself, is shown by the latter's treatment of it after a brief "liberal" flirtation under [Pyotr] Svyatopolk-Mirsky.[†] Despotism put an end to the whole liberal "spring" with a curt memorandum. Tsar Nicholas II scribbled with a pencil on a constitutional petition from the zemstvos, which he characterized as "tactless and impudent!" And that was the end of that. The liberal banquets, speeches, and resolutions were simply forbidden, and the liberals among the gentry and intelligentsia were completely at a

---

*   That is, the urban dumas and the rural zemstvos.

†   Svyatopolk-Mirsky became minister of the interior in 1904 and attempted to introduce liberal reforms—such as permitting the local zemstvos to meet regularly and lifting some restrictions on freedom of the press and religion. After accepting responsibility for the massacre in St. Petersburg of January 22, he was replaced in February 1905 by the more conservative Alexander Bulygin.

loss about what to do. They stood there perplexed and helpless. The fact remains and must be underlined with all possible emphasis that one moment before the political rebellion in Petersburg the liberal ferment had been brought to a standstill, and it visibly felt completely paralyzed by the powerful trump play made by absolutism. If the working class had not made its unexpected appearance at that moment, liberalism would have pulled down its sails again for the umpteenth time, and the whole oppositional period would have ended with a splendid triumph for absolutism. However, in a single instant, there was a complete change of scenery. The tsarist regime, with complete self-satisfaction dismissed the whole campaign of the liberals scornfully and contemptuously as nothing but scum and condemned it as "impudent," as something like a naughty child's prank. But with the entry of the proletarian masses onto the stage, even when the workers had scarcely begun to move and were drawing up their "humble petition," the regime knew that for absolutism this was a matter of life and death. And it played its final trump card right at the start, with its very first move—mass murder, open warfare against the proletariat. With that, the freedom movement was transformed at one blow into a direct confrontation between absolutism and the working class, a direct settling of accounts, and at that point the liberalism of the bourgeoisie, nobility, and intelligentsia was pushed back into second place.

This was even truer in the non-Russian provinces of the tsarist empire, particularly in Poland. Here, nationalism had fallen into a blessed sleep, no longer the powerful opposition movement of the nobility, whose last uprising had been in 1863. In "Congress Poland" in the 1860s and after, the capitalist mode of production not only broke down the separatist aspirations of the nobility but also placed the modern bourgeoisie at the pinnacle of society, and in the interest of capitalist profitmaking this bourgeoisie has become the most ardently loyal supporter of the throne. Leftover elements of the national movement have been stripped of any vital force, and only persist in an entirely dispersed form among the petty bourgeoisie and urban intelligentsia. The current revolutionary period in the tsarist empire has also become a "trial by fire" for this superficial remnant of a national movement. It turns out that not once has any stirring of vital character shown up among these remnants. It is self-evident that if ever there was a moment for a national movement to come forward, it was precisely during the period of liberal ferment inside Russia itself. It was as though that moment had been created for that very purpose. That would have been the time to take advantage of the universal ferment for the sake of national aspirations. However, during the period of open liberal protest, banquets, and resolutions Poland was precisely the only province of the tsarist empire in which the bourgeoisie, the nobility, and the intelligentsia kept themselves completely passive. No loud voice made itself heard, not even to express some liberal sentiments. No such voice came from any bourgeois or petty bourgeois stratum.

And it was only with the general uprising of the Polish working class, with that purely proletarian outpouring of solidarity with the Petersburg proletariat, only then within "Congress Poland" did a revolutionary stream join the overall flood within the tsarist empire as a whole. And this uprising was just as free of national separatism as similar risings among the Jewish, Latvian, and Armenian proletariat in recent weeks. This was a unified modern class movement of purely proletarian character, which brought together all groups of workers in the tsarist empire into one united army fighting against despotism, and thus it assured to the working class the leading position in society as the only politically active factor, and one that was fully revolutionary.

Terror[*]

Not since the successful attempt on the life of Tsar Alexander II in 1881 has any terrorist act in Russia had such political resonance as the killing of the Moscow bloodhound Sergei Romanov.[†] And, from the standpoint of moral gratification, which every upstanding and right-thinking person is bound to feel toward this deed of liberation, the assassination of Grand Duke Sergei is on the same level of importance as that of Interior Minister [Vyacheslav von] Plehve last year.[‡] People now breathe more easily and the air seems cleaner after one of the most repulsive beasts of the absolutist regime has come to such a fitting end, being put to death out on the street as a mad dog would be. These feelings are so natural for any decent civilized person that universally in our press and virtually on everyone's lips the deed in Moscow is perceived as an entirely moral act of vengeance, as retribution for crimes committed. However, the broader significance of this important development in the revolutionary battle in Russia is not exhausted by the entirely understandable feeling of moral gratification. A political judgment must be made that stands apart from one's immediate impressions and feelings about this most recent terrorist deed.

From a *political* standpoint, in the present situation we must first of all look at terror in a substantially *different* way from the way it was viewed in *earlier* times. The actual terrorist movement which preached and practiced terror as a systematic means of political struggle was born historically out of pessimism, from loss of faith in the *possibility* of a political *mass movement* and a genuine people's revolution in Russia. Terror as a system was thought of naturally as a method to be carried out only by particular individuals from among the revolutionaries and directed against particular individual representatives of the absolutist regime. It essentially stood in *opposition* to [the idea of] a *mass movement* of the working class, whether or not the terrorist fighters were aware of this themselves, whether they would admit this or preferred to keep such thoughts out of their minds.

From this standpoint and on this basis, Social Democracy has long since fought against the terrorist tactic, particularly in recent years, because it was

*   This article first appeared in the SPD newspaper *Sächsische Arbeiter-Zeitung*, No. 42, February 20, 1905. It is translated (by George Shriver) from the text in Luxemburg's *Gesammelte Werke*, Vol. 1, Part 2, pp. 519–22. The dates given are according to the Western calendar (i.e., new style), rather than the calendar then in use in Russia (old style).

†   On February 17, 1905, Grand Duke Sergei Romanov, governor-general of Moscow province, who was a member of the ruling family and one of the most reactionary representatives of the tsarist regime, was assassinated in the Kremlin by Ivan Kalyaev, a member of the Socialist Revolutionary Party.

‡   Plehve, who headed for a time the dreaded secret police, the Okhrana, served as interior minister from 1902 and was assassinated on July 28, 1904 by the Socialist Revolutionary Yegor Sazonov. In 1881, Plehve was assigned the task of investigating the murder of Tsar Alexander II.

bound to have more of a soporific and paralyzing effect, rather than rousing action—even though it might evoke strong feelings of moral satisfaction in each individual case. In effect, this method of vengeance by the terrorists invariably awakened vague hopes and expectations—especially among unclear and wavering elements—that they could rely on the miracle-working invisible arm of the terrorist "avengers." This weakened the clear understanding of the absolute necessity for, and the exceptionally decisive importance of, a mass movement among the people, a *mass revolution of the proletariat*.

The events of January 22 and the weeks following it have fundamentally changed the situation. The proletariat has already appeared on the battlefield, the gigantic power of a people's revolution has already made itself evident to the entire world, and its significance cannot be shaken by any individual act of terrorism. To be sure, political weathercocks will perhaps make their appearance in this situation also, and they will loudly assert that they are totally inspired by [the terrorist method] and place their hopes in this noisy, noble, and abrupt language of bomb throwing, and perhaps they will imagine that mass action has already played out its role sufficiently in the tsarist empire, that the *realization* and *completion* of the revolutionary period must now give way to the terrorists' duel with the remnants of a badly shaken absolutist regime. Nevertheless, it is to be hoped that such distorted views will remain limited to only a few individuals and that Social Democracy, both in Russia and in other countries, will not disregard the lessons of the weeks that have just transpired since January 22, that Social Democracy will understand and continue to profit by the fact that the lessons of the last few weeks are not merely transitory but that they *continue* to be lessons to be learned from.

And, above all, these lessons point toward the fact that in Russia *only* the people's revolution, and nothing else, is destined to bring to completion the overthrow of absolutism and to make a reality of bourgeois-democratic freedoms. In that respect, even the most successful acts of terrorism will less than ever be capable of changing anything. This is not to say, of course, that individual acts of terrorism from now on would be meaningless or useless. It is not a question of either praising terror to the skies or condemning it, but of grasping its proper role and quite limited function in the present situation. Today, after the mass people's revolution has already begun, terror is and can only be a secondary *episode* in the struggle. And this is so in two respects, in terms of space and of time. *In terms of space*, it serves only as a single sword stroke, however brilliant and lightning-like, upon a huge battlefield where the proletarian mass struggle takes place; and, *in terms of time*, it is bound and limited to a certain particular phase of the revolution by its very nature.

Terrorist acts have political significance and will find a sympathetic echo in broad circles of society only up to the point when absolutism decides to take the road of concessions. As a reply to the brutal efforts to drown the revolution in blood, the terrorist blows have a liberating impact on people's spirits. On the whole, however, when absolutism is forced to recognize the ineffectiveness of wielding the knout, and it takes a turn onto the road of constitutional concessions, even if they are weak-kneed and vacillating, at that point terror will inevitably lose support and will not find a favorable atmosphere. With the beginning of this second phase of the revolution, which may take a shorter or longer time before it sets in, the role of terror will be played out. But the revolution as a mass movement, as the rebellion of the entire proletariat, will by no means come to an end at that point. On the contrary, only then will commence the ever-more exclusively proletarian fight to push ever-more widely and broadly for the total elimination of absolutism, and to broaden as much as possible the share that the working class takes in achieving political liberation, and to assert its role in making counter moves against the unavoidable reactionary reversal of position and retrograde movement that is sure to come from the bourgeois democrats and liberal elements after the first victory of the freedom movement. In short, the proletarian revolution in Russia has all its struggles still ahead of it and must pass through all the phases of *rebellion by an entire class*, [and this will continue] until the proletariat has pushed forward this moment in history to the farthest point possible in the direction of pursuing its own class interests. On this basis and within the framework of this immense revolution of the people, individual acts of terror are the equivalent of upward sizzling bursts of flame in the midst of the mighty blazing sea of a forest fire.

The avenging hand of the terrorist can here and there accelerate the disorganization and demoralization of absolutism. But, with or without terrorism, only the massive arm of the revolutionary working class can put an end to absolutism in the tsarist empire and make freedom a reality.

Religious Procession of the Proletariat[*]

Nothing is so fitting as a time of revolution for freeing our thinking at one blow in all directions from the vision-narrowing blinders of the cliché. Real history, like the creative power of nature, is much richer and more bizarre in its twists and turns than any pedant's systematizations and classifications.

When the first tidings of the pilgrimage of the Petersburg workforce to the tsar reached ears outside of Russia, they generally stirred very mixed and undoubtedly despondent feelings. A strange image of primitive naivety, concurrent with great tragic threads, hidden behind a mystical, strange and estranging veil, was offered up to the realistic eye of the sober Europeans, who shook their head with regret at the calamitous deception of a whole people. It was only when the cannons were moved forward in the *Vassilevsky Ostrov* district, and only when we first realized the literally "bloody" earnestness with which tsarism received the peculiar procession of pilgrims, that we were forced to think of Paris, of the barricades, and of all the modern, western European reminiscences. And when we heard that in all other cities in Russia the rising took the accepted form of the general strike, including mass dissemination of Social Democratic pamphlets, we were entirely reassured that this was not an oriental caravan, but rather a modern, proletarian revolution. With all great respect for the aforesaid pamphlets, it would be a disastrous error to trick ourselves into believing that these writings alone transported the revolutionary moment into the political movement. In the Russian Revolution that we are experiencing right now, as elsewhere, the task has fallen to Social Democracy of formulating the revolutionary aspect of the proletarian rising, of guiding it towards clear expression, of liberating it from the confines of an elementary form of eruption. The revolutionary core has been present in all proceedings from the start—as present in the general strike that spread like the wind, as in the supplication of the Petersburg proletariat itself.

There is an illusion that what was actually to blame for the distressing political situation in Russia was a "misunderstanding" between the monarch and the people, a "misunderstanding" that was instigated and maintained by the systematic intrigues of "advisers" to the throne and by the entire court camarilla, who interposed themselves between the people and the misguided ruler, "the prince." This illusion by no means needs to be regarded as an exotic outgrowth

---

[*]   This article first appeared in *Neue Zeit*, 1904–1905, Vol. 1, pp. 711–14. The title in German, "Der Bittgang des Proletariats," is difficult to translate. Literally, a *Bittgang* is "a going" (*gang*) with "a request" (*Bitte*), but the term has strong religious connotations, sometimes meaning "pilgrimage." It can be rendered as "pilgrimage of supplication" or as "procession of pilgrims." J. P. Nettl gives the wording as "The proletariats' pilgrimage of grace"; see his *Rosa Luxemburg*, Vol. 2 (London and Toronto: Oxford University Press, 1966), p. 893. The article is translated (by George Shriver) from the text in Luxemburg's *Gesammelte Werke*, Vol. 1, Part 2, pp. 523–7.

of Russia's peculiar conditions and its dimly lit world of mysticism. It is not at all especially necessary for us in Germany to go hunting far out in the world to find an analogous example. There is, after all, an old but always new item that can be requisitioned out of the treasure chest of political wisdom that belongs to German *liberalism*, one which liberalism periodically narrates to itself and others, to the effect that the whole miserable state of affairs in Prussian Germany results mainly from the fact that the Kaiser is "poorly informed by his advisers," which denies him the possibility of coming to an understanding with *the people* based on true inner feelings. Nothing in this profound conception is changed by the fact that in this case what they mean by "the people" is none other than the "Free Thinker" liberals themselves and the great pain they suffer over the fact that Jewish judges are not allowed into the upper levels of officialdom and other fundamental evils of the existing social order.

But there is a vast difference between the political weight of such illusions in the heads of the liberal bourgeoisie, who are in decline—and the upward-striving modern proletariat. The theory of the "prince misled by bad advisers" is an entirely adequate political expression of the aspirations that dwell in the hearts of the German Free Thinkers of today. The pleading knee-bending before the throne and the old wives' chatter about the small blemishes that mar the beauty of this best of all possible worlds in which we live—that is the *ultimate expression* of liberal politics. When these are put together they produce a complete harmony and absolute equilibrium, which has guaranteed to the above-mentioned type of politics a hundred years of undisturbed existence, and always with the same lack of success, and yet it ensures that the liberals will evermore gaze hopefully upward, hoping that the heavenly dew of the Kaiser's blessing will descend upon them, patiently wishing to themselves all the while that the liquid that was actually coming down on them from above was a little bit different.

On the other hand, a glaring contradiction exists between the myth of the "good prince"—between that and the historical aspirations and class interests of the modern proletariat. Those who were appalled from the very first moment by the humbly pleading attitude of the people in Petersburg, the people who were damp-eyed and with great ceremony carried images with the sign of the cross in their hands when they began their march to petition the tsar—the people who are so appalled have overlooked the essence of the matter while focusing on the outward appearance, the external spectacle, in particular, the fact that the humble "petition" that this mass of people was taking to the tsar consisted in nothing other than a request that his holy majesty would kindly with his own hands as supreme autocrat surrender all his powers and abdicate as monarch "of all the Russians." It was a request to the autocrat to put an end to autocracy, a request to the wolf to please stop eating sheep, a request that from now on he should prefer tender vegetables instead of warm blood. It was a radical political program clothed in the form of a touching patriarchal idyll. It was an exertion of class pressure of the most modern kind by a proletariat that had become mature to the fullest extent, but it was decked out in the fantastic form of a colorful Bible-bangers' procession, an "amen march." And it was precisely this contradiction between the revolutionary essence expressing the interests of the proletariat and the primitive outer coating, the illusory tale of the "good prince," which was bound to end up with the flaming sparks of revolution in the streets as soon as it was tested against reality.

But this test had to be made sooner or later. Despite the entire elemental lack of clarity among the mass of the people amid stormy times, the working class pressed for this conception to be tried out and tested in practice, and it took this seriously and even sacredly, whereas the liberal bourgeoisie always had a cynical and cowardly attitude toward their "articles of faith," abandoning them on every suitable occasion. The Petersburg proletariat was serious about its faith in the tsar, and it was with astounding simplicity and great decisiveness that the workers headed for their destination in front of the autocrat's palace. Here, however, it immediately became evident that the divine graciousness of the monarchical idea absolutely does not exist—and this holds true everywhere, not only in Russia—the monarchy cannot exist without its protective screen of being misled by "bad advisers," by the court camarilla, and by the bureaucrats in general. Without this salutary screen of semi-darkness the monarch cannot hide himself from "his children," the people, "his loyal subjects." It was enough that the aroused masses had come to this idea, which was childish from the formal point of view, but in fact was frightening and dangerous—and it was enough that they should come to meet face to face with the "father of their country" and to try to make a reality out of the myth of a "social monarch" or a "social emperor." And thus this movement, with the iron law of necessity, was transformed into a confrontation between two mortal enemies, a collision of two worlds, a clash between two historical eras.

Only the indestructibly bigoted narrow-mindedness of today's Free Thinker rabble can indulge in the absurd idea that what was to blame for the revolutionary outcome of the episode on the Nevá [on January 22] was that Tsar Nicholas did not come out in a good-natured and kind way to meet with the "rabble" and lend his ear to their complaints. They are implying that if only he had done that, everything would have been fine. The theatrical performance of the Free Thinkers imagines that a hospitable reception for the proletarian procession was unfortunately disrupted by the blue pills* flying through the air. This presumably prevented the drama from ending with a truly liberal curtain call—a reconciliation between the "father of his country" and his beloved children, in which tears

---

* *Blaue Bohnen*, or "blue beans," is an archaic German colloquialism for bullets. Given that Luxemburg often uses sardonic and ornamental language, it seems appropriate to use a historical U.S. colloquialism here for bullets—blue pills.

of joy would flow together from both sides with immortal expressions of good wishes. This is a blessedly moving piece of folk theater from the "Land of If Only" [*Iffland*]—just like the plays performed countless times by German liberalism ever since those glorious days of the memorable Mayor [Karl von] Rotteck of Freiburg in 1833 right down to the present times.*

The truth is that history has already played out this particular drama on one occasion, and, in fact, it played out the beginning of the show exactly according to the liberal recipe. On October 5, 1789, the proletariat of Paris, with the women in the lead, made a procession to Versailles, so that they could personally confront their thickheaded Capetian monarch, have a few words with him face to face, and bring him back to Paris. Initially this affair transpired in a wholesome spirit and everything was quite orderly. Louis XVI gave his assurances, though with somewhat trembling lips, that he did want to return to be with his beloved Parisians "full of trust and feelings of satisfaction," and soon after that [in July 1790] a grand ceremony was held on the Champ de Mars, with oaths of mutual loyalty being exchanged along with the swearing of eternal vows. It seemed that the ceremony would never end; it was like a scene between a love-struck twelfth-grade boy and a blushing teenage girl beneath flowering lilac bushes. And yet this good-natured Louis XVI quickly evolved, in the course of his playacting with the people that had begun so idyllically, and, in the end, he totally and completely lost his fat head.

The Russian Revolution began differently, but it could easily have taken a similar turn. And one can grant to little Nicholas and his advisers that they judged more correctly than the German liberals, who are also advisers from a distant corner to an oppressive despotism, in that they grasped much more quickly the dangerous revolutionary content beneath the humble speech of the Petersburg proletariat—much more quickly, in fact, than many Western European Social Democrats, because the tsar and his advisers decided at the *very first step* taken by the proletarian petitioners to respond by using the *last trump card of despotism.*

If Nicholas and his beloved relatives and official colleagues wanted to learn something from the most recent events, the first thing they would learn is that they should not threaten the strikers and those who are openly engaged in struggle; they should not threaten *such* workers with "the most severe punishment up to and including the dungeon," but they should undertake to foster the belief in the "good but misguided prince" and disseminate it more widely among the

---

*   Karl von Rotteck, a pioneer of liberalism, served in the Baden state legislature from 1819 to 1840, first as the leader of the lower chamber, and later the leader of the upper chamber. In 1832, because of his progressive views, he was stripped of the academic chair he had held since 1798 at the University of Freiburg im Breisgau. As a result, at the beginning of 1833 he was elected mayor of Freiburg, but the Baden state government refused to certify his election. Rotteck decided not to seek election a second time because of the danger that this would trigger a conflict between the city and the state.

people. From such heretical false doctrine there would later arise at the appropriate moment the dangerous notion among the mass of the people that the "father of their country" should be confronted face to face and he should be "petitioned" for various things, the kind of things a person doesn't like to hear, such as cutting off his own head.

And we ourselves can once again learn from the Petersburg example. Among the many lessons that come to us from the Russian Revolution is to separate the content from the often-contradictory external form in revolutionary mass movements, instead of mixing them together and confusing them with one another. If it should ever occur to the proletariat anywhere to march spontaneously to the honorable legislative assembly and to government buildings with fiery resoluteness and in the most polite way to request that the political helm of state be transferred magnanimously from the hands of the ruling classes into those of the working-class masses and that, otherwise, like the Petersburg workers "we would prefer to die," and even if Pastor [Friedrich] Naumann himself marched at the head of the procession,* then we could calmly hang a placard upon the fortresses of capitalist wage slavery, the same placard that appeared resplendently on the plaza after the storming of the Bastille: "This is where the dancing was done."

---

* A friend of Max Weber, Naumann sought to develop a social liberal alternative to the Social Democratic movement by addressing issues of inequality and social justice from a middle-class perspective.

Under the Sign of Social Democracy[*]

The events of the last few weeks constitute an epoch in the history of the Polish working class, in the history of our society, and in the history of absolutism. The uprising of the Petersburg proletariat on the memorable day of January 22, suppressed with the blood of thousands by the bashi-bazouks of tsarism,[†] set off further uprisings [in the twinkling of an eye] by tens of thousands of workers throughout the empire. In virtually all provinces and territories of the tsarist state, in dozens of industrial centers, the working class walked out en masse at the first news of the Petersburg uprising and rose up with the slogans, *Down with absolutism! Long live political freedom and a Constituent Assembly!*

The Polish proletariat took its place with honor in this workers' revolution. All of Warsaw, all of Łódź, all of the Dąbrowa mining region, almost all the provinces, stood up as one, ready for an all-out battle for full political freedom. Wherever smoke rose from factory chimneys, wherever the wheels of industrial machinery were turning, wherever the hard-working hands of labor wielded hammers, everywhere there rose up at a moment's notice to join in the battle of solidarity—the gigantic army of exploited proletarians. They showed their oppressors and exploiters that neither oppression nor poverty could suppress the spirit within them, but on the contrary those things aroused in them both revolt and hatred against the yoke of capitalism and against the vile yoke imposed by the tsarist government's gang of hoodlums.

With pride and joy, Social Democracy can look upon the memorable history of this wonderful workers' revolution. Because, in this revolution, the things that our party has been saying to the Polish working people for the last twelve years, our words and teachings, have become a reality.

On January 22, the proletariat of Petersburg, having covered the paving of the streets with its blood, showed that in the fight against absolutism it stood at the front lines. And the coming-out of the whole gigantic army of workers, both Russian and Polish, in response to the call from Petersburg, showed that the Polish worker understands and feels that the Russian proletarian is his brother and comrade, the blood of his blood and the bone of his bone. In spite of all differences and distinctions of nationality that, for many years, tsardom (on the

---

[*]   This article is translated (by George Shriver and Alicja Mann) from the first two pages of *Czerwony Sztandar* (Red Flag), No. 24, March 1905. The title in Polish is "Pod znakiem Socjaldemokracji."

[†]   Bashi-bazouks were irregular troop units serving the Ottoman Empire in the nineteenth and early twentieth century. They were notorious for their brutality. In her "Junius Pamphlet" (*The Crisis of German Social Democracy*), Luxemburg used the expression "the maintenance of bashi-bazouk rule in Asia Minor." See her *Gesammelte Werke*, Vol. 4, p. 109. These irregular troop units received weapons and provisions from the government of the Ottoman Empire, but were not provided with regular pay.

one hand and Polish nationalists on the other) has tried to emphasize and instill among the working people, the workers of the entire empire formed *one single fighting army*, a single working class, aspiring to a single common goal, fighting for one and the same demand, with all their strength in common, jointly by all their means, for their common interests!

Here, at this point, it became palpably evident that in political events, economic development had welded Poland together with Russia by means of capitalist economics. During the time when Poland was led by the nobility, in the first half of the previous century, our country was a completely separate entity, an independent society that was forcibly held to Russia by the violence of the tsarist state and the absence of forces of resistance inside Poland. The entire policy of the nobility was expressed in the aim of breaking away from Russia.*

In order to create for itself a strong base of support in Poland, the tsarist government in the 1880s busily developed capitalism in our country; it raised up a new breed, the bourgeois class, nursed it along and made it rich at the expense of the blood and sweat of the Polish worker. These calculations were not disappointing. Bourgeois Poland ceased to be rebellious and insurrectionary; it became a domestic in the service of the tsarist knout. The Polish bourgeoisie

---

* The Warsaw Archiw Akt Novykh (AAN—Archive of Modern [Historical] Documents) contains a short document by Luxemburg about the history of Poland, originally written for the use of Franz Mehring. This handwritten manuscript, which could have been written in 1901 or 1902, was in the possession of Jürgen Kuczynski, who in 1952 turned it over to the Polish government. In it Luxemburg presents the following thoughts about the Polish nobility: "Everything that in Western Europe the Third Estate carried out against the nobility, here it was undertaken by the nobility itself. With the change of personnel, the methods utilized were also turned upside down. Factories producing luxury goods were supposed to bring about mass production on a scale equivalent to the period of manufacture [in Western Europe]. On the threshold of the nineteenth century there was a desire to summon cities into existence by reintroducing guilds, and to introduce an urban bourgeoisie into the political system by raising it to noble status. Legislative power was to be adapted to the needs of the times by limiting universal suffrage to the landowning nobility, and the government was to be strengthened and centralized—by the transfer of all its functions to a parliament [dominated by the nobility]. In short, they sought the salvation of Poland not in forward movement but in a return to forms that had long since been outlived. The Polish nobility was blamed for indulging itself in unheard-of class egoism. On the contrary, no other social class, to our knowledge, was ever doomed by history to such a state of self-abnegation as the Polish nobility. In the absence of a Third Estate it had to set itself against itself—like the thesis [and antithesis] of Hegel—and to fight against itself with a whole series of reforms. The Polish nobility had to, so to speak, in order to ultimately save itself as a class, dress itself in the costume of the Third Estate. But this historical costume drama, as at a Shrovetide carnival [*Fastnachtspiel*], betrayed itself in its end result. In the famous constitution of May 3, [1791], which supposedly was intended to save Poland, there now emerged, instead of modern social classes, whose spirit was supposedly expressed in the reforms [of that time], the same old two leading characters on the political stage—the upper nobility and the lesser nobility. Whereas the Polish nobility believed it could overcome itself as a class, it actually brought about only the victory of one clique (or faction) of the nobility, the lesser nobility, over the other, the upper nobility. And Poland could not be saved by that means." This document is listed in the AAN in Warsaw as item 2/1223,63/III-1, sheet 14, pp. 12–15.

married into and fused together with the Russian tsarist system, and in the process, they were jointly robbing the Polish proletariat and sucking the living juices out of it. By carrying out jointly the shameless capitalist exploitation of workers, it fused together with the Russian bourgeoisie in the joint robbing of the consumers, under the joint protection of the tsarist autocracy and its foreign and domestic policies.

These calculations were not disappointing for tsarism—the capitalism bred by tsarism in Poland eliminated the rule of the nobility, as well as the national uprisings [led by them] and all active tendencies toward separation from Russia.

But this sowing yielded quite a different crop from the one the tsarist government expected. From capitalism there grew up in Poland, as in Russia, not only a servile bourgeoisie but also a revolutionary working class. And while uniting the Polish bourgeoisie with the Russian by the same lust for enrichment through exploitation, tsarist absolutism united the Polish proletariat with the Russian by a common need for class struggle against exploitation and by a common aspiration for political freedom.

Sowing and cultivating a *single* capitalist bourgeoisie in the entire empire, promoting the interests of the exploiters regardless of national differences, also raised up a single class of the exploited without regard to differences of nationality, one single working class both in Russia and in Poland, for which freeing itself from the clutches of absolutism is a matter of life and death.

The policies of the tsarist government, with the help of the bourgeoisie, buried the aspiration toward national independence, but it bred up and cultivated a working class that in its drive for political freedom is now going to bury absolutism itself.

It is precisely this fact that has passed a death sentence upon the tsarist government in the last few weeks. This time, the soldiers, once again acting as the blind and obedient agent of the criminal tsarist regime, seem to have defeated the workers' revolution. Once again, temporarily, the gang of highway robbers prevails. But its death agony and the birth of political freedom for the 130 million suffocating under tsarism are only a matter of time, and not a long time. The uprising of the working class through the length and breadth of the tsarist empire revealed to absolutism the force that will strangle it and hurl it to the ground. This time, it is no longer a prediction for the more-or-less distant future, as stated by Social Democracy for many years, knowing the direction in which the development of social conditions was moving. This time it is no longer hundreds of proletarians inspired by socialist ideas that have entered into unequal battle, no longer thousands of the most enlightened leaders of the proletariat who have come out to demonstrate. It is now *hundreds of thousands*, the *masses* themselves, and the wide and deep sea of the proletariat, which has poured forth from its ocean bed. The working class itself, in its essential core, has risen up to fight for political freedom.

But that means it was the working class as a whole, that social and political force, that showed the world [the strength of] an unprecedented general strike in the last weeks of January and in February. When the factories, workshops, mines, streetcars, and railroads stood still, when the banks, stores, telephones ceased their activities, when the electric lights and gas lights went out, when industry, commerce, and communications were brought to a standstill—at that point both the government and the whole society immediately realized that the working class by its voluntary service under the yoke of capital was holding up the entire present-day state. No government can maintain itself or even exist if the entire working class in the entire state has decided to wage a war by any and every means and is shaking the very foundations of society to their depths.

Such a deadly weapon has not been available to any modern revolution until now. The barricade was the primary, if not the only, means of struggle in the revolutions of the nineteenth century, revolutions that served the interests of the bourgeoisie, in which the proletariat had not yet separated itself as a distinct class from the lower strata of the petty bourgeoisie, but followed their leadership into battle as a blind instrument of bourgeois rule. At present, in the Russian state, the general strike has become for the first time the initial phase of combat for this revolution, in which, also for the first time in history, the proletariat is going into battle as an independent class, conscious of its own separate interests.

With this first attempt by the Russian and the Polish proletariat to go into action with this weapon in their hands, and with the readiness to carry the fight through to the end in a life-or-death struggle, the fate of tsarist rule has already been sealed.

Absolutism understands this and feels it. Whereas in regard to the demands and resolutions of the "zemstvo" liberals the cretin-tsar contemptuously allowed himself to scribble that they were "tactless and insolent," and from on high the ministerial flunkeys ordered the liberal gentlemen to make no further mention of freedom—the news of the workers' uprising instilled mortal fear into the camp of the governmental gang of thieves. That is precisely why they are raging so furiously, why they resort to the most horrendous and hideous acts of mass murder, because they have understood that their end is drawing near, that the day of judgment is coming for them—victorious popular revolution.

Thus, just as in Russia, the coming-out of the workers also saved the honor of Polish society. Whereas in our country the bourgeois classes were moldering in the quagmire of capitalist self-enrichment while humbly kissing the knout, and our intelligentsia on the whole failed to rise to the level of even such a liberal movement as we saw in Russia, the tsarist gang of robbers could look down contemptuously on Polish society, lulling itself with the thought that it had very strong pillars of support for its rule. In the Polish press, for example in *Dziennik Poznański* [Poznań Daily], advice could be given to Tsar Nicholas, at the first news of revolution in Petersburg, that in order to save his crown and his head he should quickly come from the banks of the Nevá to a loyal place—Warsaw!*

Today, thanks to the heroic coming-out of our revolutionary working class, Poland has all at once found itself in the front ranks of the fight against absolutism and for political freedom. Already, in today's bourgeois Poland, the fates have given political leadership to the class of the most oppressed and exploited—to the Polish proletariat—just as in Russia [this has happened] for the Russian proletariat. In the last few weeks, the workers, both Polish and Russian, have given proof that they have matured enough to assume the role assigned to them by history. By their struggle, full of dedication, perseverance, and dignity, they have won themselves a place at the head of society, which until now regarded them merely as brute labor, like caryatids† holding up, on their slavishly bent-over necks, the grand edifice of the rule of capital.

The revolution has been started, but has not yet ended. In front of the united working class of the tsarist empire there stands a whole series of battles against absolutism, still to be fought. The momentary lull is merely an interval between the proletariat's first assault on the fortress of despotism and the further assaults to come. This interval should be used to intensify our agitation to the highest degree. The present situation places obligations on Social Democracy that are extraordinarily difficult and important. The first wave of general strike and workers uprising, which flowed from Petersburg through the entire empire, including through our country, was to a large extent spontaneous. Not in the sense that the workers rose up blindly, without any understanding of what was going on. On the contrary, the slogans and ideas of the struggle, which were circulated widely by Social Democracy, were so much "in the air," were such a natural expression of the workers' needs and had so much entered into the flesh and blood of the proletariat, that the only thing needed was an initial nudge for the entire mass of workers instinctively to rise up to do battle in response to the news from Petersburg. Social Democracy in our country, just as in Russia—as is usual for all true revolutionary mass movements—could barely keep up with, and give expression to, the feelings and desires of the masses, which had erupted volcanically.

---

*   *Dziennik Poznański*, No. 22, January 26, 1905, contains an article entitled "Z Warszawy" (From Warsaw), p. 3, with the following passage by Luxemburg: "As for the tsar, and indeed for his personal security and that of his family, a place could be found after the conclusion of peace ... In such a large state, and one which today is so badly torn apart, undoubtedly the Kingdom of Poland is the only place in which security would be complete, regardless of whether it was in Warsaw, Skierniewice, or Spała. It remains doubtful, however, if anyone in the circles close to him would recommend this salutary step." The newspaper *Dziennik Poznański* was published in Prussian-occupied Poznań. Spała was a small location, in central Poland, near Piotrków. Trybunalski was a hunting lodge serving the tsarist court; it was laid out in 1884, with a group of one hundred Cossacks assigned to it.

†   A caryatid is a sculpture of a female that serves as a column. The most famous examples are built into the south porch of the Erechtheion in Athens, erected in the fifth century BC.

Certainly, this mass uprising of the Petersburg working class was an undoubted surprise for Russian Social Democracy itself, aside from the fact that the outward *leadership* of this colossal political revolt was obviously not in the hands of Social Democracy. People will therefore be inclined to say the following: "Events have grown up over their heads." If by this is meant the basic idea that the elemental outpouring of this movement in its *scope* and *rapidity* has gone beyond the expectations of the agitators and also beyond the available forces and means of guiding and leading the movement, then this phrase would certainly apply to the present moment in Russia—the idea being that the Russian Social Democrats are "in over their heads" because of the overwhelming rush of events. Indeed, woe to that Social Democratic party that has *not* prepared and is not capable in a similar historical situation of summoning up its strength and stepping out onto the social stage—only *in that sense* have events "grown up over their heads." If the situation were truly beyond their capabilities, Russian Social Democracy would have failed to understand how to bring into motion a truly revolutionary *mass movement*. In general, revolutions are not summoned forth in a planned manner, thoroughly organized and well led. Such revolutions exist only in the blossoming imaginations of policemen with souls of the Puttkammer* type, the standard type of Russian or Prussian public prosecutor.

But, if the phrase "it has outgrown them; it is up over their heads" is to be understood in the sense that the *direction*, the *strength*, and the *phenomenon* of the proletarian revolution itself was a surprise for the political leaders of Russia's Social Democracy, that in the stormy course of events they had placed *their goals* far beyond what could be expected, then the fact is that the Social Democrats are precisely the *only* factor that counts in public life in the tsarist empire today, and for them the Petersburg events have *not at all* "grown up over their heads;" mentally they are fully masters of the situation.

In Petersburg, the uprising of the proletariat was spontaneous and the signal given for it was by a purely accidental leader [Father Gapon], even if the goals, the program, and thereby the *political character* of the uprising, as has been described in very precise news reports, were directly dictated by the intervention of *Social Democratic* workers. In the rest of the tsarist empire, and particularly in Poland, the initiative and the leadership of the movement from the very start was in the hands of the Social Democrats. Obviously, even here, not in the sense that the Social Democrats of their own free will conjured up a mass strike out of nowhere merely at their own discretion. They had to adjust themselves everywhere to the pressure from the workers, who in reaction to the very first news and even rumors about the events in Petersburg became greatly

---

* Robert von Puttkammer was the conservative minister of the interior in Germany who enforced Bismarck's antisocialist law and forcibly suppressed strikes during the 1870s and 1880s.

aroused and instinctively seized on the idea of solidarity action. But it was the Social Democrats who immediately gave the necessary expression to the stormy outbreaks of the masses, provided political slogans, and gave the movement a clear direction.

Now there has begun an important second phase of the revolution, one in which Social Democracy must aim at meeting events head-on in a planned way, to try as much as possible to take in its hands the helm to steer the movements of the masses and give direction to the next revolutionary action. And we can cope with these tasks only by the most persistent and strenuous *work of organization and agitation.*

On this ground, fertilized and enriched by recent events, every day ought to bring us so much work and such a good harvest in terms of the enlightenment and rallying of the workers as would require a month or even a year in different times. The more effectively and vigorously the revolutionary core succeeds now in building a road for the *party organization* to reach the masses, the quicker the victory and the fewer the casualties we will suffer in the next confrontation with absolutism. In the ordeal by fire of historical events, the program and tactics of Social Democracy have withstood the test splendidly, and our comrades can and should intensify their energy and enthusiasm ten times over, to summon the mass of the proletariat to come stand beneath our banner. And, on this banner, is written in the blood of the workers, shed in the unforgettable recent battles, for the entire Polish people and society to see—*under this sign thou shalt conquer!*

---

*   Here Luxemburg gives the Polish wording, "pod tym znakiem zwyciężysz," for the ancient motto (fourth century AD) attributed to the Roman Emperor Constantine I, *in hoc signo vinces.*

A Test Based on a Sample[*]

The recent, and still ongoing, general strike in Russia is in its scope and duration the most powerful example of this form of struggle that has ever been seen. There is really not a single industrial city in that gigantic empire in which the working class as a whole or at least those in several of the most important branches of industry have not stopped work, and in many regions, for example in Łódź and in the Dąbrowa mining region in Poland, the strike has lasted for several weeks. The strike has spread from industry to sectors of commerce and trade and to the banks. Every day there comes news, particularly from Poland, about new sectors of economic life that have been seized with the strike fever. Even insurance offices, drugstores, and photography studios have gone on strike. And in many cities, Moscow, Petersburg, and Warsaw, the police themselves are threatening to strike. Simultaneously, this giant movement is played out with every nuance from purely political and revolutionary demonstrations to purely economic wage struggles, and yet the basic tone is being set by the political demand for freedom and the demand for the *eight-hour day*, that is to say, the most important socioeconomic demand.

In its huge dimensions and in the multiplicity of accompanying features, the present movement in Russia offers a veritable mine of data [*Fundgrube*] for the study of the nature and political significance of the general strike.

In the most thoroughgoing way, the experiences of recent times have made a clean sweep of the pedantic-mechanistic conception, according to which the general strike is treated exactly like getting ready for a journey back in the days of our great grandmothers when the route was planned out years in advance and talked over thoroughly in the family circle months before it was time to bring down the trunks and load them for the journey. A real general strike, which shakes up an entire country or an entire region, cannot be organized and led that way—with "the idea of a general strike" being posed on an abstract basis as some sort of panacea, although a discussion on this basis has been going on for so long at party gatherings and in articles, just like the discussion about the "idea" of a consumers' union, until the working class has become convinced of the excellence of this "idea" and at a certain moment decided to actually begin a general strike.[†]

---

[*] This article appeared in the SPD newspaper *Sächsische Arbeiter-Zeitung*, No. 52, March 3, 1905, under the title, "Eine Probe aufs Exempel." It is translated (by George Shriver) from the text in Luxemburg's *Gesammelte Werke*, Vol. 1, Part 2, pp. 528–32. In this article, one can see what Luxemburg meant by her title—a test of various conceptions, "the idea of the general strike," against the *actual* events, i.e., "based on a sample" of current reality—namely, the general strikes in the tsarist Russian empire of January–February 1905.

[†] Luxemburg is probably referring to the German mineworkers' general strike in the Ruhr region in January–February 1905.

A mass uprising as a large-scale political and social class movement lends itself to being "made by command" as little as does a revolution. A political general strike, which can be unfolded in an orderly way, the way a screen can be unfolded in a living room and then later folded up and put away in a corner, the kind of general strike that took place at one time in Sweden, is only a demonstration, which undoubtedly has great importance as a review of the organized and disciplined forces of the proletariat, but does not represent a direct method of struggle. On the contrary, in a revolution, the general strike is only one phase, one stage in the direct struggle, and the transition from general strike to street fighting cannot be avoided any more than an exact borderline can be drawn between the one and the other.

Here again, the general strike does not flow from a preconceived *plan* worked up by Social Democracy, and it does not occur because it has been chosen as the "best" method after a long discussion. It should be noted that there is no country in which so little has been written up to now about the question of the general strike and so little discussed as in Russia and Russian-dominated Poland. It arose —as it must arise everywhere where there is a genuine revolutionary movement—of its own accord out of the economic conditions of the working class. The mass of the proletariat, in ordinary times, is welded to the chain of capital. It is tied down in factories, workplaces, and mines, and at the same time it is isolated and fragmented. If the working class wishes to undertake any kind of direct political mass action, it must before all else lay down tools and leave the factories, workplaces, and mines. Thus, the general strike is the first step and the natural initial form of every open mass action, or at any rate of every modern revolution in the streets.

On the other hand, however, the economic and social pressure of capital remains the great underlying foundation and basic fact of modern public life, and therefore, in every direct revolutionary action of the *mass of the workers* nowadays, there must be a powerful interplay between revolutionary action and the economic struggle, which by nature finds expression in a tremendous strike movement.

In this sense, the present revolution in the tsarist empire is a new phenomenon, which is likely to be far more typical for future revolutionary struggles of the European proletariat than the earlier bourgeois revolutions in France and Germany. A mass uprising of this kind never played a major role in those earlier revolutions. Certainly, in those cases the revolution expressed itself in the form of an economic slowdown, which was always a natural consequence of the political and social upheaval. However, up until now, that slowdown was only the negative expression of the disruption of the ordinary course of daily life; it made its appearance as a passive *result* of revolutionary times, but it was not by itself an active means of struggle for the revolution. This is connected with two aspects of the historical circumstances. First, neither during the time of the March Revolution [in 1848] or at the time of the great French revolution [1789–1793] was large-scale industry so highly developed and so decisive for the economic life of society as it is in present-day Russia. Second, and this is closely linked with the first factor, no modern revolution up until now has been so explicitly and exclusively *proletarian* as is the current one in the tsarist empire. In earlier revolutions the decisive factor, not only politically but also economically, was the *petty bourgeoisie*, and it goes without saying that direct action by this latter class could not take the form of a general strike. Today's revolution in Russia is not only a purely political struggle against the autocracy but also at the same time—as every workers' movement at present must be—a more-or-less class-conscious struggle against the rule of capital, and the combination of these two aspects finds its adequate expression in the enormous and powerful general strike crisis which today is shaking the gigantic Russian empire.

Therefore, this crisis is also a brilliant refutation of the pedantic conception which holds that all prospects for a revolutionary general strike can be dismissed out of hand with the dry formula that if we were to develop so "broadly" as to be able to call forth a real general strike in the whole country, it would no longer be at all necessary to do that, since we would already be strong enough to take political power and simply do away with the existing dominant social order. In Russia the totality of the conditions, which according to this conception are indispensable for a general strike to come into existence—building up trade union organizations and extending them to nearly all of the working class; a completely unrestricted right of association (i.e., the right to form or join a union); the absence of a strong modern form of militarism; well-filled trade union coffers, thoroughly well-tested union discipline; and so on and so forth— the *totality* of those conditions was lacking. In Russia, there was and still is, at any rate from the standpoint of the broad masses, what amounts to an absence of any trade unions at all; there are no union treasuries; no right of association; no training and experience on the basis of large-scale political or even economic struggles. But there *is* militarism in very brutal forms. On the other hand, despite all these circumstances, the general strike has been as absolute and as exemplary as has ever been seen in any European country; and yet, at the present moment, the people [in Russia] are not in a position to take political power and carry out a socialist transformation. Even to accomplish a political revolution, powerful and sustained struggles will still be necessary in Russia, and the general strike merely constitutes an introduction to those struggles.

At any rate, one thing is clear. This kind of powerful mass strike movement, in the *political* sense as a disruption of the entire social life of a country, is only conceivable as a *historical moment* in a revolution and therefore as a phenomenon in which Social Democracy can have exactly as much or as little room for active planning or for conscious leadership as in a street revolution, a phenomenon which itself can arise only on the foundation of a great social crisis, which affects the deepest vital interests of the broad mass of the people, but not on the basis of partial and secondary issues, such as, for example, the right to vote in elections for the Prussian Landtag.* To the ruminating academic this matter might seem to be an uncommonly important question, but the masses could never be stirred from the bottom of their hearts by that.

It is not by systematic propaganda for a general strike for its own sake, as a miracle-working form of the proletarian class struggle, and also, on the other hand, it is not by merely engaging in the beehive-type of activity of endlessly building new trade union cells, but it is by educating and awakening the masses along the lines of developing their revolutionary understanding—the understanding that in all the most vital political and social questions and decisions they can only rely on themselves, on their own direct action—it is only in this way that we ourselves lay the groundwork for that moment when the workers as a class will be ready, for the sake of their true vital interests, not only to "stop every wheel from turning" but also if necessary to shed their blood fighting in the streets. To sense the onset of such a historical moment, to take a bold initiative giving expression to that, and to lead the working class energetically and decisively through a general strike with all the consequences of that struggle, and not to stop halfway with some tricky talk about "strategic withdrawal"—that is the actual great task of conscious action to be carried out by Social Democracy.

---

*   This was the regional legislature of Prussia.

A Political Settling of the Score[*]

In the last week of January and in February, we have experienced the first period of political revolution in our country and throughout the Russian state. The most pressing need now is to ensure that our working class, as closely as it can, will become aware of the full significance of the events that have already occurred, as well as the enormity of the tasks it is still facing. For the mass of the proletariat to become aware of its own class movement and its own aspirations at any time is the main basis for, and the actual essence of, *Social Democratic agitation*.

The first fact that caused these memorable revolutionary events to catch the eyes of the world was the mass character of the fight for political liberation by the proletariat of Petersburg, and coming right after that the other regions and cities of Russia. The second fact was the immediate solidarity action of the *Polish* proletariat throughout the territory of our country, along with the proletariat of Lithuania, Latvia, and the Caucasus.

Evident for all, the vast mass of proletarians of the Russian state appeared here for the first time in the political arena, without distinction of nationality and religion. Workers who were Russians, Poles, Lithuanians, Armenians, Latvians, Jews, acted as *a single working class*, striving for one common share in a joint political purpose, a brotherhood united by the strongest ties in one common class struggle for their political and economic liberation.

For Social Democracy, which bases its program and tactics on the development of society, the occurrence of these facts was not any surprise. Even when the worker in the heart of Russia was apparently dozing under the heavy yoke of capital and despotism and gave only weak signs of protest, when in the midst of proletarian Russia only single, isolated, heroic units here and there jumped to take up the fight, and the mass seemed to be mired in lethargy, we, the Polish Social Democrats, loudly and emphatically repeated to the Polish workers—do not be discouraged by this lack of motion. The Russian proletarian will wake up to the fight and a powerful basis will emerge for him to partner with us to throw off the bondage of absolutism and launch a broad struggle for complete liberation from capitalist exploitation!

As we have pointed out to the Polish worker, the Russian proletariat belongs to a class that is his natural ally and companion, a class with which the Polish worker shares interests and *a common political task*, and the most immediate of these is the overthrow of absolutism and the winning of the broadest political freedoms. In 1894, at the first *national congress* of Social Democratic workers in Warsaw, on March 10 and 11,[†] the following resolution proposed by

---

[*] This article is translated (by George Shriver and Alicja Mann) from *Czerwony Sztandar*, No. 25, April 1905, pp. 2–5. The Polish title is "Obrachunek polityczny."

[†] The SDKP had been formed a year earlier, in 1893, through a fusion between the Union

the Executive of the Social Democracy of the Kingdom of Poland (SDKP) was unanimously adopted:

Considering:

(1) That the overthrow of the tsarist regime and winning a democratic constitution, which would ensure the working class the greatest influence on the affairs of the whole state, of each country, and of each municipality, is just as urgent a necessity for the Russian proletariat as it is for the proletariat of the Kingdom of Poland;

(2) That the Russian workers, when they have spoken, have expressed clearly that overthrowing tsarism is recognized as their political program;

(3) That joining the efforts of the proletariat, both Polish and Russian, will enable both to accelerate the fulfillment of these political tasks;

[Therefore] the First Congress of the Social Democracy of the Kingdom of Poland expresses its complete political solidarity and brotherhood with the Russian workers, considering this necessary for the mutual goal of speeding up the moment when the labor movement in Russia takes the form of a widespread mass political agitation; and in conclusion, it strongly recommends that the Russian comrades join in the mass celebration of the May Day holiday, which—despite the persecution by the same government, under whose weight all of Russia is groaning—has been established on a firm foundation in our movement and has played such a salutary role in it.

Here Social Democracy proclaimed its views at a time when the social-patriots of the PPS were persistently and tirelessly trying to convince the Polish worker that the mass of Russian workers were mindless cattle, that they are accustomed to the yoke of bondage, and that any serious help from them in the fight against absolutism cannot be expected. Similarly, just like the bourgeoisie, which is blinded by its class ignorance, [the PPS] does not see and persistently denies that from out of the clouds of capitalist domination there will slowly and unmistakably arise the historic sun of socialist liberation. In the same way, the social-patriots, blinded by their nationalistic position and petty–bourgeois chauvinism, have refused at all costs to acknowledge that the Russian proletariat is certain to, with the certainty of iron necessity, develop class consciousness and political struggle. Their entire program of rebuilding Poland, all their political existence, they based on stagnant deadness in Russia. Here is how the PPS described the social relations in Russia toward Polish workers in its newspaper *Robotnik* [Worker] in February 1894:

---

of Polish Workers and remnants of the Second Proletariat Party. Rejecting the principle of national self-determination for Poland, it defined itself largely in terms of its opposition to the policies of its main competitor on the left, the PPS.

The many years of Tatar domination over Russia left its traces in the customs of the Russian people, accustomed them to slavery, to the worship of authority, obstructing all education. Breaking free of the Tatar yoke, then merging the Russian lands into a single state—that strengthened the power of the Russian tsars, and for the eyes of the people showed the delights of their power, so that they bowed their necks humbly and without protest under the tsarist yoke.

In this way, the social-patriots have tried to destroy and silence in the Polish proletariat all faith in the revolutionary movement of the Russian proletariat. This way is the basis of telling our workers that the desire to overthrow a despotic government in Russia does not have any possibility, therefore the Polish worker should turn his back on the Russian worker and strive only for rebuilding [Poland]. Back in *January* of this year—and the Polish workers should remember this fact—in the same January when the pavements of Petersburg were covered with the blood of thousands of Russian proletarians marching for freedom, the PPS wrote in [its publication] *Przedświt* [Before the Dawn] that "the Russian worker has not yet awakened for the fight!"

This party, which calls itself a socialist and working-class party, was so full of disbelief in the power of the workers and socialism in Russia, that it felt far more related to the bourgeois *liberalism* of the Russian nobility than to the Russian labor movement. On the eve of the revolution, the PPS workers rushed to join in brotherly alliance, not with the Social Democratic Russian workers, but with *the Russian liberals*. And the spiritual kinship of our social-patriots with the Russian nobility worked to the effect that the Russian liberals, in the very same January, wrote and preached a few days before the outbreak of the revolution in Petersburg, word for word as the PPS did, that the Russian worker is not yet mature enough for such political struggle!

The Russian workers' revolution struck like a bolt from the blue on the heads of the false prophets of the PPS, breaking into splinters their twelve years of speculation about stagnation in Russia. And while, for so many years, they promised the world that at the first opportunity they would "lead a popular uprising," the Polish people, meaning the working class, did rise up—but not to rebuild Poland, but for a shared revolution with the Russian proletariat to overthrow tsarism. Polish workers showed with their January's solidarity action that the teachings of the social-patriots, which promoted for years the distinctiveness and national and political differences between the Polish and Russian workers, that their [PPS] voices were voices crying in the wilderness. The Polish proletariat did not allow itself to be driven from the class path toward nationalism, and at the first signal from Petersburg hurried to bring their lives in sacrifice for the common struggle, under a common banner!

This does not mean that the 350,000 Polish workers who with their general strike expressed their political and class solidarity with the Russian proletariat did so under the direct influence of Social Democracy. The uprising, the strike movement, was not everywhere a consciously political movement. A large part of our country's workers walked off their job, not fully knowing what the true purpose was and what the causes of this general movement were. But where the workers were aware of the *political* tasks of the moment, they were calling only for political freedom throughout the entire tsarist empire, and there was no request for the independence of Poland. At no point, even for a moment, did the workers have the illusion that they were aiming for a national uprising to "drive out the Muscovites" and to rebuild Poland.

There is not a single class or party in the entire society that would be deluded in this respect. Not a single voice is raised in the bourgeois press or in the foreign press that would claim that the recent gigantic workers' movement in our country had, even in part, the character of a national uprising. Everyone understood and saw clearly that it was not about a *national* movement, or a separatist movement, but a struggle of the proletarian *class*, in which ethnic differences disappeared, and it became only the working people, exploited and oppressed, demanding political freedom throughout the land of the tsars. Even where the emerging Polish workers were quite or half unaware of the political objectives of the movement or did not clearly understand, they tried not to denounce what they were demanding. And yet there was one great outstanding fact seen and felt by all—*solidarity with the workers' uprising in Petersburg.*

The news of the massacre in Petersburg reached the most remote parts of our country; it moved all layers of our proletariat. The close relationship of the strike movement in our country with the Petersburg events was known to all. And that fact alone already constitutes the political core of the recent general strike; this fact alone already gave the whole movement, in large part a spontaneous movement, the character of a class struggle of the proletariat for political freedom in the spirit of the program of Social Democracy and against the nationalist aspirations of the social-patriots.

That is the way it was; the movement was like all truly revolutionary mass movements, largely spontaneous and instinctive. And only reckless politicians like those of the PPS, who do not depend on an understanding of the true meaning of their own struggle, are busy throwing dust in the eyes of the bourgeois intelligentsia and with their false power blabbing about their claim that all the Polish workers "rose up at the *order of the PPS*" to strike, as the PPS wrote in its proclamation.

No Social Democratic party worthy of the name is tempted to try to command the working class, to have the workers marching in drill formation, bringing them onto the battlefield and again sending them home according to its own "decision." This kind of claim to lead the working class can be made only by the naive bourgeois intelligentsia, playing at the game of socialism, and only the most estranged among the bourgeois intelligentsia can *believe* in that like a fairy tale.

"The emancipation of the working class must be the work of the working class itself"—as Karl Marx and Friedrich Engels said in the *Communist Manifesto*.[*]

And that does not mean that some kind of committee of the intelligentsia, which has called itself imperiously a director of the labor movement, "orders" or "decides" when and how the working class is going to aim for its freedom. In reality, it only means that the broad mass of the proletariat *itself* must really understand the needs, conditions, and methods of its own liberation, and at the right moment, according to *its own will as a class*, must step up to begin to fight. Our workers did not rise up on anyone's "orders," but because their own healthy class instinct told them to; instinct awakened in the mass as a result of long years of socialist agitation and sharpened by the events of recent years and months, by war, unemployment, and the heinous crimes of absolutism. Had it not been for this strong class instinct and mood of the masses, all the party proclamations calling for a strike would have been powerless. But it is precisely the fact that the mass of workers *spontaneously* put into action the principles of Social Democracy, and the fact that this same class instinct has led it (the working class) to the views proclaimed by Social Democracy—that is the finest testament to our program and tactics that history can give.

This is not by any means to suggest that the PPS did not have any active part in calling and supporting the general strike in our country. Certainly, it took part in it, out of pure necessity, just as *all* socialist organizations throughout Russia without distinction were forced to take an active part in this general forward rush of the revolutionary working masses. But, at this point, something bad happened for the social-patriots, something that could be the worst for any political party—they were forced to take part in a movement that was going in the *direction opposite* to where they had pushed the Polish workers throughout their existence. For twelve years, they had been saying that the "Russian workers had not yet awakened." And yet, after all, they had to finally support our proletariat in its response to—a revolutionary explosion in Petersburg. They had to repeat the news of the outbreak, belying their own teachings. They were calling on Polish working people for twelve years to rebuild Poland, and, at the decisive moment, the time came for them to swallow their slogans "to oust the invaders" and support the uprising of our people—to fight for a common political freedom in all of Russia. For twelve years they tried with all their strength to shut the Polish labor movement off from the Russian one with the nationalist causeway of separateness, but finally they had to join the mad rush when the Polish labor movement followed—like a frothy mountain stream joining a larger watercourse—in the common flow of the workers' revolution in all of Russia.

---

[*]   This was stated, not in the *Communist Manifesto* of 1848, but at the time of the founding of the First International (in 1864). The German reference is: "*Die Befreiung der Arbeiterklasse muss das Werk der Arbeiterklasse selbst sein.*" See Marx's "Inaugural Address of the Working Men's International Association," in *Marx-Engels Collected Works*, Vol. 20, p. 13.

In short, the social-patriots were forced to run panting to keep pace with the mass of the Polish proletariat, trampling mercilessly on all of their flowerbeds of nationalism, which they had manicured for twelve years, trampling their program and tactics, slogans, ideals—to follow in the direction that from the beginning was calmly indicated by *Social Democracy*.

And the entire current revolution in the tsarist empire, which fills the hearts of socialists all over the world with pride and joy, the revolution that to working people sounds like the announcement of their liberation—that revolution is in fact for the PPS party the *most terrible defeat*. For twelve years, the PPS tried by every means and every device to deflect the Polish worker away from the fight for political freedom in Russia. For twelve years, the PPS tried to do this by disparaging and vilifying the Russian people and Russian Social Democracy, to separate the Polish worker from uniting politically, from merging with the Russian worker. For twelve years, the entire spirit of the PPS's work was directed toward interfering with and *preventing* the occurrence of a revolution of working people, such as we are experiencing today. And now it turns out that *all the work of the PPS in this direction was in vain*, that the operation and spirit of its program was *not revolutionary* but *reactionary*.

If the workers of the PPS had not been taught to believe blindly and uncritically in the words of the PPS's intellectual leaders, if they were able to see clearly and be fully aware of what they were doing, they would have necessarily understood that the revolution in January and the entire movement today was the *death of* the program and direction of social-patriotism.

To say this is not to engage in some sort of party boasting, which could only have importance for a group of intellectuals who delude themselves about giving orders to the working class, which a real workers' party would not do. The welfare of the workers' movement requires above all a sincere and uncompromising criticism of the errors and deviations that this movement makes, rather than covering up and masking the full truth from the workers.

The leaders of the PPS themselves clearly feel that the revolution of recent weeks has buried their nationalist work of twelve years. They also felt, just at first glance, that if they would try to give a signal for rebuilding Poland, their own workers would turn their backs on them. But, instead of honestly and openly moving onto the ground of a purely class movement on which the mass of workers stand, and giving a signal for a common political fight for freedom together with the Russian people, the social-patriots try to pull the wool over the workers' eyes and trick them.

The PPS announced in its political declaration at the beginning of the general strike a general demand for a *"Legislative Parliament in Warsaw."* But what does it mean, a "Legislative Parliament in Warsaw?"

The ordinary Polish worker understands that this is not a declaration of Poland's independence. In addition, it is clear and simple that a "Legislative

Parliament in Warsaw" cannot be born as long as the tsar's government continues to rule throughout the Russian empire. A parliament in Warsaw can appear
only as a result of the overthrow of absolutism in Russia and as part of an overall
[victory of] political freedom in Russia.

A "Legislative Parliament in Warsaw" can arise only if a Legislative
Parliament exists in Petersburg. It does not mean anything else, as common
sense tells us, but an *autonomous national self-government*. The PPS itself admits
in *Robotnik*, No. 58, that the political slogan, which it advocated was actually
national self-government. But Social Democracy, for a long time, has demanded
exactly that—national self-government, to protect the people of our country
from national oppression. But Social Democracy, as a working-class party, has
been pointing out to workers for a long time that local self-government for the
Polish nation can be won only as a part of political freedom in all of Russia and
that the class interests of our workers' demands of them to fight together with
the Russian workers for their common cause—to overthrow absolutism.

The social-patriots, forced to hide their program of rebuilding Poland,
have coughed up the slogan of national self-government, but have given it their
own chauvinist interpretation at least by being silent about political freedom in
Russia.

As a result of the heroic, glorious revolution of the Russian proletariat, they
were forced to depart from their nationalist slogan, but they took revenge at
least on the Russian workers in such a way that they told them, so to speak: "We
don't care if there, in Russia, you gain freedom or not. We want our 'Parliament
in Warsaw,' and as far as Russia is concerned, we turn our backs on Russia, and
that is that!"

They abandoned their nationalism under the pressure of the workers' movement, but in a cowardly way, not sincerely, but only halfway, and that is why they
present to the workers such political nonsense *as national self-government in
Poland without political freedom in Russia!*

In this way, the PPS leaders sacrifice in this current moment the revolutionary interests of the workers and their political awareness for the preservation of
sympathy among the petty bourgeois chauvinist intelligentsia.

But those workers who have fallen down so far as to be unaware of the direction of the PPS should finally understand today that by their participation in
our and the Russian proletariat's general movement in recent weeks, they are
actually standing on the ground of Social Democracy. Today, the first duty for
these workers is the same as the great task for all our working people—complete
liberation from the influence of ruinous nationalism and open, sincere connection to the camp of pure class struggle for the common good of the Polish and
Russian proletarians, the camp of Social Democracy.

In the Bonfire Glow of the Revolution[*]

May Day this year will, for the first time, be celebrated in the midst of a revolutionary situation—with an important detachment of the world proletarian army engaged in a direct mass struggle of huge proportions, fighting for their political rights. This circumstance should and will impart a special character to this year's May Day. Not only in the sense that the fighting workers of the tsarist empire will be remembered with a few words of sympathy in speeches and resolutions at May Day gatherings everywhere. The current Russian Revolution, if it is not merely to be acknowledged with superficial sentiments of sympathy but also to be thought about seriously by the workers internationally, [must be] recognized as *their own cause*, which in a very special way is linked up with the real meaning of the international May 1 holiday. It is a major step toward the realization of the two basic ideas of the workers' holiday, the eight-hour day, and socialism.

The *eight-hour day* became the main demand of the present revolutionary uprising in the Russian empire from the very start. Among the demands formulated by the Petersburg workers in the famous petition to the tsar, along with demands for basic political rights and liberties, the call for the immediate introduction of the eight-hour day figured prominently. In the general strike that broke out on an enormous scale throughout the empire in response to the Petersburg bloodbath, especially in Russian Poland, the eight-hour day was the most important social demand. Even later, in the second stage of the strike movement, when the general uprising as a political manifestation was temporarily suspended to make room for a long series of partial economic strikes, even here the demand for the eight-hour day was a red thread connecting the struggle for wages in all branches of industry; it set the fundamental tone for all the battles; the unifying element, and sounded the revolutionary note in all these separate struggles. Thus, the first period of the Russian Revolution up to now has manifested itself as a powerful demonstration in support of one of the two main demands of international May Day. Like no other example, it has shown how deeply the idea of the eight-hour workday has taken root in the social soil of the

---

[*] This article was published on the eve of May Day 1905—on April 29, 1905, in *Sächsische Arbeiter-Zeitung*, No. 98. The title in German is "Im Feuerschein der Revolution." It is translated (by George Shriver) from the text in Luxemburg's *Gesammelte Werke*, Vol. 1, Part. 2, pp. 537–40. Where the author uses the term *Maifeier* (literally "the May holiday"), we have often used "May Day." This of course refers to May 1, which became the annual International Workers' Day beginning in 1889, initiated by the socialist Second International. That date was chosen to honor events that first took place in the United States—mass marches in numerous cities by workers demanding the eight-hour day on May 1, 1886. The largest of those 1886 marches was in Chicago, where about 80,000 workers took part. The march was soon followed by the Haymarket incident and the subsequent legal execution, in 1887, of the socialist and anarchist leaders of the Chicago eight-hour-day movement. Italics are by Luxemburg, unless otherwise noted.

world proletariat, how very much the eight-hour day has become a question of life or death for the workers of all countries.*

No one in Russia gave any special thought in advance to linking the main political demands of the present revolution with the eight-hour day or even to placing the latter demand in the forefront. In all the agitation that had gone on previously, the main weight was placed, with a certain understandable one-sidedness, on purely political demands—the abolition of the autocracy, the calling of a Constituent Assembly, the proclamation of a republic, etc. Then the proletariat rose up en masse, and instinctively it immediately grabbed onto the main social demand, the eight-hour day, along with the political demands. The healthy instinct of the mass uprising, as though of its own accord, corrected the one-sidedness of the Social Democratic agitation, which had been focused politically, and by means of this purely proletarian international demand it transformed the formally "bourgeois" revolution into a consciously *proletarian* one. A democratic constitution, and even a republican constitution—those were slogans which in their historical content could just as well have been raised by the bourgeois classes. In a way, they actually are a kind of special adjunct belonging to "bourgeois democracy." Going only that far, the workers of Russia would have stepped onto the political stage merely "on behalf of" the bourgeoisie. In contrast, the eight-hour day is a demand that can only be raised by the working class, and it is not linked either by tradition or in its social meaning to bourgeois democracy. On the contrary, it is hated even more by the main social vehicle of bourgeois democracy in all countries—that is, the petty bourgeoisie —than by the big industrial capitalists. Thus, in Russia, the eight-hour day is not a slogan expressing the "mutuality of interests" of the proletariat and all the progressive bourgeois elements, but rather it is a slogan expressing opposition, contradiction, and conflict—a class-struggle slogan. Inseparably linked with the political-democratic demands, it nevertheless immediately indicates that the proletariat of the tsarist empire in the present revolution has with full awareness transferred its function "on behalf of" the bourgeoisie into its *opposite*, expressing its antagonism toward bourgeois society, and it is doing so as a class, as part of its effort to achieve its own ultimate liberation.

And this is where the international significance of the Russian Revolution is also found, in connection with the other central idea of May Day—the idea of making socialism a reality. The connection between the two slogans is a very close and direct one. To be sure, the eight-hour day in itself is not yet "a little taste of socialism." Formally speaking, it is merely a social reform on the basis of the capitalist economic system. When it is realized in part, as we have experienced here and there, the eight-hour day has not brought about any fundamental

---

* The same might be said today, in the second decade of the twenty-first century, about the rising demand for a livable minimum wage, to be increased as inflation increases.

change of the wage labor system but has merely raised it to a higher and more modern level. But, as a general regulation, having international legal force, which is what we are demanding, the eight-hour day would at the same time be the *most radical* social reform that can be introduced within the framework of the existing social system. It is a bourgeois social reform, but, at the same time, it is a nodal point where quantity has already begun to change into quality—that is, a "reform" which in all likelihood the victorious proletariat standing at the helm of state power would also put into effect. That is why the Russian Revolution, in which the eight-hour-day demand is setting the basic tone in such a loud and clear way, is at the same time standing under the sign of social revolution. With that, it should by no means be said that as the next product of this revolution something like the beginning of the social overturn is to be expected. On the contrary, as the next conceivable phase of the present struggle there will in all likelihood be merely a fundamental political change in the tsarist empire, and probably it will be an extremely wretched bourgeois constitution that will make its entrance.

But, beneath the surface of this purely formal political change, there will take place just as surely a very deep-going social transformation, and that will be spurred on to an unimaginable extent. And, thereby, the *international* class struggle of the proletariat. The interconnection of political and social life among the various capitalist countries is such an intensive one nowadays that the repercussions of the Russian Revolution on the social situation in Europe, and indeed in all of the so-called civilized world, will be enormous—going much deeper than the international repercussions of earlier bourgeois revolutions. It is a fruitless task to try to foresee and make prophesies about the specific forms that these repercussions will or can take. The main task is, however, to be fully clear and conscious about the fact that as a result of the current revolution in the tsarist empire there will be a powerful *acceleration* of the international class struggle, and this will confront us with new tasks and tactical challenges during a time period that will by no means be a long one—it will confront those of us who live in the countries of "old" Europe with revolutionary situations and new tactics and tasks.

It is with *this* idea and in *this* spirit that May Day should be celebrated everywhere this year. It should show that the international proletariat has grasped the most important motto: "*To be prepared is everything!*"

May Day Massacres in Russia*

May Day is the only holiday in Russia that is also celebrated by cultural associations.† The revolutionary character that this folk festival now has is made clear by the fact that the workers in Russia celebrate it on the same day as workers in the rest of the world—thirteen days before May 1st arrives in Russia according to the calendar used in the tsarist empire.

And this year on the first day of May, which happens to coincide with Easter, all of revolutionary Russia assembled to make a powerful statement against tsarism and for liberty for peoples of the empire.

But the Little Father‡ did not celebrate. He sent the troops out onto the streets and repeated what happened on Bloody Sunday in Petersburg [on January 22].

In Warsaw and in other cities of Russian Poland,§ *May Day was celebrated with the drinking of blood.* Again, peaceful demonstrators, defenseless women and children, were shot down. The official telegraph agency news reports themselves admit bluntly, without embellishment, that the troops fired without any provocation upon these pilgrims of liberty, who were exercising their sacred choice of holding a May Day procession.

This Bloody May once again passes a death sentence upon tsarism, and the entire civilized world is waiting for this sentence to be carried out.

We are in receipt of the following telegram:

Warsaw, May 1, 11 p.m.—Today a giant demonstration was called by Social Democracy. A march of 30,000 demonstrators proceeded along the following streets—Wronia, Witkowski Square, Żelazna, Jerózolimska. Eight banners were carried in the march. Many speeches were given, out on the street in the open. The demonstration continued for two hours. On Jerózolimska Avenue, around 3 p.m. a clash with the military took place [more exactly the military opened fire] with 130 people being killed, hundreds wounded, and many arrested.

---

* This report was not signed. Luxemburg's authorship can be deduced from remarks she made in a letter to Leo Jogiches of May 2, 1905. See her *Gesammelte Briefe*, Vol. 2, p. 82. The article first appeared in *Vorwärts*, No. 101a, May 2, 1905. The title in German is "Maimetzeleien in Russland." It is translated (by George Shriver) from Luxemburg's *Gesammelte Werke*, Vol. 6, p. 526.

† *Von den Kulturstaaten*—i.e., stemming from cultural tradition.

‡ That is, Tsar Nicholas II.

§ Luxemburg is referring to the events that took place at the time in Częstochowa.

Bloody May[*]

Once again, this time in *Warsaw*, the tsarist autocracy has committed the bloody abomination of mass murder of the people. Hecatombs of human lives were sacrificed by a soldiery spurred on by the authorities to vent its blood lust, hecatombs of people who for their part did not commit any acts of violence and who were merely marching down the street to demonstrate for their ideals of freedom. Women and children were murdered, unarmed workers who fled in the face of the unexpected and senseless salvos fired by the soldiers and who collapsed after being fatally shot in the back—such are the latest feats of heroism by the thugs of the tsarist regime.

The workers in Warsaw probably assumed all too trustingly that a repetition of the butchery in Petersburg on Bloody Sunday was not possible. They marched peacefully through the streets, and to begin with, the cavalry let the workers move past them peacefully, and then suddenly the unarmed, demonstrating workers saw themselves hemmed in from in front and from behind, then salvos of rifle fire along with the sabers of the Cossacks set to work to carry out the dreadful bloodbath. Far more than a hundred people were killed, and the total number of wounded is still unknown. Even the official reports from Warsaw make clear the cowardly brutality of these murdering gangsters; it was reported that soldiers forced their way into courtyards of buildings where people were trying to hide, into which people had fled trying to save themselves, and they abused them and beat them to death, but only in one case was it reported that some police were killed by a bomb thrown in self-defense. An appalling scene occurred in front of the district police station near the Church of the Cross, where a large crowd had gathered on Tuesday. Those present wanted to identify the corpses of their fathers, grown sons, and little children who had been killed and whose bodies had been brought from all over the city to the morgue at that location. But infantrymen and police crews refused admittance.

The workers are tremendously infuriated. *In many factories, there was a total work stoppage.* On Tuesday only two newspapers appeared, and on Wednesday as a sign of mourning no papers appeared at all. Military patrols are present everywhere in the city.

---

[*] This report was not signed. Judging by her letter to Leo Jogiches of May 2, 1905, it is very likely that Luxemburg was the author. See her *Gesammelte Briefe*, Vol. 2, p. 82. This item first appeared in *Vorwärts*, No. 102, 1905. The title in German is "Blutiger Mai." It is translated (by George Shriver) from Luxemburg's *Gesammelte Werke*, Vol. 6, pp. 527–8.

The Revolution in Russia [May 4, 1905]*

With regard to the number of victims of the massacre in Warsaw, the information received still varies widely, to an extraordinary extent. According to a report designated as conclusive in the *BH*,† *sixty-two* persons were killed and about *two hundred* wounded. During the night on Wednesday, [May 3], thirty-one corpses were brought from police headquarters to the cemetery and buried; in no case did the "Christian" authorities of tsarism provide coffins for laying the murdered victims to rest.

Aroused feelings in Warsaw continue to be exceedingly strong. People are waiting for the response of the authorities against the officers who gave the order for the troops to open fire. On Wednesday, several minor clashes took place between workers and police. *On Hoza Street, a police captain was severely wounded by a shot from a revolver. The newspapers, for the most part, did not appear, and the factories were at a standstill.* According to the *Kurier Warszawski* [Warsaw Courier], the leadership of the Social Democratic Party of Poland and Lithuania [the SDKPiL], because of the bloodshed, issued a declaration calling for an immediate general strike.

Martial law is also continuing in Łódź. On Tuesday [May 2], *four persons,* including two Jewish women, were *killed,* and three persons were wounded. A [police] *spy was stabbed to death* by the crowd. As of May 3, the W.T.O. [Wolff's Telegraph Office] was reporting from Łódź.

Early this morning on a public street the police station supervisor Poniatowski was *fatally wounded* by four shots fired at him by several persons.

Moscow, May 3. Last night a large crowd on Petrovsky Boulevard began to smash up a restaurant into which a station house supervisor had retreated after being struck in the face. He was defending himself against the crowd with cold steel.‡ The crowd bashed in the windows and tore off the doors while the customers fled from the restaurant in wild terror. Mounted gendarmes restored order.

THE ACTIVITIES OF SOCIAL DEMOCRACY

This report about the agitational activities of Polish Social Democracy was sent to us prior to May Day.

---

* This article, "Die Revolution in Rußland," was not signed. Judging by her letter to Leo Jogiches of May 3, 1905, it is very likely that Luxemburg compiled the reports contained in it (translating them into German where necessary), and wrote the commentaries. See her *Gesammelte Briefe*, Vol. 2, p. 86. The article first appeared in *Vorwärts*, the SPD's central party newspaper, No. 103, May 4, 1905. It is translated (by George Shriver) from Luxemburg's *Gesammelte Werke*, Vol. 6, pp. 533–6.

† *Berliner Handelsblatt*, the Berlin Newspaper of Commerce.

‡ That is, with weapon bared—*mit blanker Waffe.*

The May Day agitation this year is naturally playing a role that is quite different from all preceding years. This time the agitational literature has been extraordinarily rich. The following printed material was massively distributed by Social Democracy.*

1. A pamphlet about May Day aimed at a popular audience.
2. A large-size May Day flyer, or brochure, of eight printed pages, which analyzes and discusses the special connection between the May Day celebration this year and the revolution going on in the tsarist empire as a whole.
3. A May Day proclamation, which was printed at the party's secret printing plant inside the country, with about 75,000 copies on white paper with red lettering, and which for the first time this year was also addressed to the *agricultural proletariat*.
4. An appeal to student youth to join the May Day action.
5. A leaflet with the heading "Under the Regime of the Noose and the Bullet," which took a position against the reign of terror recently begun by the thugs of tsarism.
6. The April issue of the party's organ *Czerwony Sztandar* [Red Flag] prominently featured an article about May Day by Karl Kautsky. Besides the writings in Polish [listed above], material *in German* was distributed to the tens of thousands of German workers living in Łódź, Zgierz, Białystok, etc.
7. A May Day leaflet.
8. An *Open Letter from August Bebel* to the German working men and women living in Russian-dominated Poland and Lithuania. From this interesting document, we can reproduce only a few passages here. After Bebel describes the ultimate aims, or final goal, of Social Democracy and the present condition of the exploited and enslaved proletariat, he suggests to the German workers that they must fight for the same goals in common and in unison with the other workers of the country despite all differences of nationality, language, religion, etc. After a detailed presentation as well of the *political* program of the SDKPiL, which strives for the conquest of political freedom together with all the workers of Russia, Bebel concludes:

> German workingmen and women! These are, in brief, the most immediate demands for whose realization the Polish and Russian Social Democracy is fighting in the country as a whole, in the local region, and in the community. You too must join in this struggle and support it.
>
> German workingmen and women! Do not hesitate, but join the ranks of your fighting brothers and sisters of Polish and Russian nationality. Only by

---

* Luxemburg's "correspondent" has been listing items of "agitational literature" produced by the SDKPiL during the weeks immediately preceding May 1, 1905.

cooperating with them in a united and determined way can you win for your-self an improvement in your situation, and an existence worthy of human beings. United you are an invincible power which no opponent can overcome.[*]

9. Bebel's letter—as was reported to us—produced a wave of enthusiasm beggaring description. German workers were literally tearing the leaflets out of each other's hands.

The May Day agitational literature this time was distributed on a scale not seen before, reaching into the remotest nests in the provinces. Among the cities covered were Warsaw, Łódź, Częstochowa, Neualexandrien [New Alexandria], Lublin, Białystok, Siedlce, Żyrardów, Włocławek, Piotrków, Pruszków, Góra Kalwaria, Kaczy Dół, Alexandrov, Dobrzelin, Jeziorna, Płock, Ostrołeka, and Grójec.

THE BLOODY EVENTS IN CZĘSTOCHOWA

The following report about the goings-on in Częstochowa has reached us in addition to what is already known.

Częstochowa, April 30: The ferment among the workers in and around Częstochowa has lasted for weeks, and new fuel has been added to the fire because the factory owners are trying to renege on the concessions they made while the workers are insisting on the demands that had been agreed to. As a result, several days before May Day a strike broke out at a weaving mill and at a sheet metal rolling mill [*Walzwerk*]. Two days before May Day, the workers raised a flag on the highest smokestack of the smelter at the Handtke steel mill with this wording:

> Long live the revolution!
> Long live the Constituent Assembly!
> Long live the eight-hour day!

> —Social Democratic Party of Russian Poland and Lithuania

Mass meetings also took place, with Social Democratic orators speaking, and after that the workers marched in the streets.

On the night of April 28–29, as has already been mentioned,[†] the police and gendarmes invaded the workers barracks at the Rakow factory (a distance

---

[*] Bebel's Open Letter, dated April 9, 1905, was distributed as a May Day leaflet in German by the SDKPiL leadership. For the original German wording, see August Bebel, *Ausgewählte Reden und Schriften* (Selected Speeches and Writings), Vol. 7, Part 2: 1899–1905, edited by Anneliese Beske and Eckhard Müller (Munich: Saur, 1997), p. 784 ff.

[†] It is not clear where this was "already mentioned."

of three kilometers from the city) in order to make some arrests. The military occupied the courtyards and grounds around the factory and the workers' barracks. When the workers on the night shift found out what had happened, they rushed to the aid of their colleagues in the barracks. The factory whistle blew and the entire workplace immediately came to a standstill, while all the electric lights were extinguished. In the darkness, the workers succeeded in pushing aside the soldiers who were holding the barracks doors shut and forced their way into the barracks, where they freed those who had been arrested. Only nine of the arrestees remained in the hands of the police, and they were taken away to Częstochowa.

The workers thereupon demanded that the factory director go into the city immediately and see to it that the arrested workers were set free; if they were not freed by 8:30 a.m., all work at the factory would stop. When no answer was received by that hour, the workers downed tools, formed up in groups, and began to march toward the city to free their comrades. When news of this reached other factories in the suburbs, they also stopped work, and those strikers also joined the march.

Before reaching the city, the march encountered a squadron of cavalry, a battalion of infantry, and the police. For more than an hour and a half the workers and the military stood facing each other. Around 1 p.m. the commanding officer ordered the crowd to disperse. The workers replied that they would not leave until their comrades were released. The warning was repeated, but the workers kept pressing forward against the military.

Then the cavalry was given the order to clear the street. *The troopers rode toward the crowd, but only an isolated few rode into it; most of them did not make use of their weapons or merely fired into the air.* The crowd responded to this assault by throwing stones, which injured several soldiers. At that point, the horsemen turned around and went back, losing two carbines and three sabers. Now the workers broke into nearby buildings and from that position attacked the military with more throwing of stones. With this, the cavalry was driven back. Then the infantry was given the order to fire. *Three salvos followed.* The crowd gave way. At that point, the *police* rushed after the retreating workers, shooting at them blindly. *The soldiers, in contrast, had mostly fired into the air.*

As far as I can determine up to now, two workers were killed, two persons were badly wounded, and a thirteen-year-old boy and a woman of about twenty were less seriously wounded. *Two children were also killed* by stray bullets at a great distance from the scene of the fighting. Most of the wounded were hit by revolver shots and thus were victims of the police, who were in a raging frenzy like so many mad dogs.

The workers are now extremely embittered.

Murder in Warsaw[*]

Readers already know from telegraph agency news reports that in Warsaw on May 1 the thugs of tsarism perpetrated an unheard-of new atrocity. We have now received detailed information about this despicable and heinous act by the regime of the knout. *Murder, assassination, an ambush-type surprise attack committed with cold-blooded, deliberate intention*, committed against defenseless and peaceful masses, against women and children, against a mass of people who had appealed to the soldiers with brotherly words. The pen droops and language has no words to describe the vileness of this descent into Kalmyk-style barbarism. The only consoling aspect of the heartrending report that readers will find below is something that now clearly comes to light: the heroism of the working-class masses, their high level of political maturity, their consistency of purpose, and the powerful revolutionary energy of the proletariat—all of this shows that the bestial rule of the knout cannot continue for long; its days are surely numbered.

Warsaw, May 1, 10 p.m.—from our correspondent:

Early in the morning the day already had an extraordinary, festive appearance. All stores were closed; no carriages or streetcars were to be seen in the streets. There was a great stirring everywhere out on the streets as people moved about, a festively attired working-class public, but the bourgeois public awaited the coming events behind locked doors in their dwellings. Toward 11 a.m. a crowd of many thousands had already gathered on Wronia Street—that's where Social Democracy had scheduled the beginning of the march. Punctually at the midday hour the party speakers appeared. A worker, carried on the shoulders of others, gave a speech on the meaning of May Day and the fight against absolutism. When the speech ended, a chant went up, *Long live the eight-hour day! Long live the republic! Long live Social Democracy!* These calls were repeated by the crowd with indescribable enthusiasm. At the head of the march, a giant banner of red silk was unfolded, on which the following was spelled out in gold letters: "Away with the war!" "Long live peace!" "Long live the revolution!" "Long live the republic!" And on the reverse side of the banner: "Long live the Social Democratic Party of the Kingdom of Poland and Lithuania!" Farther back along the length of the march, seven more Social Democratic banners were carried, and among others, for the first time, a banner of the "Social Democratic Organization of Student Youth" in both Polish and Russian letters (because Russian students also belong to the Social Democratic Party in Poland).

---

[*] This report was not signed. Judging by her letter to Jogiches of May 6, 1905, it is very likely that Luxemburg was the author. See her *Gesammelte Briefe*, Vol. 2, p. 90. This item first appeared in *Vorwärts*, No. 106, May 7, 1905. The title in German is "Der Mord in Warschau." It is translated (by George Shriver) from Luxemburg's *Gesammelte Werke*, Vol. 6, pp. 539–41.

The march began. Stops were made along the way many times to hear orators who "rose to the speaker's platform" on the shoulders of workers and gave speeches. The march had swelled in the meantime to more than 20,000. In front of Witkowski Square we encountered a patrol of police and uhlans.[*] The people in the march opened a passageway through their midst for the patrol, which was thus allowed to pass through peacefully and then we marched on, also peacefully. At the corner of Złota Street[†] another comrade, a woman worker, gave a speech about the meaning of the political struggle and the fight for political freedom. Her words drew forth an enthusiastic response. At another location an orator spoke about one of the martyrs of our struggle, Marcin Kasprzak, whose name was called out and chanted by the many thousands present.[‡]

Here a patrol of mounted guardsmen watched quietly, but when the crowd began shouting revolutionary slogans in their direction, the patrol hastily withdrew. The marchers came to a halt in front of a barracks building. The soldiers began to close the windows, but reassured by the peaceful behavior of the masses, they reopened them. Then one comrade, who was held up above the mass of the crowd and addressed himself toward the windows, gave a speech in Russian to the soldiers. He spoke about the aims of the workers' movement, and about the crimes of the tsarist government, and urged the soldiers to ally themselves with the workers' movement. The soldiers responded to the speech in a friendly way, a few nodded their heads in greetings, waved their caps, and called out loudly, *Doloi samoderzhavie!* (Down with autocracy!) and *Da zdravstvuyet svoboda!* (Long live freedom!). The crowd was inspired by this and called out in Russian, *Doloi tsarya!* ("Down with the tsar!") and "Don't shoot your starving brothers!" Then this crowd of countless shining faces in untold numbers went on singing jubilantly "The Red Banner"[§] and marched on to Jerózolimska Aleja.

---

[*]   Mounted lancers.

[†]   Luxemburg actually lived on this street with her family from 1873 to 1889 and again in 1906, when she participated in the revolution in Poland.

[‡]   Kasprzak was one of the pioneers of Polish Marxism. He joined the first Proletariat Party in 1885, was arrested, spent time in prison, and escaped. After the first Proletariat Party was crushed, he helped found the second Proletariat Party in 1888. He helped introduce Luxemburg to Polish revolutionary politics when she was still a teenager, and in 1889 helped smuggle her out of Poland when her arrest was imminent. He later worked closely with her in the SDKP and SDKPiL. See Luxemburg's article in tribute to Kasprzak, "A Victim of the White Terror!" below, pp. 198–204.

[§]   "Czerwony Sztandar" ("The Red Flag/Banner") was written by the Polish socialist Bolesław Czerwieński in 1881 and set to music by Jan Kozakiewicz. The song was an adaptation of "Le Drapeau Rouge," written by the French socialist Paul Brousse in 1877 to mark the anniversary of the Paris Commune, which was sung to the melody "Le Chant du Depart." "Czerwony Sztandar" became a popular song of the Polish socialist movement and was sung at demonstrations and strikes, as well as by prisoners before execution. It was banned by the tsarist authorities. The song was used by various left-wing groups, including the PPS and SDKPiL. It is a different song from the English "Red Flag" (which is regularly sung at events of the British Labour Party) and other versions, although they share a similar name and similar sentiments. Some sources have claimed that Luxemburg was the author of a German translation of "Czerwony Sztandar" around the turn of the century. However, this is disputed in Erhard Hexelschneider, "Rosa Luxemburg und die Künste. 2 unveränderte Auflage" in *Rosa-Luxemburg-Forschungsberichte*, No. 3 (Saxony:

The public greeted us everywhere with enthusiasm. Such spirit prevailed in this enormous mass of people, who were marching so calmly and peacefully in such high spirits, and were chanting for their ideals with so much gusto, that everyone we encountered was immediately carried along with us. Even the bourgeois types watched with fascination. And so we came to Jerózolimska Aleja. And what happened there is indescribable. *Suddenly, without the slightest warning, without the slightest provocation from our side, without anything like an order to disperse, a salvo was fired at us* as we were marching unsuspectingly and singing. And then the shooting went on uninterruptedly! The march broke up in terrible panic as the cries of the dying were heard all around us, the outcry of people mortally stricken, then moaning and calls for help. We tried to save ourselves and sought sanctuary in a building at 101 Jerózolimska Aleja, climbing over a fence into a large, board-covered courtyard. But the beasts were only waiting for that! They began firing at the crowd of us who were thickly packed together in the courtyard; it was like shooting at sparrows. No exit was possible. We were in a trap. *For an entire quarter of an hour,* which seemed like an eternity to us, the shooting continued without interruption. More than fifty people fell before our eyes, and more than a hundred were seriously wounded. Those who fell were mostly women, children, and the elderly. Others sought sanctuary in the hospital building, but even there the massacre continued. I myself don't know how I came out alive. The workers are now tremendously infuriated.

Rosa-Luxemburg-Stiftung, 2007). It is, in any case, hardly plausible that a German version of the song would have been sung in Warsaw. There are several versions of Czerwieński's "Czerwony Sztandar" (for example, the PPS omitted verse two because it expressed hostility to the struggle for Polish independence) and it is impossible to know exactly which version of the song Polish workers were singing in the events Luxemburg mentions. The full version of the song is given on the front page of the SDKPiL newspaper *Czerwony Sztandar*, No. 1, November 1902.

A Year of Revolution[*]

Oh you great year! No one ever saw you [or anything like you] in our land![†]

The days May 1–4 of this current year have written the name of the Polish proletariat in the pages of revolutionary history forever, in glowing letters of fame and glory.

The May 1 demonstration and the general strike of May 4 in Warsaw were undeniably the most powerful expression up until now of the maturity and political strength of the working class, not only in our country but also in the entire tsarist empire. The workers of Warsaw celebrated in worthy fashion the first May Day of this revolutionary era and showed the whole world that they are aware of the great significance of the historical moment we are living through.

Never before has Warsaw seen such a workers' demonstration as this mass march of 20,000, a mass proceeding under the banner of Social Democracy with model order and discipline, and in the highest spirits—a mass consolidated around the seriousness of its ideas and the consciousness of its goals, hungrily absorbing every word and slogan of the Social Democratic speakers, gripped by a powerful sense of brotherhood, combined collective strength, and joyful enthusiasm.

And yet, against this peaceful march absolutism launched a criminal attack of a kind never seen before in our history. Several dozen corpses along with a hundred wounded—those were the trophies taken by the highway-robber hordes of absolutism.[‡]

---

[*] This article is translated (by George Shriver and Alicja Mann) from *Z Pola Walki*, No. 8, dated May 27, 1905. Its Polish title is "Rok rewolucji."

[†] The line of poetry quoted as an epigraph by Luxemburg is from the epic poem *Pan Tadeusz, cyli Ostatni zajazd na Litwie. Historia szlachecka z roku 1811 i 1812 we dwunastu księgach wierszem* (Pan Tadeusz or The Last Foray in Lithuania. A Tale of the Gentry during 1811–1812 in Twelve Books of Verse), written by Adam Mickiewicz, the great national poet of Poland, in the 1830s. *Pan Tadeusz* depicted the life of the Polish gentry around the time of Napoleon's 1812 invasion of Russia, which had aroused great hopes in Poland of freedom from Russian tsarist rule. Earlier, Napoleon had created the nominally independent Duchy of Warsaw after his victory over Prussia in 1807. By 1809, this Duchy had a population of over four million and included Kraków and Lublin as well as Warsaw, plus a "Polish corridor" to Gdańsk, which was made a "free city" where French troops were stationed. But most Polish lands remained under the occupation of Prussia, Austria, and Russia. Napoleon introduced a civic code and dictated a constitution for the Duchy of Warsaw, which gave the bourgeoisie legal equality with the nobility, but the nobility remained dominant in the government. Serfdom was abolished, but major restrictions on the peasants continued, to the benefit of the landowning nobility. The Duchy of Warsaw had a Polish army of 100,000, which Napoleon made use of in his 1812 invasion of Russia. Napoleon's defeat in Russia led to the fall of the Duchy of Warsaw.

[‡] See Luxemburg's articles in *Vorwärts* about the May 1 demonstration in Warsaw and the general strike there on May 4, in her *Gesammelte Werke*, Vol. 6, pp. 526–8 and 539–41. These articles

Nevertheless, victory was on the side of the unarmed working people. The attack by the government murderers, completely unjustified, was planned on high and by all indications was for the government nothing but an attempt to frighten and intimidate the workers, to deter them from such demonstrations in the future.

Dying absolutism, guided by infallible instinct, senses perfectly well the powerful effect of such peaceful demonstrations. It is aware that in the course of the unstoppable revolution, these demonstrations will occur in our country, as well as in all of Russia, and will grow like an avalanche, gathering more and more that army of conscious proletarians around the banner of Social Democracy, which eventually will smash the fortress of despotism. That is why despotism tried to stop the march of the workers—with innocent blood spilled and with the corpses of the elderly, women, and children.

But the criminal policies will fail. The working class cannot withdraw from street demonstrations because the loud but peaceful declaration of its aspirations for liberation has today become a vital necessity for the mass of the proletariat. To renounce demonstrations, to renounce mass protests against the crimes of despotism—our proletariat cannot give those up, just as it cannot give up breathing. Going out into the streets, to seek intently a sense of strength among tens of thousands under the banner of Social Democracy, and listening to the slogans of Social Democratic speakers to get some uplift and encouragement and guidance for the future—today that is the only salvation for the broadest masses of the people, who otherwise will suffocate in the terrible atmosphere of decaying absolutism. To live in such an atmosphere is [impossible for anyone but] the souls of our servile bourgeoisie, who even in the face of such horrific crimes of the government as the mass murder on May 1 are running to the halls of that same government. The revolutionary proletariat has to go out into the street, where it finds its power, which has been broken and crushed in the service of capital and under the yoke of despotism. It has to go out into the street, where its voice and outcry resound loudly and reach the broadest masses of the people, bringing to them the word of salvation.*

The revolutionary proletariat must go out into the street, which is the mother of the toilers and oppressed, because it does not have—in the society of capitalist exploitation, and under the rule of the despotic knout—anything else but the street. The proletariat must go out into the street, because only there can it gather and muster its revolutionary ranks and that is where its final showdown with absolutism will take place.

Therefore, the battle over the street is going on now, over that terrain of the workers' strength and future victory—and has been going on since May 1, this

are translated from Luxemburg's German texts in the present volume as "May Day Massacres in Russia," "Bloody May," and "Murder in Warsaw."
    *   In the Polish text the last word of this sentence is literally the word for "resurrection."

ongoing struggle between the revolutionary proletariat and the government. And the general strike of May 4 in Warsaw, a strike such as the labor movement has not seen before in our country, showed to the government and the public that Social Democracy will not depart from its chosen path, and that in response to mass slaughter, the immediate answer will be an even more powerful growth of the movement in Warsaw and other cities.

As of the first days of May, in the midst of manifestations of the greatest strength shown up to now by the revolutionary proletariat in our country, three months of an all-encompassing workers' revolution in the tsarist empire had passed—a revolution that began with the mass march and mass slaughter of the Petersburg workers.

But, at the same time, an entire *year* has gone by, a year of turbulent revolutionary struggle by the proletariat of Warsaw and of our whole country. It was April 27 last year when the memorable attack on the print shop of the Social Democrats in the Wola district struck like thunder in Warsaw.*

Marcin Kasprzak's accurate shots, which left four tsarist thugs lying dead, aroused working-class Warsaw like an electric shock. As though awaking suddenly after a long lethargic sleep, the mass of our proletariat shook itself and came to its feet in response to that desperate and heroic battle.

From then on, a new spirit inspired Warsaw, a new revolutionary flame began burning there. From then on, the initiatives of Social Democracy never stopped, but kept growing in size and strength.

Last year's May Day demonstration was followed by the street battle between Social Democratic workers and the soldiers during the fire on Grzybowska Street.

Then came the memorable demonstration by victims of the economic crisis and of unemployment, crying out for "bread and jobs," and later a demonstration against conscription, followed by the Social Democratic demonstration of many thousands against the tsarist war mobilization at the end of October [1904].†

---

*   In connection with the printing of the SDKPiL's flyer for May Day 1904, the underground printshop of the SDKPiL was surrounded by the tsarist police on April 27, 1904. When those inside the printshop broke out, four tsarist police were killed. Marcin Kasprzak took responsibility for this. In September 1905, a military court condemned him to death and he was executed in the Warsaw Citadel. For more about Kasprzak and this case see "Long Live the Revolution," below, pp. 214–16. See also Luxemburg's article in German that appears in this volume as "A Victim of the White Terror," pp. 198–204 below.

†   About 1,000 workers took part in the demonstration demanding "bread and jobs" in Warsaw on June 26, 1904, according to the report in *Czerwony Sztandar*, No. 18, June 1904, p. 3. More than half of the demonstrators joined the protest march as it proceeded down Elektoralna Street in Warsaw. The Warsaw demonstration of October 23, 1904, against the call-up for military service, was reported on in *Czerwony Sztandar*, No. 21, October 1904, pp. 3–4. The Warsaw demonstration of October 30, 1904, against the military mobilization, was also reported on in *Czerwony Sztandar*, No. 21, October 1904, pp. 4–5.

Then there began the trial of Kasprzak and [Benedykt] Gurcman* before a military court; then the trial of Władisław Feinstein-Leder and twenty other comrades, which has not yet ended.† This was accompanied by many Social Democratic actions against the war, including the widespread and effective agitation among soldiers and peasants in the Lublin area. Hundreds and thousands of leaflets were distributed by the Social Democrats at the risk of their lives in Warsaw, Łódź, Białystok, Częstochowa, Puławi, and elsewhere.

Finally, in January, Social Democracy issued a call for a general strike immediately after the news came from Petersburg, and since then the enormous strike movement has spread in our entire country, in every sector where labor is employed, a movement in which Social Democracy has played a most prominent role. That is a brief history of the unforgettable revolutionary year.

In the midst of the terrible sacrifices of the Polish proletariat, this year of revolution blazed a trail for itself.

In the midst of the poverty and devastation caused by tsarism's war in the Far East, in the midst of unemployment and hunger so severe that it drove the fathers of families to suicide, mothers to prostitution, and children to beggary; in the midst of the torments suffered by countless numbers of proletarian fighters, abused in prisons or murdered by the police and soldiers, fighters who bestrewed the streets with their dead bodies. The last despotic government is departing from the scene, leaving behind only smoldering ruins, poverty, devastation, and the bloody fumes resulting from its crimes. But, above those ruins and rising from those fumes, eventually there will emerge the dawn of political freedom in spite of everything. In the midst of such pain and sacrifices, wading through streams of its own blood and tripping over the corpses of its children, the Polish proletariat has kept on striving forward unwaveringly. This past year of struggle—from May to May—was a terrible year, but one full of heroism and glory for the workers of Poland.

A working class that can live through and overcome such a year will not stop—until the moment of victory!

---

*   Gurcman was a member of the PPS.

†   Władisław Feinstein-Leder was taken into custody in connection with the arrest of Kasprzak and Gurcman, since he was one of the organizers of the underground SDKPiL printshop in the Wola district of Warsaw. After a long hunger strike, Feinstein-Leder won his release on bail in mid-December 1904.

Two Camps*

What had to happen has happened, and every conscious worker had to have been prepared for it—an open merging of the entire Polish bourgeoisie with dying absolutism against the workers' revolution. From the beginning of the [Russo-Japanese] war and the revolutionary ferment in the tsarist empire, the Polish bourgeoisie was the home of dishonor, the only part of the disintegrating empire—with the exception of the Polish proletariat—in which the bourgeoisie retained the quietness of a funeral attendee. While in Russia, that "wild," "uncivilized" Russia, that our newspaper hacks were accustomed to look down upon, one social stratum after another stood up against the tsarist government, and the liberal nobility, professors, students, doctors, lawyers, municipal councils, one corporation after another, one congress after another, presented sharp resolutions and demands for political freedom—here in Poland, no voice was even heard.

Our nobility was silent, silent was the bourgeoisie, the petty bourgeoisie, and even the intelligentsia remained silent. Like obedient dogs, the propertied classes throughout our country were supporting the cause of absolutism by their silence. The Polish worker alone saved the honor of our country, performing valiantly with revolutionary slogans in accompaniment with the Russian Revolution. In the end, finally, our petty-bourgeois intelligentsia began to move in Warsaw; they managed to hold several "secret" rallies just to prove to the world that nationalism had led them to utter intellectual debasement. The only work of these "rallies" was to present a nonsensical and backward program for a Polish Federation without political freedom in Russia—and also to pronounce a prohibition against the class party of the proletariat, a prohibition against entering into deliberations with Social Democracy. After a while, that rabbit "action" of the Polish intelligentsia was drowned in oblivion, remaining only as a sadly humorous episode in the history of the current revolution.

Then came the second period. Our proletariat, keeping pace with the Russian, was already engaged in bloody battles with the soldiers on the streets. In Russia, the government had already ceased the liberal comedy and sharply forbade the bourgeois sectors their aspirations for freedom of expression. The pavements of Petersburg, Warsaw, Łódź, and Białystok were drenched with the blood of murdered working people.

All agreements between the bourgeois opposition element in Russian society and the government were also broken, and any hopes for reform abandoned. It was then that an entire servile pilgrimage dragged its way from Poland

---

* This article is translated (by George Shriver and Alicja Mann) from *Czerwony Sztandar*, No. 26, May 1905. The Polish title of the article is "Dwa obozy."

to Petersburg, complete with memorandums and deputations to beg the ruling murderers for mercy for our country. The Polish bourgeoisie again was nothing but a disgrace to the revolution, and ours was the only country shamelessly pleading and begging at the steps of that government, one that the whole civilized world spits at with contempt.

And after the outbreak of the general strike, when all of the working class stood with us in the fight for the overthrow of despotism, for a republic, not deterred by the heaviest casualties, our bourgeois society still tried to beg from that rogue absolutism—"a Polish school system," retaining the tsar but "Polish," and in spite of the killing of workers, it would be "Polish," and the knout would still rule, but it would be a "Polish" knout. Throughout the Russian state, it was again the only example of issuing such a disgraceful request instead of demanding reforms and political freedom.

Now, after May 1, has come a third period. Thanks to the magnificent May Day demonstration and the heroic victims sacrificed by our proletariat at that time, it now stands in the front rank of the general public revolution. At the same time our bourgeoisie, with its deputations to the governor-general, has moved openly toward an alliance with the tsarist government. It is significant that on May 10 in the anteroom of the tsarist satrap, two deputations met: one giving thanks for "religious tolerance" and the other taking up the case of the murders in May.

One should consider for a moment the meaning of that "decree on tolerance." Up until then, non-Orthodox people—Uniates,* Dukhobors,† Old Believers,‡ etc.—were forced to convert to the faith of the ruler; they were persecuted with robberies, murders, sent to Siberia, held and tortured in prisons. Now the same government of murderers has generously promised not to do robberies any more, to stop violating the religious conscience. But freedom of conscience without political freedom, without freedom of religion, is a mockery. When freedom of conscience is not based on law, on the will of the people and its representatives, then one stroke of the pen by the tsarist thugs may at any moment turn things to ruin again. Besides, the robberies, the raping of women by soldiers, the anti-Jewish incidents, and so on, were never based on "law" or a decree of the tsar. These abominations were always the simple consequence of unlimited arbitrariness on the part of the government bureaucrats and the

---

* The Uniates refers to the Eastern Catholic Churches.
† Dukhobors are a Christian sect that abhors materialism and the incessant pursuit of material wealth and advocates pacifism. It opposed both tsarism and the policies of the Orthodox Church.
‡ The Old Believers were traditionalists who broke away from the Russian Orthodox Church in the mid-1600s over its effort to align Russian church liturgy with that of the Greek Orthodox Church. The Old Believers opposed these reforms and held to traditional Russian liturgy. At the time of the 1905 Revolution, close to 10 percent of the Russian population consisted of Old Believers.

tsarist army officers, considering the life and conscience of people as nothing. Therefore, as long as this lawlessness continues, meaning as long as absolutism lasts, "freedom of conscience" and "religious tolerance" will be an outright lie, a miserable cheating comedy for gullible people! And here the Polish bourgeoisie and the Polish clergy rushed to help the thugs in this wicked comedy and this cheating.

The tsar-murderer, being guilty of thousands of crimes toward the Catholics, the Uniates, the Dukhobors, the Jews, issues a decree in that he declares that he wants henceforth to "tolerate" non-Orthodox religions, and our bourgeoisie runs to gratefully kiss his Cossack boots that just ten days earlier had trampled the corpses of Polish workers on Aleje Jerozolimskie!*

The tsarist government promises to "tolerate" the religious conscience of its "subjects" while arranging on the same day a new massacre of Jews in Zhytomyr[†]—and our bourgeois crawl like dogs under the feet of the murderers, to thank them for these generous gifts! Hallelujah! Glory be to the Lord in the highest! Absolutism, dripping with blood, has promised to be no longer exclusively "Orthodox;" it has decided to be a "Catholic" absolutism. Is that not reason enough for joy and gratitude for the Polish gentiles and the Polish Catholic clergy? Again, Poland gave the only example of such disgrace throughout the Russian state—because it was the first case, after the outbreak of the revolution, of anyone going to the tsarist government with their thanks for such a low and wicked comedy, such a parody of reform.

In Russia alone, only reactionaries properly considered as the government's agents and generally despised by all liberal and progressive sectors, such as, for instance, the gentlemen of *Moskovskie Vedomosti* [Moscow News], and perhaps only some high officials among the Orthodox priests, dare to sing hymns about the tsar's reform. And bourgeois society in Russia met with contemptuous silence that bloody mockery of dying despotism. The Polish bourgeoisie was the only one that remained silent when the Russian intelligentsia was raising loud demands for political freedom. The Polish bourgeoisie then was the only one that went to beg and submit, while in Russia the liberal and democratic sectors had only cold condemnation for the government. And now the Polish bourgeoisie is the only one that loudly gives thanks for the reforms, whose only aim is—to deceive the fighting people, to deceive public opinion and extend the death agony of this murderous despotism!

Supposedly the second deputation of "citizens" that asked for a strict inquiry into the May Day massacre was an expression of sympathy toward the murdered workers.

---

*   In English, Jerusalem Avenue in Warsaw, where workers were killed by tsarist government forces during the May 1 demonstration in 1905.

†   About twenty Jews were killed during pogroms that occurred in Zhytomyr (a town in Ukraine) on May 7 and 8, 1905. The section of the city known as "Podol" was devastated.

But our workers would be too naive if they believed that. The political meaning of this deputation was quite the opposite. The "citizens" went to the head of the tsarist government in our country with a plea, asking for a strict investigation, and they solemnly pointed out that the government alone was not to blame and that it alone was not responsible for the slaughter. By asking the ringleader of the bullies to be the judge of the May Day carnage, they admitted that they did not consider the actual perpetrators to be the culprits. Asking for a strict investigation of a case that is so frighteningly clear and simple as murder of defenseless people in broad daylight, asking for "investigation and study," where the evidence was the pools of workers' blood along with splashes of brain, crushed bones, and flesh torn to shreds, and the presenters of the evidence (the prosecutors) were the cobblestone street and the bright sun in the sky—asking this lackey of the tsar to lead the investigation in such a case is something. The citizens testified loudly that they did not believe the carnage was a conscious political act of absolutism, part of its very essence, and that it was all just a misunderstanding, a case that one needs to "investigate." In other words, by requesting an investigation, the "citizens" deliberately denied that the May Day massacre had been a confrontation between the revolutionary people and the government; they conferred upon it the random nature of an "unfortunate incident." And, above all, by going to the governor-general with a plea to investigate the May Day massacre, our bourgeoisie is declaring to the tsarist government: "We are eager to reassure you, on the day after the killing of our workers, that despite these murders, you have not stopped being for us the ruling government, that we still recognize you as the lord of our country, as the supreme judge, placed over us by the power of God's law!" That was the purpose and meaning of the deputation of the Warsaw "citizens" to the governor-general on May 10.

Giving thanks for the tsar's "religious reform" and solemnly recognizing the tsarist government's integrity despite the May Day carnage, these two deputations merged in the hallways of the castle on the Vistula River into one solid chorus of our bourgeoisie (singing) to this note: "We stand by your side, bloody tsar, and want to stand there!"

II

Big bourgeois industry, under today's capitalist conditions, is the natural political leader of the possessing classes. And here in our country today, fighting against the workers' revolution and for an open alliance with the tsar, all layers of the Polish bourgeoisie are closely grouped around the industrial bourgeoisie. For each of them, dying absolutism has something in its pocket to offer, and each of them wants to beg something for themselves after the betrayal of the revolutionary proletariat. The Polish nobility expects to bring "regional [and] local self-government" to our country.

But what is this self-government? Tsar Alexander II, back in the 1860s, after the defeat at Sevastopol,* when he had to introduce some liberal reforms to improve his almost entirely rotten tsarist empire, gave to the nobility of Russia some rights to freedom for school management, care about the health and well-being of the rural population, etc. But, for a long time already, the entire system of local self-government in Russia has fallen completely into the hands of the tsar's chinovniks† and the interior minister, who can cancel any resolution of an assembly, remove the chairmen of these assemblies and generally restrain the local government at every turn. It is precisely this destruction of local self-government by the arbitrariness of the tsarist chinovniks that was one of the main reasons for dissatisfaction and opposition among the Russian progressive nobility. So memorable is this fact that the first open request for a constitution and call for an assembly of people's representatives came from the sectors of liberal Russia. It was the voice of the assembly of the zemstvo nobility in Petersburg in November last year [1904]. And now this "local self-government," which remains only in part, and in name only, whose essence has been almost completely sucked out by absolutism, is to be generously donated—to the Polish nobility.

But the tsarist government knows exactly for whom and what to donate! Even in Russia, only affluent landowners were entitled to be elected to the local zemstvo governments. Peasants and landless persons had no participation in such local "self-government." But since the Russian nobility is largely liberal, it made use of what was permitted to the local "self-government"—improving the rural schools, spreading education among the people, building hospitals, improving roads and other means of communication, providing aid to the peasantry during crop failures, etc. In our country, the nobility does not support liberalism in any way, but the opposite is true—it is the main pillar of the most arrogant reaction. In its hands, "local self-government" will only become a new way of looting and suppressing the peasants; it will become the new scourge of God. In other words, "self-government" by the Polish nobility will become a millstone around the neck of the poor peasants. Therefore, our nobility welcomes the tsar's "local self-government" as a small partial restoration of the rights it enjoyed in the "golden era" of serfdom. So it is not surprising that the nobility stretches out its hands with joy and gratitude for the gifts of Tsar Nicholas the Last.

To the committee debating a consideration of this new benefit, the tsar's government appointed fourteen representatives of the Polish nobility, and the Polish counts rushed with their humble thanks to the bosom of their Little Father, the murderer-tsar. The deputation giving thanks for religious tolerance had already knelt at the tsar's feet, Catholic and Protestant priests fraternally

---

*   The Russian loss of Sevastapol during the Crimean War signaled its imminent defeat.
†   Chinovniks were high-ranking government bureaucrats.

united in their flunkey-type behavior of bowing to the robbers. But not only
did the bourgeoisie, nobility, and clergy enter into an open alliance with the
tsar. Our Polish intelligentsia even here remains true to its matrix—the bourgeoisie. The Polish press—from the most conservative to the progressive liberal
newspaper *Prawda* (Truth)*—began to gnash its teeth and foam at the mouth
against the revolutionary workers who had no respect for anything—neither for
the holy law of capitalist exploitation nor for the holy tsarist knout. The Polish
intelligentsia waits with its dog's eagerness, watching closely for that important
bone of grace received from bloody hands—the admission of some Pole to a
government position. And the tsarist government most likely will continue until
its very last hour to reward this Polish loyalty to the Russian knout—by granting
to some members of the Polish intelligentsia the uniform and salary of a tsarist
chinovnik. The bourgeoisie, nobility, clergy, and intelligentsia were also joined,
last of all, by our patriotic petty bourgeoisie, whose mouthpiece is the so-called
"National Democracy."

Having already abandoned its utopian program of rebuilding Poland two
years ago, this party has now openly announced a new political "program" for
a stubborn fight against the revolutionary proletariat and in defense of capital
and indirectly absolutism. In May, in the same country that saw the corpses of
murdered Polish workers on the streets of Warsaw, and the Polish bourgeoisie, nobility, and clergy [crawling] at the feet of the murderers, the National
Democracy publicly issued a proclamation to the workers, heaving bile and
spittle against "international red socialism," against "riots," against the general
strike, against demonstrations, and against the economic struggle of the workers.
Saving "national industry" and having "peace and quiet," that is to say, saving the
profits of the factory owners and preserving the rule of the tsarist government—
that is what the program of our "National Democracy" is all about today.

In this way, all other classes and social sectors in our country have joined
together against the militant working class. On one side stands the revolutionary
proletariat, and on the other, gathered together around the throne of the tsar for
his protection and their own, all of bourgeois Poland.

III

This position taken by the Polish bourgeoisie is no surprise for any class-
conscious worker familiar with the teachings of Social Democracy. Only the
social-patriotic PPS, which has been telling the workers for ten years that
Polish society is "revolutionary through and through" and that the reactionary
ugodowcy† are a mere "handful" without any influence—this same PPS stands

---

*   This publication, edited by Aleksander Świętokowsk, should not be confused with the
Russian revolutionary publication of the same name.

†   The *ugodowcy* were advocates of conciliation with tsarism.

today, in the light of recent events, like a con man who has been exposed and denounced in public.

In this betrayal of the revolutionary cause by the Polish bourgeoisie and Polish intelligentsia, the PPS itself took a very active part in giving a build-up to the servile delegation to the tsar's ministers to beg for a "Polish school system," as though this entire attempt to [undermine and defeat] the revolution politically with the swindle of a "Polish school system"—as though that were a highly revolutionary action by "society." When these servile citizens of Warsaw, led by Count [Władysław] Tyszkiewicz, had fortunately found their way into the antechambers of government ministers in Petersburg, where on the street the blood of the workers murdered there had not yet dried, at the same time the PPS was writing in its Kraków newspaper *Naprzód* on March 24: "The energetic action of society in the Kingdom [of Poland] on the question of Polonization of the school system *found itself on the very best road*—in spite of the voices of conciliationists crying in the wilderness."

And this is proved by their basing their information on none other than—*Novoye Vremya* [New Times].* This "information" was related to plans for "reform" that were expected to come from the tsar's Committee of Ministers. And in this way the PPS itself was helping to deceive the people into believing that from the tsarist government there could really come genuine reform of the school system—just as the bourgeoisie and clergy are now deceiving the people that "religious toleration" is really possible under the tsar.

Meanwhile, the PPS in its Kraków newspaper Naprzód *[Forward] even wrote with pride that this whole operation of the bourgeoisie about a "Polish school system" was the result of the activity and influence of the PPS itself. In the issue of that paper for February 22, in regard to this "operation," we read:* "The active and energetic policies of the Polish Socialist Party are beginning to bear fruit.

Thus, the PPS itself facilitated and prepared the current betrayal of the workers by the Polish intelligentsia and petty bourgeoisie, and the PPS for its part issued, at the end of January and under the pretense that this was socialism, a cunning plan for local self-government in Poland without a demand for a republic or even political freedoms in Russia. The PPS went down the same road paved earlier by certain elements of National Democracy from the time of the childish rallies in Warsaw. Following National Democracy down that road, there then came the pettybourgeois, nationalist intelligentsia, and then the nationalist PPS.

It stands to reason that the PPS cries out that it, too, wants to overthrow the tsarist regime. Only a few years ago, it had the courage at least to talk about [obtaining] "cannons" for an "uprising." The PPS fantasized that it alone was capable of overthrowing absolutism with such an uprising. But the problem is

---

* This was an extremely reactionary, pro-government Russian newspaper.

not what a particular party thinks or says, but what it actually does. What are its actual policies and actions, and what are the logical results and consequences of those policies? Today, after the beginning of the revolution in the tsarist empire, the PPS has no courage to boast about an "uprising." Restoration of a "workers' Poland" has turned into "autonomy for Poland" and "a parliament in Warsaw." This is the same old nationalism, but far more cowardly and more reactionary, because whoever demands "autonomy for Poland," without demanding at the same time, and above all, political freedoms and a republic in Russia itself, without advocating a fight for those freedoms together with the Russian proletariat, that person deceives the workers, as if "autonomy in Poland" could be anything other than part of freedom in Russia—as if this were possible without freedom from the empire, and its still-powerful sovereign, the Russian tsar. And any person who at the present moment deceives the revolutionary workers [with such talk] is really acting in the same way as the National Democrats and the whole bourgeoisie.

They all want "autonomy for Poland" without the overthrow of the tsarist regime in Russia. But such "autonomy" with the tsar, in our conditions, is nothing else but that same "local self-government" for the [Zygmunt] Krasińskis, [Aleksander] Wielopolskis, and [Stanisław] Grabskis. And asking our workers to be humble in relation to the tsar and capitalists is just like the granting of religious tolerance for our priests, like those government jobs that the Polish intelligentsia dreams about, like a "Polish school system" to be granted by the grace of the tsar, and finally, like the Polish nobility, bourgeoisie, and petty bourgeoisie organizing together for the "national" suppression of the Polish revolutionary proletariat.*

At the highest peak of such "autonomy" in Poland, with the sovereign tsar in Russia, we will see a moment when the beloved tsar will allow Polish citizens to organize armed "national guards," who will defend domestic industry and public safety on the streets of Warsaw, Łódź, and Częstochowa and "autonomously" take the place of tsarist soldiers in the murder of strikers or of demonstrating Polish workers.

This is the true meaning and essence of the "political declaration" of the PPS at the end of January, and its [call for a] "parliament in Warsaw" without any republic in Petersburg. As always, social-patriotism covers itself and its bourgeois reactionary nature, unconsciously and thoughtlessly, with the banner of socialism. "Autonomy in Poland" without a demand for a republic in Russia as a socialist program—that is an absurd, cowardly, cunning platitude. And as a reality—stated honestly, without the cover of socialism—such a platitude is the same as the current program of "National Democracy" and that of our entire bourgeoisie, which has united with the tsar.

---

*   All three were magnates of the upper nobility who supported such right-wing groups as the National Democrats.

The open unification of the bourgeois classes with absolutism, in which they reveal themselves as totally reactionary, is (in truth) only beneficial for the cause of the working class. This makes it easier for the broad working masses in our country to quickly understand that their true and constant enemy is not only dying absolutism, at whose hand the fighting workers are being killed today, but also the Polish bourgeois class, at whose hand they will be killed tomorrow.

The victory of the revolution and the overthrow of the tsarist regime will not end the fight for the workers, but only open a new era of struggle—against the bourgeoisie. And for that fight, eye-to-eye and chest-to-chest, with the class of the combined exploiters the mass of workers must hasten to get organized. Only with a united, compact, powerful Social Democratic party, conscious of the interests and objectives of the workers, can our proletariat arm itself against the future political rule of one of the most villainous and despicable, one of the most obscurantist bourgeoisies in the world.

To the Polish Intelligentsia*

Citizens! One more mass slaughter, one more crime has marked out the bloody road down which the monster of absolutism is rolling toward the abyss.

Hundreds of more sacrifices, new hecatombs of corpses—that is what the Polish working class has laid upon the altar of freedom and civilization.

And once again shame has covered the "flower of our nation," the wealthy and "highborn" citizenry [of Poland].

While the blood of those murdered on the streets of Warsaw had not yet dried, while we were burying our brothers, wives, and children, whose bodies were still twitching in the spasms of death, those other "citizens" were again sending deputations to the authorities, demanding that the governor-general start an investigation into the slaughter on May Day. They were crawling wretchedly to the chief of the gang of robbers and begging in his anteroom for "tsarist justice!"

At the same time, the reactionary scribblers were assailing us with curses and abuse—while we were fighting and dying in battle; they were like jackals pouncing on those who had fallen on the battlefield. In our country, where one's throat is tightly choked by the hand of the tsarist censorship, they attacked us more mildly, but on the other side of the border, taking advantage of "national autonomy," this retrograde backward crowd howled openly and loudly against the revolutionary proletariat and against Social Democracy, which is leading it into battle.†

Citizens! Today there are only two camps. Two roads lie open before you. The January days and the days of May, the workers' revolution that broke out in our country after the revolutionary signal from Petersburg, have divided our society into two opposing camps, have torn away the shell of national unity, which was an illusion even before that, and have clearly revealed the gulf between two distinct nations. On the one side, fighting in the ruins of despotism, openly favoring an agreement with it, are the loyal knights of capital, of privilege and exploitation. And together with them are our ex-liberals and ex-progressives, a crowd of people who have debased themselves, who dishonored our society with their servile pilgrimage to the gates of the tsar and his ministers. Also together with them are the "National Democrats," who seek to put out the fire of the workers'

---

* This appeal was published in *Czerwony Sztandar*, No. 28, May 1905, p. 10, with the title in Polish of "Do inteligencji polskiej." It is translated by George Shriver and Alicja Mann. The article was signed by the Chief Executive Committee, Social Democracy of the Kingdom of Poland and Lithuania, Warsaw, May 1905. In some respects, it is a brief restatement of points Luxemburg made in her article "Dwa Obozy" (Two Camps), in the first pages of the same May 1905 issue of *Czerwony Sztandar*, appearing here pp. 135–43.

† The reference is to the Poznań region of German-occupied Poland and especially to Galicia in Austrian-occupied Poland, where some "national autonomy" was partially permitted.

revolution with the murky water of "national unity," that is to say, "national" cowardice, who seek to betray the cause of political freedom with false currency, [the idea of maintaining a separate] "Polish school" under absolutism.

But, on the other side are we in the camp of the Polish proletariat. We whose slogan is "Revolution!" and "Death to Despotism!" We who reject reconciliation with oppression—that is unknown to us. And the writing of memorandums to the government and offering compromises—that is unknown to us. Only struggle is known to us. We who, through class unity, have become brothers with the Russian proletariat. Together with them we will pave the way, with our own blood, with our own corpses, to a republic of freedom in the whole empire and to autonomy in our country.

Citizens! There was a moment in which history offered you a grace period to think things over, a time when you alone, you yourself, could choose whether to play a modest, but meaningful role in the history of the present revolution. When the liberal and democratic intelligentsia in Russia gave the first signal for an assault on autocracy, you preserved the silence of the grave in our country. You let the revolutionary proletariat go ahead of you. And you let the reactionary bourgeoisie go ahead of you, until matters reached the point of bloody conflict. The first wave of the revolution washed over your heads.

Today the division has taken place, the die has been cast. Today there remains for you only one choice—either with us, the fighting proletariat, or with the others, the servants of capitalism and the knout. In the camp of revolution or the camp of reaction. On the side of the bayonet or on the side of the street.

Citizens! Now after the murders on May Day, silence is no longer simply inaction. *Now when the blood of the people on the paved surfaces of the streets cries out for vengeance, to remain silent is to give consent to the gang of robbers! Now those who are not with us are against us!*

Make the choice:

Here are we, the children of poverty and labor, raising high the mangled bodies of our brothers, wives, and children, we with revolutionary anthems on our lips and the red banner of socialism over our heads, we go to our deaths for your freedom and for ours.

And over there, in a dark clump, closely crowded together, are some grisly apparitions, those who favor absolutism, and over there beside them are the obsequiously hunched-over shapes of the Polish nobility and the flickering-tongued serpent brood of the reactionary press.

Citizens, make your choice! Those who are alive—let them come over quickly to us, the side of the living!

In the name of those murdered on May 1—rise up to do battle!

Death to the highway robbers' gang of absolutism!

Long live the revolution!

A Giant Demonstration in Łódź[*]

(Łódź, May 29, from our correspondent)—Yesterday there occurred an event that one might think was a dream if all of us were not still under the powerful impression of this living reality.

On Friday, [May 26,] a strike broke out at the large Grohmann plant (more than 2,000 workers). The strike was carried out with model discipline. At the same time on Friday many agitators gave speeches at the plant in both Polish and German. At noon on the same day, several workers were peacefully walking past the plant when a patrol standing nearby for no apparent reason opened fire and one of the workers, Georg Grabeżyński, fell dead right then and there while two others were *seriously wounded.*

This assassination aroused tremendous indignation among the workers. The body of the murdered comrade was immediately carried into the factory building, and the comrades watched over it day and night despite very heavy pressure from the police—and it was kept there until the time for the burial. Social Democracy immediately called for two mass gatherings at the building of the Grohmann plant for the next day—Saturday—one being held early in the morning and the other in the afternoon. At both gatherings, speeches were given by our comrades in both Polish and German about the political meaning of the incident. At the same time, feverish agitation was carried on throughout the city with the demand: *All of proletarian Łódź, turn out for the funeral of our murdered comrade!* On the same day, a proclamation to this same effect was produced and circulated by Social Democracy, and many gatherings were held in different parts of the city with between 2,000 and 3,000 taking part at each.

The burial was to take place on Sunday, that is, yesterday, at three o'clock in the afternoon. Earlier on Sunday, we held a large gathering outside of the city where political speeches were given. And the proletariat responded to our call!

By 3 p.m. a crowd of about 40,000 workers had gathered in and around the Grohmann plant. *Not a single policeman and no military personnel were to be seen.* The funeral ceremony was opened with the singing of "The Red Banner."

A speaker for Social Democracy rose to the previously prepared rostrum and in the midst of breathless silence gave a long talk about the present revolution in the tsarist empire, the common interests of the proletariat in Poland and Russia, and the aims of Social Democracy. Stormy applause and cheers greeted the ending of the speech. The enthusiasm was so great that the speaker was

* This article first appeared anonymously in the main SPD newspaper, *Vorwärts*, No. 126, May 31, 1905. According to Luxemburg's letter to Leo Jogiches of June 25 or 26, 1905, she was seeing to the publication of information about the events in Łódź (cf. her *Gesammelte Briefe* Vol. 2, p. 141). The title in German is "Eine Riesendemonstration in Łódź." It is translated (by George Shriver) from the text in Luxemburg's *Gesammelte Werke*, Vol. 6, pp. 543–5.

carried high in the air on the hands of the crowd and endlessly repeated cheers went up for him. Then a woman comrade from the Social Democratic Party spoke in German, and the German workers responded to her speech with the greatest enthusiasm. Later, there were also speeches by representatives of the PPS and the Jewish Bund and then again by Social Democratic speakers. The mood that prevailed among this enormous mass of people, the feeling of joy at being able to hold this monster gathering completely undisturbed, the total absence of the police and military, who had simply disappeared, all this together is really beyond description. *It was something never seen before in Łódź and probably in the entire tsarist empire!*

And now we lined up in rows and the entire gigantic march, with the hearse in the middle, began to move out. At the front marched the standard-bearer of the Social Democratic Party of Poland and Lithuania with a large black banner and white lettering. "Honor to the Victims of Tsarist Despotism!" and "Long Live Social Democracy!" Behind the banner came Social Democratic women with a large wreath and red ribbons, "To the Victims of Thuggery from the Comrades of Social Democracy." After the wreath, the party banner of the PPS with the wording, "Long Live Freedom! Long Live the PPS!" Farther on the standard-bearers of the Jewish Bund were marching. Then there came a *band* and after that the *hearse drawn by four horses*. After the hearse, again there were standard-bearers of Social Democracy with red banners and the wording, "Away with the War! Down with Absolutism!" After that came the countless numbers of the crowd, who soon added up to at least 50,000 workers. The funeral march crossed the following streets—Pusta, Piotrkowska, Czerwona, Wólczańska and finally came to Eckenstrasse*—and we then went on out into the fields. At every street crossing new large groups of workers had joined us. Along the way there was continuous singing of "The Red Banner" with all the different stanzas alternating with the band playing the funeral march.

From Piotrkowska Street on, the coffin was taken out of the hearse and carried on the shoulders of the workers. *And the whole way there was not a policeman or a soldier to be seen!*

Suddenly shots were heard. There was a moment of panic. But it turned out that some workers from the PPS, according to their custom, were firing revolvers, shooting in the air. In response to the universal wish of those present this was soon stopped, and the demonstration continued undisturbed to the end. At the cemetery, all told, about 80,000 people gathered, which means nearly *all of proletarian Łódź*. Then the crowd turned around and slowly made its way back to the city.

On May 30, a telegram will be sent to the bourgeois newspapers that a high-ranking police officer will be shot. The strike movement is growing.

---

*   This street was at the city limits.

The Cards Are on the Table*

Recent days have again brought another sharp turn by the tsarist government in the direction of naked and brutal reaction. No sooner had the ukase† of April 17 "on religious toleration" been issued, sending our bourgeoisie and clergy into such euphoria, and no sooner had our "citizens' deputations" unbent their necks from their grateful bows for the "kind favors" of Nicholas the Bloody, than on May 20 the citizens were given a sharp slap in the face by way of recompense. The same governor-general Maksimovich, whom they had visited to deliver their "thanks," issued his own decree cancelling the tsar's decree—of course after communicating with higher authorities—explaining that "religious toleration," which Nicholas "with his inexpressible graciousness" was kind enough to give them means in reality that the Orthodox religion will still be the dominant one, as before, and the only one that can be freely practiced. Whereas any non-Orthodox person who tries to "openly spread their beliefs" or tries to "persuade anyone else to come over to their religion" will still be prosecuted and punished, as up until now, under the strictest clauses of the penal code. "Religious toleration" by the grace of the tsar was, from the moment of its birth, already a cripple and a monstrosity. There never was any intention to give it life for more than three-quarters of a moon. The Orthodox priesthood—concerned that there would be even the slightest *pretense* of freedom of religion for Catholics, Uniates, and dissenters—immediately exerted their influence on the court circles that are utterly impoverished both morally and mentally. The man placed at the head of the commission on questions of "religious toleration" was none other than [Alexei] Ignatyev, the notorious Cerberus‡ who has always loyally served the "Orthodox" tsarist knout, and the decree by Maksimovich is the early fruit of this "rearrangement of the church flags."

Thus the savage persecution of believers in other faiths could soon flow freely and unrestrictedly, with renewed force; and thus once again showing that under absolutism there can be no "toleration," that freedom of religion, like freedom in the schools and freedom of national-cultural development, is merely a part of political freedom, and therefore the first step toward establishing "toleration" in religion, as in any other area, must be—the overthrow of absolutism.

Simultaneously with the retraction of the decree on tolerance, the tsarist government took a couple of other steps in the same spirit. By a decree of the

---

* This article is translated (by George Shriver and Alicja Mann) from the June 1905 issue of *Czerwony Sztandar*, No. 27, June 1905, pp. 1–3. The title in Polish is "Otwarte karty" (literally, "Open Cards").

† A ukase or *ukaz* in Imperial Russia was a proclamation of the tsar, government, or a religious leader (patriarch), that had the force of law. "Edict" and "decree" are adequate translations using the terminology and concepts of Roman law.

‡ In Greek mythology, a multi-headed dog that guards the gates to the underworld.

tsar on June 6, General Trepov—appointed governor of Petersburg on the day after the January 22 butchery, still so vivid in memory, for the obvious purpose of pacifying the tsar's "rebellious" capital city—this man Trepov, one of the chief pillars of reaction in its most brutal form, has now been appointed *vice minister of internal affairs* [on June 6], and with that the tsar assured him of *unlimited police and gendarme powers*, totally independent of his "boss," the prime minister.*

A special task of the new *police dictator* is to prosecute "political offenders" and to shut down the liberals' "unauthorized assemblies," and to do this without any regard for "existing laws," that is, even the "laws" of the tsar himself—in short, to stamp out the socialists and stifle the liberals.

At the same time, progress on the celebrated "constitution" was made public, being worked on by Premier [Alexander] Bulygin along the lines promised by the tsar on February 19, right after the first outbreak of revolution in Petersburg. That is to say, the tsar's minister proposes the establishment of "popular representation" on the following bases:

The only persons who can be elected to this "parliament" granted by the grace of the tsar will be owners of large and medium-sized properties, both rural and urban; in other words, only [members of] the nobility and bourgeoisie. The qualification for the right to vote is the ownership of a certain amount of property. *Poor people, the entire class of the proletariat in all of the tsardom, numbering many millions, are totally excluded from voting.* But even this assembly of the rural and urban rich would not have any influence on legislation or the government. It is to deliberate on draft laws and the budget (that is, the income and expenditures of the state), but it has only a *consultative voice.* Laws are to be enacted in reality, just as before, solely by the "State Council," that is, the chinovniksi, men appointed by the tsar—plus the tsar himself, as up until now. Lastly, the ministers are not in any way responsible for their behavior to this assembly of elected representatives of the nobility and urban bourgeoisie, and they remain, as before, purely the flunkeys of the tsar-autocrat. In the same way, the "representative assembly" cannot even call them to account or demand their dismissal; just as before, they are not in any way accountable, even if these chinovniks themselves have broken the law.

To complete this caricature of a puppet-show "assembly," having no real power or authority, being authorized only to give "advice," so that, later on, the tsar's chinovniks can use it to wipe off their boots, Bulygin's proposed "constitution" further specifies that all together this "assembly" will gather to give its advice for only two months out of the year—from November to January. There you have the entire tsarist "constitution"! An assembly can be convened, consisting of several hundred gentlemen elected from among the nobility and bourgeoisie, to blow some hot air and shoot the breeze, but the law, or rather,

---

*   Giving him a status, in his own right, equal to that of the prime minister.

the state of lawlessness, will remain as before in the hands of the tsar and the chinovniks. Absolutism remains untouched, and the knout, as ever, rules supreme!

The proposal outlined above has not yet been adopted by the Committee of Ministers, but it shows distinctly enough what absolutism is aiming for. It shows that this regime of blood has no thought of making concessions—not a single step, not an inch of ground in that direction. Together with the retraction of the decree on religious toleration, with the awarding of dictatorial power to Trepov, with the latest terrible massacres that the news is reporting from the Caucasus, with the unceasing murders committed recently against workers everywhere in the empire—all these clearly and expressively demonstrate the following: The dying beast of despotism will leap up once again to fight like a ferocious tiger for its existence, and will try once again, as in the past, with fang and claw, to preserve its criminal way of life. Already oozing gore from a hundred wounds, fatally struck from the outside by Japanese shot and shell, assailed internally by popular revolution, blinded and raging, tsarist despotism is again gathering up its last reserves of strength to wage a life-or-death battle against the revolution, to crush with fire and the sword the people who have risen up formidably to bring down upon despotism the final judgment of history.

Thus, there can be no talk of "reforms," not even farcical ones. Even our very backward bourgeoisie is making depressed and disappointed faces in response to this flagrant removal of all masks by the "most merciful" of autocrats. But also for the militant working class, this new turn by tsarism back to its old policies is an important development, whose consequences should be evaluated seriously. Since absolutism itself has chosen the road of open struggle and stubbornly persists in the defense of its existence and the inviolability of the reigning lawlessness, then the only way out of the present situation can be, not some partial reconciliation with absolutism, but only its total and complete destruction. That means, in other words, that the denouement and conclusion of the present political crisis still lies only in the hands of the revolutionary *proletariat* of the entire Russian state, just as it alone gave the present revolution its start. But this circumstance also gives hope that the political freedom that will emerge as the final result of the present crisis will have imprinted upon it the mark of the proletariat's revolutionary struggle, not that of tsarism's "liberal" chess play with the bourgeoisie.

In Russia, there exists, as is widely known, a bourgeois-noble [form] of *liberalism*, something generally unknown in our country, and there even exists a bourgeois *democracy*—elements of the petty bourgeoisie, the intelligentsia, and the nobility who are openly and sharply calling for political freedoms and the convening of a popular assembly. These circles, like all elements belonging to the property-owning classes, did not by themselves constitute a force capable of compelling absolutism to make concessions, but by the nature of things they were in a position to quickly get ready to take advantage of the workers' revolutionary battles and sacrifices. The liberal section of the Russian nobility and urban bourgeoisie has followed the development of the workers' struggle with uneasiness, regarding it only as a useful means for frightening the government and extorting concessions from it.

The class consciousness and class struggle of the proletariat developing more and more during the course of the present revolution is, in the essence of the matter, as frightening to the ruling classes in Russia as to those in Poland. Thus, the same longing for the restoration of "harmony and order" and for the quickest possible end to the current stormy period of strikes and revolutionary battles is felt nowadays in common among all bourgeois circles of the empire.

The Russian liberals—especially their most influential sector, the liberal nobility—are relying solely [on the possibility] of receiving from the government as soon as possible, and no matter how impoverished it might be, a little baby "constitution-ette," one that would assure the open rule of the liberal nobility and bourgeoisie, which would then reconcile themselves with the government right away and energetically set about alleviating the "chaos" that the "liberal" Mr. [Aleksander] Świętokowski complains so much about in [the Polish liberal newspaper] *Prawda**—that is, suppressing the revolutionary proletariat.

These expectations and this impatience of the Russian liberals were *openly* expressed in recent days by *Mr. Struve*, the official leader of the constitutional liberals, who published an "Open Letter" to the French socialist newspaper, *L'Humanité* on June 8 [1905], in which he laid out the current program of his party.†

Struve writes that what Russia needs now above all else is a *"strong government,"* in order, first, to conclude peace with Japan without making excessively great concessions, and second, to establish *"order"* inside Russia. For these purposes alone, Nicholas II ought to convene an assembly of delegates of the rural landed nobility, and that gathering would quickly name names for the tsar of men who enjoy the confidence of the country and are capable of establishing a *"strong government."* Let Nicholas II accept these men's program and entrust them with power (that means give them portfolios as government ministers).

Because Russia today needs not only freedom but also a government suitable to the requirements of both freedom and order [writes Struve].

Thus, *openly* and without shame, the liberalism of the nobility offers its services to Nicholas the Last. As for the summoning of an assembly of people's representatives elected on the basis of universal suffrage—there can be no question of that. Instead, the zemstvo liberals ask only that they themselves be

---

*   A reference to a Polish liberal newspaper.

†   At the time Struve was a member of the liberal Union of Liberation party. Later, in October 1905, he cofounded the Constitutional Democratic party. For another article by Luxemburg, written around the same time and describing Struve's "Open Letter" in fuller detail, see "Up-and-Coming Men in Russia," below, pp.167–71.

"summoned." They are ready to simply take the ministerial files from the bloody hands of the tsar, promising in return to conclude a "profitable" peace with Japan and to establish "order," that is, to suppress the workers' movement, and on top of that, even to reconcile Russia with England.

In short, Mr. Struve is trying to persuade the tsar that, to put it bluntly, Trepov is not needed at all, because the liberals themselves are capable of being "men of the iron fist."

This confession of faith by Struve shows at what a low price the Russian liberal party is prepared to sell the cause of the people's freedom to the tsar's government and how impatiently they insist that the tsar should deign to accept the services they have offered him. Since there is not a trace among us in Poland of even such an impoverished liberalism as Struve represents in Russia, our bourgeoisie and nobility would undoubtedly welcome it with shouts of joy if the demands of the Russian liberals were carried out. A "strong government" and "order"—i.e., immediately turning the bullets and bayonets of "constitutional" rule against the "rebellious" workers, who would be deprived of all rights and freedoms—that is what would await us if the demands of the bourgeoisie and nobility, both Russian and Polish, all of them loyal knights of capitalist "law and order," were to win the ear of the tsar and his advisers!

But the courtiers of liberalism will not win his ear. The very latest steps taken by absolutism show that the tsar has much more confidence in the "iron fist" of Trepov than in that of Mr. Struve, that he would rather murder the workers himself than entrust this task to "liberal" government ministers and "liberal" police chiefs.

This turn of events truly announces for us that the revolution will continue for a long time and holds, for the working class, a prospect full of heavy sacrifices as yet unheard of. But this guarantees that those sacrifices will not be in vain, that the political freedom of the future will not be merely little peacock's feathers with which liberalism wants to decorate today's despotic government.

Let us not delude ourselves that the working class could obtain the rulership after the overthrow of absolutism. We live in a capitalist society, and as long as the capitalist rules over the proletarian—who hires himself out as a wage laborer in the factory and on the land—the bourgeoisie and nobility will dominate the state politically. But if political freedoms are won completely in Russia and Poland, through the efforts of the revolutionary proletariat, then it will be grounded more solidly, and the broader the participation of the proletariat, the more will it be able, later on, to wage a strong defense of the class interests of the exploited generally against the rule of a "strong government" of the exploiters, and that can hasten the ultimate removal of the bourgeois "order" itself.

Thus, the open declaration of the latest political program of the government and the open admission of the program of the liberals reveal once again to the working class of the whole empire what its great tasks are at the present moment.

Every day, every moment of the present revolution is for the proletariat of Russia and Poland an opportunity to quickly organize itself into a strong and conscious political party—a class party—an opportunity that history will not repeat for decades to come. Under a hail of bullets from dying despotism, the working class must now arm itself for the struggle against the coming rule of the bourgeoisie.

The present revolution is costing us terrible sacrifices. May these sacrifices buy not only formal political *rights and freedoms*, which are indispensable for waging the class struggle, but also that which is most valuable, the *class consciousness and class organization* of the proletariat. May the bourgeoisie, wherever it lifts itself to a position of power, a victory gained at the hands of the workers— may it find itself facing, not groups of workers who are dispersed, disoriented, and exhausted by the struggle, but the compact class power of the proletariat, steeled and hardened in the fire of the revolution, knowing, on the day after the revolution, how to turn the blade of the struggle against the bourgeoisie with the same strength they used, the day before, to smash the governments of despotism.

The "Peaceful" Action of the PPS*

The further the cause of the present revolution has progressed and developed, the more distinctly one sphere of society after another, one political party after another, has separated itself from the fighting working class. The working class [now] stands by itself, counting only on its own strength. And the defense of its interests has become, more and more obviously to everyone, the sole task of Social Democracy.

And here something unheard of has happened. The social-patriotic PPS has come out with a special proclamation against—*the general strike*!! Since it is almost difficult to give credence to such abandonment of all good sense by a party that wishes to pass as a workers' and socialist party, we therefore quote this document in its entirety:

> Comrade workers! The class-conscious Russian workers want to celebrate May Day this Sunday [May 14]—which is May 1 by the old calendar [used in Russia]. We never retreated before from active support of the revolutionary movement in Russia—the evidence of this is our strikes in January. In the event of any serious developments in Russia we will fight jointly, even at the expense of our blood.
>
> We have already celebrated May Day. A general celebration is not such a trivial thing that you can arrange it time and time again. To overuse this method of struggle weakens our strength, which is so needed today for the final battle with tsarism. Do not give in to agitation by people who in order to gain publicity are willing to push you every day to senseless new strikes and bloody clashes that today are pointless. *Do not succumb to the pressure and terror of isolated individuals. Only the summons of the Polish Socialist Party should be obligatory for you! We should remain calm and pay no heed to any calls for another May Day celebration and a general strike.*† If the moment comes in Russia for a determined revolutionary struggle, our organization will call and request your participation. Only a planned and organized fight can lead to victory.
>
> Long live the Revolution!
> Long live the solidarity of the workers!
> —*Częstochowa Workers Committee of the Polish Socialist Party*‡

Such is the call of the PPS to the Polish working class at a time of revolution. It stands to reason that the talk about supposedly not repeating the May

---

* This article is translated (by George Shriver and Alicja Mann) from *Czerwony Sztandar*, No. 27, June 1905, pp. 7–9. The title in Polish is "Akcja 'pokojowa' PPS."

† A note by the editor of *Czerwony Sztandar* appears at this point in the original: "Emphasis added by us."

‡ A note by the editor of *Czerwony Sztandar* in the original: "The same proclamation was also issued by the Łódź Committee of the PPS."

celebration on the Russian date [i.e., May 14] is simply an excuse sucked out of someone's thumb; it is only a trumped-up disguise for this unprecedented action of opposing general strikes. Besides, to celebrate May Day in our country a second time on May 14 to protest the widespread unemployment—no one ever dreamed of that and no one agitated for that. But even if it were so, the PPS has already committed the imprudence of showing quite clearly that its intention is not to oppose some imaginary repetition of the May Day celebration on the Russian date, but to create barriers to the whole idea of the general strike. It is known that the PPS agitated in fierce opposition already, before the general strike of May 4, which (our) Social Democracy had called for to commemorate the victims killed at the May Day celebration [in Warsaw on May 1].

Therefore, the PPS proclamation is nothing other than open agitation against general strikes at the present time. "We should remain calm," "pointless strikes," "aimless bloody clashes"—that is how this party speaks today to the workers, a party that wishes to bear the name of a workers' party! When for ten years there was complete "calm" in Russia and in Poland, the PPS at that time shouted continuously for an "armed uprising," wrote about importing "small cannons" from abroad, and wondered, "Was not it the right time to lead the people to insurrection?" And now, when it can and should take action, when finally in Russia and Poland things are beginning to happen and not an imaginary "uprising" with small cannons, but a real workers' revolution—now the PPS begins to call loudly for people to "remain calm."

If the PPS had even a little sense of reality, as a genuine workers' party has, if it had any spiritual connection with the feelings and aspirations of the masses of our proletariat, then its political instinct itself would have warned it not to speak in such a shameful way in the midst of the current revolutionary moment. For who today is calling for our workers to "remain calm," who is talking about the pointlessness of general strikes? Who talks about "overusing a method of struggle?" The entire reactionary press, the reptile breed of the bourgeois press—they do. Such calls are being heard nowadays from [such capitalist publications as] the Kraków paper *Czas* [Time] and from *Gazeta Polska* [Poland's Daily], and *Słowo Polskie* [The Polish Word], and *Goniec Warszawski* [Warsaw Messenger]. The priests cry out this way in church on the orders of the Archbishop. All open enemies of the working class cry out like this, as do all open supporters of the tsarist government and the rule of capital.

To this chorus, wailing about the socialists [allegedly] terrorizing society and ruining domestic industry, the PPS has added its voice. It is not ashamed to do this and at the same time even to use the same jargon, the same words, that the reactionaries use against socialists—not only in our country but also around the world. "Do not give in to terror from isolated individuals," "do not give in to the agitation of the people who in order to gain publicity are willing to push you every day to new pointless strikes"—these words are taken straight out of articles in *Slowo Polskie* [The Polish Word] and proclamations by the party called National Democracy, barking hoarsely at the socialists and almost calling for help from the tsarist police against their agitation. These are the words that, in the German, French, and Italian parliaments, a variety of different capitalists have uttered countless times as a warning for the "poor," "misled" and "terrorized" workers, in order to separate them from the influence of Social Democracy.

There is, literally, no paper in any country that does more to put down the socialists who are trying to enlighten the workers, calling them to fight, by accusing them of trying "to gain publicity" and "terrorizing the workers." These slanders are as old as capitalist exploitation itself and the struggle of the workers for their liberation from its oppressive yoke. This foul language by all the enemies of working people, all the bourgeois slime, all police—the PPS now uses it against the agitation and struggle of the working class in our country!

Anyone, even a worker who is only slightly conscious, can understand that such action by the PPS becomes a service rendered to the tsarist government and the capitalists. Because what kind of weapon can be stronger in defense of the working class than the general strike? It is the only weapon, and the most powerful one, that can show the government and bourgeoisie that the will of the working class and its demands must be taken into account. The January general strike in Petersburg, and the January 27 general strike in our country, gave birth to today's revolution. It has shaken the foundations of absolutism. It has brought closer the time of death for the despotic government.

The strikes in our country in February and March caused a profound mobilization in the whole vast ocean of the proletariat; it mobilized them to fight for human rights; tens of thousands of the victims of exploitation and oppression were awakened from the stupor surrounding them, even our brothers working on the land, to fight for a better life. These strikes have awakened in our capitalists some respect for the despised workers and forced them to a whole range of concessions, however minor. The general strike on May Day showed the tsarist government that our working people will not calm down, will not go back to a "normal life" until the rule of the knout and the worship of the knout are overthrown. Finally, the general strike on May 4 was a worthy response of workers of Warsaw to the May 1 slaughter. It was the announcement that they were standing up for the victims murdered by the tsarist thugs—they, the proletariat of Warsaw, who hate the government murderers and are ready to fight unrelentingly against them.

In short, the general strike has so far been the most powerful weapon, and remains so in the current revolution, for raising the awareness and focusing the attention of the proletariat, and for directing its mass struggle against the capitalists and the government. To take away now from the workers in Russia and in Poland the possibility of engaging in widespread strikes at important moments of struggle, to take away from them their faith in the efficacy of these instances of mass action—if you take that away, the cause of workers' revolution will be bogged down for a long time to come. Therefore the one who today warns the workers against the general strike and urges them to "remain calm"—*such a person is acting directly on behalf of the exploiters and is acting as a supporter of the tsarist government*—whether it is a priest, thundering from the pulpit at the request of Archbishop [Vincent Theophilus Chosciak] Popiel, whether it is a scribbler for the *Goniec Warszawski* [Warsaw Messenger], or whether it is someone circulating the proclamations of the so-called National Democracy or the so-called Polish Socialist Party. It is a harmful service rendered to the tsarist government—this proclamation against general strikes. And the PPS cannot make up for this proclamation, or correct it, with "bombs" in pastry shops, not even with bombs "intended" for [Governor-General] Maksimovich.

But the best testimony of the poverty that the PPS has displayed is the fact that it ended its appeal with the following words: "If the moment comes in Russia for a determined revolutionary struggle, our organization will call and request your participation." In other words, this is what they mean: "Workers, refrain for now from mass demonstrations and revolutionary struggle, stay at home quietly, walk quietly under the yoke of capital, and when the 'decisive moment' will arrive, the PPS will send you an 'order' to turn out, and will tell you what you should do." Here we have new evidence of how totally alien the PPS is to the spirit of the mass struggle, and is simply bringing to the proletariat's class struggle a Blanquist concept, a concept commonly held in conspiratorial circles. According to these "revolutionaries," the conscious mass of the workers are not, from beginning to end, the conscious agents of their own liberation, but [instead] are called upon to appear on the scene only at the end of the fight, at some kind of "decisive moment," and at the "summons" of the so-called socialists.

It should be recognized that the National Democracy, when it urges workers with almost the same words as the PPS to "remain calm" and refrain from "pointless strikes," is acting far more honestly, and at least it does not deceive the workers with the false hope that there will be a "decisive moment" when it will summon them to revolutionary struggle.

National Democracy understands very well, just as every person with good sense today must understand, that the "decisive moment," that is, the overthrow of absolutism, *will not happen* unless the working class in our country and in the entire Russian empire is in *constant and continual mass struggle*, in preparation for that "moment." This "moment" will never happen if the workers "remain calm," sitting at home, waiting for divine mercy or orders from the PPS. Only as a result of the continuous mass actions of the revolutionary workers will there be a growing army of conscious combatants, who will then, little by little, win over a section of the soldiers. They are undermining the authority of the government, causing confusion, upset, uncertainty, and thus they are preparing the possibility of arming the working masses. They intensify the revolutionary conditions, and thus bring closer and prepare the way for that "decisive moment."

If the PPS tries to persuade the workers that this "moment" will fall from the sky all by itself, telling them to sit at home and "remain calm," then it is only contributing toward the result that this moment will never occur, that the revolutionary struggle will never develop fully as a result of disorganizing the government, that the poverty of the working class and the intimidating atmosphere [produced under] the decaying corpse of absolutism will be prolonged endlessly. "National Democracy" and other supporters of reaction know very well and do not hide the fact that to dissuade the workers from general strikes and demonstrations is *actually to dissuade them from the revolution*, from the overthrow of the tsarist government. What the PPS is actually *doing* is the same thing, differing from the bourgeois nationalists only in the fact that they tell the workers that this work *against* the revolution will supposedly result in the "decisive revolutionary battle;" that is, the PPS differs only—in that it uses this seductive revolutionary-sounding cliché.

Actually, this is not the first service provided by the PPS to knout-wielding absolutism. The same service to the government is found in every word that the PPS has been writing for the past ten years, aiming at the detachment of the Polish workers from solidarity and fraternal struggle with the Russian workers, to persuade them that in Russia there is no hope for any labor movement or for any revolution, all of it to justify its foolish utopian program of rebuilding Poland. All these reactionary acts of the PPS are simply the direct consequence of its false, nationalistic positions, revealing only the fact that the PPS is not really a workers' party, but in its whole spirit it is thoroughly an expression of the bourgeois intelligentsia and only artificially is it attached to the labor movement and socialism.

The present revolution, which has given the lie to the PPS's entire conception, has placed this party, by the very nature of things, on an inclined plane, a surface on which it has been sliding more and more quickly downhill. Now, in the true revolutionary struggle, at every step of it, it is already obvious what a fundamental difference exists between a genuine workers' party that is Social Democracy, and a party that protects petty bourgeois nationalism by using socialistic phrases, which is the PPS.

While Social Democracy is trying with all its might to explain the necessity for *mass struggle* by the proletariat, the PPS is confusing workers' minds with talk of "terror," playing in little conspiratorial "combat" circles and stunning itself with the bang of bombs, which are removing, not absolutism, but at most a few measly policemen or soldiers. While Social Democracy is exerting all its efforts toward the working class in order to explain the necessity for an independent and *separate class politics*, to explain the whole hypocrisy of bourgeois liberalism, the PPS has been in a hurry, now at the beginning of the revolution, to join in "common action" with the party of Russian *liberal nobles*, the party of the same Mr. Struve who now offers his party's services to Nicholas the Last so as to establish "order" in Russia.[*]

While Social Democracy seeks to channel all the energy and all the hopes of the workers toward a revolutionary economic and political struggle, elements of the PPS are helping the National Democratic Party to divert the workers with propaganda about "abstinence," the fight against drinking and smoking, telling them that in this way absolutism can be "impoverished." Even if the entire Kingdom of Poland refused to consume a single glass of vodka or a single cigarette *for an entire year*, this would cause a shortage to the coffers of the tsarist government of no more than 50 million roubles. But such an outcome cannot be accomplished at all by agitation, which hardly affects the multimillion-peasant mass, and certainly overestimates the great influence and importance of our serious PPS clowns, assuming that as a result of their campaigning Russian absolutism could be "emasculated" by about 5,000 roubles. Anyway, let it be up to 500,000 roubles—the whole significance of this action can be properly assessed if one realizes that during the past seventeen months absolutism has already thrown into the war effort, every month, 700 million roubles![†]

And yet the PPS boasts proudly in its Kraków newspaper *Naprzód* [Forward] that this move against drinking and smoking has found warm support "even" in the bourgeois press, not understanding in its blindness that the bourgeoisie is always willing and "even" happy to try and persuade the workers that it is not revolutionary struggle, but only "abstinence" that will improve their life.

This party that calls itself a workers' party, is helping in the midst of the current revolutionary moment to distract the workers from the revolutionary struggle against absolutism by directing their attention to the "fight against alcohol," working directly in this way to the benefit of the tsarist government!

While Social Democracy in Warsaw and in all the provinces [of the Russian-ruled Kingdom of Poland] is trying to give speeches to raise the workers' awareness of the revolutionary nature of their class, the PPS arranged for people to hold a provincial celebration of May Day in a church, [including] the singing

---

[*]   Note by the editor of *Czerwony Sztandar*: "For more about this, see the lead article in this issue." This refers to "Otwarte karty" (The Cards Are on the Table) which appeared in the same June 1905 issue of *Czerwony Sztandar* as the present article. In "Otwarte Karty" Luxemburg discussed in particular a statement by Struve published in France in early June 1905, making clear his position of offering his services to the tsarist government, along with those of his party, the liberal party of the Russian nobility. See above, pp. 148–53.

[†]   The preceding discussion about "abstinence" was sharply condemned by Jogiches, as follows: "And the dumb editor, out of unnecessary thoroughness and devotedness, inserts a superfluous passage about abstinence into the article 'Akcja ... PPS.' This disrupts the proper inner proportions [of the article] and makes a bad impression" (see Luxemburg, *Gesammelte Briefe*, Vol. 2, p. 141). In addition, as a result of errors in the typesetting of the original, incorrect figures appear in it about the losses in roubles that would be caused by a one-year consumer boycott of the tsarist government's vodka monopoly. The numbers have been corrected here.

of "God Save Poland," merging in this way into a single camp with National Democracy.*

While Social Democracy is calling on the proletariat to avenge and honor the victims of the tsarist thugs with further serious and massive revolutionary actions, such as demonstrations and general strikes, the PPS seeks to gain from some bizarre buffoonery, sounding as though it were blaspheming the poverty of the workers, and their miseries, ordering them to take a "week of mourning" by wearing a band of black crepe on their sleeves and abandoning "pleasures and amusements." As if the workers were rich bourgeois venturing several times a week to a ball with dancing, and as if without an order from the PPS, our hungry workers, in the midst of their poverty and the terrible battle they are waging, full of sacrifices—as if they indulge themselves in "pleasures and amusements!"†

And while Social Democracy, responding to the working class's own wishes, needs, and aspirations, gave expression to the workers' class struggle by calling for the great general strike of May 4, which morally overwhelmed the whole bourgeoisie and even the government's own reptile publication, *Gazeta Warszawska* [Warsaw Daily], the PPS has the audacity to issue a call expressing a desire to extinguish the fire that has spread among the revolutionary proletariat. It calls for "remaining calm" and talks about the workers [supposedly] being "terrorized." Such hatred toward the workers' party, Social Democracy, has led it (the PPS) to lose all sense of revolutionary duty of what is good for the cause of the proletariat. The PPS is ready for anything to "ruin" Social Democracy, ignoring even the fact that in this way it is playing into the hands of the tsarist government murderers!

From the very beginning of the revolution, the tactics of the PPS have ranged between clowning and betraying the revolutionary cause. Activities that might seem to be harmless, like exploding some bombs on bridges, issuing "orders" to the working class, having them wear black crepe on their sleeves and stop their "pleasures and amusements" in their basements and attics—all that betrays some characteristics of puppet shows performed by gilded youth, playing at socialism. But the PPS's activities are not playful at all—such as the exploding of bombs, the victims of which often include some very sincere persons devoted to the workers' cause, who have unfortunately been fooled by the PPS. Other examples include the PPS's alliance with the liberalism of the nobility, and last of

---

* Note by the editor of of *Czerwony Sztandar*: "PPS activists themselves described this extensively in their correspondence from Starachów, near Radom, published in the Kraków newspaper of the PPS, *Naprzód* [Forward]; see the issue for May 17, 1905."

† Note by the editor of *Czerwony Sztandar*: "PPS members again wrote at length about this in the May 18 issue of *Naprzód*, in which you can read the following, word for word: 'After two had fallen victim to the tsarist superpower in the days of May, along with a hundred others fallen in all of Poland, our local committee announces, following the example of other committees: *One week of mourning, starting May 11. No pleasure, no amusements. Outward sign of mourning: crepe [black-fabric armband] on the left sleeve.*'"

all, this proclamation against general strikes that clearly bears the mark of action that serves the government and the bourgeoisie and is harmful to the revolution.

Such freak changes and jumps are suitable only to a party whose spirit is entirely alien to the working class and does not understand at all what the workers feel nowadays, how they live, what is their spiritual mood, and most of all—what their class interests require.

And such a party has the pretentiousness to try and "give orders" to our proletariat! Such a party has the audacity to say to the workers: "Only the summons of the Polish Socialist Party should be obligatory for you!"

Fortunately, the Polish workers are already too mature politically and too class conscious for this new "rooting around" by the PPS to have any effect. Just as it was not in response to a call from the PPS that the Polish proletariat held the general strike of January 27, so too it will not now give up its revolutionary struggle on "orders" from the PPS. The only effect of the PPS's proclamation against general strikes is that the workers will see more clearly what is the essence of this party that calls on them to "remain calm" in the midst of a revolution. They understand how little the leaders of this party have in common with the spiritual and political affinities, the interests and struggles of the working class. This same appeal of the PPS is nothing more than a desperate and crazy step taken by this party, which feels that the current revolution is separating it from the workers' milieu and with each day is removing the ground from under its feet.

Honorable Gentlemen—Lawyers of Poland*

An all-Russian congress of lawyers was held in Petersburg. Here is the resolution of that congress:

> Whereas: (1) Today's bureaucratic system nationwide is not capable of satisfying the needs of the country; (2) The government itself was forced to acknowledge the necessity for the participation of elected representatives of the people in the empire-wide system; (3) Therefore, the time has come for self-government by society; (4) All attendees at the congress—however different their political and social views may be—are in agreement that our immediate task is the following: (a) Replacement of the existing bureaucratic system with a constitutional one; (b) Emancipation of all working sectors of the people from the oppression of existing economic conditions.
>
> Therefore, the congress resolves: (1) To form a political association among lawyers for the realization of the above-mentioned tasks, that is, to establish in Russia a democratic-constitutional system on the basis of universal and equal suffrage and the secret ballot; (2) To make known to the public the formation of this association.

Thus, as we see, the Russian lawyers have found their way to taking political action in that they clearly and distinctly, without mincing words, raise constitutional demands. It might be possible to find many faults in this resolution. Above all, it is not clear, because while it does go so far as to call for universal, direct, and equal suffrage with a secret ballot, it must be specified more clearly what powers a parliament elected in this way would have, and what powers the government would have, and so on and so forth. Indeed, we could see that, although the zemstvo gentlemen, for example, were in favor of universal and equal suffrage and a secret ballot, they also wanted to have a bicameral legislature, with only the lower chamber being elected in this way, while in the second or upper chamber only representatives of large property would be seated, etc. However, since laws could only be passed with the approval of both chambers, it logically follows that only those laws would be passed as are agreeable to the nobility and bourgeoisie.

The lawyers, therefore, ought to have expressed themselves a bit more clearly. In any case, the fact remains that these Russian lawyers have thrown

---

* This article appeared in *Czerwony Sztandar*, No. 27, June 1905, pp. 9–10, as part of a section of that publication with the general heading, "From Our Country," and a subsection with the general heading, "From the Life of [Our] Society." The actual Polish title of the article—aside from the general headings of the section and subsection—is "Panowie adwokaci polscy." It is translated by George Shriver and Alicja Mann.

down the gauntlet; they want to fight the tsarist regime; and that is already saying something.

How did the gentleman of the Polish bar respond to this?

They vacillated for a long time over whether or not to take part in the congress. There were those who asserted that this congress "does not have anything in common with *our interests.*" But, in the end, they did send their representatives, and they made public the following resolution:

> The Bar Association of the Kingdom of Poland constitutes a separate entity, and therefore cannot enter or join the projected Russia-wide union of lawyers. But it can enter into a relationship with the Russian Bar Association, when necessary, but only on the basis of full equality. It is necessary for the congress to recognize in regard to the Kingdom of Poland complete internal legal and administrative autonomy, based on universal, direct, and equal suffrage with the secret ballot for all citizens of the Kingdom of Poland. Representatives of the Polish Bar Association express their sympathy for the Russian constitutional movement. Its representatives will take part in the further proceedings of the congress only if the congress recognizes the necessity for autonomy for the Kingdom of Poland.

What a strange resolution! The gentlemen lawyers "express their sympathy for the Russian constitutional movement." Very lovely on their part, and we take note that at least their sympathy does not lie with the absolutist government. That is certainly a step forward, because our honorable Mr. Peplowski, "our widely known and respected attorney," for example, declines to defend socialists before a military court because he considers this "a filthy business." Another attorney, Mr. [Włodzimierz] Spasowicz, is definitely a supporter of tsarism. To "express sympathy" is all well and good, but what then? The lawyers' congress constituted itself as a political organization whose task is to fight for a constitution. The gentlemen of the Polish bar took part in the proceedings of the congress, because that congress not only recognized the autonomy of the Kingdom [of Poland] but also recognized the general right of autonomy for all nationalities in the Russian empire. But the gentlemen of the Polish bar did not join that union, because they "constitute a separate entity."

What will this "separate entity" be doing later on? It will keep on "expressing sympathy"—and will not lift a finger, will only twiddle its thumbs.

No, gentlemen of the Polish Bar Association, it is not about sympathy! When gunfire is loudly resounding in our country, when the Polish proletariat is fighting against absolutism, when blood is being spilled on the streets of Warsaw and Łódź, when a thirst for revolution has taken hold of the whole country, you have sympathy but you remain silent. Today, anyone who is not with the revolution is against it—regardless of their sympathy.

Look out, gentlemen lawyers, lest the revolution reply to you in the words of

St. John of the Apocalypse, "I know thy deeds; that they are neither hot nor cold. Since you are lukewarm, I spit thee out of my mouth."*

Truly, this is a remarkable situation. The Polish proletariat stands at the head of the proletariat in the whole Russian state. It now constitutes the vanguard of the revolution. But the Polish intelligentsia expresses its sympathy. Ha! That is too bad. Let the dead bury the dead. For those members of the intelligentsia who, nevertheless, are not satisfied with the role of "sympathizers," who are eager for active struggle, and not a passive emphasis on "separateness," who don't want to sit around twiddling their thumbs, to them we say, the road is open to join the ranks of the revolutionary proletariat. Here you will find people who are demanding autonomy for our country, but also know how to fight for autonomy by fighting against tsarism.

---

* The statement is from the Book of Revelation, 3:16 and 3:17: "I know everything you have done, and you are not hot or cold. I wish you were one or the other. But since you are lukewarm and neither cold nor hot, I will spit you out of my mouth." *Holy Bible* (New York: American Bible Society, 1995), p. 10,780.

Conference of Socialist and Revolutionary Organizations*

At the end of April, a conference of socialist and revolutionary organizations was held, called by [Father] Gapon "for the purpose of coming to an agreement on the matter of joint action against the autocracy." Our Executive Body [Zarząd—of the SDKPiL], having received the invitation to this conference along with other socialist organizations, resolved not to take part in such a gathering.

In this we were guided by the following reasons: (1) If it was a matter of coming to an agreement about giving *political direction* to "action against the autocracy," then in view of the variety of different directions being taken by the organizations likely to participate in the conference, *there could be no question* of any such unified direction; and (2) if it was a matter of coming to agreement on giving *technical* direction (that is mainly about arming the masses), then first of all, on this question our party holds a position entirely different from those held by such revolutionary organizations as for example the Socialist Revolutionary Party (SR) and the PPS. On this question, see our pamphlet *Co Dalej* [What Next?]†

Secondly, our Executive is of the opinion that truly, for a successful combination of efforts—that might come about, in general—such matters can be decided only in the course of the struggle at each particular location, whereas deliberations at gatherings of such-and-such many representatives of a dozen or so parties and sub-parties, which are either "truly" socialist or "not entirely" socialist, either actual or fictitious, cannot have any influence on the progress of the revolutionary cause.

As for Gapon's invitation, we were in a quandary about whether we should address him as "Father" or "Comrade," since yesterday's "Father" is today a Social Democrat, but tomorrow he may stand "above parties," and the day after tomorrow return to his unenlightened Orthodox peasant followers, once again

---

* This article is translated (by George Shriver and Alicja Mann) from *Czerwony Sztandar*, No. 27, June 1905, pp. 14–15.

† This refers, in part, to the article "Z doby rewolucyjnej: Co dalej?" (In Revolutionary Times: What Next?), which was published in *Czerwony Sztandar*, No. 25, April 1905, pp. 1–4. Shortly thereafter, Luxemburg published a second part of the article under the same title in a supplement to *Czerwony Sztandar*, No. 26, May 1905, pp. 1–16. For a German translation of those two parts, see Luxemburg's *Gesammelte Werke*, Vol. 1, Part 2, pp. 541–72. This two-part article from April and May of 1905 was reprinted shortly afterwards as a pamphlet published in Kraków—which is the pamphlet Luxemburg is here referring to. Later, in 1906, this work was again published as a separate pamphlet (this time in Warsaw), but as an expanded version with a new third part—and once again under same title, *Co dalej*. The full text of *Co dalej* as published in pamphlet form in Warsaw in 1906 will appear in Volume 4 of *The Complete Works of Rosa Luxemburg*.

putting on his cassock.* [And so] the Executive of our party did not make any reply, because it is of the opinion that the calling together of organizations from the entire empire to a conference by just a few particular entities is highly inappropriate and pretentious.

As the press has reported about the conference, the invitation to it was declined flatly by one section of the RSDRP, and from the conference itself four other Social Democratic organizations withdrew—the other section of the RSDRP, the Latvian SDRP, the "Bund," and the Armenian Social Democratic Workers Organization. The course taken by the conference as well as its results fully confirmed our view about the pointlessness of such "chat sessions."†

---

* In fact, this largely conforms to the trajectory of Gapon's future development. Upon fleeing Russia following the events of January 22, 1905, he drew close to the Socialist Revolutionary Party (after having extensive discussions with various leading Social Democrats in West Europe) but at the very end of 1905 he returned to Russia, whereupon he was executed by the SR when they discovered he was working for the Okhrana.

† The conference took place in Geneva on April 2–3, 1905, with the participation of eleven organizations from the tsarist empire, among them the PPS from Poland. The SDKPiL declined in advance to participate in this conference, as did the Bolshevik wing of the RSDRP. Later, the following joined in with the decision not to participate: the Menshevik wing of the RSDRP and the Bund, as well as the Social Democrats of Latvia and Armenia. The quotation cited by Luxemburg from Gapon's invitation, although not the exact wording, is from an "Open Letter" to socialist parties of the Russian state published by Gapon on February 10, 1905.

Up-and-Coming Men in Russia[*]

Recent days have brought a highly interesting and significant announcement from Russian liberalism, one that is quite relevant in that it sheds a bright light on class and party relations inside the tsarist empire in the midst of revolution.

Mr. Pyotr von Struve,[†] who is the literary representative and intellectual head of liberalism in Russia, has published an Open Letter to Jean Jaurès in Jaurès's newspaper *L'Humanité*. In this Open Letter, Struve, in the light of what might be called the definitive military collapse of tsarism,[‡] lays out, so to speak, the political platform of the Russian liberal party.

What the Russian people need most of all at this moment, according to this "leader" of Russian liberalism, is a—"*strong government*"! Mr. Struve believes he cannot emphasize enough the urgent necessity for "a strong government" and reiterates this theme many times with variations in different keys, and indeed this necessity is based on two pressing tasks that urgently require solution at the present time in the tsarist empire. First, the establishment of order; and second, and above all, the conclusion of an advantageous peace with Japan as well as the beginnings of a beneficial and at the same time "strong" foreign policy for Russia. These noble aims are more than can be handled by the present-day mindless and corrupt chinovniki of absolutism—who, according to Mr. Struve, are hopeless[§] and have caused the entire current unholy mess. Therefore what is needed to counteract this is a government made up of men with moral authority, and such gems are oh-so-easy to find and oh-so-close at hand, so that all his bloodstained Majesty need do is stretch out His Excellent hand and—here Mr. Struve makes a humble and respectful bow and whispers modestly: "I am not saying that I dare to hope that Your Majesty would place your trust in me; I am merely saying that Your Majesty *needs*, if such be Your *Will*, only to lift one little finger and in the most peaceful way your humble and obedient liberal servants would take over the portfolios of Trepov and Bułygin and would conclude a splendid peace with Japan, reconcile Russia with England, and restore calm among the revolutionary 'rabble,' who indeed, as I wrote in January, are not yet mature enough for political life, and I would ..." But Mr. Struve promises so much, so many beautiful

---

[*]   This article appeared in the *Sächsische Arbeiter-Zeitung*, No. 140, June 21, 1905. Its title in German was "Die kommenden Männer in Russland." It is translated (by George Shriver) from the text in Luxemburg's *Gesammelte Werke*, Vol. 1, Part 2, pp. 587–91.

[†]   While Struve's father used the "von" before his last name, the family being of German noble origin, Pyotr Struve himself did not use it. Nevertheless, in her text Luxemburg calls him "von Struve" for reasons of her own.

[‡]   Russia's huge Baltic Fleet had been sent in September 1904 to sail halfway around the world to the Far East to fight Japan, but after many months it arrived on the scene only to be destroyed in the battle of Tsushima Straits on May 14, 1905.

[§]   *Das Karnickel*—literally, "rabbits."

things, as future government minister under Tsar Nicholas II that we cannot by any means quote all of them here.

By the way, the quotation given above is not exactly accurate. Mr. Struve says all this, but in slightly different words: "Theoretically and abstractly speaking, nothing stands in the way to prevent the revolution from forming a government in the most peaceful way, in just as peaceful a way as [French President Émile] Loubet did yesterday when he called on M. [Maurice] Rouvier to take the place of M. [Émile] Combes, or just as peacefully as [British King] Edward VII might do tomorrow by asking Mr. [Henry] Campbell-Bannerman to replace Mr. [Arthur] Balfour. Nicholas II is as well acquainted as we are (or if he is not, he can make such acquaintance tomorrow), with the men who can be called to take the rudder for Russia, and that would mean the creation of a strong, popular, and authoritative government, a government of radical reforms. One need only convene a congress in Moscow of delegates from the zemstvos analogous to the April congress, and this congress would soon make known to Nicholas II the names of men who would enjoy the confidence of our country as a moral authority. Men who are necessary in order to form a *strong* (emphasis by Mr. Struve himself—*R.L.*) government. May Nicholas II accept the program of these men and entrust them with the helm of state. Because today Russia needs not only freedom but also the formation of a government that would be compatible with freedom and with order."

Aside from the emphasis on a "strong" government and on "order," in the outpouring above there is also a proposal that is particularly worth noting—that the government of the "revolution" be selected from the *zemstvo congress!* Since the beginning of openly expressed revolutionary unrest, and in particular since the Petersburg bloodbath, there has been a single unceasing call by the revolutionaries and by all oppositional elements—for a Constituent Assembly made up of elected representatives of the people based on universal, equal, and direct suffrage and the secret ballot. It is taken for granted by the fighting working class that the only government that can emerge from this revolution is one created by such a universally representative assembly and one that would be supported by it.

Now it turns out that, according to this liberal gentleman, the liquidation of the revolution can go ahead in a "peaceful and simple" way, that instead of an assembly representing the people, all that is needed is to call a zemstvo congress, that is, *to summon merely the class representatives of the landowning nobility*, and ministry would be formed from among these noble owners of landed property.

Further on, Mr. Struve—who it should be noted introduced himself at the beginning of his Open Letter emphatically and on an official basis as "the representative of the liberal-democratic party"—develops an extensive foreign policy program worked out in minutest detail. In good form, he passes the test as a future leading statesman and diplomat, showing that he stands as firm as a rock against the shameless demands of the slant-eyed yellow devils, yet at the same time, wise as a serpent, he proposes an alliance with Japan and, sly as a fox, also suggests reconciliation with the arch-enemy England, all the while extending a warm hand to his friend Jaurès, advocating a reaffirmation of the Franco-Russian alliance,* a reaffirmation that would assure France's rule over Cochin China.† And then he turns this new Quadruple Alliance—Russia, Japan, England, and France—against the Triple Alliance, that is, against Germany, which has been leading the Triple Alliance in its parade march into Asia Minor—because Mr. Struve wants the main base of his future foreign policy to be centered precisely on the Black Sea region.‡ Inasmuch as the leader of zemstvo liberalism wanted to make a display of his capability as an up-and-coming statesman, he has undeniably accomplished this with his barroom-style political outpouring circling the globe, and in the process he has also displayed the necessary dose of bigoted narrow-mindedness required of a statesman in that he is completely blind to the *international* trends in the world market, which have been moving with fatal logic, shifting the center of gravity of world politics and the focal point of world crises to the Far East. As a "strongman" he promises to redirect Russian diplomacy, to shove it back into the worn-out children's shoes of "Near East policy," fighting over the Bosporus.

There is something entirely different, however, which constitutes the most important aspect of the barroom-style political effusion [*Kannegiesserei*], described above. Mr. Struve's entire program centers on foreign policy, and Mr. Struve states explicitly that it is his purpose to turn the attention of all influential fighters for freedom in Russia to these problems. Today, there is no more certain or tried-and-true way of confusing the opposition to tsarism, of weakening and demoralizing it at the present moment, than to turn its gaze away from the problems of the *internal* upheaval, of the *internal* fight against absolutism, of *internal* class and party developments, and to turn it toward questions of foreign policy in the interests of the "fatherland we all have in common." Here the future liberal statesman is engaging in unfair competition, sticking his nose into the business of the present-day statesman of the knout.

The betrayal of the revolution, and of liberalism itself, by the bourgeois-liberal parties is nothing exactly new in history. To this day, every modern revolution in France and in Germany has seen the history of betrayal of the fighting people by liberal men of prominence. But, up to now at least, the betrayal did not begin until after the first victories of the revolution, when the liberal bourgeoisie already had a taste of power. What is new in the *Russian Revolution* is that liberalism already feels itself to be at the helm even before the slightest concession has been made. The Russian liberals have become "strong" statesmen

---

*   The Franco-Russian alliance was begun in 1894.

†   That is, Vietnam.

‡   Struve was interested in competing against the Triple Alliance for the spoils of the Ottoman Empire.

and "men of order," not after arriving at the Paulskirche,* but while they are already in exile in Paris—and while in Petersburg Trepov is still the master of the house! Here, once again, an iron materialist law of history is manifested in noteworthy fashion, as is the "shooting-the-breeze nature" [*Windbeutelei*] of all "ideologies" that lack firm roots in the material interests of social classes. The present behavior of zemstvo liberals stands at so much lower a level than the behavior in earlier times of the German liberals that it reveals to what an extent agrarian zemstvo liberalism, in its innermost essence, is an economically reactionary phenomenon even compared to the ever so cowardly and half-hearted liberalism of the bourgeois owners of large-scale capitalist industry. This latter type of liberalism is entirely lacking in Russia as a *class phenomenon*. The Russian Revolution has come along much too late, like a late-arriving baggage train. The devil takes the hindmost—in history, too.

For a long time now in the ranks of our German comrades, a belief in the power of Russian liberalism has been dominant, a belief that had a negative effect on a correct evaluation of the ongoing revolutionary proletarian movement in Russia and its tactics. That's how it was in January,† when several socialist factions, among them the terrorist SR Party, the national socialist Polish Socialist Party, and some other small groups met in a "bloc" with Struve's party in Paris. Many [SPD] comrades—and even the central organ [*Vorwärts*] among them—were rather surprised and very concerned about why the Russian, Polish, and Jewish Social Democratic parties categorically refused to take part in this supposed "gathering of forces."

The present turn taken by "Struvean" liberalism will, one hopes, show the advocates of "bloc" politics that precisely the interests of the struggle and of the revolution require not an alliance with such ambiguous elements, but a sharp, clear, independent working-class policy which from the very beginning would not take a friendly and trustful stand toward liberalism but would remain on the *qui vive*‡ with a watchful attitude.

In conclusion, here is a brief note *ad personam*. Mr. Struve is a former Social Democrat and a former Marxist who took the donkey's bridge of "revised" Marxism to cross over to the promised land of liberalism. His present case is one more example that if a *socialist* makes a leap away from the firm and principled worldview of Marxism, there is no stopping. Usually, one takes a fall far deeper than the bourgeois democrats and reformers. Mr. Struve has for a considerable length of time, as we have experienced, been regarded as an unreliable element even by the left-leaning bourgeois democrats in Russia, and from

---

* St. Paul's Church was a Lutheran Church in Frankfurt used as a meeting place during the German revolution of 1848–1849. It was here that the Frankfurt Assembly drew up its proposed constitution for a united Germany.
† Actually, this occurred in November 1904.
‡ That is, on the alert.

being a representative of liberalism he has evolved into being a representative merely of the extreme right-wing nobility. That is how classes and parties are unceasingly being differentiated in Russia, and this is one of the surest and most gratifying signs that the fire of revolution in the tsarist empire is not dying down but is tirelessly spreading, eating away at everything around it, so that in a matter of moments it will lick up and devour objects even when no burst of flame blazes forth with a loud crackling sound to catch the attention of the entire world.

Russian Party Controversies*

A short time ago, one of the two factions into which our sister party in Russia has regrettably been divided for approximately the past two years held a congress under the name "Third Congress of the Russian Social Democratic Labor Party."† The other faction, grouped around Axelrod, Plekhanov, and Zasulich, whose public organ is the well-known *Iskra*, did not take part in this quasi-universal congress, on the grounds that, as it explains, this "Congress" did not allow the participation of all the active local committees of the RSDRP—though such participation would obviously have to be expected of any truly unified party congress. Hence, that faction strictly adhered to the letter of the party rules, about which such a furor in the party had flared up. However, a large portion of the party organizations now did not want to abide by those rules, and this excluded the latter faction [the Mensheviks] from active collaboration in the party congress.‡

This faction has now held its own conference, after failed attempts to come to an understanding and arrange for some sort of mutual consultation with the initiators and participants in the [Bolshevik] factional "Congress," and at this [Menshevik] conference they too have made decisions and passed resolutions about questions of tactics and organization.§

We now are confronted with the fact that the Russian party, as before, is divided into two camps, although it goes without saying that they belong together, *because both* base themselves on the same program and, by and large,

---

* This article appeared in *Sächsische Arbeiter-Zeitung* No. 142, June 23, 1905. The article's title in German was "Russische Partei-streitigkeiten." It is translated (by George Shriver) from the text in Luxemburg's *Gesammelte*, Vol. 1, Part 2, pp. 592–4.

† The Third Congress of the Russian Social Democratic Labor Party took place in London, April 25–May 10, 1905 (new style). It was the first party congress of the Bolsheviks. The real founding congress of the RSDRP occurred in Brussels and London in July 30–August 23, 1903 (new style). It was called the "Second Congress," because the first attempt at a founding congress occurred in Minsk in March 1898. The 1903 congress, the real founding congress, was where the famous split between Bolsheviks and Mensheviks occurred.

‡ According to the organizational statutes of the RSDRP, the right to call a party congress was invested in the party's Council, whose chairman then was Georgi Plekhanov. Plekhanov had supported the majority at the 1903 congress, but then switched sides and joined the Mensheviks. From the late summer or fall of 1903, and continuing at the time when Luxemburg wrote this article, the Mensheviks dominated the party Council of the RSDRP as well as its newspaper *Iskra*. Since Plekhanov refused to call a party congress, the Bolsheviks took the initiative to do so themselves. An ad hoc consultative body of twenty-two representatives of Bolshevik-led party committees, most of them active *inside* Russia, issued an appeal calling on party members to speak out in support of holding a party congress and to pass resolutions to that effect. By April 1905 the overwhelming majority of party organizations had agreed that a party congress should be called, and so the "Third Congress" was held even though the party Council continued to oppose it.

§ Because of the small number who took part in the Menshevik gathering—delegates showed up from only nine party committees—it was called a "conference of active members."

on the same tactics. And, however we might deplore this fact, and in addition feel such a deep grievance about it, it is necessary, in any case, to take this split into account as a fact of life. At the very least, this deplorable conflict, which saddens us deeply, is made even worse by the way one of the two factions presents itself everywhere as the only official representative of Russian Social Democracy and tries to dismiss the other faction as merely a tiny group of incorrigible squabblers.

The "congress" faction (the so-called Lenin faction) is particularly guilty of behaving in this manner, because it has published its decisions and resolutions in German and presented them to the German public as the results of the Third Congress of the RSDRP. And, by the way, how our *party publishing house in Munich* came to place itself in the service of one of the competing factions is totally unclear to us—yet that probably is based on not being oriented accurately with regard to the situation in the Russian camp. However that may be, one of the two groups in our sister party, the RSDRP, has chosen a way to see what it can do in the given situation by making a most unintelligent move—namely, to force its rival out of the way, so to speak, and thus win recognition in the International.* It is certainly clear to everyone that this somewhat "Cossack" way of resolving a party dispute through its behavior and way of perceiving things about the faction in question (which unfortunately has made itself known a bit too widely) is not suitable for improving relations in the Russian party. On the contrary, it only further stirs up the fire. It was therefore, in our opinion, a wise word, worthy of recognition, that [Karl] Kautsky recently warned the party press in the *Leipziger Volkszeitung*, on the basis of his knowledge of persons and developments in the Russian party, that our press could complicate the situation without meaning to and make matters worse in the ranks of our Russian comrades by accepting and unwittingly reporting in a distorted way the supposedly "official" decisions of the Russian factional congress.†

Now a peculiar quid pro quo has occurred. In the *Frankfurter Volksstimme* [People's Voice of Frankfurt] of June 17, [1905], a certain comrade "Gr."‡ has come forward to acquaint the German comrades with the decisions of the

---

* Although some later commentators (as well as her critics within the official Communist movement from the mid-1920s onward) claimed that at the time Luxemburg was closer to the Mensheviks than the Bolsheviks, Luxemburg's above statement (as well as many others made in this period) shows that she was critical of both tendencies—though the Bolsheviks come in for the harsher criticism here.

† Karl Kautsky's article "Die Spaltung der russischen Sozialdemokratie" (The Split in the Russian Social Democratic Party) appeared in the *Leipziger Volkszeitung*, No. 135, June 15, 1905. For Lenin's response to Kautsky's article (written in June 1905 but apparently not published until 1931), see V. I. Lenin, *Complete Works*, Vol. 8 (Moscow: Progress Publishers, 1962), pp. 531–3.

‡ It appears that "Gr." stood for Grigori Zinoviev, a close associate of Lenin at the time and after 1917 head of the Communist International. In a letter to Zinoviev of August 24, 1909, Lenin explicitly addresses him as "Dear Gr." See V. I. Lenin, *Collected Works*, Vol. 24 (Moscow: Progress Publishers, 1974), p. 399.

supposedly "universal" Russian congress. In his article, he indignantly rejects Kautsky's suggestions, arguing that it is not at all a question of two factions, but that on one side there is the [Russian] party as a whole and on the other there are merely three misfits—Plekhanov, Axelrod, and Martov—who are making a fuss. All this is demonstrated irrefutably by "Gr."—basing himself on a report by one faction that simply denies the existence of the other faction. But that is exactly where the problem lies!

For Kautsky, it was precisely a matter of warning the German comrades in advance not to take a factional presentation of the situation for good coin, not to accept it unreservedly. Certainly, Kautsky did not mean to say—and it does not occur to us to make such an assertion—that the statements in the booklet published by [Gerhard] Birk in Munich were some sort of intentional or conscious distortions of the facts.[*] We are not about to get into a detailed evaluation of the dispute. But it is a well-known psychological phenomenon in every major party conflict that *each one* of the disputing sides sees and presents matters in its own subjective light—being honestly convinced inwardly that it is correct to the best of its knowledge—and, at the same time, is capable of laying on the table the greatest possible objective distortions. It is not a matter, then, of merely rejecting or "banning" the conception of *one* faction or its manner of presentation, but of not promoting, or giving precedence to, *either* of them by giving a one-sided presentation of the *actual* relationship of forces, and thus stirring up greater bitterness.

Whoever wishes to reconcile two disputants obviously cannot begin by declaring, before all else, that one of the two does not even exist. However, to help the two Russian factions achieve reconciliation is undoubtedly a worthy objective, toward which the German party should lend a hand as strongly as it can.

In the *Frankfurter Volksstimme*, the comrade named "Gr." also polemicizes against Kautsky precisely on this point,[†] because he considers any eventual mediation by the German party to be totally superfluous, but perhaps he will be pleasantly surprised to learn that leading comrades of the Russian faction that he takes to be the only real one—that even they themselves do not at all consider such eventual mediation superfluous, and this is the case even *after* their congress.

---

[*]   Birk, a publisher and bookseller in Munich who was associated with the SPD, published a German translation of the Third Congress of the RSDRP in 1905.

[†]   The response of "Gr." to Kautsky appeared in the June 17, 1905 issue of *Frankfurter Volksstimme*.

Strike-Revolution in Łódź*

We have received the following reports about the events in Łódź, one from June 20 and one from June 21.

(*Łódź*, June 20, from our correspondent)—Today at 6 p.m. a huge demonstration began, and lasted until 9:30 in the evening.

The Social Democratic workers of Łódź were accompanying to their final resting place the victims of tsarist thuggery who fell last Sunday. On Sunday, June 18, Social Democracy had arranged a so-called May Day–type of outing or excursion (that is, a form of mass meeting, held in the open, outside of the city, which is customary in Russian Poland). It took place in the Lagiewnik Forest, where many agitational speeches were given in front of the assembled crowd of workers. After the close of the meeting, the Social Democratic workers marched with party banners unfurled to the Zgierski Forest. Here, halfway to the city, the banners came down, and the mass march broke up into small groups that made their way separately back to the city. One group kept their banners unfurled all the way into the city. Here, on the corner of Lagiewnik and Müller streets, in the city's Baluty district, the comrades were attacked by a Cossack patrol, with *ten persons being killed and many wounded*, including a *two-year-old child*! The incident stirred up tremendous indignation among the workers. Social Democracy immediately decided to organize a funeral march for the burial of the fallen as a political protest, and at the same time began an energetic agitation in the factories. Nowadays in Warsaw and in Łódź, agitation is carried on openly in the courtyards of the factories, and when Social Democrat speakers appear there, work stops and the workers gather in the yard. Such "factory meetings," in which hundreds and even thousands of workers participate, take place *daily*—now in one factory, now in another—so that the police have given up completely on trying to fight against them, and the factory owners, out of fear of the workers, allow the meetings to go on.

By noontime on June 20, some factories had already stopped work, and during the course of the afternoon the rest of them did too. All together, the workers streamed to Church Square. Military forces were also occupying the streets so thickly that you could hardly step into the street. The greatest difficulty for the party was to get hold of the bodies of the murdered workers, which were at different locations, being watched over closely by the police. Finally, five

---

* This article first appeared anonymously, without Luxemburg's signature, in the main SPD newspaper, *Vorwärts*, No. 145, June 24, 1905. It is clearly by Luxemburg, as indicated by the fact it includes a summary of recent events culled from different press reports—a standard format used by her in her writings on the 1905 Revolution in *Vorwärts*. The title in German is "Streikrevolution in Łódź." It is translated (by George Shriver) from the text in Luxemburg's *Gesammelte Werke*, Vol. 6, pp. 546–8.

coffins were successfully brought to Brzezińska Street, and from that location the march began. Even at the start it numbered 25,000. Banners were carried at the front, a black one and two red banners of Social Democracy. Confrontation with the Cossacks seemed unavoidable at many places along the way, and at one point panic broke out in one part of the giant march. But the masses were so firm and determined that they would not give way or go back even one step. Around those who were frightened or wavering, shouts went up immediately and loudly: "Not one step back! Don't weaken! Stand firm as a rock! Make a solid wall!" And the march went on, with the singing of "The Red Banner" and the shouting of revolutionary slogans.

The conduct and mood of this enormous mass on the march, which at every corner crossed paths with a patrol of troops and police, was truly admirable. When the front of the march flowed into the cemetery, the rest of the march had to stop because only part of the huge crowd could fit in the cemetery. The orators of Social Democracy made use of that at once to give two agitational speeches, one about the political situation and the tasks of the revolution, and one about the position taken by Social Democracy toward the soldiers. The speeches were welcomed with roars of enthusiasm. In the cemetery itself, another speech was given—about the conduct of the clergy in the present revolution. Finally, the banners were rolled up and the masses dispersed in small groups without incident.

A second piece of correspondence reports about the *bloodbath* of the following day:

(*Łódź*, June 21, from our correspondent)—With awful precision a repetition of the fate of Warsaw's May Day demonstration was repeated today. *We were lured into a trap by the military in the most treacherous way.* Today another one of the victims of last Sunday's butchery was to be buried. By 6 p.m. the workers had already gathered in countless numbers in the Old City. Then it turned out that the police had gotten hold of the corpse and buried it in complete secrecy. At this news, the workers became enraged. The party wanted to call off the demonstration since the planned burial had been thwarted, but the assembled masses would not hear of leaving. Thus, the funeral march began. At Franziskaner Street, the banners were unfurled. Along the way, new masses of people kept streaming in, to join the march, and soon almost all of proletarian Łódź had gathered, and the enthusiasm knew no bounds. Along the way, the military patrols deliberately sought to stay away from our line of march, and even the police wore friendly expressions on their faces and nodded their heads at us. And so, the march succeeded in going from the wide streets of the "better" districts and entered the narrow alleys of the workers' quarter. From the behavior of the soldiers no one any longer harbored any thought of being attacked, and the workers marched trustfully onward. Now, suddenly, as we pressed into the narrow alleys, it turned out that the Cossacks were blocking the way up ahead and behind us the military had already cut off any retreat. All of the side streets were also thickly occupied by the thugs, making it impossible to escape!

And then the salvos began to crackle, without any order to disperse or the usual warning!

A terrible panic broke out. People pushed and shoved against each other in a vain attempt to get away from the murderous bullets, so that some were nearly suffocated. Many tried to escape through adjoining barbed wire fences. The gates to apartment buildings were broken down and people tried to save themselves in the courtyards. But the gangs of soldiers *fired at those in flight*, and soon there were heaps of corpses and maimed bodies lying in front of and inside the entrance halls of the buildings. It is impossible at this moment to tell the exact number of victims. *It will not be fewer than one hundred, in any case*. Right now, we don't even know how many or which of *our agitators* have fallen as victims of this butchery; only one thing is certain—we have suffered painful losses. *In response to this atrocity, Social Democracy has at this moment proclaimed a general strike for [tomorrow,] Friday, June 23.*

No detailed news about the events on Friday has become available. The telephone and telegraph systems seem not to be functioning.

The Street Battle in Łódź[*]

Tsarism is collapsing ingloriously and ignominiously in the face of the Japanese enemy, abandoning defendable fortresses and lightheartedly surrendering giant battleships and huge armies to the enemy. Meanwhile, it is celebrating victory after victory in the fight against its own people on the streets of Russia. Russia's shameful record has engraved its ineradicable marks upon the countenance of modern civilization. If there were still a public conscience in capitalist society, then the merciless horde, which crawls away in the face of an armed enemy, but which celebrates wild orgies on bloody fields of battle, which strides along, with champagne glass in hand and prostitute on arm, across a stormy sea of blood shed by the masses who have fallen in the fray, which sees in war only a means of personal enrichment, which bombs hospitals and puts on theatrical extravaganzas in honor of the kingdom of gross repulsiveness—if there were such a conscience, then this Gomorrah of Russia's rule of violence, which fires upon its own native sons, [and its] rulers would be excommunicated by the world of culture, the guilty parties would be declared free to wander over the entire globe and never find a place where they could rest because of their transgressions. But the actually existing world of culture allows its butchers to travel along with it, after as well as before, sailing down the bloody channels dug by their crimes, and they are flooded with roubles, as honorable and welcome guests at all times and in all places.

Bloody Sunday in Petersburg aroused public opinion only in passing. The frightful butchery in Warsaw troubled good souls for only a few moments. The massacres committed against the Jews, which almost every week in one place or another are carried out by the agents of the tsar, producing countless victims, have not lowered the value on stock and bond markets of loans to the Russian government, not even by a fraction. In the Caucasus, the fighting among different nationalities instigated by tsarism, which has exceeded everything of horror and repulsiveness that a wild imagination could invent—even this abomination has not been placed on the agenda of the world of culture.

To the grisly chain of "heroic" actions by the tsarist regime there now must be added, as one of the most dreadful, the *several days of street fighting* in Łódź. Yesterday we described what precipitated these gruesome events.[†] A peacefully demonstrating proletariat, which wanted simply to render the last honors to the victims of killer Cossacks, were hemmed in and trapped in narrow alleyways and then mowed down by the beasts who serve the tsar.

---

[*] This article first appeared anonymously, without Rosa Luxemburg's signature, in *Vorwärts*, No. 146, June 25, 1905. The title in German is "Die Strassenschlacht in Łódź." It is translated (by George Shriver) from Luxemburg's *Gesammelte Werke*, Vol. 6, pp. 549–52.
[†] See the article "Strike-Revolution in Łódź," above, pp. 175–7.

With admirable heroism, which makes the name of the *people* of Russia worthy of honor to the same extent that the shameful actions of the ruling family cover the name of Russia with curses and execration, the proletariat of Łódź has undertaken the attempt to arm itself against the beasts of the tsar. With a magnificent disregard for individual self-preservation, the proletariat fought for its freedom and honor. Nothing reliable or in detail is known yet about the particulars or about the prospects for the ongoing fight raging since Thursday in the streets of Łódź, an actual battle of the barricades, but the official telegraph agency itself gives us a hint of the extent of the horrors that have piled up in this major industrial city of Russian Poland. The telegraph agency's news dispatch itself estimates the number of casualties as 2,000.

In Warsaw, a general strike has also been proclaimed, without any clashes having been reported from there so far.

The civilized world looks on calmly at this horror and abomination. No one is giving aid to the noble fighters for freedom among the people of Russia, to help them against the brutal superiority in weapons of the hordes serving the tsar. But the international proletariat believes so firmly in the future of freedom and the eventual victory of *that which is human* in the human race that it will never accept the notion that such tremendous sacrifices could be in vain.

Officers in Poland are still doing what Petersburg officers most recently protested against. They are still doing the work of *hangmen* against society. But the time *must* come when no one is willing any more to be a hangman.

THE BEGINNING OF THE BARRICADE FIGHTING

We have received the following informational reports, but they do not describe the events of the last few days, which include the most recent fighting.

(Łódź, June 20, 10 p.m., from our correspondent)—*The revolution is here!* One is scarcely able to put together a report because events are rushing so swiftly one upon the other. Besides, all our agitators are busy day and night on the scene, and only with difficulty can we gather news from the various parts of the city.

First of all, a few words about yesterday's butchery. The Social Democratic standard-bearer was one of the first to fall, but he conducted himself as a true hero. Already lying on the ground with a fatal wound in his chest, he fired all the cartridges from his revolver at the Cossacks; in dying he kept holding onto the flagstaff so tightly that no one could remove it from his grasp, and the comrades covered their fallen colleague with the banner. The crowd made a passionate attempt to save the banner, but they, too, were forced to seek safety in the face of the Cossacks. The leaders of the demonstration fought with redoubled energy against the soldiery. Actually, the thugs also suffered losses; twelve Cossacks fell from their horses, either dead or badly wounded. The government reported eighteen dead on the side of the people, but, in reality, the number was twice as much. The number wounded has not yet been established, because many did not go to the hospital, but are being cared for in private homes.

This butchery was the igniting spark of the *revolution* that has started today. An enormous crowd of people gathered at the site of the bloody atrocity and *would not leave the streets all night long, despite the fact that as early as twelve midnight this unarmed crowd was constantly being shot at while they simply were standing there peacefully.* At the moment, it is still unclear how many more fell as victims to these murderous acts, because since then so many clashes have occurred that it's hard to keep an up-to-date record.

At the first moment yesterday, the mass murder of defenseless workers had a very depressing effect. The people stood around in silence at the site of the bloodshed in a downcast mood. But that lasted for only a little time. Today, from early in the morning onward, spirits were revived. The entire people are out on the streets, firm and solid, and in a fighting mood. Everywhere there's activity, and preparations for a fight.

Social Democracy already set in motion the beginnings of a general strike *today.* The factories were closed today in any case because of a Catholic holiday.* Deputations were sent by the party to talk to the shopkeepers, demanding that all stores be closed today and tomorrow. This afternoon we also had all traffic on the streetcar lines stopped. Clashes with police and Cossacks in small groups are happening without let up. *The crowd disarms the police and soldiers whenever it can.* On East Street and New City Street, several Cossacks and police agents were killed. *In the Old City, material for building barricades has been made ready*—lumber, flagstones, ladders, and the like. *At South Street and East Street, a barricade of barrels has been built.* At 9 p.m. the Cossacks began an attempt to storm this barricade. We heard two salvos, but the outcome is not yet known at the time of writing.

On East Street this afternoon, the people also *barricaded themselves in two private residential buildings* and began firing from the windows and the roofs at the military and the Cossacks and to throw stones at them. Several of the thugs have fallen. For half an hour, the buildings were fired at by the military, but the workers were under good cover and suffered no losses. Finally, the workers withdrew, over the roofs and back walls. At 7 p.m. the buildings were "taken" by the army, but there was no one in the *fortress* and there was nothing more to be found in it.

On Centre Street, the people *tore up the pavement* and heaped up some towering piles to fend off the attacks of the soldiery.

It is significant that for the most part *Cossacks* were used for direct fighting against the people. The infantry mostly stood by as a defensive force, and was not very active. It seems that the belief existed *that the infantry is none too*

---

*   The holiday was the Feast of Corpus Christi.

reliable. In fact, yesterday and today, there were several instances when small groups of soldiers fraternized with the workers. On Petrikauer Street, not far from Andreas Street, one officer led his detachment of soldiers away and said out loud to the workers, "You have nothing to fear. I will not allow any shooting."

Tomorrow (June 23) we will probably have hot and heavy fighting. The appearance of things is that the local authorities refrained from giving the order to put down the uprising, but the workers are in such a belligerent mood and so aroused that we won't get by without stubborn fighting.

In the local paper *Goniec Łódzski* [Łódź Herald], a vile and good-for-nothing article appeared in which the workers were blamed for supposedly being the first to shoot during yesterday's demonstration. *The semi-official press is spreading this despicable lie via cable to the outside world.* Therefore, it must be repeated once again—the workers have not taken a single rash or imprudent step up to now, and are not guilty of making a single provocation! *The people are defending themselves against the killer gangs.*

(Łódź, June 22, midnight, from our correspondent)—On East and South Streets the fighting at the barricades continues uninterruptedly. Both streets have been surrounded and cut off by infantry and cavalry. Artillery is also there already. In this neighborhood, all the streetlights have been shot out so that total darkness reigns. Throughout the city police and military officers are being shot at with revolvers. We urgently need help. The revolution is here.

Outbreak of Revolution in Łódź: June Days[*]

In Łódź, a sea of blood, piles of corpses, thousands injured. A terrible harvest gathered by the Angel of Death—dying tsarist absolutism.

On June 20–5, the proletariat of Łódź stood at the head of the revolution, going into the fight more powerfully, massively, persistently than has happened yet anywhere else since the outbreak of tumultuous revolution in the tsarist empire. Who caused it? Who gave the start to that June uprising in Łódź? Only people who are deaf and blind to the sufferings and desires of our working masses [can ask that], people who do not understand that a people's revolution has its own vital inner strength and spontaneous impulse, and that it moves inexorably forward. The victims of May Day and the heroism of the Warsaw proletariat awakened and stimulated the spirit of the workers in Łódź, and spurred them to fight. The Łódź workers went on strike en masse and tugged desperately at the yoke of capitalist exploitation—because they had to, because that yoke—for those awakened in spirit—had become unbearable. The fighting workers of Łódź arranged huge gatherings and demonstrations—because they had to, because awakened consciousness and class solidarity will move with irresistible force toward common mass action, toward that refreshing, uplifting feeling of power and encouragement offered to a slave of capital and a subject of the knout—when marching in a compact mass with fellow workers. The proletarians of Łódź responded to the crimes of the tsarist thugs with even bigger demonstrations because they had to, because, when spiritually awakened and reborn, the workers can no longer accept submission to violence at the hands of the oppressors, because such submission would break them spiritually, would make their faith and their strength fold up. The fighting in Łódź kept building rapidly as fights erupted on the barricades—a single chain of cause and effect. That could be interrupted only if the workers abandoned their aspirations leading them to liberation.

Despite heroic defensive battles, the proletariat of Łódź was crushed. Again, in Łódź, the same force of brutal bayonets and rifle bullets that drowned in blood the huge demonstration in Warsaw on May 1 is seemingly triumphant —the same force that stifled the January uprising of the proletariat in Petersburg.

But revolution is the only kind of war, which despite the number of failures,

---

[*] This article is translated (by George Shriver and Alicja Mann) from *Z Pola Walki*, the supplement to the monthly publication of the SDKPiL, *Czerwony Sztandar*. The supplement *Z Pola Walki* appeared occasionally throughout 1905, starting with No. 1, dated January 25, and dealing with the events of "Bloody Sunday" in St. Petersburg, which happened on January 22. The issue of *Z Pola Walki* from which this article about Łódź is translated is No. 10, dated June 30, 1905, pp. 1–2. The article's title in Polish is "Wybuch rewolucji w Łódzi," with the subhead "Dni czerwcowe" (June Days).

the revolutionaries do finally win. Absolutism triumphs in Petersburg and Warsaw and Łódź and Kishinev and the Caucasus—yet each of those victories brings absolutism fatally, inexorably, one step closer to the grave, and the working people to victory. Each of these massacres committed by absolutism disperses and spreads the sparks of hatred, rebellion, and struggle, pushes further the waves of revolution that are surging with unstoppable force, which swell ever higher and more powerfully.

In May in Warsaw, a march of 20,000 people threw the government and the bourgeoisie into a state of astonishment. A month later in Łódź, 70,000 were marching under the banner of the revolution. The Warsaw massacre of defenseless people was the culmination of an unbelievably huge mass demonstration. The bullet and bayonet triumphed over people who were fleeing, trying to save themselves from the murderous attack. In Łódź, after a month, in response to the slaughter of unarmed demonstrators, a fierce battle on the barricades began and lasted forty-eight hours. It was hard and laborious work this time for absolutism to win its "victory." For five days, from [June] 20 to 25, Łódź was the focus of continuous demonstrations, general strikes, and clashes with the soldiers—for five days in Łódź, the intensive, uninterrupted fights continued. The "laws" and the lawlessness of absolutism, and the yoke of capital, were trampled and swept away by the mass of workers, and spreading out over the city, stormy and undulating like the sea, a threatening power arose—for five days in Łódź, the Revolution was the all mighty goddess!

In that hot battle, absolutism was bound to win, inch by inch. With the help of a handful of revolvers, the heroic proletariat resisted the bandit violence of the tsar's phalanxes for two whole days, until murderous iron and deadly weariness knocked it to the ground.

Absolutism is triumphant in Łódź, deadly silence has swept away for a while the uproar of stormy revolution. The silence is interrupted by the intruding clatter of steel bayonets marching to the square of lawlessness and killings. New legions of bandits from the vicinity are pulled in. But the rivers of blood flowing on the streets of the "conquered" city call out in their silence to the people of our whole country, and of the entire empire, loud and shrill, like a bronze bell in mournful alarm. More of such "victories"—and absolutism will collapse in a simultaneous general uprising of the people in all parts of the country.

The fate of the Łódź revolutionary uprising graphically indicates the nature and conditions for victory for the revolution in the tsarist empire. Embittered, trembling, and demanding revenge against the murderers, a worker of Łódź cries out, "Weapons!" The weapons are needed; they are essential. But no weapon can give one isolated city a victory over the tsardom that rules over 130 million. As long as absolutism can bring to Łódź new battalions of soldiers from towns and villages nearby, the victory of the armed workers of Łódź is a forlorn hope. And the same is true for the workers of Warsaw, of Petersburg, of Moscow. Only when the rising becomes general, overtakes and encompasses all the major cities and leaps outward to the countryside, only then will tsarism no longer be able to bring its killer bandits from the "peaceful" villages and concentrate their oppressive force against one or several revolutionary towns, only then will victory be on the side of the people, because then even the most powerful weapons will not restore peace. Then, building up here and there, still partly suppressed, the murmur among the troops themselves will gain enough strength and courage to merge into a loud outcry of protest, shaking and breaking up the ranks of the defenders of tsarism.

The workers' revolution can overcome absolutism only when there is a widespread, simultaneous, sustained rising involving the giant mass of working people in both the towns and the villages throughout the empire. Today absolutism continues to live only because of the isolation and dispersal of the revolutionary explosions. The [problem is] that the proletariat rises up individually and sequentially in some places while in other places it has temporarily stopped its fight, or yet in others has not yet exploded.

But, in fact, with these individual outbreaks the revolution continues to live. The proletariat will abolish the rule of the knout only by a widespread general revolutionary uprising. But this general uprising of the people can only arise from individual explosions, and each such new outbreak extends the revolutionary flame, prepares and accelerates the explosion in other places, as the fighting energy of the proletariat grows in the entire country. This wearies and discourages the army, confuses the state machinery, sharpens and tightens the relations of classes and parties in the society, and fuels the overall revolutionary atmosphere. The isolated insurrection of the June rebellion of the Łódź proletariat was strangled, but in falling, it shook the foundations of the tsarist regime, just as Samson shook the pillars of the temple.

Woe to the pioneers! The revolution of the working class, which has appeared for the first time in modern history with the current revolution born in the tsarist empire, develops and becomes more powerful only through the increased consciousness and organization of the huge class of the proletariat. And the only school for this awareness and this organization is not the leadership of the bourgeoisie, as in the past in Europe, but only the result of the tireless struggle of the proletariat, its sacrifices, its blood, with which it has occupied every new position won in that fight.

The most terrible sacrifices, the greatest part of the increasing costs [of the struggle] fall upon those ranks of the proletariat that, displaying the greatest energy, consciousness, and organization, are the first to rush into battle and the first to be mowed down, because their courage rips them farther ahead of the ranks of their comrades-in-arms and brings down on them the murderous iron of the counterrevolution.

Alongside of the proletarians of Petersburg, who in January lay down wrapped in snowy winding-sheets on the pavements of the tsar's capital, along-side the proletarians of Warsaw, who with their eyes dimmed by death took a last look at the May sunshine of this year, the proletarians of Łódź have also laid down their lives on their barricades, under their scarlet banner—as pioneers of the revolution and for the emancipation of the proletariat throughout the Russian empire.

This is not the first bloody harvest to be reaped during "June Days" in the history of the working class. In the very same days of June—the 23rd, 24th, and 25th, exactly fifty-seven years ago—the *proletariat of Paris* fought a very strong battle against the government of the French bourgeoisie. In February 1848 the proletariat, together with the middle and lower strata of the bourgeoisie, had overthrown the monarchy of Louis Philippe and established a government under a republic. At that time, the Parisian proletariat believed that the republic would release them immediately from under the yoke of capital, that the republic would give the workers bread and jobs and social justice.

However, the bourgeoisie dominated the republic, which is to say that this same capitalism ruled in the republic, and the heroic proletariat of Paris, betrayed and cheated by the property-owning class, left to be the prey of poverty and unemployment, rose up in June with desperate courage to fight against the same old accursed bondage of wage slavery. For nearly four days, the battle raged in the suburbs of Paris. With unprecedented heroism, the Paris workers placed themselves behind more than 400 barricades, choosing rather to die together with their wives and children than be forced back under the yoke of capital.

The "June Days" [in 1848] ended with the defeat of the proletariat. The rampaging "victorious" bourgeoisie, after the suppression of the uprising, butchered 3,000 workers and condemned 15,000 others to penal servitude and exile. It was a real failure that removed that proletariat from the political stage for a long time. But that defeat was inevitable, because fighting heroically, the Parisian workers went into battle with the illusory hope that, in the republic of the bourgeoisie, a single armed conflict would be enough to abolish the rule of capital.

But the June defeat of the Paris proletariat was a victory for the cause of the international proletariat. Only in that terrible carnage, in that sea of its own blood, the French proletariat learned for the first time that it is a separate class, and that it can count only on itself. It learned that liberation from the hell of capital will not be given by the republic of the bourgeoisie, not even with the most heroic street battle, but by a long class fight with some help from the political rights gained in the republic. The June victims among the workers of Paris—that was the price the international proletariat had to pay to gain consciousness of its class separateness and its goals. The sea of blood, shed in June 1848 on the streets of Paris, stands between the working class and the class of exploiters all over the world.

And even today, after half a century, the June victims of the Parisian proletariat are yielding an abundant crop—the workers' revolution against tsarism. With a clear awareness of its paths and class objectives, without illusions, without fallacies, the proletarians of Russia and Poland are marching forward to storm the last stronghold of despotism, to overthrow it, and by that to speed their own liberation and that of the entire international proletariat.

On Top of the Volcano[*]

Ça ira![†]

Revolution, among other things, differs from war because its law of existence is perpetual motion—constant forward movement, developing according to its own internal logic and consistency. The revolution knows no pauses or cease-fires, unless it is in retreat.

And those supposed "revolutionaries" who are hungrily waiting only for "effects," expecting one volcanic eruption after another, are dissatisfied with the apparent pause after such acts as the barricade fight in Łódź. They consider such pauses to be merely "dead spots" in the forward march of the revolution. This proves only that, in their psychology, they are true children of the bourgeoisie, alien to the spirit of the workers' revolution.

After the Łódź uprising of the proletariat, we have so far not had in our country a second explosion of the same magnitude. However, immediately after the flare-up of the bloody battles in Łódź, there was a response in the south of Russia, a huge glow of revolutionary fire began raging in Odessa, and that was in response to the raising of the red flag of revolution on the mast of a battleship of the tsar's navy,[‡] a loud reminder that the current revolution is the unbreakable common cause of the proletariat of the whole Russian state, that the struggle in our country is more than ever part of the total revolution throughout the Russian empire.

On the other hand, in our country, two symptoms have proved that the revolution is not standing still, not stuck in place, not for a moment, but that without stopping, it is striding onward—toward victory.

The first fact is the utter bankruptcy of the tsarist terror used in Łódź. Today, it is already visible, and well known to everyone that the state of siege, the policies of force and violence, and the attempt to physically crush the heroic proletariat of Łódź after the "June Days," has *failed completely*. Despite the apparent failure of the barricade uprising, the terrible bloodshed, and the introduction of swarms of armed soldiers, the proletariat of Łódź has not lost its spirit, has not stopped

---

[*]   This article is translated (by George Shriver and Alicja Mann) from *Z Pola Walki*, No. 11, August 28, 1905. Its title in Polish is "Na wulkanie."

[†]   "We are going forward!" is from a French revolutionary song. It has the same sense as such expressions as "We shall overcome."

[‡]   A reference to the battleship *Potemkin*, one of the crown jewels of Russia's Black Sea fleet. The crew revolted against the ship's officers on June 27, 1905 over the dreadful living conditions aboard the ship, and upon taking control hoisted the red flag and declared its solidarity with the revolution. After a series of confrontations with vessels that remained loyal to the Russian Navy, the *Potemkin* sailed to the Romanian port of Constanta, where the crew was given asylum. Russia obtained the ship from Romania soon afterwards and renamed it the *Panteleimon*.

fighting. Only for a short time were the outward expressions of struggle and resistance suppressed. Today, inside Łódź, Social Democratic activity is going strong, and the struggle is striding forward. Big strikes at the Gayer factories and at other factories are new symptom of the tireless revolutionary energy of the workers in Łódź, and these may signal the nearby explosion of a new general strike.

The second fact, which has echoed loudly in the last few weeks, is the outbreak of new battles elsewhere in Łódź Province. Despite frantic efforts by the reaction, as a sign of solidarity with Łódź all the centers of labor and exploitation are standing up one after the other all across our country. Along the lines of an idea that we have advocated for a long time, street demonstrations have been taking place everywhere.

It is true that as a result of measures taken by the *tsarist authorities*, as well as the efforts of all of bourgeois "society," strikes and street demonstrations are no longer able to attain the same huge proportions as the strike in Warsaw on May 4 and the 100,000 who demonstrated in Łódź on June 21, which were capable of impressing the whole world. Nevertheless, the Polish proletariat has still been protesting *loud and strong*.

On June 26, all the working people of *Warsaw* went on strike again, and red banners appeared on its streets, and—as if just for practice in the art of revolution—barricades were erected. On June 28, 29, and 30, work stopped in *the mines*,[*] and tens of thousands of the slaves of capital remained sitting in their underground workplaces. On June 28, *Lublin* stood up.[†] On July 4 all commercial and industrial life came to a halt in *Białystok*; only gunshot after gunshot could be heard on its streets. On July 5 and 6, there were strikes in many parts of *Radom*; during July in *Kielce* [economic] life died out; and finally, on August 18, once again all of Warsaw went on strike, this time in response to the call by the Social Democratic organizations to protest the slaughter [by the tsar's troops] in Białystok. The cries "Down with the tsar!" and "Long live political freedom!" resounded through all of Poland.

Thus, the past few weeks have shown that the revolution is moving ahead with iron logic in two directions—in depth and in extent. The main centers, the old volcanoes of labor struggle—Warsaw and Łódź—inexhaustible in their huge revolutionary potential energy, not crushed by the wildest efforts of reaction, are working steadfastly on. The first leading centers of the Polish proletariat have shown that they know neither fluctuations nor fatigue. At the same time, the centers of fighting spread more and more to the provinces, tirelessly expanding the area of the revolution. And these two signs are precisely the most precious guarantee that the revolutionary cause is developing according to the laws of a healthy and strong mass movement of the proletariat.

---

[*]   For instance, the strikes that occurred in the Dabrowa basin.
[†]   That is, in Lublin, too, the workers went on strike.

In bourgeois revolutions, fatigue and exhaustion are unavoidable phenomena and are the product of historical necessity. Such revolutions, because they are bourgeois, always unconsciously overestimate their own goals; they are illusion based; they make use of the illusions of working people, who in every case push the revolutionary wave further than corresponds to the class interests of the directing bourgeoisie. Those revolutions always have a period of regression after the point of most strenuous effort.

Fatigue and exhaustion in the fight was always a psychological symptom, indicating that the breakthrough that the revolution had made had gone too far—and then it started to weaken and fail. That happened with the Great French Revolution, and the same happened with the revolutions of 1848.

Currently, tsarism and our bourgeoisie are speculating in vain on the fatigue and exhaustion of the energy of the proletariat. The workers' revolution, thanks to the leadership of Social Democracy, is aware of its roads and objectives, and the proletariat as a revolutionary class fighting today for the first time for itself, in the interest of trying to achieve its liberation, does not know, cannot know regression, or fatigue, in combat.

The last few weeks have shown again that the tsarist government and the present political order are standing on a volcano, where the old craters will continue to emit fiery streams of lava, and where new outlets will be found on the side of the volcanic crust, until they all connect and merge to form an unbroken sea of revolutionary flame, into which the leftover hulk of despotism's last government will sink without a trace.

The "Constitution" of the Knout[*]

In the situation of the revolutionary fight that has been shaking the tsarist empire already for seven months, a new fact of paramount importance has occurred in recent weeks, a fact about which the class-conscious proletariat must be very aware. It is that the tsar has "granted" the Bułygin "Constitution."

Bludgeoned by the uprising of the workers in Petersburg, followed by a continuous series of blows, absolutism was forced to seemingly make concessions. The Bułygin "constitution" is the result of the powerful revolutionary turbulence that has shaken society in Russia and in Poland since the days of the Petersburg carnage in January. It finds ever-new expression in ongoing strikes and demonstrations by the workers in violent explosions, like the uprisings in Łódź and Odessa, in some disturbances among the army and especially in the navy (such as on the battleship *Potemkin*), in the opposition movement of the Russian intelligentsia, strikes in schools etc., etc. The machinery of the despotic state has totally ceased to function in its normal manner. Despotism can maintain itself only by force, by incessant murders, individual and on a mass scale.

And now despotism has decided to try and avert the storm, that perpetual revolutionary storm, by seemingly granting a concession. The domination of the knout is threatened, and so it tries to hide behind a "constitution."

That the Bułygin "Constitution"[†] is nothing but a terrible comedy, a hideous mockery of the political freedom for which thousands of proletarians throughout the country sacrificed their blood and their lives—that is obvious at the very first glance. With their typical cynicism, the creators of this "constitution" point out loud and clear at the very outset that *autocracy* still remains the basis of the political system in the country. That is, the omnipotent reign of the tsarist knout that dominates over the life of 130 million people. But this "constitution," this monstrous brainchild of the tsarist chinovniks, is amazingly intricate and perhaps the only example in the world of despotic rule disguised in constitutional form.

The core of political freedom, as it is understood today all over the world, is the legislative authority of representatives chosen by the people. The tsar's

---

[*] This article is translated (by George Shriver and Alicja Mann) from the August 1905 issue of *Czerwony Sztandar*, No. 28, August 1905, pp. 1–4. Its title in Polish is "'Konstytucja' Knuta." Luxemburg referred to the tsarist regime as "the rule of the knout" in her writings of this period.

[†] The Bułygin Constitution was named after Alexander Bułygin, who became Russian prime minister in late January 1905 in the aftermath of Bloody Sunday. In response to the threat posed by the revolution, in February 1905 he proposed a constitution that would provide a veneer of parliamentarism while leaving real power in the hands of the tsar and his administration (it became effective in August 1905). The Bułygin Constitution provided for a merely advisory Duma (or parliament) in which workers, women, servicemen and students had no representation whatsoever. Peasants were permitted to vote, though they received far less representation than landowners.

representative body, called by this "constitution" the "State Duma," has no power to legislate, has only a consultative voice. It can give its opinions, but the whole power stays with the tsar and his ministers. The law expresses not the will of the chosen representatives, but the will of the despot, with the representatives who were chosen by the population gathering around just to talk to the wind.

The main guarantee of the influence and importance of popular representation is the responsibility of ministers and the government to the parliament. In the tsarist "constitution" it happens the other way around. The ministers do not have any responsibility toward the chosen representatives and can trample on the still-existing laws as they wish. Also, at a single word from the senate, the representatives of the public may lose their mandate and their seat in the "Duma";* at a single word from a minister, they may lose the opportunity to speak in the "Duma" to the public, to the people; at a single word from the tsar, any draft law, considered in a parliamentary session, can be removed out from under their nose and taken off the agenda. Lastly, one word from the tsar is enough at any moment to dissolve the entire "Duma" and send home the deputies for as long as the tsar wishes. At the same time, it is guaranteed that representatives of the people cannot open their mouths or discuss any draft laws that would "undermine the foundations of the governmental order"—that is, that would undermine the basis of despotism.

In this way, the parliament that is alleged to be an expression of the supreme will of the people, and which is supposed to be the law that controls the actions of the government, is in reality a gathering of humble lackeys, talking or being silent at the command of the tsarist ministers—no power, no strength, no significance, and no influence; like a Chinese screen covering the omnipotent reign of the knout.

And even those lackeys—deputies ready to follow any order of the tsar—will be elected by a small handful of the privileged nobility and the wealthy bourgeoisie. The entire multimillion proletariat, all the petty bourgeoisie, all the not-so-wealthy urban intelligentsia, the entire mass of poor, landless peasants, is excluded from participating in the elections.

Out of a population of 140 million,† nearly 139-and-a-half million will remain completely behind the fence of that "constitution" and can only watch through the gap in the fence as a couple of hundred thousand of the richest parasitic exploiters will be choosing from among themselves the representatives who will be bowing before the tsar—the despot and his gang of chinovniks.

---

* In this piece and others written in this period, Luxemburg often puts "Duma" in quotation marks, to indicate her disdain for an ineffective institution that bought off the masses when they revolted.

† On the previous page "130 million" is given for the population of the tsarist empire, as against "140 million" here. Luxemburg gives various figures for the population of the empire—in large part because the most recent (and only) imperial census was conducted in 1897. That census gave a figure of 135 million—but the number was surely higher by 1905.

And, even within these "political rights" given to a handful of oppressors of the people, absolutism succeeded with real artistry in maintaining its basic principles of rule and domination—to generate discord among different nationalities, and to encourage ignorance and superstition among the backward masses to set them against the progressive and revolutionary part of the population.

Poland, the Caucasus, and Finland are excluded from the general electoral law and are kept isolated from "the native peoples of Russia." In order to impose discord and hatred between nationalities, the chinovniks even propose to fabricate a separate and special election law for the "foreign nationalities." At the same time, across the country, a handful of representatives from the big cities—that is, from the centers of big industry, the intelligentsia, and the fighting workers—will be overwhelmed completely by a giant majority of deputies from rural areas [characterized by their] backwardness, disorganization, and political passivity. In Russia alone, out of 412 deputies in the Duma there will be only twenty-eight deputies from the cities, and from the villages 384!

The same policy of absolutism that throws the rogue gang of Caucasus Tatars* against the Armenian labor movement, or which in Chişinău instigates the scum of society against the revolutionary Jewish proletariat†—that [divide-and-rule] policy now finds its expression in this "constitutional" electoral law establishing the "Duma."

And, as a supplement to this "constitutional" cracking of the tsarist whip, the elections are to be held without freedom of assembly and speech, without freedom to form unions or freedom of the press. None of the basic, elementary constitutional rights and political freedoms prevailing today throughout the civilized world were announced. Instead, in a number of towns the symbol for celebration of this "constitution"—martial law with military courts as the triumphal gates at the entranceway to tsarist "political freedom"—will be the gallows.

On the surface, even this comedy seems to be too monstrous, too obvious, to have any practical purpose for absolutism, but it does have a purpose and even one that is very carefully designed. With such a constitution, despotism does not give up its position, not even one inch or pinch of its power. The knout remains above the legislature. But, at the same time, the knout is dressed up in a new costume. It appears that a new reality is created, along with a desire for new

---

* This refers mainly to Turkic-speaking Azerbaijani Muslims. Tatar soldiers were used in the Caucasus to attack the Armenian labor movement as part of the government's divide-and-rule policy of fomenting hostility between the predominantly Christian Armenians and Muslim Tatars. At the same time, however, the Tatars often faced discrimination and repression of their national rights by the tsarist regime. In Western Europe at the time, the term "Tatar" was most often used as an epithet, as was "Asiatic" or "Oriental."

† A reference to the numerous pogroms launched against Jews, most often with the active consent of tsarist authorities. It bears noting that Luxemburg sees such pogroms as a response to the militancy of the Jewish working class.

relationships—but all this is calculated only to cause upset and confusion in the revolutionary camp.

First of all, the tsarist government gains totally by getting on its side the wealthiest elements of the nobility and the bourgeoisie, to whom it gives the right to vote. In Russia so far, and even more so in our country,* these elements have been faithful to the bloody throne of the autocracy, but hostile in their soul toward the fighting proletariat. It is they who are getting a new privilege in the form of these new "constitutional" rights. And although these rights are a shameful comedy, they are a true gift and grace for those who do not even have any aspiration to claim such rights, except for the right to fatten themselves further with the blood and sweat of the working people. Therefore, this most reactionary part of the propertied classes, which so far has stood in silence on the sidelines in this turbulent revolution (in part out of fear of the revolution), is now calling for active and open support to the crumbling throne.

Secondly, part of the Russian nobility and bourgeoisie (as of now representing the liberal opposition) aims to overcome these [revolutionary] elements by arousing false hopes that the present monstrous parody of a constitution is an embryo that with patience and calmness could develop over time into something better. Bourgeois liberalism even in Western Europe—where it was once a giant in comparison with today's haggard liberalism of the Russian nobility—always fell into the trap set by the reactionary governments of eagerly seizing upon a sloppy, miserable "concession," [on the grounds that] one finger must be caught in order to catch the whole hand. The Russian liberal nobility will do just about anything to get out of this period of workers' revolution. It will probably agree with that "constitution" for the time being in order to satisfy and delude itself and others that from there will slowly grow true political freedom.

Absolutism expects to fool the entire mass of the politically still-unconscious rural and urban populations with this pretense of a constitution, even with the sound of that word, whose correct value they cannot yet assess. Meanwhile, millions of people in Russia and in our country do not yet understand the importance and need for universal, direct, equal, and secret voting rights. They do not know what a parliament is, what a real constitution is, what the word "republic" means, and what genuine political freedom is. Hence it is easy for the tsarist government to create the illusion that this "constitutional" mask of the knout-ocracy is actually some sort of political freedom.

Therefore, these half-conscious masses of the petty bourgeoisie, peasants, and even the masses of the workers in the cities, which today are partly ready to follow the conscious revolutionary proletariat into the fight, will tomorrow—after the beginning of the constitutional comedy—most likely rather stop and passively look forward to see what this new arrangement will bring. That is

---

* That is, Poland.

what the tsarist government is speculating on to save itself from the workers' revolution. To make an open alliance with the big bourgeoisie and nobility, to overpower the liberal opposition, to deceive the uneducated parts of the public with the pretense of a constitution with the purpose of removing them from the influence of the fighting proletariat—that is the intention of the government of Nicholas the Last, a new trick to avoid its oncoming death. As soon as this monstrosity conceived in the offices of the tsarist regime comes to life, and the comedy starts for real—then there will be heard lots of loud shouting from many directions against the fighting proletariat: "That is enough of strikes for now, enough of demonstrations and bloodshed! Now is the time to stay calm and wait to see what is possible to win in a new way, with the constitution, which we just received!" To sum up, the aim of this constitutional deception is *to create disorder and confusion in the ranks of the fighters, and at the same time, to make use of this visible and loud, although illusory symbol to interrupt and put an end to this revolutionary period and to return to "normal times," that is, to a quiet reign of the old knout in his new costume.*

Ending the string of military defeats in the Far East by concluding a peace treaty with Japan, and ending the political defeats of the internal revolution by introducing a "constitution"—those are the two tools that dying absolutism is trying to use to save its criminal life at this moment.

But these policies also visibly indicate—and this is self-evident in the present era—what should be the goal of the conscious part of the Social Democratic working class. While the goal of despotism is to end the revolutionary turbulence and restore the "peace," the main duty of the conscious proletariat must be *to maintain a state of perpetual revolution, to keep it boiling.* For this purpose, nullify all speculation by the tsarist regime aimed at deceiving and demoralizing the people with this constitutional comedy. While tsarism wants to start the "normal" and quiet course of social life by using the Bułygin "Constitution," the task of the revolutionary proletariat in Russia and Poland is to demolish this entire "constitution," and to discredit it just as it deserves.

Therefore, the plans of some Russian comrades* miss the mark completely. They are proposing that the workers take part in the electoral puppet show being organized by absolutism—even though the tsarist "constitution" does not give them any right or possibility to do that. They are creating this [illusion] for themselves, as if universal suffrage is in force—and at the same time they [imagine] that the strongest and most pronounced supporters of the revolution and the overthrow of tsarism would be elected to the "State Duma." Such a tactic might in fact either promote adaptation [to the regime] or cause the greatest confusion among the circles of less-conscious working people. To try to put into effect the universal right of voting by the people when such a voting right is

---

*   Luxemburg's criticism here is directed mainly at some of the Mensheviks.

non-existent, and the voting would be for a non-existent parliament—that is an impracticable chimera.

The broad mass of the people would never take part in such fictitious elections. We are talking about obtaining the power to exercise *real political rights*, and not about making a trial run to try out fictitious rights. Thus, if the workers took part in elections to the "Bulygin Duma"—even if they supported excellent radical candidates to this "Duma"—they would only increase the political and moral importance of this chess game of despotism, [thereby] arousing illusory hopes and expectations in the mass of the people. They would only be bringing grist to the mill of the tsarist government.

On the contrary, the task of Social Democracy, in Russia and in Poland, can only be this—to completely destroy any and all importance of both the elections and the "Duma," which is to be elected by a handful of bourgeois and noble bloodsuckers. For this purpose, [we need] scathing criticism of this "constitutional" monstrosity in order to illuminate for the broadest masses the difference between the constitutional masquerade of tsarism and real political freedom—the latter being our primary method of struggle. But that is not enough. Already the Russian democratic intelligentsia—lawyers, doctors, engineers, and so forth, organized in the so-called Union of Unions*—have called for a boycott of the tsarist "constitution." In other words, their slogan is that every honest and sincere supporter of political freedom in Russia *should not take part at all in the elections*, even when it is a question of a handful of the highly privileged who have been granted the right to vote. Anyone who takes part in the elections to this "Duma" dreamed up by the tsar's chief bureaucrats would be helping absolutism realize its plans, and therefore would be a *traitor* in regard to universal, direct, and equal suffrage and to real freedom in the state of Russia.

That slogan[†] is the one put forward by the advanced intelligentsia in Russia. But the fighting proletariat cannot be satisfied with that. The proletariat must always, as well in this case, seek to go further in its politics than the democratic

---

*   The Union of Unions (Soyuz Soyuzov) was a political organization of largely professional groups drawn from the liberal-bourgeois intelligentsia, such as physicians, lawyers, writers, journalists, pharmacists, college professors, etc. At its founding conference in Moscow in May 1905, it contained fourteen unions, of which nine consisted of groups of professionals. It also included the Union of Railroad Employees (which was a mixture of manual laborers and railroad officials), the Union of Clerks and Bookkeepers, the Union for the Achievement of Full Rights of Jews, and the Union for Equal Rights of Women. From its inception, it was led by Pavel Milyukov, a Russian liberal. The Union of Unions advocated the abolition of the monarchy, the formation of a Constituent Assembly, and the introduction of democratic governance. As the 1905 Revolution progressed, it moved to the left on some issues, calling for a boycott of the Bulygin Duma. Despite providing support for the revolution, it did not assume a leading role in it (it was much overshadowed by the soviets or workers' councils). It was disbanded in 1906 after a series of disputes between liberals and more radical elements, which had emerged in October and November 1905. The Union of Unions should not be confused with the Union of Liberation (also headed by Milyukov), which was primarily comprised of bourgeois liberals and played a less active role in the revolution.

†   That is, slogans encouraging the boycott of elections to the Duma.

elements of the bourgeoisie. For the workers, the slogan cannot be "boycott," that is, abstaining from the elections, when the workers (together with the mass of the petty bourgeoisie and the landless peasantry) have already been excluded from voting rights. But the conscious workers also cannot just sit by and look on as the electoral puppet show takes place before their eyes, after which will come the puppet show of "Duma" consultations by the tsar's flunkeys from among the nobility and bourgeoisie. Therefore, the workers must at all costs prevent this comedy from being performed.

While the more advanced intelligentsia are trying in their characteristic way to prevent the bourgeoisie and nobility from participating in this "constitutional" farce by appealing to their conscience and warning them against betrayal of the people and of freedom, the revolutionary working class must *prevent* this betrayal by taking the road of open mass struggle. Every electoral gathering arranged under the protection, supervision, and direction of the chinoviks and the tsarist police ought to become an arena into which the mass of workers, who are excluded from the right to vote, should gain access by storm through an all-out assault. [It should do so] in order to make the following slogans heard: "Down with the comedy of elections with no voters from the people! Down with the farce of a constitution of the knout! Long live universal, direct, and equal suffrage, with the secret ballot, and long live the democratic republic!"

Every voting place ought to be denounced as an outpost of absolutism, and ought to be besieged by the mass of workers, so as not to permit the privileged voters to complete their intended action of betraying the people. To disperse electoral gatherings everywhere, to prevent the elections, to render impossible the deliberations of the "State Duma" itself, to disrupt, at every step, any scheme being tried by the government and the bourgeoisie in partnership to make a reality of their joint operation of a "constitutional" comedy—that is the only plan of action corresponding to the interests of the revolutionary working class.

It is obvious that a constitution born from the knout will be guarded by the gendarmes, police, and troops. To protect those who are allowed to vote by the kindness of the tsar and the "Duma" [made up of] loyal pillars of the tsar, bullets and bayonets will be "on alert," and all attempts to prevent the "constitutional" puppet show will be accompanied by unceasing clashes between the government's thugs and the revolutionary masses of workers. But, precisely in that way, the goal and task of Social Democracy will be realized. If the entire "constitution" from the very beginning must be placed under guard by bayonets, if the "elections" can be held only to the accompaniment of loud rifle fire, if the "deputies" elected to the "Duma" are forced to crawl [to their seats] like evil doers under the protection of Cossack patrols, in that case the "constitution" will be exposed as the obvious farce that it is, as a miserable mask worn by absolutism, by that same old hated absolutism. The comedy will be defeated, illusions dispersed, the deception of the people rendered impossible. And if, in this way, the "constitution" causes a series of mass confrontations by the people against the government, then the revolution will in fact triumph over this miserable duplicity of absolutism.

Despotism wants to make use of this diplomatic maneuver precisely to put out the revolutionary fire, to initiate a phase of "peace and quiet" and normal life, [but] this will be turned into a point of departure for a new series of revolutionary outbursts. Instead of putting out the fire of the workers' revolution, this "constitution" can start it burning again with renewed force. It can add new fuel to the fire by creating disruption and spreading chaos in the reigning non-government,* [thereby] consolidating the revolutionary energy and political consciousness on the side of the working class.

By means of mass revolutionary struggle that does not permit the tsar's constitutional farce to be played out, but to convert this farce into a new, higher stage of the revolution—that is, in a nutshell, the battle tactic of the conscious proletariat against the tsarist government's tactic of fraud and swindle.

---

* By "reigning non-government," Luxemburg means the shadow of a constitutional government that will be produced by the Bułygin Constitution.

A Victim of the White Terror[*]

Once again, the accursed tsarist system has singled out a new victim for itself. Marcin Kasprzak has died a martyr's death. To describe this man's life is to recount the history of the sufferings and battles of the Polish proletariat.[†] It was a life of unlimited readiness for sacrifice, loyal devotion to the cause of the revolution, and daring deeds.

At the beginning of the 1880s the workers' movement first established a foothold in Poznań. The movement was pushed forward mainly by revolutionaries who came from Russian Poland and Galicia. Among those recruited to the new doctrine was Kasprzak, an ordinary man, a roofer by trade, a simple worker. With that tempestuous passion often found among the Poles, he plunged into the movement, and his capacity for articulate communication soon made him an influential agitator. It was not long before this youthful storm swallow ran afoul of the law. He ended up in jail on charges of *lèse majesté*.[‡] His passionate nature soon drove him to attempt an escape, in which he was successful, but from then on open activity in Prussia was not possible for him despite his Prussian citizenship, and so he began to devote himself entirely to the revolutionary cause on the other side of the border, in Russian Poland, for which he had already performed many important services.

In 1887, he showed up in Warsaw. Those were hot times. The thugs of the tsarist regime[§] had, for a short time, succeeded in creating divisions in the ranks of Polish socialists. A little while earlier, their most capable leaders had perished on the scaffold. Hundreds of fighters had been shipped off to Siberia; the party[¶] had become disorganized; police spies had an easy job of [disruption] among

---

[*] This article in memory of Kasprzak, "Ein Opfer des weißen Terrors!," first appeared in the newspaper *Leipziger Volkszeitung*, No. 210, September 11, 1905, two days after Kasprzak was hanged in Warsaw by the tsarist government. It is translated (by George Shriver) from Luxemburg's *Gesammelte Werke*, Vol. 6, pp. 553–8. The article was not signed, but is almost certainly by Luxemburg. In a letter to Jogiches of September 15, 1905, she promised an additional article about Kasprzak, which was published in Polish under the title "Niech żyje rewolucja!" ("Long Live the Revolution") in *Z pola walki*, No. 12, September 30, 1905. For the latter, see pp. 214–16 below. A copy of this article was first found in the Moscow archive RGASPI (Rossiysky Gosudarstvenny Arkhiv Sotsialno-Politicheskoi Istorii—Russian State Archive for Social and Political History), Collection 209, which contains archived material providing the basis for further volumes of Luxemburg's *Gesammelte Werke*.

[†] Luxemburg was politically and personally close to Kasprzak since she was a teenager. He played a role in introducing her to revolutionary politics and helped her flee Poland in order to avoid arrest by tsarist authorities in 1889.

[‡] That is, insulting the monarch.

[§] The Okhrana, the regime's secret police.

[¶] This refers to the First Proletariat Party, the first Marxist party in Russian-occupied Poland. It was formed in 1882. By 1886 it suffered many blows due to repression and only fragments of it existed by 1887. In 1888 Kasprzak helped form the Second Proletariat Party out of remnants of the earlier party and several other organizations.

the inexperienced workers, deprived of their leaders. In the midst of these conditions, Kasprzak took part in the immensely difficult work of reorganizing the party,* and in the process, he developed truly phenomenal skills as an agitator and organizer, but above all it was his conspiratorial talent that proved to be of such benefit to the party. He was everywhere and nowhere. Thousands of workers had seen him and heard him, they all knew "Maciej," as he called himself, but none could say where he was to be found.

Maciej had become almost a legendary figure, and in dozens of cases, when the "forces of order" succeeded in capturing one or another worker of less sturdy character, the "lawmen" kept hearing this name mentioned: Maciej had spoken at such-and-such a meeting, Maciej had distributed such-and-such pamphlets and leaflets, Maciej had organized this or that strike—but they could not catch him. Or rather, twice they already had him in their hands, but the result was only some broken teeth and busted ribs for the "preservers of order"; this man of Herculean strength and unusual agility had disappeared. For five years, he carried on this terribly exhausting activity under conditions of unbelievable deprivation.† The party was too poor to provide him with money, and regular earnings were not to be thought of; if an opportunity was found to stay overnight at some comrade's place, well and good, but if not, he spent the night under the open sky; often enough even a scrap of dry bread was lacking, because it was too dangerous to seek out a comrade, and so he endured the pangs of hunger all day.

Then something especially repulsive and horrible came his way—the party to which Kasprzak had devoted his life became untrue to itself. Once again, the party's forces had been ground down badly, and for a short time the workers movement was crippled by the brutal force and violence of the tsarist regime. At one such moment, a small group of exiles abroad dragged chaos and confusion into the picture. There arose that unclear, pseudo-socialist program which wrongly depicted as the immediate task of the socialist movement—the restoration of an independent Polish state.‡ And this ill-fated lapse into blindness by a small group of unclear minds was guilty of causing a rupture between an element among the Polish workers and the real program of Social Democracy. To this day, the sorry episode has not been overcome, as is shown by the report of the German party [the SPD] executive about its negotiations with the PPS in Prussia.§

---

* "Reorganizing" in the sense of creating a new party, the Second Proletariat Party, in which Kasprzak became coleader.

† The Second Proletariat Party went out of existence in 1893, when it merged into the Polish Socialist Party. It is the latter group that Luxemburg refers to later in this article of having betrayed Kasprzak.

‡ Both the First and Second Proletariat Party opposed demands for self-determination and independence for Poland. The PPS, on the other, supported Polish independence—a position Luxemburg's SDKP and SDKPiL always opposed.

§ Following the collapse of the Second Proletariat Party, Kasprzak joined the Polish Socialist

For Kasprzak, this development was to become the tragedy of his life. He could not go along with this mad aberration. He and a numerous group of workers in Warsaw remained true to the program of class struggle,* and that was sufficient for the new usurpers† to begin a campaign against him. And, in this personal struggle, they did not shrink from the most underhanded and criminal methods. These intriguers, lacking in all conscience, cold-bloodedly denounced him—as a police agent. He whose life had been an unbroken chain of struggle against tsarism was portrayed as an agent serving the tsar! He who daily risked his life was denounced by cowardly gangster types from ambush and from exile—who accused him of the most heinous crimes! In vain, he sought to bring these character assassins to justice, these killers of his good name, murderers of his honor. He went abroad and demanded a "court of honor," but the scoundrels wriggled out of it.‡

Of course, he found friends who helped him, but the unfavorable balance of forces could not be overcome. Again and again, the gang who were now his sworn enemies had recourse to blaming the conditions in Russia, which prevented full clarification of the matter. The scoundrels kept working away, using unfounded slander against him. It is to the credit of the *Leipziger Volkszeitung* that many years ago it had already branded this activity as a political crime being committed against an honorable man, and this occurred when the slander found believers inside the German party [the SPD] itself.§

In 1893, the unlucky man—being harried like a wild animal chased by a predator—went back to Warsaw. He wanted to dig up new proof of his innocence. But here fate caught up with him, or perhaps he had lost some of his former strength and skill, or perhaps it was only the result of unfortunate circumstances. At any rate, the forces of law and order got him in their clutches.

Party in Prussia (Polska Partia Socjalistyczna Zaboru Pruskiego, or PPS-ZP), which represented Polish Social Democrats living in German-occupied Poland. In 1903, the PPS-ZP removed his name from a list of prospective candidates for elections to the Reichstag, in part because of his support for the SKDPiL's opposition to Polish national independence.

 *   As Luxemburg saw it, any concession to "nationalist" demands for independence seriously undermined the politics of class struggle. The PPS, on the other hand (as well as many other groups in the Second International) did not see the two as incompatible.

 †   That is, those in the PPS-ZP and its parent organization, the PPS.

 ‡   Kasprzak plead his case to the SPD, but despite there being considerable support for him in the party, no action was taken, largely in order to avoid inflaming tensions with the PPS-ZP.

 §   Luxemburg is referring to an item entitled "Note from Breslau," dated August 20, 1895. The "Note from Breslau" appeared in the *Leipziger Volkszeitung*, No. 193, August 21, 1895, and stated the following: "Our Polish comrade Marcin Kasprzak, a man of great integrity, thoroughly devoted to the cause, and very much an upright person, who had been dragged into the big anti-socialist trial in Poznań in 1888, but who broke out of the Poznań prison with great skill, has recently been arrested in Breslau. At that time, Kasprzak had squeezed himself, naked, out of a cell window and then by holding on to gutters and drainpipes, outcroppings from the wall, and lighting-rod cables had worked his way to the ground." The article went on to attack the conservative newspaper *Schlesische Zug* (Silesian Express) for defending Kasprak's arrest and branding him a "nihilist and anarchist" terrorist.

In prison, he fell ill. The dreadful experiences he had lived through temporarily disrupted his sanity, and thus he was hospitalized as a mental patient. That was good luck for him, because no sooner had an escape plan ripened in this mind than he carried it out. This escape is an example of the sheer superhuman willpower of this man who had the strength and energy of a mythical hero. He leaped from a window of the mental hospital after having sawed through the bars, breaking one leg as a result of his fall and spraining the other, dislocating his shoulder, and breaking several ribs. In this condition, he dragged himself along until he found a carriage for hire. He also had to cover up his tracks, and so for half a day he traveled around the city until he was finally able to hunt up the dwelling place of a friend. After convalescing only halfway, he fled to Germany, only to end up in prison again. The Prussian prosecutor's office had an old account to settle with Kasprzak. Even then, however, the despicable slander did not die down.

To be sure, the Polish Social Democrats in Poznań received him with open arms, but the PPS kept hurling mud at their victim from behind the scenes. In 1901, the Polish and German comrades nominated him as a candidate for election to the Reichstag, thus declaring him to be worthy of the highest honor that the proletariat can offer. But even then the slanderers continued their campaign, and they would not refrain even when the SPD Executive took the matter in hand and demanded proof. No proof was forthcoming, and the SPD Executive gave the persecuted man full exoneration. But even the SPD Executive could not force the slanderers to hold their tongues.

Nevertheless, Kasprzak fought on. For him, a conspirator who had battled for so many years under such difficult conditions, it was in the end impossible to find a field of activity that was satisfying in the Prussian-occupied city of Poznań.* His path took him back to Russian-occupied Poland. There the masses of workers were moving forward again, advancing at a redoubled pace under the banner of Social Democracy, the banner of revolutionary class struggle. And that is what he was drawn to.

It was completely clear to him that, if he fell into the hands of the tsar's police thugs again, his fate would be sealed, they would take their full vengeance on him, but he did not let that stop him. He cast to the winds all reservations and warnings, but certainly he was clear in his own mind about the prospects he faced.

In 1903, he went back over there [to Russian-occupied Poland]. And once he was back in his old stamping ground, at the scene of his former battles, he demanded that he be given the most dangerous assignments.† He demanded

---

* Poznań (then called Posen) was one of the oldest cities in Poland, serving as its capital during part of the thirteenth century. It came under the control of Prussia in 1793, during the second partition of Poland.

† He made this request to the SDKPiL.

this as an honor that belonged to him, that he had earned. And at that post he fell as a hero.

On April 27, 1904, while he, along with several comrades, was at a secret printing press of the SDKPiL producing a leaflet, "the bulls" forced their way in.* Kasprzak ordered the comrades to flee while he himself took up the battle. Four of "the bulls" were to lose their lives before they managed to overcome this sole defender. In the end, he and comrade [Benedykt] Gurcman were captured; the others got away.

The tsar was victorious over Marcin Kasprzak. But the man they placed under triply reinforced guard in the Warsaw Citadel was only the shadow of the hero he had been. An impotence of the spirit overcame him, a coma-like state from which he awoke only from time to time.

And what about the slanderers? It was reported a few days ago that finally—at last!—they have laid down their weapons. On August 29, 1905, they publicly paid tribute to Kasprzak, and on August 30 the tsarist goons sat in judgment over him. And, even for this final exoneration, the martyr had only one particular circumstance to thank. One of his closest comrade-in-arms had just returned from penal exile in Siberia. The "declaration of honor" issued by the PPS is signed by Mrs. [Estera] Golde, M.D., Ignacy Daszyński, and I. Falski. The latter was an eyewitness to Kasprzak's activities from 1888 to 1892; then Falski was arrested and sent to Siberian exile. Now he has compelled the PPS, of which he is a member, to own up to the crime it has committed against his comrade-in-arms. Daszyński and Mrs. Golde were complicit in, and had collaborated in, the slander campaign for all those years, and now they hang their heads. There never was any proof of the slanderous accusations; it was all lies and deception.

The bloody verdict was handed down, and as in so many other cases was accompanied by flagrant violations of the law. Kasprzak had been acting in self-defense when he shot down the "bluecoats." But was he in full possession of his faculties when he did this? The experts doubted it. They explained, in the final round of legal proceedings in this case, that there was no question that mental illness had set in. There was no denying that this illness was afflicting him in prison. The "judge" was forced to release the victim from his clutches, for a time. Kasprzak was temporarily turned over to doctors for observation, but the authorities made sure these doctors were well aware of what the tsar wanted in this case. That was the first violation of Kasprzak's legal rights. There are two other violations of the law. The incident had occurred in Warsaw at a time when "normal conditions prevailed," but "the court" sentenced Kasprzak on the basis of martial law. That was the second violation of his rights. The defense lawyers brought up procedural violations that, according to the law, necessarily had to be reviewed by a court of appeals, but this stricture was disregarded. The tsar's

---

*   That is, thugs working for the police.

satrap in Warsaw, on the grounds of his individual plenipotentiary power, over-ruled the law. That was the third violation of Kasprzak's rights. The tsar wanted blood. His minions acted accordingly. The victim's life was forfeited.

A news report about the trial's proceedings contains one inexpressibly moving passage. Kasprzak was listening to the proceedings without any show of emotion. The defense lawyers were fighting passionately for his life—but he was not paying attention to all that anymore, he was absolutely mute and indifferent. Only at one point did he come alive. The public prosecutor was using a despicable trick, presenting the program of Social Democracy in such a way as though it ruled out any act of violence, even in extreme situations, in self-defense. The prosecutor used this to portray Kasprzak's action of putting up resistance against "the bulls" as an especially flagrant crime, and in the process this foul creature had the gall to declare: "Kasprzak is not worthy of calling himself a Social Democrat." When the poor man grasped what the prosecutor was saying, the spirit that was nearly extinguished within him flamed up once more. He arose, straightened himself up proudly and without saying a word shook a threatening fist at his detractor. To fight to defend his life—he no longer had the strength for that. But when this flunkey of the tsar attacked his honor as a worker and a socialist, a value that was for him more precious than life itself, the hero within him revived.

Equally monstrous was the sentence handed down against the second defendant. Nothing could be proven against Comrade Gurcman, neither that he had committed the slightest act of violence nor that he had taken part in the self-defense action against "the bulls." Nevertheless, he was sentenced to fifteen years of hard labor.

The representatives of German Social Democracy have raised their voices against the reign of scoundrels and the violation of rights. They presented a request to the chancellor of the German Reich* that he intercede on behalf of Kasprzak's rights [as a citizen of Prussia] on the grounds that he should prevent the legalized murder of a citizen of Germany. Kasprzak was not given a fair trial; he was murdered because legality was trampled underfoot. Prince von Bülow did not perform his duty; he did nothing to prevent this legal lynching. He made himself an accomplice in this crime of tsarism.†

---

* Von Bülow was chancellor at the time.

† [Footnote by Luxemburg] The following message was sent to Chancellor von Bülow from five SPD members of the Reichstag:

In the course of the last few days the SPD Executive members of the Reichstag present in Berlin have appealed on behalf of Kasprzak for intercession by the chancellor and the Foreign Office of the German Reich. The telegram sent to the chancellor read as follows: To the Chancellor of the German Reich, Prince von Bülow of Baden-Baden: On September 1, 1905, in Warsaw the Prussian citizen Marcin Kasprzak was sentenced to death. The defendant's lawyers appealed this sentence. The appeals court is located in St. Petersburg. Based on the state of martial law in Warsaw, the governor-general prevented the appeals documents from being sent. This

The coffin lid has closed over this victim of tsarism. A great and noble heart has ceased to beat. The name of this hero will remain unforgotten, forever inscribed in the grateful memory of the working class—Marcin Kasprzak.

---

prohibition is a violation of the rights legally guaranteed to the defendant. The undersigned are asking that the chancellor, as well as the Foreign Office, in view of the short time remaining before the sentence is to be carried out, immediately present a demand to the Russian government that it set aside the execution of the sentence and grant the defendant the rights legally belonging to him. An analogous telegram has been sent to the secretary of state of the Foreign Office. A reply is requested by the following Members of the Reichstag: [Ignaz] Auer, [Alwin] Gerisch, [Brutus] Molkenbuhr, [Wilhelm] Pfannkuch, and [Paul] Singer; No. 60 Lindenstrasse, Berlin."

Remarks at the Jena Congress on Relations Between the Party and the Trade Unions, with Reference to the 1905 Revolution in Russia [September 1905]*

Robert Schmidt has repeatedly emphasized that there can be no antithesis between the party and the unions in Germany. Actually, there ought not to be any such conflict, but if certain phenomena within the German workers' movement are likely to create and stir up such an antithesis, this very speech by Schmidt has shown us that there actually are elements working in that direction. ("Quite right!")

Because what else was the central axis of the speech by Schmidt, who asked to speak for an hour in order to explain and justify his behavior regarding the May Day celebration, but who actually used his time to undertake an unprecedented spate of badgering and baiting against *Neue Zeit* and against theory in general. ("Quite right!") In fact, this badgering was carried on with such unpleasant methods and in such an obnoxious way as we have previously encountered only from our bitterest opponents from the camp of the bourgeoisie. (Quite right!)

Kautsky is actually the person called upon to speak on behalf of *Neue Zeit*,† but he is busy right now at the Fifteenth Commission.‡ In Kautsky's absence, I feel it is my duty to present some facts to shed light on the methods Schmidt uses in his fight against *Neue Zeit*. Indeed, certain accusations have been made by *Vorwärts* in woeful tones like this: "Oh, what a shame it is that *Neue Zeit* does not work sufficiently toward the theoretical education of the masses!" *Vorwärts* is so busy that it cannot do this itself. Among those who are ready at any moment to complain that *Neue Zeit* has such a small circulation, then, we must also

---

* These remarks by Luxemburg are excerpted from the minutes of the SPD's Jena Congress, held on September 17–23, 1905. The proceedings were published as *Protokoll über die Verhandlungen des Parteitages der Sozialdemokratischen Partei Deutschlands. Abgehalten zu Jena vom 17. bis 23. September 1905* (Berlin: Vorwärts, 1905). The comments by Luxemburg are from pp. 256–7 and 269–71 of the *Protokoll* and are translated from the text in Luxemburg's *Gesammelte Werke*, Vol. 1, Part 2, pp. 595–603. Interjections from the floor are in parentheses and are often in quotation marks. Luxemburg's remarks mainly consist of rejoinders to comments by Robert Schmidt, a member of the Reichstag and leading revisionist and spokesman for the conservative views of the SPD union leaders. It is translated by George Shriver.

† At the time, Kautsky served as chief editor of *Neue Zeit*.

‡ In response to growing divisions with the SPD over attitudes toward the mass strike, the party established a "Fifteenth Commission" at its Jena Congress of September 1905 in order to look into the disagreements on this issue between different SPD newspapers, in particular *Vorwärts* and *Leipziger Volkszeitung*. The Commission rejected calls from right-wing figures that the discussion of the mass strike be shelved because it allegedly (as claimed by the rightists) represented a mere "squabble among the literati."

apparently include Robert Schmidt, but such people seize on every opportunity with the greatest zeal to work against *Neue Zeit*, to discredit it and tear it apart. Thus, Schmidt literally says it would be a blessing for the workers not to read *Neue Zeit* any more. I ask you, how can a party "comrade," a SPD delegate to the Reichstag, abase himself in such a way and say such things against *Neue Zeit*, the only theoretical publication [we have], whose purpose is to educate the German workers about socialism! ("Quite right!")

Supposedly, *Neue Zeit* has too few articles about the unions. I have here the table of contents of the articles about the unions that *Neue Zeit* published during the past year, not counting articles on the subject of the mass strike. I will go through this list with the proof right here in my hand because all this is highly relevant to the question of Robert Schmidt's truthfulness and competence in dealing with source material

During this past year, in issue No. 2 of *Neue Zeit*, [Karl] Legien wrote on the subject of the past decade of the union movement;* in issue No. 9, [Paul] Umbreit wrote on the so-called "labor chambers" [*Arbeiterkammern*];† in issue No. 20, [F.] Schnetter wrote about the "guild ideas" in the wage agreements [*Zunftgedanken in den Tarifverträgen*];‡ in issue No. 27, [Eugen] Umrath on the general strike debates; in issue No. 28, Umbreit on the enthusiasm for industrial peace; in No. 33, [Emil] Kloth on the general strike and May Day [discussions] at the trade union congress in Cologne; also in No. 33, Hermann Müller wrote about a fusion within the realm of the unions; in No. 34, Heinrich Baer on union and party; also in No. 34, Kautsky on a revision of union tactics; in No. 36, Kautsky on the Cologne union congress; in No. 41, Hoch on the Christian union movement in Germany; in No. 47, Stroebel on the unions and the spirit of socialism; [and] in No. 48, [Hermann] Fleissner on party and union. ("Hear, hear!")

At any rate, in this rather lengthy list, you will not find the names of either Robert Schmidt or [Otto] Hué, nor of one whose name has earned even greater recognition, [Adolph] von Elm. ("Well said!") If you want to find these names, you have to look, not in *Neue Zeit*, but look in *Sozialistischen Monatsheften*, or take a step farther afield and look in *Neuen Gesellschaft* [New Society], also a reformist and revisionist publication; or even farther afield in *Europa*, the now defunct publication of Messieurs Michalski and Eduard Bernstein. (Laughter and shouts of "Quite right!")

That's where they write, but not for *Neue Zeit*. And then they come along, these people who have carried their spiritual lanterns off to shine in other places

---

* At the time, Legien was chairman of the General Commission of the German Trade Unions, which was affiliated with the SPD.

† An *Arbeiterkammer* was a professional association of workers and employers, roughly equivalent to a "municipal labor exchange," in which union officials were encouraged to enter on a parity basis with the employers.

‡ That is, *Zunftgedanken*—elements found in wage agreements that were analogous to those that formerly benefited skilled master craftsmen in feudal times.

—they come here and plant themselves down and say that *Neue Zeit* doesn't have anything in it about the unions and that it would be a good thing if it wasn't read any more.

Schmidt emphasized, among other things, that if anyone did write about the unions in *Neue Zeit*, it would certainly be only some godforsaken theoretician who didn't understand anything about the practical work of the unions, and as proof he cites an article by the well-known theoretician Fleissner from Dresden (laughter), and a second article by the even better known theoretician, a journeyman baker, [H.] Fischer from Weimar (more laughter).

And what about Schmidt's understanding of how to cite source material? He read out the following sentence: "Now the striving to improve the conditions of life for workers in the state that exists *today* must quite naturally contribute to the *prolonging* of the existence of *this state*, because the better things go for the individual members of a state system, the less reason will these members have for bringing about a change of that state system." Here he quickly claps the book shut and says, Yes, you see, such are the views that are spread about by *Neue Zeit*. But this is not where the article began, and this is not where it ended.

To begin with, the author was taking up a question that was urgent at that time—whether the neutrality of the trade unions, generally speaking, was a new discovery, a "recipe" being recommended to the unions for the first time, or whether this was not in fact an old practice of the unions. The author wrote:

> The trade unions have always objected against anyone incorrectly describing them as organs of the SPD, as *Social Democratic* trade unions. The grounds for this are clear; the objectives of the unions lie in a different sphere from those of the Social Democratic Party.

The author then speaks in favor of a division of labor between the party and the unions, and then after the sentence quoted by Schmidt, the author adds the following:

> If Social Democracy now wants to carry through a change in spite of everything, it must be in the position to demonstrate convincingly that the goal it is striving for will bring further improvement for the unions—more improvements than is possible to achieve in the present society through union organizations alone.

Thus, Schmidt has simply cut the passage in half. I don't know if Schmidt was already convinced, even before he picked up this article, that it would be a good thing if *Neue Zeit* was not read so much, and therefore, accordingly, read only that one sentence torn out of context. (Laughter.) But matters stand in exactly the same way with regard to Comrade Schmidt's truthfulness, when he asserts emphatically that *Neue Zeit* is a publication specially devoted to disparaging parliamentarism. He even presents us with the frightening specter in France of conditions that have allegedly gone all to pieces, and claims that *Neue Zeit* has been working in that same direction. I would like him to show me even one single article in *Neue Zeit* where parliamentarism is disparaged.

But perhaps what Schmidt means by "disparagement of parliamentarism" is the critique of the *bourgeois* system of parliamentarism, which our program, our class point of view, obliges us to make. If that is his understanding, if he believes that it is our duty to praise the bourgeois parliamentary system to the skies, then I must certainly say that *Neue Zeit* cannot win or deserve the praise of Robert Schmidt, and I hope that in the future, as long as Kautsky edits it, it will not deserve the praise of Robert Schmidt.[*] (Applause.)

Comrade Schmidt, in his personal remarks about me, starts out by reproaching me for a lack of kindliness—that is, a courteous, friendly, comradely tone. I feel deeply touched and very contrite. Fortunately, I know a way to correct this lack, and to raise myself to a level of true and proper kindliness. (Laughter.)

To be specific, Schmidt advised the theoreticians to join the trade unions and work in them. In fact, I believe that would be very healthy for me as a way of learning about kindliness and comradeliness. Proof of this is given in an article that Comrade Hué recently published in the German mineworkers' paper.[†] At the end of his article there is a passage that can serve as a model of kindliness toward one's comrades:

> In Russia, for years, the people's freedom struggle has been raging. We have always wondered why our theoretical "general-strikers" don't immediately go to Russia to join in the fight and gather practical experience of the struggle. In Russia the workers are shedding their blood. Why aren't the theoreticians rushing to the scene of battle?—especially those who came from Russia and Poland and are now in Germany, France, or Switzerland, writing such stirringly "revolutionary" articles. For those who show such an excess of "revolutionary" energy as do our systematic promoters of the general strike—it is time for them to take a practical part in the Russian fight for freedom instead of pushing along the general strike discussion from their summer vacation resorts. Better to test things out in practice than just study them in theory.[‡] And so, off you go, you "theoreticians of the class struggle"— off to the fight for freedom in Russia!

---

[*] Because Luxemburg's speaking time had run out, she was not able to conclude her remarks on this subject until she made a renewed request to speak somewhat later during the proceedings of the Jena Congress. Her later comments follow.

[†] This paper was the *Deutsche Bergarbeiter-Zeitung*.

[‡] *"Probieren geht übers Studieren"*—a German proverb comparable to the English "the proof of the pudding is in the eating."

And then here is what Pastor Naumann had to say in his publication *Die Hilfe* [Assistance], after quoting with delight the passage above by Hué: "These words are well said! The international revolutionaries should tell us why they are not international enough to betake themselves right now to Warsaw."

In other words, Comrade Hué invites us in the most kindly and comradely fashion to go to that place where very recently the public prosecutor assisted my close party comrade, Marcin Kasprzak, to achieve the highest honor that can be rendered to any Social Democrat.*

And so I believe I have the right to hope that in the trade unions I will not only arrive at a true understanding of the fundamental principles and practical tactics of the workers' movement but also be instructed on how to maintain a genuinely kind and comradely tone in discussions among party members.

With regard to *Neue Zeit*, I have a further point I would like to make—namely, that Schmidt is heading for a big disappointment if he is hoping that *Neue Zeit* will be read as little as possible by the workers. As you know, the loveliest kind of badgering campaign already occurred once before, in 1902 in Munich. What effect did that have on the growth of *Neue Zeit*? In the first half of 1902, the number of subscribers was 3,700; and in the second half, 3,600. But in the first half of 1905, it was 4,800; and in the second half, 5,100. ("Hear, hear!")

Thus, we see that the attack by "party comrades" against *Neue Zeit* had the same effect, generally speaking, as the attacks by the bourgeois press against Social Democracy. We have grown healthier from that, and it gives us rosy cheeks. ("Well said!")

For those who do not know what the usual circulation figures are for a scholarly-theoretical review, I will add the point that *Neue Zeit*, with this number of subscriptions, is not only *not* lagging behind the best bourgeois reviews, but is ahead of them. This number of subscriptions for a scholarly publication not aimed at a mass audience must be described as "excellent."

Now a few more words about the main question before us—whether there is a conflict between the party and the unions. Comrade Hüttmann states that he doesn't understand where the attacks on the unions are coming from. He cannot imagine that there are union people who fail to stand with both feet firmly planted on the ground of the class struggle. *Facta loquuntur.*†

I want to call to your attention some leaflets that were recently circulated by the Center Party‡ against Social Democracy, in particular during the election campaign in Essen, where they capitalized on a whole series of statements

---

* Kasprzak was hanged by the tsarist government in Warsaw on September 9, 1905, ten days before the opening of the SPD's Jena Congress.

† Latin for "The facts speak for themselves."

‡ Also known as the Catholic Center Party, a right-of-center party formed in 1870 that by the 1890s favored Germany's military build-up and colonial expansion. In 1933, the party voted in favor of Hitler's Enabling Act, which enabled him to assume total power.

excerpted from the trade union press and used them against us. These statements show that many "union people," in fact, no longer stand firmly on the ground of the class struggle and that there are "unionists" who are stirring up conflicts with the party, and they exist, not purely in someone's imagination, but in *sad reality*.

The first leaflet, put out by the Center Party, is entitled "Take Off the Mask!" And here is what it says:

> A correspondent writing to the publication *Deutschlands Buchdrucker* [The Book Printers of Germany] directs a complaint against Social Democracy, charging political impotence with regard to the question of the political mass strike. He writes in issue No. 65 for this year: "Indeed with their mysticism about the political mass strike, people are only shielding an incompetent policy [based on] the Jacobin system, which at one time did help develop the agitational strength of Social Democracy, but is unsuitable for constructive political work, for real political strength in the sense of positive and lasting results. The union movement did not need the historical references by Bernstein; his utterances are only proof of the political helplessness of the party, which can move neither forward nor back, because it is bound hand and foot by an outdated program, and as a result is tied fast to its wrong politics and policies."

In a second leaflet the Center Party states:

> In issue No. 23 of *Fachgenossen* [Skilled Workers], the Social Democrat Edmund Fischer: "One may still value workers' insurance so little as to ignore the fact that today's recipient of old age or disability insurance occupies an entirely different social position compared to the grandfather of twenty-five years ago, no longer able to work, who thus became a burden on his children, or who felt it was shameful to live on social security payments. The social [security] laws are, to be sure, always the foundation structures. But they are nevertheless only the foundation, and thus they constitute the starting point for a grand edifice of human solidarity. And the effort to outdo one another in completing the construction of this grand edifice has awakened and strengthened the idea of community, of equality, of solidarity, in circles that are numbered not only among the workers, and thus this idea has contributed to the general ennoblement of spiritual life."

To this wonderful utterance the Center Party, of course, only needed to add the following comment: "Is this not an annihilating condemnation of the negative politics of Social Democracy?"

That is the way this union person gives his evaluation of the [existing] workers' insurance system, which our parliamentary delegates have never grown tired of criticizing.

Comments like these show that, in fact, there are union people who are creating a division, or fissure, making a dichotomy between Social Democratic party politics, on the one hand, and trade union practice, on the other. Actually, this split is not between the party and the unions, but exists within the unions themselves, and to a certain extent within the party as well. It is this that constitutes the split between the "revised" conception of a minority of leaders and the healthy, revolutionary conception of the mass of the workers. The mass of union members is on our side and certainly feels that it is in the interest of both the party and the unions that the workers' movement as a whole should be pervaded throughout by one and the same spirit, that the movement in all its component parts must be carried along by the spirit of socialism. (Lively agreement.) They all feel that the unions and the Social Democratic Party must say to themselves, like Bertha in *William Tell*: "There is *one* enemy before whom we all tremble, and *one* freedom that makes us all free."* (Hearty applause.)

People listening here to the previous speeches† in the debate on the question of the political mass strike must really feel like clutching their heads and asking: "Are we actually living in the year of the glorious Russian Revolution, or are we still living ten years ago?" (Voice from the hall: "Quite right!")

Day after day, we are reading news about the revolution in the papers, we are reading the telegram dispatches, but it seems as though some of us don't have eyes to see or ears to hear. There are people asking us to tell them how to make the general strike, exactly by what means, at what hour the general strike will be declared. Are you already stocked up with food and other necessities? The masses will die of hunger. Can you bear to have it on your conscience that some blood will be spilled? Yet all those people who ask such questions do not have the slightest contact with the masses or feeling for them. Otherwise, they would not worry their heads so much about the blood of the masses, because it so happens that responsibility for that lies least of all with the comrades who ask such questions.

Schmidt asks, why should we all of a sudden give up our old, tried-and-true tactic in favor of the general strike? Why should we all of sudden commit this kind of suicide? Then does Robert Schmidt not see that a time has come which was predicted to us by our great teachers, Marx and Engels, a time when evolution becomes transformed into revolution? We see the Russian Revolution, and we would be donkeys if we have learned nothing from it.

And then [Wolfgang] Heine steps up and asks Bebel, well, have you thought about the fact that in the event of a general strike not only our well-organized

---

*   This famous play by Friedrich Schiller, long considered a profound expression of the longing for freedom, was first performed in 1804.

†   These comments by Luxemburg come from later in the conference.

crafts and trades but also the unorganized masses will appear on the scene, and are you going to rein in these masses? From this one phrase* we see revealed to us Heine's entire bourgeois conception, which is a shame and a scandal for any Social Democrat. (Commotion in the hall.)

Previous revolutions, in particular that of 1848, have shown that in revolutionary situations it is not the masses who must be reined in, but the parliamentary lawyers, so that they won't betray the masses and the revolution.

Schmidt [earlier] referred to "the Belgian experiment" and to [Émile] Vandervelde's comments.† I believe that if anything has ever shown that a magnificent spontaneous mass movement could be ruined by petty-mindedness, that strike was it. And Vandervelde could not cite a single fact to refute my criticism, but instead he tried to talk his way out of it with hackneyed generalities when I demonstrated to him that this entire magnificent mass strike movement was ruined by parliamentary wheeling and dealing with the liberals.‡ (Eduard Bernstein from the floor: "Not true!" Luxemburg to Bernstein: "Oh, what do you understand about such things?" Great commotion in the hall.)

Here Heine has summoned up the specter of bloody red revolution, and has said that the blood of the German people—this was the gist of his remarks—is more precious to him than to that light-minded youngster, Bebel. I will leave aside personal questions about who has greater competence and who is more capable of taking responsibility, Bebel or the cautious and statesmanlike Heine, but surely we can see from history that all revolutions have been paid for with the blood of the people. The only difference is that, up until now, that blood has been spilled on behalf of the ruling classes, and now when we are within sight of the possibility that they might shed their blood for their own class interests, all at once there appear some cautious so-called Social Democrats who say, "No, that blood is too precious."

What we are talking about is not a matter of immediately proclaiming the revolution; it is not even a matter of proclaiming the mass strike. And if Heine, Schmidt, and [Karl] Frohme call upon us to organize the masses and educate

---

*   *Haben im Zügel*—rein them in.

†   In 1902 a general strike was called in Belgium—its first since 1893—in response to the demands of coal miners for an improvement of their living and working conditions. While Vandervelde (who at the time was chairman of the International Socialist Bureau) and other leading Belgian Social Democrats initially supported the strike, they viewed it purely in terms of obtaining electoral reforms that would widen the franchise, not as a serious effort to challenge the dominance of capital. Due to lack of widespread support the strike was defeated.

‡   During the Belgian strike of 1902, the socialists made a secret agreement with the liberals, calling off the strike in return for liberal support in changing the Belgian constitution to ensure universal suffrage, but the liberals failed to carry out their promises. As part of this agreement, the Belgian socialists conceded to the demands of the liberals to abandon the call for women's suffrage. For Luxemburg's stinging attack of this capitulation, see "A Tactical Question," in *The Rosa Luxemburg Reader*, edited by Peter Hudis and Kevin B. Anderson (New York: Monthly Review Books, pp. 233–6).

them, we will answer them that we are doing that, but we don't want to do it in their sense. (Cries of "Ach! Ach!" from the hall.)

Not in the sense of covering things up and smoothing over contradictions, as these comrades have been doing year after year and day after day. No, it is not the organization that comes before everything else, but it is above all the revolutionary spirit of enlightenment! That is much more important. Remember the time of the antisocialist "exceptional laws"! Our unions were broken to pieces, and yet they rose again from the ashes, like the phoenix. And it will be the same in the future in periods when mighty battles are fought. The most important thing is to educate the masses, and there we don't have to be as cautious as the union leaders were in Cologne. The unions must not become an end-in-themselves, thereby becoming obstructions that interfere with the workers' freedom of movement. When will you finally learn from the Russian Revolution? There the masses were driven into the revolution; not a trace of union organizations, and yet step-by-step they built and strengthened their organizations in the course of the struggle. The point is that this is a totally mechanical and non-dialectical conception, that strong organizations must always precede the struggle. The opposite is true: organizations are born out of struggle, together with class enlightenment.

In the face of all this petty-mindedness we must remind ourselves that the final words of the *Communist Manifesto* are not just a string of pretty phrases to be trotted out at public meetings, but that we are in deadly earnest when we shout out to the masses: "Workers of the world, … You have nothing to lose but your chains; you have a world to win."

"Long Live the Revolution"*

[Marcin] Kasprzak is no more. Bloody Nicholas the Last has finally prevailed over his irreconcilable foe.

Force and violence won out, falling upon the indefatigable fighter with a solid phalanx—first, of armed gendarmes, police, and plainclothesmen, then cutthroats in a prosecutor's uniform and a judge's robe, followed by traitorous doctors, and a governor-general thirsting for blood—thus the man was felled to the ground and handed over to the executioner, and thus they placed the noose around the neck of this unyielding fighter for the working class.

Kasprzak is no more. The life of a revolutionary proletarian has ended; a heroic death ended a heroic life. Twenty years of tireless struggle for the emancipation of the proletariat—in the "freedom" of Germany and in the underground of Russia under the rule of the knout, in the prisons of Poznań, Breslau, and Warsaw—in hunger and cold, in poverty and illness, caught between a rock and a hard place, sometimes stranded on a sickbed in a clinic, and under the constant threat of pursuit by gendarmes or police spies, constantly driven from place to place, without rest, without respite, a homeless proletarian. He was always inspired by a single thought—the burning desire to fight for the emancipation of his fellow proletarians, whose entire fate, the entire hell of whose existence, he had tasted throughout his own life. With [the power of his] thought he rose above and climbed beyond poverty, beyond sickness, and with iron tenacity moved toward enlightenment, toward knowledge, toward emancipation of the mind, gathering with highly focused attention every bit of enlightenment that he could attain in order to share it with others. He was not broken by any personal suffering, dozens of times leaving behind the comforts of having a beloved family—living without his wife and son, on the dangerous seas of the life of a vagabond, a footloose revolutionist—closed off all by himself, not having any especially close friends, sparing of words, but eloquent in deeds, simple and modest in the grayness of daily life, but immediately becoming an epic hero at any moment of danger or battle. That was Marcin Kasprzak.

He valued his life, offered it for humanity, and he fought with all the force of his will, unbending as steel. He defended his life against the nagaika-wielding hordes† of tsarism, defended it still when tied up and alone, thrown into a prison cell, defenseless. He defended his life like a lion till the last minute, to the last breath, during his unparalleled duel against the mobs, the life of a prisoner

---

* This article is translated (by George Shriver and Alicja Mann) from the Polish publication of the SDKPiL, *Z Pola Walki*, No. 12, September 30, 1905. The Polish phrase "Niech żyje rewolucja" (Long live the revolution) were the last words spoken by Marcin Kasprzak before his execution in Warsaw in early September 1905 in a tsarist prison.

† A nagaika is a leather whip.

against his executioners; he defended that life with his lips pursed in contempt against the streams of slander, lies, perjury, and false witness. He fought, using only the power of his spirit, like a lion-tamer among the beasts—fought to the bitter end.

And when force and violence prevailed and he had to die—he died as do only those of great spirit. His last move was to make a fist, silently threatening the flunkey of the bloody tsar sitting at the prosecutor's table. The last tune he hummed was that of "The Red Flag." His last words *"Long live the revolution!"*

A half year in the deadly dungeons of the [Warsaw] Citadel took its toll. When worn out by the struggle, the hero of the Polish proletariat finally fell into the hawk-like claws of tsarism, trembling with the thirst for blood and desire for revenge. He was only a ruin of a man with a sunken chest as the result of consumption—the disease of proletarians—with white hair prematurely frosted by suffering and superhuman efforts of his will. His silhouette, once straight and strong as an oak tree, now was the bent-over shape of an old man, and his neck was swollen with ulcers from tuberculosis. They dragged him finally, those victors of Mukden, Port Arthur, Chișinău, and Łódź, and turned him over to the executioner.

Here in the face of the scaffold, Kasprzak, for the last time straightened up his concave chest, in which only measly scraps of lung remained, straightened up his body with his last strength, and from his wheezing chest came out a hoarse voice, a voice like a sword that has been [frequently] notched and chipped in the long, exhausting battle.

And in the hallway of the gravely silent Citadel, in the gray mists of dawn, amid the heavy stamping of gendarmes' boots, one could hear for the last time some notes from the song "The Red Flag": "The butchers have long been shedding our blood …."

He sang with the last effort of his hoarse larynx, this martyr of the labor struggle. He was ready to give his blood—his last possession—after having already sacrificed his youth, strength, personal happiness, freedom, health, marital and parental tenderness, spirit and body. He was ready to give his last drop of blood for the salvation and honor of the working class.

"But there will come the day of reckoning," he continued to hum and walked onto the stage of the gallows. There he stood strong, quiet, and proud. And the deadly noose was placed around his neck, and the rope dug into the ulcerated swelling [on his neck] so as to cut off the life of this fighter. One more time Kasprzak opened his mouth, before it had to be closed forever and shouted:

Long live the revolution!

Workers! The sacrifice was great and terrible. The despotic government will be called to account, and will have to pay on the day of reckoning. Kasprzak's death is a huge bloody stain calling for vengeance. The life and death of this doubly tormented hero of the proletariat struggle will shine forever in the pages of the history of the revolution against the Russian empire, and in the pages of international socialism, like a star of the first magnitude.

Even at the last moment of his life, a human ignominy tried to poison the peace of his spirit.

Even as he was walking toward his final torment, the scoundrels came crawling to the cross.

Those who for more than twelve years made false accusations against him to impugn his honor*—they crawled, so that with their reptile hissing they could "restore his honor"; to "restore honor" to a hero and martyr—honor that they do not have themselves!

And they were in a hurry after twelve years to make it up at the last minute, so that the executioner would not be faster than they were, and thus at the last moment, when he was facing the gallows, they wanted to act because it was impossible to hold onto that slander any longer.

They were hurrying to exonerate the victim of their false accusations, to lift their false charge from their victim before the further spreading of their slander would became impossible. They were trying to save themselves from general contempt and disgrace.

These hired-assassin "socialists" were in a hurry to pass along their long-term victim, to make room for the tsar's hired assassin.

But this hideous blasphemy did not disturb the martyr's last moments. He did not see or hear anything except the light within himself that illuminated the last hour of his life—or anything except those last words, which summed up the content of his entire tortured life and his martyr's death:

Long live the revolution!

---

* For the accusations made against him, including by some in the PPS, see, "A Victim of the White Terror," pp. 198–204, above.

To Arms Against the "Constitution" of the Knout!*

Since the outbreak of the workers' revolution in the tsarist empire, there has not been a moment, so to speak, not any point at which planning and uniformity of action by the fighting proletariat of the whole country would be so urgent as it is now in the face of the approaching so-called elections to the Bulygin "State Duma."

Every thinking worker should realize that we are experiencing a turning point in the history of the present revolution. The war [with Japan] is over, and with the conclusion of peace absolutism's hands are untied so that it can gather up all its strength internally for the suppression of the revolution. Toward this goal and to inaugurate the new period, the period of "internal peace," the infamous tsarist comedy of a "constitution" in the form of a "State Duma"—that is what all this is meant to serve.

Devising this measure for the fight against the revolution is, on absolutism's side, undoubtedly a skillful step. The fate of the revolutionary struggle depends on how this "gift" will be received from the bloody hands of the knout-ocratic government in the coming months. An agreement among Social Democratic organizations from the whole tsarist empire to set up a common consolidated action in relation to this "Duma" was a necessity, and it was successfully accomplished.

The resolution adopted by the conference of delegates from Russian Social Democracy, and from the Polish, Jewish, Latvian, and Ukrainian Social Democratic organizations [on September 20–2 in Riga],[†] is completely consistent with the position we took in issue No. 28 of *Czerwony Sztandar*.[‡] The decisive point was and still is the fact that the tsarist "constitution" should not be regarded as even a pale shadow of a real concession of political rights to the people on the part of absolutism, but should be regarded as just an insulting comedy.

This "constitution" and this "Duma" are really the same absolutism, the same unlimited rule of the bayonet and the gallows, but covered with a miserable rag. So, it is clear that the interests of the proletariat, the interests of the revolution, require the *rejection* of this "gift" from the tsar and the *thwarting* of this

---

* This article is translated (by George Shriver and Alicja Mann) from *Z Pola Walki*, No. 13, October 18, 1905. Its title in Polish is "Do walki przeciw 'Konstytucji' Knuta!"

† This conference was called by the Central Committee of the RSDRP, shortly after the party's Third Congress. At the conference the Bolsheviks argued for a boycott of the Duma, whereas the Mensheviks favored participation in it. The position of the Bolsheviks—which aligned with Luxemburg's views—was adopted by the conference.

‡ See the article "The 'Constitution' of the Knout," above, pp. 190–7.

tsarist comedy. Working people in Poland and Russia must understand that the Bułygin "Duma" has basically not changed the situation even by a hair, and that as before, so now, the only hope of victory lies in the widespread emergence of a [movement] of revolutionary working people, urban and rural. To explain this to the people with all our strength, to urge them on to further tireless struggle—that is the primary obligation of Social Democracy. To dispel, and destroy with a strong fist, all illusions about an allegedly "new era," the illusion that anything can be expected from the puppet show of popular elections and parliamentary rule—that is the most immediate task of our party that stands at the head of the revolutionary struggle.

"[Our task is] to prepare an armed uprising of the people"—says the resolution adopted at that conference [of Social Democratic organizations].

But what does this mean, "to prepare a popular uprising?" Of course, the way Social Democracy understands this is not as a matter of sitting around debating about arming the masses, importing weapons, organizing "combat groups"—all these technical details are what constitute "revolutionism" for some parties, such as the PPS, but these details play only a secondary role for Social Democracy.*

To "prepare a popular uprising" means to make the masses aware of the needs and tasks of the revolutionary struggle—that is to say, to make them aware, for example, by making use of wider and wider mass gatherings and demonstrations, of more and more frequent clashes with local government forces—to prepare a merging of various sporadic outbreaks of local fighting into one popular revolutionary uprising of all the people, to spread the fight to as-yet-inactive social strata and geographical areas, to deepen and consolidate political consciousness in places where the battle has already flared up. Concerning the "State Duma," the axis of our agitational work must be to explain to the working population about the atrocities perpetrated under the continuing rule of the allegedly "constitutional" knout, and to call for mass gatherings at which the hypocrisy of tsarist policy is continually exposed and the true demands of the proletariat are continually presented.

Against a background of agitation *against* the "Duma," a tireless campaign should be developed for the convening of a Constituent Assembly, chosen by universal, equal, secret, and direct vote—a campaign for the announcement of a People's Republic based on a legislative parliament chosen by the entire population, supporting the freedom of speech, press, labor unions, free assembly, as well as free conscience and political and civil equality of all nationalities. It should be based on national self-government for Poland and for the universal arming of the people. *The entire political program of Social Democracy should*

---

* Though Luxemburg singles out the PPS here by name, it was (as she notes) the Bolsheviks who forcefully argued at the conference, "the pressing task of the moment is the preparation for an armed popular uprising." Luxemburg often criticized the Bolsheviks, at times openly and at other times implicitly, during this period for what she considered its overemphasis on armed insurrection.

be the content of that campaign, which opposes the tsar's "Duma" chess game, constantly explaining that the knout's comedy is by no means a good "step" to achieve the rights that are due to the proletariat, but on the contrary—only a way of blocking their path to attain their rights.

The struggle of the proletariat in the current situation, as in all times and stages of a revolution, is, and must be, at the same time a struggle against absolutism and a class struggle against the bourgeoisie. The "State Duma" is not only an attempt to rescue and preserve the despotic government under the pretense of a constitution, but at the same time it is the conclusion of an open alliance between despotism and the bourgeoisie against the revolutionary proletariat. The reactionary Russian bourgeoisie naturally is ready to accept the electoral privilege offered by the government. After some hesitation, the miserable liberalism of the Russian "zemstvo" nobility has also agreed to go down that slippery path designated by absolutism. The Russian liberals deceive themselves and the people with the platitude that they should "take advantage of" this first "concession" by absolutism, that sitting in the Bułygin "Duma" gives them the possibility of expanding their rights and fighting against absolutism for further rights "from the outside." The liberal nobility remains the ruling class, and this time, too, it remains faithful to itself. Although at the beginning the democratic, radical faction of the Russian intelligentsia made a firm call for boycotting the tsar's comedy—branding as a traitor to the people anybody who would participate in the "Duma" elections—now even those "intransigents" are beginning, apparently (judging from a number of reports), to sound the retreat.

Here [in Poland] we have hardly a trace of "liberalism" among those of the propertied classes. In our political life, these freshly baked groups of so-called "progressive democracy" probably still cannot be taken seriously. And the intelligentsia, for the most part, is not the most radical part of the bourgeoisie (as in Russia), but only the main support of the most reactionary party, the so-called National Democracy. Here the whole "society," with the exception of the class-conscious proletariat, is naturally rushing to the bosom of their Little Father—the "constitutional" tsar. And here, the conciliationists and the National Democratic rabble are rushing to be in the first row of those "chosen" to be in the Bułygin Duma.

The same Black Hundreds' of capitalist, aristocratic, and petty-bourgeois reactionaries—who not only did not lift a finger in the struggle for political freedom, but helped the flunkeys of the government to crack down and slander the fighting proletariat—are now rushing to gain from the tsarist "reform" by grabbing for themselves political privileges that are a result of the bloody

---

*   The "Black Hundreds" refers to xenophobic, reactionary nationalist groupings that attacked ethnic and national minorities (especially Jews) as part of an effort to intimidate opponents of tsarism. It was a well-organized movement that published a series of newspapers and organized political demonstrations and pogroms—often with the direct support of government officials.

labor struggle. These gentlemen are already hurrying and bustling, so that in the name of Polish "society," the members of the same gang of social parasites would be elected to the Bułygin "Duma." They are the same ones who during the entire revolution have disgraced the Polish people with their servile deputations to the halls of the tsarist officials, while barking at the revolutionary working class.

Therefore, for us [in Poland], even a hundred times more than in Russia, it is the duty of Social Democracy to *frustrate* the attempts at conciliationist and National Democratic vileness—as well as to counteract, with all our strength, what would be a disgrace to our country of [voting in] "elections" to the "Duma." The resolution adopted at the conference of Social Democratic parties recommends strongly the obstruction of that farce of "elections," shaming loudly those classes and strata of society that are eager to take part in the elections, branding them as traitors to political freedom and to the true interests of the people.

We do not yet know, at the time of this writing, what kind of tactic in relation to the "Duma" will eventually be applied by one of the two factions of the Russian Social Democratic Labor Party, namely, the comrades of the so-called minority.* It is very possible that they will go for a tactic recommended by their publication *Iskra* and decide not to oppose the elections, but, on the contrary, will take part in them as much as possible. As we have heard, some of these comrades—for instance in the Caucasus (Guria),† where they reportedly have support among broad layers of the peasantry—might hope to carry out campaign meetings leading up to a provincial election, and even to elect their own Social Democratic deputies to the "Duma." We have to comment that this possibility, if there is even an illusion of such a thing, should not and cannot constitute the correct tactic of Social Democracy in relation to the "Duma."

Participation in the elections by one part of Social Democracy, or *the promotion* of such participation under certain conditions—we consider this, objectively speaking, to be politically ruinous, because that tactic can lend some moral and political significance to this election farce of the tsarist regime. At the same time, this undermines what was called for in the resolution of the conference—the proletariat's *unity of action* in the whole empire.

---

* The Mensheviks.

† Guria is in the southwest region of Georgia. The Russian Empire conquered the area in the aftermath of the Russo-Turkish War of 1806–12. In 1902 the peasants of area, supported by the Social Democrats, initiated a rebellion that led to independent Gurian Republic, which lasted until 1906. It has been termed the first effort since the Paris Commune of 1871 of "socialists seizing political power and attempting to realize their vision of a new society." See Eric Lee, *The Experiment: Georgia's Forgotten Revolution, 1918–21* (London: Zed Books, 2017), p. 7. The extent of the Mensheviks' support in the region was shown after the 1917 Revolution, when they won 80 percent of the parliamentary vote in the newly independent (but short-lived) Democratic Republic of Georgia.

But it goes without saying that we do not make accusations of betrayal against Social Democrats, who with the best of intentions are recommending tactics different from ours, thinking that this serves the cause of the proletariat. We think their estimation of the interests of the working class in this case is politically mistaken and ruinous. However, condemning these comrades or stigmatizing them, from the moral point of view, obviously cannot be done. This accusation would be used only against Russian liberals and the knights of "National Demoralization," and against all bourgeois parties, which are accepting this "constitutional gift" of the knout, and which do not consider the interests of the proletariat, but only their own class interests as parasites on the proletariat.*

However, let us hope that at the decisive moment the action of the proletariat throughout the empire will be firm and uniform as much as possible, and that it will be used to achieve what is the goal of all Social Democratic organizations without exception—to turn the tsar's "constitutional" farce into a new outbreak, a more rapidly blazing and more general revolutionary fire.

As always, in such times, the tactics of Social Democracy are primarily calculated on the *political awareness* of the working people. By struggling against the Bułygin "Duma" and the farce of "elections" to the "Duma," we are bringing to the attention of the proletariat the need for revolutionary struggle as being the only way to achieve real political freedoms. Therefore, we do not delude ourselves that we can achieve through conscious action of the proletariat an immediate, once and for all, prevention of the elections and of the "Duma" becoming a reality. But the tactics of Social Democracy are not based on the direct winning of some immediate tangible results—in contrast to the tactics of that "revolutionary" adventurism that counts only on visible results in making loud noises and focusing on outward effects.†

On the contrary, Social Democracy by its very nature aims at tasks that are beyond its possibility and strength to achieve at this moment. For example, we fight constantly against militarism, even though we do not delude ourselves that we can (with the current forces of the proletariat) actually remove such a symptom of the capitalist state. Also, to take up an example from the more recent history of the revolution, we call the masses out to demonstrations, and if necessary, to fight the government to the last man, as for example in Łódź in the days of the barricades. However, we do not expect that we can ultimately win against the government in each particular case. The same goes for declaring the fight against the tsar's farcical "constitution"—we do not count in advance

---

* As she does several times during this period, Luxemburg is making a distinction between how a revolutionary tendency treats mistaken policies and ideas on the part of fellow Marxists as compared to its enemies among the bourgeoisie. She will later make a similar distinction in criticizing the Bolsheviks in 1918 (in her booklet *The Russian Revolution*) for their suppression of the democratic rights of left-wing critics of the regime.

† The terrorist tactics adopted at times by some in the PPS, and more often by the SR and anarchists, fall under Luxemburg's criticism here.

that it is possible to eliminate that comedy. But in this case, and as always, it is the *political content and moral significance* of the slogan we are advocating that is important.

By issuing the call to arms against the "Duma," a call to oppose the elections, we are making the proletariat aware in a most powerful way of how miserable the tsar's so-called constitution is. We are destroying the halo of moral and political significance around the "Duma." Even if it does come to fruition, we stigmatize it in advance as the true offspring of despotism, about to be born. We are destroying any illusions and hopes of the population in that reform granted by the grace of the tsar, and are turning their hopes and expectations toward reliance solely on mass revolutionary struggle.

On the other hand, our slogan "to arms" separates visibly and sharply the class position of the revolutionary proletariat from the bourgeoisie in our country and from liberalism in Russia—in other words, from any demagogy of the ruling classes or ruling parties. Our tactics are clearly and distinctly [showing] the outside world the real class division that exists in these political circumstances of the Duma. The entire bourgeois society is for the tsar's constitution and the elections, and the entire conscious proletariat is against them. On one side is the revolutionary struggle, on the other is the tsar's constitutional farce. That is what needs to be exposed as the truth, and that is what the tactic of Social Democracy aims to achieve.

It is enough to understand the essence of this tactic to understand just what a secondary role is played by the possibility of immediately and effectively preventing the elections from coming to fruition. If the conscious sections of the proletariat express their immediate fight against the Bulygin "constitution," if class-conscious agitation will be on the widest possible scale, then the elections for the Duma, even if they come to fruition, will be seen by the world as what they really are—a fetus, a result of rape, of hostility toward the proletariat, an alliance between the knout and the bourgeoisie, a wretched farce with which working people have nothing in common, just as they have nothing in common with absolutism.

And the reaction against this comedy, even if it does not succeed *right away* in one fell swoop, will become a reality along with all the tasks to which Social Democracy is committed—the growth of the consciousness and mass militancy of the proletariat, in proportion to the development of the struggle itself. Every instance of mass struggle by the proletariat under the banner of Social Democracy *against* the tsarist "constitution" will at the same time raise the awareness of still passive layers among the people at large about the true worth of this farce. And, at the same time, it will already be a step toward obstructing and destroying this same farce, and it will serve undoubtedly as a starting point for a series of clashes with the government that wants to protect its "constitutional" monstrosity.

The further course of the struggle and its fruitfulness will depend, as always, on the strength and the multitude of instances of struggle by the working masses. By calling on the working class to fight, by explaining the simple and clear purpose and objective of fighting, we are doing everything that is our conscious duty—directing the vanguard of the proletariat, which is precisely the task of Social Democracy.

If the "Duma" elections are to be held, let them at least be held under the cover of soldiers' bayonets. Those bayonets will strike a deadly blow against the thieves' plan of absolutism—morally and politically. Any "freedom" that has to be imposed on the people by force, any "freedom" that needs for its birth the help of bayonets dripping with blood, the bayonets of absolutism, that mortal enemy of all freedoms—such "constitutional" freedom is in advance exposed to universal laughter and contempt.

One more word. The "elections" are coming. The bourgeoisie is preparing to benefit from them. Tsarism is sharpening its bayonets to quell the people's resistance. The task of Social Democracy is not to wait until a signal for agitation and struggle is given by absolutism, [like when it] announces the elections. The proletariat must be the first to start the fight. From the very start, these shameful games should encounter revolutionary turmoil. The very first attempt of any breakthrough for the electoral comedy should be drowned out by the loud cry of the proletariat: "Down with the farce!"

There is no time to lose to begin a systematic struggle against the tsarist "constitution." What should start immediately is the broadest mass agitation, revolving around clarification of the political demands of Social Democracy and the class interests of the proletariat against the "Duma" and the elections, on the one hand, and clarifying the contradictions between the proletariat and the bourgeois parties in regard to the "Duma" and absolutism, on the other hand. That is, mass meetings, demonstrations, agitation, both written and oral, under the slogan: "Down with the farce of 'Duma' elections." All that should begin as soon as possible, before the curtain is raised. Let the "constitution" of the knout, invented in order to avert revolution, create a new explosion of flames and bring the country to a state of turbulence and militant political class struggle! Comrades, let's get to work!

A New Epoch in the Russian Revolution[*]

It really does seem as if a new epoch in the revolutionary movement in Russia is dawning. If the bureaucratic and courtly camarilla had hoped that the mass of the Russian people would sink back into a lethargy after the cessation of the curse-worthy damnable war in the Far East—the flippant instigation of which the revolution more than answered—then it will be bitterly disappointed. Tsarism's ingenious breakdown in the Far East has achieved the opposite, feeding the people's bitterness and fanning the flames of their revolutionary vigor into energetic action. The appalling bloodletting that the tsarist soldiers have carried out on the people has simply sown new seeds of hate and loathing. And the movement has certainly profited greatly in terms of coherence, organization and political insight, thanks to tireless political education work, disseminated through the medium of socialist agitation—a major transformation for a movement that had previously often flared up sporadically, without coherence, and without clear political understanding. Not only is the industrial working masses' energy for battle still undiminished, it has rather been steeled by all the battles fought and the great number of sacrifices made in them. This remains, despite the toughness of what they have had to suffer during the countless strikes, lockouts, and massacres. If we can read the signs correctly, the Russian proletariat is rearming itself for battles more decisive than any previously fought. A *universal strike* threatens to rock the whole state organism—cracking already as it is along every fault line imaginable—to its very foundations. And this time the pioneers of struggle are the *railroad employees*, who have already gone out on a general strike at many locations, including the most important localities in the empire. The thing to cheer the most in this battle is what appears to be the great measure of political clarity and energy with which the struggle to gain political freedoms is carried out.

Before the railroad workers took this most extreme step of striking against the transport network, they approached *Transport Minister Count [Mikhail] Khilkov* and the *Chairman of the Council of Ministers, Mr. [Sergei] Witte* one last time, in order to proclaim their demands and press for their fulfillment.[†] Although Mr. Witte played all the tricks in the diplomatic book, he could not avoid showing his true face when faced with the workers' concrete demands.

---

[*]   This article, "Eine neue Epoche de russischen Revolution," was not signed, but it is clearly by Luxemburg. It first appeared in *Vorwärts*, No. 251, October 26, 1905. It is translated (by Henry Holland) from Luxemburg's *Gesammelte Werke*, Vol. 6, pp. 567–73. The emphasis throughout the article (as in all others in this volume) is in Luxemburg's original.

[†]   Count Witte was finance minister from 1892 to 1903 and Chairman of the Council of Ministers from October 1905 to April 1906. He was a monarchist, but was, during certain periods, ready to accept a pact with the bourgeoisie and to grant constitutional concessions. He played a major role in suppressing the revolution.

Just in the last few days, Mr. Witte had convinced an English reporter to blow Witte's trumpet for him, by portraying himself as a progressive man with the purest intentions who would use all his influence on the tsar to push through the broadest possible freedom for the people. Despite all his slick phrases, Witte had to explain to the railroad workers' deputation that there was *no prospect of their demand for general and equal suffrage being fulfilled.* That sufficed to answer the question of the masses of whether they should engage in battle. The massive expansion of the strike was the response to Witte's tactics of appeasement. And the other groups of workers are making common cause with the striking railroaders!

Regarding the *negotiations with the ministers,* the semi-official Russian telegraph agency reports the following: Petersburg, October 24 (report by the Petersburg Telegraph Agency). A Congress of Railroad Employee Delegates held here in the city [St. Petersburg] passed a motion to send two delegations without delay to the Transport Minister and to the Chairman of the Council of Ministers; the delegations shall communicate the following demand:

> The delegates are the *true representatives of the demands of the railroad employees and workers, and also represent everyone working on the railroads.* The times in which decisions of vital significance could be decided through *administrative procedures* are over, and all the working class's demands must be *regulated through laws,* in accordance with the will of the people, and sanctioned by the whole of Russia. There is just *one single solution—an immediate proclamation of political guarantees and freedoms, and the convocation of a Constituent Assembly, elected on universal and direct suffrage.* The country should not be pushed into armed revolution, and new spilling of blood must not be permitted. The people have sacrificed enough blood, first in Manchuria and now in all towns, villages and localities of Russia. If the delegation's right to call itself the representative of all railroad personnel should be questioned, the delegation reserves the right *to teach* its contracting authority [i.e. the railroad companies and Transport Minister] about *methods to fight for a better future.*

An assembly of railroad employees held at the university and attended by 8,000 individuals passed a motion for a *general strike* from the twenty-fifth of this month and on all rail lines that lead to Petersburg.

Petersburg, October 25: The *Meeting of the Congress of Railroad Employee Delegates* opened with the reading of a *memorandum* that listed the employees' professional needs and demands. The minute-taker emphasized the necessity of sending a copy of the memorandum to Count Witte, as it contained serious questions like the creation of a Constituent Assembly:

> The congress decided to *send delegations, each of five people, with a copy of the memorandum to Witte and to the Transport Minister Count Khilkov and to await*

their reply. The delegation sent to Khilkov didn't carry this out, as it had already traveled to Peterhof to report about the incidents in Moscow. The memorandum was therefore deposited at the minister's offices, with the request to grant a personal meeting after the delegation had returned from Peterhof. Railroad workers awaited the return of the *delegation sent to Witte* with great anticipation. One member of the delegation reported that Witte had immediately received them in his cabinet rooms. He opened by saying that their discussion had to be of a *thoroughly private nature*, because the Chairman of the Council of Ministers did not have the right to accept such a memorandum. He had, however, no objections to the contents of the discussion being published. Witte remarked that the pamphlet contained *numerous demands, which no other land would be able to meet either*, but many of which were nonetheless worthy of attention. Firstly, he positioned himself *against a Constituent Assembly*, as this is impossible at present. He *repeated this several times*, arguing that *universal suffrage would give the richer classes an advantage through the option of buying votes, and was therefore not without its faults.* The idea of universal suffrage could therefore evidently not be said to proceed from the railroad workers' essential needs.

Witte went on to articulate *his recognition of freedoms of assembly and of the press*, both of which would be permitted very soon. He was surprised to discover that martial law was still in force on the railroads. This was due to a *misunderstanding*, and would be withdrawn in the next few days. Witte declared himself, moreover, to be *an opponent of the use of force and bloodletting, and a defender of freedom in the broadest sense, yet he could not predict how the strike would be stopped.* He planned to confer with Chilkov, and do everything in his power. In his opinion, the strike would first have to be cancelled before peaceful conditions could then be worked on. A *delegate* reported that Witte recognized the congress, and had expressed the wish that it become a permanent institution.

In response to a delegate's remark, that the demand for universal suffrage was not based on a momentary whim but rather on an *essential need*, and that the book trade was downright flooded with texts about universal suffrage that was a component of the demands being made throughout almost the whole of Russia, Witte replied *that there wasn't a single scholarly expert in the whole world who advocated universal suffrage.* A delegation member remarked that one shouldn't be surprised about Witte's answer here, *as he'd spoken like a real civil servant, who always skirts around a subject rather than saying anything of substance.* But in order to demonstrate character, so that demands could be pushed through, it would be necessary to postpone the next steps until October 25, when the meeting with Count Khilkov should take place. (Applause.) *As the bureaucratic machine will not give the railroad employees anything, we have to go out and take it.* And we should take that which we need. (Applause.) Another delegation member stated, "We have done our duty by compiling the demands of all employees and presenting them to the authorities. *In that moment in which the leading circles submit to the necessity of fulfilling these demands, responsibility will swing back to those who do not fulfil them.* I table the motion *to take a final decision after the meeting with Khilkov.*"

Although there were no doubts in the opinion of the assembly in relation to Witte's readiness and the extent to which they could trust his words, it decided nonetheless to wait for the results of the discussion with Khilkov, *and then made its way* as one body *to the meeting at the university.*

Even from this semi-official and doctored report, it is clear enough that the congress didn't let themselves be duped by Witte's diplomatic intrigues and his lectures about international law. This congress could correctly filter out the core among all these phrases from the tsar's darling, which is that the "broadest freedoms for the people" should still be embodied in the *ridiculous monstrosity of the Duma and that universal, equal suffrage shall not be granted under any circumstances!* No Constituent Assembly should be entrusted with creating a people's constitution, but, instead, the ridiculous representatives of higher-level bureaucracy and the corrupt moneybags shall continue to back the tsarist terror regiment and all its people-lashing, people's-soul-destroying practices, under the flimsy cover of an "advisory" body! The people certainly have seen through this perfidious plan, and refuse to take the bait placed by cooing rhetoric. They have taken up the fight with tremendous energy.

The railroad workers have immediately reacted by declaring war.

Petersburg, October 25. *Fifteen-thousand persons* took part in the assembly of *railroad employees* that was held at the university, including *workers, students* and *many women.* The assembly lasted until midnight; terroristic and rabble-rousing speeches were given, *which were met with storms of applause.*

The following semi-official reports shed light on *the expansion of the railroad workers' strike,* even though they tend more toward whitewashing rather than exaggerating events:

Moscow, October 24 (report by the Petersburg Telegraph Agency). *The railroad workers' strike is gaining ever more ground in all directions,* with the following cities now affected: Ulyanovsk, Yekaterinoslav, Kiev, Smolensk, Voronezh, Saratov, Kharkiv, Simferopol, Yaroslavl, and Nizhny Novgorod. This afternoon a crowd of 500 persons approached the goods station for the Moscow–Kursk line. The officer commanding the unit of troops occupying the station threatened to fire at the crowd, causing the throng of people to disperse. On the Moscow–Ventspils–Rybinsk line, the evening express train only got as far as Podmoskovnye Station, from where passengers had to proceed on foot to Moscow. On the Moscow–Kazan line, 2,000 people were waiting for trains to depart, the majority of them poor. They are receiving daily compensation toward living costs from the line's management. Second-class passengers are getting one rouble a day while they wait. Last night, a special train conveying the Minister of Public Works arrived on the Moscow–Petersburg line, but otherwise no trains are arriving. Today, a number of strikers attempted to stop business at the central post office, but were driven back by the troops.

Petersburg, October 25. Transport has been stopped on a large number of Polish railroads, as has rail traffic on the Petersburg–Vilnius–Virbalis line and on the Petersburg–Vilnius–Warsaw line. The German Red Cross convoy, which wanted to leave for the journey back to Germany this afternoon, has not been able to depart. Strikers have also interrupted the post service. Simple letters should be sent from Germany via the Stockholm–Turku route; the postal authorities are refusing letters and parcels sent by registered mail. A report in from Kiev states that the southwest railroads have also stopped running. A report in from the Baltic railroads Petersburg–Riga, Petersburg–Tallinn, and Jelgava–Ventspils states that railroad transport has been stopped there too.

Petersburg, October 25. Strikers have interrupted telegraphic communication between Petersburg and Kharkiv.

Warsaw, October 25. Rebels have brought transport to a halt today on the Warsaw–Petersburg railroad line, meaning no traffic is running on any of Poland's railroads with the exception of the Warsaw–Vienna line.

Warsaw, October 25. The workers of the Warsaw–Vienna railroad company have now joined the railroad workers' general strike. All traffic is coming to a halt this evening.

Yet it is not just railroad transport that has already stopped on the most important lines; concurrently, workers from other trades are preparing for mass participation in a general strike. This is reported as follows:

Warsaw, October 24. Workers in Łódź and Pabianice from a number of large factories have gone out on strike, with roughly 40,000 celebrating being on strike until now, and further work stoppages are expected. We also assume that the authorities will announce a state of siege in the Piotrków Governorate, where a railroad worker strike is threatening to break out.

Poltawa, October 25 (report from Petersburg Telegraph Agency). Here a general strike is carrying the day. High school* lessons have also been stopped. The newspapers will not appear tomorrow.

Moscow, October 25 (report from Petersburg Telegraph Agency). A congress held by the Association of Engineers has decided that all engineers, in all companies, works, factories, building construction offices, etc., are obliged to go out on strike. This component of the strike will commence today.

Moscow, October 25. The situation is getting worse by the hour. Municipal employees and workers have set the city administration a second ultimatum, wherein they threaten a general strike if their demands are not respected. Were this to happen, the situation would become even more dangerous, as then the municipal waterworks could no longer operate.

---

*   *Mittelschulen* in the original text.

Yekaterinoslav, October 24. Following on from Cossacks disbanding a meeting of school students using whips, a thousand-strong crowd gathered in front of the city hall. When troops appeared, the crowd started erecting barricades. The troops discharged their guns. A number of persons were killed or wounded. Concurrently, troops at the other end of the city in front of the Pushkin Memorial shot at striking railroad workers, killing three of them. Nine further railroad workers were wounded.

This concluding report demonstrates that the tsarist government is again working with the whip, gunpowder and lead [bullets]! We can predict that this bloodbath will not be the last one. Even Mr. Witte himself, the freedom enthusiast, has hinted that he cannot give any guarantees!

Yet despite all these sanctified means [that are part of] the divine right of kings, they shall not finish off the revolution. Through the baptism in blood that they have received, the people have been educated in revolutionary ways. Even if the movement should break down again this time, apparently without success, the workers will lead a new charge, time after time. Whether absolutism can bear these continually renewing and increasingly violent catastrophes in the long-term, is, however, a different question. The nerve of this Duma babble who have also snubbed lower-income groups inside the educated population—as they have the petit bourgeois and the peasantry—must be considered, but also the way in which they have managed to violently bind these groups to the working-class revolutionary struggle. Large parts of the intelligentsia are also taking an active part in the conflicts. The masses of the peasantry remain difficult to mobilize, but at least appear to refuse to be used as a buffer against the industrial proletarians. The last conferences of the municipal zemstvos pay testimony to this.

A particularly radical resolution was adopted by the Staritzk Zemstvo in the Tver Governorate, worded as follows:

The law concerning the "State Duma" (Gosudarstvennaja Duma) from August 6 in no way satisfies the clearly articulated wishes of Russian public opinion, and will not alter Russia's "police-bureaucratic" ordering of society. On top of that, Russian society does not possess the most elementary human and civil rights, e.g., freedom of speech and of the press, etc. A body representing the people will not be in a position to exist properly under these conditions, and will in fact be a mere shadow of a real body of this type. That is why the zemstvo assembly is protesting against the law of August 6.

Delegates sent to the Imperial Duma should follow one goal only: to transform the Duma itself on the basis of *direct, equal and secret suffrage, applied irrespective of sex, nationality and denomination, resulting in the Duma being granted law-making powers and control over activities of government organs.*

It is not superfluous to note that the local district zemstvos are *less progressive* than the *governorate* zemstvos.

This results in a situation in which Russia is now offering us the cheering stage drama of a heroic fight for freedom, after the tragedy in the Far East!* We can only hope that Western European friends of the lash will not blithely disregard this major historical lesson!

EXPANSION OF THE STRIKE MOVEMENT

Petersburg, October 25. The strike movement has again expanded. The situation is growing graver and graver still. Moscow and Petersburg are cut off entirely. The English envoy wanted to depart today, but has had to put off his departure and will leave with the first steamer sailing from Russia. His trip is connected with the Anglo-Russian Agreement. The envoy will remain in London for a considerable period in order to consult with his government about the details of the agreement. The Russian envoy in London is returning to Russia for a while for the same purpose.

Petersburg, October 25. Striking railroad workers are starting to encourage workers on lines on which traffic is still running to also stop work. A large number of medical trains, coming from theaters of war, have been halted. Yekaterinoslav is in the grips of an open revolt. The inhabitants erected barricades that the Cossacks then stormed. Many people were killed and injured by the Cossacks' volleys of bullets, although the number of victims is not yet known.

Warsaw, October 25. The revolutionary party is agitating for bringing work to an immediate halt at many factories in Warsaw and Łódź. The Polish National Democrats are warning that violent clashes could follow.

---

*   The reference is to Russia's defeat in the Russo-Japanese War.

The Revolution Advances*

The mighty struggle against tsarism has now been set al.ight across the board. The general strike by the railroad workers, at present the Russian proletariat's storm troops, has struck out explosively in every direction, halting transport throughout almost the whole country. One group of the post and telegraph civil servants has also joined the strike. This also has the effect of markedly decreasing the flow of news about events in the tsar's empire. What does get reported is evidence of the present struggle catching fire across a much wider front and with much greater determination than before.

In the country's principal cities, in Petersburg, Moscow and Warsaw, the general strike prevails. Trade is also largely quiet and even the drug stores are closed. Train stations and post offices have been occupied by the military. There is a threat that basic foodstuffs and heating fuel could run out. There have been no clashes as yet, but this is merely the calm before the storm. The bourgeoisie are panicking, and there's a general dread that awful disturbances will break out. The tsar himself is apparently in a state of utmost agitation and is determined to escape the threatening storms by fleeing abroad.

Despite this, the government persists with its politics of stubbornness. No one talks now about the convocation of a Constituent Assembly on the basis of general and equal suffrage. In its place, they really believe that they can placate the masses by handing out little cubes of sugar. Mr. Witte is going to proclaim the freedom of the press on Friday, and other "further important concessions" are being considered. But that will not be enough to fob off the people. Under the guise of press freedom, they are attempting to intoxicate the masses on a grand scale, just as the government itself has managed to leak in a corrupt kind of open-heartedness. The revolutionaries have already gone and seized press freedom for themselves anyway, as they have done for freedom of speech, despite all the spies and tsarist thugs. And what use is unlimited freedom of the press to the people, if it should not be the means to fight to gain the rights to legislate, that they are currently demanding? That is why the "liberal" Mr. Witte's methods of baiting and placating will only serve to pour oil on the flames, and fan the flames of the masses' "covetousness" even further.

Tsarism has missed its chance. Too often has it used false promises to fool the people, and too frequently has it brutally administered blue pills to those demanding bread and freedom. The former naive trust in Little Father Tsar

---

* Although this article, "Der Vormarsch der Revolution," was unsigned, Luxemburg's authorship can be verified based on her letter to Jogiches of September 29, 1905, and in particular her letter to Jogiches of October 6, 1905. See Luxemburg's *Gesammelte Briefe*, Vol. 2, pp. 177 and 183. The article first appeared in *Vorwärts*, No. 252, October 27, 1905. It is translated (by Henry Holland) from Luxemburg's *Gesammelte Werke*, Vol. 6, pp. 574–8.

is, since the Petersburg blood bath, long buried, and the amount of respect accorded to the power of bureaucracy and the bayonets is no less shaken. The proletariat and those bourgeois classes that have united themselves with it are utterly resolved. If absolutism wants to try its luck in a bloody test of its power, then the folk will not even shirk street battles!

IN AN ARMORED TRAIN AGAINST THE STRIKERS

Scherl's newspaper* received the following from Petersburg on October 26: On the Nicholas line, five versts† from Petersburg, a 5,000-strong bunch of striking workers began to destroy the railroad line, aiming at stopping every connection to Moscow. The telegraph and telephone connections were destroyed in the same manner. Just as this had been achieved, the postal train from Moscow came flying toward them—the train driver noticed the demolition job and was able to stop the train on time. The raging crowd gave the train's staff a good hiding, yet did not touch the passengers. They shut off the engine's steam, and the travelers had to hike on foot to Petersburg, their hand luggage on their backs. Military staff dispatched an armored train to repair the demolished railroad, with the railroad-cars at the front and the locomotive at the back.‡ The soldiers were ready to shoot immediately, if the strikers harassed them. Engineers were able to repair the rail line.

ON MOSCOW'S STREET BATTLES

The previously cited paper received the news yesterday that Count Khilkov, the Transport Minister, wanted to leave the city yesterday evening, but nobody was prepared either to drive the locomotive, or to accompany the train. Whereupon the minister stated that he would drive the train himself. After a small train had been made available, Khilkov got everything in the train ready for departure, and then got into the locomotive. However, a group of rebels then shot at the train, forcing Khilkov to turn back. It was not until midnight that the count was able to finally leave the city. The railroad workers are now starting to proceed more actively. They are using violence to thwart every attempt to restore traffic. The clashes with the military and the police result in heavy street battles. Work has been stopped in the main post office in all departments since yesterday evening; the telegraph office continues to function, but only under strong military protection. The destruction of the waterworks had triggered

---

*   Luxemburg means the *Berliner Lokal-Anzeiger*, published in August Scherl's publishing house from 1833 onward and called "the Scandal Advertiser" by the workers.
†   An obsolete Russian unit of length, equal to 1.0668 kilometers.
‡   Luxemburg had written "decision" (Beschluß) rather than "back" or "conclusion" (Schluß) in her original text.

a panic, but now, after a short interruption, they are working again. Water is available. However, the water workers are saying they would now strike, if the revolutionary leaders demanded that of them. Municipal workers and lower-level employees are threatening more general strike action, to include nursing staff at municipal hospitals and technicians at the central electricity works. October 28 will be the decisive day. Many engineers have already gone out on strike, as have all pharmacists. The police have closed down the Pharmaceutical Society and sealed off their local meeting hall. A number of pharmacists have been arrested. The employees are also prepared to join the movement.* Workers have walked out in many factories starting from today, including in the brandy distillery. Terrible ferment is everywhere. Colossal meetings and assemblies are taking place daily, especially at the university. Political leaders consider that the time is ripe for a general strike, and open revolution may become reality inside the shortest space of time.

A telegram submitted to the Petersburg Correspondent yesterday evening reports about the character of this mass movement. Following a motion at the mass assembly at the university yesterday, all workers on all Petersburg railroads have joined the strike today. The workers from the Putilov Works† assembled this evening, and will probably join the strike on Monday. Everything has been proceeding peacefully until now, with the leaders seeking to avoid street skirmishes. All train stations are now guarded by troops, and gendarmerie patrols are moving through the streets. People are expecting a general hike in foodstuff prices that, in case the strike goes on for long, could lead to conflicts on the street in the end. The atmosphere among the workers is very sophisticated, and the mass assemblies held recently at the higher education institutions have contributed considerably to this. Speeches with utterly revolutionary contents are made at these assemblies.

For the first time, the new movement is assuming forms of a really deep-reaching mass movement. The government, which had intended to publicize the four freedoms and legislation for the Duma, has now postponed this action. The current railroad workers' strike has put it into a state of substantial anxiety, and it is now discussing ways and means of emancipating itself from the current situation. It now also appears to be tending toward the use of violent means. Witte continues to take the stage in the name of moderate liberalism, but the speech he gave yesterday made an extremely bad impression.

---

* Many of these pharmaceutical workers in this period became part of the Union of Unions.
† The Putilov Iron Works was a major metal and machine-making factory that employed 12,000 at the time of the revolution. Workers there had already gone out on strike in early January 1905, presaging the revolutionary upsurge. Many Putilov workers were part of Father Gapon's march to the Winter Palace later that month, and several were killed in the ensuing massacre.

DREADING THE IDEA OF PROLETARIAN RULE

London, October 26 (Laffan's News Agency).* The *Times* reports from Petersburg that panic is spreading throughout Petersburg's population. People fear that the government could be toppled, and that the rule of the proletariat could be announced. Open outrage dominates proceedings in southern Russia. The workers are putting up barricades and barbed wire fences.

THE TSAR FLEES ABROAD:

London, October 26. The *Standard* reports from Petersburg, that the tsar, currently in Peterhof, is considering leaving for Denmark, where he wants to stay for two months, in order to recover after the recent excitement. Provisionally, the tsar plans to remain with his family in Denmark until Christmas. During his absence, Witte is to be trusted with the widest powers of attorney and to be equipped with a regent's decision-making powers.

According to one interpretation, the tsar intends to recover from his over-strained nerves in Darmstadt.† The only strange thing is that he envisages his stay abroad as only lasting two months. Has he really tricked himself into thinking that peace will have come back to Russia inside two months? The kind of revolution that has broken out in Russia nurtures itself by stretching for years and assuming an ever-more radical character. Little Father should rather use his idleness abroad to study the English and the French revolutions!

WITTE AS PROPHET?

London, October 26 (Laffan's News Agency). According to a report from Petersburg in the *Daily Mail*, Count Witte concluded a speech held before a delegation of strikers on Tuesday by stating, "I only see two ways out of the present situation. Both are bloody. The state must either use military force to suppress the revolt, or civil war between the people and the rebels must be declared—as it is not entirely impossible, that the current breaches of the peace could lead to the fall of the Russian government."

It is quite possible that Witte thinks things of this sort, but it does seem pretty improbable that he should have articulated it so frankly to the strikers!

THE STRIKE EXPANDS

Wolff's [Telegraph Office] communicates the following semi-official Russian news items:

---

*   This was a news agency founded by William MacKay Laffan, who at the time was owner of the *New York Sun* newspaper.

†   A city in western Germany.

Petersburg, October 26. The rebellion spread this morning into the world of trade, meaning that stores were shut.

Petersburg, October 26. All warehouses and stores are closed in the Vassilevsky-Ostrov district. The post and telegraph offices are under military guard. The printing works are still operating.

Moscow, October 26. The situation gets worse by the day, with the number of fluctuating protests constantly growing. The Muscovite Rayon has reserves of coal for his factories for a month, and there is only enough wood to last for the next ten days. All drug stores were closed yesterday.

Petersburg, October 26 (report by the Petersburg Telegraph Agency). At an assembly of railroad employees held yesterday evening, they announced that the administrative staff of the southeast lines in Vologda have also joined the strike, together with the First Societies of Local Lines.

Kharkiv, October 26. Two thousand people assembled in the university barricaded themselves inside after seeing that military forces had surrounded the building; they were released after long negotiations between the professors and the military authorities. Participants then continued the planned assembly in the open air with the approval of state forces.

Kursk, October 26. After receiving the strikers' demands, governmental institutions—along with other, self-governing institutions—have suspended their activities.

Catastrophe Impending?[*]

The unbearable revolutionary tension in Russia has been raised one notch higher. The general strike has already expanded in a colossal fashion. Railroad transport is down in the whole of the tsarist empire. In addition to the railroad workers' general strike, the rest of the workers have joined the general strike in numerous cities, including *Petersburg, Moscow, Warsaw, Łódź, Kiev, Kharkiv, Samara,* and so on. It is said that over a million workers are now currently on strike. Due to the complete transport standstill, and due to the strike itself, food-stuffs have become scarce and prices have shot up. This is causing the ferment to constantly increase, with people expecting a bloody civil war to break out any hour now. Despite this, the government thinks it can still rely on its bayonets. Trepov, minister of police, is said to have promised to now be in a position to paralyze any violent attack in Petersburg, and to break resistance in the provincial cities. The only condition to blame for the strike's rapid spread is the badly organized provincial police force that has also not been informing him, Trepov, sufficiently, right up to the latest present hour, and which has not always carried out his orders correctly. This chief police thug's way of seeing things—as perverse as it is brutal—matches with the impudent threat Trepov has made to Petersburg's population. This runs as follows:

> Rumors of forthcoming mass disturbances have stirred up the capital's population. Measures for the maintenance of order have been taken. I therefore request that these rumors should not be believed. Any possible attempts to incite disturbance will be suppressed immediately in the most energetic way possible and shall not be allowed to spread. If during this suppression the same mobs of the people resist, then troops and police shall, in accordance with my order, not fire at first into the air but will rather immediately shoot at the crowd, and will not be saving bullets. I announce this in order that anyone taking part in the assemblies concerned with inciting disturbance knows what will await them; but also so that the sensible part of the populace stays away.

The question is whether this puffed-up police terror will break down ignominiously when push comes to shove. Considering the intensity of the movement that has taken hold of all of the people in the capital cities, it certainly is an open question, whether police and troops will not actually end up fraternizing with the people in the end.

---

* Although this article, "Vor der Katastrophe," was published anonymously, Luxemburg's authorship can be presumed based on her letters to Jogiches from September 29, 1905 onward, and in particular her letter to Jogiches of October 6, 1905. See Luxemburg's *Gesammelte Briefe*, Vol. 2, p. 177 and 183. The article first appeared in *Vorwärts*, No. 253, October 28, 1905. It is translated (by Henry Holland) from Luxemburg's *Gesammelte Werke*, Vol. 6, pp. 579–84.

A Russian correspondent reports:

It is impossible to generalize accurately about the mood among the troops. As a *symptom* however, it is remarkable that an officer held a speech on Wednesday at an assembly of railroad workers, in which he declared that *the officers do not want to serve absolutism, they want to serve the people.* He demanded the separation of the army from the hated gendarmerie and police force, and went on to divide the troops into three categories—those who would follow orders to shoot at the people, those who would refuse to do so, and, finally, *those soldiers who would shoot at the soldiers who had shot first.* A *soldier* spoke after the officer, declaring that because absolutism had betrayed the fatherland, "*it is a soldier's duty to fight for the fatherland against absolutism.*"

According to a report in Scherl's paper, the *Petersburg Police* are also in a state of ferment. "*Floods* of lower-level police officers *have put in resignation requests,* and have also been holding *meetings;* their situation should be improved as quickly as possible."

It would definitely be premature to want to lose oneself in prophecies about a general mutiny in the army, but it deserves mention that in all revolutions that have taken hold of all circles of the population, the army has proven itself to be unreliable. On top of that, tsarism is receiving an omen through the renewed ...

DISTURBANCES IN THE BLACK SEA FLEET

As reported from *Odessa,* disturbing news has reached us here from Sevastopol. According to these communications, the battleship *Potemkin* from the Black Sea Fleet was *set on fire* on Wednesday by arsonists *and was completely destroyed by the flames.* Concurrently, a mutiny broke out against the officers among the crew of the Battleship *Empress Catherine II.* The same thing happened in a company of the Fortress Artillery. It was only with great difficulty that both mutinies could be suppressed. *Four hundred men were arrested.*

THE TSAR'S MANIFESTO* IS PUBLISHED TODAY

This should represent the cashing in on the promise to grant the people *freedom of assembly,* yet considering the twelve extra points stipulated in the *exemptions,* it is unlikely to have anything beyond a minimal impact. It is, indeed, particularly worth considering that official overseers whom the government will

---

* Faced with the political general strike, the tsarist government felt forced to grant constitutional concessions. In the tsar's manifesto of October 30, 1905, he promised to grant civil freedoms, to extend the franchise of those entitled to vote for the Duma, and to grant legislative power to the Duma. However, these were only promises.

dispatch to any assembly that has been *registered three days in advance*, will be *carrying with them clever powers of attorney to close the aforementioned assemblies*. The fairly dark mood in Petersburg, as depicted in a telegram in the *Day* newspaper, chimes with these developments:

> *We stand here, on the eve of the revolution,* which can break out over us in all its terror at any moment. All city inhabitants are in the grip of an indescribable anxiety that cannot *be expelled by the decree from Governor-General Trepov today,* which reasserts that all measures for the immediate crushing of any resistance have already been taken.

FIRES RAGE IN WARSAW

Wolff's [Telegraph] Office communicates the following official report. Since yesterday, telegrams sent to Russia are the subject of considerable delays. Connecting lines to Warsaw, Odessa, and Kiev have been disturbed. (Fires raging in Warsaw.) Another report claims that one whole district is in flames.

MOSCOW WITHOUT WATER AND GAS

Moscow, October 27. From today, there is no water and no gas. The streetcars are running only with a single carriage and only on a few lines. The bakeries are almost all closed. Those that are still open are selling their last bread and will then close too. Neither the zemstvo nor the municipal administration is functioning. Many private institutes, offices and warehouses have also suspended business. In an appeal to the population, the governor regrets that the agitation of malicious persons has filled the workers with hate; and he generally disseminates calming messages. The military is set up at posts everywhere in the city, armed with orders to fire at even the smallest crowd of people if they take the least possible step toward violent activities.

STREET BATTLES IN KHARKIV

Kharkiv, October 26 (report by the Petersburg Telegraph Agency). The telegraph service has restarted, making it possible to give a description of *events since October 24.* Several assemblies of workers were held at the university on October 24. During one of these assemblies, news arrived of the death of a student called Constantinidi, who had been wounded by a patrol unit; accompanying this, news arrived of acts of violence committed by holligans. When the assembly heard that troops were about to arrive, *it was decided to barricade the university and defend it with weapons.* Barricades were built from telegraph poles, cobblestones, cables, etc. The area that was cordoned off included the cathedral, the university and the court buildings. The court archive was badly damaged, its floor strewn with papers. The assembly then turned the university into a fortress, with doors and windows barricaded by masses of stones, coals and beams. *The crowd gathered there numbered roughly 3,000 people.* Many red flags bearing revolutionary slogans were flying from the roofs. Field hospitals were set up at three points in the city. *In the afternoon, a heavy container arrived carrying firearms and other arms that were shared out among the rebels.* Concurrently, people joined up in gangs in the city for plundering weapon stores, one of which was robbed down to the last gun. *Dragoons firing from a sheltered position shot at the crowd.* Ten people were killed, many wounded. Later, 300 people carried out a patriotic demonstration with a picture of the tsar and Russian national flags. These pro-manifesto demonstrators smashed up an ambulance that was coming toward them and beat up the doctors and stretcher-bearers as well as individual students, before striking out at workers who were moving toward the university—but the patriotic crowd were *forced to disperse by the workers' revolver shots.*

This led workers to smash the windows of the editorial office of the reactionary newspaper *Yuzhnyl Krai* [Southern Area], which also houses the official municipal newssheet. Some tramps made use of the general confusion in more distant districts of the city that had been deserted by the police, by attempting to loot shops and beating up passing people. A state of siege was declared covering the university district. The governor handed over commanding powers to Lieutenant General Mau. A committee for public welfare, which had just newly convened and consisted of the city's most respected citizens, led the negotiations with the governor.

In the meantime, troops arrived from other nearby municipalities. With the approval of the governor, the welfare committee formed a *militia of armed workers and students* for the maintenance of order in the city. The citizens greeted the militia with cheers. From individual points in the city, the troops shot at the militia, wounding several persons. The welfare committee negotiated with Lieutenant General Mau to agree to conditions for handing over the university. Mau proposed the following conditions: Those persons currently barricaded inside the university would have to clear the barricades without using weapons, and would be allowed to neither sing nor cry out in the process. *After that, they would not be hindered in joining up with their mates, who were gathering for a big meeting on Skobelev Square.* The weapons had to be handed over to the university administration. The people who barricaded themselves inside the university accepted the conditions, and left their fighting posts peaceably. Troops then occupied St. Paul's Square. The crowd jammed in behind the troops and greeted the figures coming out, escorted by a squadron of dragoons, with loud cries of support. The students and workers made their way in a long procession to Skobelev Square, where an assembly was held that went on until 6 p.m. Then everything broke up peacefully. There were no further clashes with the troops, even though isolated shots could be heard again in the evening.

So, all this happened on October 24. A different, later report stated that rebels had proclaimed the Republic in Kharkiv. As more troops had been directed to the city, it was probable that bloody clashes would result.

Petersburg, October 26. *Workers in the new admiralty* employed on the construction of the warships Bayan, Gilyak, Pallada and Chivinetz have, alongside *workers from the marine workshops*, gone on strike. Furthermore, civil servants from the Directorate-General of State Railroads in the Ministry of Railroads have gone on strike, as have the civil servants from the Zemstvo Administration of the Petersburg Governorate.

The Social Democratic Party's leadership organized the sale of firearms to the strikers; twenty-five cartridges were handed out with every gun.

Petersburg, October 26. The university was the stage for a few hours this evening for a large *gathering of the people*. Around 20,000 *people* gathered in the main hall, in the smaller halls and in the large courtyard, including representatives of *all social estates, professions and classes of [wage] earners*. The assemblies passed in a thoroughly peaceful fashion. The speakers' ruminations were met with loud cheers of approval everywhere. In the courtyard, leaders of the party of action encouraged those present to clarify our current circumstances *through use of armed force*. What had until now been partial strikes had developed itself into a mighty, unified strike of the Russian people. This, everyone's *general strike*, is the revolution. The government's side had turned its weapons against the people. Nothing else could help in achieving clarity in the situation, apart from *using armed force for the people's side*. During the speeches, demands from the Social Democratic Worker's Committee were disseminated. The assemblies went on into the night.

Warsaw, October 26. Ar*med bands ambushed the newspaper printing works*, destroyed the presses and attempted to prevent printing. The *Kurjer Warzawski* [Warsaw Courier] was printed nonetheless, albeit with a long delay. Other bigger newspapers were not printed at all. The *foodstuff prices are increasing here and in Łódź rapidly*, a coal shortage looms, the situation is tense. *The general strike in all factories is starting tomorrow.*

In *Pabianice*, the first *disturbances* have broken out. The military fired off several rounds, hitting several persons. More details are not available at present.

Petersburg, October 27 (report by the Petersburg Telegraph Agency). Telegrams received in the night bring *disturbing news* from *Minsk, Kiev and Saratov*. In Kiev, the newspapers have joined the strike with the exception of the *Kievlyanin* paper. *All drug stores are closed in Saratov. The city is without lighting.* Instead of newspapers, the only thing that is "published" now is telegrams. Saratov's Duma has organized a committee to protect its citizens.

Petersburg, October 27. In the sitting held yesterday of the *professional associations*, the *pharmacists, doctors, advocates, and other professional groups* decided *to join the strike on October 28.* The typesetters passed the motion only to set newspapers edited in a revolutionary spirit. All schools are closed until October 31 in accordance with an official order.

Zlatoust, October 26. The railroad workers' strike that broke out here yesterday has turned into a general strike today. Transport had to be stopped.

Krasnoyarsk, October 26. A strike has broken out on the Siberian Railroad that is planned to continue until Tuesday.

Samara, October 27. During clashes with a *crowd numbering several thousand, troops fired at an assembly of peaceful citizens.* A public conversation continues, labeling the convocation of a *Constituent Assembly* as the only means of pacifying the country.

Łódź, October 27. The streetcar system is at a standstill. Due to the suspension of rail transport, Łódź is cut off from the outside world and no post has arrived for the last two days. Basic foodstuffs, petrol and coal are rising in price; the city is peaceful.

Dnipropetrovsk, October 27 (report by the Petersburg Telegraph Agency). After solicitations by the citizens, the authorities have removed the troops from the streets. The intensified military guard in the city has now been withdrawn. The authorities are permitting assemblies again. Trade is coming back to life. The burials of the victims of the disturbances are taking place without incident.

The Russian Volcano[*]

A nightmarish feeling is steadily taking possession of Russian's ruling clique, a feeling that one is moving across the crater of a rumbling volcano, that although the pulsating crust has not yet been blown open, this terrible eruption could happen any second now. The rumor that the tsar is considering fleeing proves resilient. Apparently, his yacht lies at anchor ready to sail, its steam engine ticking over, ready to bring the foremost of the accused to safety, if catastrophe should break out. The situation in all centers of the revolution has intensified since yesterday. The strike has become even more general and the bitterness is boiling ever hotter.

We have received no news at all today from Kharkiv, where revolutionaries are set to proclaim a republican government—such silence clearly a sign of calamity. Yet revolutionaries also intend to form a revolutionary government in *Moscow*, the empire's second city. Moscow factory owners have bowed to necessity by joining the call for basic human rights and by stating their readiness to allow the workers to use their factories for assemblies. In *Petersburg* and *Moscow*, where the general strike has reached absolute proportions, the people are in council in massive assemblies as to which further next steps must be taken.[†] While people are determined to do their utmost to avoid utilizing violence, the people are also just as resolutely determined to use the weapon of stopping work with the toughest ruthlessness. It seems that plans are being made for all eventualities, as a large number of revolvers have also been handed out in Petersburg.

Bloody clashes have broken out again in several cities. The municipal theater is in flames in *Tallinn* and armed masses are preventing the fire brigade from extinguishing the fire.

The *railroad workers' strike* has stretched out beyond the European rail network to take in the large Asian lines. Employees on the Trans-Baikal Railroad and on the Central Asian Railroad have joined their European brothers' strike movement! Proof indeed of the all-encompassing manner in which the idea of revolutionary struggle has taken hold of the masses!

---

[*] Although this article, "Der russische Vulkan," was published anonymously, Luxemburg's authorship can be presumed based on her letters to Leo Jogiches from September 29, 1905 onward, and in particular her letters to Jogiches from October 6, 1905 onward. See Luxemburg's *Gesammelte Briefe*, Vol. 2, pp. 177 and 178. The article first appeared in *Vorwärts*, No. 254, October 29, 1905. It is translated (by Henry Holland) from Luxemburg's *Gesammelte Werke*, Vol. 6, pp. 585–9.

[†] This is an indirect reference to the soviets—the spontaneously generated, decentralized and democratic forms of workers' self-organization that had a major impact on the 1905 Revolution.

FREEDOM OF ASSEMBLY RESTRICTED!

The proclamation regarding freedom of assembly that supposedly should, as far as possible, take account of the people's wishes, has been exposed not as an extension, but even rather as a shameless worsening of the current situation:

The Imperial Decree* extending the law concerning public assemblies contains *fundamental restrictions* compared to current regulations. Assemblies must be *registered three days in advance* and their *purpose* must be stated *in detail*. A government representative has to be allowed entry to assemblies, who is entitled to demand the name of every single speaker from the chairperson, and to *close down the assembly. Open air* assemblies are *forbidden*. If these regulations are violated, an assembly's chairperson can be punished with a *prison sentence of up to three months* and with a 300-rouble fine; *the remaining participants* could face up to one month in prison and a fine of 100 roubles.

The people naturally scorn these regulations. Mass meetings are being held everywhere in Petersburg. Sixty-thousand people took part in these yesterday, with a different report even talking about *120,000 persons*. Various *officers* present explained that the liberal cause could *count on the support of at least two-thirds of the troops*. Even the *flag-bearers among the reservists* have come together to voice protest against the current system of government, as have *lawyers, engineers, writers, bank civil servants,* and so on. The revolutionary committee has received a large quantity of revolvers and cartridges which it has sold to the workers at cheap prices—each worker gets twenty-five cartridges free. The electrical works at Helios are on strike, leaving many private flats and half the city without light. Prices of foodstuffs continue to rise. The *water-works have been sealed off,* leaving the district of Vassilevsky-Ostrov without water. *No newspapers* will be published tomorrow, as the typesetters are on strike again.

THE SITUATION IN PETERSBURG

Petersburg, October 28. The military has occupied the state banks and the Imperial Rents Office. All these institutions are still working today, as are the private banks, with business continuing as usual. Business people are still frequenting the stock exchange, but not much business is being done as the supply side is missing. The Finland Railroad has started operating again under a military guard. Simple foreign correspondence will be transported at present via Helsinki, Turku and Stockholm. Apart from numerous military patrols, inner-city streets make their familiar impression on the viewer. First aid posts and stands for bandaging the wounded have been set up at many points in the city. *All pharmacies have joined the strikers, resulting in a complete stop in the sale of*

---

* This is a reference to the tsar's manifesto of October 1905.

medicines. Petersburg's attorneys and their assistants wish to *join with the mass of workers* and also to force the closure of the district courts, in order to then hold people's meetings in the court halls. *The attorneys moved through the court premises, forcing the civil servants to leave the building and to suspend their duties.* When the throngs of people then wanted to penetrate into the court in order to hold their assemblies, *they were forcibly dispersed by military and police.* A pharmacist located on Sergiyev Street that had opened again for business was looted and smashed up.

London, October 28 (Laffan's News Agency). The *Daily Telegraph's* Petersburg correspondent announces, in the form of a telegram, their conviction that *tsardom together with its reactionary forces and its out-of-date form of government will belong to the historical past before next Monday already*, and that Russia will have taken its place among the European constitutional states. According to a report in the *Times* from a private individual in Petersburg, Witte's appointment as prime minister will be signed today, Saturday.* Liberal leaders who have not previously held official posts will win places in Witte's cabinet. *General Trepov* will also take control of a ministry, while the current finance minister, [Vladimir] Kokovtsov, and the present minister of teaching, Glazov, will retire from government.

THE AUTHORITIES ARE BECOMING POLITE!

The *Day* reports from Kiev: Civil servants on the southwest railroads have been on strike since Monday, and technical staff is not exempted. While trains are still running to Odessa and Podvolotszka, these are the only trains still moving in the whole of Russia. Unsettling dispatches are being disseminated, and civil society is extremely intimidated. Assemblies are taking place at the university, consisting of students, civil servants, women and other seditious elements. *The authorities' public appearances are marked by unparalleled politeness and consideration.* Shops and banks on the main streets are closed. Military forces are spread out throughout the city, and train stations, government counting houses and the Imperial Bank are being guarded by the military, yet an atmosphere of utter peace prevails everywhere. The younger section of the representatives of the lawyers and the judicial civil servants demanded of the President of the Court that he *suspend every judicial process.*

---

* Terrified at the prospect that the revolution threatened an imminent collapse of the regime, Tsar Nicholas II—after initially favoring a harsh military crackdown to "restore order"—was prevailed upon to appoint the liberal-minded Witte as prime minister, in October 1905. Witte was constantly frustrated by a refusal on the part of tsar and the royal family to accept genuine political reforms, and in 1906 he was forced from power by reactionary hardliners.

THE LITTLE FATHER PACKS HIS BAGS

London, October 28. The *Standard* reports from Petersburg that the stock exchange's *extremely serious stance* led to that same institution announcing, *based on sound information,* that a member of the tsar's circle has given the order to *keep the imperial yacht's steam engine ticking over.* This order also applies to several warships that would accompany the yacht in order to bring *the tsar and the imperial family to Germany,* come what may.

GOVERNMENT BOND SCHEME FOILED!

A Russian correspondent reports: The present revolutionary movement in Russia—for which only the peculiar actions of the Russian possessors of power can be held to blame—has already bequeathed a bouquet of obstacles to the Russian government, which it now will not be easy to overcome. These do not only include what have become well-publicized political demands of the workers and of Russia's leading parties, but also the endeavor *to shake conclusively the whole present regime from the horribly burdened shoulders of the Russian people, whatever it costs.* In order to *rob* the Russian government of that vital factor, *monetary support,* an outstanding party is now agitating for the Russian people to refuse to recognize Russian government bonds from today's date. We would explain the motivation behind such a strategy as follows. Persons who are in no way adventurists, who are highly respected not only in Russia but also abroad, request that they be permitted to submit the following communication to the public concerning financial politics—*each bond, which should be cashed in at present, will be immediately refuted,* because no state can lend the Russian government money in the current period, seeing that the people and the Russian bureaucracy are battling each other, and no one knows which side represents the Russian nation. If the French Republic is inclined to support Russian autocracy, that it is her right, but that, in turn, gives the Russian people the right, *not to recognize the liabilities which its enemy has acquired* in order to keep the people in slavery. In no case will the Russian people recognize bonds that the Russian government has issued since the start of the civil war, regardless of which type they may be.

The revolution really has shaken Russia's credit ratings, to such an extent that no new bonds are possible, as is evidenced in the following *official* report from Petersburg:

Petersburg, October 28 (report by Petersburg Telegraph Agency). The Finance Minister has made a statement on his own initiative after representatives of international banking visited the city. This statement was made prior to any statement on behalf of the international bankers, and with regard to internal circumstances in Russia that could not fail to have a negative effect on the behavior of the European money markets vis-à-vis Russian market values. In this context, the Finance Minister proposed *that further negotiations concerning the planned credit packages be postponed until a change has occurred in the aforementioned circumstances*, and until foreign money markets start behaving favorably in relation to Russian market values.

STREET BATTLES IN TALLINN

Tallinn, October 28 (report by Petersburg Telegraph Agency). Repeated clashes with the police and the troops took place last night. *Eight people are reported as killed in the clashes, with forty wounded.* Mobs armed with rifles and revolvers prevented the fire brigade from extinguishing the municipal theater that had been set on fire.

Moscow, October 28. Moscow factory owners communicated via a delegation to the governor-general that they consider the imposition of martial law to be undesirable. By contrast, they consider it necessary to allow the workers to hold assemblies in factories, moreover to organize the Imperial Duma on libertarian principles, and finally, to grant the people basic freedoms.

Moscow, October 28 (report by Petersburg Telegraph Agency). All banks, businesses, restaurants and theaters are closed, and trade on the stock exchange is not taking place. They are about to close the university. *The Duma passed a motion to announce its own permanence.* The gas works have discontinued operations.

Irkutsk, October 28 (report by Petersburg Telegraph Agency). The employees of the Trans-Baikal Railroad have gone out on strike.

Ashkhabad, October 28 (report by Petersburg Telegraph Agency). The employees of the Central Asian Railroad have stopped work.

The Revolution in Russia [October 31, 1905][*]

Up until now, the explosion that many sides have anticipated in the principal cities has not occurred. Police and military authorities seem to only have avoided street battles in several cities by bowing to the conditions of the masses of the people; by letting the imprisoned go free and allowing the demonstrators complete hegemony on the streets. Whether or not this lenience betrays the powerlessness of authority, whether the police and troops could not be trusted, or whether an unusual restraint was imposed because it was thought that hunger would drive the strikers back into the factories in the end, cannot be clearly discerned. It is, however, probable, that possibly reckoning on hunger forcing the breakdown of the movement is an error. The crisis is by no means over, and moves daily into a more acute phase. Not only does the general strike hold its own everywhere, it continues to stretch and expand.

Now, for example, 100,000 workers are striking in both the city and region of Łódź. The spirit that possesses the souls of these workers is evident not only from their heroic perseverance in the strike, but also from the contents of their proclamations, and the applause that greets their revolutionary speeches. Wide classes of the intelligentsia and of the bourgeoisie are being torn forth toward the same revolutionary decisiveness by the workers' imposing methods. Which is why it is extremely likely, if the tsarist representatives don't manage to agree upon last minute, far-reaching concessions, that heavy street fighting can be expected.

However, there appear to be valid reasons for assuming that, if it comes to clashes, the trust in the armed forces is shaky. Sources say that hundreds of soldiers have been arrested in Łódź, because they refused to shoot at the demonstrators. Similar happenings are reported from other localities. And it is not only the sons of the working people who appear to have gained consciousness of the disgraceful role that is imposed upon them—many officers are also said to be contributing to revolutionary propaganda.

---

* This article, originally entitled "Die Revolution in Rußland," is translated (by Henry Holland) from Luxemburg's *Gesammelte Werke*, Vol. 6, pp. 590–5. Although the article is unsigned, Luxemburg certainly is the author. It accords with the agreement reached with the party executive on October 23, 1905, about which she wrote to Jogiches on October 24–5, 1905: "As you can see, we have to count on me having these two lead articles for the *Vorwärts* weighing me down from now on, but on top of that, e.g., K. K. [Karl Kautsky] [is] demanding that I should direct the Russian section [of *Vorwärts*], albeit only via working from home (through notes)—so that means rather a lot of work." See Luxemburg's *Gesammelte Briefe*, Vol. 2, pp. 213–14. Luxemburg became the leading political editor of *Vorwärts*, with responsibility for the column "The Revolution in Russia" from the end of October. On November 1, 1905, she wrote to Jogiches: "You see, since yesterday I've been involved with *Vorwärts* on a daily basis, having to start from four in the afternoon. It is evident that *the wagon is stuck in the mud*, and I have to help energetically to get it out. Yesterday I wrote the lead article on the spot and worked through all telegrams about Russia. Today I'm going to write the lead article again on Russia." See *Gesammelte Briefe*, Vol. 2, pp. 228 and 235.

And this is how a Russian correspondent reports about the following
Pamphlet of the Revolutionary Officers:

Comrades! We are experiencing a difficult and earnest moment in our fatherland's
interior politics. At the very least, it would be dishonest to stand apart as a cold-
blooded and non-empathetic observer while this series of incisive experiences
unfold, happenings that fly over us faster than the wind, and catch up all classes of
society, from the lowest of the low to the highest of the high, in their wake. Each
and every social class of our fatherland offered up its representatives, gifted warriors for this shared, holy, dear and now-unstoppable cause, the liberation of our
fatherland and of the people from the Tatar-Turkish despotism of the disreputable,
florid, hyper-thieving, spiritually and morally desensitized bureaucrats of every
rank and position, from the field usher—the drunk, thief and robber of soldiers
in a company—to the general of supplies, from the master-sentinel, who accepts
"small gifts" for forbidden "enterprises," to the powerful police leaders, who have to
receive "visiting presents" according to their rank, from the popes who steal from
the peasants, to that creature, who twists Christian teaching in Russia, and martyrs
130 million people in religious and moral terms, and whose name is [Konstantine]
Pobedonostsev.*

And what is happening now in holy Russia? The blood of brothers is being spilled
everywhere! The whole of Europe is shaken by an impression of scandalous bestial
acts. And we, the representatives of a well-organized and tremendous power, continue to sleep in our swamp—with its thick crust on top of us—of caste interests,
small-minded office politics, romantic adventures, staged historical plays—a small
garrison's iniquities! Comrades! We are playing a despicable and unworthy role. We,
who are so proud of our officers' honor, we, who form the height of the armed forces
of a country who has trusted to us the protection of the inviolability of our imperial territory and of the moral and material interests of the nation, we, who in our
vocation should hold high the flag of the chivalrous virtues of protecting the weak,
and of supporting the rule of law, the legal system, and justice—what are we now?
Where have we been brought to recently by our utterly shaken government, which
continues to only consist of a heap of creatures—omnipotent purely as a result of
our incomprehensible support—courtiers, knights, cowering behind the ramparts,
and at its head a policeman, with a nightstick in his hand and a nagaika† down
his boots?

And we're meant to serve such a government? A government that is bankrupt
and beaten in all positions of domestic and foreign politics, a government, which
curses and humiliates us, not only as army officers but also as human beings, which,

---

*   Throughout his career, but especially during the 1905 Revolution, Pobedonostsev was an
extremely reactionary figure that sought to "cleanse" Russia of non–Christian Orthodox denomi-
nations and peoples, most of all the Jews.

†   Nagaika was a short, thick whip often used by Cossacks.

with its dreadfulness, tactlessness, baseness and cruelty of soul, insults us, only to hide behind our bayonets and cannons in moments of utter confusion and panic. Is such a government worthy of our support, a government by the police force, a government of violence, despotism, of theft and of murder?

Comrades, enough! Reflect and remember how they maltreat us every minute and every step of the way. One hint from some miscreant from the gendarmes or the police, stating that the public is "restless," suffices to lead us demonstratively onto the streets to curse and violate the embittered crowd that then expresses its hate against us. We are kept under arms without a break, and left prey to the uncontrollable power of the police, who do with us as they will, as if we were their servants, and servants without honor or a sense of shame at that.

Comrades! We cannot reanimate the colossal corpse of autocracy, which has started to rot, and all our bayonets are nothing in comparison to the people's cudgel. We therefore do not want to wait for the end of autocracy, but to cross over instead to the side of truth, of the law, of the oppressed people, before it is too late. The well-being of the people is our well-being, the happiness of the nation is our happiness, and its unhappiness is our unhappiness. We therefore want to stretch out our hand to our younger brothers in order to drive away our common enemy, insulter and oppressor. Comrades, arise!

CATCHING UP WITH THE TSAR, OR A DEMONSTRATION OF THE FLEET

A private dispatch brings us the following report from Kiel. The *Schleswig-Holst[einische] Volkszeitung* has reported: The *Third Torpedo Boat Division*, *Lübeck*, the turbine cruiser and the *Hamburg* cruiser all received commands yesterday, via an *imperial cabinet order*, to be ready to sail. The cruiser *Hamburg* and the torpedo boats would pick up the royal family in Peterhof; the cruiser *Lübeck* would be stationed in Klaipeda, in order to ensure the safety of the route. The royal family would then be transported to *Kiel*.

This attention-grabbing headline has meanwhile reached several Berlin papers. Yet one interpretation is that the flotilla has set sail in order to *protect the German embassy,* as that latter institution is *already lost at sea.*

The deployment of the German aid fleet—did Russia request it, or does it result from Germany's own initiative?—casts a very dim light on the Russian situation. Have we come to this, that the "Admiral Over the Peaceful Ocean" has to be saved from the wrath of his own people by foreign ships? As it happens, it is highly probable that the tsar will feel even safer in Copenhagen than he would in Kiel.

Yet we do not want to suppress a final assumption in this regard. Perhaps the purpose of dispatching the fleet has been completely misunderstood, as it possibly has nothing to do with saving the tsar. Perhaps it rather has to do with a demonstration of the fleet against the impertinent maltreatment of both Germans at the hands of those same brazen border Cossacks,* who later threatened to arrest the district commissioners leading the investigation [against them].

VICTIMS OF FREEDOM

Odessa, October 30. It is impossible to determine the numbers of victims of yesterday's disturbances with any degree of accuracy, as the cemetery and hospital administrations are *strictly banned from giving out information.* The police removed the corpses and the wounded themselves, the number of which must be *very substantial. The authorities are showing no confidence in the infantry,* and are confining them to barracks; *they are only using Cossacks and the gendarmerie.* From behind a barricade, a student shouted to a group of Cossacks rushing by that instead of shooting at their brothers, who are fighting for the freedom of a common fatherland, they'd do better joining the fighters instead. *To which the Cossacks responded with four salvos, killing one person and injuring around forty.* Whereupon the remaining persons—numbering several hundred, and until this point still uninjured—dove, chased by the Cossacks, into the nearest houses, barging into strangers' apartments or hiding themselves in the lofts, or on the rooftops. Turning many private apartments into field hospitals in the process.

Kiev, October 29. Despite the governor-general threatening to bombard the city, *the revolutionary movement endures.* At the university, the military and a large crowd of the people *clashed.* More than *1,000 persons were wounded.* The authorities arrested the leader of the radical party, Attorney Ratner. News from the provinces is alarming. There are reports of *large-scale bloodshed* in *Poltava.*

THE FERMENT GROWS

Moscow, October 28 (report by the Petersburg Telegraph Agency). *The excitement among the population persists.* This morning, the authorities' lackeys forced *all stores to close,* with the exception of the little colonial goods stores. *Clashes with the police* broke out at several locations, particularly at the Panagia Portaitissa Gate, *where many people were wounded. Armed students have barricaded the university and are guarding it.* In the interior of the building a group of students are ready to go into action, in case a bunch of reactionaries from the Okhotny district of the city—who already mugged and mistreated students this morning—should renew their attacks. The telephone service in the city is suspended. Members of several theaters are contributing to the political strike. After an enquiry from the city administration, workers' delegates have declared their readiness to ensure that the operations of the municipal waterworks will be

---

* Luxemburg is referring to an incident in which some German citizens were illegally abused by Cossacks.

resumed, but only under the condition that the workers have complete control over the waterworks, that these workers may select appropriate engineers, and that they have the right to themselves determine when they interrupt operations. The city administration plans to communicate their response this evening. A large assembly took place at 3 p.m. this afternoon, with participation from the local council, representatives from the zemstvo, the nobility and academic societies, the press, and, finally, associations and executives of all parties. In passionate talks, the speakers argued for the armed struggle and the introduction of a welfare committee. Telegraphic communication with Petersburg is only possible through a single wire from the governor-general's house. Various groups of workers, particularly the printers, have joined the strike.

Warsaw, October 30. Today, the factories, banks and other institutes are closed. Streetcars are thrown over or set alight from time to time. Strikes are starting in provincial cities. The situation is especially critical in the city and region of Łódź. *Over 100,000 workers are celebrating there. In the Suwałki Governorate, armed bands have destroyed eleven shops that enjoyed the monopoly on spirits.*

Warsaw, October 30. *A gendarme has been* killed in the *suburb of Praga.*

Łódź, October 30. All the stores are closed here. A few businesses that had opened were smashed up. *Several thousand workers processed through the streets and tore up flags* that had been hoisted to mark the court holiday today. Military patrols fired off blanks. *A bloody confrontation is expected.*

Łódź, October 29. *Three bombs were discovered* today during a house search. The owners were arrested after firing at the police.

Warsaw, October 29. Employees of the Vistula Railroads have responded to management demands to recommence work by stating that this cannot be negotiated, *until their delegates, imprisoned in Petersburg, are released.* Newspapers in the city weren't published; special supplements with the dispatches from the Petersburg agencies were the only thing that was published; these supplements have to pass a particularly strict censor. The authorities have officially informed local homeowners that they will be held responsible for excesses that take place in their houses.

Riga, October 29. *The excitement continues to grow.* All educational institutions, warehouses and factories are closed. The streets have been filled with workers, who impede every form of transport. All business is at a standstill. *A colonel has been shot on the street.*

WORKERS' DEMANDS IN PETERSBURG

A sitting of the *municipal Duma* was held on Sunday in Petersburg. The public had packed in tightly; the entrances were manned by numerous police officers. *Thirty workers' delegates* presented themselves before the Duma, lodging the following petitions:

(1) The workers insist upon their general, well-known demand for *rights of freedom*. (2) The city should provide for *nourishment for the workers* for the duration of the strike. (3) Although the workers do not want to see the water supply being destroyed, they demand the immediate withdrawal of the troops guarding the *water supply*. If this doesn't happen, the water supply should be destroyed. (4) In the future, the city should no longer carry the costs either for the state police, or for the Cossacks, who are deployed against the citizens. (5) The city should guarantee the *personal safety* of the delegates, as it is possible that the governor-general will order their arrest. (6) The city should give the workers weapons and constitute a *citizens' militia*, enabling the workers to guarantee peace, safety and order. The Duma promised to give its response to these demands by Tuesday. The strike was also proclaimed yesterday on the Finland railroad from Petersburg to Beloostrov,* on the Russia–Finland border.

WILL A REAL CONSTITUTION BE GRANTED?

Petersburg, October 30 (report by the Petersburg Telegraph Agency). An *imperial* manifesto is due to be published this evening, appointing *Count Witte* as *prime minister*, charged with the task of unifying functions of government that will in turn grant bourgeois freedoms, a *law-enacting* Duma and the *extension of the right to vote*.

STREET FIGHTS

Petersburg, October 30. Reports continue to reach us *from the provinces* regarding the *spread of the strike* and the ferment, which has led to *bloody clashes* in several localities. In the Baltic Sea Provinces, *Riga* and *Tallinn* are the stage for bloody scenes. Several confrontations with the troops occurred yesterday in Riga, with injuries inflicted by shots and by close-combat weapons. In Tallinn, the rebels passed the motion to enforce their political demands at all costs. During the confrontation, troops fired off two salvos, *killing forty-five persons and wounding roughly the same number again*. In *Odessa*, the disturbances took on a much more serious character, with the military blocking off any access to the university. The mass of workers flooded into the streets, closed the shops, cafés and restaurants, and threw over streetcar compartments. The police removed the field hospitals from the city. On Richelieu Street, Cossacks *clashed substantially* with rebels, *who had erected barricades*. Several people were wounded. *Barricades* were also constructed at other points in the city, *and around twenty persons were killed and roughly 200 wounded*. The Cossacks took down the barricades toward evening, but access to the port remains blocked by the military.

---

* Lenin was later to return to Russia during the 1917 Revolution through this very same railway station in Beloostrov.

Our Task[*]

Our party is extending itself outward and expanding ever-more powerfully, and ever-larger masses of people are taking refuge under its banners, in the full realization that only our party guarantees the unqualified representation of the interests of the people. It is drawing one new region after another into the sphere of its political activity, and its field of operations is constantly widening. But with this enlargement of our party's fighting terrain, the number and complexity of the tasks of our press are also increasing, along with the duties and political responsibilities of our press, especially at the present moment when on the political horizon of the autocratic empire next door to ours the thunderclouds of revolution are building and the flicker of lightning heralds the outbreak of a storm that will smash Russian absolutism to pieces, destroying the strongest bulwark of reaction in Europe. At such a moment one question presses itself forward: What task does our press have to fulfill? What is the proper way for it to serve as the leader and standard-bearer in the struggles of the day and to respond correctly to the demands that will confront it? It is especially fitting that the new editorial board, as it begins its work, should take up a serious question: What is our task? And how will we fulfill it to the extent that the available forces and resources permit?

Our tasks are primarily of two kinds—to bring new troops to our banner and to turn these new recruits into class-struggle fighters who will stand their ground in the difficult battles that await us, taking their position surely and firmly on the basis of Marx's theory. The second task is almost harder than the first. The wretchedness and dreariness of our political situation in Germany, the leaden weight of feudal hangovers—which this new German Reich, in spite of its swiftly advancing industrialization has dragged along with it—the increasing burden of a militarist system that has been developed to the utmost and a foreign policy and naval construction policy that has imposed monstrous sacrifices in blood and money on us in exchange for worthless colonial wastelands, and in addition to that the absence of any large party advocating definite liberal-democratic principles. All these factors have produced even in bourgeois circles a general dissatisfaction with the

*   This article first appeared in *Vorwärts*, No. 256, November 1, 1905. Its title in German is "Unsere Aufgabe." It is translated (by George Shriver) from Luxemburg's *Gesammelte Werke*, Vol. 6, pp. 596–9. This lead article in *Vorwärts* is a statement of purpose on behalf of the new editorial board of *Vorwärts*, which Luxemburg discussed in a letter to Jogiches of November 1, 1905 (see her *Gesammelte Briefe*, Vol. 2, p. 228). After the death of Wilhelm Liebknecht, *Vorwärts* came closer to the revisionist elements in the SPD, and in 1905 it sided with the opponents of the mass strike, thus stirring indignation among the majority of SPD members. This issue figured largely at the SPD's Jena Congress (September 1905), which established the "Fifteenth Commission" to look into the issue. After the Commission rejected the revisionist arguments against the mass strike, *Vorwärts* published a statement of resignation by six of its editors (which included supporters of Eduard Bernstein, such as Kurt Eisner). A new editorial board was established at that point, with Luxemburg as the "responsible editor." Her position began on November 1, 1905.

political conditions [in Germany], and this provides a splendid field for recruitment, for our agitational campaigns to enlist new members. It is thus an actual
fact, demonstrated to us not only by electoral statistics but also by the increased
number of subscribers to our party press, that the breadth of our support has
grown to a tremendous extent. However, this expansion of our influence does
not correspond, as all sensible people will recognize, to a deepening of the theoretical level of our party. Our newly recruited supporters for the most part still
carry with them strong remnants of their earlier conceptions, and the demands
for their collaboration tend to monopolize them as soon as they join our ranks,
so that very little time remains to them for political work on their own behalf, for
going more deeply into the world of socialist concepts and ideas.

Our main task should be to try to help correct this lack of theoretical consolidation for the good of the newly recruited members, so as to make themselves a
part of the Social Democratic proletariat and to be fully aware of themselves as
class-struggle fighters who see the political events of the day from the proletarian
class standpoint and have learned to understand them that way. The introduction
to theoretical subtleties, educating the new recruits in the scientific teachings
bequeathed to us by the great masters who preceded us—this can never be the
primary task of a daily newspaper, which helps to lead the struggle in all areas,
which must counter the positions held by every opponent of ours and must
defend our own positions, and which, furthermore, must deal with new tasks
that arise daily, events of the day of the most varied kind. This task [of theoretical
education] properly belongs to our theoretical weekly *Die Neue Zeit*; however,
it will be a good thing if we direct our attention toward printing editorials more
frequently than has been done up to now—editorials that will not just make some
passing references but will deal with various political situations and newly arising
questions in their historical-economic context, explaining their significance and
presenting them as examples of theory applied in practice. Special consideration
should be given in this regard to the revolutionary movement in Russia.

Nevertheless, purely theoretical clarification will by no means be neglected.
As soon as the new editorial board is running smoothly, the previous theoretical
supplement of *Vorwärts*, which has seldom appeared in recent times, will again
begin to appear more frequently—even if not every week.

And along with detailed critical commentaries on outstanding newly published literature in the fields of social science, history, politics, and *belles lettres*,
we would also run short popular-science articles. Besides that, now and then [we
would like] to arrange for critical commentary on particularly notable events in
our party, and occasionally to offer brief critical commentary about the most
important questions of principle and tactics that arise, so that our readers will
obtain a definite picture—even if of course only on a restricted scale because of
space limitations—of the intellectual life of our party press.

The union movement is acquiring ever-greater significance. In the immediate and direct economic conflict between capital and labor, we see more and more a mirror image of the class struggle of the proletariat as a whole. Battles involving principles of previously unsuspected dimension have developed out of the wage struggles of the past few decades. Not for the sake of winning higher wages or shorter hours alone does the goal-conscious proletariat of today, organized in unions and conscious of its purpose, come onto the field of battle. No, it is demanding recognition of the principle that the seller of labor power also must have a say in determining the price of labor power. But the employers as a class are determined to hold fast to the crude and long-outlived standpoint taken by rulers and slave-masters in bygone days, demanding that the government provide guarantees for the employers, who are also trying to make use of the legislative power [to serve their own interests]. And as economic development makes the individual capitalist more powerful, as capital organizes itself more tightly, the more it subjugates the state power to itself and manages to influence legislation more and more in its own favor, to that same extent do social struggles acquire ever-greater scope and strength, making clear to the most backward and shortsighted worker how little the union member can neglect the political movement and how little Social Democracy can neglect union organization. Thus, to demonstrate this over and over again with examples from the life of society—that will also be one of our primary tasks.

In order to make more space for the goals described above, reports about purely sensational matters should be kept to a minimum and abbreviated as much as possible.

At first, this program will be implemented bit by bit. The editorial board has been substantially altered as a result of the events of the last few weeks. Three members of the former editorial board have turned to new fields of activity, and three new people have joined the editorial team. In such cases, some time is always needed before a smoothly functioning collaboration is worked out. Besides that, the editorial board is not yet fully staffed. The necessary number of people has not yet been added to the board. But we all have the firm intention to apply our full strength to the tasks before us, and where there is firm will and determination, much can be accomplished.* But we also need the support of all the forces of intellect and spirit in our party, especially of the workers of Berlin. We count on their help.†

---

* Kautsky wrote on a visitor's card to Luxemburg on Saturday, October 28, 1905: "Dear Rosa, The interregnum comes to an end tomorrow, and you are festively, that is, officially, hereby invited as a collaborator to be part of the new editorial board. Be there tomorrow, Sunday, 10 a.m., at an editorial session that will regulate everything else. Your first duty: a lead article will be expected from you on Tuesday [October 31]. You yourself will work out everything else, together with the others. Long live the revolution in all corners and ends of the earth. Yours, K.K." The text of Kautsky's card is found in Luxemburg's *Gesammelte Briefe*, Vol. 2, p. 225.
† The following were members of the editorial board in addition to Luxemburg: Hans Block, Georg Davidsohn, Wilhelm Düwell, Arthur Stadthagen, Carl Wermuth, Heinrich Cunow, Heinrich Ströbel and Fritz Kunert.

The New Constitutional Manifesto of Nicholas the Last*

From the tsarist empire, the telegraph brings news that yesterday the tsar signed a manifesto offering the prospect of a new constitution.† The famous "Duma" is supposed to be given legislative powers, and "those classes of the population that are now completely deprived of electoral rights" are to be granted the right to vote. Also, the granting of personal inviolability and freedoms of conscience, speech, assembly, and association are supposed to be proclaimed. According to assurances by correspondents working for the privately owned bourgeois press and news dispatches from the semi-official Russian press, the population of the tsarist empire broke out into loud rejoicing and shed bright tears of joy in response to these magnanimous promises made by the supposedly beloved Father of His People to his "loyal subjects" (that phrase, "loyal subjects," was actually used in Bloody Nicholas's manifesto!).

We are not in a position at this moment to verify the accuracy or reliability of these news reports. But our inclination in any case is to assume that the reception given to this "resounding" constitutional manifesto from a ruler virtually being held captive at Peterhof‡ by the masses of the people—who are embittered in the extreme and are ready to fight with the utmost determination—was given not so much with tears of joy as with the same kind of grim silence and rumble of anger as the fighting masses of Berlin [in March 1848] responded to the "words of reassurance" from the royal palace: "It is the king's will that ..."§

Thus far, what has come from the blood-smeared hands of the absolutist Angel of Death¶ is not *freedom* but mere *promises*, not yet any *deeds* but only *words*. There are no grounds at hand for rejoicing or for trumpeting fanfares of victory. In all previous revolutions, in fact, the road from liberal words to liberal deeds has always passed over mountains of corpses, through further battles and terrible sacrifices—with the final outcome always remaining in doubt.

---

* This article, "Da neue Verfassungsmanifest Nikolaus' des Letzten," was not signed. It follows the lead article, "Unsere Aufgabe" (Our Task), on the front page of *Vorwärts*, No. 256, November 1, 1905. Luxemburg indicated her authorship in a letter to Jogiches, also on November 1. See her *Gesammelte Briefe* Vol. 2, p. 228. It is translated (by George Shriver) from Luxemburg's *Gesammelte Werke*, Vol. 6, pp. 601–3.

† An English translation of the tsar's manifesto may be found in Sidney Harcave, *The Russian Revolution of 1905*, pp. 195–6. Elections to the Bułygin Duma were scheduled to be held by January 15, 1906, based on another manifesto issued by the tsar in August 1905.

‡ The Peterhof Palace in St. Petersburg was one of the places the tsar was residing in at the time.

§ Faced with an unexpected revolutionary outburst in March 1848, Prussian king Friedrich Wilhelm IV announced plans for a constitution, freedom of the press, and other reforms. These promises were quickly reversed as he moved in the weeks afterwards to suppress the revolution.

¶ That is, Nicholas II.

In general and for the most part, the concept of "revolution" is perceived from the vulgar and flatfooted police standpoint in the same way as it appears in the narrow-minded outlook of today's bourgeoisie: as a series of external adversities for the police and legal system. They would always want to assume that once liberal freedoms were actually granted, along with a *truly* modern constitution, the revolution in Russia would come to an end.

The enormous crisis going on openly and palpably in the tsarist empire since January of this year is above all an internal *social process*, the rise and development of a new society within the womb of the old, and here, too, the liberating female, "la Révolution," is not so much the mother as merely the *midwife* of the new society.

What the limited bourgeois view sees as the sole aim and meaning of the whole crisis—a liberal constitutional order, a state governed by the "rule of law" in the modern sense—is only the outward expression and product of a deep and ongoing social upheaval-cum-transformation, the shifting and rearrangement of relations among classes, parties, and social strata, processes that have been taking place within the womb of the old society of tsarist Russia.

And, therefore, the promised "granting" of constitutional liberties—even if, we repeat, these words were to become deeds—would fail by far to mark the *close* of the revolutionary era, but rather it would merely begin *another stage* in this era, in which new classes would form parties, which would develop and ripen. This would by no means bring to a standstill their elaboration of many-sided positions and struggles for the exercise of power. On the contrary, it would for the first time fully open the way for such processes.

Thus, if yesterday's constitutional manifesto issued by the last "tsar of all the Russias" were to become a reality, then a new phase of revolutionary struggles would begin tomorrow—perhaps one of much longer duration. And who knows whether it would be less uncompromising than the previous phase of struggles of the working class against the half-baked bourgeois, agrarian, liberal, democratic, and other aspirants to political power and dominance? It [will still] struggle for the establishment, maintenance, expansion and utilization of the rights achieved through its enormous sacrifices.

And yet, in a certain sense, we actually can celebrate! Not a premature and childish victory celebration in the spirit of liberalism, which rejoices at every apparent victory, even if the final outcome is still uncertain—and does so above all as an excuse for withdrawing from the field of battle. No, we really can celebrate, based on recognition of what has been accomplished in a real sense at the present moment. And we can do this even if the agonized blurting out of tsarist promises on a temporary basis is nothing more than a vain attempt by despotism to prolong its doomed existence by stealing one more moment of reprieve. Because now that this manifesto has been announced in such clear-cut terms, it cannot be taken back. It represents a swansong compared to the previous manifesto issued by the tsar [in August]; *it tolls the death knell for the entire construct and concept of the "Bułygin Duma."* Even before "elections" could be held for that monster sired by frivolous fellows from the tsar's regime of blood, that supposed "representative body of the people," the entire farce of the "Bułygin Duma" was knocked to pieces and blown away by the unanimous rebellion of the urban proletariat throughout the tsarist empire, from Petersburg to Odessa, from Warsaw and Łódź to Krasnoyarsk. It was trampled and ground underfoot, and turned into nothing!

The people have been spared the slow agony of a journey through gradual stages, of having its patience tried by a war of frogs and mice* against the bloody absolutist regime. The road to real freedom has been shortened, opened, and cleared in truly revolutionary fashion.

And this is, without a doubt, the work of the class-conscious vanguard of the proletariat of Russia, the work of Social Democracy!

Just when that memorable first week of January 1905 started the sudden powerful upsurge of the Petersburg proletariat (and immediately after that the massive upsurge of the proletariat of all the industrial cities in the Russian empire)—and just when the "liberal" and "democratic" banquet threatened to run into the ground through its own inadequacy and inner uncertainty— the decisive intervention, the raising of the proletarian fist, brought about one good shove that sent the cart rolling forward again. And so, too, now, just at the moment when Russian liberalism and democracy were ready to stumble over a mere straw (the "Bułygin Duma") and cause the work of the revolution to collapse and fall into decline for a substantial length of time, the men of the zemstvos (and with them many other "democratic" heroes) were getting ready, with much moaning and groaning, to bite the sour apple of the "Bułygin Duma." At first, they had rejected it with disdain, [but now will] take part with good grace in the "election," while issuing many fine consoling and reassuring statements about the glorious liberal "thunderous speech" they intended to blast forth—even though, actually, their lips will be sealed by a ban on publication. This liberal "thunder rumbling" supposedly is in defense of and for the benefit of the people, who would remain on the outside as onlookers [*Zaungäste*].

It was at this point that the urban working class—now under the conscious and firm leadership of Social Democracy—rose up and said: "No, dear sirs, we prefer to establish some order here, with our own hands." And one week

---

* Luxemburg is here using a phrase that Marx employed in response to the infighting among the exiles from the 1848 Revolution. See "Heroes of the Exile," in *Marx-Engels Collected Works*, Vol. 11 (New York: International Publishers, 1979), p. 310: "And the very fact that they fought each other so bitterly led each to believe in the importance of the other. Anyone who wishes to pursue the study of this great war between the frogs and the mice will find all the decisive original documents in the *New-Yorker Schnellpost*."

of intensive agitation and tremendous mass strikes was enough to leave all the promised splendor of the "Bułygin Duma" lying in the dust.

Appearing on the field of battle for the second time with a colossal upsurge at the decisive moment, the industrial proletariat of Russia has shown today, just as it did in the first act of the revolution, that it *actually carries the load* for the entire revolution and is in fact its *only reliable load-bearer.*

It was also this proletariat that, during the entire interim period, kept the fire of the revolution going by means of a never-ending guerrilla war. It nourished the revolution with the blood of the working class, keeping it on the right course from the beginning up to this very day, reigniting the revolution over and over again with countless sacrifices.

The revolution in the tsarist empire is still far from having exhausted its strength. It still has powerful forces in reserve. Absolutism has already lost one trump card after another from its hand. *Meanwhile, the peasant masses have not really stepped onto the stage, and the revolts in the army have not led to any decisive breakthrough!* The most difficult and most important work of the revolution has been done, and the first crucial breaches in the bulwark of tsarism have been made, by the industrial proletariat with the use of its strength and power alone. This has been solely the result of the action of the urban workers.

And how quickly the young giant has grown and stretched itself out! One may well recall the semi-fantastical, mystical image of the proletarian trudging on his pilgrimage to the tsar's palace on the River Nevá, peacefully and defenselessly, with his wife and child, carrying icons and church banners, only nine months ago—and at the same time one can compare that to the swift, thoroughgoing, purposeful actions carried out by the workers during these last weeks and their unbreakable determination to destroy the "Duma" comedy of the tsarists.

Some may say that the activity of Social Democracy in the tsarist empire thus far has been too incoherent and inadequate—and yet *its* work, *its* agitation during the interim period was undeniably the driving force behind this miraculous political growth and ripening of the proletariat, and *its call to action* gave the signal for the outbreak of this latest decisive battle.

Gone are the icons and prophets. All the mists and fogs of illusion have been dispersed. Clear and certain of its goal, with a fully matured outlook, the proletariat of Russia is on the job, fighting for its own emancipation, engaging in *class struggle* for its own interests. And because the class-conscious workers through their heroic actions thus far have assured themselves leadership of the mass of the people in the coming battles of this ongoing revolution, we have every reason to celebrate and to cry out with full confidence: Ça ira!" "We are moving on!"

---

* The Polish equivalent of *ça ira!* would be "Iidziemy naprzód" ("We're moving forward"). In other eras, similar phrases have been used: "*We shall overcome!*" and "*Venceremos!*"

"Powder Dry, Sword Well Sharpened"*

The critical test for the political value and merit of a party is not how it conducts itself before the battle, and not even during the battle, but *after* it. Marx observed as long ago as his *Eighteenth Brumaire of Louis Napoleon* that the premature "self-satisfied howling about victory with which Messieurs the Democrats congratulate each other"† is a sure and infallible sign that a crashing fiasco for the revolution is imminent. In all modern revolutions, this has been a constant, a standard phenomenon, and of course the present moment is no exception— especially in reference to news of the latest manifesto issued by the tsar. Our German liberalism doesn't go along with the idea of revolution, and it hasn't for a long time, but all the more zealously does it assume the role of "self-aware" "victory howler," one who sees as his most urgent task to persuade those who are fighting (and to do this at every even halfway suitable opportunity) to trust in faith, hope, and charity, and above all, *to disarm*. It goes without saying that there must unfailingly be present a "certain man" upon whom all hopes and aspirations from now on can be concentrated, a man who will set everything right, guarantee liberty, restore order, but above all among the miracles he will perform must be *to bring peace to the land*. Witte and peace—that is the magic political formula of German liberalism today, with which it wishes to calm the billowing waves of revolution and conjure them away.

The Mosse *Daily* cries out: "*Russia now needs peace above all!*"‡

"*Russia needs peace above all!*" explains the tsar's premier [Witte], following the lead of the German Free Thinkers.§ He lectures to a deputation from the Petersburg press and in great haste forms a cabinet for the regime made up of former members of the government and new liberals "aspiring" to perform along the same old lines, once in office.

"*Russia needs peace above all!*" That is what the troop patrols explain, basing themselves on the tsar's manifesto, to the crowds of demonstrating workers,

---

* This article, "Da Pulver trocken, das Schwert geschliffen," first appeared in *Vorwärts*, No. 257, November 2, 1905. It is translated (by George Shriver) from Luxemburg's *Gesammelte Werke*, Vol. 6, pp. 604–6. The article was not signed, but it is clear that she is the author based on Luxemburg's letter to Jogiches of November 1, 1905. See her *Gesammelte Briefe*, Vol. 2, p. 228.

† See *The Eighteenth Brumaire of Louis Bonaparte*, in *Marx-Engels Collected Works*, Vol. 11, p. 107: "It was enough to hear the self-complacent howl of victory with which Messieurs the Democrats congratulated each other on the beneficial consequences of the second Sunday in May 1852"—the day that the term of Louis Bonaparte was supposed to expire. This was of course followed by the "fiasco" of Napoleon III's seizure of power.

‡ Rudolf Mosse was the publisher of the *Berliner Tageszeitung* (Berlin Daily), which was linked with the liberal Free Thinkers Association.

§ The German Free Thinkers Association was formed in 1881 by followers of the positivist philosopher Ludwig Büchner. Atheistic and materialist in orientation, it nevertheless opposed revolutionary action by the working class.

and they leave the pavement covered with dead and wounded in Petersburg, Moscow, Warsaw, Sosnowiec, Kiev, Kazan, Chişinău, Poltava, Bialystok ...*

"*Russia after the manifesto needs peace above all!*" That is what the gangs of plainclothes police in Odessa declare as they contrive and plot their massacres against the Jews.

"*Russia needs peace above all!*" That is what the bands of Cossack cavalry shout, coming up from behind and carrying out a bloodbath among the unarmed and defenseless population.

And "Russia needs peace above all!" is what the *Russian liberals* will also declare today or tomorrow as well. That is why the commentaries of German liberalism about the events in the tsarist empire are worthy of note—because the stirrings in the soul of today's down-at-the-heel Western European bourgeois liberalism reflect with unfailing accuracy the stirrings in the soul of "youthful" Russian liberalism. This Russian liberalism is something that grew out of the discontent and frustration of a section of the Russian nobility who were the owners of large landholdings, expressing their protests against arbitrary police rule and against an economic policy dominated by the chinovniki. And to a large extent, it even exceeds the incomparable German liberalism in its wretchedness. The few genuinely bourgeois and big-capitalist elements in Russia, which in the course of the latest revolutionary crisis joined the call for fundamental reform, for a "cultural reform" in the state structure, did not do so out of a Platonic love of "freedom," but out of a very practical dissatisfaction with the turmoil and troubles that tsarism was no longer able to overcome. It is not the knout that bothers them anymore, but the opposite, the *impotence and ineffectiveness* of the knout against the "power of the street." It is not against the regime of blood in itself but merely against its ineffectiveness, which has ultimately become unbearable for the bourgeoisie.

In addition, as a third element of the bourgeois freedom movement in Russia, there comes under consideration the wavering, inwardly uncertain stratum of the bourgeois-democratic *intelligentsia*, which by nature has "two souls contending in its breast"† and which in all its activity regularly swings like a pendulum between the "lovers of order" among the liberal nobility and the revolutionary workers' movement. That such a dubious liberalism basing itself on such heterogeneous elements is an unreliable ally—that will probably make itself evident once again in the very next moment.

In revolutionary times people, classes, and events come to a head with remarkable speed. The tsar's manifesto has produced nothing at all in the way of positive achievements, and yet it has already, as if overnight, brought about a major shift in the situation, in the constellation of forces on the field of battle.

---

* The ellipsis is in the original.
† A famous phrase from *Faust*; Goethe was one of Luxemburg's favorite authors.

From all the partial news reports that have come from the empire of the blood-stained "constitutional" manifesto there emerges an approximate picture of the state of affairs from which one must conclude, guided by fighting instinct and historical experience, the following:

The Russian freedom movement now faces a profoundly serious and decisive moment. The news of the constitutional manifesto coming along with the news of rampages by the murderous gangs of tsarist thuggery will be used by the liberal elements to put the workers' movement in paralysis, using the watchword, "*peace and order.*" And it will use this slogan of peace and order, as soon as tomorrow perhaps, in order to drown the revolution in blood under the leadership of the "liberal premier." All of bourgeois society, with few exceptions, will take the manifesto as an excuse to arouse "hopes and expectations" following the tried-and-true example of our German "victory howlers" of liberalism. The revolutionary working class in Russia must *march alone* in its further path along the road ahead, relying solely on itself, its own strength, its own determination, its own tenacity, its own unwavering steadfastness and refusal to be frightened or intimidated. At this moment, for the class-conscious proletariat in the tsarist empire, as for the fighting proletariat everywhere and always, the watchword remains: "Keep your powder dry and your sword well sharpened!"*

---

* The phrase originates from Oliver Cromwell, who reportedly voiced it to his troops during his campaign against Ireland in the 1600s. However, the actual phrase used by him was, "Put your trust in God; but mind to keep your powder dry."

The Tsar's "Constitution," Modified by Mass Murder[*]

The third day since the appearance of the "constitutional manifesto" has gone by. The last traces of enthusiasm aroused by the manifesto, as played up by the official telegraph dispatches, have been drowned in the streams of bloodshed by citizens attacked by the wild beasts of tsarism. Distrust has once again proved itself to be the true democratic virtue, and the tactic of Social Democracy [expressed in the phrase] "arms at the ready!" has proved to be the only correct tactic. Even the liberal "folk" who yesterday "were so wonderfully intoxicated" have changed their mood and are now saying, "Ouch, what a hangover."

And no wonder! From all the cities, all the regions, from every corner of the empire come news reports of murder and looting, anti-Jewish rampages, and other bestial excesses by the police, the Cossacks, and the soldiers. Tsarism has resorted once again to its "tried-and-true," favorite method of fighting against the revolutionary movement of the proletariat. It has stirred up the dregs of society, the "fifth estate," the lumpenproletariat, to try to drown the vanguard of the working class in a sea of blood. *Against the general strike, generalized murder!*—that is the tactic of tsarism, as has become undeniably clear in the last three days.

And the massacres, the anti-Jewish pogroms, the "patriotic" demonstrations by police agents aimed as provocations against the population—all of this broke out so immediately after the publication of the manifesto, so suddenly, with such vehemence, so universally and so simultaneously that it is simply impossible that all this was merely "*pure coincidence*." It cannot be seen as anything but the implementation of a carefully worked out plan. The bloody news coming in from all parts of the empire leads with compelling logic to the inescapable conclusion:

Mass murder, pogroms, and the constitutional manifesto are all details of a single fiendish plan worked out by tsarism in its death agony. The liberal elements and those in the broader circles of the population who remain confused have fallen for this plan of making use of the manifesto, which costs nothing to the regime except empty promises and is aimed at winning over those

---

[*]   The title of this article in the original German is "Die zaristische 'Verfassung,' gemildert von den Massenmord." We have given a fairly literal rendering of the title. An alternative translation might be: "From the Tsar, a 'Constitution' with a Qualifying Condition—Mass Murder." The article first appeared in *Vorwärts*, No. 258, November 3, 1905. It is translated (by George Shriver) from Luxemburg's *Gesammelte Werke*, Vol. 6, pp. 609–15. The article was not signed, but in all likelihood is by Luxemburg. On November 1 she wrote to Jogiches: "The SPD executive decided to pay twenty marks for a lead article and five marks daily for the Russia section, and for brief notices ten pfennigs per line." This amounted to about 350 marks per month (See Luxemburg's *Gesammelte Briefe*, Vol. 2, pp. 228, 235).

elements and quieting them down. But the intention was at the same time to suppress and hold down the revolutionary workers' movement by means of a general attack bringing to bear the holy trinity—cavalry, infantry, artillery—and employing the active assistance of the dregs of the population. This, then, is the finely tuned plan of the tsarist regime, to judge from all the evidence. It is a repetition of the June Days [of 1848 in France] à *la Cossaque*—in the true Russian manner—that was undoubtedly the aim of the tsar's "constitutional manifesto."

And now we see that the correctness of the word of warning issued by Social Democracy—"*Do not disarm! Keep fighting all along the line and as hard as we can!*"—has been brilliantly confirmed. The workers, with their combat readiness and decisive rejection of the manifesto swindle succeeded immediately in dampening the enthusiasm [for it] in broader circles of the population. They prevented all wavering, and thus strengthened their own fighting positions. Dead and wounded cover the pavements by the hundreds in the tsarist "constitutional state," but *politically*, victory is on the side of the proletariat. It has placed itself at the head of the discontented population as a whole, the battle goes on, and the latest bloody attempt by absolutism to save itself has fallen flat. This certainly is the last "manifesto" of the last tsar, which only for a few hours awoke confidence and hope among certain layers of the population. But its final effect has merely been that in the face of its own bankruptcy it managed to bury an earlier swindle operation put forward by the same tsarist regime—[that is,] the so-called constitutional proposal for the Bułygin Duma.* The method of "calming people down"† used against the revolution has merely awakened a new powerful upturn of the revolution—that is the old familiar logic of final desperate attempts at saving itself employed by every dying form of government and society.

ALL-RUSSIA MASS MURDER

Petersburg, November 2 (report from the Petersburg Telegraph Agency). As was reported from *Poltava* on November 1, *Cossacks attacked a number of people who had peacefully gathered in front of the prison, where the police chief had allowed them to call a gathering*, so that they could be present at the promised release of political detainees. A number of persons *were severely wounded, some of them fatally, with twenty-eight wounded* being taken to the hospital, others to their homes. Great fear and *profound embitterment* prevail among the population. From several other cities, namely Bialystok, Kiev, and Pskov, it was reported that *disturbances and unrest were bloodily suppressed by the troops.*

---

  * As indicated earlier, the Bułygin Duma would have been a purely consultative "parliament" based on extremely restricted voting rights, essentially window dressing for a continued all-powerful monarchy.

  † "*Beruhigungsmittel*" in the original, which can also be translated as "tranquilizing device."

Petersburg, November 2. The Petersburg Telegraph Agency reports the following from Minsk, under yesterday's date: A crowd numbering about 10,000 people held a demonstration today in front of the prison and demanded, along with a threat to storm the prison, that political prisoners be freed. When the crowd subsequently began new demonstrations in front of the railroad station and demanded that the soldiers leave and fired revolver shots at them, the crowd was dispersed by a *salvo.* As a result, a number of persons were *killed* or *wounded.*

PLUNDERING BY SOLDIERS AND POLICE

Petersburg, November 1. The Petersburg Telegraph Agency reports the following from *Kazan: Plundering and bloodletting* prevailed today on Mozvenskaya Street. Shots were fired at the district court and the chess club buildings, on which occasion a number of persons were wounded and many high school students were injured. *Pools of blood covered the snow, and this was mainly in front of the seminary.* Wild excesses, to which the stores especially fell victim, took place late in the evening when only police and Cossacks were still on the streets. Telephone calls for help from the owners of the stores to the police administration remained without any results. An eyewitness confirms that the soldiers were plundering and that the assistant police chief threatened to shoot at them when he intervened to put an end to this misconduct. Many stores, private homes, and even public buildings were riddled with bullet holes. It is impossible to determine who led this activity, but it is certain that *the police and Cossacks were unleashed without any plan or definite orders. They were shooting blindly without any provocation at peaceful pedestrians in the streets.* In the zemstvo hospital twenty-five wounded persons were lying there, being cared for. *The indignation of the public is universal, even among convinced conservatives, who condemn the behavior of the police in the sharpest manner.* They had misbehaved when no higher authority was present. The members of the municipal council appealed to the governor. The latter explained that the police chief had exceeded his authority and that a judicial investigation against him had begun. The troops and the Cossacks were ordered not to come out of the barracks, and the municipal administration may organize a militia. Those who had been arrested had their freedom restored. A large crowd of people marched on the police station, and there they took away whatever weapons they could find and brought them to the municipal council building.

"CONSERVATIVE" PROVOCATIONS

Moscow, November 1 (report from the Petersburg Telegraph Agency). *Social Democratic orators [explained that they] would recognize complete victory only if all political demands were met.* Gatherings for the purpose of *arming a people's militia* are underway. In the city, the *liberals(?)** are organizing marches with red banners, during which revolutionary songs are sung. The conservatives* (that is the Black Hundred gangs of the police*), carrying banners with the colors of the national flag along with a portrait of the tsar, are also organizing demonstrations at which the national anthem is sung.* Yesterday a conflict broke out between two such marches at the Iverskaya Gate. The conservatives were put to flight by the liberals who fired shots at them. A confrontation also occurred on Myasnitskaya Street *between a number of printers on the one hand and some dragoons and Cossacks on the other. Ten of the demonstrators were wounded by the unsheathed weapons of the troops. The crowd organized demonstrations further on in front of the Technical School, where the widow of the veterinarian [Nikolai] Bauman was killed by shots* that were aimed at the crowd gathered around the coffin of Bauman.[†]

AN "AMNESTY" AMID STREAMS OF BLOOD

Warsaw, November 2 (from a private dispatch to *Vorwärts*). Yesterday morning large assemblies of people gathered and at first were suppressed by the police. In the process seven persons were shot and killed and several wounded. In the afternoon, the patrols were withdrawn. At once large crowds of people marched through the streets singing. Amid universal jubilation, Social Democratic speeches were made and appeals were distributed. The people and the military seemed to be united in brotherhood. In the evening the streets were brightly lighted. Large crowds of marchers appeared on Theatre Square. The theatrical performance was interrupted, and the orchestra played for the crowd from the balcony of the theater building. The crowd demanded of the police chief Myers that all those arrested for political "crimes" should be freed, and 400 persons were set free. But the crowd demanded that all prisoners be freed, and assumed a threatening attitude. Suddenly Cossacks appeared, and also dragoons. They attacked the crowd with weapons bared. Six people were killed, twenty-three badly wounded, and several slightly wounded. Scenes of repulsive horror ensued.

IN SOUTHERN RUSSIA AND IN RUSSIAN CENTRAL ASIA

Petersburg, November 2 (W.T.O.).[‡] From *Rostov-on-Don* it was reported that an attempt made yesterday by the clergy to calm down the good people by

---

  *   The parenthetical question mark is in the original.
  †   Bauman was a popular Moscow Bolshevik assassinated by the Black Hundreds during the days immediately following the tsar's "constitutional manifesto," shortly after he was released from prison. The enormous funeral procession honoring him and bearing his coffin to a cemetery is described in Sidney Harcave, *The Russian Revolution of 1905*, p. 200.
  ‡   Wolff's Telegraph Office.

holding a church procession remained unsuccessful. Excesses became ever-more serious; plundering continued, and the city found itself in the hands of the people. *Shooting began immediately. The hospitals became filled with dead and wounded.* It is dangerous to go out into the streets; several houses are in flames. From *Kazan* it was reported that *a militia consisting of 400 workers and students has been formed, bearing weapons* that were taken from the police. During the night, the troops of this militia patrolled the streets. Nowhere was there any disturbance of the peace.

From *Kurgan* and *Tashkent* it was reported that *the military used armed force to disperse peaceful demonstrations, and many persons were wounded in the process.*

MASSACRES OF JEWS

Petersburg, November 2 (report from the Petersburg Telegraph Agency). From several provincial cities, in particular *Rostov-on-Don, Kiev, Novgorod, and Kherson*, news dispatches have arrived here, reporting that among the population *a growing bitterness against the Jews* is making itself evident. The Jews were blamed for behaving in an antipatriotic manner, for causing disturbances of the peace by political agitation, and for instigating and leading the revolutionary movement. *In the cities mentioned above, houses and stores belonging to Jews were plundered and some of them were set on fire. Many persons were killed or wounded.*

Petersburg, November 2 (report from the Petersburg Telegraph Agency). *The plundering of the houses and stores of Israelites* on the main streets of *Novgorod* happened because some of the Jews (i.e., the Social Democratic workers) organized a demonstration. The Jews were marching around the city with red banners and giving revolutionary speeches.

Kiev, November 1. The attacks on Jews [*Judenhetze*] began here at midnight on Tuesday.[*] The houses around the market were burned down. *Not a single Jewish store was spared.* The riffraff stole goods from the stores, *with the police themselves participating.* The plundering began again on Wednesday evening. The Jews fired from the balconies of their houses, shooting at the troops and the so-called loyals (i.e., the plundering mob), who returned the fire. The riffraff forcibly broke into several houses and *threw the Jews out onto the street.* The latter threatened bloody vengeance against the Christians on Thursday. The dwelling places of a number of wealthy Jews were demolished, among them those of Baron [Horace] Günzburg and the well-known industrialists Brodsky, Zaitsev, and Epstein.

---

[*] The tsar's "constitutional" manifesto, signed on Sunday evening, did not become widely known until Monday, October 31, 1905.

THE STRUGGLE GOES FURTHER ALL ALONG THE LINE

Moscow, November 2 (report from the Petersburg Telegraph Agency). Numerous gatherings, or assemblies, were held here today at which the tsar's manifesto was criticized and the point was made that it offered no satisfactory guarantees. Without exception, people hold the view that it is necessary to win the guarantees, which are being demanded unconditionally, and especially that they can be won *through the pressure of walkouts and strikes*. Social Democratic speakers perceived that they had won a complete victory above all by demanding full satisfaction of all political demands. Gatherings for the purpose of *arming a people's militia* are also underway.

Riga, November 2. Yesterday's huge rally, which was anticipated with such great alarm, was attended by about 50,000 persons, but it proceeded peacefully. A resolution was adopted *to continue the general strike*, with the exception of businesses supplying food, until such time as the promises made by the manifesto were successfully guaranteed. Yesterday there arrived the first railroad train from Petersburg [since the end of the rail strike].

Moscow, November 2. At a meeting of lawyers, a decision was made to demand the dismissal of Trepov and legal prosecution against the Metropolitan of Moscow for preaching anti-canonical sermons calling for attacks against the opposition. Further, a resolution was adopted to approach the State Duma with a request that it form a people's militia and, if the Duma refused, to take steps in that direction themselves. Today traffic resumed on rail lines from Moscow to Kursk–Kiev–Voronezh, to Ryazan and the Urals, and to Vyazma.

FIRST GENERAL STRIKE IN FINLAND

Helsinki, November 2. The situation continues to be very serious. *The universal walkout has spread even to the police.* Public services for the preservation of order generally will be maintained by a militia consisting of students and workers. Coffeehouses have been transformed into meeting places. *Yesterday the governor and the senate, in the presence of a huge crowd, officially submitted their resignations.*

Copenhagen, November 2. The telegraph administration reports as follows: Telegraphic communications between Fredericia [in Denmark] and Petersburg have been *broken off by the strikers*. The connection between Fredericia and Libau still exists. Libau is connected with Petersburg.

Stockholm, November 2. [The Swedish paper] *Svenska Dagbladet* reports as follows: According to telegrams to shipping companies here, *maritime communications with Finland have been broken off because of the general strike.*

Helsinki, November 2. In all the cities of Finland, for the maintenance of order, *citizens' guards* will be organized. The voice of the people has been raised up high.

Helsinki, November 2. A deputation has demanded that the governor-general [of Finland] resign from his post. He replied that as a soldier he could not do so without permission from the monarch, but he vowed to submit his request for permission to the emperor immediately.

A telegram from Wolff's Telegraph Office brings the following "reassuring" news: Petersburg, November 2. *The strike committee has decided to end the strike at twelve noon tomorrow.* This is a questionable report, which, without further confirmation, is not to be believed.

ABSOLUTISM IS ASKING FOR CONFIDENCE, AND MAKING THREATS

Petersburg, November 2 (report from the Petersburg Telegraph Agency). Today there appeared a *government communiqué* in which the regime appealed to that section of the Russian population which loves law and order and expressed the hope that society would support the government in its effort to introduce a new system of public order, which society had long been demanding and which would be possible only after the full restoration of order. The communiqué stated further on *that certain elements were attempting to undermine confidence in the regime and cause popular unrest.* If, nevertheless, a majority of the people come to the aid of the government, a rapid improvement of the situation will occur. However, if that does not happen, the government *does not take responsibility for any negative consequences,* and [in that case] the tasks that stand before us would be carried out less quickly than would be desirable.

Freedom Is Born in the Tsar's Empire[*]

What does the tsarist "state-of-law" look like at this very moment? Pacifying "communiqués"—with the simultaneous imposition of the state of siege—an amnesty for political criminals—with the exception of warriors from the whole current period of revolution—decrees about press freedom—while knifing peaceful citizens to the ground—and the "unassailable principles" of the constitutional manifesto—accompanied by a general outbreak of mob violence against the Jews. This, indeed, is the kingdom of the "freedom-granting" knout.

Yet this grotesque piece of theater is merely the logical expression of the situation's inner contradictions. With a struggle, absolutism can still keep its head above water for a few moments, but only by making libertarian promises and concessions. Yet these concessions signify a denial of its own self, as tsarism's means of survival consist purely of so many means of destruction. That is why we don't progress beyond these mere promises, and as these naturally only serve to fire up the revolution anew, instead of pacifying, such libertarian promises are followed with deadly certainty by relapses into the naked terror regime of the whip.

Despite this, *political freedom has in fact already been born in Russia*—amid the muddle of tsarism's breakdown—and this freedom is growing by the hour. It has not been "granted" by absolutism, but rather consolidated by the workers under Social Democratic leadership. Mass assemblies in the streets of all major cities have become a daily occurrence. The papers are already being published in several cities—including Warsaw—without any censorship, which they have freed themselves from by the work of their own hands. Prisoners have been liberated by a storming mass of people. Political freedom has been *forcibly put into practice* through the decisiveness of the urban, class-conscious, working class. In order to grasp the inner logic and *developmental process* running through the events, we need to be able to see through the colorful picture of contradictory news, through the *details* to the meaning of individual moments, and on, to penetrate the meaning of the *phases* of the revolution—phases which are now being measured in *days* and hours. *The revolution in Russia triumphs as a movement of the modern, metropolitan workforce*—this proves true not only with regard to this revolution's general contents, but also to each of its steps, in each individual moment!

---

* This article was first published in Luxemburg' *Vorwärts* column "The Revolution in Russia," No. 259, November 4, 1905, under the title "Die Geburt der Freiheit im Zarenreich." It is translated (by Henry Holland) from Luxemburg's *Gesammelte Werke*, Vol. 6, pp. 616–20.

THE AMNESTY

Peterhof, November 3 (report by the Petersburg Telegraph Agency). An imperial ukase regarding the granting of an amnesty has been signed.

Petersburg, November 3. The government approved the amnesty that had been demanded, and which has already been signed by the tsar. *Those prisoners sentenced for political attacks after 1899 are excluded from the amnesty(!!).*

MURDERING SCOUNDRELS WORRYING ABOUT MORALITY

Petersburg, November 3 (report by the Petersburg Telegraph Agency). A government communiqué explains how participating in street demonstrations needs now to be seen completely differently, in light of the October 30 *manifesto* creating *non-negotiable foundations* for the development of Russian life, based on rule of law and on the legal system. Such participation can only benefit the forces of disorder, which is why *the participation of school students* from middle and lower-level institutions of learning at such rallies *should be condemned on moral grounds.* Even if society's attention were not already focused on such participation, the state would still be threatened by a growing number of people whose *respect for authority and order* is being radically shaken in the classroom already. The government is calling on all citizens to observe self-discipline and to busy themselves with peaceful activities.

THE PRESS DECREE

Petersburg, November 3. *The public can view the exact wording of the decree granting press freedom* in the editorial office of the *Novoye Vremya* [New Times]. Count Witte requested of the chief editors of the Petersburg papers that they evaluate its contents and, if necessary, make proposals to him for changes. The chief editors will subsequently meet Count Witte this evening to discuss the matter.

STATE OF SIEGE IN ODESSA!

Odessa, November 3. The imposition of the state of siege stipulates that no one is allowed to be seen on the street after 7 p.m., that anyone who appears at a window or on a balcony after this time will be shot at, and that light must be extinguished in houses at 9 p.m. Yesterday, police and troops confiscated arms from over 5,000 persons who were carrying revolvers.

Petersburg, November 3 (report by the Petersburg Telegraph Agency). The *censorship* of the newspapers' official telegrams has been rescinded.

RIOTS AGAINST JEWS AND A MASSACRE

Petersburg, November 3 (report by the Petersburg Telegraph Agency). New information reached us during the night about attacks against Jews. In *Smolensk*, the city's autonomous administration managed to dampen down the violence by intervening energetically. In *Rostov-on-Don*, several streets look now like piles of ruins and the new market has been burned down. *The attacks against the Jews are continuing in Mariopol, in Donetsk* and in *Kiev*, where grenades were also thrown at Cossacks. *Twelve persons were killed* and *forty-four wounded* in Kiev yesterday.

In *Poltava*, a crowd of the people penetrated into the prison, during which *thirty-eight persons were wounded*. Disturbances also arose in *Uman*, with demonstrators demanding the release of political prisoners.

Warsaw, November 3. *Demonstrations on the streets* lasted until well into the night. A military post in the Saxon Gardens was attacked by revolver shots, which it responded to by firing off a salvo. *Many persons were killed or wounded*.

INSURRECTION IN SOUTH RUSSIA

Petersburg, November 3. Reports in from *Mykolaiv* state that *open unrest* reigns throughout the city. Machine-gun fire can be heard on the streets, where *numerous dead* and *wounded* are lying around. About 200 grenades have been thrown, causing a large number of people to lose their lives, or leaving them horribly maimed. There is no consolation to be found anywhere in the city.

INSURRECTION IN ALL THE PROVINCES

Petersburg, November 2. The latest telegrams from the provinces report on sometimes more, sometimes fewer, *disturbances* today and yesterday. The military intervened in many cities, leading to more *deaths and injuries*, principally in *Kaluga, Grodno, Rybinsk, Tver, Minsk, Kurgan, Bialystok, Baku,* and *Sevastopol*. Clashes also broke out between members of different political parties in many cities. Other telegrams reported on the continuance of disturbances directed *against the Jews*, in Ryeshin, Vitebsk, Romny, Kiev, Vilnius, Kirovohrad, *and particularly* Odessa, where *plainclothes police officers* were recognized.

THE FUNERAL PROCESSION OF THE TSARIST "CONSTITUTION"

Tallinn, November 2 (report by the Petersburg Telegraph Agency). A crowd of around 30,000 persons remained today for several hours on the spot where *the participants in the rallies fell, after they had been shot by troops*. The crowd sang laments beside the *thirty-eight coffins* that were laid out there. The streetlights and the houses were hung with black cloth and with innumerable wreathes of mourning. Candles could be seen burning in the windows, as the funeral procession stretched out for several kilometers. The city authorities contributed to this act of grieving, and shops and public institutions were closed.

Minsk, November 1 (report by the Petersburg Telegraph Agency). *Burials are taking place here almost on an* hourly *basis of people who have fallen victim to the latest disturbances. The corpses are driven away on droshkies. Fifty-four corpses were lying on the Jewish cemetery. The workers have imposed a three-day mourning period for those who have been killed. Work has been suspended in public institutions.*

IN POLAND

Warsaw, November 3 (private dispatch to *Vorwärts*). People are printing newspapers without censorship. Social Democracy is holding *large meetings of the people in all districts*, at which it is calling for resilience in the struggle, and in the general strike. The speeches are greeted by tremendous cheering by the population. "National democratic" and the hypocritical "god-fearing" tendencies are agitating against Social Democracy with all their strength, while admonishing for the maintenance of peace and for giving up the general strike.

Częstochowa, November 3 (private telegram to *Vorwärts*). *The general strike continues.* Social Democracy is able to have its pamphlets printed in a legal printing works. Yesterday red posters could be seen hung up throughout the city: "The Social Democracy of Poland and Lithuania invites the working people to a large assembly of the people at the municipal merchant's casino." The police allowed the posters to stay hanging. The assembly took place with over 2,000 participants. The speakers were met with thunderous applause. Colossal assemblies of the people also took place on the streets.

Przybiernów, November 3 (private telegram to *Vorwärts*). The legal printing works has been occupied by the Social Democrats who continue to work for the party. Pamphlets are now being printed and disseminated in an entirely open manner. *The general strike continues.* Mass meetings are taking place frequently, for example in the colliery house of the Count Renard pit. Social Democracy has publicized its solution—*immediate formation of a people's militia!* The workers are arming themselves as far as possible.

IN THE CAUCASUS

Petersburg, November 3. According to reports from *Baku*, the strike is continuing in the Caucasus. Railroad infrastructure between Tbilisi and Peti has been destroyed by the rebels and transport has been suspended.

IN FINLAND

Helsinki, November 3. The city administration has formed a welfare committee and has explained to the *strike committee* that they see themselves as now in a position to take over the maintenance of order, for which purpose 10,000 marks shall be made available. Moreover, the city administration has voted in a board of three members that will meet twice daily, which the strike committee should turn to in case of important questions.

Helsinki, November 2. At an assembly held yesterday, the motion was passed *to continue the strike until all political demands had been fulfilled.* The governor-general stated that he would send the list of demands to Petersburg today and promised to withdraw military patrols, *because order is being maintained better than ever* and the citizens' militia is sending out their own strong patrols. The minister of police submitted his request to resign. Gendarmes left the municipality of Hanko after their weapons had been removed. Gendarmes in Hämeenlinna fled to their barracks, as was also the case in Turku. The governor of Turku sent the military back, and promised that he no longer wanted to use it.

MARTIAL LAW IMPOSED

A private dispatch from the *Berl[iner] Zeitung* newspaper reports: Martial law was imposed in *Rostov-on-Don* yesterday. This measure has proven favorable, as at least some peace has prevailed in the city since then. It has not yet been possible to reestablish railroad transport.

RAILROAD TRANSPORT AT A STANDSTILL.

Katowice, November 3 (W.T.O.).* *Official report.* All railroad transport in Russia is at a *standstill.*

The *Vossischen Zeitung* has received the following: *Petersburg,* November 3. The *workers' committee* publishes the *News [Izvestia] of the Workers' Deputies Council* on a daily basis,† which is then also published in a four-page format in the *Voss[ischen] Zeitung.* Issue No. 3 from today includes the following appeal:

As we consider it necessary for the workers to be able to *organize* themselves as well as possible on the basis of the successes already achieved, and in order to arm themselves for the final struggle concerning the convocation of a Constituent Assembly,

---

*   Wollf's Telegraphic Office.

†   Although Luxemburg refers to this as a workers' "council" in the German—as "*des Arbeiterdeputiertenrates*"—instead of using the Russian term "soviet," the reference here is to that very institution.

for the purpose of founding a *democratic republic*, we call now for a *suspension of the strike*. It should be *recommenced* as soon as the right time has arrived. Furthermore, typesetters are being requested to only work in papers whose editors commit themselves to allowing the newspaper to be published *without considering the orders of the censor.*

The Revolution in Russia [November 5, 1905]*

THE FOURTH DAY OF LOOTING AND SLAUGHTER

Kiev, November 4. *Uproar and looting has been the order of the day here* for four days now already. The military shoots at *Jewish houses*, because the Jews resisted the looting by force of arms. The manager of the Imperial Bank branch telegraphed Witte to communicate that the military's passive attitude meant that Witte had to refuse any responsibility for the protection of the bank. This telegram motivated the arrest of around 190 looters, a measure which has scared the looters somewhat and has led to a decrease in the robberies.

THE REACTION STARTS TO MOVE!

Moscow, November 5. The *Monarchist Party*† publishes a declaration, in which it explains its intention to use all means to support autocracy in Russia. This is the same party that spreads the claims that the Constitutional Manifesto is a forgery made by Witte. The *Moskovskiye Vedemosti* [Moscow News], this party's organ, has published an extremely brisk attack against Count Witte.

ONLY TWO WOUNDED!

Warsaw, November 3 (report by the Petersburg Telegraph Agency). *Only two persons have been wounded today.* Teachers at municipal schools have passed a motion to teach in Polish from this moment on. A large assembly of railroad civil servants passed a motion *to strike for as long as it takes for all the people's wishes to be fulfilled.*

CHIȘINĂU‡ IN FLAMES!

London, November 4. According to reports from Odessa, *Chișinău* is said to have been completely destroyed by fire. On Friday, street battles raged for the whole day in Odessa, between the liberals and the so-called loyalists. *The number of dead and wounded is* estimated at around 500. The German and the

---

* These notes were published in Luxemburg's column "The Revolution in Russia" in *Vorwärts*. The original title of the article is "Die Revolution in Rußland"—one of many articles that she published under the same title in 1905. It is translated (by Henry Holland) from Luxemburg's *Gesammelte Werke*, Vol. 6, pp. 625–8.

† This is a reference to the Russian Monarchist Union, a far-right organization that was founded in February 1905 to provide support for the tsarist authorities. It especially targeted Jews for attack, which it held responsible for the revolution.

‡ Then known as Kishinev, a major city in what is now Moldova. At the time, it was the capital of the province of Moldavia, which the tsars had conquered from the Ottoman Turkish rulers of Romania.

French consuls requested their superior authorities to send the ships stationed in the Bosphorus.

Odessa, November 4. During the course of yesterday, the *outrages of the mob* continued. A large number of Jewish shops, including large businesses in central streets, were looted; several of the city's factories have been burned to the ground. The hospitals are spilling over with the wounded. Again, several persons have been killed. The consulates and the hotels are guarded by troops.

Reports of severe mob outrages have also been received from *Chişinău,* Nikolaev, Sevastopol, Rostov, and Kirovohrad, crimes principally directed against Jewish businesses and shops.

Petersburg, November 4 (report by the Petersburg Telegraph Agency). Reports from the provinces sound more peaceful. In Rostov, where the disturbances have caused damages to the value of millions, railroad transport has restarted. In Riga, a rally took place yesterday with 150,000 persons participating. Speeches about the significance of the manifesto were held in seven languages from thirty-four stages. People greeted the troops with shouts of "Long live the army!" Railroad transport has recommenced in Novorossiysk.

THE AMNESTY

Has now been proclaimed. A *telegram* reports the following from *Petersburg,* November 4, 11:24 a.m: The enacting of the amnesty also covers, among other contents, all crimes carried out against the person of the emperor or against other members of the imperial household up to and including October 30. Further, it also covers the crime of participation in secret societies formed with the purpose of overthrowing the current order.

The ukase lists specific categories of persons sentenced for political crimes, who will *receive a full pardon;* for other persons sentenced for severe crimes, *major reductions of sentence* will come into force; *persons sentenced for minor political misdemeanors will receive a full pardon.*

THE GENERAL STRIKE SHALL CONTINUE!

Riga. The situation here has still not improved. A meeting of the people held yesterday evening passed the motion *to continue the general strike.* This has been followed by the closure of numerous pharmacies. Disturbing news is arriving continuously from the provinces.

THE PEOPLE'S MILITIA

The *Russian Correspondence* reports: "Voluntary Protection of the People." According to a notice in the *Novoye Vremya* [New Times], a "voluntary people's guard" has formed in Russia, consisting of around 100,000 members. The delegates of the Moscow section of this "voluntary" institution have recently submitted an address to the tsar, in which they express their thanks for the establishing of the Imperial Duma, and ask him to accept the gift of a painting of a saint from them. It would be very interesting to find out how many members of this "liberal guard" are employed by the police department.

SLAUGHTER OF THE JEWS

Petersburg, November 3. The *semi-official* Petersburg Telegraph Agency reports: according to a telegram from *Tomsk*, troops supporting the terrorist party attacked a gathering of liberals today. The liberals fled into a railroad administration building. *Shots were fired by both sides.* When, during the course of the evening, the building was set alight, a battalion received the order to attack, which lead to numerous persons being wounded. The theater was also vandalized and smashed up.

In *Batumi* today, a clash erupted between demonstrators and the military, in which people were both killed and wounded.

In *Moscow*, the governor issued a declaration today, admonishing the population to desist from further demonstrations and to take up again their familiar ways of life, so that they could enjoy the fruits of the new decree.

GERMAN IMPERIAL PROPERTY IN DANGER

Frankfurt am Main, November 4. In light of disturbances in recent days in Odessa, Rostov and other Russian cities, which have also threatened both the lives and the property of German imperial citizens, the imperial government has been in dialogue with the Russian government, as announced previously, in order to ensure special protection for the aforementioned imperial citizens. This request was then met, while the battles in Batumi raged. (*Frankf[urter] Zeitung*)

Of course! The imperial government is rather quicker to react to protect the threatened "property" of imperial German business people and other bourgeois, compared to when the issue at hand is the *life* of a noble revolutionary and proletarian, like Kasprzak!

THREATS

As reported from *Saratov*, the governor announced today that he would suppress all disturbances and lootings by force of arms. Revolutionaries held speeches despite this announcement, containing sharp attacks against the emperor, which were then followed by looting of the Jews' apartments and shops. A grenade was thrown at the troops and revolver shots were fired off. The military returned fire, injuring people in the process.

In Kiev, too, the governor announced that he would crush any attempt to initiate disturbances.

As reported from *Yaroslavl*, the population has been rioting against school students and the Jews for three days now. Jewish houses and shops were looted out entirely.

At assemblies in *Ivanovo* and *Voznesensk*, clashes broke out today with Cossacks.

From *Odessa, Kiev, Yevpatoria*, and numerous other cities, reports have been received that pogroms took place in these localities yesterday, *directed against the Jews*.

The Murderous Cads of the "Constitutional State"*

BUŁYGIN GOES—TREPOV STAYS

After the secret tsarist constitution has been shown to be politically bankrupt, it is natural that the father of the infamous "Imperial Duma" follows his child into the kingdom of the shades.† Bułygin's farewell‡ also means the farewell to the swindle of the constitution. Trepov will indeed remain as lord over the situation, which means the blatant rule-of-the-sword, slaughters of the Jews, and mass murders in public squares.

Petersburg, November 4 (report by the Petersburg Telegraph Agency). An imperial ukase accepts the request from *Bułygin, Minister of the Interior, to be relieved of his post. [Pytor] Durnovo,*§ who had been Bułygin's aide until now, will temporarily fill Bułygin's post.

Petersburg, November 5. The city Duma spent the whole day yesterday informing themselves about the means *with which they could prevent the spilling of blood at the funeral ceremony today.* In this, the Duma turned for support to *Witte*, who declared that he *would permit the rally, and that in any case it was not in his remit to dispose of the troops.* Whereupon the Duma decided to publish an appeal to the population, and sent a delegation to *Trepov.*

A BLOODBATH FOILED

A mass demonstration of the workers was planned for November 5 in Petersburg, to correspond with the burial of the victims of the tsar's thugs. Trepov evidently prepared to turn this opportunity into a bloodbath, a general slaughter of the revolutionary working class in the capital city. The workers' leaders decided, however—correctly recognizing tsarism's intentions—to only go into decisive battle at a point that would be favorable for the working class, a point in time when the armament of the proletarian militias of the people would be more complete.

---

* These news posts were published in Luxemburg's *Vorwärts* column "The Revolution in Russia," in issue No. 261, November 7, 1905, under the title "Der Verfassungstaat der Mordbuben." It is translated (by Henry Holland) from Luxemburg's *Gesammelte* Werke, Vol. 6, pp. 629–32.

† A reference to a famous scene in the ballet *La Bayadère* by Marius Petipa, in which Solor (the warrior) enters into a dream-like euphoria in contemplating his lover, the temple maiden Nikiya, and sees her spirit amid the peaks of the Himalayas called "the kingdom of the shades." It was first performed by the Imperial Ballet at the Imperial Bolshoi Kamenny Theatre in St. Petersburg on February 4, 1877.

‡ Bułygin was fired as minister of the interior on October 30, 1905 (new style), after the government proved unable to contain the strike wave that swept Russia in September and October. The tsar appointed in his place a far more reactionary figure, Durnovo.

§ Durnovo served as minister of the interior from October 30, 1905 to April 22, 1906.

Petersburg, November 4 (report by the Petersburg Telegraph Agency). The Council [Soviet] of Workers' Deputies has *cancelled* the rally planned for Petersburg for Sunday, *and reserves the right to schedule this rally for a later point of time, when it would seem advisable to the committee.*

THE COUNTERREVOLUTION MOBILIZES REACTIONARY ELEMENTS

Petersburg, November 6. A *government communiqué* invites the authors of the disturbances to apply *moderation*, and calls for *loyal subjects to contribute to the pacification of the country. The government expresses its wish to be able to rely on the majority of the population, prudent as they are and focused on peace, in its implementation of the reforms.* Knowing that this majority holds dear Russia's future development based on civic freedoms and on territorial integrity. The government is counting especially on the support of the *press*, which must grasp that the current situation demands a unification of the mental power of the whole of the people.

Moscow, November 5 (report by the Petersburg Telegraph Agency). *Several students, chased by a crowd of reactionaries*, fled into a college for engineers and shot from here at their attackers, who were smashing in the college's windows with stones. *Cossacks were called*, who surrounded the building.

Warsaw, November 5. The *"national democratic"* and *"loyal"* elements of the bourgeois, nobility and petit bourgeois have organized a large demonstration today under the motto of *"unity of the people"* and *enmity against the Social Democratic "agitation of the people."*

THE COUNTERREVOLUTION MOBILIZES MEN OF THE CLOTH

Petersburg, November 5. The synod has commanded *the orthodox clergy to block the population's struggle*, as it degenerates into a civil war, *with all means at its disposal.* Warsaw's governor-general has been informed by telegraph that *the immediate release of Catholic clergy*, confined to monasteries due to religious offenses by order of the civil authorities, would be appropriate.

THE COUNTERREVOLUTION ORGANIZES ARSON AND MURDER

Baku, November 5 (report by the Petersburg Telegraph Agency). While *conservative Russian and Muslim workers* (or, to put it in real German: police stooges) *with national flags and pictures of the emperor* organized a rally, other individuals shot at and threw grenades at houses of Armenians. *Whereupon the agitated "workers" set fire to the house of an Armenian; the fire spread to twenty further houses.*

The "pro-manifesto party"* *looted four shops.* During these proceedings, roughly *twenty persons were killed or injured* and several of the looters were arrested.

Tbilisi, November 5 (report by the Petersburg Telegraph Agency). When *a number of reactionaries with pictures of the emperor moved through the city today,* revolver shots and grenades were targeted at them. *Troops who were accompanying the procession responded to the shooting by killing ten persons and wounding around thirty.*

Tbilisi, November 5 (report by the Petersburg Telegraph Agency). Yesterday, during *alternating reactionary and revolutionary rallies in Vladikavkaz,* both parties collided. Both sides fired off shots, *killing four persons and injuring seventeen.*

Ivanovo-Voznesensk, November 5 (report by the Petersburg Telegraph Agency). Disturbances directed *against the Jews* commenced today. Numerous houses with shops attached to them were looted; and Jews were also *killed and wounded.*

Warsaw, November 5. A few pathetic miscreants, who intended to call for a pogrom against the Jews, were battered to death by the workers.

Warsaw, November 6. Persons arriving here from the scene report that the scenes of terror in *Kiev* continue. *People are looting both day and night, and the rabble is ruling the streets, without intervention by either military or the police.*

Moscow, November 6. As reported in the *Russkoye Slovo* [Russian Word] from *Odessa,* looting continued throughout the whole city yesterday. Gangs of felons roamed the streets carrying out all manner of *atrocities. Children were torn away from their mothers and cut up into bits.* Doctors, nurses and priests were killed in the presence *of plainclothes police agents;* everything going was looted and stolen to the last. We can assume that the disturbances were *organized* by *police spies.*

THE GENERAL STRIKE PERSISTS!

Brest, November 5. Delegates from the *workers in the arsenal* voted in principle *for the general strike.*

Łódź, November 4. On order of the authorities here in the city, forty-nine detainees have been released from prison. *The strike is holding out.*

Moscow, November 4 (report by the Petersburg Telegraph Agency). *All restaurants and hostelries selling meals* are closed because of the *food workers' strike.*

---

*   Presumably, the Russian Monarchist Union.

THE LABOR PARTY IN FINLAND DOMINATES THE SITUATION!

Helsinki, November 5. *After negotiations between the bourgeois Constitutional [Democratic Party]* and the Labor Party,† the latter published an ultimatum today, in which it stated that it would vote in a provisional government and would offer the Constitutional [Democratic] Party two seats in this government. The Constitutional [Democratic Party] has refused meanwhile to take part in such a government.*

THE PROLETARIAN "DICTATORSHIP"

Przybiernów, November 5 (private dispatch to *Vorwärts*). Here, in the Dąbrowa Region, Social Democracy has constituted a kind of "provisional government." Countless representatives from all classes of citizens come to the office, opened in all haste, to request permission to hold meetings, to inquire about directives and news, and to receive the latest proclamations. The working class is ceaselessly putting on huge meetings.

THE INSURRECTION AMONG SAILORS AND SOLDIERS

This semi-official telegram reports:

Tbilisi, November 4. *Participants at a patriotic* (that means organized by police stooges) *rally*, who paraded through the streets of *Baku* with a picture of the emperor, were ambushed by twenty *sailors from the Caspian Fleet*, armed with carbine guns. The sailors were disarmed and arrested by the *troops accompanying the demonstrators.*

Shots aimed at Russian and Tatar pro-manifesto supporters came from *houses lived in by Armenians*, which were then *put under cannon fire.*

Kronstadt, November 5. *A crowd of sailors, soldiers, and workers* looted several buildings (probably *public* buildings—the editors) this evening. The military, which had been sent to suppress these breaches of the peace, fired *off many shots and cordoned off a number of streets.*

The *Berliner Zeitung* receives the following telegraph from Paris. *As reported in Le Matin, a whole regiment of infantry has gone over to join the revolutionaries in Liepāja. A division of Cossacks, which wanted to move against the crowd, was forced to flee by the mutineers.*

---

* The right-of-center Constitutional Democratic Party was founded on October 12–18, 1905, through a merger of several liberal organizations. It was also known as the Party of People's Freedom. Its politics mirrored those of the Russian Constitutional Democrats, or Kadeks.

† This refers to the Social Democratic Party of Finland (Soumen Sosialidemokraattinen Puolue), founded at Albo in 1899. Prior to 1903 it was known as the Finnish Labor Party (Suomen Työväenpuolue).

PARTIAL RECOMMENCEMENT OF RAILROAD TRANSPORT

Berlin, November 5. The Bromberg Railroad Division has made the following statement: They are now again accepting goods intended for transit to Russia via Prostki, *but only those intended for stations on the southwest railroads, with the exceptions of Odessa and Kiev.*

Warsaw, November 6. *The first train* arrived yesterday *from Petersburg*, with further trains following today. According to rumors, this means that the Poles should be entitled to significant concessions. (The government obviously wants to win over the "well-meaning elements," in order to use them against the working class in Poland.)

The Political Mass Strike[*]

That the political mass strike as a means of workers' struggle, which we have recently been able to observe, has so quickly gained recognition is unique among the phenomena of party life. It is unique not just among party comrades but also among researchers. What is remarkable is not the question's novelty, because, quite the opposite of being new, it has been under discussion for a very long time—even causing vehement arguments at international congresses twelve years ago. It was also discussed within our party, with the conversation tending toward whether the mass strike could, for example, be used to fight for universal suffrage in the Prussian parliament. What is remarkable is the way in which the mass strike has been suddenly included as a means of class struggle.

Not too long ago, this method was seen as something foreign to the proletarian-socialist class struggle, something inessential that couldn't even be discussed,[†] and now we share the feeling that the political mass strike is no lifeless being, but represents rather one bit of a lively conflict. What led to such a rapid turnaround? The Russian Revolution! In Russia people also used to share the same views about the political mass strike as held by us. Although people knew very well that revolution would break out in Russia and that this would only run its course with the use of force, people didn't know which form this would take. Now, after the glorious 22 of January which has inscribed itself with golden letters into the history books, we can clearly see which form the violent struggle for the overthrowing of Russian absolutism is taking. The size of the success of the political mass strike, as used in the Russian Revolution, has brought about this turnaround in how people perceive this political instrument.

What lies behind the fact that slogans of the political mass strike capture our attention so suddenly and so immediately? It must be a large realignment in class relations, causing workers to look instinctively for new weapons with which to fight their battles. In short, two opposing tendencies have surfaced inside our party recently, one exemplified in the person of Eduard Bernstein, the diligent propagandist of the politically demonstrative mass strike, the other personified in Dr. [Raphael] Friedeberg.[‡] In the political mass strike, Bernstein sees the tool

---

[*]   This speech of November 7, 1905 was given at a public assembly in the polling office of Leipzig City Center—a so-called "House of the People." It was first published in *Vorwärts*, No. 259, November 8, 1905. It is translated (by Henry Holland) from Luxemburg's *Gesammelte Werke*, Vol. 6, pp. 633–7.

[†]   The main reason being that the mass strike was generally associated with the political perspective of anarchism.

[‡]   Although Friedeberg began his career in the SPD associated with the moderate wing of

for fighting for political rights and for fighting off the ruling class's constant theft of such rights. The opposite position has its base in the trade unions and found its expression in the Cologne Congress,* the summary of its argument running as follows: The general strike is something very dangerous and ruinous for the workers' movement.

The more it seems that each position rules out the tenability of the other, the more erroneous this assumption actually turns out to be. Instead, they proceed from the same foundation, an anarchistic worldview, which observes things hanging in the air. According to the anarchistic perspective, a general strike—which certainly is the anarchists' cure-all—can be generated, or ended, or refused, just as the workers want it. This conception of the mass strike does not see it as a product of historical development and necessity, but rather as a means that can be applied, or indeed ignored arbitrarily, at any time. The same logic finds its expression when the trade unions and leaders declare that we don't want the general strike at all, and reckon that they have banished it from this world with a ten-line resolution. This is the same conception that states that the tactics—which means the methods—used in class struggle are not inter-linked with the theory or the aims of that conflict, so they can be alternated or applied arbitrarily. This is the whole ahistorical, bourgeois way of conceptual-izing things. Our opportunistic comrades take up the same position when they say that although principles must be protected, tactics do not have to take their lead from them.

Marxist socialists have an utterly different conception of things. If you were to ask one of these beings if they supported the general strike, then you would not get a yes or no answer, as you would from the anarchists, but rather the response that we would first need to familiarize ourselves with the relations, to see whether such a method was demanded by historical necessity. The incorpo-ration of such a method into the weapons of class struggle does not, as we see, depend on whether individuals want it or don't want it; instead, it is develop-ments in relations that force this method onto the workers.

We are moving toward the highest escalation of societal relations. We should not permit ourselves to lose sight of foreign politics. The Russo-Japanese War has led to a colossal realignment in relations between powers. It has pushed

---

the party, by 1904 he worked closely with the Free Association of German Trade Unions (FVdG), a left-wing (and more militant) rival to the SPD-associated Free Trade Unions. In 1904–1905 he strongly argued for the adoption of the mass strike by the SPD. He left the SPD in 1907 and became an adherent to what he called "anarcho-socialism."

* The Fifth Congress of the Trade Unions of Germany took place in Cologne from May 22–7, 1905. A resolution at the Congress stated: "The Congress regards the general strike, as rep-resented by anarchists and other people without any experience in the area of economic battle, as not worthy of discussion; furthermore, the congress warns the workers not to be delayed in the small, daily work of strengthening workers' organizations by taking in and disseminating such ideas."

Asia's young military power into the foreground and has made an essential contribution to toppling Russian absolutism. Since 1895, when Japan was cheated out of the fruits of its victory,* the major powers brought about an inner, larger aggravation of the circumstances in the Far East. Until then the hotspot of international politics was beside the Bosphorus. However, since 1895 the Far East has caught our attention.† This proves that the old world politics and world-economics—as Marx called it‡—have stepped over the borders of Europe and the world hotspot has relocated to the Far East.

Given that [Jean] Jaurès bases his peace propaganda on the peoples' increasing insight, due to peace prevailing in Europe for the last thirty years, one look at the global political situation—at the major powers' increasing escalation against each other, at the insane rearmament—shows us how wrong and shortsighted Jaurès' politics is. The Russo-Japanese War showed us that this was not the end of martial struggles, but rather just the beginning of a new phase.§ Due to its victories and position of prominence, Japan will become the object of severe attacks launched by the old powers, during which we [Germany], as events at the fortresses in Jiaozhou have illustrated,¶ will no longer be mere spectators but rather participants. Which precipitates, in its turn, growing rearmament on land and on the sea, and new import duties and taxes in domestic politics; this causes a situation of permanent famine, as already exists in certain regions of Germany. The starving classes of the population, forced to nourish themselves from fungi, demonstrate the monstrous cleft between the capitalists' lifestyle, and the lifestyle of the "beneficiaries" of capital.

---

* The Sino-Japanese war for domination in Korea ended with a peace favorable to Japan at the Treaty of Shimonseki on April 17, 1895, which forced China to recognize the independence of Korea and to cede Taiwan, the Pescadores Islands, and the Liaodong Peninsula in Manchuria to Japan. However, the combined intervention of Russia, France, and Germany—all worried about Japanese expansion in East Asia—forced Japan shortly afterward to return the Liaodong Peninsula to China.

† Luxemburg is referring to herself and other anti-imperialists within the Second International. As she put it in a letter to Jogiches of January 9, 1899: "Around 1895 a basic change occurred: the Japanese opened the Chinese doors and European politics, driven by capitalist and state interests, intruded into Asia. Constantinople moved into the background. Here the conflict between states, and with it the development of politics, had an extended field before it: the conquest and partition of all of Asia became the goal which European politics pursued." See Luxemburg's *Gesammelte Briefe*, Vol. 1, p. 250.

‡ Marx spoke of the historic task of bourgeois society as the creation of a world market—and along with it, globally driven political and economic policies—from as early as the *Communist Manifesto*.

§ Luxemburg had been arguing since the late 1890s that events like the Sino-Japanese War signaled the beginning of a new series of military conflicts between states that would sooner or later upset the relatively peaceful conditions that Europe had enjoyed since the end of the Napoleonic Wars—a prescient forecast of what was to come in 1914.

¶ On November 14, 1897, Germany annexed the region of Jiaozhou, China. In a treaty on March 6, 1898, the Chinese government was forced to lease Jiaozhou Bay to the German Empire for ninety-nine years, as a naval base, and to concede the hinterland of Shandong.

When viewed from either socio-climatic corner—the Ruhr conurbation and the Saxony-Thuringia textile industry,* with its starving, boundlessly exploited proletarians, who remind us of the first pioneers of the class struggle, the silk weavers of Lyon[†]—this scenario demonstrates to us how things really stand; but they also show us the impotence and limitations of the trade union movement.

There is no difference at all between the situation of Lyon's silk weavers in the first third of the last century and our present day. We can see the big social struggle coming already, and on top of that the repercussions of the Russian Revolution, as has already been seen in Austria.[‡]

The Russian Revolution has to mean an escalation of class struggles, whether these are victorious or not. In case of victory, the revolution will certainly not create a socialist paradise, but it will—if accompanied by the creation of a modern, bourgeois state-of-law—trigger class struggles within the party with a mighty bang. From that point on, the political struggle in all modern countries will storm ahead, opening up a new era for Europe. Even if we only focus on international escalation in the Far East, [it is clear that] we are moving toward large political battles. The struggle that German Social Democracy has led until now was a role model for all other countries,[§] but we need to be conscious that it was solely tailored for parliamentarianism, and guaranteed power for us in this area. The escalation of the struggle and the application of new methods go hand-in-hand with realignment of power relations between the masses on the outside, and their representatives. The consciousness of the masses, who know that they must fight for their rights on the streets, shows that the question of whether the mass strike is useful or harmful, is hypothetical. This question will become just as superfluous as the question that used to be asked, of whether one should take part in parliamentary life or not.

Characteristic for adversaries of the political mass strike are [Karl] Frohme's[¶]

* This refers firstly to the miners' strike in the Ruhr from January 7 to February 19, 1905, consisting of around 215,000 miners. They demanded the eight-hour day, higher wages, guarantees for pit safety, and the elimination of all repression of political activity. Strikes and lockouts of 36,000 textile and tanner workers in Gera, Glauchau, Greiz, Meerane and other locations in Saxony-Thuringia in the fight for higher wages took place from October 20 to November 28, 1905. The executive of the Association of Textile Workers broke off the strike, without gains having been achieved.

† The silk weavers of Lyon rose up in April 1834, under the leadership of French proletarian secret organizations, demanding the banishment of poverty and the construction of a "social" republic. Parisian workers followed their examples. After intensive fights across the barricades, the rebels succumbed to the superior strength of the military.

‡ Under pressure from large workers' demonstrations for a democratic voting law in the whole of Austria, and partly in response to the Russian Revolution, the Austrian government announced the introduction of universal and equal suffrage in November 1905.

§ The numerous parties of the Second International were largely modeled along the lines of the SPD's Erfurt Program of 1891, which centered on the distinction between "minimum" and "maximum" demands.

¶ According to the *Hamburger Echo* of August 30, 1905, Karl Frohme lectured on the subject

deliberations at a meeting in Hamburg, where he urgently warned against playing with fire, what with this mass of explosive substance currently piled around us. All questions regarding what should be used to shut up the striking masses, etc., have apparently already been answered by Russia's practical example.

The anxiety of the unions that such struggle brings suffering or even ruination into their organizations bears witness to ignorance about these struggles, which have actually become historically necessary. It sure is a worrying sign that people in the German trade union movement are starting to look at the form [of struggle] as if it were the main issue. The petrified monsters in the English trade unions should be a cautionary tale for us all.

All organizations destroyed by the Antisocialist Laws,* including the Organization of Book Printers, who had to bow before a certain clause, came out of that same struggle strengthened tenfold. When the revolution broke out, the Russian workers had next to no organization at all—and now? Now they have trained the masses to the point that work can be stopped in an instant, one minute in this city, the next minute in the next. Today they have organizations, and although still in the first phase of construction, their core is good. We might wish the German trade unions had something of their spirit. (Quite right!)

It is evident from these deliberations that we cannot grasp things in a one-sided, mechanical fashion, and that, above all, we cannot just pay heed to domestic politics, but must also follow foreign developments.

If today, as a result of one of those well-known, sudden decisions, Russian despotism should end up being saved by German bayonets, then the German working class couldn't watch passively while the Russian people are cheated out of the prize for their struggles; they would have to take a stand, and allow the situation to teach them which method to use.

The mass strike does not *have* to be used in seizing the right to vote—it depends entirely on the situation.

But the working class must be informed about all these proceedings, so that they deserve to be called revolutionaries! Readiness is everything! (Thunderous applause, lasting a long time.)

---

of "General Strike and Political Mass Strike" on August 29, 1905 at a meeting of the wages office for joiners. He strictly rejected the political mass strike by categorizing it as an anarchist method of struggle.

* The Antisocialist Laws in Germany, in effect from 1878 to 1890, banned dozens of socialist periodicals and book publishers. It did not however ban the SPD directly, and the party made rapid gains in membership and parliamentary representation after its suspension.

The Tsar Breaks His Word Again[*]

The semi-official Russian Telegraph Agency has now communicated the guidelines covering the draft of the new voting law.

Petersburg, November 7. The *Council of Ministers* is now putting forward *additional conditions* for *elections* to the new *Imperial D[uma]*. These state that the right to vote be granted to landlords who pay a *rent tax* of at least the *third* category; to business people, who pay *second* category business tax *and* possess a *leaving certificate from a higher education institution*; to civil servants who draw a salary of *at least 1,200 roubles* in the principal cities, or at least *900 roubles* in all other localities; and to *property owners, with real estate of an estimated worth of at least 300 roubles* in towns of up to 25,000 inhabitants, or an estimated worth of at least 1,000 roubles in towns with more than 25,000 inhabitants. There *will be twenty-one workers' representatives in the D[uma], meaning roughly one for every 250,000 workers*. A district system will elect workers' representatives. The *number of members in the D[uma] will increase to 600*. The Council of Ministers has ended the negotiations about provisions concerning the abolition of preventive censorship.

This is how the tsar cashes in the promise that he made on October 30 in such a solemn manner. Back then, he promised to "*appoint those classes of the population who at present go entirely without suffrage*, whereby the *continuing development of the principle of universal suffrage* will be left up to the newly founded institution with law-making powers." Incorporating those classes into the voting system who have lived without rights up to the present day actually consists of extending voting rights to the *middle* classes of the citizenry and of the civil servants. The petty bourgeois and the lower civil servants are *excluded* from the right to vote, just as before. To top that, "granting" voting rights to 7.25 million proletarians and giving them a whole twenty-one representatives in a 600-seat D[uma] is something worse than a bad joke! This "concession" is rather a mockery of the working class, which in its struggle for freedom in the service of culture has had to shed so much of its noble blood.

That a "universal" voting law of this sort will be interpreted as something other than a shocking provocation was unquestionably the claim of the "liberal" Mr. *Witte* himself. If the struggle is continued and new slaughters take place, then this sad statesman and lackey of the tsar must take responsibility for the spilling of blood!

---

[*]   This unsigned report about proceedings in Russia was certainly penned by Luxemburg. This article first appeared in *Vorwärts*, No. 262, November 8, 1905, under the title "Neuer Wortbuch des Zaren." It is translated (by Henry Holland) from Luxemburg's *Gesammelte Werke*, Vol. 6, pp. 638–40.

WITTE'S ONLY SUPPORT

Mr. Witte knows—too well, as it happens—that the new draft voting law can only unleash a new, violent outbreak of revolution. He's banking in cold blood on new butchery as the most natural kind of manipulation. He considers the D[uma] far less a sure bet than the bestial bloodletting of his friend *Trepov*, the commanding leader of the Cossack bloodhounds, the ringleader of the appalling butcheries of the Jews, the puller-of-strings behind the arson attacks and murderous pogroms, executed by a caste of pimps and felons. As reported in *Novoye Vremya* [New Times], Witte explained to the representatives from the zemstvo offices and from municipal administrations that the government needed some part of society as a pillar of support. He made it understood that he was hoping for a favorable result at the zemstvo congress on November 19; even though he also didn't view the Imperial D[uma] as a cure for all ills, the convocation of the long-demanded Constituent Assembly on the basis of universal suffrage was at present impossible. Witte went on to remark that the number of people against the current reforms was very numerous indeed. The only person who supported him was—Trepov.

This is how the revolution will run its course, sweeping aside Butcher Trepov and Political Conman Witte as it goes!

THE ATROCITY OF "ORDER" IN ODESSA

According to telegrams received in London, a total of 3,500 persons are said to have been killed and around 12,000 wounded in Odessa. According to further reports, all hospitals, half-a-dozen of the larger school buildings, many clinics, and also private houses are full of the wounded. In the suburb of Moldavanka, 1,000 corpses and wounded lay on the street between Saturday at midnight and the following Sunday afternoon. The authorities then picked these up and threw the corpses in large mass graves. In the Jewish quarter, the mob carried out unbelievable atrocities. The elderly, women, and toddlers were massacred, many children were strangled, and hundreds of them were thrown alive out of the windows of high houses. Trepov's gangs of stranglers tortured the victims to death by hammering nails into their heads, pressing out their eyes, cutting off their ears, and tearing out their tongues with pliers, while the innards of many women were also torn out; old and sick people who hid in the cellars were soaked in petrol and burned alive. These frenzies were organized and led by police and soldiers. In the private clinics alone, over 300 children were treated for saber wounds inflicted by soldiers to their heads and shoulders. The damages to property in Odessa are estimated at 20 million marks.

Odessa, November 7. The Chairman of the Chamber of Commerce sent an urgent telegram to the Finance Minister, informing him that the looting and felonies are still going on, and that these are severely damaging trade. A complete ruin of the trade situation is now unavoidable. A number of businesses and banks did open yesterday, but had to close again at eight o'clock, when the disturbances began again. The Chairman of the Chamber of Commerce sent Witte a second telegram in which he beseeched him to save his hometown. No answer has yet been received from Witte. The town of Bilhorod-Dnistrovskyi* near Odessa is in flames. Anti-Semitic movements are continuing in the Odessa District. Agitators are moving through the countryside, explaining to the people that the tsar has signed an ukase, which permits robbing and murdering Jews. As a result of this, numerous anti-Jewish pogroms have taken place.

MARTIAL LAW IN THE CAUCASUS

Petersburg, November 6. War is dominating the Caucasus. The Transcaucasian Railroad has been brought to a halt. Military reinforcements must reach their goal on foot. Seventeen bridges have been destroyed. Railroad tracks have been torn up at forty locations and the telegraph lines are out of service. Georgia and Dagestan are cut off from the rest of the world. The whole male population of the Caucasus is in possession of arms (*The Daily Mail*).

---

* This town in Ukraine was known as Akkerman in Luxemburg's time, which is how it is referred to in the original text.

A Conservative General as a "Revolutionary"*

The year 1905 has been wonderful. It has transformed the world. While it used to take many years to reform relationships between states and peoples from the bottom up, this year's done that with one blow.

The settling of peace between Russia and Japan,† an event that in earlier times would hardly have affected relations to the non-participating states, has conjured up a revolutionary force, which has changed the face of the world. In the Far East, Russia—whose autocrat was still telegraphed to just a few years ago as the "Admiral of the Pacific Ocean"‡—has disappeared from the political stage. It now must resign its place to Japan, its vanquisher, which now moreover has become the hegemon of the whole of Asia, strengthened through its alliance with England, which guarantees both powers sea, land and trade dominance for an indeterminable period.

The Treaty of Portsmouth has also, however, sent waves crashing over to Europe, forcing all old relations off their tracks. The Triple Alliance, an alliance existing for decades§ for protection and defense between Germany, Austria-Hungary, and Italy, which had seemed the surest guarantee of European peace, only still exists on paper.

If misfortune should have it that tomorrow or the day after tomorrow war should break out between Germany on the one side and France and England on the other—which can no longer count as entirely impossible, since no state has ever lost a question of international significance as much as Germany did on the Moroccan question¶—neither Austria-Hungary nor Italy would order even

---

* This article, "Ein konservativer Generals 'Revolutionist,'" published anonymously, first appeared in *Vorwärts*, No. 267, November 9, 1905. It is translated (by Henry Holland) from Luxemburg's *Gesammelte Werke*, Vol. 6, pp. 641–5.

† The Russo-Japanese War of 1904–05 ended in September 1905 with Russia's defeat. The Portsmouth Peace Treaty of September 5, 1905 solidified Japan's dominance by formally acknowledging its control of Korea and southern Manchuria. The U.S. played a major role during the negotiations to end the war, especially in preventing Japan from obtaining reparations from the Russian Empire. The U.S. also had its conquest of the Philippines recognized by the major powers as a result of the treaty.

‡ According to newspaper reports, Wilhelm II telegraphed Nicholas II in summer 1902, after visiting the tsar in Tallinn, addressing the telegram to "the Admiral of the Atlantic Ocean and the Admiral of the Pacific Ocean."

§ The Triple Alliance between Germany, Austria-Hungary, and Italy was first formed in 1882 and was renewed periodically up to the outbreak of World War I in 1914. Each of them promised support to the other two in the event of war.

¶ The German Navy arrived in Tangiers on March 31, 1905, demanding concessions for the German exploitation of raw materials. This was blocked by France, which claimed the same rights for itself, strengthening its position in Morocco. This provocation resulted in a crisis in international relations, ending with Germany's almost complete isolation in 1906.

a single man to march in aid of Germany. Germany must count itself lucky that its "hereditary friend" Russia, whose friendship culminated in the founding of the "Franco-Russian" alliance, is now being rummaged around by the revolution, otherwise it would find common cause with France and England against Germany. The hour would never be so opportune as this one for Russia, in such a war, to execute the robbery, desired for a long time, of Prussia's Baltic Sea Provinces.* Since Russia has met with a border it cannot climb over, it will now seek to attain in the west what it has been denied in the east, ports on the sea. The possession of the Bosphorus and the Prussian Baltic Sea Provinces are, from now on, the aim of its desires. This has also been clearly, and quite self-evidently, recognized by Count Witte, who also confirmed these facts in a recent interview to which little attention was made, by commenting that Russia will now seek to obtain in the west what remains denied to it in the east. He is content that his country should pursue this new task.

You would have to be afflicted by a complete loss of sight to be able to overlook how perilous this situation is for Germany on the Wilhemstrasse or in the Hohenzollern Residence on the Spree.† All attempts, however desperate, to commit themselves to the tsar—who is living in intense fear of his own people—through all imaginable duties of the lover will do nothing, absolutely nothing, to change the facts as described.

Just as in the course of a year, through the aforementioned proceedings, the external situation of the European states has escalated extraordinarily, bringing the danger of a big European war nearer than it has been since 1871, so has the domestic development of large and until now backward states taken a mighty step forward.

The Russian Revolution, which under the leadership of Social Democracy has shaped things in an ever mightier and deeper way, has made possible that which only recently was regarded as impossible. Russian despotism is falling right now, and the only thing that can take its place is a new, modern Russia. It should be able to surprise the Western European states in a myriad of ways through the creation of new institutions, just as its revolution has surprised Europe and the world.

Yet the new Russia also threatens the old Prussia right into the marrow of its existence, that old Prussia, under the brutal domination and subjugation of the Junkers and of pseudo-constitutionalism. A democratic Russia in the east and a republican France in the west make two neighbors, which will inevitably bring Prussian rule by the Junkers and police to its knees. This is about you! Which is what Mr. [Karl Heinrich] Schönstedt said presciently, when defending Russian

---

* This refers to the area around Memel (today Klaipeda) as well as East Prussia. Large portions of the latter were ultimately incorporated into the Soviet Union, at the end of World War II in 1945. It remains part of Russia today, known as the Kaliningrad Corridor.

† The Kaiser's Berlin place of residence.

police spies and mutual favors in the Prussian justice system on Russia's behalf.* Mr. Schönstedt will also soon belong to the has-beens.

The immediate reaction to events in Russia has been to set off great excitement among the proletariat of its neighboring states. In Hungary, the shameful class- and nationality-based dominance of the Magyars has been shaken by the proletariat—still relatively weak because of a lack of large-scale industrial development—under Social Democracy's leadership.† This attack has, it must be said, been aided by a conflict between the Hungarian king, the Austrian Kaiser,‡ and the Hungarian aristocracy and bourgeoisie. The latter groups are aiming at unlimited political domination.

Despairing that he might not be victorious in this battle, and bearing in mind the limited power of the rump of the ruling classes that is still favorably disposed toward him, old Franz Joseph, nearing the end of his days, gets the sublime idea to try to solve things through universal suffrage—to drive out the devil with the help of the deep blue sea.

Kaiser Franz Joseph and his Hungarian Ministry have become the *comrades-in-union* of Hungarian Social Democracy, and are now all pulling on the same rope, in endeavoring to push through universal, equal, direct and secret voting rights in Hungary. We can only say that world history is not getting the joke here! To top that, an old warhorse has stepped up to lead the cabinet, to represent the Austrian Kaiser and the Hungarian king, a man who until now would much more likely have dreamed of administering blue pills in bullet form against Social Democracy at the head of his soldiers, than walking with her arm-in-arm in the fight against the nobles and the bourgeoisie of Hungary.

But the old warhorse has got used to the new situation surprisingly smoothly, giving a speech during the last days of October about universal suffrage and about his program, which astonishes in its radicalism.

His speech included the following:

The question of parliamentary reform has matured in the eyes of public opinion, based on the recognition that current relations are not merely untenable from the perspective of political and societal balance, but also, and to a greater degree, from the perspective that the precondition of existence and the living aim of parliamentarianism is to purposefully care for the interests, rights, and social and economic endeavors of all classes in society. And whosoever observes the degeneration of our public conditions with eyes that will see, cannot register the causal link that exists

---

*   At the time Schönstedt served as the Prussian minister of justice.

†   A one-day mass strike had taken place in Hungary on September 15, 1905, including street demonstrations in which over 100,000 participated. In October–November 1905, forceful strikes and demonstrations for universal suffrage were initiated in Austria-Hungary.

‡   The Emperor of Austria and King of Hungary at the time was Francis Joseph I, who ruled the "dual monarchy" of Austria-Hungary until 1916.

between the anachronism of a far-too-tightly defined right to vote, and parliament's sterility.

Because what is the characteristic tendency of Hungarian parliamentarianism in recent years? On the one hand, the most urgent and living sociopolitical interests are entirely neglected and receive no consideration whatsoever from the people's representatives, while on the other hand, the parliament wastes the country's precious time on fruitless debates concerning constitutional law, and in a querulous splitting of hairs. That mid-sized real estate falls apart, that smaller-sized real estate is destroyed, and that the number of dwarf-sized pieces of land is growing in a frightening fashion [seems not to trouble parliament] ... A parliament, voted for by a group that artificially shuts out the largest part of the people *is unable to experience any receptivity for their true needs*, and a parliament that does not feel as if it depends on what is under it, *feels itself divested of that task of representing the people, which consists of understanding, and the loving care of the interests of wide sections of the population ...*

And a disentangling, a real disentangling, of such a type that doesn't just stop at the symptoms of the illness but which reaches down to its ultimate causes and cures the evil at the root, such a disentangling can only and solely be achieved through such a reform of parliament, *inserting again the interest and the will of the people into parliament. No one* who has fulfilled their duties in relation to the state *may be excluded* from exercising their political rights, and therefore, my honorable gentlemen, the government has placed the right to vote, to be carried out in a universal, secret, communal, and immediate fashion, at the head of its program ...

In conclusion, [Géza] Fejérváry commented: "*It is a fact that there can be no national largesse without democratic and social progress,* and there can be no social and democratic progress without an intelligent development of national forces, ready to make sacrifices ...*"*

We can look in vain for a general in Prussia-Germany who is able to speak with such cleverness and wisdom to an assembly. Herr [Fürst Bernhard] von Bülow, for instance?[†]

Hungarian Social Democracy is pursuing its struggle for a universal, equal and secret right to vote, based on direct election, in the half of the empire known as Cisleithania.[‡] And what do you know? Hardly have the demands been voiced, and there's the Austrian Prime Minister, Herr [Paul Freiherr] von Gautsch,

---

[*]   Fejérváry at the time was Prime Minister of the Kingdom of Hungary.

[†]   Luxemburg is being ironic here by referring to a known reactionary who was a major architect of Germany's imperialist expansion overseas.

[‡]   Cisleithania was the unofficial name given to the northern and western part of the Austro-Hungarian Empire—that is, the section that did not consist of the Kingdom of Hungary or its possessions in the Balkans.

stating that the government is drafting a proposal related to the introduction of the universal right to vote.

What the Hungarian king promises the Hungarian people as a life-saving way of anchoring himself amid state and societal misery, cannot be denied the people by the embodiment of the same person in the other half of the empire, the Austrian Kaiser. Events have their own logic.

But as the proletariat in Russia and Austria-Hungary are demanding their civil rights in the manner described, can the working class in Prussia and North Germany go on with the guns still pointed to the ground, allowing a jaunty class of Junkers and a swanky bourgeoisie to deprive them of their self-evident rights as citizens?

Does the Prussian and North German working class (the southern German states already have the universal, equal and secret right to vote, based upon direct election, except Bavaria, which is in the middle of consultations to introduce this right for the state parliament elections)—which is the equal, in terms of intelligence and political education of any working class in the world, and which, in terms of numbers, strength, and productivity, constitutes the primary factor behind the country's economic development, and no less so behind its military and maritime power—does this working class want to remain the pariah inside the state?

Is it not expected that this working class should sell the very health inside their bones, when the mistakes of the governing have ignited the European war, in order to defend a fatherland, which they actually shouldn't care about since they are entirely lacking rights ? Whoever has duties should also have rights. Are not governments and the ruling classes already considering how the burdens on the working classes can be increased again, to honor the holy cows of militarism and naval expansionism? And all of that at a point in time at which the gift of new import duties is upon us, meaning further price rises for the most essential foodstuffs.

The question presses itself upon the working class of Prussia and North Germany: What now?

We can be certain that Prussian and North German workers will not achieve universal, equal and secret voting rights, under direct elections, with the same ease as the workers of Hungary and Austria, but facing the enemies' stronger power is an incomparably stronger and politically better trained proletariat.

We are talking about a struggle using peaceful means for the primary and most important civil right. How best this struggle can be led to success must be determined by special committees, which have to be carried out by the relevant organizations and their leaders.

The Revolution in Russia [November 9, 1905]*

THE COUNTERREVOLUTION AT WORK

Here is some correspondence: *Petersburg*, November 8. Gen. Trepov will remain at all his posts.† The person he has to thank for this is [the Dowager Empress] Maria Fyodorovna.‡ She stands at the head of the reactionary clique of grand dukes of the Romanov family.

Petersburg, November 8 (report from the Petersburg Telegraph Agency). A government communiqué condemns the attempts of some newspapers, using the general unrest as a pretext, to shake the authority of the *upper echelons of the military*, and it points out that in the general evaluation of the activities of the troops there is no difference of opinion between military and civilian administrative officials. Also, the majority of society, when evaluating the situation calmly and impartially, will recognize the services of the troops in pacifying the entire country.

THE SABER AND THE ASPERGILLUM§

Saratov, November 7 (report from the Petersburg Telegraph Agency). The population, which to some extent had already calmed down or had become calmer, has once again been strongly aroused by a proclamation from Bishop Hermogen of Saratov.¶ In this proclamation *the bishop has demanded acts of violence against the enemies of the state*; he includes among these the male and female *high school students.***

REIGN OF TERROR OF THE COSSACKS

Moscow, November 8. The Union of Unions founded by the liberals of Moscow†† has sent a telegram to Count Witte calling for removal of the Cossacks stationed in Moscow, asking him to send them out of the city because of their acts of violence.

---

* This article, "Die Revolution in Rußland," is from *Vorwärts*, No. 263, November 9, 1905. It is translated (by George Shriver) from Luxemburg's *Gesammelte Werke*, Vol. 6, pp. 646–9.

† Dmitry Trepov had been chief of police in Moscow since 1896. In April 1905 he became chief of police of all Russia.

‡ Fyodorovna was the widow of Tsar Alexander III and mother of Nicholas II, the reigning monarch of the time.

§ A perforated container for sprinkling holy water.

¶ In Russian, Germogen; from the Greek, Hermogenes (born of Hermes).

** That is, students attending a *gimnaziya*, high school with a curriculum providing an academic education, rather than technical or vocational training.

†† Although the Union of Unions was founded by liberals such as P. N. Milyukov, some sections within it adopted more radical positions during the 1905 Revolution.

MASSACRES OF JEWS

As has been reported from Bucharest, acts of violence against Jews are continuing in Bessarabia. One town has been entirely destroyed by fire, and all the Jewish inhabitants there have perished. The city of Izmail on the Danube is in flames.

London, November 8. According to reliable sources in Russia, the estimate of casualties resulting from the rampages against Jews in southern Russian comes to 15,000 dead and the number of wounded is upwards of 100,000.

Petersburg, November 7. Witte's first official action as president of the council of ministers was the dismissal of eleven governors, in whose territories the anti-Semitic rampages took the worst form.

THE REVOLUTION MARCHES ON

London, November 8. According to a report from Petersburg in the *Daily Mail*, five towns in Finland—Uleaborg, Christinestad, Jacobstad, Nikolaistad, and Nystad—are *in the hands of the rebels*. The Russian occupation of the fortress of Sveaborg took place without a single stroke of the sword.

IN THE CAUCASUS

Batumi, November 7 (report from the Petersburg Telegraph Agency). Stores and businesses have been closed. The pupils of all schools remain barred from receiving any instruction. Social Democratic sources claim that during the destruction of the railroad line at the station of Sady Vakho, eighteen people were killed and four were wounded.

On November 2, the people's militia in the town of Nassakirali attacked the district police chief, who was accompanied by 120 Cossacks. *The fighting lasted for seventeen hours, and 105 Cossacks fell. The town's police chief was definitely killed.* Only four members of the militia fell in the fighting.

Warsaw, November 8 (from a private telegram received by *Vorwärts*). The agitation against the Social Democrats by groups headed by the clergy and by the National Democrats is becoming stronger and stronger. The tumult caused by the "Nationalists" has made it impossible to hold meetings of the workers. In spite of this, the workers have declared themselves in favor of *continuing the struggle*.

HKT-IST DRIVEL*

The bourgeois press is talking drivel about "agitation for a Greater Poland," which is supposedly now raging in Russian Poland, and it bases this allegation on reports being widely circulated by rumor that the *commanding officers of* [German] *troops on the eastern border,* in Upper Silesia, have been under orders for a long time to take all necessary measures to *"nip in the bud* any Greater Poland initiatives being undertaken on Prussian soil."

At any rate, the pretext has been chosen in an extremely unskillful manner, because the "Greater Poland" agitation in Russian Poland is just as much a *product of the bloody-minded fantasies of the HKT-ist witch hunters* as is the alleged "Greater Poland" movement in the Poznań region and in Upper Silesia. The HKT-ist reactionaries know very well that the political tendency in Russian Poland called "National Democratic, papist, and anti-Semitic" serves the cause of *counterrevolution* just as much as the [Wojciech] Korfanty party in [German] Upper Silesia does. In the recent election battle in [German-occupied] Kattowitz,† the German right-wing party headed by Korfanty‡ played its strongest trump card against the German Social Democratic Party's campaign by accusing the SPD of supporting "the excesses of the Russian Revolution."§

If German troops are actually mobilized on the Russian border that should not be seen as a preventive measure against an imaginary "danger of a Greater Poland" but as an extremely incautious provocation against the workers' revolution in Russia and in Russian Poland, and this must be emphatically called to account by the German working class.

---

* The German adjective *Hakatistisch* (HKT-ist) is formed from the first initials of the last names of three men, Ferdinand von Hansemann, Hermann Kennemann, and Heinrich von Tildemann-Seeheim (*Ha-, Ka-, Ti-*). Those three Junkers, East Prussian owners of large landed estates, were encouraged by Wilhelm II in 1894 to found an expansionist-colonialist movement among German settler-colonists in areas now belonging to Poland, especially aimed at taking over lands owned by the Polish nobility in the German-occupied part of Poland. In 1899, the HKT-ists adopted the organizational name "German East Marches Society" (Deutscher Ostmarkenverein). Writers from the Ostmarkenverien regularly referred to Poles as "non-white" and posited a racial dichotomy between "white Germans" and "black Poles" and called for the ethnic cleansing of the latter. Many of its members later become supporters of the Nazis.

† Polish spelling, Katowice.

‡ Korfanty was a Polish activist and politician in Upper Silesia (then a part of Germany) of Christian-Democratic persuasion. In 1901, he became editor of *Górnoślązak* (The Upper Silesian), which advocated on behalf of the rights of Poles living in Germany from a conservative, antisocialist position.

§ For a detailed account of the election campaign in Upper Silesia, in the German-occupied part of Poland, see Luxemburg's article "Zur Wahl in Kattowitz-Zabrze" ("On the Election in the Kattowitz-Zabrze Region," *Gesammelte Werke*, Vol. 6, 564–6.

A BELATED ECHO OF THE KÖNIGSBERG DISGRACE[*]

Our Königsberg party newspaper writes as follows: *Irony of World History*. Our Comrade *Skubik* reports by telegram that he has been freed from prison in Riga. The case against him was to be tried in Petersburg in the near future. Now this "dangerous man" accused of "high treason" is free, while here in Prussia the persons who allegedly supported him in his "treasonous efforts" still find themselves under lock and key, and they are presently serving a three-month prison sentence that was handed down against them in the Königsberg trial. *That trial was intended as an effort to save Russian absolutism.* The friends of the tsar suffered a severe defeat at that time. Now with the freeing of Comrade Skubik that defeat has become even more annihilating. That's how it was bound to be.

FOR THE RUSSIAN REVOLUTION

On Saturday in *Amsterdam*, at the *People's Palace*, a grand demonstration of sympathy for the Russian Revolution took place. This meeting, which was attended by 5,000 people, unanimously adopted the following resolution: "This assembly sends its greetings to the Russian workers, who are heroically fighting against absolutism. We greet them as new comrades-in-arms in the struggle by workers of all countries against the social system of capitalism, and we call upon the workers of the Netherlands to provide strong support financially for the ongoing revolution in the tsarist empire."

London, November 6. Yesterday, in spite of rain and fog, a rather large demonstration took place at Trafalgar Square, called by the Social Democratic Federation in order to make known the sympathy of English workers for their fighting brothers and sisters in Russia. The following resolution was adopted: "This gathering sends fraternal greetings to our Russian comrades, who at present are engaged in a titanic battle against despotism and bureaucracy. We hope that their brilliant exertions, their cool-headedness and boldness, and the circumspection with which they have treated the tsar's [constitutional] promises —all this will quickly lead to the emancipation of Russia, so that the Russian workers will be placed in the position to make a reality of their economic emancipation amid the bright light shed by liberty. We greet with joy the imminent

---

[*]   In July 1904, a trial was held in Königsberg, capital of East Prussia near the border with the Russian empire, in which nine German Social Democrats were accused of "high treason" for smuggling anti-tsarist literature into the Russian empire. Among the defense lawyers was Karl Liebknecht, later to win fame together with Luxemburg as outstanding opponents of German participation in World War I. In the end, none of the defendants was convicted of "high treason," and only three defendants were convicted of the minor charge of "membership in a secret society." See Luxemburg's article about the Königsberg trial, "Der russische Terroristen-Prozeß," *Gesammelte Werke*, Vol. 6, pp. 494–8.

collapse of tsarism, which has always been the bulwark of reaction and a danger to peace in Europe."

RAIL SERVICE

Königsberg, November 7. The management of the royal [German] railroads wishes to make known that passenger and rail service has been reopened on the following routes connecting with the Wirballen–Petersburg railroad line;[*] The Libau–Romny line via Koshedary; the Riga–Orel line via Dvinsk; and the Windau–Rybinsk line via Rieshitza,[†] connecting with the Nikolai line going through Pskov and Gatchina to St. Petersburg. The other connecting routes are still closed [shut down by the rail strike]. For the time being Grajewo[‡] is transferring freight destined for stations on the rail lines of Russia's southwest, with the exception of Kiev and Odessa, as well as freight destined for the Polesye line, the Moscow–Brest line, and the Kharkiv–Nikolaev line. Passenger service through Grajewo has been restored only for stations on the rail lines of Russia's southwest.

Warsaw, November 7. On the Warsaw–Petersburg rail line, regular operations have been restored. The shutdown of the Warsaw–Vienna rail line and the Vistula lines will probably continue for a few more days. The general strike is gradually coming to an end. Meanwhile in Łódź today the Cossacks killed six.

---

[*] Wirballen (now Virbalis in Lithuania) was a railroad town on the border between East Prussia and the Russian empire; it was a point at which the German rail network connected with the Russian rail network on the rail line going from Königsberg to St. Petersburg.

[†] Rieshitza appears to be the German spelling for a town near Dvinsk (Daugavpils), in the southeast of present-day Latvia. The Libau–Mitaw–Rieshitza railroad ran from the Baltic port of Libau (now Liepāja , Latvia), its westernmost point, through Mitau (now Jelgava, Latvia), through Riga (the largest Baltic port in Latvia), to Dvinsk (now Daugavpils, Latvia), its southeastern endpoint. This railroad connected a few miles northeast of Dvinsk with the rail line to St. Petersburg.

[‡] Grajewo was a Polish rail town in Russian-occupied Poland on the border with East Prussia, at a point where the rail network of Germany connected with that of the Russian empire.

The Revolution in Russia [November 10, 1905]*

A busy fumbling back and forth within the court camarilla, a swindlers' intrigue between Witte and Trepov behind the scenes, personnel changes that had already been decided in advance within the ruling group, the organization of entirely new tsarist ministries to satisfy another bunch in the ruling house engaged in mutual toleration of thievery from one another, and the general plundering of the people—and all of that in the wake of the people's mighty onslaught of the last few weeks. One almost doesn't know which is greater—the stupidity or the scandalous nature of these worthy representatives of the last bastion of the absolutist divine right of kings in Europe. A half-hearted amnesty, an "expanded" suffrage, with the exclusion of the rural proletariat, the petty bourgeoisie, and [the workers,] *those who took part in the recent revolutionary strikes*; the replacement of Trepov, the Russian Cavaignac,† with some other willing tool of the camarilla, some other from among the tsar's degenerate brood; and at the same time, massacres of Jews and mass murder without end. These are the means by which absolutism, which has been shot to pieces, thinks it can help itself out of this difficult spot! And so, with iron tread the revolution continues on its way. The proletariat is feverishly arming itself for new battles. It is likely to be scarcely a matter of weeks before one more confrontation all along the line will give a powerful shove forward toward a final decision, and perhaps even will bring about the final decision.

MINOR REPAIRS

Petersburg, November 9 (report from the Petersburg Telegraph Agency). By order of the tsar a separate Ministry of Commerce and Labor has been created. The man in charge of the chief administration for agriculture [Pjotr Christianovich] Schwanebach, pending acceptance of his request for resignation, has been named to the Council of State. Another member of the Council of State, [Pavel] Lobko, pending acceptance of his resignation, will be named state comptroller under the adjutant general. Prince Khilkov was awarded the Order of Alexander Nevsky, set in diamonds. The tsar sent handwritten notes to Grand Duke Vladimir [Alexandronovich]; the former finance minister, [Vladimir Niokolajevich] Kokovtsov; Prince Khilkov; and Lobko.

---

* This article first appeared in *Vorwärts*, No. 264, November 29, 1905. Originally entitled "Die Revolution in Rußland," it is translated (by George Shriver) from Luxemburg's *Gesammelte Werke*, Vol. 6, pp. 650–3.

† Louis-Eugene Cavaignac was the French general who suppressed the June Uprising in France of 1848.

Petersburg, November 9. *The Holy Synod* will be transformed into a patriarchate: the present metropolitan of Petersburg will be named patriarch.

Petersburg, November 9. The state council will sign a law establishing *an official Press Bureau*, similar to the organization that Bismarck in his day introduced into Germany.

Petersburg, November 9. Nominations have not yet been made for the Interior Ministry or the Ministry of Education. The decision to have the Council of Ministers function efficiently as a businesslike cabinet was approved by the tsar. *Trepov*, according to one report, will submit his resignation. Supposedly the Grand Duke Nikolai Nikolayevich will take his place.

Laffan News Agency reports as follows: *London*, November 9. General Trepov, according to the Petersburg correspondent of the *Daily Telegraph*, has offered to resign five times, but has always been asked by Witte to remain in office.

ELECTION LAW

With a piece of correspondence from Russia comes this news: It has been decided that only those workers' candidates will be allowed to run for the State Duma *as have been active as workers the entire preceding year*. Likewise, only permanently employed factory workers can run as candidates, not those who are employed in agriculture part of the year.

MASSACRES OF JEWS

The rampages by the Black Hundreds, and the riffraff incited by them, against the Jews are continuing in the whole vast stretch of central, southern, and western Russia. Prince Eristo,* who belongs to the Union of Unions, intends to make it clear for the people through leaflets and articles that the current rampages and anti-Jewish massacres have been organized by the Russian government.

THE FIRST SOCIAL DEMOCRATIC NEWSPAPER IN PETERSBURG

Petersburg, November 9. Today the first issue of a Social Democratic paper, *Novaya Zhizn* [New Life] appeared here. The editorial board is said to have close ties with *Maxim Gorky.*†

Wolff's Telegraph Office reports: In the first issue of its newspaper the Social Democratic Party is publishing its program, which corresponds in general to the Erfurt Program of the Social Democratic Party of Germany.

---

*   Prince Eristo was a pen name of Aleksei Peshkov, better known by his other pen name, Maxim Gorky.

†   *Novaya Zhizn* was the first legal Bolshevik daily newspaper. It was published from October to December 1905.

THE STRUGGLE CONTINUES

From *Torun* comes this report: The strike committee here has *banned shipping* on the Vistula [River], which until then had been moving unhindered. The pontoon bridges at Plock and Wloclawek have been abandoned by the authorities and taken over by the strikers. With control of the bridges, the strikers have gained the means of enforcing the ban on shipping. The steamboats from Danzig* and from here are at the same time refraining from leaving from here for Warsaw.

Riga, November 9. The striking *railroad workers* have been fired. A railroad battalion has refused to serve. *School pupils* have forced the closing of all educational institutions. Troops have prevented a planned attempt on the life of the local police chief. The detective here had to flee because of death threats.

Petersburg, November 9. A gendarme officer banned an attempted meeting by workers of the Moscow railroad line. As a result, the workers succeeded in having this officer dismissed, because otherwise they would organize a *general railroad strike*.

Petersburg, November 9. According to reports reaching here from Kronstadt, but not yet confirmed, a bitter conflict took place last night in Kronstadt. It is said that the infantry fired their weapons and machine guns were reported to have been put to use. The city is said to be in flames and the inhabitants to have fled. The telephone connection with Petersburg has been broken off, but the telegraph is still functioning.

PEOPLE'S MILITIA

The "temporary" governor-general of *Courland*, Lieutenant General Boeckmann, has himself formed a "citizens' guard" defense force to protect the city of *Jelqaua* and has granted the most far-reaching concessions to the population.

Katowice, November 9 (private telegram to *Vorwärts*). In neighboring Grasnowice, the Social Democracy in cooperation with the local citizenry has formed a committee to organize a people's militia. Only workers are to be armed. People wanted to immediately disarm the police and gendarmes, but they were nowhere to be found in the entire district. People's assemblies numbering from 10,000 to 15,000 take place daily.

PARTY CONFLICTS

In Petersburg a second organization of *constitutional monarchists* has been formed, and has made it known through the major Petersburg newspapers that any and every "movement" that *opposes the person of the tsar and every demand for a republic will be forcibly suppressed*.

---

* Today's Gdańsk.

The democratic-liberal Union of Unions has publicly appealed to the population of Russia to demand *complete amnesty*, because it has become clear that the amnesty granted by the tsar is not satisfactory, having been issued on a highly restrictive basis, and that up to this very moment countless "political offenders" are still languishing in prison.

SABER RATTLING ON THE BORDER

Those sweet darlings of the HKT-ist movement* have been proven right in their suspicions. According to the *Schle[ische] Zug* [Silesian Express] [in the Prussian-occupied part of Poland's Upper Silesia], the state legislature of the Katowice region has been authorized to "freely take measures" in the event of threats against the border by strikers or revolutionaries, to immediately call up military units sufficient for the defense [of the border].

As has been reported, the Cossacks and other uniformed thieves employed by the Little Father, with their brazen excesses, have continually caused disturbances and uneasiness along the Prussian border, but now have been "driven into their mouseholes" by the revolutionaries.

The purpose of this totally groundless saber rattling derives solely from a desire to seriously "disturb" the class-conscious German workers whose hearts and minds are totally in sympathy with the revolutionary movement "over there." One would not think it necessary even for the sake of "combat readiness," especially with this technique of simply inventing stuff, to stir up the general state of alarm, which is bad enough already.

---

* For more on the "HKT Movement," see footnote *, on page 300, above.

After the Bankruptcy of Absolutism*

The Communists, therefore, are practically *the most advanced and resolute* section of the working-class parties of every country, that section which *pushes forward all others* ...

—*The Communist Manifesto†*

The recent railroad strike in Russia, which suddenly brought about a new turn in the course of the revolution, has now moved off stage for the time being. With that, a particular phase of the revolution has come to a close. The question is this: what situation has now been created and what further course of events is to be expected?

Observed superficially, the tsarist empire at this moment presents the appearance of being a wasteland of chaos, a hodgepodge of highly contradictory phenomena, in which the bourgeois press wanders erratically, including the German liberal press with its customary tendency to lose its head [*Kopflosigkeit*], to rejoice all filled with hope at every news report about the "endeavors" of its beloved Witte, and immediately thereafter to again shut down, deeply disturbed at the news of another pogrom against the Jews. In reality, the outward-appearing chaos of conditions in Russia is only a characteristically adequate expression of the particular internal relations that have been created during the last two weeks among the existing social and political forces.

The railroad strike, which became the signal for a universal walkout in all the cities of the giant empire, demolished with a single blow the latest attempt of absolutism to hide itself behind the spindly frame of a "Duma" constitution. The tsarist government was forced by the colossal and unanimous onslaught of the working class, whose general strike brought all the machinery of state and all of public life to a standstill—forced to come out with wide-ranging promises of real parliamentary liberties, but by that very action, absolutism actually submitted its resignation. With this latest constitutional manifesto—even though it remains merely a piece of paper—it gave notice of its own bankruptcy as a system of government. This piece of paper is not really the proclamation of a constitution, but it is a statement of abdication.

---

*   This article, whose title is "Nach dem Bankrott des Absoplutismus," was not signed, but it is one in a series of lead editorials by Luxemburg as chief editor of *Vorwärts*, this one appearing in the issue No. 265 of November 11, 1905. A copy of it is found in RGASPI in Moscow, in collection 209, in which documents are archived that were intended for further volumes of the (incomplete) German-language Luxemburg *Collected Works* that was edited by Paul Frölich (in the 1920s) and authorized for publication by Clara Zetkin and Adolf Warski. It is translated (by George Shriver) from Luxemburg's *Gesammelte Werke*, Vol. 6, pp. 654–7.
    †   See *Manifesto of the Communist Party*, in *Marx-Engels Collected Works* (New York: International Publishers, 1976), p. 497.

Absolutism has abdicated. It no longer exists in reality. But the political form that the new Russia will and must take has not yet been decided. And this is surely not so because of Mr. Witte along with [Ivan Logginovich] Goremykin or some other "worthy gentleman" of that sort—it is not because they have failed to make themselves clear or because "someone" in Peterhof has "lost his head," as the Mosse press groans despairingly.*

The *power relations* among *classes and parties* do not give a damn about the petty scoundrels of the court camarilla and their lively games of intrigue because those power relations are caught up in a rapid and shifting process of change. The new Russia, as a social and political construction on which the political constitution will be fastened like a fully finished roof, is now caught up in a process of becoming. And this process of inner differentiation and clarification has been given a powerful push forward by the railroad strike and the general strike.

The moderately liberal, constitutional-monarchist zemstvo party—which was always available and willing to engage in horse-trading with absolutism, and which was pushed to the fore during the recent period (when a relatively moderate atmosphere of calm prevailed and the street revolution experienced a lull)—has now suddenly been shoved into the background again. The "statesmanlike wisdom" and "moderation" of the liberals falls silent, terrified by the powerful entrance which "the street" has made upon the scene.

The intermediate stratum of radical-democratic bourgeois intelligentsia has been swept along together with the onslaught of the workers. Today the intelligentsia energetically supports the general strike of the proletariat and its radical demands.

The recent battles have so greatly altered the physiognomy of the opposing camps that today the call for universal, direct, and equal suffrage is a firm demand advocated by *all* oppositional parties.

But the working class, for its part, has at the same time been pushed further ahead with a powerful thrust, by its own movement of the last few weeks. Because of the inner logic of the struggle, the action of the proletariat, its demands, and its conduct have become ever-more determined and radical. The *demand for a republic* has now come to the forefront of proletarian action. Whereas in the previous period, from January to October, the convening of a Constituent Assembly based on universal suffrage was the watchword of the mass movement, the central slogan is now *a republican form of government*. Of course, the call for a republic was always part of the program of the Social Democratic parties, from long ago, and was always faithfully referred to in the writings and speeches of

---

* The "Mosse press" refers to the publications owned by a German newspaper mogul, Rudolf Mosse, who was allied with the liberal Free Thinkers. Mosse founded the *Berliner Tageblatt* (Berlin Daily) in 1871, and in 1891, also in Berlin, the *Volkszeitung* (People's Paper), which openly expressed agreement with the Free Thinkers on domestic issues.

Social Democracy.* For the masses, however, and in the living struggle, this demand was for the time being a kind of schematic abstraction devoid of substance. Only the forward strides of the revolution itself, and the leftward shift of the whole situation, have driven the proletariat en masse beyond the initial demand for universal suffrage and a Constituent Assembly and have made the demand for a republic the focal point of the struggle today.

On the one hand, it is precisely the political freedoms authoritatively won in the streets by the proletariat itself and already put into practice—it is because of these that the mere slogan "Constituent Assembly" has been bypassed. In the most important large cities and industrial centers, the working class has already realized for itself the most elementary rights and freedoms that were expected from the Constituent Assembly. Unrestricted mass gatherings, giant demonstrations, speeches made directly to the people, Social Democratic writings openly produced and distributed, the Social Democratic parties coming forward openly as legally recognized powers, and here and there, for example in the Sosnowiec coal basin, a literal dictatorship of the working class—all these [realities] have with compelling logic driven the working class toward ever-more radical and resolute demands.

On the other hand, Social Democracy instinctively and in accordance with its nature takes up the sharpest demands, makes its political position and its demands as sharply pointed as possible in order to maintain its role as the force that drives all others onward, in distinction from the bourgeois-liberal and democratic groups. On the basis of the demand for a republic, it can be expected that subsequent struggles between parties and classes, between the working class on the one hand and the bourgeois liberals on the other, will be the ground on which the battle will be fought.

To the philistine, the demand for a republic in yesterday's empire of the tsars surely appears unrealistic and foolhardy. To the so-called "practical politician" and Social Democratic "statesman," it is an irresponsibly "dogmatic form of fanaticism." Many a Western Social Democrat until recently still regarded it as the task of the working class to serve as a support and stabilizer for anxious and jittery Russian liberalism and to console itself with the melancholy realization that in the present period, after all, it is the bourgeoisie and not the proletariat which has been decreed by fate and divine providence to assume political power.†

---

* All of the tendencies of Russian Social Democracy up to 1905, from the Bundists to the Mensheviks and Bolsheviks, argued that Russia's economic and social backwardness meant that the demand for a democratic republic was the foremost task facing the workers' movement—not the creation of a socialist society, which lay in the distant future. The demand for a republic had also been central to the approach taken earlier by most nineteenth-century West European socialists (including Marx), which held that the socialist class struggle could best be advanced within a democratic political context.

† The issue in dispute was over whether the struggle for a democratic republic will be led by the liberal bourgeoisie (as was the case with the 1848 Revolutions) or the proletariat. Luxemburg,

This statesmanlike wisdom is dictated from the perspective of the small frog in the pond, as it has shown itself to be in the present struggle as in every other previous one. Obviously, to the fighting proletariat in Russia it does not occur for an instant that it is on the verge of winning some sort of socialist paradise. Rather, it understands very well that on the day after the revolution the helm of state will fall into the hands of those who are now parasites upon the revolution, the bourgeoisie and the nobility.

However, it is the inner logic of the events themselves that pushes the fighting proletariat onward to express its radical class position in the form of ever sharper and more determined political demands and *in this way* to drive the bourgeois opposition forward as far as possible, to the outermost point reachable by the revolutionary wave. And you know, if one follows attentively the course of the Russian Revolution up until now, everything has gone literally according to the old, much-pooh-poohed "schema" of Marxism. It is nothing other than the very politics of Marx taken from the *Communist Manifesto* and from the March Revolution of 1848, which before our eyes sixty years later is becoming reality in Russia, together with "vestiges of Blanquism," and the "utopian" demand for a republic.

Still there remains the inexhaustible treasure of political lessons that can be taken from the flying sparks of the Russian Revolution, lessons that have not yet been learned by the international proletariat. But the self-evident history of this revolution already speaks with a voice of thunder—the voice of Marx. And whoever has lost the ability to understand and recognize the living truth of Marx's spirit here in the sandy wastes of bourgeois parliamentarianism has only to go there to learn in Russia!

like Lenin and Trotsky, held the latter position. For Luxemburg, the 1905 Russian Revolution proceeds from the point at which the 1848 Revolutions *ended*—not from where they began.

The Revolution in Russia
[November 11, 1905]*

TURMOIL IN THE NAVY

In Kronstadt, the struggle is raging on an enormous scale. Here is what the news dispatches report:

Petersburg, November 10. The crew of the 14th Naval Squadron, which is garrisoned in the center of the city of Kronstadt, mutinied and demolished everything in its barracks. The Fourth Uhlan Regiment, which was landed in Kronstadt, was immediately met with fixed bayonets. Most of the troops went over to the revolutionaries, and the marine infantry also mutinied. Regular soldiers and ordinary civilians were without any reason fired upon by the rebels. The number of casualties is not yet known. Stores were looted of almost everything, and were also set on fire.

Paris, November 10. According to a late-night dispatch from the Petersburg correspondent of *Le Matin*, sailors on one of the warships of Kronstadt have bombarded the Cossacks who were landed on the beach. Also, several forts were firing at random, and the fear is that they too have joined the rebels.

Paris, November 10. From Petersburg, the *Petit Parisien* reports that the news from Kronstadt has aroused the greatest anxiety here. The Peterhof Dragoon Regiment, which belongs to the category of crack troops, gave itself up to the rebels without a struggle. A regiment of cavalry lancers was almost completely wiped out in one terrible battle.

Petersburg, November 10. *In Kronstadt there are altogether about 25,000 military in revolt. People fear that the mutineers will succeed in taking over one of the ships in the harbor and will then bombard Peterhof.†*

Paris, November 10. *Le Matin* reports from Kronstadt the following: At 5 p.m. half of the city was already in flames; any help was impossible. The tsar himself gave the order to mercilessly suppress the rebellion. There is fear that the fire will spread to the arsenal, where munitions are stored in large quantities, and that would cause a terrible explosion. All available troops have been sent from Petersburg to Kronstadt.

Petersburg, November 9. *A thick layer of smoke lies over Kronstadt, through which one can see the red-hot glow of occasional smoldering patches. Inside*

---

* This article, "Die Revolution Rußland," was first published in *Vorwärts*, No. 265, November 11, 1905. It is translated (by Henry Holland) from Luxemburg's *Gesammelte Werke*, Vol. 6, pp. 658–60. This article is one of a series in which Luxemburg comments on the Kronstadt uprising of early-to-mid November 1905. In citing news reports about this over the course of roughly one week, she points out that the reports are often unclear and contradictory.

† Peterhof was the main residence of the tsar.

Kronstadt, eight military depots in the naval fortress are in flames. It is impossible to enter the city. Telegraph reception is cut off. Telegraph poles have been torn down for a distance of six kilometers outside of Kronstadt. Telephone connections have also been interrupted. The last phone message was the report that a steamer with 150 sailors on board was encountered, which was being sent to Petersburg to be imprisoned because of their participation in the disorders of the past week. Turning over these sailors to the naval authorities in Kronstadt was the most recent official act of General Trepov. *But, during the trip, the sailors overpowered their guards, and the steamer sailed back to Kronstadt harbor under the red flag, completely in the hands of the rebels.* Soldiers and sailors gathered in solid ranks to greet the arrival of the returnees. Then they all united to carry out an uprising *against the officers and officials of the tsar, and two hours later the city and fortress of Kronstadt were entirely in their hands.*

London, November 10. As the Petersburg correspondent of the *Times* has learned from reliable sources, *those in control of a warship anchored outside of Kronstadt* are firing at Cossacks on the shore. The forts are keeping up an irregular fire. It is assumed that *some of them have also mutinied. The Winter Palace will be readied most hastily for receiving the tsar because the region around Kronstadt [and Peterhof] is not secure.*

THE TSARIST REGIME HAS LOST ITS HEAD,
AND IS "REASSURING" EVERYONE

Kronstadt, November 9 (report from the Petersburg Telegraph Agency). The news about unrest in Kronstadt is exaggerated, and the fires in the city are out. Units of infantry, artillery, and Cossacks are patrolling the streets. The disturbances have not been renewed and were caused by rabble. They are being energetically suppressed.

Petersburg, November 9 (report from the Petersburg Telegraph Agency). From all parts of the country reassuring news is being received. The governor-general of Moscow has made an appeal to the population in which he calls for calm and proclaims that he could take the law into his own hands; he swears to punish and he is determined to restore order. In Keltsy, rail traffic has been restored. In Volsk, a commission has been appointed to look into the causes of the events of the last few days. In Irkutsk, schools have been reopened and the streets are still occupied by the military. The uprising in Mariinsk has been ended. Peace and quiet reign in Theodosia, and the stores have been opened. The schools in Kiev will be reopened on November 14. News about the full restoration of order comes from all the cities of Finland. In Helsinki and three other cities, the tsar's manifesto has been received with great joy. The uprising has been ended and rail traffic resumed. In Helsinki, the senate with the consent of the governor-general has voted to pay 160,000 marks to the National

Guard and the workers who performed police service in the city during the uprising.

SYMPTOMS OF "THE RESTORATION OF ORDER"

Riga, November 10. *The curator has announced the closure of all public schools and middle schools* with the exception of the Polytechnic Institute.

Petersburg, November 10. The *Union of Unions* has published an appeal to its fellow citizens to take energetic action against assaults upon the Jews. *All crews of the naval group in Kronstadt took part in the rebellion along with the commandos in training. The firing lasted for over twelve hours.* The number of mutineers mounted to several thousand, a large part of whom were drunk. During the night from November 7 through November 8, fires broke out in many parts of the city. Fire department crews were hindered in their activity by the sailors. Order was restored yesterday afternoon. The mutineers were divided among themselves, and the group favoring peace among them gained the upper hand. The sailors are now distributing appeals calling for peace to be restored. Yesterday evening thousands of sailors carrying white flags marched through the city, in many parts of which machine-gun emplacements have been set up.

The Revolution in Russia
[November 12, 1905]*

MARTIAL LAW IN KRONSTADT

According to the "reassuring" news reports of the semi-official agencies, the following official statement has been made: *Petersburg*, Nov. 10 (report from the Petersburg Telegraph Agency). *Today martial law was imposed on Kronstadt.*

TURMOIL IN THE NAVY IS ONGOING

London, November 11. According to reports received here from Petersburg a *revolution* broke out *among the sailors of the 14th and 18th Naval Squadrons, who are part of the garrison.* Consequently, guard troops occupied the barracks of the sailors.

The [London] *Daily Mail* reports as follows: *Petersburg*, November 10. *During the fighting in Kronstadt, more than 300 men perished in the flames. The number of wounded was mounting toward 1,500.*

MARTIAL LAW IN POLAND

Petersburg, November 10 (report from the Petersburg Telegraph Agency). *The decision has been made to declare martial law† in the entire territory of the Kingdom of Poland.*

ALL SCHOOLS CLOSED

Petersburg, November 10 (report from the Petersburg Telegraph Agency). *In all the cities of Russia the universities* and *all higher educational institutions have been closed.* The ministry of education has made known in this connection that no time has been set for the reopening of the schools. *Secondary schools also* will be closed for an indefinite period.

---

* This article first appeared in *Vorwärts*, No. 266, November 12, 1905, under the regular section heading used by Rosa Luxemburg: "Die Revolution in RuBland." It is translated (by Henry Holland) from Luxemburg's *Gesammelte Werke*, Vol. 6, pp. 661–3.

† Luxemburg uses two different terms to describe what is often referred to in English as a single term, a "state of emergency." "Kriegszustand" is often translated "state of war" and "Belagerungszustand" as "state of siege" or "state of occupation".

MASSACRE OF PRISONERS

Chișinău,* November 11. Last night there occurred an uprising in a prison here, during the course of which the prison was set on fire. Troops that were hurriedly called in *fired a salvo at the rebelling prisoners, causing the deaths of several prisoners, and also there were many wounded.*

THE NEW CABINET

Petersburg, November 10 (report from the Petersburg Telegraph Agency). Today a decree of the tsar was published naming the following as ministers: [Ivan Pavlovich] Shipov, finances; [Vassili Ivanovich] Tmiryazev, commerce; [Klaudi Semjonowich] Nemeshayev, means of communication [i.e., railroads]; [Dmitri Alexandrovich] Filosofov, imperial comptroller; [Nikolai Nikolayevich] Kutler, agriculture. The resignation of the vice president of the Academy of Arts, Count [Ivan Ivanovich Graf] Tolstoy, was accepted.

Of these "worthy gentleman" only Shipov is known as a politically active liberal, indeed as the leader of liberalism's most moderate right wing. This new bunch, it goes without saying, will be greeted by the public with absolute disgust, just as the previous pseudo-liberal combinations were.

A different news dispatch reports that even Shipov has declined to take part in this bloody farce.

Petersburg, November 10 (report from the Petersburg Telegraph Agency). Shipov, the zemstvo representative who received an invitation to enter Witte's cabinet, has declined this offer and gave his reason as follows: At the present time, the entry of representatives of various social groups into the cabinet can have great significance only if these representatives have come to an understanding among themselves as to program. But if only one of them is taken, then it is impossible that this representative can do anything useful for the cabinet, especially because the imperial treasury is a sphere that is entirely foreign to me.

STRUVE AND WITTE

According to information from Petersburg received from a correspondent there, Pyotr von Struve, publisher of the journal *Osvobozhdenie* [Liberation] that is produced in Paris, has been invited by Witte, who sent a handwritten letter to Struve, to come to Petersburg and publish his newspaper there.

Thus, the ex-Marxist Struve may soon be able to put into practice his clamorous agitation for a "strong regime."

---

* Luxemburg gives the phonetic spelling "Kishinyov," which correctly reflects the Russian pronunciation of the city's name, now called Chișinău.

SOCIAL DEMOCRATIC DICTATORSHIP

Das Kleine Journal has published the following correspondence about the Dąbrowa* coal-mining region, which is inhabited by 80,000 workers.

From Sosnowiec, in the Dabrowa coal basin: The rule of the workers, that is, of the Social Democratic parties, has gained the upper hand. No one dares to disobey their orders, not even the local authorities or the military. Their latest achievement is the formation of a workers' militia, which on Monday begins operation in Sosnoswiec, and Będzin and Dąbrowa will soon follow its example. In Sosnowiec, a workers' delegation sought out the police chief Kronenberg and notified him that their own police would now oversee matters of public safety. When he was asked to provide weapons for the "people's militia," Herr Kronenberg could not suggest anything against it. He merely indicated that this matter was not within his jurisdiction. The Social Democratic committees behave as though they intend in all seriousness to take over the police stations and city hall, and to have their own authorities occupy them. These parties have cancelled the payment of taxes. To make up for that, various citizens have been fined by the committees because they defied the orders of the parties or have committed offenses against the workers. At the printing establishments of Sosnowiec, which have been occupied by the Social Democrats, so that the owners have no say at this time, three journals are being published, including one in Russian that is intended for the soldiers, to win them over to the workers' movement. It should also be noted that in the surrounding area no one has disturbed public security. Thus far, the strikers have been letting housewives purchase meat in Modrzew and bring it back across the border.†

CONCERNING PROPAGANDA

Concerning reports by the tsarist government, we have received the following note: The news reports from Kronstadt, which is in a state of total revolution, should be treated with the greatest caution, as should all telegraph dispatches about the Russian Revolution. The dispatches about the events in Kronstadt, as readers must have noticed, have been extremely contradictory and unclear. This is because the telegraph works exclusively in the interests of the government, and its aim is to discredit the revolutionaries in the eyes of public opinion.

What is now being reported sounds strikingly similar to what was reported in the spring of 1871 in and around Paris about the fighting against the commune; the same lack of clarity, the same exaggeration, the same lies and prevarication. At that time, it was the bandit chief of the "forces of order" at Versailles, the dwarf [Adolphe] Thiers, who prevaricated to the world about the

---

*   In the original, this is given as the German name of the town, Dabrowa.
†   That is, from the Prussian-ruled part of Poland's Upper Silesia.

events in and around Paris. Today this prevarication is being committed by two Russian telegraph agencies, one under the influence of Witte, the other under that of Trepov. It is these agencies that weave the web of lies. No matter how hard they fight against each other, both agencies have the same interest in this given instance: To keep the world in the dark about the true nature of the revolution, particularly when, as in Kronstadt, the last bastions of power, the army and navy, are involved. *Therefore, caution!*

Large Landowners and the Revolution[*]

It still cannot be predicted what course events in Russia will take, but in any case one cannot expect that the revolution will come to an end any time soon. The contradiction between the impoverished condition of the working masses in the tsarist empire and the awareness they have gained of their strength is too great. It must drive them forward over and over again until either they have exhausted their strength or a substantial improvement of their living conditions has been achieved. After longer or shorter pauses, the revolution is bound to flare up anew over and over for years to come.

But the longer it continues the more certain it is to set the rest of Europe in motion, above all the neighboring countries. Austria, which is completely fragmented internally, with an unstable government and a fiery proletariat, was the first to be affected.[†] But will this movement stop short of Germany? Certainly not. Such enormous upheavals as those in Russia cannot go by without leaving a trace and affecting the other nations of the world (especially in the age of global commerce), other nations in which class contradictions have already reached the highest level of tension even without that. It is inevitable that Germany, too, will begin to stir, but in saying that, we can say nothing definite about what forms the movement will take. That does not depend on us but upon numerous conditions that we do not control. At this point we wish to abstract from the circumstances of *foreign policy*, in whose recesses powerful conflicts are hidden, and restrict ourselves for now to the prospects of domestic policy. Here we find the most powerful impulse driving toward a policy of severe conflict to be *the class of large landowners*.

If the government remains the obedient servant of the large landowners, it will be playing a dangerous game, because then it will be doing everything toward making the forms of the class struggle more brutal, even though to serve its own interests right now it must act in as conciliatory a way as possible.

It is not a very promising sign that the government has remained completely passive with regard to the *meat shortage*. In the interests of serving the large landowners the government has turned the mass of the population against the

---

   * This article, entitled in German as "Agrarier und Revolution," first appeared in the November 14, 1905, issue of *Vorwärts*, No. 267, November 14, 1905. It is translated (by Henry Holland) from Luxemburg's *Gesammelte Werke*, Vol. 6, pp. 664–7. This article was not signed. It belongs to the category of leading articles by the chief editor of *Vorwärts*.

   † In October–November 1905, powerful strikes and street demonstrations occurred in Austria-Hungary, demanding universal suffrage. This movement, in which tens of thousands took part, spread across the regions of Galicia, Tyrol, Mähren, and Krain, among others. Slogans put forward by Social Democracy such as "We will speak Russian to them!" and "Long live the general strike!" were taken up. The unrest spread to the army and navy as well. The government promised in February 1906 to submit a bill for electoral reform to Parliament. An electoral law, which in many respects was quite restricted, was finally approved in January 1907.

government itself. The rise in the cost of living cannot be disregarded, because it threatens to rise still further as a result of the events in Russia. The peasant and the proletarian in Russia have until now suffered from malnutrition. That has been demonstrated in countless ways for a long time. Now the revolution offers them the possibility of obtaining the food that they themselves produce, of obtaining it to consume it for themselves rather than see it exported. There is sure to be a reduced quantity of food exported from Russia, especially since the latest harvest in many parts of the Russian empire has been a total disaster.

In this situation, the implementation of the new tariff serving the interests of the bread profiteers is supposed to begin, and yet there are still fellows who have the gall to raise their voices in support of a tariff war against America.* At a time when we can count less and less on Russian grain and petroleum in the period immediately ahead, we are supposed to make the import of petroleum and grain from America impossible! A tariff war with the United States would be a sense-less proposition under any circumstances. Its costs would have to be paid above all by the proletariat, and its benefits—if there even were such a thing—would fall into the hands exclusively of the bread profiteers. But to think of what a tariff war with America at the time of the Russian Revolution would mean for the proletariat—this would be to advocate a highly dubious proposition. In fact, it would be senseless folly.

At a time when the cost of living is rising more and more, wages remain at the same old level. It was only the big strikes by the best-organized strata of the working class that has prevented the cost of living from rising even more in the recent period. In our own ranks, there has been much dispute over whether such strikes as that of the miners or the strike in the Berlin electrical industry ended in defeat or not. The answer to the question depends on which side of the strug-gle one places the emphasis on. The strikes ended in defeat to the extent that they did not attain their goals of forcing the employers to improve the material conditions of the workers. However, they ended in victory to the extent that the union organizations were not weakened, but actually were strengthened by these strikes. The workers are not discouraged or demoralized, but are in a more pug-nacious mood than ever. Thus, these strikes constitute the introduction to new and larger battles, which will be so much more bitterly fought to the extent that the success of our Russian brothers is greater and thereby the mood of combat readiness among the fighting workers will be greater. Also, the more successful the government's policy is for the large landowners, the sharper the workers feel

---

*   When Witte served as finance minister in the 1890s, he oversaw the introduction of a series of high tariffs in order to promote domestic Russian industry. The implementation of the new tariff on wheat was meant to discourage the import of American grain as part of a similar effort to promote the domestic economy. Unlike Russia at the time, American wheat production was becoming highly mechanized, resulting in a much lower cost of production than its Russian equivalent.

the goad of poverty, the higher the cost of living rises, and the more unsatisfactory the level of wages becomes. All this is certain to pour oil on the fire.

But along with the energetic fight for higher wages in industry we can also expect, in the springtime of the coming year, a strong *movement among the agricultural workers in the region to the east of the Elbe*. The big landowners to the east of the Elbe will not be able to retain their workers. They will flee from the region and go into industry. They will have to replace them with immigrants from the east, namely from Poland, from the Russian- and Austrian-ruled parts of Poland. But in the coming spring the Polish agricultural worker will be an entirely different type of person from what he has been in the past. He has behind him a year of revolution, he has lost the habit of bowing down to the gendarme, and he has seen the lord of the manor tremble before him. If he crosses the border into Prussia again as a "guest worker,"* he will no longer come as a strikebreaker but as a revolutionary agitator. But even if he does not come back, if he remains at home during the coming year in order to fight for a better life on his native soil, even then the spirit that inspires him will not stop at the black and white border fence. In the coming spring, the big landowners will have to count on dealing with people goaded by poverty and with movements fighting for higher wages.

As ever, they will resort to the brutal use of force again this time, and they will appeal to the fact that agricultural workers do not have freedom of association,† and they will rely on the anti-Polish hostility of the government. But that which in previous years was barely working as an intimidating factor any longer, must today in the vicinity of the Russian Revolution serve directly as a provocation to the rural proletariat. With the fire burning in the neighbor's house and with the sparks flying, nothing is more vulnerable to fire here than the thatched roofs of our landowners.

Will the government leaders of Germany with their brutal instincts strike at the fire wildly so that the sparks fly in all directions and a new fire is thus kindled all the more easily? The internal, domestic policy of Germany is now at a stage at which the government can, by acting in a timely manner, turn the flowing stream into a peaceful channel. *A tariff policy that is friendly toward the proletariat, giving up anti-Polish harassment*, passing a far-reaching law providing *protection* to the workers which will lead to a *legalized eight-hour day*, the right of association for *agricultural workers*, and last but not least an electoral law providing *equal suffrage and the secret ballot for the state assemblies*—those are measures that the government leaders can provide and that will work well for them so that the intensification of class contradictions in Germany will be fought out in less intensified form than in our neighboring countries.

---

*   That is, a migrant worker.
†   That is, the right to form a union.

But will the government of Germany have the strength, the courage, and the intelligence to shake off the pressure from the landowning class in order to introduce an era of reforms like this on its own initiative? Who among us today would trust that the Prussian German regime would have such wisdom? But really that is up to the government. We do not have to rack our brains over its problems.

Nevertheless, a big moment has come not only for them but also for us. The stagnation that has hemmed us in for so long is weakening. We are heading toward an era of large and powerful mass movements, an era in which big decisive reforms can be pushed through. In particular, we must advocate the demands listed above with greater energy than ever before. We must show the government of Germany that the German proletariat lays claim to the same rights being demanded in Russia and that are being won there in bloody struggles. If the government insists on pursuing its policy favoring the large landowners, this lack of vision will be no different from the mindless brutality of slave-owners who are accustomed to treating their enslaved subjects like cattle, and then we will oppose them with the power of our revolutionary ideals.

The Revolution in Russia [November 14, 1905]*

THE LATEST BUTCHERY

The *Standard* reports about a terrible bloodbath carried out against peaceful demonstrators by Cossacks in *Tallinn*.† *London,* November 13: Several thousand citizens had gathered in Tallinn to hear political speeches about the current situation in Russia. The assembly was conducted in an utterly calm and peaceful manner. Suddenly Cossacks came crashing in to the scene, to break up the participants. But instead of riding into the crowd, the Cossacks immediately fired off *several rounds of bullets,* and only then rode into the fleeing crowd. *Five hundred persons were killed on the spot, including many women.*

AGAINST DEVOLUTION FOR POLAND

Petersburg, November 12 (report by the Petersburg Telegraph Agency). An official communiqué reminds us of the imperial ukase from December 25, 1905 that establishes the foundations for a *step-by-step renewal of the civic life of Russian* subjects, and goes on to state that the measures decided upon herein also apply to the subjects of *Polish* nationality. Based on these measures, *the laws of exceptionality were abolished,* which restricted this nationality's untrammeled development and established rights for it equal to those that the Russian population is subject to. Reforms followed affecting schools, zemstvos and municipal and juridical administrations, all determined in accordance with the minister committee's legislation from June 16, and by the ukase stipulations from April 30 concerning religious freedoms. Moreover, the following was also extended to cover Poland—*general measures for the convocation of a Duma of the Imperial Empire* and the introduction of *right of assembly.* Finally, on October 30, the Poles were recognized as *free citizens* and thereby offered the full possibility of actually demonstrating their capability for taking part in the great, creative task. Forgetting entirely sensitive lessons previously learned, the Polish politicians who lead the national movement in the Kingdom of Poland announced intentions that are as equally *dangerous* for the Polish population as they are *shameless* in their opposition to the *Russian Empire,* in their aim to *separate from*

---

* This article was published in *Vorwärts,* No. 267, November 14, 1905, under the title "Die Revolution in Rußland." It is translated (by Henry Holland) from Luxemburg's *Gesammelte Werke,* Vol. 6, pp. 668–71.

† From its founding in the thirteenth century to 1918, this important city in Estonia was known as Reval—which is the name used here by Luxemburg. We instead provide the modern name of the city.

the latter. They reject the idea of working together with the Russian people in the Duma and demand, through a series of motions and assemblies, full autonomy for Poland with a special institution representing the people, by aiming for a reconstruction of the Kingdom of Poland.

They consist internally of two parties, the socialists and the nationalists.* Yet both parties agree to strive after these same ends that also exist in the heads of the numerous writers, publicists, and orators who seek to carry the population along with them. In various towns in the region of Vistula,† many marches have taken place accompanied by Polish flags and the singing of revolutionary Polish national songs. Simultaneously, they have started to high-handedly suppress the language of the state, even where its use is ordered through law. In particular localities, gangs of workers and peasants are looting schools, state brandy distilleries, and communal institutions, destroying all correspondence written in Russian in the process.

The government will *not tolerate* that the *empire's integrity be violated.* The insurgents' projects and deeds force the government to state in the clearest possible terms, that as long as new breaches of the peace in the Vistula region are not restrained, and as long as the part of the population that follows the political agitators does not desist from its illusions, *not one of the well-intentioned deeds from the manifestos of August 19‡ and October 30 will be permitted to benefit this region.* It is, of course, impossible to talk of the realization of peaceful principles in a country that finds itself in a state of rebellion. With the purpose of re-establishing order, a number of districts in the Vistula region have been declared to be under a *state of martial law;* the future of the Polish people lies in its own hands. The government that is willing to maintain the Polish people's national rights—as extended in the newest legislative acts—in the future, will wait for the people to distance themselves from the political agitation that has taken hold of the Kingdom of Poland; and the government warns the people against embarking on a path whose danger they have unfortunately experienced on previous occasions.

Petersburg, November 12 (report by the Petersburg Telegraph Agency). Count *Witte* has received *declarations* from various parts of Poland concerning the *full autonomy of Poland.* These included a telegram from Kalisz on the 11th of this month, informing him how a well-attended assembly in that city had decided that *only the introduction of a constitution for Poland, and full legislative and administrative autonomy,* coupled with autonomy in the education and legal systems, and the establishment of a national parliament in Warsaw on the basis of universal, equal and secret suffrage, could lead to healthy development

---

*   That is, the left-wing PPS and right-wing National Democrats, respectively.

†   In the original, Luxemburg gives the German name of the region and river, the Weichsel. We provide here the modern name.

‡   In the original, the date of August 18 is given.

for the country. A telegram from Radom gives Witte a report on an assembly of inhabitants from the town and its surrounds that had come down on the side of autonomy, and had decided to demand the immediate convocation of a Constituent Assembly based on universal and equal suffrage.

So, we see that tsarism is attempting to crush the nationalist movement by provisionally *denying* the Polish people those rights and freedoms it had just *promised*. A form of politics that can naturally only be counterproductive.

A GERMAN INTERVENTION?

The *Times* correspondent in Petersburg reports that the continuation of the general strike in Poland is certain to ensure the arrival of Polish autonomy. Despite the imposition of martial law, the Russian government has still decided to operate with *too great a willingness to concede* in its relations with Poland, because it *mistrusts Germany* and fears a *German meddling* in Polish affairs.

The *Standard* also published a report about the possibility of an intentional intervention on behalf of Germany. [Kaiser] Wilhelm II reached an agreement with *Austria* six months ago to send troops to Poland in case *Russia proves no longer man enough to meet the situation*. Although Austria will not be able to take part in the intervention because of the disorientating events in Hungary, they are aware that Wilhelm II is committed to just such an intervention. According to the latter, this would not be the case of an intervention against *the will* of tsarism, but rather one *for the benefit* of Little Father Tsar.

Both interpretations are equally wrong. It seems inconceivable that Wilhelm II, who has so often and with such emphasis stressed his love of freedom, could think of meddling in the Russian turmoil even for a moment, *the outcome of which remains so utterly unforeseeable*. The results of such an intervention could be *downright disastrous* for the German government in the current situation. In any case, the English reports are merely intended to provoke a German disclaimer.

SOCIAL DEMOCRACY AND THE AGITATION AGAINST THE JEWS

Today's issue of the *Zeit am Montag* [Monday Times] reports from Petersburg that the new Social Democratic newspaper *Novaya Zhizn* [New Life], published under Gorky's editorship, is said to have called for the slaughter of Jews. But it has itself expressed doubts as to the correctness of this news. This is, of course, based on a grotesquely comical quid pro quo. The Social Democratic newspaper* had—in its first issue that we have in front of us—reprinted a leaflet by

---

* In any case, since *Novaya Zhizn* was a newspaper of the Bolsheviks, it is hardly credible that it would have called for any "slaughter of the Jews."

the so-called Black Hundreds, in order to document the rabble-rousing activities of these police scum. The Black Hundreds called for the slaughter of Jews in this leaflet. That is how the newspaper exposed and nailed the police's agitation and the "tools they use," in a way that could not be misunderstood by anyone in possession of their normal facilities.

FOR RUSSIAN FREEDOM

London, November 9 (author's comment). Yesterday a public assembly took place in the Queens Hall, called by the Social Democratic Federation to express its sympathy with the Russian proletariat. Excellent speeches were held by the comrades [Harry] *Quelch, J. F. Green,* [Henry] *Hyndman,* John Williams, Herbert Burrows and Jack Williams. Green hoped that Nicholas II would meet the same fate as did Charles I and Louis XVI.* Hyndman referred to the economic reasons pushing forward an all-encompassing revolution in Russia. Quelch maintained that if the King of England should send gunboats to protect the tsar, English workers would answer with a general strike. The assembly closed by adopting a sympathy resolution. A collection resulted in a total of 350 marks.

---

*   Both of these monarchs were executed as a result of revolutions.

The Revolution in Russia [November 15, 1905]*

[ARTHUR JAMES] BALFOUR'S† PROTEST AGAINST
THE SLAUGHTER OF THE JEWS

London, November 14. In an assembly of Jews held yesterday in Memory Hall to voice protest about the riots against Jews in Russia, the following telegram from *Balfour* was read out: His majesty's government has heard the news of the *massacre of Jews* with regret and *outrage*, and has already *taken measures that seem suitable to mitigating the effects of this adversity.* Similar telegrams have also been received from Lord [Archibald Philip Primrose] *Rosebery*, [Joseph Austin] *Chamberlain*, [Herbert Henry] *Asquith*, the *Archbishops* of *Canterbury‡* and *Westminster,§* and other respected personalities.

There is as yet no news stating that the *German* government intends to take the tsar to task about these bestial slaughters!

Our *conservative organs of the press* have greeted this shameless carnage by almost bursting with joy—although we know it was set up by that tsarist blood-hound Trepov and carried out largely by soldiers and police officers.

WITTE'S THREAT!

Petersburg, November 14. As reported in *Nasha Zhizn* [Our Life], Count Witte, at a reception for a delegation of all Polish social classes, stated the following: "*The government is not considering granting concessions to the Poles* as this people's *lack of readiness for reforms has become strikingly evident.* It is now clear that *only a little pile of revolutionaries want reforms.*" Witte went on to remind his audience that *we could still be in for a reaction.*

Petersburg, November 14. The progressive newspapers have *condemned* the government's pronouncement about Poland. *Rus'* [Russia]¶ writes that the pronouncement directly results from the bureaucratism of Witte's cabinet, and demands that representatives of society be incorporated into the cabinet in

---

* This article, originally entitled "Die Revolution in Rußland," was published in *Vorwärts*, No. 268, November 15, 1905. It is translated (by Henry Holland) from Luxemburg's *Gesammelte Werke*, Vol. 6, pp. 684–6.

† At the time Balfour was British prime minister, a position he held from 1902 until December 1905.

‡ The Archbishop of Canterbury at the time was Randall Davidson.

§ The Archbishop of Westminister at the time was Francis Bourne.

¶ *Rus'* (Russia) was a liberal newspaper published in St. Petersburg from 1903 to 1908, with intervals under different names—*Rus'* (Russia), *Molva* (Hearsay), and *Dvadtsaty Vek* (The Twentieth Century).

whichever form: it is dangerous to delay. *Syn Otechestva* [Son of the Fatherland]* compares the government's paralysis inside the empire to Witte's decisive approach in relation to Poland, drawing the conclusion that when dealing with a defenseless population Witte is given free rein, but when faced with the real bearers of power, his hands are tied. *Nasha Zhizn* disputes that any Polish party has demanded the separation of Poland from Russia until now. *Novoye Vremya* [New Times] appeals to the Pole's prudence and tact not to aggravate Russian–Polish relations on the eve of the convocation of the Imperial Duma.

CONSTITUTIONAL PROMISES AND DICTATORSHIP BY THE SWORD

Petersburg, November 14 (report by the Petersburg Telegraph Agency). In accordance with the *intention* announced by the emperor in the October 30 manifesto *to extend voting rights to those classes of the people* who at present don't have them, the Council of Ministers is currently working on conditions for this extension that should be published *as soon as possible.* After which the elections for the Imperial Duma will take place without delay.

Petersburg, November 14. The *military instructions* approved by the emperor for the *general adjutants,* who are being dispatched to the governorates of Chernihiv, Saratov, and Tambov to restore order, will be published today. These military instructions grant the dispatched persons general command over troops and police units in the respective governorates; *place all government and municipal authorities under their charge* with the exception of the court and inspection authorities; and grant the general adjutants the rights *to have any persons who appear to be capable of endangering public order arrested, to close trade and industrial companies, to suppress newspapers, and to issue obligatory decrees for the maintenance of public order.*

MARTIAL LAW IN KRONSTADT?

Den [The Day] newspaper has received the following news from Petersburg: the inquiry into the Kronstadt revolts is approaching its close. *The heroes of this drama are due to be shot*—yet all classes of society are raising their voices, warning against carrying out these death penalties *that could lead to inconceivable consequences* in this terrible time of ferment. First, the clergy, in the form of the much-talked-about priest and writer [Grigori Spiridonovich] Petrov,[†] wants to plead for clemency from the tsar for the mutineers, then almost *the whole of the press in the capital takes a stand against carrying out the death penalties,*

---

*   *Syn Otechestva* was a newspaper published during parts of 1904 and 1905. It should not be confused with the literary journal of the same name published in the first half of the nineteenth century.

†   Luxemburg's reference to Petrov is to a leading advocate at the time of "Christian socialism."

and finally the residents of Kronstadt gather signatures for a petition penned with the same sentiments. The Kronstadt citizens had always lived peacefully together with the sailors until now. All these protests should serve to prove to the government that the mutineering sailors have less guilt in the matter than the government itself, whose indolence created the conditions inside the naval system that ultimately led to this explosion.

EIGHT-HOUR DAY IN PETERSBURG

Petersburg, November 14. Workers want to introduce the eight-hour daily working period into several factories in the city already.

UPRISING IN VLADIVOSTOK

London, November 14. According to reports that have reached us via Japan and Shanghai, the *population in Vladivostok is in a full state of uprising.* Heavy street battles are taking place between the insurgents and the troops. Many people have lost their lives in these clashes. The foreign inhabitants have solicited their governments to send warships to Vladivostok for their protection. Proceedings in Vladivostok are distracting attention from the fact that now news is obtainable about events in Siberia between Tomsk and Vladivostok. We believe, however, that Siberia is also shaken by revolutionary turmoil.

The Revolution in Russia
[November 16, 1905]*

THE BATTLE FLAMES UP ANEW!

Imposing a state of siege over Poland—by citing the fabricated pretext of a national movement—with the purpose of injuring the elite troops of the current revolution in the tsar's empire, the class-conscious Polish proletariat, and isolating them from the Russian proletariat by applying unequal treatment—has produced the opposite result. The struggle is breaking out in complete unanimity, and in brotherly solidarity, both in Poland *and* in Petersburg with renewed vehemence!

The dispatches report: *Petersburg*, November 15. The newspapers in the city published a *motion* adopted yesterday by the *Petersburg Council [Soviet] of Workers' Deputies*, according to which a *general political strike should start* today at noon, as a sign of solidarity with the Kronstadt mutineers and with the revolutionary proletariat [of Poland]. This *motion* carries the revolutionary motto, "*Scrap military courts, the death penalty, and martial law, in Poland and in the whole empire.*"

Petersburg, November 15 (report by the Petersburg Telegraph Agency). Rebels halted transport on the Warsaw and Baltic railroads at noon because of the general strike that has broken out anew. The express train to Chernyshevskoye has not departed.

Petersburg, November 15 (B.H.). The measures taken by the government against Poland have ignited great excitement among the population. Most newspapers have published sharply critical expressions of protest, and observe that serious consequences would be the result.

Warsaw, November 14 (Private telegram to *Vorwärts*). Social Democracy has announced that the response to the imposition of a state of martial law is to proceed with the general strike at all costs.

Warsaw, November 15 (B.H.). Yesterday 500 bank employees held an assembly in the stock exchange, deciding to continue the strike. The management of the gasworks communicated that there would soon be a shortage of coal, and that as a result the production of lighting gas would have to be discontinued soon. Disturbances continue in the city.

---

*   This article was first published in *Vorwärts*, No. 269, November 16, 1905. Originally entitled "Die Revolution in Rußland," it is translated (by Henry Holland) from Luxemburg's *Gesammelte Werke*, Vol. 6, pp. 687–90.

REBELLION IN THE MARINES

Just as the admirable *Potemkin* revolt in Odessa influenced the navy in Kronstadt, it is now obvious that the tremendous revolt of the Kronstadt sailors has echoed in the Far East—in *Vladivostok*. The thunderclouds over the heads of absolutism are charged with sallow flashes of lightening from one end of the huge empire to the other, while the thunder grumbles ever-more audibly.

London, November 15. Telegrams reporting from *Vladivostok* via *Shanghai* that *soldiers and sailors have risen up* and set fire to the city that is now completely destroyed. Merchants and the rest of the population fled onto the ships lying at anchor in Vladivostok bay. More than fifty ships laden with provisions are anchored in the bay. Further ships await loading. They will all be prevented from sailing. *Askold*, the Russian cruiser, set sail on Tuesday from Shanghai and is said to be bound for Vladivostok. The other Russian warships anchored at Shanghai—the *Mandyur*, the *Gromboi*, and the *Bobr*—have received orders to sail with all possible speed to Vladivostok to suppress the disturbances there. As reported by the *Morning Post* in Shanghai, the breaches of order in Vladivostok have already ceased.

Petersburg, November 15. The rumor that circulated for two days about a mutiny of sailors and artillerymen in Vladivostok has been confirmed by a wire report to the *Novoye Vremya* [New Times]. The city has been looted and set alight. On the first day of the disturbances, around *300 mutineers were killed.* The same paper explains that from a juridical point of view it would not be impossible to talk of a mutiny in Kronstadt, because superior officers were not present during proceedings, and these were exclusively a matter of excesses and lootings carried out in a drunken state, i.e., crimes that are not punished by the death penalty.

The well-informed reader, whose attention we particularly want to direct toward the letter from Petersburg reprinted for today's issue, will know how to distinguish, in the aforementioned wire-reports, between the news of a mutiny of sailors and soldiers [on the one hand], and the frightening stories about murder, arson, and looting [on the other]. These crimes and atrocities are exclusively the work of the government and its organs.

THE MOOD AMONG THE OFFICERS

We have received the following from Petersburg: A number of officers from the regiments of the guards, Russia's most gentlemanly regiments, published the following letter in the Petersburg papers:

Lieutenant Frolov, who voluntarily took on the role of executioner against a defenseless crowd, by giving the order to shoot that resulted in hundreds of people being wounded, *has violated the honor of military uniform.* We request Lieutenant Frolov to voluntarily present himself in front of a civil court within the space of one month. Should Frolov not fulfill our wish by the required date, *he will be boycotted by all officers in the capital,* as will be the whole body of officers in the mounted Regiment of the Guards who tolerate *such* officers. All officers of this regiment would then be expelled as members of the various associations, and none of these officers would have their salutes reciprocated.

CLOSED SCHOOLS, MUTINEERING REGIMENTS, AND PEASANT DISTURBANCES

The semi-official Petersburg Agency, which goes to every effort to spread "sedative news" daily, is forced to present the following news bouquet about the general state of the tsar's empire today: *Petersburg,* November 14 (report by the Petersburg Telegraph Agency). We have received the following reports from the *interior of the empire:* In Kharkiv, the university's governing committee has decided *not to restart* lectures until martial law has been rescinded. In Nizhny Novgorod, complete calm prevails. In Kutaisi, the governor-general has informed a Duma delegation about the imperial steward's order not to transport troops sent to Guria. In *Vladikavkaz,* the disturbances *inside the Apsheronsky regiment* have stopped, and the garrison has been strengthened by a *regiment of Cossacks.* In Chita, Krasnoyarsk and Morchansk, where anti-Semitic disturbances had been expected(!), calm prevails. In the *Chernihiv* Province, *peasant revolts* have taken place. Inhabitants from several villages looted a farm and set it alight. They then attacked two further villages, but were forced back. The *military has been deployed* to the localities affected. *Similar occurrences* have been reported from the *Samara* Province, and *serious disturbances* have erupted in *Yeravan.* Around 700 Armenians attacked a Tatar village, killing 400 inhabitants, setting the houses alight, and driving the cattle away. The *military* has also been deployed to this locality.

PETERSBURG'S SECOND SOCIAL DEMOCRATIC NEWSPAPER

Aside from *Novaya Zhizn* [New Life] which was founded just a few days ago by our Petersburg comrades,[*] a second party paper, *Nachalo* [The Beginning],[†] should also appear soon. The announcement in the bourgeois Petersburg papers stated that alongside well-known Russian party authors like Plekhanov, Zasulich, [Julius] Martov, and [Alexander] Parvus, German Social Democrats will also

---

[*]   A reference to the Bolsheviks, who published *Novaya Zhizn.*
[†]   *Nachalo* was a newspaper founded on November 13, 1905 by Leon Trotsky in alliance with a number of leading Mensheviks. It quickly became one of most popular publications among workers involved in the soviets. It should not be confused with an earlier publication under the same name, which briefly appeared in 1899 as a journal of the "legal Marxists" such as Pyotr Struve.

write for the new Russian partner publication: *August Bebel, K. Kautsky, Rosa Luxemburg, Franz Mehring*, and Comrade *Victor Adler* in Vienna.

Warsaw. The magazine *Glos* [Voice], which had been published with the sub-heading *Organ of Social Democracy for Poland and Lithuania*, has been *banned*.

PROTEST AGAINST THE EXECUTION OF 300 MUTINEERING SAILORS

Petersburg, November 15. The newspapers have published a series of *letters from private individuals* vigorously protesting the execution of 300 mutineering sailors in Kronstadt, and demanding that the mutineers be brought before a *civil court* for a new trial.

The Truth About Kronstadt[*]

A veritable downpour of contradictory news dispatches about the events in Kronstadt came out of Russia during the past week. The main trend of the semi-official reporting from the tsarist empire crassly and crudely made this point—the rebellion in Kronstadt should be seen by the Western European public as an orgy by mindlessly drunken sailors, as a series of hair-raising atrocities committed by a raging mob. That's how the sailors' rebellion is supposed to be presented to the public—as a chaotic outbreak of unbridled and criminal brute instinct.

Obviously, the *working-class* public in Germany, as elsewhere, knew very well what to make of this attempt at the molding of public opinion. It yearned for a more truthful account of what had happened.

We are now in a position to describe with the greatest exactitude the actual events in Kronstadt. Below we present a letter from Petersburg. It gives an account of the Kronstadt days that will make the blood boil in anyone who has not fallen into the depravity of a wild beast. Yes indeed!

Excesses by riffraff, wild chaos caused by an outbreak of criminal brute instincts, murder and pillage did occur for several days in the naval fortress that guards the entrance to the tsarist capital city. Smoking ruins do mark the way taken by this monstrous orgy. But the bestial riffraff who celebrated this orgy of violence were not the sailors, and were not the fighting proletarians of Kronstadt. They were the Black Hundreds, the tools of the tsarist regime, its shameful roughnecks and thugs, who wanted to use murder, robbery, arson, and pillage to suppress, befoul, and discredit one of the most magnificent expressions of the political class struggle in this revolution.

Corruption and moral decay arise in any expiring form of state or society as an accompanying phenomenon that occurs by natural necessity. However, the scoundrels of the tsarist regime, in their last, desperate struggle for existence, have developed such an unparalleled level of cynical depravity that by comparison the merciless brutes of France's *ancien regime* and even Louis Bonaparte's notorious Society of December 10[†] seem to form a gallery of mythical heroes from antiquity.

Petersburg, November 10 (from our correspondent). Events are now rushing and crowding one on top of the other at such a pace that it is almost impossible to keep up with them. In order to make them into a coherent picture illustrating

---

 * This article first appeared in *Vorwärts*, No. 269, November 16, 1905, under the title "Die Wahrheit über Kronstadt." It is translated (by George Shriver) from Luxemburg's *Gesammelte Werke*, Vol. 6, pp. 691–4.

 † The Society of December 10 was founded by Louis Bonaparte in 1849 of lumpenproletarian elements with the aim of harassing and intimidating opponents of the government.

the actual state of affairs, we want to emphasize some important points after the fact, after the series of events has taken place—or rather, after the *reversal* of the series of events. We begin with the events by which, in the last few days, "all good souls" have been most deeply shaken, the colossal uprising of the sailors in Kronstadt.

For the past two years, an organization of Russian Social Democracy has existed among the sailors of Kronstadt. It has enjoyed great influence and has carried on systematic agitation. The rebellion of the crew of the *Potemkin* in its day* made a strong impression on the sailors of Kronstadt. Several sailors who were Social Democrats were transferred from the Black Sea Fleet to Kronstadt after those memorable events. The intention was to weaken their "rebellious" influence, but they, of course, continued their agitational activity even more vigorously. Finally, a short time ago, the 18th Garde Equipage was sent away from Petersburg to be "isolated" at Kronstadt in the same way, because it too had been infected by the "plague" of Social Democracy. It was this "equipage" that put out the first call for the Kronstadt uprising.

The massive movement of most recent times was initiated by a great majority, in which 10,000 sailors took part. Sailors themselves took the floor at the mass meeting and were the main speakers. They spoke about the special burdens borne by sailors as well as the general political situation in the Russian empire.

Finally, a list of demands was drawn up consisting of eighteen points, excessive length of service being one of them. The demand was to reduce the number of years of service in the navy from seven to five years. Also, sailors' pay was to be increased from 22.5 kopecks per month to four roubles; better treatment of sailors by officers with respect for their human dignity was also demanded; in addition, the mass meeting called for freedom of speech and the press, the right of assembly and of association, and freedom of conscience, as well as universal, equal, and direct suffrage, and the right to vote for a representative body with legislative powers, etc.

This enormous assembly at the same time declared itself in favor of the need to participate in the general revolutionary proletarian struggle in the whole Russian empire, so as to achieve the downfall of absolutism. After the close of the meeting, in which a mood of the greatest enthusiasm prevailed but also an atmosphere of order and tranquility, the sailors lined up to form a huge column and began a mass march through the city, with Social Democratic banners and the singing of revolutionary songs, again maintaining the greatest order.

A number of *artillery troops* also took part in the mass meeting. The authorities, using that as an excuse, carried out a number of arrests immediately after the meeting. They didn't dare touch the gigantic mass of the sailors, although forty artillerymen were sent off to be placed under lock and key. However, the

---

*   The *Potemkin* mutiny began on June 15, 1905.

sailors would not tolerate this. Together with some of the *harbor workers*, they went to the railroad station, intervened, and set their artillerymen comrades free. In the process an actual confrontation took place between the allied sailors and workers, on the one hand, and the soldiers on the other. However, the course of the confrontation remained more-or-less free from bloodshed, because the soldiers themselves were wavering, for the most part, and did not want to open fire on the sailors.

Then when the sailors had been victorious and the conduct of the ground troops had shown they were unreliable—that was when the Black Hundreds organizations immediately set to work. At their head was the "miracle-maker," John of Kronstadt,* who has close connections with the court camarilla. Many other priests are associated with him, as well as the upper ranks of the officer corps. They hurriedly began to round up lumpen elements, police informers, plainclothesmen, other police agents and hangers-on. Instantly, a "patriotic force" took shape, with the portrait of the tsar being carried in front along with priests singing hymns, and behind them came a procession of the dregs of Kronstadt society, most of them drunk thanks to the Judas-type "pieces of silver" handed down from on high to these lumpen elements. The pious, patriotic procession marched forth with the crowd breaking into liquor stores and private homes. The "defenders of order" plundered and stole like ordinary thieves.

This lumpen procession was directed openly and with obvious intent against the peaceful and orderly march of the sailors and harbor workers. A clash developed between the two forces. Since the sailors were competently getting the better of the riffraff, two detachments of regular troops were sent most urgently from Petersburg. It goes without saying that the lumpen elements were meant to serve only the purposes of provocation. It was up to the soldiers to carry out the massacre of the sailors. A regiment of dragoons and a regiment of guards cavalry arrived—*with machine guns*. But, here too, the previous experience was repeated. The troops wavered. The soldiers did not want to shoot; they allowed themselves to be disarmed without resistance. In this way, victory remained on the side of the sailors and harbor workers, who had also gained possession of machine guns.

Embittered to an extreme by the officers' infamous provocations—the officers openly inciting the Black Hundreds [to attack the sailors]—the latter now directed machine-gun fire against the officers' club, began bombardment of the forts, and commandeered a battleship. The situation thus became extremely precarious for the officers and the priests. They huddled in abject terror. For two

---

*   John of Kronstad (in Russian, Ioann Kronshtadsky) was an orthodox priest of deeply conservative and anti-Semitic convictions. In 1903, he accused the Jews of being responsible for the pogrom launched against them in Kisinev. In the same year, he helped introduce Tsar Nicholas II to Rasputin. During and after the 1905 Revolution, his followers, called the Ionnitsy, assisted the pogroms launched by the Black Hundreds.

full days, the sailors were the masters of the city. And no excesses at all occurred during those forty-eight hours, not the slightest infringement against the peaceful population. Meanwhile, however, the Black Hundreds chiefs set a plan into operation. Suddenly a terrible fire broke out in the city. The police agents had *started fires at thirty-two places simultaneously*. Not only plainclothesmen but openly uniformed police were seen setting the fires. A terrible panic began, amid indescribable chaos. In wild anxiety, [part of] the population fled to Petersburg. There, citizens stormed into the editorial offices [of newspapers] and recounted the foregoing—they *swore* that not one sailor had taken part in the arson. These inhabitants of Kronstadt knew quite exactly that the fires had been set by agents of the regime. The riffraff had simultaneously begun to steal and to pillage, as they always did, of course; those drunken gangs, those "defenders of law and order," broke into private dwellings and celebrated their orgies. In the midst of this utter and complete chaos, an entire division of troops sent from Petersburg broke into Kronstadt, and a bloody battle began in which the sailors and harbor workers were finally "defeated."

This battle and this victory [of the reactionaries] must be made an eternal memory in history, just like those other "victories"—the anti-Jewish pogroms in Chișinău and Odessa. Nevertheless, one thing at least is clear—the throne of the Romanovs is being preserved today by the last true "pillars of society," the drunken police spies and their plundering hangers-on.

The State of Siege in Poland[*]

The revolution marches on its path with impeccable logic. Each new violent trick performed by absolutism in decline becomes the starting point for a new violent outbreak of the struggle.

The state-of-occupation imposed over Poland has triggered a return to the general strike, first in Petersburg, then in Moscow and in the whole of Russia. For now, the giant, the tsar's empire, lies chained and powerless on the ground, while the "strong arm" of the revolutionary, class-conscious proletariat rises into a clenched fist, and the state of siege in Poland metamorphoses into a state of siege that the working class imposes on tsarism.

This brilliant action, carried out by the Petersburg proletariat, is particularly remarkable for being the first solidarity initiative for which the signal came from Petersburg. In the previous periods of revolution, it was usually the other way round. The Polish working class responded to every initiative undertaken by their Russian brothers in the struggle, as they did to every plot directed against them by the ruling band of rogues, with passionate declarations of solidarity. January 22 turned into a signal for a series of general strikes in the whole of Russian Poland. There were immediate, lively responses in Poland to the Moscow railroad workers' strike. In contrast, the grandiose May Day celebrations in Warsaw, and the bloody battles of the Polish working class in Łódź, have not generated reactions or active support in Russia proper until this day. This is certainly not due to the Russian proletariat lacking feelings of fraternity, or of the deepest sympathy and political insight. It was much rather the case that the proletarian masses in Petersburg and Moscow were not yet mobile or disciplined enough to fall into line straight away when the order was given. The movements of the masses were more of a spontaneous and elemental nature, a real systematic and purposeful *leadership* of Social Democracy did not yet exist in Russia, the preconditions for mass action, stemming from a free decision, had not yet been established. And what a turnaround now! Within hours of the announcement of the state of siege in Poland, the leading Petersburg workers' organization passed a motion calling for solidarity action with the Polish proletariat, and the masses are thus mobilized within hours, trains at a standstill, the factories quiet, and the general strike executed impeccably. This current action has only been made possible by the revolution's quick marching step, facilitating

---

[*]   Although this article is unsigned, Luxemburg is clearly the author. A transcript can be found in the Moscow RGASPI, Find Number 209, documents archived for the unfinished German-language *Collected Works of Rosa Luxemburg*, published by Clara Zetkin and Adolf Warski and edited by Paul Fröhlich between 1923 and 1928. The article first appeared in *Vorwärts*, No. 270, November 17, 1905, under the title "Der Belagerungszustand in Polen." It is translated (by Henry Holland) from Luxemburg's *Gesammelte Werke*, Vol. 6, pp. 695–8.

massive progress in political training, in the masses' readiness to fight, and in the leading influence of Social Democracy since those January days. Our angst-ridden opponents of the idea of the political mass strike, who meaunder on with such smugness about the necessary discipline and training for the masses, can now demonstrate—faced with the tremendous, continuing work of the proletariat's political training, amid the fire of battle—if they possess the political warrior's most indispensable ability, *the ability to learn.*

At least the Petersburg workers, however, are able to display a high degree of political maturity, particularly in their resolution that specifically calls for a solidarity rally for the revolutionary Polish *proletariat*, not just for solidarity with "Poland," which was the old, standard phrasing. The attempt by the tsarist bashi-bazouk that they, as it happens, share with our own "liberal" HKT,* is nothing but a mendacious and crude speculative attempt to graft the bogeyman of national antimonies together with "national ferment," in order to suffocate the proletariat's revolutionary class movement.

The tsarist government needs the state-of-emergence and the fantastical, scare-mongering pictures of the "Polish danger" for two reasons. First, to scare the living daylights into the Russian liberals [by evoking] the supposed state-endangering tendencies of "the Poles," so that sympathies for the revolutionary movement will be cooled among people who are, at the bottom of their hearts, good "patriots"—[the latter being] people who gush about the "integrity" of the empire of the knout. Secondly, they use the pretense of a "national ferment" to violently quiet the purely political class struggle of the Polish proletariat.

In reality, there's not a trace of a national movement today inside the Russian part of Poland, in the sense of aspiring toward the reestablishment of an independent Polish state.† The obsequious brave warriors and the capitalist moneybags of Russian Poland are way in front even of the *Russian* reactionaries in terms of their "loyalty" to the hegemony of the knout. Weren't *Poland's* bourgeois classes the only ones who sent deputations to the government after the butchery on January 22 in Petersburg and after the Cossack mass murder on May 1 ... with expressions of gratitude for the hypocritical Ukase on Tolerance on Religious Matters? Even the moderate Russian liberals greeted this with cold disdain! Was it not a Polish agribusiness newspaper, the *Dziennik Posnański* [Poznań Daily] that—during the eventful days in January—gave Tsar Nicholas the advice, not intended ironically, that he should save his evidently wobbly head and the crown by making with all speed for Warsaw, the sole place of refuge in which the "parties of order" could offer him absolute security? Poland's bourgeois classes do now stand with both feet on the solid ground of capitalist reality, which has

---

*   The German East Marches Society (Deutscher Ostmarkenverein), or HKT, which advocated a policy of racist ethnic cleansing of Poles living in the German Empire.

†   This is a contentious claim that many in Poland at the time—and not solely those in such groups as the PPS—would have taken sharp issue with.

long since transformed the old nationalist-rebel Poland into a devout factory of exclusively beautiful soul of capitalist profit.* And the effects of this capitalistic transformation process go so deep, that Poland is the only province during this whole revolutionary period of the history of the tsar's empire in which the bourgeois classes have not shown the faintest sign of stirring for freedom. No trace here of either bourgeois or agrarian liberalism that takes the stage in Russia proper in such a pathetic form, and no trace of bourgeois democracy among urban intelligentsia circles. It has been the proletariat, entirely on its own and against all bourgeois classes and groups, which has made Poland into one of the mightiest furnaces of the Russian Revolution. It has fought under the flag of a clearly delineated *class struggle*, and in the spirit of class solidarity that belongs together with the Russian working class.

The one party in Poland, who until only a few years ago represented the Polish national solution for the reestablishment of Poland, and who, until recently, eked out their pitiful existence primarily in Galicia—this so-called "National Democracy," a catch-all for the petty bourgeoisie and for anti-Semitism—officially renounced their program in 1904, concurrent to the start of the revolution in the tsar's empire, labeling it "utopian."† Today in Poland, they play the role of absolutism's voluntary helper, putting all their urgency into founding "national" yellow trade unions,‡ and in battling against Polish Social Democracy.§ This was the same "national" party that only weeks ago wrote the following words under the title of "Industry of the Fatherland Ruined" in their organ *Slowo Polskie* [The Word of Poland], blind as they were with rage about the general strike that was choreographed by Social Democracy. From *Slowo Polskie*: "*The time is finally ripe for us to openly announce that we hate Russian absolutism much less than Polish Social Democracy ...*"

The other party that previously stood for the national Polish solution, the Polish Socialist Party, made an official announcement three months ago. It has joined the ranks of those accepting that a Polish national rising is completely utopian in Poland today. The last, weak remains of the old Polish nationalist movement have disappeared in the strong waves of the general proletarian revolution in the tsar's empire, in which all workers are united in one army, without regard for nationality and sharing a common goal—the achievement of political freedom in the whole of the tsar's empire. "National" cant in Poland today

---

*   Luxemburg had earlier sought to demonstrate this claim through her 1897 work, *The Industrial Development of Poland*. See *The Complete Works or Rosa Luxemburg, Vol. I: Economic Writings 1*, edited by Peter Hudis (London and New York: Verso Books, 2013), pp. 1–78.

†   Luxemburg is here referring to the right-wing National Democratic Party of Roman Dmowski, which was founded in 1897 as a vehicle for Polish nationalism.

‡   These are fake unions that serve the interest of the employers, not the workers.

§   Luxemburg no doubt has in mind the group's virulent opposition to her SDKPiL. It should be noted, however, that the National Democratic Party also fiercely opposed left-wing tendencies that supported Polish national independence, such as the PPS.

only serves as a cover for the bloodiest reaction as wielded by both the Polish bourgeoisie and the petty bourgeoisie, as well as functioning as a smug pretense for the regime of the lash's violent escapades. In just this way, the large "nationalist" demonstrations that were arranged recently in Warsaw by the "noblest and the best," presented only one solution. Long live the people's unity—against "class-agitating" Social Democracy, they say; they passionately wish that the recent lackey-like "deputations" of the Polish bourgeoisie toward Petersburg will pacify the Polish proletariat as quickly as possible. And this is to be facilitated by granting the weakest possible freedoms regarding autonomy, re-establishing the desired "peace" and "order," and throttling revolutionary Social Democracy in the process.

But both sets of speculations—from the Polish reactionaries on the one side, and from the tsarist whip-bearers on the other—are wrong again. The bourgeoisie's "unity demonstration" in Warsaw has fanned the flames of party and class struggle in Poland to even greater heights. And the very state of siege that was aimed at isolating the Polish proletariat from the Russian Revolution has motivated the revolutionary Russian proletariat to carry out the first purposeful and strong action of solidarity for their Polish class comrades!

Not a single day without new moral victories, and not a single hour without the revolution making new progress! It is a joy to be alive!

The Revolution in Russia
[November 17, 1905]*

THE UNWRITTEN CONSTITUTION

The situation is escalating at this very moment in Russia and particularly in Petersburg to such a degree that we can expect that a state of siege will also be imposed on the capital on the Neva any day now. The bandits of tsarism evidently want to make a desperate attempt to stop, with violence, the revolution that is storming forward. But that is the very characteristic thing that a revolution does. Without waiting for the government's decisions and the "legal" pen strokes of lawyers' chambers, political freedom in all areas of public life has won through so strongly, that, amid the *Sturm und Drang*,† a way back can no longer exist.

A specific press law has not been issued; formally speaking, censorship exists in all its old rigor. A new law is due to be published soon, providing a substantial easing of the regulations surrounding the founding of newspapers. For Russian papers an announcement will now only have to be made fourteen days before the first issue; for non-Russian papers the stipulated period will be three months. In fact, a level of freedom prevails in the press in Petersburg, Moscow and Warsaw, which in the Prussian-German *Rechsstaat* "state-of-rights"‡ can still only be dreamt of. No paper even bothers about the censor anymore, as they simply ignore it. Editorial teams respond to strong warnings by the board-of-censors by stating that censorship contradicts the tsarist constitutional manifesto, and is therefore illegal. This leaves an oppositional press dominated by political criticism voiced in the sharpest of tones; political caricature and political wit are cleaning their guns without the least inhibition. In this atmosphere of fresh air, the differentiation of the press along party lines becomes more lucid by the day. A whole series of radical workers' papers have already been published in Petersburg, including: *Golos Naroda* [People's Voice], *Rabochaya Gazeta* [Workers' Gazette]; and *Russkaya Gazeta* [Russian Gazette]. We have already spoken about the founding of two unambiguously

---

*   This article first appeared in *Vorwärts*, No. 270, November 17, 1905, under the title "Die Revolution in Rußland." It is translated (by Henry Holland) from Luxemburg's *Gesammelte Werke*, Vol. 6, pp. 699–702.

†   This literally means "storm and drive." That phrase was popularized by the literary movement in German of the late eighteenth century of the same name, which broke from neoclassical artistic forms by extolling emotions, individuality, and subjectivity over the prevailing order of rationalism.

‡   *Reichstaat* is generally analogous to the Anglo-American concept of "state-of-law," although with an emphasis on moral rightness. It is this moral dimension—and the lack of it in the Prussian-German state—that Luxemburg is stressing.

Social Democratic party papers in Petersburg.* The way in which the reading public has received the Social Democratic papers is significant in determining Social Democracy's political and intellectual position of power in the current revolution. When *Novaya Zhyzn* [New Life]—that was founded with decidedly modest financial means—was published for the first time, the whole print run of 100,000 copies was sold out in Petersburg alone within only a couple of hours, meaning that a new edition had to be printed at night for the provinces. The public surged into the offices of the new paper in such numbers to register for a subscription, that there was a thronging queue of people outside all day, as if it were a theatere box office. The first issue included the official party program of Russian Social Democracy as a supplement to a publication that included an artistically splendid satirical sketch by [Evgeny Nikolayevich] Chirikov, *The Eagle and The Hen*†—symbolizing the proletariat and the liberals. The issue was of course "sequestered'" in proper fashion, which did not stop it being disseminated. The second party newspaper, due to appear shortly, will surely receive a similar reception. The demand for the living, printed word of the leading revolutionary party of the proletariat has become so enormous that several party newspapers could exist healthily beside each other, as polemical arguments between them are unthinkable in the present environment. Regarding the circumstances in which the press currently, it is revealing that the organ *Slovo* (The Word)—previously progressive but in recent times an ultra-reactionary rag of agitation—has been forced to close. The reason for this utterly involuntary farewell is that Petersburg typesetters refused to put together these filthy sheets. The *Post* and other papers of this caliber should count themselves lucky that they don't publish in Petersburg.

NEW STRUGGLES IN PETERSBURG

Petersburg, November 15. The authorities are *preparing for heavy street battles.* Whole batteries of *machine guns* are being moved into position. *Civil society is fleeing. All ships currently bound for abroad are full of refugees,* mostly full of women and children. They are sailing at high speed *toward German ports.* The workers have *threatened that an armed gathering of half-a-million people* will take place on Thursday afternoon. Ninety-nine thousand people stopped working on Wednesday. Strong troop divisions prevent assemblies, but numerous gatherings

---

*   This is a reference to *Novaya Zhyzn* (New Life) and *Nachalo* (The Beginning), the former published by the Bolsheviks, the latter primarily by those grouped around Leon Trotsky.
†   Chirikov joined the revolutionary movement in the 1880s and became an important exponent of Russian realism by 1900. In 1903, he authored the famous play *The Jews* and worked closely with Maxim Gorky during the 1905 Revolution. In *The Eagle and the Hen*, an eagle that is raised by chickens takes himself to be a chicken, until an owl convinces him to fly and spread his wings—much as the proletariat at first identifies with the liberals until it has the chance to "spread its wings" and fly on its own.

take place anyway, which formulate unanimous motions in favor of the armed struggle.

Petersburg, November 16. A number of former Minister of the Interior civil servants from Plehve's period of office* are heading the workers' movement that has broken out again—civil servants, who have since become socialists. They are of great service to the workers because of their comprehensive knowledge of the various branches of the administrative apparatus. We estimate the total number of strikers *at 700,000.* Darkness cloaked half of Petersburg's streets from yesterday evening onwards because of the gas workers' strike.

A PROCLAMATION FROM WITTE

Petersburg, November 16 (report by the Petersburg Telegraph Agency). Count Witte directed a telegram with the following content to the workers at all factories and other works:

> *Brothers, workers!* Take up your work again and stop taking part in disturbances! Have compassion with your women and children and desist from listening to advice from the evil-minded! The emperor has commanded us to address ourselves to the question of the workers with exceptional interest, and for this purpose we have created a trade and industry ministry that will bring about fair relations between the companies and the workers. Give us time. *I will do everything I can for you, in the realm of what is possible.* Listen to the word of a man who loves you and who wishes you well.
>
> Count Witte

The Petersburg workers will prefer to do themselves what they consider necessary, instead of relying on this windbag Witte!

LYNCH-MOB JUSTICE AND PEASANT REVOLTS

Laffan News Agency reports from Petersburg:

A summary execution was carried out early on Thursday on a *civil servant of the legal chambers* who was accused of inciting to participation in a *pogrom against the Jews.* A number of workers surrounded him on the street, commenced a formal interrogation with him, and subsequently sentenced him to death. Workers *shot* him on the spot with a revolver before dispersing. Terrible *atrocities* have been committed in *Burgade* and *Danutzery* in Bessarabia against the *Jews,* with girls and women dragged naked through the streets and abused in the vilest possible way.

---

* Vyacheslav von Plehve was Russian interior minister from April 1902. A firm opponent of liberal hopes, he was assassinated by the Socialist Revolutionary Yegor Sazonov on July 28, 1904.

The mob poured petrol over the Chief Rabbi of Chişinău *and burned him alive.* In the provinces of *Saratov,* Yekaterinoslav, Tambov and other regions *the peasants* are revolting *in their thousands, plundering the estates and murdering the estate owners.* The tsar has sent special legally authorized representatives to "pacify" the peasants.

Land mines have been found buried beneath the tracks on the Warsaw–Vienna line.

The minister of the admiralty, Admiral [Alexei Alexeyevich] Birilev, has been advised *to execute as few participants from the Kronstadt mutinies as possible.* The *sailors have announced that they would kill one officer for every executed mutineer, and would start that process with Admiral Birilev.* The officers are threatening to desert, in case the authorities pronounce mass death sentences against the mutineers.

TSARIST EXPRESSION OF TRUST IN THE ODESSA THUGS

London, November 15 (Laffan's News Agency). General [Alexander Vassiliyevich] *Kaulbars,* Odessa's military governor, authorized the *Standard's* correspondent in that city—by way of his adjutant, Colonel von Rever—that not only were reports about the general's imminent *resignation without foundation,* but that the tsar had even sent him a telegram *worded in an especially gracious manner,* in which the general's actions during the most recent disturbances in Odessa were appreciated and acknowledged.

The *Standard's* correspondent noted that in light of the damning judgment that has been cast upon General Kaulbar from all sides, he, the correspondent, would refrain from commenting on the tsar's telegram.

THE INSURRECTION IN VLADIVOSTOK

London, November 16 (Laffan's News Agency). According to reports arriving via Shanghai, around *800 persons have been killed or wounded* during the disturbances in Vladivostok. Insurrectionists burned the whole of the business district to the ground. It is impossible at present to estimate the cost of the damage.

The Revolution in Russia [November 18, 1905]*

News of *peasant unrest* is the recurring chorus during these most recent days of the revolution's history. As yet, this news arrives sparingly, bit by isolated bit; as yet, the unrest is limited to the central zone of the tsar's empire, the provinces of Kursk, Smolensk, and Saratov. Yet these are but the forerunners to a general eruption of peasant revolts, which, growing constantly, will ultimately rattle the entire empire like a terrible earthquake. Since time immemorial, the Russian agrarian movements have had the peculiar tendency that—as soon as they have made a start—they soon acquire an epidemic character, growing rapidly to enormous dimensions despite the cruelest of repressive measures. The last, large peasant unrest dates from the time immediately prior to the outbreak of the current period of revolution.† This peaked in the mighty revolt in Ryazan Province,‡ crushed militarily and with bestial cruelty by Prince [Ivan Mikhailovich] Obolensky.§ This was still under Plehve's political direction, when the tsar's regiments with their Cossackian odiousness still believed they could go on celebrating their orgies of violence unhindered.

Straight after that the thunderstorm broke. But instead of acting as a signal for the immediate explosion of general peasant unrest, the movement of revolution restricted itself exclusively to the urban proletariat. The grandiose, revolutionary actions of the Russian masses have been, until now, exclusively the accomplishment of the industrial working class, a reality that manifests itself externally in the *general strike* as the dominant form of struggle. The workers' movement's next reflex was for the rebellion in the *armed forces* to take the stage—the Potemkin revolts, the risings in Kronstadt and Vladivostok,¶ the wavering and disorganization of the land troops. And only now, as the third member of the club, is the storm gathering gradually around the peasant's rising.**

---

* This article first appeared in *Vorwärts*, No. 271, November 18, 1905, entitled "Die Revolution in Rußland." It is translated (by Henry Holland) from Luxemburg's *Gesammelte Werke*, Vol. 6, pp. 703–7.

† Peasant unrest flamed up from March to May 1902 in a number of regions, such as the provinces of Voronezh, Kutaisi, Poltava, and Kharkiv, before it was suppressed by force of arms.

‡ For an analysis of these peasant revolts of 1902, sparked largely by the inability of peasants to pay their arrears in taxes and payments for land allotments, see Sidney Hargrave's *The Russian Revolution*, pp. 20ff.

§ Obolensky at the time was an Imperial Russian lieutenant general. In 1910, he was assassinated by revolutionaries in St. Petersburg.

¶ The sailors' uprising took place in Vladivostok on November 12 and 13, 1905 and was beaten down by tsarist troops.

** The unprecedented series of peasant revolts in 1905 included 219 peasant uprisings in October, 796 uprisings in November, and 575 uprisings in December.

The mass rural revolt will of course carry a whole new element with it into the general revolution, at first causing a major realignment of its character. Regarding the homogeneity and clarity of its endeavors and its goals, the peasant movement is of course not in the least comparable with the proletarian movement in industrial cities. Inside the peasant unrest, petty-bourgeois utopian aspirations of peasants experiencing land poverty walk side by side with the modern economic demands of the rural proletariat, who [illegible word]* in their turn, voice political opposition against the terrible pressure of chinovnik economics, and against the tax system, and militarism—all these manifold demands are mixed up together. In saying that, we should point out that the structure and composition of the rural population differs widely in the various regions of the huge empire. Additionally, the work of socialists educating and organizing the masses in these rural backwaters is much more recent and of an incomparably narrower extent than in the industrial cities. It can only be the revolution, the struggle itself, that will soon enable people among the peasantry to catch up on what is lacking, as the industrial proletariat has done already, in terms of inner clarity, in terms of the work of disciplining, organizing, and, ultimately, *of differentiating according to class position*—as can now be achieved in an abbreviated process. This process of development, in the revolution's interior, certainly will vent its spleen in many still more vehement explosions, as a natural part of the peasant movement. But the final capital of the peasant unrests will simultaneously be the epilogue to the fall of old, tsarist Russia. The alarm bells that ring out now from church towers of rebellious village parishes in the Kursk, Saratov and Smolensk districts, will turn into bells for the death of absolutism and for all the social and political venality that cling to that apparatus.

The immediate effect on the general situation of the peasant unrest that is now beginning will be an escalation of class and party opposition in the environment of struggle that has prevailed until now. The agrarian-noble liberalism of the zemstvos, shocked by the red cockerel, will press even more energetically for the quickest possible conclusion to the revolution. That will leave the urban proletariat even more isolated in its revolutionary forward march. On the other hand, it will be necessary, in accordance with [its] nature, for it to attempt to grab hold of the leadership of the peasant masses. The tasks of the class-conscious workers in Russia thus grow mightily by the day. The Russian Revolution is already assigning these workers the same task in miniature that it always placed upon the shoulders of the international proletariat in its world-historical career—to be the shock troops of the totality of the working people, to be the whole enormous army of the exploited and the oppressed.

---

*   This bracketed comment is made by the editors of the *Gesammelte Werke*, and refers to the original.

PEASANT UNREST

Petersburg, November 17. Agrarian unrest is persisting in the provinces, particularly in *Kursk Province,* and is assuming ever-greater dimensions. Peasants destroyed Count Apraksin's properties, setting fire to buildings, and wounding the count and his spouse. Other domains in the surrounding region have been looted and set on fire in similar fashion.

Petersburg, November 16 (report by the Petersburg Telegraph Agency). A Council of Ministers was held today in Tsarskoye Selo under the chair of the emperor, at which the peasant question was due to be discussed.

TARDY ATTEMPTS AT PACIFICATION

Petersburg, November 17 (report by the Petersburg Telegraph Agency). The authorities have issued a most urgent decree, reducing all categories of purchase of property duties for peasants by half from January 14, 1906, and cancelling them entirely from January 14, 1907, onward. The Peasant Agrarian Bank has been instructed to make it easier for peasants to buy land through the bank, and to increase the bank's capital for this purpose, while granting bigger privileges in relation to loans.

THE GENERAL STRIKE

Petersburg, November 17. The telephone service was stopped at noon today. The telegraph civil servants are still negotiating on joining the strike. As regards the railroads, only the Finland line and the short stretch to Tsarskoye Selo are still operating. The bakers intend to join the strike on Sunday. During a night meeting, the strike committee passed a motion that they would persist in their strike until a democratic government, based on universal suffrage and direct elections, has taken power. The workers decided to do without Witte's sympathies.

Petersburg, November 16 (report by the Petersburg Telegraph Agency). The city is quiet. The staff of a number of drug stores have joined the strike. The newspapers have not been published. At the electricity works, the strikers have been replaced by sailors. The Nikolai Railroad ceased operations at 3 p.m.

Moscow, November 16 (report by the Petersburg Telegraph Agency). The workers are averse to the strike as proposed by the Council [Soviet] of Workers' Deputies. The majority refuse to strike for the cause of Poland. (This is only the *semi-official* report. It is more probable that, first, a general strike will be organized in Moscow.)

Warsaw, November 16. The sale of Polish daily papers has been prohibited by the governor-general. Local stores were open for the whole day today, and work should recommence in all factories tomorrow.

Chişinău, November 16. Workers' organizations in the city have proclaimed the *general strike* to start on *Monday.*

REVOLUTION IN THE ARMED FORCES

Petersburg, November 16. Military assemblies have taken place in the strike-riven regions of *Moscow* and *Baku,* at which the resolution of the *general strike committee* was accepted. The *Naval and Quartermaster Guards* in Petersburg also conducted a meeting, at which they declared themselves united with the committee's program. The sole non-official paper that is being published is the *Strike Board News,* published, as it is, beyond the reach of any *censor.*

THEY WOULD NOT DARE!

Petersburg, November 16. The declaration of a state of war, announced yesterday, has not come about.

Petersburg, November 16 (report of the Petersburg Telegraph Agency). A report in from Kutaisi states that the authorities have rescinded the state of siege imposed on Georgia.

ON THE EIGHT-HOUR DAY

The Petersburg Workers' Council* most recently passed a motion to introduce the eight-hour day into all factories and establishments, by means of a large and encompassing action. Declarations of this purpose have been made from the workers to company management, leading to a big panic among the magnates of capital. They are rounding up industrialists for an assembly, in order to throw out the workers' "impudent presumption."

Petersburg, November 16 (report by the Petersburg Telegraph Agency). An association of [employer] representatives from seventy-two factories in the greater Petersburg region declared unanimously—after sitting in council—that they consider the eight-hour day demanded by the workers to be impossible, as it would ruin the works and leave the workers without bread. In similar companies in Europe, with the exception of England, a working day is ten to twelve-and-a-half hours work, and in those works dependent on blast furnaces, everyone works in two shifts, each of twelve hours. The working day in Russia is no longer than in the rest of Europe, whereas Russia has more public holidays. The profits gained from Russian workers are three percent less than the average in Europe. Shortening the daily working time would lead to industry's total ruin and would

---

*   This was the most important soviet during the Russian Revolution. Here, as elsewhere in her writings of 1905, Luxemburg refers to the institution by its German name—*Arbeiterräte*—instead of using the Russian term *soviet.*

make any form of competition with the European factories impossible, until they would also reduce their working time by the same amount. Russian companies have higher overheads—they claim—because both raw materials and machines are much more expensive in Russia, and because the Russian factories compensate their workers for accidents suffered, which is not the case in other countries. The majority of the Russian people are already suffering from large-scale want. Shortening the working time would push up the price of the products, thus exacerbating the peasants' destitution. The Association of Representatives passed the motion to close the factories in case the workers didn't back down from their demand for an eight-hour working day.

The remark specifically about the Russian company owners' "lower profits" is impudence born out of droll naiveté. It is a generally known and officially proven fact that the gentlemen in, for example, the textile industry, pocket *on average* 40 percent, while their chums in the iron and mining industries bag 50, 60 or even higher percentages of "pure profit." The Petersburg workforce will certainly not let itself be flustered by the braggarts' talk of those "suffering from want."

MILITARY DICTATORSHIP IN SIGHT?

Petersburg, November 17. The tsar has announced his intention, in case the present situation worsens, to appoint Grand Duke Mikhailovich as military dictator with the broadest possible legal powers.

The Revolution in Russia [November 19, 1905]*

THE VIOLENT BLOWS OF REACTION

Petersburg, November 18. Tonight, the police forcibly seized the printing plant of the workers' newspaper *Izvestia* [News].† The entire workforce was arrested on charges of *lèse majesté*. The workers' committee‡ remains firm in its determination to continue publication of the paper.

THE SEMI-OFFICIAL NEWS AGENCY KEEPS TRYING TO "CALM PEOPLE DOWN"

Petersburg, November 18 (report from the Petersburg Telegraph Agency). The mayor is warning the population not to listen to the call of the Council of Workers' Deputies to begin a new walkout. Yesterday's attempt by the Engineers' Association to persuade bank employees to join the strike remained without results. Today all banks were open.

THE GENERAL STRIKE

Petersburg, November 18. Five hundred and twenty factories, including some that are run by the government, are affected by the walkout. The number of workers on strike is 113,000. Work stopped completely in four enterprises owned or operated by the state.

Warsaw, November 18. Social Democracy§ has decided to proclaim a general strike if the state of siege in Poland is not lifted.

Warsaw, November 18. Last night a bomb was thrown at a squadron of Cossacks, but without having any effect.

Warsaw, November 18. About 1,000 workers from the Staranowice Metal Works, who did not know that the railroad strike had been ended, stopped a mixed train⁵ on the transfer line to Ostrowice and forced it to go back. The telegraph system was disrupted and a bridge was rendered inoperable. Rail traffic was interrupted.

---

* This article first appeared in *Vorwärts*, No. 272, November 19, 1905, under the title "Die Revolution in Rußland." It is translated (by George Shriver) from Luxemburg's *Gesammelte Werke*, Vol. 6, pp. 708–9.
† *Izvestia* was the newspaper published by the St. Petersburg Soviet of Workers' Deputies.
‡ That is, the soviet.
§ That is, the SDKPiL.
⁵ A combined passenger and freight train.

Katowice, November 18. The railroad administration reports as follows: The first train from Katowice to Warsaw [after the rail strike was ended] departed successfully at 10:35 this morning. Riding on that train was a commission charged with negotiating the restoration of passenger and freight service to Warsaw.

THE WORTHY GENTLEMAN AND MAN OF HONOR LETS THE MASK SLIP

Petersburg, November 18. Count Witte has opened up a vigorous campaign against the revolutionaries. He sent representatives from the new Ministry of Commerce and Labor to the workers, instructing his representatives to say that the ministry was at the workers' service, but that they *must separate themselves from the revolutionary organizations.* The workers refused, and the revolutionary executive committee [of the St. Petersburg Soviet] issued a *counterproposal calling for social revolution.* It simultaneously sent representatives to summon the Social Democratic Party together with the ranks of the Social Revolutionaries. Count Witte replied with the threat that *martial law would be imposed.*

Petersburg, November 18. Special precautionary measures have been taken for the protection of Count Witte(!).*

THE RAMPAGING OF THE "BLACK HUNDREDS" IN VLADIVOSTOK

Tokyo, November 17. A Japanese businessman who arrived in Moji from Vladivostok on board the German steamship *Arcadia* recounted the following details about the *disturbances in Vladivostok.* The insurgents were *40,000 strong.* Among them were officers and crewmen from two warships in the harbor. They set fire to all buildings of any significance in the city, culminating in the burning of the headquarters of the German firm Kuntz & Alberts. The mutineers directed machine-gun fire at any steamships attempting to leave the harbor. However, a mishap occurred among those guarding the harbor, and the *Arcadia* was able to slip out. It goes without saying that the burning of buildings was not done by the mutineers, but by a police-directed mob that was unleashed upon them just as in Kronstadt and everywhere else.

MILITARY REBELLION IN HARBIN†

From London there comes a telegraph news dispatch, as follows: *London*, November 18. According to reports that reached here by way of Vladivostok and Tokyo, a mutiny broke out among the troops in Harbin—one worse than

---

* Luxemburg's exclamation point.
† Harbin is a major city in Manchuria. Russia had sent a sizable military force into the region during the Russo-Japanese War.

the mutiny in Vladivostok. The rebelling soldiers plundered and burned government property as well as people's homes, and they killed many officers who had resorted to arms to try and restore order. The rebels committed horrifying acts of violence and sought their victims among European as well as Chinese residents. The latest news reaching Vladivostok was that the mutiny in Harbin was still going on.

The Revolution in Russia
[November 21, 1905]*

ON THE AGRARIAN REVOLUTION IN RUSSIA

We have received the following: A peasants' congress of the Moscow governorate took place for the first time in May this year, a result of an initiative of zemstvo statisticians and agronomists. This congress decreed that an All-Russian Peasants' Association must be founded. This association's inaugural congress, covering the whole of Russia, took place in Moscow in mid-August. Present were one hundred peasants from twenty-two governorates. Official representatives from the Social Democratic Party and from the Party of Socialist Revolutionaries also took part in the negotiations. The congress sent its warmest thanks to its brothers—workers fighting in the cities for political freedom—and lent their support to the political demands of Russian labor.

The following resolution was passed on the agrarian question:

(1) Private ownership of land and soil shall be rescinded.
(2) Lands belonging to the monasteries, the church, and the aristocracy (i.e., the crown) shall be confiscated without compensation.
(3) The land of large landowners shall be confiscated, in part with compensation, in part without.
(4) The conditions under which the land of large landowners shall be confiscated are to be set by the Constituent Assembly.

With regard to the further activities of the Peasant's Association, *Novoye Vremya*† [New Times] published the following notice on November 9, 1905:

The office of the All-Russian Peasant's Association started work today by preparing material for the upcoming peasant's congress for the whole of Russia. The office is sending out calls for contributions together with a complete draft resolution for the parishes. The peasants are requested to discuss this draft and pass parish resolutions relevant to it. The draft recommends clear statements supporting universal suffrage, including women's suffrage; a direct and secret ballot; the abolition of the estates of the realm;‡ self-administration in the administration of the *volosts*;§ auton-

---

* This article first appeared in *Vorwärts*, No. 273, November 21, 1905, under the title "Die Revolution in Rußland." It is translated (by Henry Holland) from Luxemburg's *Gesammelte Werke*, Vol. 6, 710–13.

† This publication should not be confused with the more recent paper called *Novoye Vremya*, which has been published in Russian and German since 1991.

‡ Intended as a means to end social stratification.

§ A district made up of five to ten villages.

omous districts, in which members of all social estates have legal equality; a reform of the administration at district, governorate and province level, with the functions of these administrative bodies handed over to the zemstvos, voted on the basis of universal suffrage; and the transfer of all landed estates belonging to the state, the aristocracy, the monasteries, the church and private landowners into the ownership of the people, on condition that the land may only be used by those who cultivate it with their own work, or the work of their families. Indirect taxes on consumer goods must be repealed along with excise duty on matches, sugar etc., and be replaced by income tax. All children of both sexes and of school age must be educated at the state's expense.

The draft concludes with a demand for the release of all peasants who have suffered as a result of the agrarian unrest.

> Concerning the conditions under which land and soil shall be transferred into the people's ownership, the Peasants' Association office argues that these should be determined by freely elected people's representatives. We have received information that thousands of signed parish resolutions, compiled in accordance with the aforesaid demands, have already been sent to the office from various Russian regions.

The communications above are highly important. Agrarian communism runs in the veins of the Russian peasants. The news just in from central Russia of mass peasant risings in the last few days shows to what extent communist ideas are present among the peasantry. The idea of common ownership of land and soil is not yet foreign to Russian peasants; it has only been a few generations since the transfer of Russian land and soil from parish into private ownership.* The main grab of parish lands was carried out by aristocrats, who then took possession of the best estates, exactly as happened in England, France, and Germany; in recent centuries, most notably in East Elbia† and Mecklenburg. The abolition of serfdom in Russia at the beginning of the 1860s was another occasion that forced the peasants to take a nasty knock, in a similar fashion to the so-called emancipation of the peasants in Prussia in 1810.‡ The Russian peasant is still suffering

---

* Luxemburg develops this point in much greater detail in her *Introduction to Political Economy* and her anthropological and ethnographic studies on the developing world, composed when she was taught at the SPD's school in Berlin from 1907 to 1914. See *The Complete Works of Rosa Luxemburg, Vol. I: Economic Writings 1*, pp. 146–300.

† *Ostelbien* or East Elbia refers to the German territories to the east of the Elbe river, especially the Prussian lands of Brandenburg, Pomerania, and Silesia, which had been shaped by a long history of conservatism, serfdom, and Protestantism.

‡ Following its defeat by Napoleon in 1806, Prussia embarked on a series of military, administrative, and social reforms, one of which was the abolition of serfdom throughout the kingdom. Peasants were allowed to appropriate lands on which they worked, provided they paid for it—which most could not do. As a result, many were forced to surrender control of their land to absentee landlords, which made the situation worse than before.

very badly under these blows today, and he now believes the hour has come to reclaim what was stolen from him by his lords during centuries of thralldom.

If ever such a revolutionary movement was to arise in Germany, this would probably take root east of the Elbe, with the peasants and day laborers setting the priority on transferring the lords' lands, their latifundia,* into communal possession. It would be easier to carry out an agricultural revolution in East Elbia than anywhere else in Germany.

Petersburg. November 19. *Unrest among the peasants* is increasing. In the Stary Oskol district of Kursk Province, seventeen estates have been plundered and set alight. Infantry and Cossacks have been sent in. The governorates of Kursk and Penza, where unrest among peasants has also occurred, are said to have increased their defensive measures.

THE ZEMSTVO LIBERAL LORDS

Moscow, September 19. The Congress of Zemstvos and Municipalities opened this afternoon. [Ivan Illyich] Petrunkevich was voted president, Shepkin and [Alexander Alexandrovich] Saveliev vice-presidents. Twenty-six governorates and thirty-nine cities are represented; twenty-three Polish delegates are also present. [Fyodor] Golovin spoke first and explained that the manifesto of October 30 had not answered all demands, *but one must fight against anarchy.* [E.W.] Roberti made the point that the consultations existed to establish whether the congress *could support the government, and if so, under which conditions.* Several speakers, including the mayor of Saratov, Nemirovsky, insisted that *Witte must be helped to pacify the countryside, and that all details be left up to the Duma*(!). Nemirovsky spoke about the specter *of peasant unrest*(!) adding that the only cure was *to unite with Witte.* Count [Pyotr Alexandrovich] Heyden said it was essential that the government did not tie itself in knots with their contradictions. Freedom has been declared simultaneously with an imposition of a state of siege, and general adjutants have been furnished with unlimited powers. *Yes, a strong display of power is necessary at present,* he said, but only one that is *good*, and based on the rule of law. Those temporary laws aimed at achieving freedom are more important *than questions of electoral law that would be worked out in the Duma*(!). The city of Stavropol's representative, [Vassili Semjonovich] Abramov, spoke against meeting Witte, arguing that the October 30 manifesto has been rescinded. Rodichev followed, stating that the government has neither grasped the current situation, nor does it understand the manifesto of October 30; it should not proceed through actions *and* down the legal avenue at the same time. However, *if the government requires support, then one must help it,*

---

* A large landed estate or ranch, as in ancient Rome or more recently in Spain or Latin America, typically worked by slaves or serfs.

on condition of its most solemn promise to separate itself from reactionary tendencies. *One has to help the government* to bring the fundamental legal content behind October 30 into force; but first—according to Rodichev—the government has to take action to generate trust.

The negotiations were then postponed until the following day.

THE COMPOSITION OF THE BOURGEOIS-LIBERAL PARTY

Tartu, November 19 (report from the Petersburg Telegraph Agency). The Baltic Constitutional Party is on the verge of splitting. In its program, published today in Russian, German, and Estonian, the party demands the maintenance of *strong state power* to carry out reforms and to protect bourgeois freedom. Moreover, the program demands long-term political and economic reforms to benefit the working classes; provision for the poor; fair taxation; autonomy for urban and peasant organs of self-administration; and permission for national languages to be used in the autonomous universities, and in government and parish institutions.

ARRESTS

Warsaw, November 19. Numerous arrests have been carried out among the intelligentsia. The news that Frau Dr. [Estera] Golde had been shot has fortunately turned out to be false, as we suspected.

THE ASSEMBLY IN RECESS

Petersburg, November 18. *The strike committee* [of the Petersburg Council (Soviet) of Workers' Deputies] has today adopted the following resolution: The strike of railroad workers and other workers from Petersburg has proven to the government that the implementation of brutal measures such as the implementation of the death penalty—and declarations of martial war—will always be met by active resistance from the working class. The strike has proven that our power lies in growth, so if the committee decides one day that offering the government a decisive battle is necessary, we would triumph. The committee also proposes ending the strike on November 20 at noon, and then continues: *From now on the comrades will gather their strength.* If it is considered necessary to strike again, then all railroad workers will down tools simultaneously, and for as long as it takes for the government to grant all their political and economic demands.

Delegates representing the workers will hold an assembly on November 19 to discuss ending the strike on November 20.

The Revolution in Russia
[November 22, 1905]*

THE LIBERALS START TO WAVER

Every judicious observer of party relationships in Russia should have been able to predict what is happening now, a matter referred to many times in this column—*the Russian "liberals" are changing sides already to join the counter-revolution!* These upright citizens had already taken sides after the Bułyginist†miscarriage of the first "Duma" project. Their participation in elections—conducted under an electoral law akin to a bloodstained Cossack parody of the Prussian and Austrian systems of electoral injustice—cemented their resolve to bring the period of open and revolutionary mass conflicts to a close. The grandiose and unanimous rising of the urban proletariat, and the unprecedented general strike called by the railroad workers, shook the racketeer band of tsarism and all liberal circles for a while. The absolute ruler of all police spies and pimps coughed up a new constitutional manifesto, but the gentlemen liberals merely made faces and held their tongues, as implacable as rock when faced with the demand of at least granting universal and equal suffrage.

And now the general strike has ended, for the simple reason that a single general strike cannot continue indefinitely. In smashing the "Duma" smugness it has done its job, and now the class-conscious proletariat is gathering strength and ordering its ranks, before swinging to deliver a new and yet more conclusive blow. This momentary laying down of arms is sufficient for both the absolutist Black Hundreds and the liberals to recover, and for them to swing, more decisively than before, to join the counterrevolution. As soon as the first *shock* resulting from the proletariat's display of power is over, the *angst* and the *hatred* of property owners and of the privileged toward revolutionary high-handedness comes into its own. And just as the greatest manifestation of the industrial proletariat known to date exits, the dreadful spectere of the *peasants' revolt* takes the stage! The result of this rapid transformation is the *Zemstvo Congress* currently taking place in Moscow.

One after the other, from north and south and east and west, the gentlemen representatives of the zemstvo rush in with hasty, trembling votes of confidence for the remnants of absolutism, for this government of arsonists, thieves, and contract cut-throat killers; and of [today's] Louis [XVI].‡ Landowners, threatened

---

    * This article first appeared in *Vorwärts*, No. 274, November 22, 1905, under the title "Die Revolution in Rußland." It is translated (by Henry Holland) from Luxemburg's *Gesammelte Werke*, Vol. 6, pp. 714–16.
    † A reference to Alexander Bułygin's shaping of the so-called "Bułygin Constitution" in response to the Revolution of 1905.
    ‡ French king Louis XVI (1754–93), whose absolutist regime was overthrown during the French Revolution of 1789–1799. He was executed in 1793.

and quivering with angst, are seeking shelter under the zemstvos' wings against the revolution, in which, just in accordance with the *Communist Manifesto's* old recipe, the *question of ownership* is being pushed ever-more into the foreground. Just as the government gang have done, the gentlemen liberals have chosen the same "constitutional" cover as the medium of transition to the hegemony of counterrevolution—shifting the constitutional question, including the question of electoral law, onto the "Duma," elected through unjust elections by curiae* to the exclusion of the revolutionary mass proletariat, and to the exclusion of the democratic intelligentsia. The concessions of the last manifesto shall yet again remain a tsarist lie, the "Duma" shall take power as a result of a sham electoral law, and in that house, in the name of "the people's will," the people shall get another square blow to the head.†

This whole lovely sum will most certainly be nullified by the determined attitude of the proletariat, and by the peasants' movement, whose momentum cannot now be stopped. The *Zemstvo Congress* is itself an important symptom for the ferocity of class and party struggle that will soon take pole position in the Russian Revolution. The emergence of two camps becomes ever clearer. More and more peasants and members of the armed forces are moving under the banner of the industrial proletariat, while all bourgeois elements of the opposition move ever-more openly under the banner of "order." This can only serve the cause of both the revolution and the proletariat. History wants to serve us up the purest wine. So much the better.

THE SECOND DAY OF THE ZEMSTVO CONGRESS

Moscow, November 20. The *Zemstvo Congress* is continuing its negotiations today about relations with the government and with Count Witte. The representatives from Chernihiv and Saratov tabled the motion to *grant the government a vote of confidence* on condition that they convene a Constituent Assembly. The representative from Orel stated that he would only grant the government a vote of confidence if they abolished state of emergency legislation. The representative from Stavropol drew attention to *the threat posed by the agrarian movement*, and added that *this movement is going to destroy Russian civilization*(!). A Saratov representative countered that claim, explaining this movement is no cause for concern; the peasants are being *led by agitators. The initiators of this unrest must be treated with contempt*, and an objection must be voiced against the strikes. Prince [Pyotr Nikolaiyevich] Trubetzkoi added that *if the congress didn't support*

* *Kurienwahlrecht*, or election by curia, was used in the Austro-Hungarian Empire between 1861–1907 as the legal basis of dividing the electorate into different classes. Luxemburg uses this term to illustrate that this system gives a structural advantage to the traditional elites and thus denigrates democratic aspirations.

† Another reference to France's last monarch, King Louis XVI of France, who came to be seen by many in the French population as the epitome of tyranny.

the government it would generate the impression that everyone was dissatisfied with the manifesto of October 30(!!). Everyone must rally round this manifesto, *as the alternative is a rule of terror.* Redner proposed requesting the government to build a commission made up of *representatives from the zemstvos, the towns and cities, and upper secondary schools, who should draft an electoral law for the Imperial Duma.* The Kazan representative then added that the population is *against the Constituent Assembly*(!). The Petersburg representative moved for *support for the government and a period of waiting for the Duma to meet,* that being the only institution suitable for *creating laws to protect freedom.* The Novgorod representative tabled the motion that the fundamentals of the October 30 manifesto be accepted, and that we align *ourselves with the government.* This was seconded by a representative from Saratov. The Tver representative only wanted to grant the government a vote of confidence under certain conditions. The sitting was then postponed until the following day.

The congress for peasants is composed largely of town-dwellers, low-level employees, and journalists, with only a small group of peasants themselves. The managing director of a petrol company has been chairing this conference.

Petersburg, November 20 (report from Petersburg Telegraph Agency). In Kostroma an assembly of the Constitutional Party passed a motion that *all zemstvos and municipal authorities must attest to their confidence in Count Witte,* that being the only method of pacifying the disturbances and strikes.

ON THE STATE OF SIEGE

Łódź. November 20. A number of confectioner's shops were occupied by the army this evening; all guests were interrogated and many were arrested.

THE JAPANESE DEFEND RUSSIAN "ORDER"

The *Daily Telegraph* reports *from Nagasaki*: Peace has been re-established on Russian prisoner transport ships. Admiral [Zinovy Petrovich] Rozhestvensky decided to dispense with further Japanese protection. However, Japanese torpedo boats are still guarding the transport steamer Tambov that went to sea today. Disaffection is evident among Russian prisoners in Kokura, Fuknoka, Kurume, and Kurmamoto.

REPARATIONS FOR CHINA

Washington, November 21. China has demanded reparations worth 20 million dollars in compensation for the damages that China incurred during the Russo-Japanese war.*

---

* The Portsmouth Conference of 1905 ended the war without providing for reparations, as initially demanded by both China and Japan.

The Revolution in Russia
[November 24, 1905]*

THE LIBERAL "PILLARS OF ORDER"

The Zemstvo Congress has made an official statement against the formation of the Constituent Assembly! The "liberal" gentlemen have thereby cemented their alliance with the tsarist government, and have accepted the government's plan to strangle constitutional change in the *Duma*, sidestepping a National Constituent Assembly† that would have been elected by *all* of the people in the process. Of course, none of this will have any impact on the revolution's path. The *workers* are sticking calmly to their battle plan, and are preparing for a new and decisive battle across the board in December or January.

Moscow, November 21 (report from the Petersburg Telegraph Agency). The Zemstvos Congress and the municipalities. In the continuing consultations about the position to be adopted in the negotiations with Witte's ministry, the Polish speakers Dborotworsky and [Alexander Robertovich] Lednitzki stated that they were prepared to reach agreement on the condition that martial law be rescinded in Poland, that primary schools be allowed to teach in Polish, and that this language be re-introduced in administrative and public institutions. Lednitzki protested vehemently against the claim that Poland was considering separating itself from Russia. [Mikhail Alexandrovich] Stachovitch, representative from the town of Jelatz, proposed supporting the government only on the condition that elections to the Duma—which he requested be called a representative rather than a Constituent Assembly—be held on the basis of universal suffrage, *and* on the condition that the death penalty be abolished. *Prince Volkonski from Ryazan warned the assembly against overblown demands.* If the majority were to decide publicly against supporting the government, then he would propose *that the minority form themselves into a group and put themselves at the disposal of Witte's ministry.* [Vasili Vassilyevich] Klimov from Ryazan said that the people will always be for the tsar, and that *a National Constituent Assembly is only necessary for Social Democrats.* Stachovitch, Marshal of the

---

* This article first appeared in *Vorwärts*, No. 275, November 24, 1905, under the title "Die Revolution in Rußland." It is translated (by Henry Holland) from Luxemburg's *Gesammelte Werke*, Vol. 6, pp. 717–20.

† Luxemburg uses *Konstituante*, rather than *konstituierende Versammlung*, to make a direct reference to the National Constituent Assembly in France, in July 1789, in German called *die Konstituante*. It ended the traditional system that gave equal weight to the three social estates (clergy, nobility, and the so-called third estate) in the assembly. This traditional system of pre-revolutionary France amounted to the third estate being at a huge structural disadvantage, despite representing by far the largest amount of people.

Nobility, referred to the example of the Finns, who, if they *had received a promise from the Chamber of Representatives would have stopped the revolution immediately.* The assembly should, he said, *wait for* the new constitution, based on the October 30 manifesto. Prince Pavel Dolgurokov proposed *support for Witte's ministry. All other speakers elaborated on the same thoughts*; only Shepkin stated that Witte's ministry has proven itself incapable during the last three weeks of delivering to the country the new freedoms guaranteed by the monarch. It must now either be swept aside, or be forced to grant these freedoms inside three days.

Moscow, November 22 (report from the Petersburg Telegraph Agency). The congress has received telegrams from various associations, zemstvo administrations and other bodies in the provinces, *all stating that supporting the government is a must and positioning themselves against the Constituent Assembly.*

Petersburg, November 22 (report from the Petersburg Telegraph Agency). Prime Minister Count Witte received telegrams from *municipal councils* in Kazan and Astrakhan, and from the stock exchanges in Rybinsk and Samara, in which these bodies declared their preference to *support a government* founded based on the manifesto of October 30.

Petersburg, November 22. Count Witte received a lengthy telegram from the members of the Zemstvo Congress in Moscow, communicating their readiness to *support him in order to restore order.* A delegation of members from the Zemstvo Congress will receive an audience with the tsar in the near future. Rumor has it that *numerous ministerial portfolios will be distributed among zemstvo men.*

These "liberal" *mamelukes* are getting what they deserved!

MARTIAL LAW AND BLUE PILLS FOR THE PEASANTS

Petersburg, November 22 (report from Petersburg Telegraph Agency). *A state of increased protection* has been declared in the governorates of *Chernihiv, Tambov, Penza,* and *Kursk,* in the municipalities of *Balashov, Serdobsk, Petrovsk, Atkarsk,* and *Saratov,* as it has in the governorate of Saratov and the city of Saratov.

Petersburg, November 23. The *agrarian movement* in the provinces of Tambov and Voronezh is growing in size. That prompted the vice-governor to order the *arrests* of a number of rabble-rousing peasants, and for an even larger number of them *to be shot.* The *troops carried out these orders, resulting in the shooting of over 100 peasants and the wounding of many others.* The peasants destroyed dwellings and demanded that the landowners relinquish their land; at which the owners fled into the cities.

---

*   By using this metaphor, Luxemburg not merely conceptualizes the role of liberals as mercenaries for the status quo, but frames them as a special kind of "owned slaves" analogous to the Mamelukes in the Islamic empires in the Middle East and India; she wants the reader to know that they are dangerous slaves, who could seize power.

STILL A STATE OF SIEGE

Petersburg, November 23. The governor of Livonia, present in the city, explained to Count Witte that order could only be maintained by imposing a state of war.

THE STRUGGLE CONTINUES!

Report in from *Warsaw*: A large public assembly took place yesterday in the workshops of the Warsaw–Vienna railroad, with 10,000 participants. They passed a motion that *unless the government repeals martial law in Poland by January 1, 1906, a general strike for the whole of Poland will be declared.*

Petersburg, November 22. A number of state manufactories were closed, and the workers made redundant, *because the workers refused to return to work.* The government went on to communicate that these industrial establishments will remain closed permanently, if the workers don't relent.

Helsinki, November 23 (Wolff's Telegraph Office). At a meeting of the *Labor Party** the motion was passed by 191 votes to 96 that the party *will not participate in elections for regional parliaments.* If necessary, a *general strike* should be declared.

FERMENTATION IN THE ARMY AND NAVY

Petersburg, November 23. According to reports received by the Admiral Office, there is *much unrest among the crews of the two Russian cruisers that have reached Saigon.* General [Nikolai P.] Linevich has also reported concurrently in a similar vein that agitators among the troops in Manchuria have also attempted insurrections.

THE "ADMINISTRATIVE ROUTE" TO A CONSTITUTIONAL COMEDY

Petersburg, November 22. Today the tsar chaired the first complete meeting of the new cabinet assembled by Count Witte, in Tsarskoye Selo. The tsar reportedly signed two edicts during the meeting, giving more form to the promises made by him in his manifesto, aimed at transforming *freedoms of assembly and of the press into permanent constitutional measures.*

---

*   This refers to the Finnish Labor Party, which changed its name to the Social Democratic Party in 1903. Its leftwing was led by O. Kuusinen and Y. Sirola. Luxemburg later met with some of its leaders during her stay in Finland in 1906.

TSARIST LIBERALISM HIT BY HARD BLOW!

London, November 23. The Petersburg correspondent of the *Standard* reports that *Count Witte has had a stroke*. His left arm *is paralyzed*. The prime minister has also been suffering under *dizzy spells*. Hours have passed in which people have seriously worried about Witte's life. It appears unlikely that Count Witte will remain in office for long. The same report can be found in the Parisian *Le Matin*.

Mosse and Auntie Voß* will be tearing their hair out—how can world history move at all without Witte?

---

* Luxemburg is referring to the newspaper *Berliner Tageblatt*, produced by the newspaper publisher Rudolf Mosse and holding close links to the liberal Free Thinkers' Association (*Freisinnige Vereinigung*). "Auntie Voß" is the name for the *Vossische Zeitung*, a daily liberal-bourgeois paper. The name derives from the founding publisher and bookseller Christian Friedrich Voß.

The Solution to the Problem*

In the tsarist empire, the cause of the revolution is marching on with iron logic. At this moment, the phase of peasant uprisings has begun, and thus the revolution has planted its flag in the countryside as well. Up to now, since the beginning of this period of revolution, the peasants in Russia have remained silent. The urban industrial proletariat, influenced for a decade and a half by the tireless educational efforts of Social Democracy,† was the first to appear on the scene and has carried on the struggle alone. Until now it has remained the sole bearer of this immense revolution, and it has been destined, owing to its class position in society, to remain the most clear-sighted, the most resolute, and the farthest going, and therefore it has taken the *leading part* within the ever-growing revolutionary army in Russia. But even *before* the mass of the peasants [began to move], the cause of the urban proletariat was joined by elements of *the military* on both land and sea. The memorable insurrection on the battleship *Potemkin*, and then the uprising of the Kronstadt sailors near the very portals of the tsar's residence, and immediately after that the revolt of the troops in Vladivostok and Harbin—this series of explosions showed that a powerful ferment was underway throughout the Russian navy, in the south, in the north, and in the Far East.

And nowhere was it a matter of some raging outburst of wild and mindless passion, a lie that the semi-official Russian news agencies were in the habit of bruiting about, and that lie found docile and willing belief from our bourgeois press, with the "liberal" newspapers leading the pack.

No, it is the spirit of political enlightenment, of proletarian consciousness, the product of *Social Democratic* educational work—that was what found expression in the so-called "mutinies" of the Russian sailors up until now. On the battleship *Potemkin* and at Kronstadt it was people from Social Democratic organizations who marched at the forefront of the movement. The clear and distinct formulation of demands of an explicitly political nature, and at the same time of a proletarian character, left its mark on the rebellions in all cases, the mark of revolutionary activity that is class conscious through and through. And if all these rebellions were accompanied by the dark shadow of arson, murder, drunkenness [*Suff*], and plundering, this was not done by the "mutinous" sailors.

---

* This article was first published in *Die Gleichheit*, No. 24, November 24, 1905, pp. 139–40, with the German title "Die Lösung der Frage." It is translated (by Henry Holland) from Luxemburg's *Gesammelte Werke*, Vol. 1, Part 2, pp. 619–22.

† Although the first empire-wide Social Democratic party was not established in Russia until 1897 (with the Jewish Bund) and the RSDRP in 1898, earlier Social Democratic parties and groupings existed on a regional and local basis, such as the Proletariat I and II parties (founded in 1882 and 1888, respectively) and the St. Petersburg League of Struggle for the Emancipation of the Working Class (founded in 1895). Informal Social Democratic groupings in the form of study circles and other formations also existed by the late 1880s.

It has already become known to the whole world that it was the hoodlum gangs of the tsarist regime,* which by systematic prompting and encouragement on the part of the police and the priests sought to drown the revolutionary upsurge in blood, to drown the rebellious sailors and the industrial workers in the cities beneath a foul wave of criminal actions. Murder, arson, and pillage were set into motion not by the "mutinous" sailors but by hired "pillars of law and order" organized by the absolutist regime as a means of combating the sailors' rebellion.

But it is not only in the navy but also among the ground troops serving Nicholas the Last that the seeds of revolution are ripening with every passing hour. Already when absolutism attempted to suppress the sailors' revolts with the use of gleaming weaponry, in many instances the troops refused to fire. Twice this happened with the regiments sent to Kronstadt to butcher the rebel sailors. In the cities, the troops repeatedly refused to obey orders during encounters with demonstrating workers. In Moscow during the memorable mass funeral procession in honor of the Social Democratic leader [Nicholai] Bauman, who was assassinated by the sharks of the tsarist regime, among the 200,000 who marched, the military was massively represented. A group of high-ranking officers with sabers drawn formed the honor guard around the Social Democratic banner at the head of the demonstration. A living chain of people formed a line of marshals on both sides of the giant procession with workers, students, women, soldiers, and officers in bright, multicolored alternation, their arms stretched out and their hands clasped together. It was not only in the ranks of the ordinary soldiers but also in officer circles that the forward-looking revolutionary component raised their voices ever-more sharply against the willing cutthroats of the tsarist regime. The military as a whole, brought to a state of breathlessness by the fiery and feverish agitation of the Social Democrats, every day becomes less reliable, less and less serviceable as a support for this autocracy in the process of collapse.

In this way, one of the most important tactical questions finds its solution, a problem that has given terrible headaches to the opportunists who try to make calculations about the class struggle both here in Germany and everywhere. How can any mass action of the modern working class, whether it be a series of ever-larger street demonstrations or a mass strike, count on success, [they ask,] because after all, we, the unarmed proletariat, will run up against the iron wall of militarism with its gleaming steel bayonets and we are entirely powerless against that. And thus, we are constantly being appealed to by those who cannot imagine any mass action of the workers other than in the framework of the stodgy old milieu, the cold atmosphere of everyday parliamentary peace and quiet. Over and over again, they forget that serious mass action by the proletariat in and of itself cannot take place other than in a revolutionary situation, in

---

    *   Among which were the Black Hundreds.

a situation that has already brought the entire mass of the people and the entire country into a state of ferment.

If that is so, then even the "iron wall of bayonets" can be seen from an entirely different point of view, because in times of revolution, when the cause of the fighting proletariat has become the cause of all working people, the cause of all the oppressed and exploited, in that situation there awakens in the heart of the soldier—the citizen, the son of the people, the proletarian. Those who in their thinking *oppose* the present-day military as an unchangeably hostile force to the people's revolution forget that the revolution draws the military itself into its whirlpool; they forget that behind the external noise and alarm of revolutionary struggle is hidden its most powerful, and socially and historically its most important side, *the political educational work of the revolution.* And this work becomes fulfilled not only among the mass of the working class but also in the broader strata of the population, the peasantry, the petty bourgeoisie, and also among that part of the masses who are dressed in the "king's uniform."

The Russian events have shown once again that *the revolution, which brings up new political and social problems, also brings a solution to those problems, carrying them in its bosom.* The Russian Revolution once again is simultaneously a warning to those of little faith in our own ranks and a warning to the ruling classes who propose more and more military and naval projects, and who thereby, not only in Russia, are calling up spirits to the social surface which they themselves one day will not know how to banish.

The Revolution in Russia
[November 25, 1905]*

At present, all sides are preparing and arming themselves for new and tough battles. The Zemstvo Congress that has just closed has given the liberal position a clear and unmistakable form. The formal refusal to convene a Constituent Assembly—meaning that constitutional competence is handed over to the ordinary "Duma," and the decision to support the government to put this new "constitution" into place—is a gauntlet thrown at the feet of the working class and Social Democracy. There will be tough battles, sooner or later, between Social Democracy and the constitutional monarchists, who expect a constitution from this government of the Black Hundreds, and want to enforce freedom with that government, rather than with the "street." The longer the peasants' unrest continues, the nastier these battles will be. The first flaming glow of the peasants' rising has already been enough to cause agrarian liberalism to flee. Fear of revolution was the reoccurring tone of all speeches at the congress. Now the gentlemen are pushing for new Duma elections to be held as quickly as possible, so that "order" can be restored. Rest assured: when *these* liberal men finally have their hands on their portfolios and power, they will put absolutism to shame, in their ruthless use of violence against the revolutionary working class and the peasants! ...† Meanwhile urban workers prepare feverishly for further battles. The whole energy of Social Democracy in Russia as in Poland is now focused on *the organization* of the masses. Priorities here are founding a legal *party press*, creating legal or semi-legal *trade unions*, and in so doing legalizing the *political* organization of Social Democracy. New problems of tactics and organization turn up almost constantly, and so the work of inner clarification and consolidation of class struggle continues, tirelessly, unheeded from the outside and indeed invisible, especially to foreign countries. The revolution isn't resting on her laurels for a second. In those moments, when she, the revolution, isn't fighting any noisy battles, and the world is not full of the clang of steel upon steel, then she's carrying out the more *important* part of her historical work. She forms classes and parties, deepens the political consciousness and organizes; she separates that which is socially distinct and unites that which belongs together. And the conscious bearer of this revolutionary work is, for the first time ever, *Social Democracy.*

---

* This article first appeared in *Vorwärts*, No. 276, November 25, 1905, under the title "Die Revolution in Rußland." It is translated (by Henry Holland) from Luxemburg's *Gesammelte Werke*, Vol. 6, pp. 721–4.

† The ellipsis is in Luxemburg's original.

THE ZEMSTVO CONGRESS

Moscow, November 24 (report from the Petersburg Telegraph Agency). The congress of the zemstvos and the municipalities has refused the *convening of a Constituent Assembly*, and supports the constituent functions of the first assembly of the Duma.

Moscow, November 24. The Zemstvo and Municipalities Congress demands that numerous ministers subordinate themselves to the Council of Ministers, with the exception of the minister of the imperial court. Support for direct and universal suffrage was carried by a two-thirds majority vote at the congress.

BOURGEOIS ORGANIZATION

A congress of business people and industrialists from the whole of Russia will take place soon in *Moscow*, as the *Russian Courier* reports. This congress should agree the program for the Party of Trade and Industry in the Imperial Duma.[*]

The political flag of Russia's future "national liberals" is flying in the name of extremely high excise duty, the weakest type of constitutionalism and agitation against the workers. That much is clear already.

THE FIGHT GOES ON

Petersburg, November 24. A number of factory owners have decided to stop work again tomorrow, because the workers are still refusing to withdraw their demand for an eight-hour day.

Petersburg, November 23. [Alexei Alexeyevich] Birilev, minister of the navy, will allow the works on the Neva to open again tomorrow, Friday, after a period of closure. He stated that the workers should be granted one last opportunity to return to work. Most other industrial works in Petersburg will remain closed until the start of next week. They want to see how the workers position themselves in relation to the government's measures. *The official number of unemployed workers in Petersburg is currently 60,000.*

Petersburg, November 24. The final year of the engineering school *has gone on strike*, in response to the sacking of a liberal head teacher. Workers at the new Admiral Shipping Yard are boycotting their new boss, Admiral [Konstantin] Kuzmich.[†]

---

[*]   The Party of Trade and Industry was founded in 1905 after the publication of the tsar's manifesto on October 30 (New Style). It was a counter-revolutionary party representing big money in Russia's central industrial regions, and collapsed in 1906.

[†]   Kuzmich had been appointed chief of the port of Saint Petersburg shortly before this. In May 1906, he was killed in an act of revolutionary terror.

THE AGITATORS' CLUB

The *Russian Courier* has received the following: A new *Association of Factory Owners* has formed in *Moscow*. The Association wants to raise around *ten million marks* in capital, to which every industrialist will contribute from their turnover. The Association's purpose is to *combat strikes through mutual support and mutual assurance of each other's businesses.*

Petersburg, November 24. The Association of Printworks Owners decided not to pay employees taking industrial action for the duration of the strike. The Moscow Tram Companies decided the same. Reports in from Moscow state that newspaper-sellers have boycotted the Vetschernaja Pochta [Evening Post] newspaper, and thoroughly damaged its printworks yesterday.

Moscow, November 23. Striking workers smashed up the Bostanshoglo tobacco factory along with a number of other buildings, and tipped over a tram carriage. In *Busuluk*, in the Samara Governorate, disturbances developed out of a *conflict between police and army recruits.* Led by artisans, this rabble (i.e., police trash)* went on the rampage and released twenty-one convicted criminals. Looting of shops was only prevented with much effort.

Moscow, November 24. The telephone workers have gone on strike, in protest against long working hours. There are also concerns that a new strike may break out on the Nikolaev railroad.

THE RAILROAD WORKER'S STRIKE CONTINUES

Breslau, November 23. As communicated by the Breslau railroad management, *goods trains to Russia* via Grajewo are currently *blocked*, as is the Balachany–Baku–Sucharany line, part of the Trans-Caucasian Railroad. On the lines to Nizhny-Novgorod, and on the Moscow–Kazan railroad lines beyond that, the goods bound for Siberian stations have been stored temporarily, until further transport is possible.

HELP NEEDED!

Just in from *Moscow*: The *strike commission's finances* appear to be so depleted that strikers haven't received a single kopeck in the last few days from the strike fund, despite all best efforts.

Warsaw, November 24. *Courland's governor* has issued an order to all military governors in which all persons who organize assemblies are to be seen as insurrectionists, and that such assemblies are to be entirely prohibited. If however assemblies do take place, then these are to be *dispersed with force.* Telegraph officers in *Piotrków* are instructed not to forward telegrams to Witte or to the

---

* Luxemburg suggests that the police were using agent provocateurs to incite violence.

tsar if they contain personal content. In Łódź, *7,000–8,000 workers are striking in thirty-seven factories.* Twelve students have been arrested in *Doubrava.*

THE REBELLION IN THE NAVY

Brăila, November 24. Despite the Russian consul's intervention, the Russian ships lying here at anchor cannot steam off to Bessarabia and Killa *because mutinying sailors have declared that they don't want to return to Russia.* Another Russian steamer carrying numerous Russian revolutionaries on board, which had planned to pick up sailors from the *Potemkin* so that they couldn't participate in the revolution in Russia, has now been ordered not to land.

COSSACKS AGAINST COSSACKS

A correspondent here has received the following: A large assembly of Don Cossacks was held during the last few days in Moscow. This assembly passed a motion demanding that the government: (1) Prosecute all Cossacks who have shot at defenseless citizens; (2) permanently divest the Cossacks from police office; (3) send back all thirteen Cossack regiments currently in central Russia to their home by the river Don.

THE SUCCESS OF KRONSTADT

The unrest among sailors in Kronstadt has led to the Navy Department deciding to reduce the period of naval service—until now, seven years—by two whole years. The navy will, moreover, be entirely restructured.

The Revolution in Russia
[November 26, 1905]*

POLISH AUTONOMY AND THE LIBERALS

Moscow, November 24 (report from the Petersburg Telegraph Agency). The office of the Zemstvo Congress proposed further consultation with regard to the draft resolution *on the Polish question*, and voted wholeheartedly in support of a previous congress decision concerning Polish autonomy. Not only had the decision in question nothing to do with the separation of Poland, no, indeed *the opposite was true; it was necessary to secure the power and indivisibility of the empire.* That is why the reasons for the introduction of the state of siege in Poland as set out in the communiqué do not match the facts. The Congress perceives the following measures to be urgent: (1) Repeal of the state of siege in Poland; (2) submitting the question of Polish autonomy to the first Russian National Assembly, with the condition that the empire remain united; (3) introduction forthwith of the Polish language into primary schools, parish courts, and in matters brought before justices of the peace.† The negotiations commence this evening at 10 p.m.

Moscow, November 25 (report from the Petersburg Telegraph Agency). The Polish question was debated yesterday during proceedings of the congress of zemstvos and municipalities. *Struve*, the editor of the newspaper *Osvobozhdenie* [Freedom] demanded liberal administration and autonomy for Poland, now in the throes of the same anarchy as has spread through the rest of the empire. There is no need to fear foreign interference in this process. *All Russians would be united against this.* Prince Dolgurokov stated that autonomy did not mean separation, and even [Vasily Danilovich] Katkov is not supporting autonomy. The debate was suspended at midnight.

UNIVERSAL SUFFRAGE

An urgent telegram sent to the *Russkiye Vedomosti* [Russian News] reports the Russian government's decision *to introduce a universal, secret, and equal electoral law for the elections of people's representatives as soon as possible.* More detailed information should be published soon.

Like music to my ears ...

---

* This article first appeared in *Vorwärts*, No. 277, November 26, 1905, under the title "Die Revolution in Rußland." It is translated (by Henry Holland) from Luxemburg's *Gesammelte Werke*, Vol. 6, pp. 725–7.

† Luxemburg uses the term *Friedensgericht* at this point, denoting the type of court, rather than specifying which type of judge would hear such cases. "Justice of the peace" is, however, an adequate translation for the level of the judiciary that Luxemburg is describing.

WITTE IN THE STORM

The *Russian Correspondent* received the following telegram from Petersburg: Have found out from best sources that Witte is in very difficult position because [Pyotr Nikolayevich] Durnovo* is now following Trepov and the reactionaries, and has the tsar's heartfelt approval in this.

THE FIGHT GOES ON!

A private dispatch from the *Berliner Tageblatt* reports: *Moscow*, November 24. *A new strike movement* is beginning here in earnest. The fact that waiting staff, housemaids, and telephonists are striking is relatively harmless. But *serious disturbances* have been taking place since yesterday evening in a number of factories on the edge of the city, work has been stopped, and many *factory buildings have been totally destroyed*. To top that, rumors are circulating that we can expect a *new general railroad strike* to begin on December 4.

Petersburg, November 24. The new ministry for Trade and Labor has researched a set of *strike statistics*. According to these, 119,000 men stopped work on declaring the latest strike in Petersburg, and 10,000 men went on striking after the industrial action had been declared finished. *At present, 23,000 men in Petersburg and 51,260 men in Moscow are on strike.*

Riga, November 25. The atmosphere in the region surrounding Riga grows ever-more threatening. *Revolutionary peasants* are occupying the sources of Riga's water supply. The local railroad to Stopmannsdorf has been totally destroyed, the tracks torn up, the telegraph lines have been cut, and civil servants have been taken prisoner. A variety of peasant parishes have declared themselves to be independent [by creating] communally administered districts, having chased out the civil servants.

Petersburg, November 25. The newssheet *Nasha Zhizn* [Our Life] describes the outbreak of revolts in *Irkutsk* as well as the spread of unrest in Poland. In *Moscow* striking workers are roaming the streets. The residents of the *Balashov* district have sent General Bakanov a telegram in which they complain about Cossack excesses. *The Cossacks robbed, looted, and dismembered residents. In Rostov, 500 workers roamed the streets, toppling over tram carriages, at which shop owners closed their shops and industrialists stopped production.* The workers

---

*   On October 23, 1905, Durnovo succeeded Bulygin as interior minister. He was deeply conservative and opposed any democratic opening. He left office in 1906 after the departure of Witte from the government. Later, in 1914, he sent the tsar a memorandum that predicted the outcome of World War I with remarkable accuracy: "A general European war is mortally dangerous both for Russia and Germany, no matter who wins ... [T]here must inevitably break out in the defeated country a social revolution which, by the very nature of things, will spread to the country of the victor ... An especially favorable soil for social upheavals is found in Russia, where the masses undoubtedly profess, unconsciously, the principles of socialism."

decided to organize a *protest strike* lasting forty hours, to protest against the massacre of workers by Cossacks.

FOR THE EIGHT-HOUR DAY

Petersburg, November 25. The agitation in support of the eight-hour working day has so far produced the following results—five factories have fired 1,700 workers, while seven other factories have announced redundancies. The new Admiral shipyard, the Baltic shipyard, and a few others are still operating under the old conditions. Workers have gone back to work in the Putilov armaments plant and in almost all the factories in the Narva and Moscow districts, in order to develop their organization.

THE REBELLION IN THE ARMY

London, November 25. According to the *Standard*, the Manchurian Army is facing an open insurgency; apparently, soldiers have set the city of Harbin on fire.* (It was not the soldiers, of course, but rather the Black Hundreds, led on by the police.—The editors)†

IN VLADIVOSTOK

The Berliner Zeitung has discovered that the following telegram was sent to [Nikolai] Linevich‡ a few days ago: The revolts of troops that began in and around Vladivostok on November 13, and raged in an uncanny way for several days, *are still going on. Half of the city* has been, at various locations, *burned to the ground, ravaged, and looted.*

THE REBELLION IN THE NAVY

Sevastopol, November 25 (report by the Petersburg Telegraph Agency). Unrest has broken out among the sailors stationed here, and among the soldiers of the *Brest* Regiment. Signs of unrest are also visible among the *port workers.*

---

* Russia at the time was still in competition with Japan over control of Manchuria and had sent a sizable ground force into the region near the end of the Russo-Japanese War. It was one of the factors the led the Japanese government, concerned that its troops were stretched too thin in the area, to agree to the settlement that ended the war.

† The editors of *Vorwärts* inserted the sentence in parentheses into the original article.

‡ At the time, Linevich was adjutant general of the Imperial Russian Army in the Far East.

The Revolution in Russia
[November 28, 1905]*

The storm of revolution pounds against the shaking ruins of absolutism, wave after wave. No sooner has the urban proletariat stepped off center stage for a moment in order to equip itself with better defenses and more deadly weapons, than the military rebellion steps into the limelight, as if everyone were following a detailed field plan. *Sevastopol in the hands of revolutionary marines! Hurrah!* The thunder is everywhere and the valley of tsarism is kettling† in a full circle: Sevastopol, Odessa, Kronstadt, Vladivostok, Sevastopol! The "bad circle" of old Russia has been squared, and there is no escape. These aren't blind and primitive outbreaks of protest as some in the West, including Social Democrats, might think. Sevastopol and Odessa are old; age counts now in Russia after just *a few* years. They are *strongholds of Social Democratic agitation.* On board the *Potemkin,* Social Democracy was at the wheel. *Organized* Social Democratic sailors are leading the rising in Sevastopol today.

We received the following *private dispatch* yesterday. *Sevastopol, November 26, 8:40 p.m. An imposing and peaceful demonstration of soldiers and sailors has just taken place, demanding improved conditions, the discharge of reservists, and political freedoms. The commanding officer, who threatened to shoot at the demonstrators, has been arrested. The field guns, previously planted in the ground, were removed by the cannoneers. The situation is extremely tense but the men's earnest and calm behavior means we can expect a peaceful conclusion.*

We, however, do not share this hope. It is deadly certain that tsarist henchmen will turn to murder and arson carried out by police trash to drown the military's triumphant movement in a wave of dirt and crime.

Semi-official dispatches report from *Petersburg,* November 27. *Novoye Vremy* [New Times] reports from Sevastopol. Deputies from the ironclad ship the *Panteleimon* (formerly *Potemkin*) and from the cruiser *Ochakov* were present at gatherings in the marines' barracks; other warships anchored in the roadstead did not answer the mutineers' request to join them.

The Brest Regiment disassociated itself from the mutineers and marched toward the camp where all loyal troop units have gathered together. Military high command awaited further developments. The water supply is now guarded by the military; the Jewish population has fled.

---

 * This article first appeared in *Vorwärts,* No. 278, November 28, 1905, under the title "Die Revolution in Rußland." It is translated (by Henry Holland) from Luxemburg's *Gesammelte Werke,* Vol. 6, pp. 728–30.
 † Kettling is a police tactic for controlling demonstrators by corralling them in a circle with but one way out—the one controlled by the police.

The newssheet *Rus'* [Russia] has received reports that mutineers had imprisoned Commanding Officer Neplyev and General Syednikov, but have now released them both. Commanding officers and other officers on the warships have been arrested. *The artillery joined the revolutionary movement.* A Lithuanian regiment arrived in Odessa from Simferopol. Troops have also marched in from Pavlograd. Admiral [Grigoriy Pavlovich] Chukhnin handed over command to the commander of corps, General [Alexander Niokayevich] Möller-Sakomelski. *A company of sappers has also gone over to the mutineers, and the mutineers have expressed solidarity for the workers. In the evening, all ships sent delegations to express sympathy for the mutineers. The railroad lines have been torn up as far as Inkerman.*

Petersburg, November 26. According to Admiral Chukhnin, the mutiny among the sailors of the Black Sea Fleet is taking on an earnest character, as a result of continuous socialist propaganda. There have, however, been no reports of excess violence or plundering of civilians.

Sevastopol, November 26. The mutinying sailors sent Admiral Pisarevsky a coffin accompanied with the demand that he leave the city within three days. The dimensions of the mutiny are growing by the hour.

Sevastopol, November 26. The situation is extremely serious and people are now hoping that looting can be averted. Sailors, soldiers, and workers are organizing street processions with red flags at their head.

THE ECHO FROM THE FAR EAST

Vladivostok, November 27 (report by the Petersburg Telegraph Agency). Trouble is *fermenting increasingly* among the *soldiers* who have returned from the war in Japan. They are dissatisfied, with the vast majority of them facing delays in their transport back home; new convoys of POWs from Japan are arriving regularly. Yesterday, a soldier in Port Arthur refused demonstratively to salute an officer, and lambasted him instead with abuse. The officer responded by fatally stabbing the soldier. To revenge their comrade's death, the soldiers attempted to burn down the officer's casino, in which four officers were residing, who made use of their revolvers. Three officers were killed, one wounded. The number of wounded soldiers is not known. Cossacks restored peace. Forty-seven of the insurgent soldiers were imprisoned, including seven ringleaders.

THE GENERAL STRIKE: THE LATEST WAVE

Petersburg, November 26. *The strike is continuing to spread.* The workers are demolishing factories and private houses on a daily basis. (Surely an official "mix-up": government thugs, not workers.) The losses caused by strike unrest during the last few days have been calculated at approximately 1 million roubles.

The machine works in Kolomnash will be closed on November 28; around 6,000 men who make up the workforce will be sacked. *The tram workers' strike goes on.*

Petersburg, November 26. The number of people on strike in Petersburg has now reached 24,000.

THE PEASANTS' REVOLT SPREADS!

Petersburg, November 26. Agrarian unrest has now spread into the governorates of Nashazizu and Smolensk. In the Voronezh governorate, peasants have set the Duke of Oldenburg's property on fire.

The *Local Advertiser* has printed the following private dispatch: *Moscow,* November 26. The peasants' union is holding its congress of delegates here this week. Roughly 160 delegates are participating. The debates have been filled with a pure revolutionary spirit and conducted with great passion. The main subjects on the agenda have been lifting the peasant class economically and agrarian reform. The congress demanded the *communalization of land and soil* and the *convening of a Constituent Assembly,* whose task it should be to execute the transfer of land to the masses through legislative channels. If this demand goes unmet, the peasants want to *boycott all estate owners; declare an agrarian general strike; and refuse to hand over any tax-payments, remount horses or reservists.* The peasants would, in the case of unmet demands, seize all investments in savings banks and other banks, and would force brandy stalls to close.

Victorious Days for the Constitutional Manifesto*

TAKEN FROM THE RUSSIAN NEWSPAPER *RUS'* [RUSSIA]†

Yes—our people have today fought their way through to their first large and well-deserved victory. It was not easy to achieve. Many rough days of combat lie before us. The real work is only just beginning, thought I, traveling in the evening to the telegraph station, to get news to distant exiles; the day has come, thought I, because of which so many of our best and most selfless players will now be locked into a cruel fight with despotic powers.

The day of victory has dawned; yet how much discomfort, sorrow, unhappiness, desire, and suffering were present in the camps of the combatants and of the defeated, and how much calm atrocity, and how much cold and brazen scorn on behalf of the powerful victors! One thinks, unintentionally, of the fallen victims of this battle. [Stepan] Balmashov, the young, modest eighteen-year old, still almost a child, who, after being sentenced to death by hanging, refused to sign an appeal for clemency.‡ He did not want to request anything from people who, in his eyes, had no right to judge him. In his last letter to his mother, he wrote the following comforting words: "I sacrifice my life for the poor and oppressed of my people," and went on with steadiness and certainty into death.

Is he the only one? There have been so many! We will make them pay for it! ... God! They who have fallen in desperate battles, none of them can see anything! They are no longer with us! There are so many of them! They are all in their grave.

The day of freedom and victory darkens for me ...

Yet what cries are these? A few cavalry guards and all around them a cheering mass, waving leaflets toward them and pressing in hard against the horses. What is this? A mutiny? No, the soldiers are bending down out of the saddles, and stretching out their hands, which others are rushing to meet in peace-loving fashion, to joyfully shake those hands. "Peace has been agreed! Peace between the people and the army!"—is what I assume they said.

---

* This article first appeared in *Vorwärts*, No. 278, November 28, 1905, under the title "Die Siegestage des Verfassungsmanifestes." It is translated (by Henry Holland) from Luxemburg's *Gesammelte Werke*, Vol. 6, pp. 731–41.

† Luxemburg published this emotional eyewitness account (taken from the publication *Rus'*) as a supplement to her column "The Revolution in Russia." Shortly after she became editor-in-chief of *Vorwärts*, she resolved (on November 1, 1905) to use supplements of the paper for more popular, middlebrow essays.

‡ A member of the Socialist Revolutionary Party, Balmashov assassinated Internal Affairs Minister Dmitry Sipyagin on April 2, 1902. After refusing to ask for clemency, on the grounds that "the method of combating a terrorist seems to me inhumane and cruel, but it's inevitable with the current regime," he was executed in May 1903.

Children, enough; you are not going to shoot at us now; peace and the people's will have arrived; now you are ours, and dear to us. A man shouted out from
the throng, "Do you think we would enjoy shooting you? Do you really believe
we wanted to burden our souls with sins! We were ordered to do it! Didn't it
pain us to go into battles against our own people, against our brothers and our
relatives? We aren't hangmen, we are Christians like yourselves! How our souls
are exhausted now! Thanks be to the Creator!" roared the soldiers festively with
tears in their eyes, touched and overjoyed. Just as the crowd of people surrounding them were doing.

Quickly reunited! Moments of grace! I thought to myself.

How much despicable power and shameful shamelessness does it take to
throw one part of the folk against the other, one armed and the other unarmed.
Thank God that our army has now been relieved of this disgrace. The officers
are probably just as happy. A heavy dishonor hung over them, particularly over
the guards.

Thank God! Our brave soldiers will no longer follow orders from commissars and district overseers to shoot and kill unarmed and innocent children of
our people! Thank God!

I straightaway sent a message via telegraph that the fortress of slavery had
given itself up to the people; it had capitulated. The exiles, however, would not
be cheered by this news that they hadn't mentioned in their manifestos. So I
decided to head for the editorial office.

From there we journeyed on to the technological institute, where there was
shooting, or so the editors said.

So, we journey. "Why are they shooting?" I asked my escort, as we sat down
in the carriage. A bomb's been thrown at the police patrol who claim that the
bomb originated from the inner parts of the institute, although it is completely
obvious that the bomb was thrown from the street, with all the signs suggesting
an agent provocateur. The leaders of the movement had made a binding resolution to use no violent measures whatsoever. Somebody, ignoring this fact, gave
the order to shoot in through the windows of the building, where professors and
students had locked themselves in.

We journey. The streets are full of life. Manifesto flyers and pamphlets are
being distributed and sold everywhere.

Yet this turnaround has cost us all astonishingly little blood, remarked my
escort.

I disagree with you. What about Manchuria! That loss of 300,000 Russian
men* is the bloodbath into which this criminal regime is now sinking. The criminals in power will never let go of that regime without blood being let. Only

---

* This refers to the Russian losses incurred in the Russo-Japanese War between January 1904
and September 1905.

when we are stained all over by the blood of innocent victims, covered in ignominy and odium, only then will they start to lose the ground beneath their feet,
and relinquish power out of weak hands, which the folk will then take into their
pure and unstained hands. As our imperial pensioners followed the tracks of
numerous adventurers and vagabonds, like Bezobrazov, for example, the former
stadtholder* in the Far East, or Alexeyev and others, and soaked the Chinese soil
in the people's blood, then they could have done the same here, and could have
been forced here on Russian soil to defend their noble existence on the backs of
oppressed humanity. Yet now the innocent blood of the people, shed in the Far
East, has flowed over to us, the heart of the people foaming over in its red waves,
igniting a holy fury that hits back powerfully through the shameless windows of
grandiose palaces.

"Indeed! Quite true!" my escort replied.

"Get back! Back! Transport into this area is not permitted," gestured the
police on the bridge toward us.

We got down from the coach and continued on foot. We saw Cossacks with
a nagaika, gendarmes, commissars, constables walking their beats, and patrols
of policemen. In short, everything that still stank of the rot, the mildew, and the
bodily decay of the old regime.

The rumor proved true. A bomb had been thrown by an unknown person
who then quickly disappeared. The military responded by opening atrocious fire
on the university's windows, behind which innocent people were located.

We returned together to the paper's copy room, and parted around four, as
none of us had wanted to leave earlier.

Yet all this is still original and relevant! Through almost a year-and-a-half,
the whole of freethinking Russia awaited and hungered after this resurrection, in
dark and damp prison cells, carefully guarded by Plehve's heavies.†

And now! ... But what kind of song is that?! ... Continually interrupting my
thoughts.

A huge crowd of people had gathered at the police cordon, harmoniously
and reverently singing a song to honor the victims who had fallen on January 22,
[1905], singing, with exposed faces. The red flag waved in the air like a banner.
I happened to be present. The melancholy sounds of the prayer-like song triggered terrible pictures in my brain. It was around five o'clock in the evening.
Already dark, a crowd of roughly 300 people had gathered on the bridge, where
a company of soldiers had positioned itself. Horrible street fights had taken place
only shortly before this, initiated by the military in Alexander Park, beside the
Petrovsky Bridge, and at other locations in the city. Voices chanted unceasingly

---

    *   A provincial executive.
    †   A reference to Vyacheslav von Plehve, director of the police of Imperial Russia and one of
the most reactionary of government ministers. He was assassinated by a member of the SR Combat
Group in 1904.

from the crowd, "Executioners! *Oprichnina!* Shame on you! Murdering your own brothers! Murderers! Executioners! Shame on you! Executioners!"

Each of these words flew, precisely because of their biting fairness, like a direct slap in the face of the officer standing next to his company. But that brutal nature receives only the pain of the insult, and not the shame that is so well deserved.

"Disperse or I'll fire!" he screamed, evidently losing his self-possession.

"Executioner! Murderer! Go on then, fire!" … came the reply from the mob, not moving an inch.

The signal from the horn resounded. The soldiers shouldered their guns.

A shudder passed through one part of the crowd. Yet others who had worked themselves up into an ecstasy assuaged them, crying, "Stop! Stop, brothers! Then let the executioners shoot us down unarmed, we are not moving from the stop. Let our blood pour down over their heads! Murderers! Killers! Yes, their own brothers! Murderers! Killers!" Many raised their arms and stood, as if petrified, in this position.

A burst of fire rang out.

As if mowed down, the dead and wounded fell to the earth.

The groans of the wounded and the moans of the dying filled the air. Everyone who could still move turned to flee. Another burst of fire resounded into the backs of the fleeing crowd. The murderers had completed their work.

A few hours previously, however, on the same day and in the same place, an even more outrageous scene had played out in front of my eyes.

Around midday, a squadron of guards in white uniforms rode toward a crowd of workers gathered on the Petrovsky Bridge.

Their officers rode out ahead and, in thunderous tones, demanded that the workers disperse. Whereupon several workers stepped out of the crowd, revealed their faces and turned to greet the officers: "Honorable gentlemen! We gather here to go to the tsar as to our own father in flesh and blood, to entreat him to help us, and to lay our petition at his feet. God knows we don't mean any harm. Look, we have come with our women and children!" In saying this, they gestured at the masses standing behind them, in which women and children really were to be found.

Yet the officers repeated the strict order to disperse.

"We cannot just clear away without having delivered our request that our Father Tsar alleviate our destitution. That is what we promised each other," replied the workers, humble and yet steadfast.

---

*   The Oprichnina was a murderous group of government agents, similar to a secret police organization, used by Ivan the Terrible between 1565 and 1572, aimed at breaking the power of the boyars, the old families of the Russian nobility. Individual members of the Oprichnina were called Oprichniks.

The officer gave the signal to attack.

"We are still going to our Dear Father, even if he beats us!" shouted the workers in response.

And, again, the horn was blown.

With brandished swords glinting and held high, the soldiers galloped directly into the crowd.

Everyone ducked out the way, pushing themselves back against the railings. But nobody escaped. The front rows bowed their heads humbly, some falling to their knees; in the back rows was a woman cradling a suckling child.

"Then those who deride the Cross should strike us!"—a woman's voice was to be heard—"but we shall still reach our Dear Father."

In a single galloping burst the horses reached the edge of the crowd, and stood as if rooted to the spot.

The soldiers found it impossible to decide to slash down onto the humbly bent workers' heads; the swords hung in the air. "We really aren't executioners, charged with murdering defenseless people," is what the soldiers were probably thinking.

And the feeling was palpable that none of them had the heart to inflict suffering on defenseless and innocent people.

My eyes suddenly came to rest on the head of a venerable old man, on whose neck, stretched out far in front of him, the veins stood out like streaks. He was supporting himself on the knee of a young worker standing in front of him; I couldn't see his face. I could only see this long, scrawny neck, lunging out of a brown knitted coat. A life of distress, penury, and squalor could be read along the whole line of that neck.

The old man awaited his fate with the others.

A deathly silence descended on the scene.

Everyone was waiting for a great moment. Good seemed to have triumphed over evil. Yet then something wild, blood curdling and unspeakable happened ...

The officer swung his sword ... and came down onto the long, scrawny, humbly bent forward neck of the stooped old man. The old man swayed and collapsed, covered with blood. His head hit the ground and I saw how his red blood discolored the white snow.

This was read as a signal. The soldiers immediately began to swing their swords, right and left. The first rows fell, including the woman with the suckling child. The rest, pressed back against the railings, didn't know where to flee in their terrible fear. Many threw themselves into the Moyka, and you saw them being smashed to pieces on the ice.

The animalized horde was chasing them now with their swords drawn. I, too, was pulled into this side of the throng. I had a long fur coat on and stepped forward slowly, covering my eyes with my left hand. Roughly ten paces in front of me, I observed a woman on the sidewalk. She had covered her face with both hands and was sobbing hysterically.

The whole crowd was far ahead, being chased by the bloodthirsty and sinister thugs. Screams of despair and the ring of swords melted into each other and rose up to the heavens ...

Then I suddenly noticed the trot of a single horse behind me. A mighty saber stroke down onto my back almost knocked me to the ground. I looked round. Left of me was standing the same officer who had been the first to land his blow on the old man's long, thin neck.

He had a wild and awful face, blotchy, black and red from his nervous brutality. "Move, you heap of sh—, when you are ordered to!" ... he blurted out, hoarsely. I replied simply, "Murderer!" and again he raised his sword, wanted to bring it rushing down on top of me, but slashed into the wall instead; the horse was shaken and reared up. But what was that? He swung out at the crying woman who was walking in front of me. Wounded on the head, she collapsed to the ground.

That is how the loyal and devoted servants of the tsar dealt with the people who had come to their father to issue a complaint about their suffering and destitution.

I have seen and lived through many burdensome and, yes, even terrible things in my life. Yet never have I felt such a horrible feeling of disgust and revulsion as I felt at watching this merciless slaying of unhappy and defenseless—do you hear, defenseless—people, and for what? For being so naive and trusting as to go with their supplications to their "Dear Father," the tsar? ...

We had gone to see the emperor, but had been met with showers of bullets and saber blows. That is why the tsar no longer exists for us!—shouted the workers on their way home that day. Yes, that was the day on which the criminals in power laid the foundation stone for the people's revolution. On that day, they eradicated the last remaining faith that the people's hearts had held for them.

The final dull and heavy sounds of the funeral songs died out in the air.

Quaking, I reflected on the onerous pictures that had engraved themselves into my memory.

The songs fell silent.

A simple worker swung himself up onto an empty cart and began to speak loudly.

He spoke of freedom and reminded the people of the fallen victims who had fought for freedom, and who had been felled by the horde of enemies of the people. A light breeze moved through the red flag.

Whereupon a student climbed up onto the "tribune." He spoke of the huge part that the proletariat had played in the movement and applauded this. Many, many speeches followed. After which, people set out toward the Morskaya, the red flag fluttering at their head.

"Stop! Stop!"—and everyone stood where they were. It was a moving meeting. Another speaker rose to speak. Drawing our attention to the fact, that this was only the first success, and that the next bigger, tougher and more difficult fight was only now beginning, he proposed taking an oath on this very spot to those who had fallen, to those who had lost their lives, that no one would put down arms until a total victory had been won. Everyone raised their hands, "We swear! We swear," the cry ringing through the air fraternally. The meeting started to move forward again. We came across armed troops, who shook hands with lots of us in a comradely and friendly way, each declaring to the other that they were enemies no longer. And, again, someone shouted, "Halt!"—and the meeting came to a standstill. One speaker was lifted up; he pointed out that while we here were openly greeting freedom, many of its defenders were still thirsting for it behind damp and dark prison walls ... "We will not go back to work until they have given us back our friends and our comrades in freedom." "No, no!" came the response, as if from a single throat. The red flag waved and started to move. We reached Marinsky Square. The red banner drew to a halt in front of the Nicholas I monument. A great number of speeches were made, interrupted by cries of "Onward!" At the end a worker read out a poem that emphasized that we could not shy away from casualties. "The wood will be turned over; the earth however will be covered with new seeds, from which new rows of warriors will sprout, over the graves of the fallen brothers." As if in answer to these last words, the Marseillaise thundered out of a thousand throats. The bronze figure of the mighty emperor was wrapped in nocturnal gloom. The meeting started to move again. I followed it with my eyes, the red flag flying over their heads, still visible until it disappeared in the light, bright distance of illuminated streets ...

THE FIRST OF NOVEMBER

The second day of freedom awoke in a good mood. Cheerful rays of morning light woke up the city. I made my way to the Nevsky Prospect where I immediately encountered a procession. A colossal crowd of people strode with most exemplary discipline toward the Winter Palace, red flags unfurled high above them. Freedom songs and worker's songs were sung unceasingly. Everyone's facial expressions looked cheerful and courageous, yes even the earthy colored worker's faces, eaten up by worries, appeared to be covered with the color of life, as if they were feeling a foretaste of a better life.

All those who met the procession doffed their hats. Various slogans could be read on the flags, including, "Freedom and land to the people!" A quite different phenomenon could be encountered beside an inn, moving under a flag with three colors, upon which was written, "Long live freedom and the emperor!" I moved closer to this procession. From their outer appearance, you could be fairly sure that this was a bunch of hucksters and petty bourgeois. They were very excited. They were evidently worried about violence breaking out, yet no one was stupid enough to start any trouble. But then one of them suddenly grabbed a boy with a red band on his arm and began to hit him, tearing at the armband. Others stood up for the boy and a brawl broke out. The three-colored flags were yanked down, torn to shreds and trod into the dirt. Red flags were hoisted in their stead. Then the demonstration proceeded. Apart from this incident, which, it was said, recurred three times, the discipline was exemplary. One demonstration followed the next, the various demonstrations meeting and congratulating each other. A meeting made up of a few hundred red flags took place under the roof of Kazan Cathedral. Around 5 p.m. all demonstrators joined up to form a superb sight, the like of which had never been seen before. It really was an uplifting picture—thousands and yet more thousands of people standing with their heads bare to the sky under the baldachin* of the red flag. Neither armed troops nor commissars were to be seen. That is possibly why the discipline was so exemplary.

There were no drunks to be seen and no sounds to be heard disturbing the day's festiveness. Holding hands, as if they wanted to reinforce their unity, the proletariat moved forward in uniform rows with the youths, who were learning as they walked. Now and then songs of freedom emerged out of the compact mass. At last we reached the Anichkov Palace—at which nobody looked, as if obeying orders. Now it seemed as if the sounds were ringing out more self-confidently, more mightily and more festively than ever before. I looked to my right. The lonely windows of Grand Duke Sergei Alexandrovich Romanov's majestic palace† looked down, black and empty, gloomy. A moving mass of red flags proceeded solemnly below, rolled out full length by the wind. The whole time we heard demands shouted out of the crowd, that we should go directly to the political prisoners to liberate them. The movement's leaders, however, refused to permit these demands, by attempting to convince the mass that the liberation had to take place through peaceful means; the weapons should only be taken up in case of emergencies. But, for now, the unarmed crowd's demands were to be answered by bayonet thrusts and volleys of bullets.

Whereupon the mobile meeting turned and made its way, entirely disciplined, to the university, from which everyone only parted company late into the night. This day together with all that had gone before it proves loud and clear how conscious the proletarians are of their aim, how excellent their political education has been. One hundred thousand workers took part in the strike movement in Petersburg and its surrounds. Yet no one could have complained about disorder. No violations, no attacks on private property, despite the rapid

---

* A ceremonial canopy of stone, metal, or fabric, over an altar, throne, or doorway.

† Grand Duke Sergei Romanov was the uncle of Nicholas II and an influential figure in the government. He was an extremely conservative figure who was responsible for evicting 20,000 Jews from Moscow. In 1905 he moved into the ornate Neskuchnoye Palace.

development of poverty and destitution as a result of the stagnation of every source of income. The movement's leaders tirelessly stressed the necessity of maintaining order, without exception. Doing the opposite would have played straight into the hands of the police. The movement drew a special and exclusive power from this. You truly would have been correct in saying, "Praise and honor to our working people!" And yet despite the masses' tactful behavior, blood did flow again. The Trepov system,* in all its power and glory, was back in the limelight. The Japanese principle of tough generals, who certainly didn't want to spare bullets when using them against Russians, came completely into its own. Thanks to these inhuman principles we again had a number of innocent human victims to lament. The Trepov system remains in full force in despite of this, which we regret utterly. The same Trepov system intends to whip up confusion among the people, so that it can win its stripes by oppressing them. That same system, thanks to which any half-decent standard of security for citizens either on the streets or in their own houses is impossible, can only disappear by toppling its creator.

Late that same evening I was back in the newspaper office.

Come down onto the street. Now a quite different picture is unfolding in front of you. The workers had already returned to their dwellings. The city was back in the hands of the police and the Black Hundreds. What a booze-up and what street brawls!

Three lumpen holding hands came up to me—or so my escort tells me—and asked coarsely, "Tell us then, are you in bed with the 'reds' too? Talk, and if you are we'll punch your face in."

I struck one, and all three drunks fell to the ground. We went out onto the street, where around fifty drunk lowlifes were jeering, screaming, and rushing forward, carrying national flags. It was frankly painful to see the Russian flag in such hands as theirs. I moved on toward the Winter Palace.

An officer of the guards, dressed with embarrassing elegance, was leading a patrol; he had been encircled by a heap of men, demanding to hear the national anthem.

At the head of the heap there stood or rather swayed a typically drunken hero from the Black Hundreds, who had clasped the officer's hand while gesticulating wildly, and, pressing firmly, wheezed out incoherent words: "We're walking together to our Dear Father tsar, we have come to see him, to tell him what we think, and now we have joined up with you lot, the military, to form a voluntary personal body guard for the emperor. We'll get those red rogues on

---

* The "Trepov system" is named after Dimitri Feodorovich Trepov, head of the Moscow Police, governor-general of Petersburg, as well as Russian assistant interior minister. He benefited from the support of Tsar Nicholas II and was notorious for his hardline approach to any protesters. During the revolution of 1905, Trepov promoted repressive measures, which, however, failed to contain the revolutionary momentum.

the floor and then they'll be sorry!" All these words came out of his mouth comically mixed up with various other choice expletives, an embarrassment to the ear. I watched this scene and began to laugh aloud.

The officer noticed and turned to me aggressively, "What business have you here?"

I looked back at him and at the bunch of lumpen chatting in a friendly way to the shining officer and went home, without saying another word. Screams coming from the drunken bounders rang out into the nocturnal dark for a long time that night.

The next day, November 2, I saw with my own eyes how gendarmes and Cossacks, falling into fits of grim rage, jumped down onto sidewalks and set to work on peaceful passing individuals and groups with their truncheons, acting with an inhuman bestiality.

Having reached the editing room, I received visits from many eyewitnesses and wounded persons, who reported similar scenes to me, voicing complaint about them. Solid and well-off-looking people also arrived, who just happened to have been passing through the streets when they were met by the Cossacks' truncheon blows and were wounded.

The Trepov system was evidently still in force, just as before. The people who had come were outraged and indignant.

Why, ladies and gentlemen, are you so indignant? After the events of January 22 there's absolutely nothing left, I replied, that is able to throw me into a state of indignation or of astonishment.

Do think about it! All this happened after the constitution had been granted, after freedom of speech and the press, the inviolability of individual personality and other high-sounding words had been spoken, and now we're back to the nagaika?!—that's how my outraged visitors saw matters.

Permit it, you must permit me to say it! We still have neither constitution nor these freedoms. We still have nothing but promises of all these good deeds to come. But we already had all these promises on December 25, 1904, and after December 25 came January 22, 1905. Look here: on October 30, they were making us promises, and then on the first and second of November they were giving us the nagaika, and other such treats. "What's illogical about that?" I said, to convince and calm my visitors. They were angry at me, although I had told them the truth. We were right to have stopped believing in such promises long ago; too many, far too many, have been made and not kept. Yet I remain convinced from the bottom of my soul that the hour will come—and come soon enough—in which all promises will be kept, and some more besides. We now have a secure guarantee. This is anchored neither in pledges that can be broken again tomorrow, nor in the personality of a prime minister, who can be removed from power tomorrow, and even banished to the remotest location, as the menial souls of the court toadies have long wished it. No, a guarantee that can keep promises is anchored in the people themselves, who've now had opportunity to show their strength, and who are definitely in a position to go and take that which has been promised them, thanks to their unbreakable will and their overwhelming power.

The Revolution in Russia
[November 29, 1905]*

The sailors are still holding the city of *Sevastopol*. Measures for the maintenance of peace have been adopted. The city is a model of law and order, and
the game of chess that the counterrevolution is playing is met with force and
energy, but without any excesses. The government does not even dare to use
regular troops against the mutineers after the fiasco in Kronstadt, as the soldiers would then change sides straight away to join the sailors, rather than
butcher them. At this very moment, the tsar's servants are contemplating
ways to subvert, through some miscreant trick, the real law and order now in
place in Sevastopol, to change that into tsarist and pious anarchy, and orgies of
violence.

The semi-official Petersburg Telegraph Agency reports: *Sevastopol*,
November 27. *Peace at present in the city.* The officers and crews of the *Ochakov*
cruiser have been forced to leave the ship. On the *Rostislav*, an ironclad, and on
the *Tri Sviatitelia* [The Three Hierarchs], the crews have remained calm, and
have shown no inclination to join the mutineers. *A battalion of reservists has
made common cause with the sailors.* A state of siege has been imposed on the
fortress settlement. *The sailors perform their law-abiding duties without officers,
patrol through the town, and arrest those comrades who do not have permits to
leave the barracks.*

Petersburg, November 28. Telegraph communication with Sevastopol has
been restored. According to reports that arrived in the afternoon, the sailors'
and soldiers' demands are purely economic, resulting in Count Witte's dispatch
of a representative to Sevastopol who will report back to him about the current
situation. Although the mutineering soldiers and sailors have occupied not just
the whole city but the arsenal as well, *order has not been disrupted.* The sailors
can uphold order without the officers.

A report in Laffan's News Agency states: *Petersburg*, November 28. The
military authorities in Sevastopol have reported to the government that isolation and exhaustion can be the only means of suppressing revolt in the coastal
fortress. *The military authorities are of the opinion that using troops against the
mutineers would be an unsafe method.*

Sevastopol, November 28 (report from the Petersburg Telegraph Agency).
The deadline given to mutineers to surrender expired today. Lieutenant Schmidt,
elected and intent on revolution, took command of the *Ochakov* cruiser. The

---

* This article first appeared in *Vorwärts*, No. 279, November 29, 1905, under the title "Die
Revolution in Rußland." It is translated (by Henry Holland) from Luxemburg's *Gesammelte Werke*,
Vol. 6, pp. 742–4.

town's *Duma* has turned with an urgent request toward Petersburg for measures to be taken *to save the city.*

The "liberal" moneybags are trembling under the sailors' peaceful dictatorship, and long for the protection of the arsonists and looters from the Black Hundreds!

LOCKOUT TACTICS

For some time, the industrial bourgeoisie in Petersburg have ever-more blatantly been using the tactic of lockouts against the revolutionary proletariat, to make it crumble in the face of hunger and to scare it away from further general strikes. According to reports of the Petersburg correspondent of the *Daily Telegraph*, 50,000 workers in Petersburg are already unemployed. Now the semi-official wire has just brought in the following news: *Petersburg*, November 27 (report from the Petersburg Telegraph Agency). *Reportedly, thirty-three factories with a total of 75,000 workers have announced their dismissals to the latter.*

This provocation on the part of the troublemakers will not, of course, constrain the revolutionary actions of the working class, but on the contrary will pour oil onto the flames, and lend the struggle a class character more clearly than ever.

Following telegraphic announcement: *The Council [Soviet] of Workers' Deputies* has decided to force the reopening of the locked Petersburg factories *through an all-Russian strike*, and, for this purpose, to *initiate agitation* in all centers of urban and rural population, in the army, and in the naval fleet.

THE PEASANTS' CONGRESS

The peasants' congress passed this motion: (1) *To boycott* the Duma; (2) to designate all those who took part in the elections of representatives to the Duma as enemies of the people; (3) to start widespread electoral agitation straight away, so that representatives can be voted into the constituent people's assembly without religious discrimination, on the basis of a secret and direct ballot; (4) to divide Russia up into electoral districts.

SOLUTION TO THE PEASANT QUESTION

Moscow, November 28 (report by the Petersburg Telegraph Agency). The whole Congress of Peasants' Councils—which had just drawn to a close—was arrested yesterday. *Chirikov and* [Vladimir Germanovich] *Tann, two writers who both preach an open uprising, were among the number of those arrested.*

"LIBERAL" LOVE AFFAIRS

Petersburg, November 28. According to newspaper reports, Count Witte has communicated to urban zemstvo delegates that he considers it necessary to bestow on one of the zemstvo delegates the portfolio for minister of the interior.

PRESS FREEDOM

Petersburg, November 28. The publisher and editor of the satirical magazine *Pulemyot* [Machine-gun Fire], Shebuyev, was *arrested yesterday.**

Samara, November 27 (report from Petersburg Telegraph Agency). *A number of prisoners were killed or wounded during disturbances in a city prison;* a few have fled.

---

*   *Pulemyot* pioneered such graphic elements as montage, which later proved highly influential in the work of such pathbreaking filmmakers as Sergei Eisenstein.

The Revolution in Russia [November 30, 1905]*

The revolutionary movement has taken a new developmental step: *General Strike of Post and Telegraph Workers*, the latest report in from Russia. In this very moment, the tsar's empire has again been cut off from the outside world, and absolutism is under a state of siege, not due to the railroad workers' actions, but because of the post and telegraph personnel. This grouping is now for the first time striding onto the battlefield of the revolution, with this independent and general action. The admirable unity and rapidity of this action is just as remarkable as what triggered it. The civil servants at the postal service and the telegraphy have been sympathizing with the battling proletariat for a long while. When the general strikes came, they mostly joined forces with the workers. In the last few weeks, during the industrial workers' all-encompassing and feverish push toward *organization*, the post and telegraph civil servants followed in their footsteps, and have wanted to create a solid form of professional organization. The government grasped how dangerous this undertaking was, and so they thought they could submit their "minions," the civil servants, to a measure they would never dare to try on the industrial workers. A terse ukase was published in the last few days, forbidding government civil servants to partake in any form of labor-based union.

But here again the message is—too late! The Russian civil servants, once so shy and self-effacing, are now also sensing the strength and revolutionary fire in their veins, flowing out from the mighty and heroic proletarian class struggle. In answer to the ukase, a motion proposing an immediate general strike was passed and also carried out! In the whole huge empire, tens of thousands, hundreds of thousands of revolutionaries started to move as if they were *one man*, with a degree of organization and discipline that we in Germany can still only dream of.† What progress since January 22! The industrial proletarians, organized and focused on their aims, the rebellious and politically conscious army and marines, the sturdy and spirited battling civil servants …

---

* This article first appeared in *Vorwärts*, No. 280, November 30, 1905, under the title "Die Revolution in Rußland." It is translated (by Henry Holland) from Luxemburg's *Gesammelte Werke*, Vol. 6, pp. 745–7.

† This is a rather remarkable statement, given the pride which most German socialists had toward their highly organized party and trade union movement—and how much and how often they looked down upon their Russian brethren for being "backward" and "unorganized." The point was sure to be noticed by many readers of *Vorwärts*.

And again, we must face up to a great historical truth—the revolution achieves as much education and organization within a few weeks as would require decades, using methods typical for "times of peace." Yes, the revolution achieves that which cannot be achieved at all when history jogs along at its normal trot; she, the revolution, shakes up the whole social body, which then resettles into quite new layers. It is she who has suddenly turned the class of the industrial proletariat into the leader and load-bearer of the whole shake-up today, despite this class being statistically speaking so "weak." The various movements of the civil service, the petty bourgeoisie, the liberal intelligentsia, the peasantry, the army and the navy are all manifestations of the working class's revolutionary action, under the leadership of Social Democracy.

Moscow, November 29. Early yesterday morning the civil servants were moved to telegraph Prime Minister Witte, to demand their wishes be fulfilled within twelve hours. The catalysts were the repressive measures forced through by Durnovo, minister of the interior, against post and telegraph civil servants, coupled with the ban on labor organization within this group and the dismissal of twenty-five organizers of this union. On not receiving any reply from Petersburg, the civil servants went out on strike. The Moscow–Petersburg telephone connection is already disconnected.

Petersburg, November 29. The post and telegraph civil servants are striking in all main centers of the empire—in Siberia, Kharkiv, Odessa, Rostov, Riga, Liepāja, etc.

Berlin, November 29 (Wolff's Telegraph Office). Official Report. A large number of connections with Russia have been interrupted since this afternoon.

THE GENERAL STRIKE SPREADS

Warsaw, November 29. The general strike has broken out in and around Dąbrowa Górnicza.

Petersburg, November 20. The Council [Soviet] of Workers' Delegates has decided to direct an appeal to all friends of freedom, to the railroad workers, to the post and telegraph civil servants, to the army and the fleet, in which all addressees are requested to support the workers. The reason for the appeal is the lockouts effecting 100,000 workers.

Petersburg, November 29 (H.O.).* *The situation here is darkening. The ferment among the military is taking on serious manifestations.* Numerous families are preparing to leave the city, causing the passport office to be overrun. The American ambassador has already submitted a vehement complaint to the Foreign Minister regarding the assault on Bleß, the embassy's secretary.

---

* Probably Hirsch's Office, a news agency

SEVASTOPOL HOLDS OUT

Sevastopol, November 29. The governor-general's flank adjutant telegraphed that no disorder has broken out until now. *The mutineers are keeping quiet,* but there are worries that the city will be *under fire* during the course of today, because the order to the fleet to steam off has not arrived.

THE NEW PARTY PAPER

The first issue of our related Russian paper *Nachalo* [The Beginning] was published on the 26th of this month.* The paper bears the subtitle, "Organ of the Russian Social Democratic Workers' Party," and the headline, "Proletarians of the World, Unite!" The party newspaper, printed in broadsheet format, pulsates from start to finish with the revolutionary life of the worker's movement, with articles and reports on the revolution's next tasks: the strikes, struggle for the eight-hour day, and developments in trade union and political organization. We're talking about reports from all sides, from all corners and ends of the empire. You just need to pick up a single issue of the party paper to see and experience the whole of Russia as a bubbling volcano, and the proletarian class struggle is its life-giving fire!

We send our mighty colleagues in Petersburg our most heartfelt fraternal greetings!

---

* Actually, it began publication a few days earlier, on November 13, as Luxemburg had earlier reported.

Lieutenant Schmidt*

The bloody ambush wasn't long in coming! Absolutism has been forced into firing on its own ironclad ships to send them up in flames, and into bombing its own barracks. The disciplined lads in Sevastopol have been crushed in a dreadful fight—crews who followed repeated official instructions received through the tsarist government *canaille*† to maintain *absolute peace and order*, men who didn't initiate the slightest disturbance! This time the pack of rogues didn't even have the time or opportunity to stage, through their footmen—pick-pockets, pimps, and spies—an orgy of violence, the responsibility for which they could have then pinned onto the "mutinous" sailors. Not a trace of "guilt" can be found on the blank signs of the revolutionary dictatorship in Sevastopol. The banner was flying, in broad daylight, for the *political and revolutionary* rising against the nagaika regime. And it was for *this* crime alone that the cowardly band of runaways from Liuyang, Shenyang, and Port Arthur‡ suffocated their own people in Sevastopol under a sea of blood, in a naked and public duel to preserve their own criminal existence!

The Sevastopol rising has fallen in the same way that the Potemkin and Kronstadt risings have fallen. But their fall has shaken the pillars of absolutism like Samson shook the pillars of his prison. We may still need a few more crushed risings, but the whole building of old, tsarist Russia will collapse, in the end, down onto the stupid *canaille* and their forfeited heads.

The figure of a man is rising, in revolutionary glory, out of the foundation of Sevastopol's stupendous rebellion, a man, who though yesterday was barely known in public, now appears as one of those heroes who only reveal their greatness in revolutionary times, and, confronted by gigantic moments, are tossed up on to the peak of things.

Barely ten days have passed since Lieutenant Schmidt suddenly became a beloved and popular people's tribune,§ at a most unexpected occasion. Tellingly, this occasion was the day of the funeral for the *victims of the most recent tsarist constitutional manifesto.*

---

* This unsigned article belongs to the lead articles written by Luxemburg as chief editor of *Vorwärts*. It first appeared in *Vorwärts*, No. 281, December 1, 1905. It is translated (by Henry Holland) from Luxemburg's *Gesammelte Werke*, Vol. 6, pp. 748–52.

† This French loanword means "the lowest class of vulgar people." This is a typical technique in her writings on the 1905 Russian Revolution—taking terms that were normally used in an abusive way against the proletariat and using them instead against the tsarist government or its supporters.

‡ These were main theaters of the Russo-Japanese War, 1904–1905.

§ Luxemburg is making a conscious reference to a number of leaders of the French Revolution who were given the titles of "Tribune of the People" or "Plebeian Tribunes." These in turn are modern variants of the Latin *Tribunus plebis*, which was the first office of the Roman state open to the lower classes (known as plebeians). During the Roman Republic it was the most important check on the power of the Roman Senate.

The funeral in Sevastopol on October 20 was extraordinary, with inhabitants from the whole municipality taking part. Peaceful residents were buried, who had organized a peaceful action in front of the prison in the night in which the tsarist manifesto was announced, resulting in troops shooting them. Order at the funerals was maintained impeccably, despite the tens of thousands in the crowd. Thanks to an energetic intervention by the city council, military and police were not present. After the dead had been given up unto the earth, and the mayor and others had held excellent speeches, Marine Lieutenant [Pyotr] Schmidt walked up to the grave. His appearance heightened the concentration among the thick mass of crowd, several thousand strong, crammed together on the neighboring hill. In the few days of "freedom" that had just passed, Schmidt had proven himself to be a political agitator and first-class speaker, deserving of great hopes. Although not a city councilor, the mayor had invited Schmidt to take part in meetings, and this advisory voice of his had won him popularity in the city in no time at all. Schmidt displayed a vibrant efficacy in this new function; he had already initiated political meetings among the intelligentsia prior to the manifesto. After a deathly silence had descended, the speaker began in a quiet voice, exhausted from his grueling and relentless agitation work, and moved by deep convictions:

> It is behooving, at the graveside, only to offer prayers, but prayers are equal to the words of love and the holy oath that I want to take with you here today. When joy filled the souls of the deceased at whose graves we stand through the rising sun of freedom, their next impulse was to hurry as fast as possible to those languishing in prison, who had fought for freedom, and who now, in the hour of huge and widespread exultation were denied this greatest possession. They hurried to tell the prisoners of the glad tidings they were bearing. They requested their release and were killed for this request. They wanted to share this highest of life's possessions—freedom—and were robbed of their lives for doing so ... Terrible and unprecedented crime! Huge and irredeemable suffering! And now their souls are gazing down at us and ask, silently, "What will you do with this possession, of which we have been robbed forever? How will you make use of your freedom? Can you promise us that we'll be the last victims of despotism?" And we must calm the restless souls of the deceased, we must promise them that. And I swear to them, his voice sounding out louder, that we'll never give up so much of an inch of the human rights we have won for ourselves!*
>
> I swear, said the speaker, his hand raised, *I swear*, resounded many thousands of voices. We promise them, that we will devote our whole work, our whole soul and even our lives for the retention of our freedom. I swear! *I swear!* repeated the

---

* As often occurs in these articles which cite press dispatches and reports on events relevant to the 1905 Revolution, Luxemburg here inserts a half-sentence of her own into Schmidt's comments.

crowd. We promise them, that we'll devote all our force, our life in its entirety to the working and destitute people! I swear!—*I swear!*—rang out the crowd's reply. Sobs could be heard. "We promise, that from this point on there will no longer be Jew or Armenian or Tatar among us, but that we will be equal and free brothers of the great and free Russia. I swear!" And the "*I swear*" repeated by the people rolled all around the surrounding hills. We promise them, that we will see this thing through and obtain universal and equal suffrage for everyone! I swear! And the people shouted threateningly: "*I swear!*"

And in front of the people stood no longer a speaker but a mighty tribune, who the 10,000-strong crowd was prepared to follow. "We promise them"—the words like ore from the lips of the speaker—"that if we are not granted universal suffrage, then we'll declare the general strike in Russia. I swear!" the speaker concluded. "*I swear!*" sounded like thunder over the earth. The speaker had finished; he was kissed and embraced. A simple soldier wrapped his arms around his neck, forgetting all discipline and the speaker's officer's rank. Schmidt disappeared into the crowd. That same evening Lieutenant Schmidt was taken prisoner on order of the commanding officer General Chukhnin, and transferred like a criminal with a cloth over him to the ironclad ship *Tri Sviatitelia*. Six days later, the ironclad *Tri Sviatitelia* hoisted the red banner of the revolution.

Lieutenant Schmidt is lying fatally wounded. He fell as a true Tribune of the People, as the tough pioneer of the Russian proletariat. The international proletariat will follow his call to decisively settle accounts with *every* form of oppression and servitude endured by the poor and the exploited, and, by contemplating the heroic Russian sacrifices at the Battle of Sevastopol.

Slovo [The Word], a Petersburg publication, carries the following report about the Battle of Sevastopol: The same naval officer *Schmidt* discussed above was declared commanding officer of the revolutionary forces by the mutineers. Admiral *Chukhnin*, commanding officer of the Black Sea Fleet was in charge of the loyal government forces. As the battle began, the mutineers appeared to have the better chances of victory by far. The revolutionary commanding officer Schmidt united *ten warships* and *three northern forts on land* under his command. The remainder of the fleet, the southern forts, and the coastal artillery kept faith with their oath of duty.

The mutineers opened heavy fire onto the city at 3 p.m. Because there was no return fire whatsoever, the mutineers were convinced they had taken the city. Schmidt sent *two parliamentarians with a white flag* to Admiral Chukhnin to demand his surrender. Chukhnin had both emissaries of the revolutionaries *arrested*(!), and then ordered his side to *open fire against the mutineers*. For the next two hours, from 3:30 to 5:30 p.m., a *proper battle ensued, both on land and at sea*. While the ten warships under Schmidt's command bombarded the city, the revolutionary sailors and troops proceeded from the Lazarev barracks, which they had barricaded themselves into, in order to attack the city from the landward side. The use of artillery caused devastation on both sides. The projectiles from the mutineer's warships fell on the city, destroying many houses and killing numerous persons on the streets. The inhabitants fled into basements and other safe hiding holes. The mutineers appeared to be aiming at public buildings; it was the admiralty offices that incurred most damage. Several churches were also completely demolished, probably because their towers offered an easy target.

Elsewhere, the southern forts supported by the so-called coastal artillery were successful in their fire against the revolutionary fleet. The *Ochakov*, a cruise ship that the mutineers had taken, was hit at several places below the waterline and started to burn.

According to a dispatch from the *Publisher's Press* in Odessa, the ship sank soon after the end of the battle. *Dnepr*, a warship, and a separate torpedo boat were also hit by numerous shots and, after an hour, they sank. The battleship *Panteleimon* (formerly *Potemkin*) was badly damaged.

Schmidt himself was fatally wounded and surrendered with his ships at 5:30 pm.* Meanwhile, two loyal government regiments had forced back the sailors from the Lazarev barracks incurring serious losses, and then went on the attack against the three northern forts that were in the hands of the mutineers. Both regiments stormed the forts and captured them with a bayonet charge. Large numbers of mutineers lost their lives in this hand-to-hand fighting.

The official version of this carnage was as follows. *Petersburg*, November 30. Report in from Sevastopol, yesterday, at 3 p.m., the Black Sea squadron that had joined in common cause with the *Ochakov* cruiser, and had replaced the saltire with the red flag, was ordered to surrender by signals from the shore. The answer was a refusal. *At which the artillery batteries on the north side received*

---

* On March 10, 1906, issue No. 58 of *Vorwärts* published two columns of detailed notes that Lieutenant Schmidt had made during his time spent in the Casemate Prison in Fort Oshakiv awaiting the execution of his death sentence. These included the following editorial comment: "According to this self-portrait, *Lieutenant Schmidt* appears to have been more of a utopian idealist, than a clear thinking and decisive man of action." People aiming at revenge would grow up out of his blood, which (as Schmidt wrote) "no longer feel any false sentimentality toward a bestial opponent." Issue No. 67 of *Vorwärts* on March 21, 1906 reprinted the report from the *Den* [The Day], about Schmidt's execution: "Lieutenant Schmidt alongside the sailors Chastnikov, Gladkov, and Antonenko was shot at 4 a.m., by a firing squad of sixty sailors from the *Terets*, a gunboat; these sailors were in turn backed up by a platoon of infantry. Schmidt was very composed and asked his defense counsel to take down as fact that he'd never given men orders to shoot, and therefore did not have any human lives on his conscience. He spent his final hours writing letters to his sister, Frau Isbach, and to his sons. The execution was carried out on the Island of Beresand, when dusk was already falling. Schmidt walked quickly toward the place of execution and requested that no hood should be put over his face, nor that his hands should be tied to the post. He then said a moving farewell to the sailors and soldiers and shouted, 'A long life to you! Fire!' Schmidt only fell at the third volley of bullets. The corpses of the four executed were laid in prepared coffins and were buried hastily, right there and then."

the order to open fire on the squadron; however, these batteries had also decided to make common cause with the squadron and started to open fire on the city, especially on the batteries on the south side. (A malicious lie, naturally. The rebellious squadron had absolutely no reason to fire at *"the city."*) *Lieutenant Schmidt* commanded the squadron. Half of the city is destroyed, but the squadron has also suffered badly. *The* Ochakov *and the* Dnester *were run onto a sandbank, and* the *Potemkin* is badly damaged. Several torpedo boats have also run aground. *The Brest Regiment undertook an assault against the artillery batteries* in order to silence them. After *Lieutenant Schmidt was fatally wounded* at 5 p.m., the mutineers surrendered.

THE ECHO

The Petersburg correspondent of the *Daily Telegraph* reported that a new *mutiny* had broken out in *Liepāja*. A new mutiny is also reported to be underway in *Kronstadt.**

IN PETERSBURG

The *Berliner Tageblatt* has received the following: The chief of police in the city has ordered the Cossacks to continue disarming the workers, resulting in lots of bloody clashes. Danger is fermenting among the postal workers, and a widespread strike has been repressed only through use of military violence.

Petersburg, November 30. No news from the provinces at present, because communication lines have been completely destroyed. The workers have stated that the political, general strike will commence on Monday, December 4.

---

*   Here Luxemburg is referring to Kronstadt, located thirty kilometers west of Petersburg—not to be confused with the Romanian city of Brașov, which was still referred to as Kronstadt in German during Luxemburg's lifetime.

The Revolution in Russia [December 2, 1905]*

THE GLORIOUS BATTLE

The *Petersburg Naval Staff* has published the following telegram that the minister of war received yesterday from the commanding officer of the Odessa military district, Vice Admiral Chukhnin, with the following report dated November 29:

On November 28, it seemed like we would defeat the mutiny without engaging in battle. We circled the mutinying battalion with troops and issued them a final demand to surrender immediately and unconditionally. The mutineers however engaged us in battle, by commandeering the *Svirepy* [The Grim One], a torpedo boat destroyer, along with three other torpedo boats, all of which approached the *Ochakov*. All these ships together with the *Ochakov* hoisted the red flag. Whereupon the *Ochakov* hoisted the signal, "Schmidt is commanding the fleet." Schmidt proceeded to go on board the torpedo boat destroyer *Svirepy* to be met with cries of "hurrah" as he sailed along in front of the squadron—without, however, receiving a reply from the same. Then Schmidt changed course toward the port and released the persons whom he had ordered to be arrested.

During the morning, armed battalions of mutineers commandeered smaller boats in the port. Later the ironclad *Panteleimon* (formerly the *Potemkin*) was taken over by armed battalions working in boats from the *Ochakov* cruiser, though it had been disarmed before the seizure. The officers were taken prisoner and brought on board the *Ochakov*. Nothing could be done to counter the mutineers' actions because the fleet had been disarmed as a result of an order by the commanding officer of the VII Corps. Further mutineer advances took place through the afternoon and the situation grew even more serious. The ships that were moored in the south bay were taken and the red flag was hoisted over them. The first plan of action now had to be scrapped and new decisive measures taken. The mutineers had brought the captured officers on board the *Ochakov* in the hope that they wouldn't fire against so many officers.

Schmidt explained to the captured officers that as soon as the opposing troops commenced hostilities, he would have them hung. At 3:30 p.m. field guns opened fire on the ships in the south bay that had hoisted the red flag and on the remaining sea vessels of the mutineers; the red flag was lowered immediately. Schmidt signaled, "I have a large number of captured officers." After one of the mutineers' vessels was sunk, the *Ochakov* began to fire. The fire was immediately returned by the batteries on the north side and by the ships in the squadron. The *Svirepy*, the cruiser *Pamiat*

*   This article first appeared in *Vorwärts*, No. 282, December 2, 1905, under the title "Die Revolution in Rußland." It is translated (by Henry Holland) from Luxemburg's *Gesammelte Werke*, Vol. 6, pp. 753–6.

Merkuria, the ironclad *Rostislav,* and the mine-cruiser *Captain Sacken* put the torpedo boat destroyer under heavy fire, which was soon put out of the battle. Two other torpedo boats were also put out of action, one of which sank. The *Ochakov* had hardly fired six rounds before hoisting the white flag, whereupon the squadron ceased firing at it. Fire had broken out on board the *Ochakov* and boats had been sent out to rescue the crew. Schmidt, disguised as a sailor, tried to flee but was arrested. A minelayer carrying 300 blockade mines that was moored in the south bay was sunk right at the start of battle by its own crew, because of fears that the mines could explode.

THE MILITARY IN REFRESHING REVOLT

Petersburg, December 1. According to the latest reports, numerous soldiers belonging to the Cuirassiers, the Hussars,* and the Rifles have been arrested in Tsarskoye Selo because they had complained about bad treatment.

Petersburg, November 30. According to rumors spreading everywhere throughout the city, *an officers' assembly* took place yesterday in the Nicholas *Staff College*, with permission of the academy director. The officers gathered pronounced their sympathy with the mighty freedom movement currently moving through the whole of Russia. Today disturbances have broken out in the Second Guard Sappers Battalion. The men are demanding the release of a mate of theirs, under arrest since yesterday.

The telegraph office in the city has just gone out on strike.

Riga, December 1. The ferment that broke out in the garrison of the city has been quashed. The strike of post and telegraph workers has spread through the city. Letter and telegraph communication for private persons has been completely stopped. Telegraphists from Daugavpils are working on the Petersburg line and secret police have been employed to deliver the post. The foreign consulates have taken a whole range of precautionary measures for their respective citizens. In case of emergency, these should be shipped out of the city.

TRADE UNION ORGANIZATION STRIDES FORWARD

Moscow, November 30 (report by the Petersburg Telegraph Agency). Today the *chairman of the Union of Café Workers*, Pudovsky, was arrested. Pudovsky has been leading this union's strike movement. The police president stated that all members of the Moscow strike committee would be arrested and deported. *Vperiod* [Forward], the newly founded newspaper representing the proletariat's interests, will be allowed to publish.

---

* Cuirassier refers to an armored cavalry detachment. The term comes from the French word "*cuirasse*," which refers to the breastplate of armor worn by the cavalrymen. Hussars refers to members of a light cavalry.

Warsaw, December 1 (Wolff's Telegraph Office). *Martial law in Poland was suspended today.*

TSARISM'S BASTILLE

The following facts have been taken from a report by *Melshin* published in *Syn Otechestva* [Son of the Fatherland] concerning the most atrocious torture chamber in the tsar's empire—the *Shlisselburg Fortress.*[*] This was reorganized as a political prison on August 13, 1884, for which a special gendarmerie admin-istration was created, whose civil servants received double salaries. It cost the state 75,000 roubles annually to maintain the fortress. Anyone imprisoned here was subjected to total isolation. They were allowed neither to knock nor to sing nor to whistle nor to walk quickly. In the prison's first years the iron beds were even removed from the cells during the day, so that even the sick had to lie down on the cold floor. There were no books in the fortress. The sick lay in their cells and died there. Their comrades weren't even allowed in to see the dying, who had lost their senses under the influence of the despotic regime. The laughter and the screams of the mad often led the other detainees to despair. *Sixty-seven detainees*—"the worst criminals"—have been housed inside its walls from 1884 to the present day. Of these, *thirteen have been executed*, and these are: Rogachev, Stromberg, Ulyanov, Generalov, Ossipanov, Andreyushkin, Shlevayev, Michin, Minakov, Balmashkov, Kalayev, Gershkovitch and Vasilyev. *Three took their own lives*: Klimenko and Grachevski, who poured petrol over himself and died in terrible pain; and Sophia Ginsburg, who cut her wrists with a shard of glass from the lampshade. *Sixteen detainees* died as a result *of lunacy, tuberculosis and scurvy. Two* can be found right now in the Kanashian lunatic asylum. After release, *three* former detainees *committed suicide.*

It is not possible to recount all the atrocities that were played out in the silence of this torture chamber. For example, Balmashkov's corpse was thrown after execution into a hole filled with caustic lime over which was placed a stack of chopped wood. Similar "monuments" were placed over the graves of Gershkovich and Vasilyev, who were executed last summer. In one wing of the Schlisselburg Fortress, an "unknown person" was *bricked in*, whose fate remains a secret to this very day. Despite the "Constitutional Manifesto" from October 17,[†] *five* victims are still languishing in the Schlisselburg Fortress: Karpovich, Gershuni, Melnikov, Sazonov and Silkorsky.

But the day is coming soon … O that it may come quickly, really quickly!

---

[*]   The Fortress was founded in the fourteenth century. After the area came under Russian control under Peter the Great (in 1702), it became a high-security prison.

[†]   October 30 in new style.

The Revolution in Russia [December 3, 1905]*

As a result of the telegraph strikes very little news is reaching us from Russia. The scanty bit that we do have arrives much delayed after many detours.

MR. WITTE DROPS HIS MASK

A delegation of the striking post and telegraph civil servants presented themselves on December 1 to Count *Witte, but were not permitted entry.* Witte communicated that the strike of the post and telegraph civil servants would not be tolerated in any civilized country and recommended that the delegation appeal to "their immediate superiors."

The "liberal" mediating role of the prime minister is all played out. Faced with strong revolutionary action, he is through with the softly-softly approach.

THE TSAR'S EMPIRE IS CUT OFF

Copenhagen, December 2 (Wolff's Telegraph Office).† As communicated by the telegraph office in the city, *the telegraphic connection with Russia has been completely down since* 4 p.m. this afternoon.

THE DYING SOUNDS OF THE BATTLE OF SEVASTOPOL

Petersburg, December 2 (report by the Petersburg Telegraph Agency). A telegram has been received from Lieutenant General Möller-Sakomelsky dated December 1 concerning the events at Sevastopol, which states the military mutiny is over; the new troops are behaving impeccably; more than 2,000 of the insurgents have been taken prisoner. *The attitude of the inhabitants, particularly the Jews and the revolutionaries, is disturbing; they are mocking and upsetting the officers.*

Vienna, December 2. In contradiction to the semi-official reports, private reports from Moscow that have reached us here maintain that *skirmishes are still continuing in Sevastopol.* A heavy mood of panic dominates Odessa, where pogroms against the Jews are feared. *The regiment of sappers stationed in that city has mutinied.* General Kaulbars has threatened the Moscow papers with taking the toughest measures against them if they continue to publish "misleading reports." The academic senate has communicated to the city's captain of armed

* This article first appeared in *Vorwärts,* No. 283, December 3, 1905, under the title "Die Revolution in Rußland." It is translated (by Henry Holland) from Luxemburg's *Gesammelte Werke,* Vol. 6, pp. 757–60.
† '

forces that if the closure of the university is not retracted within twenty-four hours then it will be reopened with use of force.

THE BLACK HUNDREDS SET TO WORK

Kiev, December 2. New disturbances have broken out here. The mob in Podol looted shops and the military had to intervene. The rabble threatened to attack the intelligentsia and the consulates, leading the governor to take strict precautionary measures. The streets are occupied by the military.

THE MILITARY AND THE DEBTS OF TSARISM

The *Daily Mail*, normally very unreliable, reports that the central strike committee has passed a motion intending to paralyze the government by stopping loans reaching the Russian empire. The committee stated that bonds that the government had taken out abroad would be declared void if the present government were toppled. Moreover, the committee is working on a plan that would use force to bring all the government's gold into its own possession(!).

The last statement sounds adventurous. However, the fact that a future revolutionary government would not dream of* paying off absolutism's debts to the gentlemen bankers in Western Europe is so obvious that it can be taken as read, and does not particularly need to be "decided upon."

A HOAX

The *Hirsch Office* is spreading the following news: *Petersburg*, December 2. In the first issue of the new Social Democratic paper published yesterday, the socialist leader *Plekhanov* warns against continuing the revolution, the long duration of which carries with it a threat for our culture—a claim that Struve agrees with. The article created a lot of attention and was discussed in a sympathetic manner in the liberal papers.

This is of course a hoax. We do not know which "new Social Democratic paper" is meant in this case. *Nachalo* [The Beginning] was published on November 26 already and doesn't contain a single article by Plekhanov. In any case, it is impossible that Comrade Plekhanov can have made the statements attributed to him above. At the very most, it is perhaps possible—if there's any substance whatsoever to the rumors—that Plekhanov has warned against overstretching the general strike as a method. But even this seems extremely implausible.

---

* In the German, the word used is *"beifallen,"* in the sense of *occur to*, "It would not occur to them."

THE RUSSIAN REVOLUTION IN THE EYES OF THE ENGLISH

London, November 29. The English press and particularly the monthly periodicals like to display their generosity in the face of important occasions and events. Generous, that is, from a liberal point of view. Yet the traditions of English liberalism came into being in momentous times. This is why its followers are capable of interpreting historical happenings in an historical way. Nowhere is this clearer than in their judgment of Social Democracy. It wouldn't be in the least bit an exaggeration to say that Russian Social Democracy's recent achievements have cast a light on the socialist movement here of a kind never seen before. The English are always impressed by the art of organization—voluntary organization of political and social movements and parties. And our Russian comrades are the sole organized force in the Russian turmoil. We cannot, however, deny the fact that England is now sliding into a mood similar to that which broke out in England soon after the French Revolution had begun. [Edmund] Burke's* spirit is awaking.

The article "Europe and the Russian Revolution" in the December issue of the *Fortnightly* [*Review*]† is written in this spirit and uses all that Burke is capable of. But it still contains some thoughts that might be of interest for us. They concern the political mass strike, which the writer simply calls the general strike. After examining Russia's economic development over the last fifteen years, and describing the formation of industries and the proletariat, the author comments:

This was the situation brought to a head by the methods of the New Revolution. The general strike preached for years by German socialists as the *ultimo ratio* of the proletariat seemed an idea so abstract, a contingency so remote, that it excited the satire rather than the apprehensions of constituted authority and its defenders. In the last days of October it appeared in Russia in practical application as the most portentous and terrible instrument ever employed by political agitation. Up to that moment [Edward] Gibbon's famous argument that a hundred thousand disciplined men ready to strike toward any point can hold down a hundred million of more-or-less disconnected subjects seemed to have lost little of its validity. Railways, telegraphs, and telephones in Russia as in India seemed only to have increased the ability of a central authority to concentrate toward any point and to crush opposition with the greater rapidity. In Russia, a comparatively small minority has proved its ability to dislocate at a blow the machinery upon which modern government depends in all its operations. The towns in Russia are but dots upon the map. Yet

---

* Edmund Burke was a prominent opponent of the French Revolution of 1789. Luxemburg is suggesting that British liberalism may well respond to the 1905 Revolution as Russian liberals did—by distancing themselves from it.

† *Fortnightly Review* was an influential English magazine founded in 1865 by Anthony Trollope and other prominent intellectual figures. It offered literary and political pieces from a conservative as well as liberal perspective until 1954, when it ceased publication.

they are the points of junction—the screws and rivets that keep the whole apparatus of the state together. Without them the fabric of bureaucracy itself falls asunder. Militarism cannot mobilize. It becomes a question whether its army corps can be fed. The pressure upon the strikers themselves is extreme and exhausting. When their funds are exhausted, they must resume work or starve. But the intense power of their tactics extorts concession from a government not supported by an active and dominant public opinion ... The general strike in practical operation is obviously by far the most important phenomenon of politics since the French Revolution. *

The article is written under the pseudonym of *Perseus*.† Judging by his style, he used to write in the same monthly journal using the pseudonym *Calchas*, and has an important position in the Foreign Office.

---

* In the article, Luxemburg provides a German translation of the following statement in *Fortnightly Review*. We provide here the English original.

† We have been unable to identity the author who used the pseudonym of Perseus.

The Revolution in Russia [December 5, 1905]*

The post and telegraph civil servants' general strike is continuing. The repeal of martial law in Poland, with the obvious purpose of at least getting the Polish post and telegraph workers to resume work and therefore restart foreign communications, has failed utterly, at least for the time being. Solidarity between civil servants throughout the empire is holding its ground against the government's maneuvers and threats. We're particularly glad to note that post and telegraph civil servants *in Finland* are holding strong for the common cause.

Contrary to earlier reports by the German papers, the same *liberal papers* heading the pack which stated that the postal strike was starting to "die away" two days ago already, have to report the exact opposite today, with downcast faces. The strike is in fact continually spreading, now that the *railroad telegraphists* are preparing to join the movement. Simultaneously with this, fresh waves of general strikes among the *industrial workers* are expected to break out in Petersburg and other cities. And, finally, not a single day goes by without new reports of rebellion in the armed forces. Revolutionary ferment has even shoved its way forward into the circles of the military "aristocracy"—the tsar's own guard. Open revolt has broken out in the immediate personal surroundings of the last tsar, at Peterhof and at Tsarskoye Selo.

A private dispatch has reached me via several hands from Wolff's [Telegraph] Office from Petersburg, dated December 2, describing the situation as follows: The cable service to Denmark has been suspended, and telegraph communication with Finland has been interrupted. Telegraphic civil servants working for the railroads are refusing to transport both government and private telegrams, but they have stated, on the other hand, that they are prepared to forward telegrams concerning train transport. If the railroads' telegraphic civil servants also suspend this service, as is expected any hour, then all train services will also have to be suspended. The whole progressive press is demanding the resignation of Durnovo, minister of the interior, who is being held responsible for these heightened tensions. It is generally believed that profound events await us in the days to come. The Social Democrats and the revolutionaries want to use this opportunity to declare the general strike in all regions. The government is determined to crush all revolts ruthlessly. Apart from numerous patrols by the cavalry, the Cossacks, and the infantry, a lively yet still normal impression can be gained from the street. The population is stocking up on groceries. Twenty-five men from the tsar's Preobrazhensky Guard have been arrested, and fifteen

---

* This article first appeared in *Vorwärts*, No. 284, December 5, 1905, under the title "Die Revolution in Rußland." It is translated (by Henry Holland) from Luxemburg's *Gesammelte Werke*, Vol. 6, pp. 761–4.

of them interned in the Peter and Paul Fortress. Neither newspapers nor letters have been delivered for several days.

PROLETARIANS OF ALL NATIONALITIES

Stockholm, December 3. According to reports received from Helsinki, *the striking Finnish telegraph civil servants* have adopted a resolution, voicing protest against the attempt to suppress freedom of association, despite this being authorized by the tsar. *The Finnish civil servants express their solidarity with the Association of Post and Telegraph Civil Servants*, and contemplate remaining on strike until the Association's central office in Moscow declares the strike finished.

Stockholm, December 3. As communicated by the telegraph exchange in Stockholm, the Finland–Russian telegraph line is continually interrupted. Telegrams are being forwarded once a day by post to Uusikaupunki.

Petersburg, December 2. The banks in the city have stated that, until further notice, they are collecting all simple letters addressed to them from the Chernyshevskoye post office daily, using their own post personnel.

THE COUNTERREVOLUTION EMIGRATES

Many "better-off" families in *Warsaw* are leaving the city so quickly that it seems like they are fleeing because of the upcoming general strike, which the railroad employees also want to join. The passport offices are literally occupied.

The tsarist capital is completely cut off from the world. Due to the suspension of all telegraphic connections with the provinces, only very few reports are available about events playing out there. According to reports received by letter from Warsaw, the striking telegraph civil servants are threatening to destroy all telegraph lines if the authorities were to carry out reprisals against them. The same source states, moreover, that large conflagrations have broken out in Moscow, set in reality by the police, but blamed upon the striking workers.

As a last resort, the counterrevolution is trying to utilize the peasants' movement for its ends and against the revolution.

What is new are the mass proclamations from the reactionary side distributed among the peasant population, calling on these people to fight back against revolutionary agitation and the "Polish danger," as this could cause nothing less than the destruction of the whole Russian empire. The peasants, however, aren't buying this poppycock. The serf knows very well what he wants.

WHAT THE MARINES ARE DEMANDING

As reported from Odessa, the Sevastopol sailors are demanding the following: abolition of the death penalty, a wage rise, a four-year military service, and the convocation of the Constituent Assembly. There is unrest in the city's garrison.

The headquarters of both factions of the Russian Party have sent the following letter to the International Socialist Bureau:

> Dear Comrades!
>
> The huge Russian Revolution finds itself in a very serious situation. The government is attempting to apply the tools of Reaction, already tested in 1863. Following Polish demands for the autonomy indispensable for achieving free, cultural self-determination, the tsar's government has responded by imposing a state of siege over the whole of Poland, with the intention of putting wind to the flames of national hatred between Russian and Poland, and thereby using this chauvinism to strike down the revolution. These tsarist politics are winning support from the other semi-absolutist powers. Wilhelm II's Prussian government is mobilizing its army on its eastern border, and we must seriously expect this army will be sent into Russia to subjugate the Polish people.
>
> The struggle of the Russian Revolution, the whole of humanity's struggle, is in danger! The Russian proletariat supports their Polish brothers for the violence that has been done against them, through energetic protest. We call on you, dear comrades, that you would wish to communicate those measures you intend to take to protect against this danger, and to support the Russian people—should this danger actually come into being.
>
> Yours with party and comradely greetings!
>
> The Central Committee and the Organization Commission
> of the Social Democratic Labor Party of Russia

A letter worded in similar fashion has also been dispatched to the leaders of the German party.

It is obvious that the International Socialist Bureau,[*] alongside the German party leadership, can only articulate the deepest outrage regarding all of absolutism's acts of violence. The most effective *method* against the tsarist government speculating on national antipathies being unleashed, lies in the hands of Russian and Polish proletarians themselves—a determined, fraternal class solidarity, which until now has so happily stood up against the chauvinism of their ruling classes. And, this time, these tactics have borne fruit again—*martial law has been rescinded in Poland for the last two days.* As a result of the Russian government facing up to its purposelessness and from the admirable solidarity actions of the post and telegraph civil servants in Poland as in Russia, it is forcing the government into retreat! As regards the saber rattling on the *German imperial*

---

[*]   The central bureau of the Second International.

border, unequivocal messages coming from accountable positions make clear that German Social Democracy would rise to the last man against a possible military intervention, which would benefit Russian tsarism. Meaning we can expect simple common sense in the leading circles to ensure that provoking their *own* working class in such a manner will not even be considered.

The Revolution in Russia [December 6, 1905]*

The post and telegraph civil servants' general strike is continuing in outstanding fashion! Accordingly, we have access to hardly any telegraphic reports from Russia. Private letters are the only way in which sparse news is emerging from the country, prompting the *Vossische Zeitung*† [Voß's Newspaper] to publish the following letter from Riga, dated December 3: The *post and telegraph civil servants'* strike action continues. Tensions have escalated more than they have been defused. The civil servants are in a state of excitement about Count Witte's refusal to receive a delegation of their association, directing them instead to their immediate superiors. Strong processes are also in flow among the railroad workers. They are not satisfied with the directive concerning a salary rise to up to 15,000,000 roubles, and continue to present *political demands*. They have reportedly sent a telegram to Count Witte, written in a very particular tone, demanding *the convening of a Constituent Assembly*. The railroad is at present maintaining private post communication using delivery staff, but these workers are personally under threat. The departing delivery workers are being observed at stations by whole throngs of postal civil servants. Persons carrying bundles of letters are stopped by the postal civil servants and are stopped from entering the stations by use of threat. Some letters are, however, still being smuggled through.

How sensitive the tsar's empire is to the effects of the post and telegraph strike can be seen in this private letter to the *Local Advertiser* in Petersburg, from December 3: The state is suffering huge losses because of this strike. The total number of letters, money and registered items, transfers, packets, and paper slips that the postal offices of this city have to process daily stands at 530,000 items; if the loss for telegrams is also included in the calculation, measured at c. 13,000 daily, then just the Petersburg post service alone is losing at least half-a-million roubles daily because of the strike. The striking post and telegraph civil servants held an assembly on Saturday to discuss their situation, with 2,000 members participating. *It was decided to stay strong, to continue the strike and to force the government into concessions.* The next goal is to achieve the release of detained delegates. The strikers are being supported by a strike committee and may well soon be able to celebrate the strike's twentieth day, just like their Moscow colleagues. This assembly was attended by the president of the Council [Soviet] of Workers' Deputies, representatives of various political parties, and a delegation from the Moscow Post and Telegraph Congress, who Count Witte had refused

---

*   This article first appeared in *Vorwärts*, No. 285, December 6, 1905, under the title "Die Revolution in Rußland." It is translated (by Henry Holland) from Luxemburg's *Gesammelte Werke*, Vol. 6, pp. 765–9.

†   A liberal, Berlin-based newspaper.

to receive. The assembly went on to pass the motion *not to attend the handing over of pay packets* scheduled for today, Sunday. The total number of strikers in Petersburg alone is now 6,000.

Meanwhile, the *railroad strike* continues, gradually, to spread. This is underlined by two telegraphic reports: *Kiev,* December 5. Telegraphic communication began again yesterday, a service supplied by two retired civil servants and two girls. *Railroad transport on the southwestern railroads has, on the contrary, been stopped entirely, including the Kiev, Odessa, and Sevastopol lines.*

Haparanda, December 4. The *Svenska Telegrambyrå* has received a report from Tornio that a *new railroad worker strike has broken out in Finland,* triggered by the convention of the senate. At present the strike is stretching as far as Hämeenlinna, but will probably *spread over the entire railroad network.*

THE REVOLUTION IN THE ARMED FORCES

The rebellion inside the military is now spreading so violently that reports of "mutinies" or individual regiments, of arrests and of bloody battles follow hot on the heels of each other. That being said, we can trace out the following logical link in the development of the movement; the whole thing was started by *crews of marines.* The land troops used against them were enthused by the revolutionary flame, in the very process of suppressing their comrades in the fleet. While the troops more-or-less allowed themselves to be used as the tsar's slaves against the workers' demonstrations, things started to seriously breakdown when they were sent against the marines. And now the land troops are rebelling themselves, and the government has to deploy Cossacks to pacify them. This means, however, that the same whole game will be replayed. The Cossacks, who have always proven their worth as bloodthirsty beasts against the people, start to go to pieces when they are deployed systematically against *soldiers.*

And so, consequentially, the revolutionary fire puts down roots from social class to social class, from one pillar of absolutism to the next. The apparently insoluble tasks of the revolution appear to solve themselves through the revolution's own progression. Of course, the seeds of enlightenment, *sown by Social Democracy* through tough and tireless work, are starting to mature everywhere amid this. But it is primarily the inner, iron laws of revolution that have suddenly made whole new classes receptive and fertile for these seeds, classes that until yesterday appeared to us as thankless and stony ground.

At present, the south Russian city of *Kiev** is the center of a violent military revolt. As our readers learned from yesterday's issue, a *state of emergency will be declared tomorrow.* Again, the reason for this is a movement among the troops.

---

*   Kiev is, of course, in Ukraine. Luxemburg never acknowledged, however, calls for Ukrainian independence and self-determination, and repeatedly referred to it as Russian.

The *Russian Correspondence* newspaper received the following description of events in Kiev: On December 1, at 7 a.m. *a company of engineers* began the strike in Kiev. As the whole Russian people are also doing, they demanded absolute freedom, not just on paper, but also in real life. Spreading from the barracks, they drew more and more soldiers into the strike. Several brigades kept their distance and didn't unite with them. At 4 p.m., the soldiers moved toward the Kehivanek smelting works, whose workers are organized in a Social Democratic way, to hold a general meeting. The Asor Brigade then shot at our comrades, killing thirty and wounding many. Cossacks wanted to fight against the striking soldiers the next morning, but when the strike leader stated that several soldiers were wounded, the Cossacks withdrew. General Draque directed some words toward the striking soldiers, who read aloud the strike demands comprising thirty-five points in reply. Principally they demanded exemption from service duties in the reserves, reduction of service period, decent treatment, improvements in food and clothing, and a political Constituent Assembly. After which, they sang the Marseillaise. There was a shortage of food supplies in the barracks during the two days on which the meetings took place. The soldiers moved through the streets playing music. The population gave them food supplies during the night, for which many were arrested. On December 2, all newspapers were confiscated apart from the Kiev organ of the Black Hundreds. The revolutionary committee declared the general strike, in protest against the slaughter. Workers and soldiers organized meetings at the Polytechnic Institute in daily anticipation of significant events. The solemn burial of the dead soldiers took place on the 3rd, the crowd being dispersed by the Asor Brigade. The city is extremely unsettled. A state of siege will be declared tomorrow. The Polytechnic Institute is closed and surrounded by soldiers. The newspapers are not being published.

We have received, in addition, the following reports:

Kraków, December 5. According to reports from *Warsaw*, the 46th Infantry Regiment is refusing to carry out further police services.

Warsaw, December 5. A mutiny has broken out among the garrison in *Osovze*. In *Grodno*, numerous mutineers of that town's artillery regiment have been arrested. The infantry are mutinying in Kharkiv. Recruits are refusing to swear the oath of allegiance.

THE MILITARY UPRISING IN VORONEZH

Den [The Day] newspaper prints the following telegraphic report: *Voronezh*, December 2. The penal battalion's local and military prison in the suburb of Pridacha was set on fire yesterday by military prisoners and mutinying soldiers from the penal battalion. The fire spread to a row of shops. The mutineers marched toward the state prison to release the prisoners in line, led by their band, but were held up by regular troops at the bridge that leads from the town toward the state prison, which was by now in flames. Volleys fired out the windows by prisoners prevented the fire brigade from extinguishing the flames … The prison was surrounded by troops. After the exchange of fire, some of the mutineers from the penal battalions were taken prisoner. Another group of these mutineers is now fleeing; another has been surrounded.

This description is, of course, colored in the way these semi-official Russian reports are. What is certain is that the disturbances among those in Voronezh have, as everywhere, a decidedly political character.

A DAFT HOAX

The *Daily Telegraph* has published the following nonsense, filed by its Petersburg correspondent: The German Social Democrats have urgently advised their Russian kindred spirits against nihilistic actions, yet the Russians, more urgently in need of money than good advice, have decisively rejected this warning.

Not one single word in the whole report is true, of course.

FINAL NEWS AND DISPATCHES ON THE REVOLUTION IN RUSSIA

Petersburg, December 5. The following news has at last arrived via *Chernyshevskoye,* supposedly from "private parties," but in reality probably spread in semi-official fashion by the Russian *government.* They must be considered with caution. General Möller-Sakomelski, Commanding Officer of the 7th Army Corps, as reported by *Rus',* has stated that four sailors and three revolutionaries have been killed during the closure of the Sevastopol barracks. Two thousand men have surrendered, including 1,600 sailors and 400 others mostly comprised of agitators in civilian dress, with the rest made up of infantrymen. Even though these 400 men also had access to weapons, a large *deficit of organization* was evident in their actions. The city is now quiet again. A large group of portal workers is prepared to start work again and unrest on the streets is not expected. Despite their large number and excellent arms, the mutineers didn't display excessive energy but merely some clumsiness. This was why loss of life was much lower than during any other clashes with badly armed or unarmed groups of folk. *(This contradicts newer reports according to which 1,800 sailors have fallen!)* The investigative commission has begun its work. Sailors and sappers were the main groups in the mutiny, alongside private persons, principally Jews. One soldier from the Brechen regiment fell and two men are wounded. On the revolutionaries' side, three men are dead and four sailors wounded, however a rumor doing the rounds suggests *that the number that the inhabitants succeeded in wounding is substantially higher.*

The Petersburg garrison has had major reinforcements in the last few days. In case unrest occurs, the city has been divided into four sections, whose command has been assigned to the generals *Osserov, Lubensky, Schirm*, and *Trotsky*. As of December 3, these four sections were manned by forty-two battalions, fifteen squadrons, sixteen *sotnia** of Cossacks and twelve machine guns. A strong military presence has been deployed in the post and telegraph offices, and in the factories.

An assembly of post and telegraph civil servants was stopped that same evening by mounted soldiers and Cossacks hitting out with nagaika. The Chairman of Workers Deputies appealed to the post and telegraph civil servants in the pages of *Rus'*, relaying a statement made by the city's chief of police, in which he explained that he was following orders from above. *A single stone thrown, or one shot, he said, and the crowd will be dispersed forcibly using machine-gun fire.* The appeal ended with the call not to slacken in the struggle until total victory has been achieved.

The military district court sentenced the persons who participated in the plot against *General Trepov* to four to ten years forced labor.[†]

Petersburg, December 5 (received via *Chernyshevskoye* from the Petersburg Telegraph Agency). According to figures gathered in an inspection of the factories, *the number of unemployed factory workers in Petersburg currently stands at 28,000.* As reported in the papers, preparations are being made for the reopening of the eleven sections of the workers' associations organized by *Priest Gapon*, closed after the disturbances in January. The return of the sequestrated sums of money should also occur in the near future. The Socialist Revolutionary Party has already begun their campaign against the workers' associations and *Gapon*. The Socialist Revolutionary Party passed a resolution stating that the measures proposed by *Struve* and *Gapon* could only lead to ruin for the workers.[‡]

The *Paper for Trade and Industry* has been informed by a reliable source that *the government supports the project of universal suffrage.* (Presumably to raise the slumping exchange rate of the "Russians" again by making promises![§]) The situation in Petersburg is unchanged. Martial law has been declared in the city and municipal region of Kiev, because disturbances have broken out there.

According to the *Rus'*, the Imperial Duma should convene by January 28 at the latest.

---

[*]   This is a Russian term meaning military units of 100 men.

[†]   At the time Trepov was considered among the most reactionary members of the government; he regularly urged Nicholas II to use violent measures against protesters. Although his removal from power was one of the promises of the October Manifesto, he was appointed by Nicholas II as commander of the imperial palace.

[‡]   When Gapon returned to Russia at the end of 1905, he entered into discussions with the government that were mediated by Pyotr Struve. The SR party, with which Gapon had earlier had friendly relations, now began to denounce him.

[§]   This parenthetical sentence was introduced into the article by the editors of *Vorwärts*.

The Political Mass Strike[*]

The police managed to surpass themselves to begin with, refusing entrance not only to members of the press, but also to the speaker. It was only after a heated exchange that the excluded lecturer managed to penetrate into the hall by way of smaller side paths. After Comrade *Luxemburg* touched upon this incident in her introduction with a few sarcastic remarks, she moved on to discuss how the German working class has shown an enthusiastic and general interest in the political mass strike recently. Until a short while ago, German Social Democracy had considered this method of combat taboo. Sudden turning points of this kind in valuing a particular political solution always possess the symptomatic meaning that deep realignments have occurred in social relations, being what Hegel calls the turning point of quantity into a new quality.

What is of most value, according to Luxemburg,[†] is the *sheer interest* in the debate about the political mass strike—and it really is irrelevant whether this or that comrade, or this or that party newspaper positions itself against the political mass strike. The German working class has suddenly turned with passionate interest toward this slogan, without their leaders or specific bodies having shown any interest. We simply need to recall the Trade Union Congress in Cologne.[‡] There, trade union representatives—the *crème de la crème* of a trade union class of civil servants for the whole of Germany—passed the resolution that not only should the political mass strike not be considered, but that merely discussing the issue should be *forbidden*. Although Comrade [Theodor] Bömelburg protested against this interpretation of the resolution, the *Grundstein* [Foundation Stone][§] writes nonetheless: "Despite Jena, and in keeping with our previous position, we will not consider using the political mass strike, and yes, we refuse any form of discussion about it."

Such motions only reveal that particular persons work with a certain touching notion, deceiving themselves into thinking they can really direct the action, and also the inaction of the workers, by pronouncing a tsar-like ukase over the people: "You should keep your mouths shut!" Yet it's been proven that the working masses are now ahead of their so-called leaders, and are seeing with

---

[*] This was given as a speech by Luxemburg to a "Meeting of the People" sponsored by Social Democratic Women of Berlin. It was first published, based on as newspaper report, in *Vorwärts*, No. 287, December 8, 1905, under the title "Der politische Massenstreik." It is translated (by Henry Holland) from Luxemburg's *Gesammelte Werke*, Vol. 6, pp. 770–4.

[†] Since this speech is presented as taken down by a reporter, in several instances Luxemburg is referred to in the third person.

[‡] The May 1905 Trade Union Congress not only opposed adopting the strategy of mass strike but also forbid its discussion.

[§] *Der Grundstein* was a journal for masons, quarrymen, and related professions, published fortnightly in Hamburg from October 1, 1875.

more clarity. (Applause.) Our future does not lie in the infallibility of our leadership, i.e., in civil service circles, but in the large masses themselves. Every time we're faced with a new question about tactics and principles, we've got to be clear about which general and theoretical foundation we're working with, both to deal with these questions and to research the matter.

There are, in this vein, various positions regarding the mass strike. On the one hand, there is Comrade [Raphael] Friedeberg and his zealous preaching of the mass and general strike in his sense of the word. Friedeberg is opposed by the rigidly dismissive viewpoint of the trade unions, as discussed above. We can say that both parties spring from the same theoretical ground, which we can label anarchistic. Typical for anarchist thinking is to see the tasks of political struggle detached from economic and social development, and exclusively from a speculative perspective, as if floating in thin air. Only by using such unencumbered speculation can you believe that a mass strike is something you conjure up. Neither position views the mass strike from the perspective of historical necessity, but rather chooses to see it as a tool of struggle, to be used *arbitrarily*. You could say that they treat the mass strike as a kind of pocketknife that you always carry, to flick out or fold away again as the situation demands.*

Social Democracy's position, based, as usual, on historical fundamentals, differentiates itself unequivocally from this trivial postulation, as it does in all questions of theory and tactics. Social Democracy does not ask: "Is it daring, or rather useful, to experiment with the mass strike? Shall we use it, or shall we not?" Based on its materialist approach to history, Social Democracy poses the question thusly: "When we glance at the current and forthcoming development of class contradictions in contemporary society, and reach our conclusions from that, will the mass strike take place as a historical necessity, as a historical form of class struggle—or not?" When posed in this way, the question need no longer engage with many of the objections raised by the opponents of the mass strike.

The speaker then branched off to talk about *Weltpolitik*† and sketched the situation in the Far East resulting from the last war between Russia and Japan, in order to conclude that we must expect even bloodier wars to come.‡ Sooner or later, even Germany will no longer be an observer, but rather a sharer in this suffering. Plans are afoot to turn Kiautschou into a naval fortress,§ and the

---

* Luxemburg will later use this exact formulation in *The Mass Strike, the Political Party, and the Trade Unions*, in 1906. See *The Complete Works of Rosa Luxemburg, Vol. IV: Political Writings 2* (London and New York: Verso Books, forthcoming).

† The foreign policy adopted by Germany after 1891, which stressed the need for Germany to develop as an international power and secure colonies in the developing world. It represented a rejection of Bismarck's earlier Realpolitik, based on ensuring a stable balance of power between the major nation-states.

‡ A prescient forecast of what was to come with World War I.

§ Kiautschou, on the southern coast of Shandong Peninsular in China, became a German leased territory seized from China in 1898.

powers behind that project are working toward a sea war.˙ Antagonism between the great powers has grown, and what is the other side of this same coin? Army and navy expansion, new trade tariffs, new taxes, and a new exploitation of the masses—antagonisms between classes, in both Germany and in other states, will be exacerbated!

To that should be added a new factor that must have a huge influence—revolutionary Russia. Its effects have already been demonstrated in social struggles in other countries. You just need to take a look at the struggle for suffrage in Austria and in Saxony.† Those are the sparks that have sprung across from the great sea of flames in the east. You would have to be struck down by stupidity to such an extent that it contravenes even police law—or better, to be afflicted by the police's sort of blindness—not to grasp that more and more sparks will leap this gap every day.

Turning to the Russian Revolution, the speaker elucidated the way things stand in Russia today, arguing that the only form the revolution could create was that of a liberated, democratized, and *bourgeois* Russia. Social Democracy, the party with which we are fraternally joined, is leading the Russian proletariat. The new Russia will carry the molten lava of the class-conscious proletariat within it. New conflicts will arise and attempts to throw off the capitalist yoke will follow.

The rest of Europe will feel the effects. The Russian Revolution is not just an epoch for the Russian people, but also a milestone in world history. It is a prologue for other revolutions, which will develop by necessity, and which can have no other conclusion than the much maligned and previously ridiculed dictatorship of the proletariat.‡ The speaker didn't want to engage in making vague prophecies. What she was saying was nothing other than wholly sober conclusions drawn from cool observation of both the Russian Revolution, and of the international context of class struggles in all other countries.

And what's the situation regarding the political mass strike here in Germany? A conclusion can be drawn from the course of development world politics has taken in the last ten years, and from the development of the Russian Revolution in the last few years. Antagonisms between classes in all capitalist countries will be ratcheted up to an incredible degree, and the mass of workers will no

---

*   This refers to those in the German government and military who had concluded that the policy of *Weltpolitik* could succeed only if Germany underwent a massive build-up of its naval forces—even if that should risk war with other European powers.

†   In November and December 1905, a struggle involving tens of thousands of participants took place in Saxony, against the then-current three-class suffrage system, and for the implementation of a democratic voting system with which to elect the state parliament. Bloody clashes with the police took place in Dresden.

‡   Luxemburg's comment is clearly aimed against reformist elements in the Second International, including but not restricted to Bernstein, who dismissed the importance of this critical Marxian concept. In doing so, she is pointing to the *permanent* character of the ongoing Russian Revolution.

longer be able to meekly put up with class hegemony—with all its humiliation and misery—as it does now. We can rather expect turbulent confrontations and direct battles with the ruling classes.

Having said that, the working class—having committed itself to a larger, communal struggle—will have to come out of slavery up to the surface, up out of the workshop, the factory and the mine. Downing tools and going out on strike in this manner is the natural first step for this class. It certainly would be possible to learn from the application of the mass strike in Russia; although there's no place where it is *less discussed* than in Russia right now. The Russian Revolution has demonstrated that the mass strike has become historically necessary for the working class when it stirs into action. The time will also arrive in Germany, when the mass strike is seen as an irrefutable method of struggle.

The speaker [then] protested against the fact that she and others are depicted as opponents of parliamentarism among certain circles of comrades. Whether and to what extent *parliamentarism* should be seen as a form of working-class struggle can't be decided by us, but only by the path of historical development. But precisely because of this situation, the mass strike shouldn't be seen as the sole means of achieving bliss, even though it can be of excellent service to the workers' movement under particular historical preconditions. The ruling classes are currently doing their best to prevent from us fighting our battles inside the house of parliamentarism, by stripping us of the means to do so. It isn't radical Marxists who want to destroy parliamentarism—it's rather the bolstered and toughened forces of reaction that are doing their best to strip us of the means [to use parliamentary methods]. We are almost compelled from without to turn to other means and methods.

While a mass strike can neither be forbidden nor arbitrarily triggered, as it always depends on the historical situation, let's not lapse so far into fatalism as to say that every mass strike can only be sent down to us from heaven. It certainly is the case that if a strike is to be carried out according to plan, it has to be the result of a motion of the organized workforce. It is exclusively the situation that demands a mass strike in the first place, which cannot be ushered in through a motion. The main thing is that Social Democracy is ready and waiting should such a situation come about, and capable of acting as the vanguard of the masses.

The speaker then proceeded to tackle several of the well-known objections that have been brought up against the mass strike, by Comrade Frohme in the *Hamburger Echo* for example, and from trade union leaders and other individual comrades in the party. She also spoke out against seeing the trade unions as an end in themselves. Marxists are against these particular tactics and *not* against the trade unions in general. Marx saw the trade unions as an essential weapon for the workforce. However, the trade unions should also not be degraded to the status of a slave of the tools that the workforce is using for its liberation. It should be pointed out that nothing is as fruitful for the idea of organization as an open and intense class struggle. Not only would the trade union organizations together with the political organizations have nothing to fear in the case of a mass strike in Germany, this event would be a rebirth for them, and they would move on from it strengthened tenfold.

The question has been raised: "Would the unorganized masses follow us [in this mass strike]?" This again is a question that would solve itself in the process of playing the game, when individuals come down from agonizing on their pedestals, to the ground of the mass strike as a historical necessity. When we reach that point, we will also have arrived at a situation in which every word uttered by the organized party will also be taken up and followed by the not-yet-organized part of the proletariat. When the situation demands that the mass strike is a necessity, then that in itself will install clarity in the proletariat, etc.

After refuting Wolfgang Heine's critique—"caution worthy of a state attorney [should be shown]"—the speaker summarized her own standpoint together once more, as elucidated above. She then closed her lecture that had been interrupted by applause on several occasions, with an admonishment that is as valid for Social Democracy as it is for every warrior: "What counts is being prepared!" (A storm of long-lasting applause.)

During the final section of her speech, Comrade *Luxemburg* took Mr. [Eric] Mühsam thoroughly to task,* which again earned her strong applause.

With thunderous cheers for international Social Democracy emancipating the world's peoples that followed hard on the heels of cheers for Comrade Luxemburg herself, the impressive assembly closed.

---

* Erich Mühsam had polemicized against Luxemburg from an anarchist standpoint. He was later to be one of the main leaders of the ill-fated Bavarian Soviet Republic of 1919.

The Revolution in Russia [December 7, 1905]*

The post and telegraph civil servants' strike action is holding strong. Most of the telegraph wires between Petersburg and Moscow have been cut. All railroad stations in Petersburg are being guarded by troops. Railroad stations in most cities are overflowing with freight cars leaving the capital that cannot be unloaded because of the workers' strike. The unemployed are leaving the capital and Moscow and are moving to the villages to escape a potential famine. This means that revolutionary agitation will of course be spread in increased measure to the surrounding countryside. While that is going on, absolutism is under threat of a *financial crash*.

There is most serious concern about the government's financial situation in Petersburg, as the *Times* reports from the city. The semi-official newspapers are publishing reports on the rich profits being made from the brandy monopoly, written in an almost ecstatic tone, forecasting an income from this source of over a million marks for next year. It is believed in Petersburg that these articles betray the government's intention to *mortgage the brandy monopoly to German banks*. The presence of Fischl, authorized signatory from the Berlin Banking House Mendelssohn in the city, adds weight to this belief. We can at any rate assume that the "outstanding revenues" from the brandy monopoly can at best be traced to the Black Hundreds' copious consumption, which the government pays for out of its very own pocket.

As regards the workers and peasants, it has just been ascertained that their brandy consumption has dropped noticeably during the last year of revolution. If the German banks are willing to enter into this pretty business, then we can count on it being a resounding flop. Priest *Gapon* has apparently turned up in Petersburg again, his presence—as has usually been the case to date—only causing bewilderment and tensions inside the workers' movement.

As reported in the Russian papers, preparations are being made for the reopening of the eleven sections of the workers' associations organized by Priest *Gapon*, closed after the disturbances in January. The return of the sequestrated sums of money should also occur in the near future. The Socialist Revolutionary Party has already begun its campaign against the "workers' association" and Gapon. The Socialist Revolutionary Party passed a resolution stating that the measures proposed by Struve and Gapon could only lead to ruin for the workers.

We cannot rule out the possibility that the government is now intentionally reopening the Gaponist clubs and associations to spread chaos and confusion in proletarian circles. *The railroad strike* continues to draw nearer. As reported by

---

* This article first appeared in *Vorwärts*, No. 286, December 7, 1905, under the title "Die Revolution in Rußland." It is translated (by Henry Holland) from Luxemburg's *Gesammelte Werke*, Vol. 6, pp. 775–8.

a Lviv dispatch from Petersburg, an assembly of railroad civil servants passed a resolution yesterday, that if the post service's central board did not retract numerous redundancies, then they would go out on strike. *The general strike has broken out in Nikolaev.*

The peasant uprisings are also continuing, as is proven by the sparse news that still reaches us from Russia. As stated by *Laffan's* News Agency: peasants have looted a large estate in the *Penza Province* belonging to Prince Naryshkin, son-in-law of Count Witte's. The stately home and other estate buildings were destroyed.

Paris, December 5. The *Journal* reports from Petersburg that a total of 60,000 workers are currently on strike. A local assembly passed the resolution to continue the strike under all circumstances. Clashes continue on the streets.

TSARISM AND ITS FOREIGN RELATIONS

The good old days of Aranjuez* are gone, in which Russia was seen "as the strongest bulwark of international reaction!" Now the capitalist states are barricading themselves off from Russia as fast as they can, and with that from the dangerous revolutionary horde. A whole series of telegrams illustrate the majestic picture— the tsar's old empire, going up in the revolution's huge sea of flames, cut off from the world, viewed with horror and mistrust by the other "powers!" ...

Washington, December 5 (report by *Laffan's News Agency*). The State Department has not received any news from the American embassy in Russia for the last two days.

Constantinople, December 5 (report from the Vienna Telegraph Office). As a result of events in Odessa and Sevastopol, and in ports where the arrival of revolutionary ships is to be feared in the aftermath of the *Potemkin* affair, the same measures have been taken for the Bosporus as were ordered while the *Potemkin* affair lasted. Several torpedo boats are stationed at the entrance to the Bosporus.

Stockholm, December 5. The *Aftonbladet* reports that the Marine Ministry will send two warships to Russia to protect Swedish subjects. The *Psilander*, a torpedo boat destroyer, will sail tomorrow to Petersburg. A second torpedo boat destroyer shall be sent to Riga along with a merchant steamship, to be available for the Swedish consul in that city.

Vienna, December 6 (H.O.).† Despite the Austro-Hungarian ambassador's intervention in Petersburg, the Russian government is refusing to grant claims that the injuries incurred by Austrian or other citizens during the disturbances

---

*   Aranjuez, in central Spain, was the site of a palatial residence of the King of Spain in the eighteenth century. In 1808 it was the site of the Mutiny of Aranjuez, a popular uprising against King Charles IV, which was largely a response to an economic crisis that resulted in a sharp drop of industrial production.

†   From Hirsch's Office, a press agency.

should be compensated. The government points out that those concerned could sue in court in accordance with Russian law.

AN APPEAL TO HUMANITY

In *Mainz*, in the big hall of the Liedertafel,* an assembly of more than 1,000 people was held on the evening of December 5. A committee had invited numerous city councilors; the member of the regional parliament, Dr. Schmidt; Dr. [Eduard] David, the member of the Reichstag; as well as representatives from all political parties. After introductory talks by Mr. [Eugen] Leviné from Petersburg and Prof. Staudinger from Darmstadt, the following resolution was passed unanimously:

> The assembly meeting on December 5, 1905 in the large hall of Liedertafel in Mainz expresses its utmost indignation concerning the thousands in Russia who, under the eyes of the authorities, can be murdered, maimed and robbed of their property. The assembly declares the atrocities that have taken place cast derision on the achievements of civilization, and hopes that all of decent humankind will share its indignation. We expect that the pressure of public opinion makes a repetition of such experiences impossible, and that the unfortunate victims receive their share of moral support from the cultured states, particularly through the endorsement of equality of rights for all citizens of one state.

There is much talk here of "humanity" and "public opinion." The fact is that the hard-fought *proletarian class struggle* is the only protection against the bestiality of absolutism, and not these two very problematic powers, blurred as they are in their conception by the bourgeois.

NICHOLAS'S FINAL "SWISS GUARD"

Petersburg, December 5 (via Chernyshevskoye, from the Petersburg Telegraph Agency). A regimental party of the *Semionovsky Guard Regiment* was celebrated yesterday in *Tsarskoye Selo*, at which Tsar Nicholas addressed the troops, highly praising *their proven loyalty to duty*. At a breakfast with the officer, the tsar *proposed a toast to the officer corps*. He thanked the regiments again for their exemplary services and concluded with the wish that the Semionov regiment may always remain so strongly united as it was currently showing itself to be.

---

* A major concert hall, which hosted performances by Gustav Mahler and many other important composers.

The Revolution in Russia [December 8, 1905]*

The striking post and telegraph workers are fighting bravely on. The Russian government continues to have to rely on the services of police spies and similar "volunteers for work." A telegram received from Petersburg via Chernyshevskoye reports: The industrial action of the post and telegraph workers is continuing as strongly as ever. The strikers are in good cheer and are convinced that their stamina will lead to their demands being met. Count Witte supports these, and the only obstacle now is Durnovo.† Meanwhile the postal service continues to function as well as it can through support from 2,000 volunteers from the general public. There's been a lot of movement around the postal building for a number of days now; patrols marching up and down and Cossacks riding in rows attract many curious gazes. Mounted patrols pass through the grounds of the imperial residence day and night.

An assembly of post and telegraph workers decided *to extend the strike*.

A second telegram confirms: *Petersburg*, December 6 (Via Chernyshevskoye). The situation in Petersburg is unchanged. The striking post and telegraph workers maintain that they want to force Durnovo's resignation. Expressions of solidarity and donations are flowing in considerable measure toward them. *The Association of State Civil Servants also expressed its support for the strivings of the post and telegraph workers, through a resolution with many signatures.*

In the meantime, as reported in delayed telegrams from the Petersburg Telegraph Agency, the government is attempting to fan the fire's flames through new acts of violence:

Vladimir, December 3 (from the Petersburg Telegraph Agency, via Eidtkuhnen). *Two students and seven telegraph workers have been arrested here due to participation in the strike.*

Moscow, December 5 (from the Petersburg Telegraph Agency, via Eidtkuhnen). *One part* of the imprisoned members of the Association of Post and Telegraph Workers *was released.*

THE THREAT OF A GENERAL STRIKE IS WORKING!

The extent to which the working class is teaching absolutism through their wonderfully coordinated general strike action can be seen from the following case, as

---

* This article first appeared in *Vorwärts*, No. 287, December 8, 1905, under the title "Die Revolution in Rußland." It is translated (by Henry Holland) from Luxemburg's *Gesammelte Werke*, Vol. 6, pp. 779–81.

† Pyotr Nikolayevich Durnovo, minister of the interior, had banned the All-Russian Association of Post and Telegraph Employees. In response, the congress of the association called a protest strike on November 15.

reported in *Rus'*. The engineer Sokolov and several other railroad workers were handed over by the commanding officers of Fort Kushk (Transcaspia) to a war court, and were then sentenced to death. When the president of the Samarashian Railway Committee got news of this, he reported it to the Central Railway Office in Moscow with the statement, that, should the sentence be carried out, a general railroad strike would break out immediately. A direct wire with the demand that the death sentence be rescinded followed from Moscow to Count Witte, to the ministers of transport and of war, and to the Russian General Staff, as well as to a number of other railroad companies. The transport minister responded by informing the railroad companies that the execution of the sentence was temporarily suspended.

The Petersburg Telegraph Agency added that neither Count Witte nor the minister of war had been informed about the sentence. The latter immediately after receiving the information sent enquiries to Kushk, Ashkhabad, and Tashkent and simultaneously ordered, in the event that the sentence had in fact been pronounced, that the enforcement of the sentence be postponed. The fact that no official announcement has been made can be attributed to the telegraph workers strike.

A ROLE MODEL FOR CLASS SOLIDARITY

As reported to the *Frankfurter Zeitung*: Petersburg, December 7. The Moscow Association of Book Printer Assistants has declared that it is not able to support current individual economic strikes, because the whole proletariat is arming itself for the political general strike, which should be the final blow to topple the government.

Priest Gapon now even appears to feel himself that his game is up. As a telegram reports: *Petersburg*, December 7. Priest Gapon has decided to leave Russia and intends to take up permanent residence in Paris.

A NEW ACT OF TERROR

The Socialist Revolutionary Party appears to be making use of terrorism again after a long pause. As the *Daily Telegraph* reported, the *former minister of war, General Zakharov*, was shot while visiting Saratov Province to pacify the insurgent peasants, by a woman belonging to one of the revolutionary parties. The woman entered the house of the governor of Saratov, and demanded to speak with the general who was residing there. Once in front of Zakharov she fired three shots at him, killing him on the spot.

Saratov, December 5 (via Chernyshevskoye from the Petersburg Telegraph Agency). The woman who shot the former minister of war, Adjutant General Zakharov, in the governor's house, was arrested and stated that she had carried out a sentence ordered by the mobile, military wing of the Socialist Revolutionary Party.

Such individual acts of terror are, however, of only inferior significance, now that the whole huge mass of the proletariat is conducting the fight.

MARTIAL LAW: NO END IN SIGHT

Petersburg, December 6 (report from the Petersburg Telegraph Agency via Chernyshevskoye). Martial law has been imposed on the Livonia Province.

The Revolution in Russia [December 9, 1905]*

The post and telegraph civil servants strike continues! This, despite the fact that the tsarist government is doing all it can to trick observers abroad into thinking that the strike is "dying down," such as in distributing the following telegram:

> The government's decisive attitude and the Association of Post and Telegraph Civil Servants joining the Council [Soviet] of Workers' Deputies, which has caused a split among the striking post and telegraph civil servants, appear to be directing the strike toward its end. The Council of Ministers, who met yesterday, also reflects this position by sticking to their decision not to authorize the Association of Post and Telegraph Civil Servants. The local director of the post service ordered 200 postal civil servants to be evicted from flats situated in post office buildings, along with the sackings of 332 civil servants who work in post offices, and 800 delivery postmen. The postmen will be re-employed again immediately, as will the civil servants on supplicating to the authorities, in as far as the extent of their individual strike participation allows this.

Yesterday, on December 6, one group of civil servants went back to work. The Finnish post and telegraph civil servants have telegrammed to reject joining the Russian workers.

News like this about the strike "dying down" has been coming out of Russia since the very first days of the strike movement. The *Berliner Tageblatt* has published the following private telegram from Petersburg: Despite post services operating in the city, their whole work seems more like a game that, as long as the provinces continue to strike, can only have purely local relevance. The telegraph service resumed work in individual municipalities yesterday. However, most business people and banks aren't making use of postal services, but are sending their post via couriers either toward the border, or to the municipalities of the interior. The business situation has become extremely critical. The four percent pensions listed on Wednesday's stock market at seventy-four were actually being bought at sixty, although this rate will not be registered. We can assume that the strike will stretch out for a number of days yet.

The delegates of the Council of Workers returned yesterday from various Russian municipalities. The conclusion of their journeys being that an all-Russian strike on the anniversary of Bloody Sunday is now certain. On this day, all organizations will be brought to a standstill for weeks and the last battle between the proletariat and the government will commence.

---

* This article first appeared in *Vorwärts*, No. 288, December 9, 1905, under the title "Die Revolution in Rußland." It is translated (by Henry Holland) from Luxemburg's *Gesammelte Werke*, Vol. 6, pp. 782–5.

THE SOLDIERS' REVOLT

Vossische newspaper reports from Warsaw: The troops from the Grochov regiment stationed in the city were ordered to report without weapons to the barracks' courtyard. Here Cossacks surrounded them. They were searched one by one. On many was apparently found the revolutionary *Soldatsky Listok* [Soldier's Newspaper]. All of these men have been imprisoned. The *postal strike* has now expanded to include the *Railroad Mail Service*. The post railcars are no longer being connected to the trains, because there are no civil servants present to sort the letters. They are being taken across the border by a trainee motivated by friendliness.

A report by *Laffan's News Agency* states: *Petersburg*, December 6. At the session yesterday of the *Socialist Revolutionary Party* emissaries returning from the south reported that troops there are prepared to rise up against the tsar and are just waiting for a sign from Petersburg. According to telegrams received here, the city of *Novorossiysk* is now in the hands of mutinying troops, as is the city of *Yekatertinador* in the Caucuses, where soldiers are occupying the arsenal and 16,000 guns have been distributed among the workers from that city and from Novorossiysk. A similar movement has broken out anew in Sevastopol.

Tokyo, December 7 (*Laffan's News Agency*). A report in the *Asahi* newspaper confirms that the city of *Harbin* was in flames on November 30. The supply lines for the Russian troops were cut and the city plundered by the Chinese.

Warsaw, December 8. Reports have reached us from Łódź that the revolutionary movement among the troops is making significant gains. Numerous breaches of discipline are taking place every day.

We have, in addition, received the following reports:

Petersburg, December 8. The *resignation of the minister of justice* will be officially announced within the next few days. This will not weaken the cabinet's position (a fine statement from a "cabinet" no longer sitting!). The minister of justice's successor has not yet been declared.

Warsaw, December 8. According to telegrams from Petersburg, numerous private banks have informed the finance minister that they will be forced to close their businesses if the postal civil servants' strike were to continue even longer.

A HOAX, PROBABLY

Petersburg, December 9. The leaders of the revolutionary movement have reportedly already *sentenced Priest Gapon to death*, through accusing him of having been won over to tsarism.* Priest Gapon's so-called "trip abroad" was

---

* Gapon fled abroad in the aftermath of Bloody Sunday and was at first welcomed by numerous Russian revolutionaries living in exile (such as Plekhanov, Lenin, and Kropotkin). He also

nothing less than a veritable flight from his erstwhile colleagues. Gapon has apparently already crossed the German border, with the intention of heading to France.

A HUMOROUS REPORT

A semi-official telegram from Petersburg reads as follows: *Petersburg*, December 8. Everything quiet here. All rumors circulating abroad are unfounded. The workforce is tired of striking and is returning to work everywhere for the same old conditions. And in the military discipline is returning too.

WITTE: AT HIS WIT'S END

The *Frankfurter Zug* [Frankfurt Train] newspaper reports: Witte, whose response to the zemstvo delegation's petition is being withheld from the government's program, has turned toward joining the reactionary camp. His reception of the zemstvo delegation demonstrated his definitive break with the liberals. However, at this moment in time, the reactionaries find other personalities within the reactionary tendency more pleasant and easier to deal with than Witte, who they don't necessarily trust. At present, it is Durnovo who has the best chances, declaring that the only men and parties with whom the government could join forces are the infamous reactionary Count Dobrinsky (Tule) and the Agrarian Association, whose congress is in Moscow right now. It is as if a large revolutionary outbreak should be engendered, only for it to be mercilessly crushed by cannons and canister shot.

This would be a foreseeable end to this skating on thin ice, which the darling of German liberalism performs with such virtuosity.

HANNIBAL ANTE PORTAS!*

Nicholas cannot even get peace from the general strike inside his own palace. As our Russian correspondent reports: A strike has broken out among the servants, cooks, and other employees in the tsar's palace in *Tsarskoye Selo*. They are demanding a pay-rise. The court minister has accepted all the strikers' demands.

---

developed close ties with the Socialist Revolutionary Party. Upon his return to Russia at the end of 1905, however, he contacted the tsarist secret police, the Okhrana, and offered his services to them. While his motives for doing so are unclear, he may have thought that re-establishing a connection with the regime could help the workers' cause. He was executed shortly after his return to Russia, in March 1906, by the SR.

*   Roman saying: "Hannibal is at the Gates!"

THE PRESS IN THE COURTS

Both of the party newspapers in Petersburg have to fight legal actions at present.

On December 21 in Petersburg the well-known Russian author [Nikolai Maximovich] *Minsky*, the editor of *Novaya Zhyn* [New Life], will be tried for the "distribution of revolutionary propaganda." This propaganda consists of the fact that the Russian Social Democratic program was inserted into the first issue of our partner newspaper. Minsky will be defended by Grusenberg, a well-known attorney. The trial is open to the public. It is the first time in Russia that a political trial will take place in the public eye.

In January 1906, a similar process will start against the editor of another Social Democratic newspaper *Nachalo* [The Beginning].

AN EXAMPLE WORTH EMULATING

The municipal councilors in Poznań passed a resolution at their last meeting requesting the magistrate to issue an order, through which 2,000 marks for victims of the Russian disturbances would be allocated.

The Revolution in Russia
[December 10, 1905]*

The strike continues. There is almost no news available from Russia apart from the Petersburg Agency's own reassurances ... that the strike is almost over, traffic and communication lines "normal," and everything's in the finest order. At least they haven't lost their sense of humor yet in Petersburg, even if it is only gallows humor.

The English papers report: 100,000 Petersburg workers are now armed with guns. Two million revolvers have been distributed across the entire empire. Weapons deliveries from revolutionaries abroad have been turned down by leaders of the uprising, with the reasoning that there will be sufficient rifles available in the imperial arsenals.

The Union of Unions has sent an ultimatum to Count Witte, regarding the report that a number of participants in the Sevastopol mutinies are due to be shot. The Union is threatening a general strike unless the sentence is immediately suspended.

According to further reports received, the mutiny of the Russian troops began in Harbin on November 12, and spread from there. About 10,000 soldiers took part in the mutiny. They caused chaos on the streets, looted most of the Chinese shops and set fire to the government's mills, the barracks, and the other imperial buildings. Clashes arose during which many persons were killed.

We have also received the following reports:

Kiev, December 9. The second *Infantry Regiment* is mutinying in Proskurov. Squads are refusing to serve and are destroying equipment.

Odessa, December 9. According to private reports from Sevastopol, *Lieutenant Schmidt* has not yet been executed. Accompanied by a very strong escort, he was removed yesterday from the Ochakov fortress. Further reports from Sevastopol state that the editor of the local paper *Krimsky-Vestnik* [The Crimean Herald] was forced, under threat of execution, to publish an article portraying the Jews and revolutionaries as being the initiators of the last uprisings. The military is preventing dispatches from leaving Sevastopol.

Petersburg, December 9. Rumors are circulating in the city that Durnovo has submitted his resignation.

Petersburg, December 9. The Association of Ministerial Civil Servants issued a proclamation, vehemently demanding freedom of association, which stated,

---

* This article first appeared in *Vorwärts*, No. 289, December 10, 1905, under the title "Die Revolution in Rußland." It is translated (by Henry Holland) from Luxemburg's *Gesammelte Werke*, Vol. 6, pp. 786–7.

further: "Down with tyranny and with the reactionary ministers who've caused all the suffering that has come upon our land."

TSARIST FINANCES

Paris, December 9. *Le Matin* reports: Rouvier did not state at the Council of Ministers that the Russian warrant service was covered for two or three *years* through the sums deposited in the banks, but rather for two or three *semesters*.

Revolutionary Days in Moscow[*]

When, in times to come, historians of the great Russian Revolution recount the incidents of the October Days, which form a milestone in the course of this revolution, they will have, in the first instance, to draw attention to the happenings in Moscow. Russia's revolutionary proletariat has dumbfounded the whole world with its feeling for solidarity, its political maturity, its colossal power, and its heroic deeds capable of standing up to the counterrevolution's cruelty and crafty moves. It is, however, particularly the *Moscow* proletariat that has won eternal glory in the battles of these memorable October weeks! In Moscow of all places, in our old Mother Moscow, now seen as the fortress of orthodox reaction, there was no burning of members of the intelligentsia as in Tomsk and Tver, no bloody orgies started by the Black Hundreds, and no massacres of the Jews. The reason why the Russian government and the militias' undertakings have gone awry is obviously the powerful organization and political education of the Moscow proletariat.

It is impossible to give a brief summary of the incidents in October in Moscow; they are too immense to squeeze into the frame of a newspaper article. We would like therefore to simply give a short overview and to select a few dramatic moments from this battle of the titans, in the form that *participants* described them to us.[†]

When on October 9 a strike of all railroad officials and workers of the Moscow railroad district broke out, no one could tell, nor even could the comrades in the Moscow committees foresee, that this strike would spawn a situation that would lead, quick as lightning, to a catastrophe for the absolutist state order and to the pronouncement of a constitution. [It is] what the Russian intelligentsia, the Russian proletariat, and all those freedom fighters who met death on the gallows, in the prisons, and in the Siberian tundra and taiga during the last century and longer, had striven for. It was thought that the strike would stretch itself over three to five days but would then collapse. Yet it was only the bourgeoisie and the proletariat, not yet knowing their own strength, which managed to fool themselves in this regard. News of the Moscow strikes broke like a huge wave over the whole of Russia. By the next day, transport in the whole of central Russia had started to falter, and on the day after that nothing moved on the railroads between Petersburg and Odessa, from the Caucasus and mid-Asia to east

---

[*] Although no name appeared with this article, Luxemburg was most probably the author. Its content, diction, and the use of eyewitness accounts is very similar to what is contained in her other writings of the period in *Vorwärts*. The article first appeared in *Vorwärts*, No. 289, December 10, 1905, under the title "Die Revolutionstage in Moskau." It is translated (by Henry Holland) from Luxemburg's *Gesammelte Werke*, Vol. 6, pp. 788–92.

[†] The rest of this article is a summary of a report Luxemburg received from a participant in the Moscow protests.

Siberia. Trains remained in stations en route, amid fields, and everywhere the news of the strike reached them. The situation turned serious and the Moscow bourgeoisie were seized by a great panic. Current stocks of flour, meat, coal, and wood were ascertained, prices shot up uncannily, and people started hoarding in a feverish fashion.

After two further days had passed, municipal government officials joined the strike. The city appeared to be extinct. Gas and electric lights were extinguished, the trams slowed down to a stop, the slaughterhouses closed, the hospitals emptied of both caretakers and doctors. The phone network was put out of order. The wildest rumors circulated through the city. People hurried to supply themselves with water and guns, while the shops locked their doors and boarded up their windows. The papers were the only things to appear and always brought news of more and more fresh strikes. The pharmacists downed tools, and the pharmacies and drugstores had to close. A dirty black liquid streamed out of the water pipes; the water board was also on strike! And, finally, post and telegraph workers came into the fold. Moscow was cut off from the whole world. Wireless telegraphy, which now connects Petersburg and Moscow, had not yet been installed.

The city lay there dead. The Tulerskaya and Neglinny Lanes, the equivalent of Berlin's Friedrichstrasse and Leipzigerstrasse, were empty. Only the echo of horses' hooves from wide patrols of Cossacks and dragoons rang out. Civilians hardly dared to leave the house and there was barely a soul to be seen when evening came.

Yet despite this outer silence, life in the interior and in the inner city pulsated hotly. The first public assemblies were held with thousands of people in university lecture halls, the Polytechnic [and] Mine Surveyors Institute, the conservatories, the engineers' college, etc. Thousands upon thousands of workers from the locked factories, university and college students, final grade high school students from the boys' and girls' high schools, officials from the national and private banks, officers and common soldiers, their epaulets adorned with handkerchiefs, businessmen, female peasants in simple headscarves, young lads and old grandmothers, gentlemen in expensive furs and men in shabby *chuiken*[*]—all flowed to the meetings. A new epoch in the life of society had begun, a new breeze was in the air. A single stroke had transformed freedom into reality.

And what had brought about this transformation? Social Democracy. The meetings began around nine in the morning and stretched on until midnight. Between ten and twelve meetings took place simultaneously in the various lecture halls of the university. The speakers swapped around every two hours, and the speeches all had roughly the same content. "Down with the tsar!" rang out from all the stages, and the thousand-headed audience applauded in response.

---

* Cheap clothing worn by the Russian poor.

Passions were set alight. Freedom of speech knew no limits. The population was high on this dearest possession of cultured people and of citizens, hitherto never experienced; free speech, open, revolutionary struggle. And where did all of this happen? In "loyal Mother Moscow," in the heart of old Russia, in the fortress of tsarism and clericalism.

The Moscow movement was led by the committee of the Social Democratic Party, the party also responsible for the initiative behind the mass meetings. As chance would have it, a crowd of non-resident comrades from other municipalities were staying in Moscow at that time, and were immediately pulled into the work. The authority of the party grew enormously. A wide range of resolutions and motions proposed by Social Democratic speakers were passed unanimously. An example of this authority can be gleaned if I mention that I was often voted as a chairperson of the gatherings,* even though the masses didn't know me personally, simply on the authority of Social Democracy in itself, the force that I presented myself as speaking for. Let us sketch a picture of one such gathering:

It is 9 a.m. The dining hall in the boarding house of the Institute of Mine Surveyors is packed tight. Three thousand to four thousand people are present. Above us on the second floor another meeting is taking place—workers from the Prochovondshen Factory. In the canteen of the main institute the post and telegraph workers are also holding a meeting, simultaneous to ours. The railroad workers are in the drawing and drafting room, municipal officials in a different room, and in the auditorium a general meeting of the people is taking place. A student of the Mine Surveyors Institute is busy keeping order. "Comrades!" he says, addressing the gathering, "I propose as chairperson a member of the Social Democratic Party," and points to me.† Everyone claps. As I get up onto the stage one member of the Black Hundreds who has sneaked in shouts out in protest: "The vote's invalid, down with him!" screams the individual. "Off with him, off!" shout out a few more of their comrades from the back rows. "If you support the Social Democratic chairperson, please raise your hand now!" shouts out the student loudly. The whole auditorium raises their hands as if one. "And who against?" Nobody moves. "It's not right!" cries out a single voice. There is commotion throughout the auditorium. "Police plant!" "Black [Hundred] scum!" "Comrades"—I'm doing my best to shout loudly—"by voting for me as chairperson you also transferred power to me to lead this assembly. Calm down. I recommend that the person causing the disturbances be removed!" Four comrades grab the rowdy representative of the Black Hundreds and accompany him to the door.

---

* Since this consists of Luxemburg's summary of a report, she is not referring to herself here. She did not leave Germany for Russia until the very end of 1905.

† Luxemburg is, again, not referring to herself, but rather providing an image of the events occurring in the mass meetings.

The auditorium is full of tension. Everyone is on edge. Many have not slept for nights on end, a situation ripe for rapid provocations. Panic can ensue very easily, and many people could fall victim to it. "Comrades!" I say, "a few members of the Black Hundreds are present here, and they will try to break up this meeting. Do not be scared. Our armed 'worker troops' are also present." "Bravo!" rang out the response through the wide hall. Everyone's enjoying the fight and is overtly thirsting to perform heroic deeds. The meeting commences with a number of facts concerning the progress of the Moscow strike and the Russian situation being read out. The reports are presented passionately. The audience interrupts the speaker with cries of joy. Next, our comrades take the stage and give impassioned speeches, hot with rage. And truly, our speakers, our agitators have done a good job. Hail to you, friends ready for sacrifice! You've carried the huge struggle on your shoulders! Each of our speakers had to get up to speak five, six or more times every day. Often without having eaten the whole day, without having slept at night, dripping sweat, tired and hoarse they hurried from the university to the Mine Surveyors Institute, from there to the conservatory, to the Polytechnic and so on, talking everywhere with all their might and the deepest enthusiasm, firing people up and explaining things. We also had to organize the "workers' army," to work on agendas for meetings, to attend conferences at which both fractions—the "majority party" and the "minority party"*—worked with each other in order to agree upon joint public appearances. Out on the street, however, our speakers were blatantly chased and threatened by members of the Black [Hundreds]. Whole sections of them came in the evening to wait in front of the various assembly rooms, and went for the speakers as soon as they stepped out onto the street. The chases and the fist-fights didn't however stop the comrades from going on working and influencing things. Their reward was to see whole troops of the proletariat marching in rank and file, not scared of the nagaika, bullets, or machine guns, following Social Democracy at every word and wave of the hand.

We had not yet been supplied with weapons, and had to warn the proletariat to avoid clashes with the military. This didn't stop the workers from wanting, although unarmed, to engage the troops in combat, wishing to defend their freedom not with their guns but with their bare breasts. "Comrades! The hour of the armed uprising has not yet come. Don't let them provoke you into straying from the path. Do not go as lambs to the slaughter. We will call you ourselves when the decisive hour of battle comes. In the meantime, organize and arm yourselves, agitate, and be prepared for the moment that matters." That is how we spoke to represent our committee. Both "majority" and "minority" faction speakers called for arms to be used in the near future. Large sums of money were

---

* The Bolsheviks were the majority faction of the RSDRP, while the minority faction the Mensheviks.

gathered for the armaments. At gates and at doors, in the corridors and in the halls, collectors could be seen everywhere, shouting, "Comrades! Give money for arms!" And alongside the copper, silver, and gold coins that were thrown into the hat, 100 rouble notes were also thrown. Ladies took off brilliant earrings, bracelets, rings, and golden necklaces, and threw them into the collecting hats. Some threw their full purses in. Even daggers and revolvers were passed over to the collectors. These were great moments, the greatness of which cannot be entirely captured on these pages.

The Revolution in Russia
[December 12, 1905]*

The camp of tsarist counterrevolutionaries is behaving like headless chickens, in a way apparently unparalleled in history. In the face of the obvious breakdown of the whole state machinery of absolutism, the stupid thugs cling rigidly to the inalienable vested right of the nagaika, still believing that [the truncheon] can impress somebody. A daily briefing from Minister Durnovo states categorically that the Association of Post and Telegraph Civil Servants will not be tolerated under any circumstances! Those civil servants who continue to strike will be "dismissed from service" at all costs, while those who "initiate disturbances" and cause damage to the networks and to expensive equipment will be prosecuted in court. Actions of this type would mean "public insurgency and rebellion." Five hundred thousand roubles were allocated to support post and telegraph civil servants in mid-November. In distributing these funds, only those civil servants returning to duty will qualify, who have previously been recognized for their "industriousness." They are intending to add insult to very real injury, and to bribe the rebellious slaves of the state with "support."

These clumsy bellows of the reaction serve of course only to fire up the strikers. An assembly was held in *Petersburg*, attended by 2,000 people, in which a *continuation of strike action* was voted for by all but one participant.

The executive committee of the Council [Soviet] of Workers' Deputies adopted a resolution, which declared that, in light of the unavoidable breakdown of the old system, it would be to the proletariat's advantage to postpone the decisive blow. The Petersburg Workers' Deputies Council is therefore not yet giving the signal for the *general strike*.

Rus' reports on December 7 that those considering *establishing a military dictatorship* in Tsarskoye Selo have postponed introducing that institution until a larger uprising should break out. According to rumors circulating, the Black Hundreds are planning a rally, during which the Petersburg newspaper printing houses will be raided.

All these rumors should lead us to expect longer and more acute fighting in Russia. Yet it does give us the chance to see for the umpteenth time *who* is the author of the bloodshed, the abominations and the civil war, *who* is doing the provoking, and *who* is deliberately stretching out and exacerbating this terrible crisis—is it the revolutionary mass of folk, or is it the blindness, the selfishness, and the criminal lack of discernment displayed by the guards of the current "order"?

---

* This article first appeared in *Vorwärts*, No. 290, December 12, 1905, under the title "Die Revolution in Rußland." It is translated (by Henry Holland) from Luxemburg's *Gesammelte Werke*, Vol. 6, pp. 793–5.

THE PEASANTS' WAR

Petersburg, December 10 (via Chernyshevskoye). The peasants' disturbances are taking on ever-more threatening dimensions, and some have now begun in the immediate vicinity of the *Moscow–Kursk* railroad. The peasants are not only setting fire to country residences but are also threatening the train stations. (As reported, please note, by the semi-official telegraph agency.) The empire's "peaceful population" can see no other remedy for the "soothing of troubled souls" than the rapid convention of the Imperial Duma. In answer to requests of this sort, Count Witte replied that the Imperial Duma would assemble soon. An alteration to the voting law has however not yet been announced. In a similar vein, *the world of trade* is protesting against Durnovo's position in the post and telegraph strike, which has already led to unrest on the streets of Moscow. The arrests of the organizers and the office members of the Association of Post and Telegraph Civil Servants in Moscow will more likely nourish the movement than cause it to stall.

From Moscow, *Novoye Vremya* [New Times] telegraphs: The stock exchange is very troubled by reports from Vyshny Volochyok, where workers have threatened factory overseers with death and have already stabbed one. (Obviously a semi-official, fake news item.) In the factory in Tver, workers have decided to take on the leadership of the works.

THE MILITARY REBELLION

The *Frankfurter Zeitung* has received this report: *Petersburg,* December 11. General Linevich has recommended that the army be withdrawn rapidly, *otherwise military revolts in the Far East are unavoidable.*

On the tenth of this month, the following report from *Warsaw*: Mutinies in individual parts of the military are now happening more often in Poland. Yesterday afternoon three military bands paraded through the city, playing peace songs and followed by a large crowd of folk bearing red flags. That evening, the fourth battalion of the Keksholm regiment of the Austrian Kaiser's Royal Guard mutinied; it has been locked into the barracks. It is said that a large rally is being planned for tomorrow from the military's side.

As reported from *Moscow,* the troops there are divided into two camps, one of which is loyal, the other—and the more significant—being revolutionary minded.

The officers of the latter camp attend meetings in uniform, at which they give speeches.

THE REVOLUTION IN RUSSIA   439

THE POLICE FORCE IN REBELLION

Warsaw, December 10. *Police officers* in the city have gone out on strike. The Chief of Police responded by removing all of them from their posts.

RAILROAD WORKER STRIKE BREWING

In *Riga*, an assembly of *railroad civil servants* was dispersed on Friday evening, using armed force. Machine guns were also put to use for this purpose. *The number of dead is said to be significant.* Machine guns have also been moved into position in the street. *The train connection between Riga and Petersburg has been suspended.*

A NEW PARTY NEWSPAPER

The prospectus for the first big daily newspaper of Social Democracy, which should be published in the next few days, has been sent to us from *Warsaw*. The paper will be called *Trybuna Ludowa* [People's Tribune], and can count among its staff Bebel, Kautsky, [Paul] Singer, Clara Zetkin, and further leaders of French and Dutch Social Democracy.

We send the new comrades our most heartfelt, fraternal greetings!

The Revolution in Russia
[December 13, 1905]*

The counterrevolution is intentionally pushing for a catastrophe. According to a telegraphic circular ordered by Durnovo, all post and telegraph civil servants are to be made redundant and then employed anew. In this context, we have to expect a railroad strike as a consequence.

The general railroad strike declared in Warsaw has not yet broken out. However, a general decision in the whole of Russia in that direction is to be expected. In the meantime, military revolts are spreading further and further. After *garrison reservists* in the fortress at *Brest-Litovsk* appeared in a state of utmost agitation, circa 1,000 men were discharged and sent home.

THE LEADING ORGANIZATIONS AT THEIR POSTS

The *Local Advertiser* publishes the following private dispatch: *Petersburg*, evening, December 11 (via Chernyshevskoye). Following the arrest of [Pyotr Alexeyevich] Khrustalev-Nosar, the president of the Council [Soviet] of Workers' Deputies, an extraordinary meeting was convened to determine how the Council should react to the arrest. It was proposed that the general strike should be orchestrated with all available means. A majority of the members opposed the motion, however, stating that a local strike would be pointless, and if one wanted to declare the general strike, then all of Russia's trains would have to be pulled into the effort, which the railway delegates judge to be an unsuitable measure at present. The delegates from the Post and Telegraph Association insisted that their strike be carried out first. Finally, a resolution was adopted, in which, in response to the arrest of the president of the Council of Workers' Deputies, an appeal is to go out for the whole of society to protest, while the *proletariat*, on the other hand, will be called upon to commence *the armed struggle*. Also present at the meeting were *delegates from the Guard Fleet Equipage*, who declared their solidarity with the workers. They are prepared to stand up for the people's cause at the decisive moment. For the time being, the sailors are spreading propaganda among their young comrades. Khrustalev-Nosar's arrest is said to have resulted from a whole series of articles that the Council of Workers' Deputies published in the workers' papers, containing defamations against the tsar(!), as well as calling on the military and the people to take up the armed struggle.

---

* This article first appeared in *Vorwärts*, No. 291, December 13, 1905, under the title "Die Revolution in Rußland." It is translated (by Henry Holland) from Luxemburg's *Gesammelte Werke*, Vol. 6, pp. 796–8.

The extraordinary meeting of the Worker's Council ended with its chair voicing the assurance that *it will not be long until the proletariat rules over Petersburg.*

FRIEDRICH ENGELS' JUDGMENT FROM 1883 ABOUT THE RUSSIAN REVOLUTION

In a letter from 1883, the well-known Russian socialist *Hermann Lopatin* shared with one of his friends* the content of a conversation he had with *Engels*, in which the latter clearly laid down his views regarding the task of the revolutionary party in Russia.

Lopatin gave his friend the following report:

> We debated at length and in depth about circumstances in Russia and made efforts to become clear on this point—on how, in all probability, the political and social rebirth of Russia would unfold. According to Engels, Russia was the French kingdom of the present century. Russia was fully entitled to possess the revolutionary initiative for new social transformation and for new birth. The fall of tsarism, which will tear away the last pillar supporting absolute monarchism in Europe, will simultaneously generate a new combination of European states, will shake up Austria, and will give all other countries a violent and decisive shove, resulting in radical, interior changes ... It is very doubtful whether Germany will risk sending its troops to Russia to protect and maintain tsarism, using the chaos inside Russia as a pretext. If Germany really would dare do that, so much the better: then that would mean both the certain fall of the current regime and the beginning of a new era.†

KREUZ-ZEITUNG'S RIFFRAFF WRITING ABOUT TSARIST RIFFRAFF

A public meeting took place in a room in parliament yesterday, convened by Professors Harnack and Bergmann with the aim of initiating a relief operation for Germans who have incurred damage in the Russian turmoil. Around 200 gentlemen from the "best circles" were in attendance, including many from the armed forces. Facing this esteemed and "brilliant" audience, Prof. [Theodor] Schiemann from the *Kreuz-Zeitung* gave his best in presenting the following:

---

*   The friend was Mariya Oshanina, a leading Russian Populist who was a member of the Executive Committee of Narodnaya Volya (People's Will) in the early 1880s and the leading woman theoretician of the Populists.

†   See Lopatin's "Letter to Mariya Oshanina," in *Marx-Engels Collected Works*, Vol. 26 (New York: International Publishers, 1990), p. 591–3. Lopatin was one of the first Marxists in Russia, having studied Marx's work as early as 1868. He met with Marx in 1870 and assisted in the translation into Russian of Volume One of *Capital*. Closely associated with the Populist movement, Lopatin was exiled to Siberia after his return to Russia, but escaped in 1883 and made his way to Paris and then London, where he met with Engels.

"Utterly horrible catastrophes are to be expected. Russian governmental power is failing. The riffraff are getting braver by the day." Schiemann sees the future through very pessimistic eyes. "Mutiny in the military, robbery, and murder are becoming increasingly rampant. It is known that a very large number of Russians have already fled to Germany." Simply terrible!

The Revolution in Russia
[December 14, 1905]*

After barely six hours of service, telegraphic links with the tsarist empire were suspended again at midnight, due to a damaged line in combination with the Danish cable service stopping work. The post and telegraph strike continues in Moscow just as before. The strikers are receiving sizable donations from civil society. There are clashes everyday with the police and the military. The executive committee of the *Petersburg Section of the Post and Telegraph Association* adopted a resolution that declared that the Association would continue to exist on the basis of the manifesto of October 30, despite Durnovo's daily briefings. The rebels are not the post and telegraph employees, the rebel is Durnovo, in his contravention of the imperial manifesto. Rumors are spreading on the Moscow exchange about significant bankruptcies. Bloody fistfights have erupted in *Novgorod* Province. At the train station in Voromenka, the police, provoked by the peasants, sent for the public prosecutor and the military. Seven "agitators" were arrested and are being charged with "incitement to mutiny."

From the factory town of Orekhovo near Moscow, *a bloody confrontation between workers and Cossacks* has been reported. Three Cossacks were shot to death.

The party paper *Novaya Zhizn* [New Life] reports that Khrustalev-Nosar, chairman of the Council [Soviet] of Workers' Deputies is being held in the Peter and Paul Fortress, where measures have been taken in the event that the workers attempt to free him. The main gate has been closed, cannons have been positioned in the outer courtyard and sentry duty has been reinforced.

Private reports from *Riga* describe the situation there as being extremely serious. *A cannon has been installed at the train station, a machine gun* at the post office. The military is however seen as not being reliable. The city is apparently under the rule of Latvian Social Democrats.

Rus' has published a telegram signed by the Sixth Sapper Brigade in Moscow, in which they communicate that troops who finished their service this year or last year have requested a discharge; this request remains unanswered. They would therefore like to again draw attention to their request and remark that, in the event of receiving negative notice, *they reserve the right of freedom of action.* They will wait until the twelfth of this month.

---

* This article first appeared in *Vorwärts*, No. 292, December 14, 1905, under the title "Die Revolution in Rußland." It is translated (by Henry Holland) from Luxemburg's *Gesammelte Werke*, Vol. 6, pp. 799–801.

MARTIAL LAW EXTENDED FURTHER

Petersburg, December 12 (report of the Petersburg Telegraph Agency via Chernyshevskoye). The governors-general, governors and captains of municipalities in regions not currently covered by the state of emergency received authorization to issue mandatory provisions for a maximum of three months should the public order be threatened. They are, furthermore, authorized to impose administrative sentences and to forbid the influx of foreign weapons, particularly from Finland; private sales of weapons may also be forbidden.

PROVOKING THE COUNTERREVOLUTION

Petersburg, December 13. The government has comprehensively rejected the proposals to convene a Constituent Assembly, which would examine the possibilities of universal and equal suffrage.

PEASANT UNREST

A report from *Odessa* in the *Standard* describes how peasant unrest has now extended over the *whole of south Russia*.

REVOLTS IN THE MILITARY

Petersburg, December 12 (report by Laffan's News Agency). Travelers from *Kharkiv* report that the Bialystok and Okhotsk regiments have mutinied.

Petersburg, December 13. A report received from *Kharkiv* states that the revolutionary party is agitating in a most energetic way in military circles.

The *railroad workers* in Odessa have decided *to join the general strike* because of the arrest of the worker's delegation in Petersburg.

And we have received the following letter from *Mr. Gapon*:

Most Honorable Editors!

Forced recently to leave Russia for a limited period, I found in issues 285 and 287 of *Vorwärts* a number of lines about me, well suited to presenting the motives that lead me to take this step in the wrong light. It is not true in the least that I left Russia because I felt, as *Vorwärts* stated, that my role in the Russian Revolution had played itself out. No, it was rather the risk of being grabbed by government thugs at any moment, i.e., of being thus cut off from the mission I had undertaken, that motivated my decision to leave. I have, on top of that, a number of what are purely business dealings to carry out on behalf of the workers that have stayed loyal to me, during my stay abroad.

I remain loyal to the fundamental principles of international socialism and will do so in the future; it is only in the realization of these principles that I cut a path that narrow-minded doctrinaires perceive as damaging to the worker's cause, and which isn't seen as such by the folk of the socialist-revolutionary *deed*. Be that as it may, I would like to ask for one thing. Do not grant any significance to any interviews about my supposed plans and intentions, as I have to date not discussed these with anyone outside but with my own organization, nor am I disposed to do so in the future.

Geneva, December 9, 1905[*]
With socialistic greetings,
Georgi Gapon

---

[*]   Shortly after penning these lines, Gapon returned to Russia.

The Revolution in Russia
[December 15, 1905]*

THE KREUZ-ZEITUNG'S IDEALS FULFILLED

A *new strike law* is expected in the next few days.

It is said that the new strike law will permit economic but not political strikes, and fixes penalties for the initiators, alongside incentives for those willing to work who don't join the strike. Strike participation by state civil servants is "absolutely prohibited."

Tsarism still doesn't get it. Name me one single person who cares about what it permits and what it forbids!

PATCHING UP ABSOLUTISM

Petersburg, December 14 (reported via Chernyshevskoye by the Petersburg Telegraph Agency). Today the Council of Ministers will conclude their negotiations regarding the workers' associations' law. According to the law passed by the Council of Ministers, dissolution or closure of these associations can now only be ordered as a result of court cases, and not as previously through administrative procedure, through the Ministry of the Interior, the province governors, or the police, etc. As yet, the law has a temporary character, advancing slowly to publication in the next few weeks simultaneous with an overall law concerning rights of association.

Petersburg, December 13 (via Chernyshevskoye). The *Government Herald* reports that the newly finished voting law will shortly be presented to the tsar.

MILITARY REVOLTS

Moscow papers report insurrections in the city among the Sapper Reserves Battalion, in the artillerymen's barracks, in the Kursk Garrison, and among reservists in Siberia. Troops in Irkutsk refused sentry duty. The Moscow paper *Nasha Zhizn* [Our Life] reports: the insurrection among the troops in Kiev continues. Soldiers are fraternizing with students and workers on the streets and are asking the people to be forgiven for firing on them during the disturbances. Accompanied by the sounds of military music, two regiments paraded alongside workers together through the streets.

---

* This article first appeared in *Vorwärts*, No. 293, December 15, 1905, under the title "Die Revolution in Rußland." It is translated (by Henry Holland) from Luxemburg's *Gesammelte Werke*, Vol. 6, pp. 802–4.

Warsaw, December 14. *Police officers* from the first municipal district have gone on strike.

REVOLUTIONARY TACTICS

Representatives of the Councils [Soviets] of Worker's Deputies gathered in Moscow have decided together with the radical parties *to prevent all partial strikes*, because they compromise the general strike that the workers are arming themselves for.

WHAT THE GERMAN PETTY BOURGEOIS COULD LEARN

Chosen from many similar reader's epistles, the paper *Rus'* has published the following letter:

> Honorable Editor!
>
> My janitor tells me that some of the latest letters I received were delivered to my house by an officer, while others were delivered by a lady. I would like to inform the post office that I do not want to receive any letters brought to me by such government lackeys, and then these people are nothing other than strikebreakers. I want to receive my letters from the striking postal civil servants themselves, but not before their victory. The post service has no right to send me these intruders. In the future, I will refuse them.
>
> With most sincere regards
N.N.

Would *German* "citizens" behave in such a manner if *our state's slaves* from the imperial post and telegraph service were involved in a political conflict of this nature?

We have received the following letter from the *striking post and telegraph civil servants in Odessa*:

> We have read the following in *Nachalo* [The Beginning], a St. Petersburg paper, in issue No. 9 from November 24/December 7: The international bank received a registered parcel from Berlin on November 22/December 5, addressed to the office of the Russian Association of the Post and Telegraph Civil Servants. Due to not knowing the address of the office, the bank director returned the packet to the head of post and telegraph information, Mr. Sevastianov, who is keeping the parcel to one side.
>
> If a parcel such as this really does need to be sent to the address given above, we would like to strongly request the dispatcher to make the same enquiries as to where the parcel has got to, and, in case of confirmation, to send the newspaper article

printed above, along with the respective registered delivery directly to the offices or to the editors of any libertarian newspaper.

With comradely greetings,
The Odessa office of the Pan-Russian Association
of Post and Telegraph Civil Servants
Buchheim, Senior Engineer
Trusov, Engineer
Didrichson, Senior Mechanic
M. Gofman, Mechanic
Knyazev, Civil Servant
Malinovsky, Civil Servant
B. Popovsky, Civil Servant
Odessa, November 28, December 10, 1905

The real issue here is obviously the embezzlement of financial aid coming from abroad for the strikers by thieving fingers in the tsarist government. The warning issued by our brave comrades in Russia certainly will *not* vanish without effect. The donors will now be vigilant about giving their church dimes to anyone other than *safe persons*.

The Revolution in Russia
[December 16, 1905]*

The revolution is currently dominated by military revolts. The "uprising" is spreading so violently in what was until now the guard protecting absolutism, that the greatest optimist on earth wouldn't have thought it possible just a few months ago. Marines, land troops, privates, officers up to the highest circles of nobles of the guard, Cossacks, border soldiers, yes, even constables and other law enforcement officers: all caught up in the purest rebellion. And we're talking about a peaceful uprising of the slaves previously sewn into the "tsar's tunic," one which is purposeful about its political aims and highly honorable in its outer appearance. Economic and political demands are being formulated everywhere. It is a general awakening of the spirit of citizenship and of proletarian class spirit. The following reports bear witness to that.

Petersburg, December 12 (Laffin's News Agency). From Moscow, *Rus'* has received the following threatening news about the mood within the city's military. According to these reports, communicated by telephone: Officers and men from all categories of weapon regiments, including the Cossacks, held a meeting, at which they decided to construct a general register of the complaints of all the Moscow garrisons. A *mass military assembly* will be organized for this purpose. Three hundred soldiers in Moscow who accompany prisoners' transports have also joined the *walkout*, after it became known to them that their comrades in Kursk had done the same. The striking soldiers in both cities demand *better treatment and political rights*. The first demand has already been met by the authorities, yet the soldiers' strike is still continuing.

The third *sotnia* [century, or hundred] of the first *regiment of Don Cossacks* has produced a series of demands of an economic nature. These people received doubled rations *immediately*, yet had their lances and guns removed from them simultaneously. (Which is the best proof that this isn't just about "economic demands!"—The editor.)†

Petersburg, December 14 (from a private correspondent, via Chernyshevskoye). The papers contain reports about disturbances among the sappers in Warsaw. In Lublin, troops from the Ryazan infantry regiments organized *a rally with red flags*. The papers report about plans among resident troops to instigate an officer's evening and to found *a progressive military paper* in 1906. On the Austrian border, 600 men from the *Border Guards* went on strike.

---

* This article first appeared in *Vorwärts*, No. 294, December 16, 1905, under the title "Die Revolution in Rußland." It is translated (by Henry Holland) from Luxemburg's *Gesammelte Werke*, Vol. 6, pp. 805–7.

† This parenthetical sentence was introduced in the original by the editors of *Vorwärts*.

In *Sevastopol* on the ninth of this month, an extraordinary general meeting of *all marine officers* from the 14th equipage of the Black Sea Fleet was held, at which the following resolutions were passed:

> (1) The marine officers wish that no blood be shed. (2) They wish not to leave the port of Sevastopol. (3) They regret that thanks to the tactless role played by Admiral Chukhnin, who ignored the officers' wishes, the sailors have lost trust in their superiors. (4) They insist that the sailors' economic demands be fulfilled. (5) They ask the tsar that the mutinying sailors not be handed over to a drumhead court martial, but rather be tried in a public military court with a civil defense attorney being permitted. (6) They demand Admiral Chukhnin's demotion and the *convention of an assembly of all Black Sea Fleet officers*, which should adopt resolutions on the various questions regarding the reorganization of the Black Sea Fleet.

Disturbances have broken out in the Troitsko-Sergiyevsky infantry regiment in Moscow. The soldiers demand: (1) Reservists be discharged from active service immediately. (2) Better food. (3) A rise in salary. (4) Better clothing. (5) Decent treatment by the officers. (The semi-official news services regularly hush up political demands, as was the case during the uprising of the Sevastopol marines.)

APPEAL OF THE RUSSIAN RAILROAD WORKERS
TO THE MANCHURIAN ARMY

The Russian military administration is attempting to bend the rumors about the Manchurian Army that have surfaced in the last few days to its own purposes, presenting the story as if the dissatisfaction was confined to those reservists striving to return home and was unavoidable due to the various strikes and the poor service potential of the Siberian railroad. Now the *Central Office of Striking Russian Railroaders* has launched an action of agitation to benefit the soldiers striving for home, with the result that telegraphic messages are coming in from almost all Russian train stations on this and the other side of the Urals, stating that the Russian railroad workers are prepared to make all necessary arrangements to bring the Manchurian Army back to Russia. This written appeal, just now distributed at all Russian stations and sent to Harbin on the twelfth of this month, is of interest in this context:

> Comrades, soldiers! Don't believe the fallacious claims of General [Ivan Pavlovich] *Nadarov* and your other superiors who state that it is the railroaders who have blocked your passage home. They are defrauding you in order to defame all of us, and to hide the truly guilty ones into the bargain. Comrades, soldiers! We railroad workers hereby declare that we will, irrespective of the strike, bring each one of you back home; we have never refused to do this and we will not refuse to transport you

home in the future either. We are with you and for you! We demand that they bring you home immediately. We demand freedom and the truth! Down with drumhead court martials! Down with the death penalty! Long live the fraternity of soldiers! We ask you comrades to distribute this telegram in all divisions of Manchurian troops, so that they know who their friend is and who their enemy.

SOCIAL DEMOCRATIC RULE IN RIGA

Petersburg, December 14 (via Chernyshevskoye from a private correspondent). *Riga is completely cut off from the rest of the empire.* According to the scarce information available to us, *all factories are on strike there.* Only the waterworks and the electricity stations are still in service. Armed workers are even preventing wheeled transport on the streets. Goods deliveries are only possible via water routes. Workers' guards prevent entry into the city. *Because of a lack of troops, martial law exists only on paper.*

Syn Otechestva [Son of the Fatherland] publishes the following telegram from the Livonian governor Sveginshev to the minister of the interior:

Riga, December 10. The commands of all river steamers are on strike. There is therefore no contact with the incoming steamers. A cruiser and two torpedo boats are needed here. The Baltic railroad service has been suspended in the districts affected by the strike. Troops must be sent by water. Necessary to send a significant mass of troops rapidly. Your couriers have been intercepted.

The same paper reports that the Latvians (i.e., *the peasants.*—The editor.)* streamed into Riga and *joined forces with the workers.* Government buildings are said to be in flames. Train station service and telegraph service are said to be in the hands of the insurgents. Warships have departed to Liepāja from Riga.

The news of the conflagrations proves—if it is not invented—that in Riga too the last "guard" of the last Nicholas—the Black Hundreds—is trying to save throne and altar.

---

* This parenthetical phrase was introduced in the original by the editors of *Vorwärts*.

The Revolution in Russia
[December 17, 1905]*

The Council [Soviet] of Workers' Deputies, the Central Committee of the Peasants' Congress, the Organizing Committee of the Social Democratic Labor Party,† and the Central Committee of the Party of Social Revolutionaries have published a "manifesto" in which the following is declared, after preliminary criticism of the government and the economic situation: Neither redemption payments‡ nor other state taxes will be paid; that by agreement only gold will be accepted for purchases and payment of wages, while for payments of less than five roubles only hard cash will be accepted; that deposits at the savings banks and at the Imperial Bank will be withdrawn, and these will be demanded in gold; and finally, that payments for loans that were concluded during the period in which the government found itself in a state of open war with the people are declared invalid.

The workers who have demonstrated their power and their decisiveness are now being courted by the middle classes. The English papers report: Workers' and peasants' associations are preparing to start a common parliament in January. The Union of Unions is attempting to gather the socialists around it and has drummed up support by also having passed a resolution approving of an armed uprising.

The progressive papers are continuing to argue for an alliance between all leftist parties, to which are counted the Constitutional Democrats, Radicals, Social Democrats and Social Revolutionaries; an alliance with the anarchists (of which there are only one or two dozen in Russia—The editor.§) remains however out of the question, as this would even be rejected by the Socialist Revolutionaries. Until now, the socialists have reacted to the moderate parties' accommodating gestures with extreme contempt.

---

* This article first appeared in *Vorwärts*, No. 295, December 17, 1905, under the title "Die Revolution in Rußland." It is translated (by Henry Holland) from Luxemburg's *Gesammelte Werke*, Vol. 6, pp. 808–10.

† That is, the RSDRP.

‡ This mandated that serfs must pay the landowner for their allocation of land in a series of redemption payments, which, in turn, were used to compensate the landowners with bonds. Seventy-five percent of the total sum would be advanced by the government to the landowner and peasants would repay the money plus interest. These payments were cancelled in 1907.

§ This parenthetical phrase was introduced in the original by the editors of *Vorwärts*. The claim was far from accurate.

UPROAR IN THE ARMY

The *Daily Telegraph* reports: The latest telegram of the commander in chief of the Manchurian Army, General Linevich, to the Ministry of War in Petersburg, runs as follows: "I cannot combat the growth and spread of revolutionary propaganda in the army. Over half the army is mutinying at present. The reservists are demanding to be conveyed home immediately and don't want to accept any paper money. Request telegraphic instructions. Urgently." A response was wired from Petersburg via Europe and Vladivostok, with unknown contents.

The charge sheet against Ship's Lieutenant Schmidt, who led the mutiny in the Black Sea Fleet, includes charges punishable with the death penalty. The charge sheet includes the following daily briefing, which is said to have been issued by Lieutenant Schmidt on November 28.

> To the Mayor of Sevastopol! Today I issued the following telegram to His Majesty the Emperor: the glorious fleet of the Black Sea, which remains deeply loyal to the nation, entreats you, sir, to convene an assembly to grant us a constitution without delay; and, in so doing, the fleet ceases to obey your ministers.
>
> (Signed) Fleet Commander Schmidt.

(Please see our supplement today about the Sevastopol uprising—The editor.)*

Petersburg, December 16. According to reports from *Rostov-on-Don*, large disturbances have broken out there. The town garrison, loyal to the tsar, used their weapons to deal with the disturbers of the peace. In so doing, *300 persons were either killed or injured.* Ship workers in Rostov have sunk some ships carrying weapons, and burned others. This caused heavy losses for the merchants. The banks have refused to pay out deposits, while the better-off residents are fleeing from the municipality.

THE "PACIFICATION" OF THE PEASANTS

A correspondent of the very moderate Petersburg paper *Nasha Zhizn* [Our Life] describes in his paper how the insurgent peasants are being "pacified" in the district of Borisoglebsk in Tambov Province. A number of excerpts from his interesting letter deserve to be reprinted here: A telephone system has been introduced throughout the district of Borrisoglebsk, states our author, possessing the idiosyncrasy that when one user talks, his conversation can be listened to by all other users. Thanks to this, all police secrets are now known in the district. This is how it became known that a supervisory official told Polonsky, the state captain, that, "We'll take much more grain off the peasants than even they were able to take from the estate owners."

---

*   This parenthetical phrase was introduced in the original by the editors of *Vorwärts*.

Cavalry Master Ilyushkin, who commands a battalion of Cossacks, gives his subordinate, F. Shcherbinin, who is on his way to the Votochy Oleshky, the following order (via telephone): Be conscious of the fact of what has to be done. Do not drive into the village, otherwise you'll be cut off. If it should prove necessary for the peasants to come out of the village, *then set fire to the village from the edge.* Demand that the grain be handed over. In case of refusal, give the order to fire—first into the air, then at the peasants. *You generally must make an effort to scare the living daylights out of them;* set fire to dung so that there's flames and sparks, then spread out through the whole village and *smash in the window panes.*

Lieutenant Shcherbinin then phoned his wife to communicate the impressions the "pacification" had made on him: *"Blood is flowing everywhere, everything's up in flames and we're beating, stabbing and shooting."*

"EDUCATED" SPIES

A group of agents from the infamous "Protective Division," tasked with spying on and sniffing out everything, have sent our sister paper in Petersburg, *Novaya Zhizn* [New Life], a letter, demonstrating that even the political spies have caught the "plague of revolution." At first the editors of *Novaya Zhizn* doubted the correctness of these statements, but some fact-checking ascertained that there really are "educated" elements among the agents. The interesting letter reads as follows:

We, the educated agents, despise you (i.e., the government) and communicate to you our outrage, because the full weight of your criminal deeds oppress us educated agents. It is our vocation to protect humanity(!) from terrorism(!), but not to act as terrorists ourselves. It must surely suffice for you that while you conceal yourselves behind our backs, you force us to follow society's every step. But no, you who have made the most of our hunger and the hunger of our families to get us into your hands, you force us to terrorize society on top of that. It is not society but rather you who calls up terror.

You, tyrannizers of humanity, even though you hired us to protect humanity, now you've forced us to carry out your demonic plans, you monsters, who know that when a person falls into your hands they are lost. Be that as it may, and even if society looks down on us as thugs, you nevertheless have been unable to kill our souls. We all belong to the whole and together we will fight for human freedom. You know that if we leave your ranks that there's not a single place that will take us on. We are forced to wander lost like Judas. May our blood and suffering therefore rest upon your shoulders and the shoulders of your descendants. Yet we, too, are proletarians, and we will die fighting in the ranks of the proletariat against you, you monsters.

The letter is written in a very ungrammatical fashion, but it is exactly that which testifies to its authenticity.

Visitors to Moscow's stock exchange have decided not to pay any taxes if the government continues to take action against the striking post and telegraph civil servants.

The Truth About Sevastopol*

We have received the following precise report from our private correspondent in Sevastopol about the glorious marine uprising in the city, which has been presented in entirely the wrong light in the German bourgeois press and in the semi-official Russian telegrams:

Sevastopol, November 30, 1905. I wish in the following to give a short sketch of the momentous events that have played out here in recent weeks.

On the day after the "Freedom Manifesto" of October 31, a crowd of 10,000 gathered here to a tremendous meeting, and then proceeded to the prison to release the political prisoners. Members of the military hiding in the prison opened fire on the crowd, killing eight and wounding around twenty.

Two days later an ostentatious burial for the fallen took place, which numerous revolutionary organizations attended. Speeches were held beside open graves. Captain (Second Class) *Pyotr Schmidt* gave one of the best speeches. He thereupon was arrested on order of the Commanding Chief of the Black Sea Fleet, Admiral Chukhnin.

Every Sunday over the next four weeks, meetings took place on Sea Boulevard, where the immediate demands of the revolutionary parties were explained to the people. Admiral Chukhnin strictly forbade the sailors and soldiers to take part in these meetings, and posted patrols at the entrances to the boulevard for this purpose. Embittered by this order, the sailors and soldiers organized meetings in the barracks and on the warships moored at Sevastopol, where the local Social Democrats had been energetically agitating. Schmidt, who had been released again after two weeks [of] prison, was now thrust by events into the foreground, and played a most lively role in the subsequent developments.

Starting on November 21, daily meetings were held on the square between the marine barracks (i.e., the barracks of the sailors currently stationed on land) and the barracks of the Brest infantry regiment. Ferment among the sailors swelled. At first the government organs adopted a "wait-and-see" attitude. On November 24, another meeting was held. Rear Admiral Pisarevsky then issued an order to the detachment of sailors from the so-called battle company, who were carrying out regular duties for that specific weekday, to disperse the assembly by firing on it. Petrov, a sailor who heard the order, without pausing, shot at Pisarevsky and Stein, the army officer, with the words, "Better that you two should die, then that thousands should die because of you." Pisarevsky was seriously injured, while Stein died that same night.

* This unsigned article first appeared in *Vorwärts*, No. 295, December 17, 1905, entitled "Die Wahrheit über Sewastopol." It is translated (by Henry Holland) from Luxemburg's *Gesammelte Werke*, Vol. 6, pp. 811–18.

On Saturday [November] 25, the sailors of the fleet barracks gathered yet again. The soldiers from the *Brest Infantry Regiment* joined them as did one group of port workers, and they all paraded in a tremendous demonstration to the sounds of the sailors' band, cheered on by elated locals, toward the barracks of the Bialystok infantry regiment—a substantial distance—to win its soldiers for their cause. En route the radicals encountered the *Bialystok regiment* suited for battle, and a company of artillery. The Bialystok regiment's band trumpeted out the national anthem and the regiment displayed their guns. In order to emphasize that the demonstration was thoroughly peaceful, the radical marine band also started up with "God Save the Tsar." Whereupon the Bialystok regiment and the artillery turned around and headed for the field camps located outside the city. The demonstrators remained together even longer, conducted a meeting in front of the barracks of the Brest Infantry Regiment and then returned to the marine barracks.

The government meanwhile was aiming to isolate the sailors as far as possible and win back the soldiers of the Brest Infantry Regiment, who remained largely unaffected by propaganda. No tried and trusted methods could help this time. On Saturday night the military chaplains were mobilized, brandy was shared out among the soldiers, and these soldiers, now drunk in a double sense of the word, were fired up against their brothers, the sailors fighting for freedom. During the night, a new oath of loyalty was taken from the soldiers and the officers of the regiments. Those who hadn't appeared in the barracks in the preceding days again took control of the command of these men.

While this was going on, the sailors formulated the following seventeen demands and presented them to the authorities: (1) Sailors and soldiers imprisoned for political reasons should be released, their safety guaranteed, and all sailors handed over to a public court. (2) All so-called battle companies and Cossacks are to be removed from the city. Abolition of martial law. Abolition of the death penalty. (3) Immunity for persons in the delegations. (4) Complete freedom outside hours of [military] duty. The right to visit all public houses and assemblies. (5) Establishment of libraries and reading rooms at the state's expense. Subscriptions to books, newspapers and journals according to the soldiers' wishes. (6) Polite treatment of the men by the officers; they should address them with the polite [Russian] form of "you." Abolition of use of titles outside hours of duty. (8) Reduction of the service period for soldiers down to two years (at present three years eight months), for sailors down to four years (at present seven years). (10) Immediate discharge of all reservists and of all soldiers who have finished serving their period of active duty. (17) The officers should give the men two hours of lessons of a general nature during their period of service.

Points 7, 9, and 11 to 16 [not listed above] are purely economic demands, like raising salaries, annual leave of one month's duration, pensions for invalids, and regulation of clothing and nutrition. Extra work should be carried out not by the soldiers but by paid workers; a prohibition on using soldiers for purposes of domestic service, etc.

In addition to these points, the sailors and soldiers are formally supporting all-Russian demands for: (1) The immediate convocation of a Constituent Assembly on the basis of a universal, direct, equal, and secret right to vote; and (2) support of the eight-hour working day.

The sailors' program was distributed everywhere on Monday, November 14, and posted on street corners.

The sailors had repeatedly requested that Admiral Chukhnin appear at the marine barracks to listen to their demands. Yet, although they gave guarantees for his personal safety and although a special patrol was even sent for his protection to the field camp where the general was stationed, Chukhnin did not appear.

The officers of the marine barracks (the so-called Lazarev barracks) should have withdrawn from the barracks by Saturday, November 12. Discipline was maintained by the sailors themselves in an exemplary fashion. Patrols traversed through the city and arrested any sailors who had left barracks without a permit. The brandy shops were closed and you couldn't see a single drunk anywhere; a rare phenomenon in Russia on a public holiday. A sailor who was wandering soberly through the streets with a brandy bottle in his hand was immediately taken to the cells by a passing patrol. The influence of Social Democracy on the men's conduct was unmistakable, with the result that the types of excess that would have given the authorities the desired reason to go in and establish "order" were entirely avoided. The "mutineers" tried to emphasize their desire for peace at every opportunity.

On Sunday afternoon, an extremely large meeting took place on Sea Boulevard, this time with sailors and soldiers participating. Captain Schmidt delivered a mesmerizing speech, in which he solicited support for the second all-Russian political mass strike. Sunday and Monday passed in an utterly peaceful manner.

On Monday, the revolutionary sailors disseminated an appeal in which they requested the local population to remain peaceful and not believe rumors that were being maliciously spread suggesting that they intended to encourage looting in the city. The sailors reassured the population that the highest degree of public order would be maintained and that they would only conduct an armed entry into the city to protect its inhabitants in case the Black Hundreds should dare organize rabble-rousing against the Jews, or engage in general looting.

This appeal made the best possible impression on the population and aroused even warmer sympathy for the battling sailors. Their impeccable conduct was rewarded with unanimous praise, and sailors passing in the streets were greeted by many locals with handshakes and friendly smiles. The atmosphere was one of elevation and reliability. Not a single sign indicated that the sailors' movement would meet with such a bloody end. Despite all this, many inhabitants did flee to the surrounding settlements, scared after the events in Kronstadt and Vladivostok. The closure of shops, ordered by the chief of police with regard to the demonstration on November 15, in conjunction with the state of siege declared on the fortress of Sevastopol on November 27, played a large part in intimidating the already terrified inhabitants still further.

In the context thus described, November 28 drew nearer, a day that has now become one to commemorate in Russia's history. It was a Tuesday, a clear, sunny day. The armored cruiser *Ochakov* was situated in the outer roadstead alongside four torpedo boats that were sailing with it. The ironclad battleship *Panteleimon* (formerly named *Potemkin*) was located a certain distance away from the *Ochakov*. On Monday already, thirty marine officers had been arrested from the ranks of the sailors and brought aboard the *Ochakov*, because it was reasonably believed that the presence of the officers would encourage the government to guide the conflict toward a peaceful resolution. A number of civil servants attached to the marines, who had made themselves unpopular during their period of service, had also been arrested and interned in the Lazarev barracks. The arrests were carried out by the patrols in the most correct manner possible, and nothing could be found wanting in the courtesy with which the internees were treated.

Early on Tuesday morning, a delegation of insurgent sailors from the marine barracks made their way on a small steamship to the *Ochakov* cruiser, where they were greeted with a loud hurrah. The *Ochakov* hoisted the red flag. Shortly after, the delegation, led by Schmidt and protected by a torpedo boat destroyer, the *Svirepy*, made its way toward the [ship] *Prut*. On board were found the sailors imprisoned in the course of the disturbances in June 1905 on the *Potemkin*, *Prut*, and *Georgi Pobedonostsev*. A large number of prisoners were released, without any resistance whatsoever by the guards, and were brought aboard the *Ochakov* to the sounds of roaring cheers. When the steamer with the emancipated prisoners sailed past the *Potemkin*, it was greeted enthusiastically by the latter's crew, and shortly afterwards, at around 1 p.m., the *Potemkin* also hoisted the red, revolutionary flag.

While this was going on, the following occurred aboard the five other ironclad battleships—the *Rostilav*, *Tri Sviatitelia* [The Three Hierarchs], *Dvenadsat Apostolov* [The Twelve Apostles], *Sinop*, and *Chesma*, as well as the cruiser *Pamiat Merkuria* [Mercury's Memory] and other small ships. A steamer with a delegation of marine officers sailed along the front of the whole fleet (with the exception of the *Ochakov* and the *Potemkin*, which were stationed some distance away), and paused beside every single ship. The officers on board the steamer informed the sailors that part of their economic demands had already been met and promised to do their best so that their outstanding demands would also be satisfied. The backward and gullible section of the crew took the officer's empty promises at face value, while the politically organized sailors, on the other hand, found themselves to be in the minority and unable to sway the mass. This led to a rift in the sailors' ranks, which resulted in a fistfight among the crew on the *Rostislav*. At first, the red flag was hoisted on the *Rostislav*, which sparked a lively debate; it was then taken down and torn up, and the patriotic, white and blue St. Andrew's Cross was hoisted [in its place].* By about 1 p.m., all the aforementioned ships had hoisted the St. Andrew's Cross. In the meantime, the Lazarev barracks, located on a hill and visible for miles, had unfurled the red flag. The two parties now faced each other, ready for battle. Admiral Chukhnin held the supreme command of the fleet loyal to the government, while Captain Schmidt, positioned on the *Ochakov*, had taken supreme command of the revolutionary fleet. The situation became critical, and the population awaited the events to come with bated breath, oscillating between fear and hope.

Their patience wasn't to be tried for too long. At around 3:45 p.m., the first shots rang out.

Around 3 p.m., the *Uralets*, a revolutionary steam cutter with a delegation of sailors on board, sailed alongside the *Terets*, a gunboat loyal to the government. The latter was reportedly encouraged (through signals) to join the revolutionary fleet. According to a different account, the *Uralets* is said to have had the locking tappets for the firearms on board—which had been purloined by the officers and only now rediscovered—and the ship wanted to bring these to the *Potemkin*. It is at any rate irrefutable that the loyal-to-the-government *Terets* gunboat opened fire and *not the "mutineers."* It is moreover important to record that the first shots from the government side *did not come from the crew, but rather from officers on the Terets*. The *Uralets* incurred damage and was not able to continue sailing. The injured onboard the *Uralets* were brought away immediately by a steamer which hurried to the scene, accompanied by the revolutionary torpedo boat destroyer *Svirepy*; the steamer even managed to tow the *Uralets* into port.

Meanwhile the crew of the *Bug*, a loyal-to-government minelayer located near the *Terets*—and loaded with 340 blockade mines containing more than 1,200 pood† of nitrocellulose—opened the ship's lowering devices right at the start of battle; and in full view, the *Bug* sunk within half an hour up to the tip of the mast. This deed earned the crew the highest and most deserved praise, because if the mines had exploded the whole portion of the city around the bay would have been flattened, and countless human lives would have been lost.

At the same time, the ironclads *Rostislav* and *Tri Sviatitelia* and the cruiser *Pamiat Merkuria*, as well as the batteries on the north side, opened fire against the revolutionary *Ochakov*, while the *Svirepy* was put out of battle by shots from the *Terets*. The *Svirepy*'s helmsman was killed as the *Pamiat Merkuria* swept by,

---

* The St. Andrews flag, consisting of intersecting blue crosses against a white background, had been the official flag of the Russian Navy since 1712. It was eliminated following the Bolshevik seizure of power in 1918.

† A pood is an old Russian measurement, roughly equal to 16.38 kilograms.

which placed the defenseless *Svirepy* under heavy fire, *killing the entire crew.* A part of the *Svirepy*'s crew who *threw themselves into the water* were killed by shotguns. Meanwhile, fire had broken out on board the *Ochakov* and its crew felt compelled to hoist the white flag as a sign of surrender. Yet the *Ochakov* was *shot at for another ten minutes*, contravening all rules of war, because of a supposed "misunderstanding." Moreover, revolutionary torpedo boats *268* and *270* were incapacitated, and Captain Schmidt was arrested on the latter.

The remainder of the crew of the *Ochakov* jumped into the water during the battle, and the crowd that gathered on Sea Boulevard attempted to rescue the drowning men by sending out boats. At first, the authorities behaved shamelessly during the rescue. Not content with not taking the least part in the rescue action, and not providing a single government boat for it, they also attempted to obstruct the movement of the lifeboats in all sorts of ways. It is an undisputable fact that a private boat which rescued sailors from torpedo boat *270* and wanted to return to the shore was annihilated by two shots from the loyal-to-the-tsar cruiser *Pamiat Merkuria*—causing both rescuers and those being rescued to forfeit their lives! None of the thirty-three officers held prisoner on board the *Ochakov* were killed; a government boat rescued them soon after the battle ended. Only later, after the battle, when fire was still raging on the *Ochakov*, did the authorities find enough humane feeling in themselves to send out boats to pick up those who had jumped from the ship into the water.

And there were other outrageous happenings during the battle that must be recorded. A crowd of between sixty and one hundred people were gathered on Sea Boulevard during the cannonade when someone from the crowd suddenly unfolded a red flag. Immediately, the ironclad *Rostilav* thundered out two cannon shots in the direction of the crowd, which luckily killed no one (the missiles burst some distance from their target).

At 4:19 p.m. the government ships began a veritable bombardment of the marine barracks, using machine-gun fire that was uninterrupted for twenty-one minutes. (It is public knowledge that the telegrams of the tsarist thugs have spread the lie that the *revolutionary crews* carried out the bombardment on the city, a lie that was then spread by the trusting bourgeois foreign press.—The editors of *Vorwärts*.) After that, the fire died down considerably, with scattered cannon shots being fired at the marine barracks only every hour. The Lazarev barracks were then stormed around 2:30 a.m. on Wednesday morning, with the support of heavy cannon fire, and at 4:00 a.m. the 1,600 freedom fighters were forced to surrender themselves and numerous artillery to government troops.

The *Ochakov* was ablaze the whole night through. No one had lifted a finger to put out the fire. The ship *with the remaining fighters who had stayed* on it was left to a terrible death in flames. The sinister and yet striking image attracted hundreds of shocked observers on the shore, who followed the sporadic detonations coming from the ship with anxious horror. By Wednesday morning the blaze was finished and the *Ochakov* utterly burned out. The tsar had won the first sea battle in two whole years.

The city of Sevastopol seemed to be extinct on the morning that followed; nobody dared to go out. Only a few unshakable people opened their shops. Yet at noon everything was already quickly locked up again, as rumors spread that a pogrom against the Jews and the intelligentsia was about to break out immediately. Luckily the rumor did not prove to be true. The "men of order" considered it better to postpone the continuation of the thieving murders for a while yet.

The panic that took hold of the inhabitants during the bombardment is indescribable. Folk lost their heads entirely, and sought refuge in basements and other hideaways. Others lunged out into the streets, throwing themselves onto the ground, or hiding themselves behind trees, fences, and walls. Much of the city's infrastructure only suffered mildly. The only buildings to incur serious damage were a number of houses standing on the banks of the sea. Telegraph, postal [service], ship, and railroad lines were all entirely suspended during the days of battle. On the Thursday after the bombardment, the railroad reopened transport for a number of hours. The train station overflowed with swarms of fleeing residents who had abandoned all possessions to at least save their lives.

At this stage, it is not possible to determine the exact numbers of casualties. As far as one can establish, only four to six persons are said to have been killed in the Lasarev barracks, while on the *Ochakov* at the very least one hundred men were killed. Others drowned, many are suffering from burns, and many have been driven mad.

And that is the history and the end of the sailors' uprising in Sevastopol, which began so peacefully and prudently!

It is impossible to register this crime committed by absolutism and its murderous apprentices in words alone. It sticks out brashly amid all the bleak, shameful marks of tsarist despotism and perfidy, unique in its own way.

The history of the Russian freedom movement, well able to tell tales of countless suffering, will enshrine the fallen heroes of Sevastopol eternally in its memory.

The Revolution in Russia
[December 19, 1905]*

Despite military revolts and uproar in the civil service, despite the peasants' uprising and the workers' struggle, the tsarist camarilla is clinging stubbornly to its provocative position. It is preparing itself for one last, desperate attempt, in which it will go against all working people, against its own civil servants and military, in order to help the "Black [Hundreds]"† keep their hands on the tiller—the tsarists only aided by naked anarchy. Durnovo and his consorts are counting on the *weariness* of society, and on the revolution *exhausting itself*. They hope to stir up the still stupid masses and the bourgeois business world against the "disturbers of the peace." They are already making public threats *to incite bands of murderers to attack the striking post and telegraph civil servants!* They are denouncing the revolutionary uprising of proletarians and peasants in Livonia as a national uprising with the purpose of seceding from the empire, in order to spur on "patriotic instincts" against Social Democratic labor in Riga and Kaunas, and against the peasants who are showing solidarity with them. And, finally, they also deem it to be an opportune moment to dare to strike out violently and publicly against press freedom and against organized labor.

The arrests of the Council [Soviet] of Workers' Deputies in Petersburg alongside the temporary ban on a long series of papers are a direct provocation against the revolutionaries. The government believes that the workers are at present not ready for a mass strike, and therefore wants *to force* them into striking out prematurely through brutal provocations. It is impossible to mistake how serious the situation is. The outcome of the struggle can no longer be doubted. A government has never been able to exist by supporting themselves on the lumpenproletariat as the only "class" in open insurrection against the working class. The counterrevolution's cheeky and blind haughtiness will in itself prolong the struggle excessively, and will force it to take on the most extreme and bloody forms. Absolutism prefers to leave the whole empire in ruins, in a terrible chaos, rather than abdicate. Yet the anarchists of absolutism will have to make way for the Social Democrats' planned, revolutionary course in the end!

---

* This article first appeared in *Vorwärts*, No. 296, December 19, 1905, under the title "Die Revolution in Rußland." It is translated (by Henry Holland) from Luxemburg's *Gesammelte Werke*, Vol. 6, pp. 819–23.

† Several times in this article Luxemburg uses the term "Schwarzen Banden" (Black Bands), but it is clear from the context that she is referring to the reactionary groupings known as the Black Hundreds.

THE VIOLENT BLOW

Petersburg, December 16 (via Chernyshevskoye, from a private correspondent). The building in which the Council [Soviet] of Workers' Deputies operates was surrounded by troops yesterday. The police arrested thirty deputies who were transported away in closed cars guarded by Cossacks.

Petersburg, December 18 (report by the Petersburg Telegraph Agency). The arrest of the Council [Soviet] of Workers' Deputies has made a big impression on the workers. Yesterday a series of advisory meetings were held in various districts, principally in those in which the workers live, in order to vote in a new soviet executive committee and to debate the question of the general strike. Moves to activate the general strike have also taken place in Moscow, as is reported from the city. Generally, people are not convinced that the general strike can succeed under present conditions. All but 32 of the 268 persons arrested on Saturday evening at the meeting of the Council [Soviet] of Workers' Deputies have been released; the thirty-two did not want to give their names.

PRESS FREEDOM

Petersburg, December 17. The *Government Herald* writes: After the manifesto was published on October 30, editors and publishers from many local newspapers and journals founded an association to protect the freedom of the printed word and passed a resolution to ignore the law. Some press organs breached all limits and permitted the type of article to be printed, the publication of which, according to the criminal law code, amounts to a serious crime. As a result of this, charges have been brought regarding a total of ninety-two infringements of the criminal code in both imperial seats between November 5 and December 15; moreover, charges have been brought to justices of the peace against all the periodicals, based on the new, temporary rules about the press.

Moscow, December 16 (report from the Petersburg Telegraph Agency). Mr. Skirmund, the editor of the Socialist Revolutionary paper *Borba* [The Struggle] has been arrested.

THE BLACK [HUNDREDS'] THREATS

Petersburg, December 17 (report from the Petersburg Telegraph Agency). The government has received information from several sides, claiming that the population is so devastated by the railroad workers' strike, and so shaken up by the same, that a new strike would push them into acts of violence against the railroaders, which would also unfortunately cause innocent people to suffer. In the light of the disturbances still dominant in many localities, *the government would consider it difficult to restore order, in case the population let themselves be sucked into violent acts against the striking railroaders.*

REVOLUTIONARY RISING IN LIVONIA

Kaunas, December 17 (telegram from the Petersburg Telegraph Agency). We are
receiving official reports from all districts concerning the Lithuanian uprising;
this is an insurgency against the present authorities. Government institutions
and schools have been demolished everywhere. The civil servants have fled. As
has already been pointed out, the Catholic clergy have agitated for the Orthodox
Church's lands to be confiscated, and for all Russians to be expelled from
Lithuania. The "Old Believers" prayer houses have also been demolished. Armed
groups raided Old Believers' villages. Russian staff members were mistreated on
the railroad between Liepāja and Romny. Railroad transport is restricted due to
the concentration of troops; flight units have been formed from tri-service air
force, army and naval troops, but the total troop numbers are low.

THE STRIKE LAW

Petersburg, December 17 (sent via Chernyshevskoye by the Petersburg Telegraph
Agency). The tsar has sanctioned the measures developed by the Ministers'
Council and debated in the Imperial Council against the strikes. Incitement to
strike on the railroads and at telegraph stations will be punished by prison sentences of between eight and sixteen months. Persons who commence a strike
will be interned for four to sixteen months. Persons who enjoy constitutional
law privileges who decide of their own accord to stop work will be punished
with three weeks to three months solitary confinement or with a prison sentence of four to sixteen months. The court can, furthermore, order the defendant
to be dismissed from their post. Attempts to achieve a walkout through use of
violence or threats will result in prison sentences of three to sixteen months.
Participation in societies that aim to induce strikes is punishable by imprisonment in a fortress for between one year four months and four years, with the
loss of certain professional rights and responsibilities. Salaries will not be paid
during the unauthorized work stoppage. Employees whose health is damaged
by strikers during the strike will receive compensation, or a pension if they have
been incapacitated and are now unable to work; if they have been killed or have
had serious injuries inflicted on them, their families will be provided for.

THE STRIKE GOES ON

Yekaterinoslav, December 16 (via Chernyshevskoye). The postal civil servants
walked out of work this afternoon. The mailmen didn't show up for work, and
destroyed mailboxes instead, grabbing a cart carrying mail sacks and tearing
open the letters. The police intervened and in the ensuing skirmish, two policemen were wounded by revolver shots.

MILITARY REVOLTS

Moscow, December 16 (via Chernyshevskoye). An assembly of the Rostov Grenadier Regiment was held in the city, with representatives of various parties taking part. The meeting was chaired by a committee of twenty soldiers, without any breaches of the peace. The regiment's commander has handed in his notice. A battalion from the Astrakhan regiment is stationed in the same barracks as the Rostov regiment. Units from the Rostov regiment prevented units from the Astrakhan regiment from carrying out their duties. The Rostov regiment's officers consulted with each other the whole day long. The soldiers' demands were delivered to the Division Commander; he promised to forward them to the highest authorities. The Rostov regiment instructed an appeal to be sent out to all regiments, in which the regiments were encouraged to join the movement, to remove the current commanders, and to fight for the freedom of the army. Answers should be issued until December 19. The Rostov regiment then immediately adopted a motion to organize a military demonstration to pass through all streets.

Moscow, December 17 (report by the Petersburg Telegraph Agency). The Rostov regiment has surrendered. Soldiers from the Mitrailleuse* Company surrendered first, followed by the third and fourth parts of the dissatisfied battalion. It is noteworthy that they did this in the presence of representatives from the extremist parties. The remaining soldiers will follow their example. Ten ringleaders were arrested, including Shabarov, the soldiers' superior. A few significant demands have been granted, including the inviolability of letters to the soldiers, an increase in rations, and a regular payment of wages.

The *Local Advertiser* reports that Lieutenant Schmidt has been released from fortress imprisonment.

THE ANARCHISTS IN RUSSIA

A group of anarchists in Petersburg—there are only a few dozen anarchists in the whole of Russia†—had approached the Council [Soviet] of Workers' Deputies Workers' with the request, based on the representation of other parties, including the Social Democrats, that a delegate from the "anarchist party" also be represented. The Council [Soviet] of Workers' Deputies responded that a couple of anarchists in Russia don't make a party and refused them participation. The

---

*   A mitrailleuse is a type of volley gun with multiple rifle barrels that can fire either multiple rounds at once or several rounds in rapid succession. It was originally invented in Belgium.

†   This was not accurate; at the time, there were a considerable number of anarchists in Russia, even if far fewer than the number of Marxists. For a study of the role played by the anarchists in the 1905 Revolution, see Paul Avrich, *The Russian Anarchists* (Chico, CA: AK Press, 2005).

wording of their response is the same as how the anarchists are treated by all socialist congresses in Europe.*

This led to a storm of indignation among the anarchists. A different anarchist group published a strong polemic in the bourgeois paper *Rus'* against the Workers' Delegates Council, and reprimanded the first anarchist group who had begged for admission, thereby heaping the guilt of an alarming violation of anarchistic "principles" upon themselves. The anarchists declare that a Russian workers' struggle led and organized by Social Democracy is a reactionary phenomenon, spawned by the bourgeoisie! [According to them,] all that Social Democracy does is to drive forward the logical further development and idealization of "statist and social barriers, within which people suffocate." Social Democracy's struggle for democratic freedoms is merely the continuation and perpetuation of the slavery of absolutism! ...† It is not uninteresting to note that the anarchists, in their confusion—and moreover in the *reactionary* nature of this confusion—tar everything with the same brush, including the fact that the truly revolutionary movement in Russia is as strongly opposed to them as it is in Western Europe.

---

* A sizable section of the German Social Democratic Party actually consisted of anarchists until 1895, when their tendency (known as "Die Junge") was expelled from it.

† The ellipsis is contained in the original text of Luxemburg; it does not represent material that was removed from publication.

The Revolution in Russia
[December 20, 1905]*

THE RUSSIAN POSTAL-SLAVE'S FIGHT FOR FREEDOM OF ASSOCIATION

One of the most striking impressions thrown up by the current revolution in Russia is the incomparable and admirable general strike of the post and telegraph civil servants. Here, too, the basis of the strike is a desire for *economic* emancipation, a protest against the terrible exploitation of the lower civil servants. But it is precisely that which grants the *political* wrestling which has sprouted out of the revolt against the exploitative system such strength of purchase, such insuperable revolutionary force. The Russian postal slaves' fight for freedom of association is in terms of its character just one aspect of the general proletarian class struggle.

The following letter gives a closer picture of this from the capital of the tsar's empire: *Petersburg*, December 15 (our own comment). To understand the spring that is released by the current general revolt of the post and telegraph civil servants, it is above all necessary to emphasize the purely fiscal character that has dominated the Russian postal service since time immemorial. The postal service, this large cultural factor behind intellectual and economic progress, is simply regarded as a pumping plant instructed with filling the insatiable imperial purse. A few examples of this: While in the United States of America the post and telegraph service has only brought financial *losses* for the Union in recent years, e.g., to the sum of 17.6 million dollars in 1894 and 11.4 million dollars in 1897, the postal service in Russia (whose inhabitants only send one-twentieth of the mail consignments that the Americans send) produced an income of 4.4 million roubles already in 1884, which continued to rise, reaching an income of 19.1 million roubles by 1903. Total Russian income from the post and telegraph service in 1903 stood at 58.2 million roubles. Meaning that the postal administration, with operational costs of 39.1 million roubles, made a "pure profit" of 19.1 million roubles, i.e., around 50 percent of capital!!

This usurious pure profit made from the postal service is only made possible by the unimaginable exploitation of the post and telegraph civil servants, particularly the lower civil servants. While the United States has, for example, 71,000 post offices, Russia, with a population of three times the size, has only 8,861 post offices, including all the train stations and district offices that take in and deliver simple correspondence. While there is one post office for every 887 inhabitants in the United States, one post office in Russia has to cover 10,000 inhabitants!

---

*   This article first appeared in *Vorwärts*, No. 297, December 20, 1905, under the title "Die Revolution in Rußland." It is translated (by Henry Holland) from Luxemburg's *Gesammelte Werke*, Vol. 6, pp. 824–7.

The result is that the relatively small quantity of post and telegraph civil servants are burdened with excessive work in comparison to their capacities. The length of the civil servants' working day is not fixed, and they sometimes have to work twelve-hour shifts or longer, depending on the workload. The situation is even worse for the 19,300 *delivery* and auxiliary staff, who have now become the strike movement's backbone. A mailman's working day lasts from 7 a.m. to 8 p.m., almost without a break. A postal worker sorts the incoming post four or five times a day, and delivers that post four or five times a day. The mailman's bag, a sack with letters, newspapers, and magazines carried on their back—all that weighs more than a pood in total sometimes, i.e., more than forty pounds.

While the real workers in the post and telegraph service get a few paltry dimes as salary and collapse under an unbearable workload—particularly on public holidays like Christmas, Easter, and New Year when they have ten times their normal work—the higher and top-level civil servants, who have almost nothing to do, are catered for in the finest fashion. A department head gets, for example, 2,800 roubles (6,000 marks) annually, with a bonus at Easter, two bonuses annually for "cures," ongoing bonuses for their children's education, etc.—endless bonuses, in other words.

Determining the size of the pension, the level of pay raise with a transfer to Siberia, etc.—all of this is in the hands of the higher levels of the bureaucracy, completely at their discretion, and it is here that the biggest abuse of power occurs. There is no one with whom the lower civil servants can seek protection.

These pariahs of the bureaucracy, these lowest level post and telegraph civil servants, patiently accepted their fate for a long time. But at last the hour of emancipation struck for them, too. They, too, were caught up in the revolutionary movement of the whole proletariat. Following the example of the Social Democratic workforce, they immediately grabbed hold of the first and indispensable tool of liberation—of *organization*. The postal civil servants understood that an alliance of the exploited was the first precondition for improving their situation. An All-Russian Association of Post and Telegraph Civil Servants was formed. The slaves of the state who had been stepped on for so long joined the association with flames of enthusiasm. The government on their part understood just as quickly that the *organized* postal civil servants had wrested themselves free of their despotism, and issued thereupon a fight to the death against the association. The postal civil servants threw off their gloves and now the fight about *freedom of* association has been raging for weeks, a right that the state's slaves, now awakened to their human dignity, will no longer have wrested from them.

But the civil servants' general strike is not just about freedom of association. They are taking a full part in the general revolutionary struggle for political freedom. Their immediate demand is the convocation of the Constituent Assembly on the basis of a universal, equal, director, and secret ballot; other demands include rights of assembly and of association, and calls for freedom of the press and of speech.

Their economic demands are modest in the extreme. The postal civil servants demand a minimum monthly salary, firstly for the civil servants of 50 roubles (108 marks), for lower-level workers of 30 roubles (63 marks), and 25 roubles for the auxiliary staff. Do you know who these auxiliary staff members are? They are called "pupils." But they aren't fifteen- or sixteen-year-old boys. The "pupils" are bearded fathers with kids, who currently get 10 roubles (20 marks) a month and have to work twelve hours a day! They remain "pupils" for many, many years. Beside these wage demands, the civil servants are also demanding pension and incapacity packages.

The sympathies and the active help of both the proletariat and of bourgeois democracy lie with these battling civil servants. At the office of the Post and Telegraph Association in Moscow, thousands of bourgeois families have registered their willingness to nourish one civil servant during the strike. Large sums of money are streaming into the strike headquarters from all sides.

However, there are also "volunteers" who apply for postal service to help the government out of this jam. But please note that these are not traitors out of the postal civil servants' ranks. No, these are people from the "best" circles of society. In this fashion, the following gentlemen are working in Petersburg as post-assistants and mailmen: *Chamberlain* Kosuakov, *Baron* M. Velio, *Baron* von Rapp, *Baron* von Steiger, *General* L. Adamovich, *Major General* A. Hauke, the *Princess* Gaparin, the *Baroness* M. Medem, and the *lady-in-waiting* E. Pandeleyava, etc., etc.

These aren't strikebreakers. These are people who have clearly recognized the opposition between their class interests and those of the battling proletariat. Their "voluntary service" is that of blatant class struggle, and that is why we're not afraid of it. The courage in our ranks is unshaken. We shall overcome, we shall most certainly overcome.

THE "MUTINEERS" SHOULD BE GIVEN A SOAPING

Petersburg, December 19 (report from the Petersburg Telegraph Agency). A daily briefing in the military section reveals that an imperial command from December 19 has ordered better food and a wage increase for units from all tri-service troops. Furthermore, warm blankets, bed linen, and *soap* should be delivered to the troops.

SEMI-OFFICIAL DECEPTIONS

The following report, which has "a lie" written all over it, is being distributed by the Russian government gang: *Petersburg*, December 19. The investigation into Khrustalyov-Nosar, president of the workers' committees, has discovered that Khrustalyov-Nosar had made all necessary preparations for taking Witte prisoner(!). Twenty sacked postal civil servants have registered with the revolutionary committee in order to attempt to assassinate Durnovo(!). The government's announcement is making a favorable impressions and isn't being seen as a reactionary act(!), but rather as proof of the government's determination to restore order and to introduce the constitution(!).

READY TO FIGHT

Petersburg, December 19. The executive committee of the Council [Soviet] of Workers' Deputies, which had to interrupt its meeting yesterday due to fear of arrest, has issued an appeal together with the Union of Unions, in which they declare that the current government is threatening to plunge the country into danger. They will rise to meet the battle that the government has begun. Methods of combat will depend on what the government does next. For the time being, all forces should be mobilized, to be ready for the general strike when such a strike is announced.

Riga, December 17 (report from the Petersburg Telegraph Agency). Peace is currently presiding over the city and its environs. The general strike lasted for three days, without clashes, attacks or acts of violence resulting from it. The complete lack of news did however generate anxiety among the population. Now everything is slowly getting back to normal; and rumors are of course circulating, saying that a new strike will probably break out. The rumors circulated in Petersburg and abroad about destruction and arson in Riga can probably be traced back to reports about extremely serious rioting in the provinces, where, it is said, arson, murders, and other acts of violence have occurred, and many estates, leased estates, and stately homes, have been completely destroyed.

FURTHER PROVOCATIONS

Petersburg, December 19 (report from the Petersburg Telegraph Agency). Martial law has been imposed in the Suwałki governorate covering the districts of Vladislavovo, Mariopol, Volkovyshky (*sic!*), and Kolvary.

The Revolution in Russia
[December 20, 1905]*

Formally, today's revolution in Russia is the ultimate offshoot of the Great French Revolution of a hundred years ago. The entire past century essentially accomplished only the work bequeathed to it by the aforesaid great historical upheaval—the establishment of the class rule of the modern bourgeoisie, capitalism, in all countries.

In the first act of this century-long crisis, this truly authentic revolution undermined the feudal society of the Middle Ages, turned it upside down, shook it, carved it up roughly into the classes of modern society, illuminated to a significant extent the goals [of these new classes] along with their social and political programs, and in the end overturned feudalism in all of Europe—with the help of the Napoleonic wars.

In subsequent stages the internal class division of modern bourgeois society, which had begun with the Great French Revolution, was carried further—in class struggle and through class struggle. In the period of Restoration [1815–30], high finance took the helm of state into its own hands, but the July Revolution [of 1830] put an end to that. In the July Revolution, the big industrial bourgeoisie came to power, and then it fell thanks to the February Revolution [of 1848]. The February Revolution finally gave power to the broad masses of the medium and lower strata of the petty bourgeoisie in the form of today's Third Republic. Here the modern class rule of the bourgeoisie achieved its final form and fullest development. But meanwhile, in the midst of all these internal struggles of the bourgeoisie, there arose a new cleavage—the deep divide between the entire bourgeois society and the modern working class. The birth and maturation of this class contradiction, in parallel with the internal class conflicts among the bourgeoisie, also extended through the history of the entire century.

The Great French Revolution already saw the first general shaking up of all the elements, and together with all the internal conflicts of bourgeois society, it also brought to the surface the proletariat and its ideal—communism. The brief reign of "the Mountain" [in 1792–1793], the highest point of the revolution, marked the first historical debut of the modern proletariat. However, this

---

    *   This article was first published in the Warsaw-based Polish periodical *Trybuna Ludowa* (Tribune of the People) on December 20, 1905, under the title "Rewolucja w Rosji" (The Revolution in Russia). *Trybuna Ludowa* was a legal publication during December 1905, after Tsar Nicholas II's October Manifesto promised constitutional reforms in the midst of the general strike of October 1905. But that freedom of the press did not last long, coming to an end early in 1906. Many years later, in 1959, this article was reprinted in a Polish selection of Luxemburg's writings (*Wybór Pism*—Selected Works). A German version of the article, not accompanied by any date, appeared in Luxemburg's *Gesammelte Werke*, Vol. 2, pp. 5–10. It is translated (by George Shriver and Alicja Mann) from the Polish original.

proletariat did not step onto the stage of history independently, but was wrapped in the folds of the lower strata of the petty bourgeoisie and together with those strata constituted what was called "the people," whose hostility toward bourgeois society found expression in the poorly understood form of the antagonism of the "people's republic" toward constitutional monarchy.

In the February Revolution and in the terrible carnage of the June Days [of 1848] the proletariat as a class separated itself completely from the lower strata of the petty bourgeoisie and for the first time became conscious that within bourgeois society it was an entirely distinct class, which had to rely on its own strength and which was the mortal enemy of the existing society. In this way modern bourgeois society took shape in France and the work begun by the Great Revolution was completed.

While these main acts of the historical drama of capitalist society were played out in France, the history of Germany, Austria, and Italy was reflected in those acts—as was the history of all modern countries in the capitalist world.

There is nothing more foolish and absurd than when modern revolutions are viewed as nationally limited occurrences, as events that, with all their power, have an effect only within the borders of the country concerned, and that, on the other hand, they exert only a more-or-less weak effect on "neighboring countries"—because of their status as "neighbors." Bourgeois society, capitalism, is an international phenomenon, a worldwide form of human society. There are not a multitude of bourgeois societies, or kinds of capitalism, as there are modern states and nations. Rather, there is only one international society, one capitalism, and the seemingly separate and independent existence of particular countries behind state borders in the presence of this single, indivisible worldwide economy is only one of the contradictions of capitalism. And also, for this reason, all modern revolutions are, as a matter of fact, *international*. All of it is one and the same prolonged bourgeois revolution, which in various acts was played out across all of Europe from 1789 to 1848 and which established the modern class rule of the bourgeoisie *on an international basis*.

Seemingly, the Russian state itself was an exception to that worldwide revolution. Here it appeared that medieval absolutism was able to persist as a leftover monument of the precapitalist era. But now, even in Russia, absolutism has already been crushed by the revolution [of 1905]. What we are living through today is no longer a battle of the revolution against the ruling system of absolutism, but a struggle between the remnants of absolutism, which survive in a formal sense, a struggle between them and the modern form of political liberty, which has become a living reality. And along with that, there is a battle among classes and parties over the limits of, and constitutional arrangements for, that political liberty.

The Russian Revolution, from the formal standpoint, as we have seen, is an ultimate offshoot of the era of *bourgeois* revolutions in Europe. Its most immediate task, according to outward appearances, is the creation of a modern-capitalist society under the open class rule of the bourgeoisie. However, the fact that Russia seemed to be isolated and closed off for the duration of an entire century and did not take part in the general European upheaval means that the revolution in Russia, which from the formal standpoint is bourgeois, is actually not at all the work of the bourgeoisie but of the working class. This means that the working class is no longer just an appendage of the lower petty bourgeoisie, as in all the [modern] revolutions up to now, but is coming forward and taking action independently, fully aware of its own particular class interests and aims—that is, as a class of workers led by Social Democracy.

To a large extent, the present revolution in Russia is linked directly to the slaughter in Paris in June 1848—to the days when, for the first time, the division between the proletariat and the entire bourgeois society became a reality, when at a single blow that division was put into effect as an accomplished fact.

In this way, today's Russian Revolution contains within itself a greater contradiction than any of the preceding revolutions. It was not the bourgeoisie in this case who won the modern political forms of class rule by capital; rather, it was the working class that obtained them in spite of the bourgeoisie. Although—or rather, because—the working class for the first time entered the arena as an independent, class-conscious social stratum, it did not have those utopian socialist illusions with which it had come forward in alliance with the lower elements of the petty bourgeoisie in the bourgeois revolutions of the past. In Russia, the proletariat does not now have as its goal the establishment of socialism—it wants only to establish the capitalist-bourgeois preconditions for socialism. But at the same time, the workers have left their distinctive mark on bourgeois society, because this society took its moment of origin directly from the hands of the class-conscious proletariat. In truth, the working class has not set itself the task of the immediate introduction of socialism, but even farther from its thoughts is the establishment of an inviolable and untroubled rule by capital of the kind that emerged from the bourgeois revolutions of the past century in the West.

Rather than that, the proletariat in Russia is waging a battle simultaneously against absolutism and against capitalism; it is demanding the forms of bourgeois democracy, but it wants them *for itself*, for the purposes of the proletarian class struggle. The proletariat is demanding *the eight-hour day*, a people's militia, and a republic—propositions directed toward bourgeois society, not socialist [demands].

However, these demands [are] so subversive of the rule of capital that they can be regarded as forms that are transitional to the dictatorship of the proletariat. The proletariat in Russia is fighting for the implementation of the most elementary *bourgeois* constitutional rights—the rights of assembly and of association, the right to form coalitions, and freedom of the press. And even today in the whirlpool of revolution the proletariat is making use of these bourgeois freedoms with the aim of creating its own more powerful class organizations, both economic and political—unions in the plants and factories and Social Democratic organizations. Thus, while one class—the bourgeoisie—formally is permitted to rule, it comes out of this revolution in an unprecedentedly weak condition, and the class that has formally been suppressed—the proletariat—turns out to be unprecedentedly strong.

In this way today's revolution in Russia, *as far as its essential content is concerned*, has gone far beyond the other revolutions before this time, and in its methods it has nothing in common either with the bourgeois revolutions of the past or with the struggles of the modern proletariat at present—parliamentary struggles. It has created a new method of struggle corresponding to its proletarian character—the revolutionary mass strike. First, in its essential content, and then in its method, it is a completely new type of revolution.

Formally it is bourgeois-democratic, [but] in its essence it is proletarian-socialist, and thus this revolution, from the standpoint of its content and method, has become a *transitional form*—in transition from the bourgeois-democratic revolutions of the past to the proletarian revolutions of the future, in which the question will already be posed of the dictatorship of the proletariat and the implementation of socialism.

Thus, it is a distinctly defined type of revolution, not only logically but also *historically*, a form resulting from the given balance of class and social forces. The society that has emerged from this revolution in Russia is so much of its own special kind that it cannot be the same as the societies that resulted from the earlier revolutions in the West in the year 1848.

The strength, organization, and class consciousness of the proletariat will be so strongly developed in Russia after the revolution that the framework of "normal" bourgeois society will be disrupted at every turn. At the same time, the weakness and downheartedness of the bourgeoisie, which senses its own coming downfall, completely devoid of any political and revolutionary past, produces a combination of forces in which a steady and stable class rule by the bourgeoisie will be constantly shaken. A new phase in the history of bourgeois society is therefore also beginning, and because of this disruption of the balance of class forces, it will constantly give way to troubled and stormy times; and those stormy times, with more or less lengthy pauses between them, times which may be more or less violent, can lead to no other outcome than social revolution—the dictatorship of the proletariat.

All of this applies most of all to Russia. However, just as the massacres on the pavements of Paris in the French revolutions also shaped the destinies of Russia and all of Europe, in the same way today on the streets of St. Petersburg, Moscow, and Warsaw, the fate not only of Russian society but of the whole capitalist world is being decided.

The revolution in Russia and the unique social creation produced by it are also bound to shift the relationship of class forces at a single stroke in Germany and in the whole world.

The Russian Revolution has closed an approximately sixty-year period of peaceful parliamentary rule by the bourgeoisie. With the Russian Revolution, we enter a period of transition between capitalist and socialist society. How *long* this period will last is a matter of interest not only to political forecasters of the weather. For the class-conscious international proletariat, it is important only to keep an ever sharper, clarifying eye on the near future as this emancipatory era unfolds, and to understand that in the thunderstorms ahead it must grow with equal speed, in steadfastness, consciousness, and heroism as the Russian proletariat is growing today before our eyes with each passing day and hour.

Before Decisive Battle*

The situation in the revolutionary empire is very serious. The side of the reaction is readying itself for one last violent blow, by violently interrupting the peaceful and deadly serious creative work of revolution, attempting to draw the proletariat into battle, before it can choose the timeliest moment for itself. The working class, and all the social classes who are gathered around its struggle— the military, the marine crews, the lower government officials, and so-called liberal professions—are all plunged passionately into the task of *organization*. Labor organizations and political organizations germinate and shoot from the old tundra of the tsarist empire, now thawing in the heat of revolutionary fire. Political education and organization—those are the two tasks, or better said, single task, which has swallowed up all revolutionary energies in the last few weeks. To await the fruits of this most noble cultural labor, to first allow the working people to be granted the indestructible defenses of *organization*, is precisely that which the cabal of courtiers gathered round the tsar's sinking throne wish to prevent. And now the counterrevolution is pushing for a bloodbath and for military dictatorship as its last refuge, because the crusade across the country of the Black Hundreds, the *lumpenproletariat*, has finally failed, because revolutionary *thoughts* and revolutionary *organization*—even in the armed forces—have emerged victorious out of the confusion and anarchy that absolutism had set in motion.

It is important, in this moment full of responsibility, to listen to that party standing on the crest of events in Russia, the leadership of developments in its hands. *Nachalo* [The Beginning], one of the official Petersburg party organs of our Russian twin party, has published the following leading article on the situation in Russia:†

> The reaction mobilizes her forces. She descends from her luxurious, glittering palaces into the dark cellars to search among the mud and the dirt that capitalist society had produced, for allies in her defense of "holy" rights—exploitation and despotism without barriers. The reaction disarms that ever-growing part of the army whose heart starts to beat in time with the masses. The reaction floods the major cities with

---

*   Although no name is identified with this article, it is clearly by Luxemburg. The article first appeared in *Vorwärts*, No. 298, December 21, 1905, entitled "Vor der Entscheidungsschlacht." It is translated (by Henry Holland) from Luxemburg's *Gesammelte Werke*, Vol. 6, pp. 828–31.

†   *Nachalo*, founded by Alexander Parvus, Julius Martov, and Leon Trotsky, was de facto Trotsky's newspaper. The lead article from *Nachalo* quoted here can therefore be taken as being written by Trotsky. See Bernd Florath, "'Es ist ein Lust zu leben!' Rosa Luxemburg als Redakteurin des sozialdemokratischen Vorwärts über die russische Revolution 1905," in *Lesearten marxistischer Theorie mit Beiträgen über Anton Ackermann, Otto Bauer, Ferdinand Lassalle, Rosa Luxemburg, Georg Plechanow*, edited by Wladislaw Hedeler (Berlin: Helle Panke, 1996).

that other part of the military, to which the hot life-breath of revolutionary storm has not yet seeped through thick barrack walls. She expresses thanks to the Cossacks for "loyal service," who, after enduring a humiliating fiasco in their looting raids in Manchuria, now wish to indemnify themselves through looting raids in their own fatherland. She, the reaction, blesses with holy water and images of the saints her "new troops," who are willingly up in arms against youthful freedom, in order to reinstate ancient slavery. She poses the tricolor of absolutism as a question, and writers her own answer upon it—*military dictatorship!*

And the frightful spectere of military dictatorship is haunting the whole empire, making the "citizens" tremble, i.e., those classes of civil society who value their immediate, material privileges above all else, and who therefore hate the revolution and the reaction's reign of violence in equal measure.

Yet though the reaction may stand threateningly tall, may mobilize her beloved troops, may dare to play violent and insolent tricks like arresting the leaders of the labor movement, the proletariat can coolly claim: *I'm not afraid of either reaction or military dictatorship, not in the least!*

The facts are clear—the reaction can no longer succeed. And if this cabal of courtiers, these officers of the guard, these heroic heroes in the fight against defenseless people should succeed in moving the government into taking the crazy decision of imposing a military dictatorship over Russia, *then this government's remaining days in rule would be counted in days, and no longer in weeks.*

The reaction can no longer succeed. She is no longer capable of staging a bloodbath in Petersburg or in Moscow, as she was still able to do just a while ago in the provinces. Certainly, individuals like [generals] Neidhardt or Kaulbars are still to be found in Petersburg or Moscow, just waiting for their chance to dip their hands into the blood of the defenseless people. But the government can no longer find a sufficient number of stooges among the *populations* of Petersburg and Moscow to carry out their criminal plans. The whole fiasco of the Black Hundreds' "patriotic demonstrations," organized in Petersburg and in Moscow under the egis of the metropolitan elite themselves, were fewer than 1,500 people; [that so few] wanted to gather under its banner has proven clear enough this lack of resources. Only one last option is open to the government—a direct and brutal slaying of the defenseless population by the *soldateska,*⸳ which would only work on condition that the military in Petersburg and Moscow still has sufficient persons of such character. But such butchery would certainly spell the last day of the absolutist regime *today already*, a day in which government representatives would be gambling with their own heads and would lose them.

Yes, the reaction can stage a bloodbath. But she cannot succeed, as she no longer has the strength to do so. The proletariat opposes her, having got a hold on its own interests, having recognized its goal, a goal that is welded together through

---

*   This pejorative Italian word means an unleashed, lawless mob of soldiers.

the powerful bonds of class solidarity and *organization*. The peasants oppose her, with their demands for a radical solution to the land question, a solution that is unthinkable without the revolution winning. All those parts of democracy oppose her, in whose hands all the threads are concentrated, which determine the function and coherence of the mechanism of the state. Railroads, post, telegraph and telephone networks will refuse to offer absolutism their services, in that moment in which it composes itself before the celebrations, after temporary victory of a St. Bartholomew's Day massacre* variety. An ever-increasing section of the army is opposed to her, leading to the ever-more frequent occurrence that the reaction's hired hands so refuse to do their "duty" that even those whose vocation it is to fight the revolution—yes, even the police and police spies—refuse this fight. And, finally, international capital also opposes her, with its profit and greed, and which, exclusively concerned with its percentage returns, is literally panting for "law and order." International capital, of course, mistrusts the revolution, but mistrusts the reaction all the more, a reaction who has already shown herself powerless in her efforts to restore "order" and in her efforts to guarantee those returns with which Russia is burdened through the thieving economy of absolutism, to the advantage of international finance.

Capitalism has pulled together the most remote and manifold parts of the Russian empire with tight ropes. The class movement of the proletariat has poured these material and economic relationships, this molten steel, into the lively form of a united political struggle of the working class. The proletariat's leading role in the struggle for Russian freedom has brought unity, certainty of purpose, and organization into the emancipatory waves that are washing through the empire.

A bloodbath in Petersburg would send a signal today already for a general uprising in the provinces. And a triumph for the soldateska in Petersburg would spell their ultimate defeat in the provinces. The international stock exchange would reward a "victory" for absolutism in Petersburg by striking the absolutist government off the list of institutions with the best credit ratings, the list of those best able to meet debt payments. This government, still kept alive by the international exchange, would die in the very moment in which its suckling mother withdrew her trust.

That is why we don't need to worry about the revolution's fate. That is why we don't need to worry—on the condition, of course, that the absolutist government has not gone completely mad, and decides to throw itself into the abyss of a military dictatorship and a bloodbath.

The government can land, at the most, in its impotent rage, a few isolated blows on the head of the emancipatory movement of the proletariat, and she can bet on it, that the working class will hesitate before answering these—not wanting to be disturbed from its great task of self-organization and preparation for the day to come

* The St. Bartholomew's Day massacre took place in 1572 with targeted assassinations and a wave of Catholic mob violence directed against French Calvinist Protestants (the Huguenots).

of open battle right down the line. Nevertheless, the government will not and cannot dare to put those bloody plans into practice born of the criminal fantasy of that cabal of courtiers.

And if they do dare, nonetheless … well, then they'll see that not the revolution but rather absolutism will choke in the blood that is shed.

That is why the proletariat need not fear the reaction and their assaults. And that is why we can call out to all fearful souls: *Do not be scared!* Hurry instead with all your strength to help the proletariat then win we shall, come what may!

The Revolution in Russia
[December 21, 1905]*

The government drives forward following Durnovo's line,† in order to provoke. Arrests of well-known labor movement leaders continue. Dying absolutism is going for broke, and wants to violently incite decisive battle before labor considers itself strong enough to conquer. Despite all these provocations, the leading organizations are maintaining a calm and solid stance. The rumors peddled by the bourgeois press about an attempt at a general strike that is already failed are all lies, just as the rumors are about atrocities committed by *workers* in Riga or about the "red guard" in Finland. The reader will discover from reports received by the comrades affected that the public is being deceived about the chaos and anarchy, through semi-official telegrams and the bourgeois correspondents' own accord. In reality, we're discussing utterly focused political and economic endeavors, which nonetheless do wish to suffocate *absolutism* in a general chaos of bloodshed and looting.

Alexandrov, December 20 (from a private correspondent). We have received the following from Warsaw: The chairman of the Warsaw Association of Railroad Workers, Moracewicz, *has been arrested* today. The Association reacted by passing a motion through which a strike of the civil servants on the Vistula Railroad will begin on Friday.

Kiev, December 20. Several *members of the Congress of South Russian Revolutionaries* were *arrested* recently. The police have forbidden all assemblies, with the exception of the Christian Social Association. The Black Hundreds have for their part called for nine massacres of the Jews. Reports in from various municipalities in Bessarabia say that the police themselves have called for the Jews to be persecuted. Disturbances have also broken out recently in Odessa.

ORGANIZATION IN THE MILITARY

Petersburg, December 19. The new Social Democratic workers' paper *Severny Golos* [Voice of the North]‡ out today publishes an appeal of the *Central Committee of the All-Russian Association of Military Persons of all Branches*, in which officers, units, and officers of the guards of the army and of the fleet

---

* This article first appeared in *Vorwärts*, No. 298, December 21, 1905, under the title "Die Revolution in Rußland." It is translated (by Henry Holland) from Luxemburg's *Gesammelte Werke*, Vol. 6, pp. 832–6.

† That is, a line of increased repression.

‡ *Severny Golos* was a legal daily newspaper of the RDSRP that began publication in St. Petersburg on December 19, 1905. It was jointly edited by the Bolsheviks and the Mensheviks. The tsarist government closed it down after its third issue, on December 21, 1905.

are called upon to join the Association. This has the purpose of supporting the freedom movement, and, as its final goal, the convening of a Constituent Assembly on the basis of a universal, direct, and secret franchise; and the realization of a new ordering of the state and of military reform, as worked out by this assembly. The Association's tactics will consist of not using armed forces against the freedom fighters, maintaining order, protecting all citizens against acts of violence, preventing rabble-rousing and the realization of an all-Russian strike in the army. As the final act in its activities, the Association promises to help all those people who suffer because of their participation in the same.

A HOAX

A *Laffan's News Agency* cable from *London* states: as reported in the *Daily Telegraph*, that Vera Zasulich, who had to spend more than a quarter of a century abroad, is said to be among the workers' delegates arrested by the police in Petersburg. Along with the well-known revolutionaries [Vladmir Lvovich] Burzev, Plekhanov, and Tschernov, she is one of the party's finest speakers.

Comrade Plekhanov is most definitely abroad, in Switzerland to be precise;* and it is very much to be doubted whether Comrade Zasulich even took part in the Workers' Delegates Council.† The whole report looks like a hoax.

PREPARATIONS FOR THE GENERAL STRIKE

Petersburg, December 20. The *railroad workers* in Moscow have decided to join the *general strike*. Consequently, the Workers' Deputies Council in the city ordered the strike to begin today at noon, as had been promised. *This report still needs to be confirmed.*

As has been reported to the *Novoye Vremya* [New Times] (a reactionary paper) from Moscow, representatives of the revolutionary parties penned a manifesto yesterday, in which workers and troops called for the founding of a democratic republic. The tone of this manifesto is said to be so "challenging" that even radical papers have decided not to publish it.

Petersburg, December 20. The *general strike* should begin here tomorrow at noon. In Moscow, electric streetcar employees have been on strike since this morning.

Petersburg, December 20. In the session yesterday of the Union of Unions, it was communicated that disturbances have broken out again in Sevastopol. Kharkiv is said to be in the hands of insurgent persons who have voted in a

---

*   Plekhanov was one of the few leaders of the Russian Marxist movement not to return to Russia during the 1905 Revolution.

†   Although still a committed Marxist, Zasulich's active involvement in revolutionary politics had already begun to wane by the end of 1905.

new Duma; the latter has transferred 10,000 roubles to the rebels. According to a report from *Slovo*, an official report has been received from Tbilisi that bloody clashes have again been taking place there between Armenians and Tatars since the twelfth of this month, after the steward had granted the request from the Armenians for 500 guns to build a militia with. Both the troops and society are demanding that this militia be disarmed. The troops have used their own initiative to start this disarmament. Panic is dominating the city. The same paper reports from Yaroslavl that 600 armed workers have occupied the Kornsinkinshen factory and have declared it as the property of the proletariat.

Petersburg, December 20. The response from the labor leaders in Moscow reached us yesterday. It is favorable news for the general strike, meaning that the strike could be declared without delay.

Warsaw, December 20. *The leaders of the post and telegraph strike* have been arrested; the telegraph line between Moscow and Petersburg has been reconnected.

The *Vossische Zeitung* [Voß's Newspaper] writes: *Civil War in Finland?* Preparations are being made for unusual happenings, as reported in the letter that has reached us from Helsinki. The "red guard" representing labor and the "white guard" organized by the bourgeoisie are standing, armed, facing each other. The price of weapons has increased sharply and there's hardly one revolver left for sale in the whole of Finland. If skirmishes break out today already, during the opening of parliament, and if these should be won by the Labor Party, a declaration of the Finnish Republic cannot be ruled out. The workers' paper *Tuomier* already carried the mysterious remark a few days ago that the "red guard" doesn't exist to protect the parliament or to maintain order in the city, but is rather envisaged "for other purposes." The main issue is that the workers don't want to represent the Finnish parliament as a representation of the people, since this institution is well known for being elected by the votes of the bourgeois estates.

AN APPEAL FROM THE FINNISH SOCIAL DEMOCRATS

We have received the following letter:

The Social Democratic Party of Finland hereby sends all party comrades in all countries their greetings. It cannot have escaped the notice of the politically educated section of the public that despite all the upper classes' complaints, a deep divide dominates the Finnish people. This threatens to render fruitless the efforts to achieve political freedom, for which all forces should have worked together. Not only is capitalism getting more threatening by the day, and workers more exploited by wage slavery than ever, but massive political oppression also prevails. This becomes thinkable and even natural only in a country where a large majority of the people cannot express their will in a real body that represents the people. Dissatisfaction with these unacceptable conditions has expressed itself in ever-more powerful demonstrations in the last few years. Last spring, Finland's parliament—a four-chamber representative system cobbled together in the most miserable way—refused to recognize universal suffrage for the bourgeois estate and the peasants. It was only thanks to the clear course taken by the workers' organizations that the ensuing demonstrations were prevented from spilling over into public riots.

The most recent occurrences in Russia have significantly accelerated our political development, and demands for the convention of a Constituent Assembly were frequently voiced during the course of the general strike carried out in October.

However, the ruling classes' machinations, coupled with a solidarity deficit, prevented these demands from being met. However, then came the tsar's splendid manifesto in October, which put the question of universal, egalitarian, and direct franchise back on the agenda. Since then, no proposal against the principle of universal suffrage has come forth, and all ruling parties have spoken out at large party assemblies where large majorities favor the one-chamber system.* Disquieting symptoms can nevertheless be observed, particularly inside the Old Swedish faction† that exercises decisive influence on the composition of the nobility and of the bourgeois estate, and in part also upon the estates of the clergy and the peasants, through the powerful and rich voters who support it. The message is becoming ever clearer that the ruling class intends to use a two-chamber system as a defensive wall in order to save their class privileges, whereby our proletarian interests and democratic progressive reforms will of course be compromised in a most sensitive manner.

To save the people from this dangerous threat, the Social Democratic Party is preparing to *proclaim a new general strike* the moment that the vital interests of the people [risk] being decided by the shortcomings of this class parliament.‡ We trust that the members of the international Social Democratic organizations in all countries will understand that we are preparing ourselves for a test of strength that is entirely based on our program—and is also unavoidable. In doing so, representatives of the Finnish party are hereby appealing to the international community in the hope that by communicating our appeal, we receive support for an endeavor that may soon be necessary and justified. In this way, Finland's proletariat can win the

---

* This is because a one-chamber system, as against a four-chamber system that weighs votes differently depending on social status and class, comes closest to the democratic principle of "one man, one vote."

† Most of Finland was a part of the Kingdom of Sweden from the thirteenth century to 1809, when the Finnish-speaking areas of Sweden were ceded to the Russian Empire. A significant and influential Swedish-speaking minority remained. Swedish was the language of the cultural and educational elite well into the 1920s.

‡ That is, a parliament designed to thwart popular representation and ensure the dominance of the ruling classes.

most basic freedoms and political rights, and thereby be better equipped to join the huge international army of Social Democracy in future battles.

Helsinki, December 13, 1905

Emil Perttilai, August Rissanen, Recording Clerks

Yrio E. Sirola, Party Secretary

THE REVOLUTIONARY RISING IN LIVONIA

Jelgava, December 15, 1905 (editor's remarks). The news about the "atrocities" carried out by revolutionaries in the city, and diligently distributed by the reactionary press, are utter lies. The real story is of an entirely calm general strike movement of local labor led by Social Democracy. Excesses against estate owners are only occurring in a few individual villages and landed estates, as everywhere in the Russian empire, as an unavoidable consequence of the brutal attitude of the estate owners and of government civil servants.

The strike began in Jelgava on Saturday, December 9. It was announced with the forethought that the general Russian mass strike was about to begin—a precondition that has not, as yet, materialized. The rumor that the striking workers are said to have stormed the castle in Jelgava is, like all the other spine-chilling tales, a work of fantasy. It is also a fairy story that "revolutionary" Livonia has proclaimed itself a "free republic." The program of the city's workers is exactly the same as in the rest of Russia, a democratic republic covering the whole Russian empire.

Knyasev, the new governor of Courland, resorted to the usual notorious "energetic methods." On the Saturday and Sunday, drunken Cossacks lashed out at demonstrators, and on Monday, December 11, people were shot at solely for laughing when a Cossack officer fell from his horse. While the officer was getting up again he shouted at his Cossacks the command to shoot, and they began shooting without delay. Several persons were killed, and between twenty and thirty wounded. The Cossacks lashed out mercilessly at the crowds who had wanted to save themselves by hiding in the yards of the surrounding houses, surrounding these yards, and aiming at the houses in which anyone was to be seen at the windows.

The local, loyal-to-the-tsar Germans are bitter to the point of desperation.[*] They bring the Cossacks beer and food, and are boisterously pleased to have found the "right protection" at last.

The Jews are worried that the new governor will fall back on the infamous trick of incitement to violence against them, though it is hardly possible that he

---

[*]   Livonia, now split between Latvia and Estonia, possessed a substantial German-speaking ethnic minority since the Middle Ages. They formed an important part of the ruling class of Livonia, which explains their support for tsarism and opposition to the Russian Revolution.

should succeed in doing this, as revolutionary labor is too heavy a weight among the population to let something like that pass without punishment.

The military is overstretched and rushes from one place to the next without a moment's peace in order to suffocate the movement growing constantly throughout the land.

The Revolution in Russia
[December 22, 1905]*

START OF THE GENERAL STRIKE!

Moscow, December 20. The life of society draws to a halt as a result of the universal work stoppage. The electric streetcar service is suspended. The senior office civil servants from the city council and the zemstvos will walk out this afternoon. Production has stopped in a number of larger factories; *50,000 workers are celebrating. Not a single printing house is working*, so *no newspapers* will appear tomorrow. And tomorrow most *schools will also be closed*, and the pupils let out for their Christmas vacation already. The wine stalls are closed. The *Association of Engineers* has joined the strike. The *bank employees* will probably join the work stoppage tomorrow. Because the *central electricity stations* are not working, the city is *without lighting*. *Theaters and clubs are closed*. In the post offices, operations have to be *suspended* in the evening because of deficient lighting. A *Congress of Post and Telegraph civil servants* decided *to join the general strike*. Many shops were closed at midday already, while others had to be closed in the evening because electric lighting was unavailable.

Many workers and workers' deputies were arrested today. Strikers' assemblies were *forcibly dispersed* by Cossacks.

The printers from the printing house owned by [Ivan Dmitriyevich] Sytin, the publisher of *Russkoye Slovo* [The Russian Word], arrested Sytin and the editors of *Slovo* today, and produced *the first issue of the paper of the Workers' Deputies Council* at the printers, which contained an appeal to the people, *to organize the armed revolution*. The Social Democratic paper *Borba* [The Struggle],† which had also carried a revolutionary appeal, has been *impounded*. Representatives from the *Union of Unions* in the city have decided *to join the strike*, in order to support the proletariat's revolution.

Petersburg, December 20 (report by the Petersburg Telegraph Agency). The strike committee of the *Nicholas Railway civil servants* has decided *to announce their strike* tomorrow morning at noon.

Warsaw, December 20. The Petersburg Railroad Workers' Committee has forwarded the communiqué to the Warsaw railroad workers, *that the strike will begin tonight at midnight*. The city's *fire brigade* also went *on strike* yesterday. Cavalry patrols are moving through the streets. Business people state that trade is at a complete standstill.

---

* This article first appeared in *Vorwärts*, No. 299, December 22, 1905, under the title "Die Revolution in Rußland." It is translated (by Henry Holland) from Luxemburg's *Gesammelte Werke*, Vol. 6, pp. 837–8.

† *Borba* was published by the Socialist Revolutionary Party.

Petersburg, December 20 (report by the Petersburg Telegraph Agency). As reported from *Moscow,* employees from all rail lines in the city went on strike today at noon; all strikers are *armed.* The governor-general has *declared a state of heightened security* in the city.

Dnipropetrovsk, December 20. The *general strike* has been proclaimed on the Dnipropetrovskian railroad. Every single transport is suspended.

The *Berliner Tageblatt* publishes the following private dispatch from Petersburg: Because the Petersburg Worker's Council Executive Committee is dependent on Moscow, the general strike will only begin here today at noon. There are still some voices in the freedom movement camp—like Professor [Pavel] *Milyukov's** for example—who are warning the Workers' Council [Soviet] to stop before taking this step, before it is too late. Milyukov publicly articulates his fear that the strike will fail because the workers are tired of striking. Similarly, Pyotr Struve gave a public lecture yesterday, speaking about the powerlessness of the revolutionary parties, and emphasizing that the telegraph and postal service strike has done more harm than good to the revolutionary cause.

These liberal gentlemen's raven cries will of course have no influence on the battling proletarian masses. The stone has started to roll!

The *Workers' Deputies Council* has brought out its newspaper, in which it calls for an immediate battle against the government and explains that this battle is firmly decided upon—and that it will not be the last. The appeal continues:

Yet the government is throwing down their last cards, the *army* and *the financiers. Yet the cards have already been played!* We take on this fight, knowing that Witte's government isn't in a condition to push on with their slippery game. Witte's government has conjured up this battle prematurely. *May innocent blood, which will have to flow, be on his hands! We declare the general strike! Fight to the last drop of blood!*

---

*   Pavel Milyukov was the leader of the Constitutional Democratic Party (CD), known colloquially as "the Cadets," a liberal party committed at first to a constitutional monarchy and later to a republic. Members included progressive landowners, representatives from the bourgeoisie, and members of the intelligentsia. Milyukov was also instrumental in helping form the Union of Unions in 1905, but the group began to come apart at the end of 1905 over conflicts between liberal and more radical elements.

The Revolution in Russia
[December 23, 1905]*

THE GENERAL STRIKE STRIDES FORWARD

Petersburg, December 22. The telegraphic communication with Moscow is suspended. The strike began this afternoon in 220 factories. Seventy thousand workers, roughly one-third of the total workforce, are out on strike.

Petersburg, December 22. The strike, which began yesterday afternoon, is spreading. The noon train to Chernyshevskoye set out under strong military escort. The district in which the Imperial Bank and the department stores are located is being strongly guarded. Infantry patrols move through the streets.

THE BLACK HUNDREDS AT WORK

Moscow, December 21 (report in the Petersburg Telegraph Agency). Striking railroad workers have been attacked by wagon drivers. Many of the wagon drivers' horses were killed in the resulting street brawl. Members of the Workers' Deputies Office have been arrested. Several acts of violence have been carried out by the mob against revolutionary speakers and students. The strikers want to force the post and telegraph civil servants into joining the strike, too. According to a motion of the Association of Bank Civil Servants, all private banks are closed, as are all warehouses, shops, and theaters. A group of 300 men moved through the streets, forcing bars and restaurants to close their premises.

The report yesterday from *Kharkiv* had been confirmed. Two hundred and fifty soldiers from the Starobyelsk and Lebeinsk regiments took part in the rally yesterday with red flags. The troops sent against the crowd could ignore their instruction as regards the breachers of the peace—and did not fire. The revolutionaries turned that to their own advantage.

Moscow, December 21 (report from the Petersburg Telegraph Agency). An assembly of 12,000 people took place today in the premises of the aquarium. Infantry, dragoons, gendarmerie, Cossacks, and police occupied the exits and demanded that the people locked in hand over their weapons.

Moscow, December 22. At a meeting of striking railroad workers, a motion was passed allowing one train with grain per day to depart to the provinces under threat.

Petersburg, December 22. New disturbances have broken out in Tbilisi. The Germans in Kokzen have formed a civil defense force.

Petersburg, December 22. Shaparov, the leader of the mutineers in Rostov,

* This article first appeared in *Vorwärts*, No. 300, December 23, 1905, under the title "Die Revolution in Rußland." It is translated (by Henry Holland) from Luxemburg's *Gesammelte Werke*, Vol. 6, pp. 839–41.

is said to have escaped from prison. According to reports in from Kharkiv, Rostov is apparently really in the hands of the insurgents. Reports have also been received from Sevastopol of trouble fermenting.

IN LIVONIA

Petersburg, December 22. As has been reported from Ryeshiza, in the governorate of Vitebsk, that section of the region lying along the Livonian border is on strike. Catholic Latvians living in the region are being terrorized by Livonian tribes. Spurred on by agitators, they defy state authority and call for the removal of the regional state leaders. Peasant disturbances are underway in the rest of the region. As has been reported by telegraph to *Novoye Vremya* [New Times] from Riga, by tearing up the tracks at night, rebels have caused a military train carrying sappers that had been deployed to Riga to derail—whereby five men were killed and twenty wounded. The sappers had to retreat to Dünaburg. In the vicinity of Kockenhusen station, the aides of Peterson—the regional boss—were put before a people's court together with Peterson's managing director and killed in an atrocious manner. A strong troop detachment with artillery has arrived in Riga from Tuckum. It threatens to punish the city in an exemplary way if those guilty of the massacre of the garrison aren't handed over.

Riga, December 21. Six citizens of the German Empire, Lieutenant Habenicht, Bader (a teacher), Wotrich (a hunter), Hetmer, Schneepel, and Gerul (a domestic servant), who were being held by the insurgents, have been let free. Lieutenant Habenicht is still definitely in the city, while the others have returned to Germany.

Riga, December 21 (report by the Petersburg Telegraph Agency). Eight mitrailleuses have arrived from Petersburg. Gendarmes from various railroad stations, who have arrived unarmed, report that the insurgents have taken their weapons from them. Insurgents attacked a train transporting coined gold for the state bank in the vicinity of Walk. These were, however, chased away by troops who rushed to the scene, so that the train could make it to Riga and the gold be handed over, unscathed, to the bank.

A NEW CHILDREN'S CRUSADE?

We receive the following interesting piece of news from a reliable source: *Stettin*, December 21. On Saturday a steamer left from Stettin for Riga with 150 armed German students on board, sailing to assist their fellow countrymen in Livonia. The steamer is called *Ostsee* and is scheduled to reach Riga on Tuesday.

If the news is accurate, then world history will certainly weave a laurel wreath as hats for this corps of valorous little German boys, rushing to help the Junkers* cornered in Russia.

---

* Luxemburg is referring to the fact that many of the ethnic Germans living in the area were large landowners.

The Germans in the Baltic Provinces[*]

All the bourgeois papers are full of shocking news about atrocities carried out by the "Latvians" in the Russian Baltic provinces. Tears are flowing everywhere about the poor German victims of the Latvian people's rustic wickedness. Collections have already been organized for these victims, and the nation's noblest and finest—from whom not the faintest touch of human sympathy could be extracted after the outrageous atrocities committed by *Cossacks* against defenseless Russian people—are now besides themselves with pious rage because of the mistreatment endured by their compatriots. And yet no one has either tackled or answered the following question, from any point of view: From where did these sudden outbreaks of hatred against the Germans in the Baltic provinces erupt? *Who* are these *Germans* and *who* are these *Latvians* who are currently engaged in open civil war with each other? The following private correspondence from Livonia gives us ample answers to these *decisive* questions:

Riga, December 18. You already know fine and well that the first news reports about developments here that have been trumpeted out into the world feature colossal exaggerations, and generally give an utterly unclear picture of developments. There were no signs of murders or conflagrations, either here in Riga or in other *municipalities*. Labor had simply announced a general strike and then acted on that, because Latvian Social Democracy assumed that this had already been announced for the whole of Russia. The outstanding discipline by which the workers here followed Social Democracy's watchwords, bringing the whole life of industry and trade to a standstill, was certainly capable of putting the bourgeoisie into real shock—and also of making them furious. Yet that in itself is not enough to explain the general panic. Another movement needs to be examined in this context, *our rural movement*. It needs first to be said, that here in the Baltic provinces, in the heart of the countryside, utterly unique relationships rule the day. The prevailing form of land ownership is the highest rung on the ladder of chivalric large land ownership, i.e., clearly a latifundia economy.

In *Livonia*, for example, about one-third of the whole land area consists of large pieces of land, owned by the aristocracy, while the same people own roughly *half* of the same type of estates in *Courland*. There is, opposite to these, a large mass of the *rural proletariat*, exploited in an inhuman way through the system by which leased land is procured from the latifundia estates. And yet the lot of the east Prussian

---

[*]   This article is unsigned, but is most probably from Luxemburg. It is similar in structure to her column "The Revolution in Russia," through which she often informed her readers about revolutionary events in Riga, and about the problems of nationalism. The article first appeared in *Vorwärts*, No. 300, December 23, 1905, entitled "Die Deutschen in den Ostseeprovinzen." It is translated (by Henry Holland) from Luxemburg's *Gesammelte Werke*, Vol. 6, pp. 842–4.

"bonded servants" still sometimes appears enviable in comparison to the Helot* existence of rural workers in Livonia and Courland. What, however, colors this purely class relationship in a peculiar way is the fact that the whole of the landowning aristocracy are, without exception, *German Junkers*, while the rural proletariat is *Latvian*. Religion is irrelevant here. Both Latvians and Germans are Lutheran. And the difference of nationality would of course normally be irrelevant, because rural Latvian folk are very good-tempered and not bothered about anyone's nationality. It is only the Germans who have made themselves hated for being brutal owners of the latifundia. Because, as far as the *Germans* were concerned, national hatred did of course play a part. They didn't just treat the poor Latvian peasants with the usual Junker inconsideration, but also displayed the full disdain of the "hegemonic nationality." And, in fact, from the perspective of the Latvian peasant, the rulers for decades weren't the Russian Cossacks but rather the German owners of feudal estates who treated the rural population like despicable slaves without any rights. It must be added that the Protestant *clergy* also rank among the large landowners here. These aren't the typical Lutheran country pastors like in other northern countries. No, the gentlemen clergy here sit together at the same heavily laden table with the Junkers, with whom they are intermarried and interbred, and help these aristocrats break the backs of the Latvian country folk twice and thrice, keeping them hostage to the system.

This ruling Junker caste was until very recently content with Russian absolutism's rule-of-the-lash, as were the German bourgeoisie in the municipalities, who were no less industrious in nourishing themselves through the exploitation of the *Latvian* industrial workers. Of course, the misters grumbled loudly about the *Russification* of schools and civil society. Yet it was their own brutal class rule that had created the very situation whereby the Russification of the schools could enable poor Latvian people to attend middle- and higher-level schools for the first time! As long as the German Junkers lorded over the teaching system, the sons of Latvian people were not allowed to slip through the gates of the higher-level schools! All in all, however, the Baltic noble families had and have such strong connections and influence at the tsarist court in Petersburg that the peasants were entirely within their power.

The Social Democratic movement increased rapidly in recent years, at first in the *municipalities*. January 22 of this year was the starting signal for a series of general strikes executed in impeccable fashion in Riga, Tallinn, and Jelgava, etc. Social Democracy started to gradually spread its sphere of influence in the heart of the countryside. And then, when the first signs could be seen that the slaves wanted to raise "their hackles," the Baltic German Junkers immediately pulled all strings in Petersburg at their disposal to obtain "increased protection" over the people in Livonia and in Courland. All these lords "of this and that" painted such a threatening picture of the situation in the Baltic provinces for the tsarist camarilla that they

---

*   The Helots were the slave class of ancient Sparta.

naturally found willing listeners among the government of the knout, who "blessed" these lands by imposing martial law right at the start of the year.

One example may serve as demonstrative for many to describe how the Junkers began to champion their "holy rights" with the help of the nagaika. In spring of this year—I cannot recall the date more exactly at this moment in time—one of the mighty of this German Junker clan, *Prince* [Anatoly Pavlovich] *Lieven*, set out to "pacify" all peasants in the whole region. *With a detachment of Cossacks*, he suddenly ambushed the village of *Szagarren*, which still belongs to the governorate of Kaunas but is close to the border, and ordered all the peasants to be *flogged*. A bookkeeper by the name of Janson was also whipped on the order of this superior human being. Because Szagarren actually belonged to the estate of the Russian prince Naryshkin and the violent Junker happened to stroll into another wolf's territory, Naryshkin brought charges concerning the Cossack raid before the Qadi court,* and Prince Lieven was given seven days house arrest. And that is how a German aristocrat does business, with the support of martial law and with the help of the Cossacks.

It is not hard to imagine what hatred and fury have stored themselves up in the hearts of Latvian country people in the course of these last months! The current uprising is over nothing more than repaying their debts. The people's readiness to use violence exactly matches the long years of violent exploitation and repression by the German Junkers. The brutal "gentlemen" are simply harvesting the hatred that they sowed among their slaves. Prince Lieven, the hero of Szagarren, was, as we see, one of the first victims to be killed. And yet there are also other ways in which the Junkers are harvesting the fruit of their own seed. The long condition of war, houses for Cossacks in the villages—all this has *shaken up rural workers politically*, and has *revolutionized* them. This educational experience has enabled the Latvian peasants to quickly grasp what urban Social Democracy had tried earlier with the greatest effort to make clear to them. Now the peasants understand that they must hate both the Junkers and absolutism, and that their closest ally is the urban worker. The atrocities of the rural unrest are the work of the German Junkers, yet the political education crystallizing out of the unrest, and now being strongly expressed, is the work of Latvian Social Democracy. Masses of rural workers are now streaming into our midst under the universal banner of a democratic republic for the whole empire.

---

* The writer is here ironically comparing justice in this area to an Islamic "Qadi" Court, which was responsible for the application of Islamic law at the bequest of the Caliph. The comparison is somewhat misleading, however, since over time Qadi judges enjoyed a great degree of autonomy—largely because the law applied by them was not seen as the creation of the ruler or Caliph, but rather as derived from Islamic texts that required close and careful debate and interpretation.

The Revolution in Russia
[December 24, 1905]*

The International Socialist Bureau has forwarded the following appeal to us:

To the workers of all countries!

January 22 will be the first anniversary of the decision by Nicholas II and his advisers to massacre the workers, who had demonstrated unarmed to request an end to the despicable war, an improvement in their unbearable conditions, and the granting of the most basic human rights that the proletariat already possesses in all other countries.

This day of January 22 is a decisive date in the Russian Revolution. This was the day which opened wide the eyes of the people. It annihilated all illusions of those who still believed in the tsar's good will. It ultimately gave the signal for outright battle, for a fight to the death between the working class and the last supporters of a regime that has long been damned by the consciences of all honest humans.

In vain, tsarism attempts to escape its destiny through initiating new crimes. He, tsarism, mobilizes the Cossacks; he arms and organizes the *Black [Hundreds]*; he stirs up sinister characters against the Jews, against Armenians, against the intelligentsia, against everyone whose opinions, nationality or race brands them as an enemy of the bureaucracy and of absolutism. The revolutionary proletariat has been resisting and opposing these despicable politics for a year now, with the most wonderful exertion of effort that a people have ever used in a struggle for liberation.

The whole empire is in the grip of a continuous revolution. Strikes after strikes. Not a single month goes by without new efforts that tear new concessions from the tsar, preparing the ground for his final fall, and making that unavoidable. During the days that followed January 22, a strike of 600,000 workers takes place in Poland,† which soon spreads to the whole empire, with the slogan "Death or freedom!" shouted out as a type of solution. Kalyayev executes Grand Duke Sergius. The working class rejects the tentative efforts of the Shidlovsky Commission and of Kokovtsov, the finance minister.‡ Peasants' revolts break out, and rural folk appropriate the

---

* This article first appeared in *Vorwärts*, No. 301, December 24, 1905, under the title "Die Revolution in Rußland." It is translated (by Henry Holland) from Luxemburg's *Gesammelte Werke*, Vol. 6, pp. 851–6.

† The Polish strike occurred on January 28, 1905.

‡ On January 29, 1905, faced with the growing strike movement, the tsarist government formed the Shidlovsky Commission. According to the official press release, it was intended to resolve the causes of the popular dissatisfaction. Vladimir Kokovtsov was finance minister in Sergei Witte's cabinet from February 5 to October 24, 1905.

manorial estates, whose owners have fled to the cities. The sailors of the *Potemkin* join the people's struggle, and the flag of the "International"* is hoisted on the tsar's ships. Groups of soldiers, their number growing by the day, refuse to shoot down their brothers. Military high command exposes the Manchurian Army to the most ghastly suffering, a scandal indeed—and then doesn't dare to recall them. Political parties come out into the open for the first time. Promises are made to them, and they are promised concessions. The tsar proclaims his "unshakable will" to convene a national assembly, yet one selected only by nobles and the rich, with the whole of the working class and the educated intelligentsia excluded. He orders the revolution's unforgettable heroes to be hung—Vasilev, Gershkovich, Kasprzak, Krause, Chmelbitzky, Nikoforov, and others. He orders Petrov, Titov, Adamenko, Tchrony, Mocheslover, and other comrades in the outraged fleet to be shot. But the martyrs' blood is rich in blessings. The continually growing socialist movement unites the urban proletariat, the rural folk, and the liberal elements of the bourgeoisie in an act of mighty, communal effort, or through ravishing violence. The general strike breaks out in all large municipalities. Transport routes are disrupted and Russia gets cut off from the rest of the world. The government is hit by the railroaders strike in the heart of its being, and, after several days of futile resistance, Nicholas II recognizes his defeat in solemn style with the *manifesto of October 30*, in which he announces new concessions.

The history of this year of 1905 has made the value of Russian socialism clear to the world. It has shown the prophecy articulated at the international congress in Paris in 1889 to be true: "The revolutionary movement will be victorious in Russia as a workers' movement or it will not be victorious at all."[†] But now, thanks to the willingness to sacrifice, thanks to the proletariat's devotion and heroic courage, that movement is now certain of victory, and already, everywhere in Europe, the inescapable breakdown of tsarism is shaking all supporters of the reaction at their foundations. Yet the work is incomplete. If the revolution has already triumphed in people's minds, then she has, as a material fact, only just begun. The proletariat will have to continue their struggle for months and maybe for years, before Russian Socialism can celebrate a decisive victory.

In this struggle, which is also our struggle, the Russian proletariat has to be able to rely on our moral support and just as much on the material support of the whole International. It also entirely matches with our conception that the comrades in the United States have sought to move the affiliated parties to celebrate this historic day, January 22, in festive fashion—through a spirited appeal to the International Socialist Bureau.

---

[*] That is, the red flag of revolution.

[†] Plekhanov had stated years earlier: "To conclude, I repeat and emphasize: *the revolutionary movement* in Russia will *triumph as a workers' movement*, or it will never *triumph*." See *Protokoll des Internationalen Arbeiter-Congresses zu Paris. Abgehalten vom 14. bis 20 Juli 1889* (Nürnberg: Wörlein, 1890), p. 63.

We're convinced that our proposal will fall everywhere on friendly ears, where a socialist consciousness has been woken. And that our guiding message should read thus: *On Monday, January 22, or at least on the evening before (Sunday), all associations of all affiliated socialist parties will hold mass gatherings, and, where possible, parades. The speakers, designated in advance, will remember the heroic struggle of our Russian brothers, and a collection of money will be organized, in order to aid with all means those fighting against tsarism for the holy cause of freedom. The collections should be conveyed to the central organization of the affiliated parties or to the International Socialist Bureau.*

Down with autocracy! Long Live international Socialism!

The International Socialist Bureau: Argentina: A. Cambier, M. Ugarte; Australia: H. Dierks; Bohemia: A. Nemec, F. Soucu; Bulgaria: G. Kirkov; N. Sakasov; Denmark: P. Knudsen, C. M. Olsen; Germany: A. Bebel, P. Singer; England:[*] H. Hyndman, J. Keir Hardie; France: J. Jaurès, E. Vaillant; Holland: P. Troelstra, H. van Kol; Italy: E. Ferri, F. Turati; Japan: Sen Katayama; Luxembourg: Dr. Welter; Norway: A. Eriksen, Olav Kringen; Austria: Dr. V. Adler, F. Skaret; Portugal: A. Guecco; Switzerland: O. Rapin; Sweden: H. Branting, C. Wickman; Serbia: B. Stoyanovitch; Spain: P. Igselias, F. Mora; Hungary: E. Garami, J. Weltner; United States: D. de Leon, M. Hilquit.
The Executive Committee (Belgium):
Eduard Anseele. Émile Vandervelde. Camille Huysmans, Secretary.[†]

THE GENERAL STRIKE IN PETERSBURG

Petersburg, December 23 (report from the Petersburg Telegraph Agency). Today 82,000 workers who are subjected to the factory inspectorate are on strike; this is two-thirds of this category of workers.

THE COUNTERREVOLUTION'S VIOLENT TRICKS

The police stopped all forms of assembly in Petersburg yesterday, and the office of the Association of Workers' Deputy Councils was forcibly dispersed. Then, in the evening, the Employees' Association Council was broken up too. Numerous persons were arrested yesterday. Police and military surrounded a house in the district of Vasilevsky-Ostrov, where they suspected a sitting of the executive

---

[*] The document was less than accurate here, since the two delegates represented not just English but *British* socialism. Keir Hardie was himself of Scottish origin.

[†] See *Archivalische Forschungen zur Geschichte der deutschen Arbeiterbewegung*, Vol. 2/V: *Die Russische Revolution von 1905–1907 im Spiegel der deutschen Presse*, edited by Leo Stern (Berlin: Rütten & Loening 1961), p. 1137. See also *Bureau Socialiste International. Comptes Rendus des Réunions Manifestes et Circulaires. Vol. I 1900–1907*, edited by Georges Haupt (Paris: La Haye, 1969).

committee was taking place. Almost all the house's residents were arrested and carted off to the police station, where further mistreatment occurred.

Petersburg, December 22 (report from the Petersburg Telegraph Agency). A government communiqué encourages the capital's population *not to lose its nerve regarding* the announcement of the general strike. All precautionary measures have been taken to guard against serious disturbances, and all those that are still developing *will be nipped in the bud.* The governors of those governorates in which martial law has not been imposed have been permitted to act independently on the authority that has been granted to them, by granting petitions from large landowners who request authorization *to build police stations at their own cost.*

THE BATTLE OF THE MOSCOW BARRICADES

Moscow, December 22. This evening, a detachment of dragoons on Strastnoi Square were forced into responding to shots from the workers' guard by (!) (semi-official report), *releasing a salvo.** *Eight workers* and *two dragoons* were wounded. Soon after, workers installed barbed wire defenses here and on the old Triumph Square, and cordoned off the sidewalk with store signs. Cavalry and infantry dispersed the crowd by firing into the air. At 11 p.m., troops stormed the *barricade* built on Tverskoy Boulevard from three rows of wire, iron doors, and planks, etc. By midnight the street was free again. *Eleven workers were wounded* in battle.

Moscow, December 22 (report from the Petersburg Telegraph Agency). According to precise investigations, *seventy people were arrested* from the 10,000 persons at the *aquarium,* all of whom were surrounded by troops. After verification of their identity and after their revolvers were taken from them, these people were set free again. Many daggers, revolvers, and knives were found in the garden. Two persons were injured due to carelessness.

Today gatherings were held *around red flags* in many squares, at which *speeches were held.* Cossacks and dragoons dispersed the crowds. *Scuffles* broke out on one square. The police *arrested forty-two persons,* including both male and female students. As these were being transported to the police station, *the crowd attacked the transport, and fired off a number of revolver shots;* one policeman was injured.

Moscow, December 23 (report by the Petersburg Telegraph Agency). In the office of the political police, two bombs destroyed the wall, the ceiling, and the interior. A law enforcement officer and a member of the uniformed police were killed, and one soldier was wounded.

---

*   We have reproduced here Luxemburg's idiosyncratic literary technique of placing an exclamation mark *before* a piece of information. She does this to warn her readers that the information she has just provided comes from a semi-official report and should therefore be treated with skepticism.

IN THE PROVINCES

Petersburg, December 23. The Petersburg Telegraph Agency disseminates the following report: The factory workers are on strike in *Kostroma*, while in *Vilnius*, the Vilnius–Baranovichi and Baranovichi–Bialystok lines of the Lithuanian railroad network are still running. The Luninez to Rovno, and Luninez to Pinsk routes are however on strike. In the north, it was principally the Baranovichi Railroad Brigade who refused to join the strike. In *Rostov-on-Don, lots of railroad routes* stopped work yesterday. Today, tools were downed on the trams, in the printing presses, and in many factories and workshops. In *Saratov*, the railroad workshops on the Ryazan–Ural route have been celebrating. In *Kiev*, the complete network of the Southeast Railroad is joining the strikers today.

IN SOUTH RUSSIA

Report in from *Lviv*: According to reports received here, *transport should be brought to a halt* today on the south Russian railroads.

MARTIAL LAW IN POLAND

Alexandrovo, December 22 (from a private correspondent). Martial law war has been reintroduced *in the whole kingdom of Poland.*

Warsaw, December 22 (private report from *Vorwärts*). The party paper *Trybuna Ludowa* [People's Tribune] is being seized, issue by issue. Today the printer was forced to sign a declaration stating that he would no longer print the paper. Several arrests have been carried out among reporting and editing staff. The manuscripts of issue No. 5 have been sequestrated. We will self-evidently begin publishing a new paper in the next few days.

Tallinn, December 23. All the factories and workshops here have been *closed.* Several agitators have been arrested. For their part, the *railroaders have decided to go on strike.*

Petersburg, December 23. Two battalions of guards and a machine-gun detachment have arrived in Tallinn. From Petersburg, the Empress's Ulanen Guard, infantry, artillery, and machine guns are being deployed to Riga.

The Revolution in Russia
[December 28, 1905]*

STREET FIGHTS IN MOSCOW

Moscow, December 24 (report from the Petersburg Telegraph Agency). Today the insurgents rebuilt the *barricades* at all the points where they were destroyed yesterday. Brest Street is full of barricades right up to the train station. Cannons have been brought into action again on Strastnoi Square. At the Patriarch Ponds, on Bronnya Street, at Karetnyi Rjad, the Petrovka, and the Tverskaya, rebels are exchanging fire with troops. In the plundered Von Thorbeck arsenal, an "infernal machine" exploded last night, causing the neighboring Hotel Metropole to be set on fire.[†] The fire was soon extinguished. An attempt made to plunder the Van Brabetz arsenal turned out, however, to be unsuccessful. The shooting let up this morning. Two hundred had been counted wounded by early this morning. The number of dead has not yet been determined. The artillery has been firing against the barricades since early this morning. Firemen set fire to the barricades. Clashes, which kicked off on the Tverskaya and on other streets, became particularly heavy on the Tverskaya Boulevard and the surrounding streets. The rebels wounded twenty gendarmes. There were also clashes in the suburbs this evening. A bomb was thrown on the Sretenka. The stations are occupied by troops. The Union of Unions passed a motion to maintain the general strike, but not to participate in the armed rebellion.

Moscow, December 25 (report from the Petersburg Telegraph Agency). Three hundred men from a revolutionary militia arrived here this morning at around 11 a.m. on a special train into Perovo station belonging to the Moscow–Kazaner railroad: 2,000 striking workers gathered in this railroad's locomotive depot, including a few hundred men belonging to revolutionary militias. The crowd then occupied a neighboring grocery store, and shot at troops standing beside the station, who returned cannon shot. At around 1 p.m., the building burned down in which the grocery store was housed. Meanwhile, revolutionaries in the Yaroslavl railroad workshops fired at the Nikolayevsky railway station, in the vicinity of the store. A detachment of grenadiers responded from the roof of the station. Lyubertsy and Perovo stations, where red flags are flying, are currently in revolutionary hands.

---

* This article first appeared in *Vorwärts*, No. 302, December 28, 1905, under the title "Die Revolution in Rußland." It is translated (by Henry Holland) from Luxemburg's *Gesammelte Werke*, Vol. 6, pp. 857–61. It is based on reports from December 23 to 27, 1905. *Vorwärts* had stated on December 24, 1905, that the next issue would be published on December 28.

† An "infernal machine" was a term used in the nineteenth and early twentieth centuries for a type of explosive device used for military or terrorist purposes and detonated by a timer or sensor.

THE BATTLE GOES ON

The *Local Advertiser* publishes the following private report: *Petersburg*, December 26, 11:40 p.m. Terrible news has arrived from Moscow about the street battles from the last few days. Around *10,000 dead and wounded* are said to have been counted in the city. *The battle is still going on*, especially around the train stations and the factories of the Prokhorovs, where 3,000 armed workers engaged in combat with the military who wanted to disarm them.[*] The battle lasted all day long, resulting in many dead and wounded. Then the revolutionaries fired at the prison, whereupon the military guard returned fire. The revolutionaries are building barricades ceaselessly, which the artillery then shoots down. The military is staying loyal to the government; the soldiers who haven't sworn the loyalty oath are locked into their barracks. The instigators intend *to build a ring of barricades around the center of the city*, in the hope that the military will finally join them. The artillery destroys the barricades with grenades, while the fire brigade sets light to wooden obstacles. During one meeting with 10,000 participants, it was said that soldiers were also present. It was proposed to give them an ovation, applauding their attendance. Yet in doing that, a rumor started, spreading the misunderstanding that the military were coming, and a terrible panic ensued. Everyone started running away, leading many to be crushed and wounded. It was decided during the meeting to lock up Admiral Dubasov, the governor-general of Moscow, and the city's chief of police, Baron Medem.

The following report from London: *London*, December 27, 12:20 p.m. According to the latest news that has arrived in Petersburg by railroad via Odessa and from Moscow, as telegraphed to the *Times*, the *revolutionaries have captured the Sukharev Tower* on Sadovaya Street and have positioned machine guns there. On the Red Square, enormous crowds have gathered, where *a heavy battle* is being fought out. The First Don Cossacks, the Tver Dragoons, and the Resoizer Infantry have *mutinied* and are being held under arrest at barracks. Attempts to capture Nikolayevsky station failed. At least 2,000 persons had been killed by Sunday. On Monday, Admiral Dubasov telegraphed that *15,000 persons are dead and wounded*, with him calling the situation *very serious*. According to the latest news, the situation has not essentially changed. The revolutionaries are not making progress, but they are not yet showing any *signs of exhaustion*.

GENERAL STRIKE AND STREET BATTLES IN SOUTH RUSSIA

Petersburg, December 27. The Petersburg Telegraph Agency disseminates the following report: The *general* strike began in *Kharkiv* on the twenty-fifth of this

---

[*]   Timofei Prokhorov and Konstantin Prokhorov were co-owners of the famous Three Mountains Factory in Moscow. For more on this, see Boris B. Gorshkov, *Russia's Factory Children: State, Society, and Law, 1800–1917* (University of Pittsburgh Press, 2009), p. 161.

month. Artillery fired two shells destroying the walls of the Helfreich factory, where workers had locked themselves in. Workers rushed to the scene from the locomotive factory to relieve their comrades, and threw two bombs. There were also armed clashes at the train station and in the middle of the city. According to the official report, *nine persons were killed*, more than 200 wounded, and 138 arrested. There were many disturbances during the night. A strike broke out yesterday in *Odessa*. Even the pharmacists are on strike. Work has stopped in the port. Steamers cancelled their trips. Goods trains are not departing: passenger trains are traveling as far as Zhmerynka. The port workers have decided to protect the population in the event of disturbances. At *Kozaityn Station* clashes erupted between workers and troops. *Six rail employees* were *killed*, and roughly *fifteen wounded*. The *arrests* are continuing in *Saratov*.

Kiev, December 27. Attempts to initiate a *general strike* have succeeded. Factories, schools, [drivers of] horse-carriages, and railroad administrations are all striking; the newspapers, too, are absent. On three separate occasions during recent nights, the gendarmerie forced entry into the apartments of the most highly regarded families and searched the properties. The *mass arrests* have continued. This has caused such a stir that the general public has killed two spies on the streets, in broad daylight. The military have posted sentries on all streets. The Black Hoard is being held at the ready; they have slaughtered two Jews. *A bloody confrontation* played itself out at the train station, between revolutionaries, strikebreakers, and the military.

BLOODY BATTLES IN CENTRAL RUSSIA

Tambov, December 24 (report from the Petersburg Telegraph Agency). The cities of Tambov and Kozlov and the administrative districts belonging to them have been declared to be under the rule of martial law. A *state of siege* has been imposed on more than ten other municipalities and their districts. The brigadier, Lieutenant General Klawer, has been granted the authority and powers of the governor-general. Bombs and weapons were sequestered during the *arrest* of a crowd of armed people.

GENERAL STRIKE AND STREET BATTLES IN THE CAUCASUS

Tbilisi, December 26. Here, the Mohammedans and the Armenians* have *agreed peace with each other*, while the *strike of the postal civil servants*, however, continues and has developed into a *general strike* since yesterday. The Social Democrats have seized the railroad. Transports have been reduced to a bare

---

    * To authentically convey Luxemburg's original tone, we have used the archaic term "Mohammedans" here, as Luxemburg writes "die Mohamedaner" at this point in her original text.

minimum. Street battles are taking place in other localities between Socialists and Cossacks.

UPRISING IN LIVONIA

Königsberg in Prussia, December 26. The following news has been received from Liepāja via Chernyshevskoye. by courier and from a reliable source, and dated December 23. From it we conclude that the situation in Liepāja must be seen as very serious. Due to the strike of the post, telegraph, and rail civil servants, which recommenced recently, the city is more-or-less entirely cut off from the rest of the country and from abroad. Utter anarchy prevails in rural areas, and remote country districts are in complete disarray.

SEMI-OFFICIAL PACIFYING LIES

Petersburg, December 27 (report from the Petersburg Telegraph Agency). All newspapers appear again in the city today; a large section of the factory workers is still on strike. Murders of police officers in working-class districts occur often, and small clashes with Cossacks also occur. Operations have not yet started on all routes of some rail companies, for example on the Baltic Railroad. Attempts are being made on the border to disrupt services on the Warsaw Railroad. Government circles are of the opinion, as communicated in *Slovo* [The Word], that peace will be restored in Moscow in two or three days. The destruction caused by cannon shot is very large indeed. Yesterday evening, the closure of the sprawling Ushnerov printing works was begun, in which insurgents had held police officers and other persons captive. The bombardment was still continuing at 11 p.m.

ARRESTS

Petersburg, December 26 (report from the Petersburg Telegraph Agency). During a meeting last night, the whole general staff of Petersburg's "armed cohorts" was arrested: a total of forty-nine men including Engineer Schulman, the staff leader. The authorities sequestered plans, official papers, infernal machines, and other weapons.

Petersburg, December 23 (report from the Petersburg Telegraph Agency). In view of the strike, all assemblies of a public or private character in the city at which political or economic matters are discussed have been forbidden until further notice.

TSARISM'S NEW STILLBIRTH

The *right to vote for the Imperial Duma* has been granted to the following categories by imperial ukase: (1) Owners of real estate which is liable to taxation, providing that they have owned the same for at least one year; (2) owners of industrial enterprises which are liable to taxation; (3) persons who pay personal property tax; (4) persons who pay business tax; (5) persons who possess a property in their own name; (6) persons who receive a salary from the state, the zemstvos, municipal councils, or the railroads; these persons also have the right to participate in the urban voters' conferences. Workers from factories with fifty or more workers have the right to send delegates into the electoral assemblies on the following basis: workers from factories that employ between fifty and 1,000 workers may send one delegate; and workers from factories that employ over 1,000 workers may send one delegate per 1,000 workers. The actual voters will then be voted by these delegates.

The first Duma sitting can be opened after the senate has published a list containing at least half of the total number of members of the senate. The emperor* has ordered the votes to be speeded up, so that the minister of the interior can take measures ensuring that the Duma can assemble as quickly as possible, and so that the same institution can announce special instructions concerning co-option votes.

---

*   That is, Tsar Nicholas II.

The Revolution in Russia [December 29, 1905]*

THE BATTLES IN MOSCOW

… continue in an unimaginably bitter fashion. According to the latest reports, troops haven't succeeded in the slightest in defeating the heroic, battling revolutionaries. It even appears open to question whether the government will be able to conquer the insurgency at all. According to the admissions of the terrorists in the government, the Cossacks have been carrying out monstrous and bestial acts.

The reports state: *London*, December 27 (report in *Den* [The Day]). The following was telegraphed via Petersburg: The revolutionaries' fight is continuing with *unabated energy*. Alongside Cossacks and the police, infantry were also used against them today. They consist of 60,000 students, workers, skilled manual workers, and unemployed persons, in possession of *six machine guns* of the latest type. They are fighting in three detachments and *the women* are excelling due to their outstanding *bravery*. The fighting today has been extraordinarily heavy. A spark-gap telegraph system is planned between Petersburg and Moscow. The whole Ural railroad is in the hands of the insurgents.

Moscow, December 27. Wolff's Telegraph Office. The revolutionary militia's front stretches from Kazanskaya station and runs for roughly ten kilometers. Because the districts captured through use of barricades have been extended so considerably, *the government troops' advance has been impeded*. Artillery was used in the early hours of the afternoon against the insurgents, who are now into their fourth day of imposing a state of siege on the city. Barricades continued to be built up at new points and now surround the city. Revolutionaries suddenly appeared in the Alexander Garden in the Kremlin and exchanged fire with soldiers, during which two soldiers and three revolutionaries fell. Only the Nicholas Rail is working from all the rail companies in the Moscow railroad hub.

Petersburg, December 28 (report in *Den* [The Day]). The Semyonovsky Lifeguard Regiment that was deployed to Moscow is under the command of General Stackelberg, who also brought important orders for Admiral Dubasov, the governor-general of that city. The Semyonovsky Regiment is taking three days rations, and 195,000 cartridges with it.

The insurgency has now spread to the areas surrounding Moscow, *parts of the military are totally exhausted*, and many officers have had to resign their

---

* This article first appeared in *Vorwärts*, No. 303, December 29, 1905, under the title "Die Revolution in Rußland." It is translated (by Henry Holland) from Luxemburg's *Gesammelte Werke*, Vol. 6, pp. 862–4. The article is based on reports received until December 28, 1905, the date that she left for Warsaw in order to take part in the revolution there.

commands because they were having *nervous breakdowns*. It still has not proved possible to defeat the revolutionaries. The number of armed revolutionaries is still very considerable; four English-made machine guns in their possession are in constant use. *Thirty houses were demolished yesterday.* The city is on fire at various points because of the dreadful artillery fire. *A large proportion of the inhabitants have perished in the flames;* whoever managed to escape *was showered with bullets, causing many victims to fall.* The cannonade lasted for the whole day yesterday. Theft and plundering are the order of the day.

Petersburg, December 27 (report by Laffa's News Agency). Following on from the disarming of the proletariat in Petersburg, a regiment was dispatched from here to Moscow today, and a brigade of artillery to Riga. This morning troops surrounded houses inhabited by 3,000 workers from the Putilov works, taking over 1,000 revolvers and roughly 100 rifles off them.

Moscow's governor communicated to the minister of the interior that replacements must be found for the Cossacks. *They are receiving strong vodka rations* so that they can cope with the strains of day and night shifts without a break, *but as a result they are entirely out of their minds and are killing undiscerningly everything they meet.*

GENERAL STRIKE

Petersburg, December 28. The general strike has broken out in *Vilnius, Radom, Brest, and numerous other provincial cities.* The police in Kiev discovered a bomb factory in an apartment, and impounded three finished and many unfinished bombs. The First Army Corps, arriving back from Manchuria, is being transported straight to the Baltic provinces to restore order. A regiment of guards has left from Petersburg to Moscow to suppress the disturbances there. The import of grain and pulses has stopped entirely; many trading companies have stopped their payments.

DERAILING TRAINS

Petersburg, December 28 (report in the Petersburg Telegraph Agency). Several casualties occurred on the Baltic Railroad in the night of the twenty-seventh of this month. Sometime after midnight, *the locomotive of a passenger train plunged into water* from a bridge near Raussick, seventy-one kilometers from Tallinn, because the tracks had been torn up. The number of victims is unknown. Because the telegraph system is disrupted, it was not yet possible to confirm whether or not the rumor that a military train with horseman's guard units *traveling* to Tallinn has had an accident. In the same night *two goods trains traveling to Petersburg derailed near Narva, one after each other.* The trains' carriages were *destroyed.* In this case, too, the "accident" was intended with malice.

ROBBERY OF A MUNICIPAL PAYMENT CENTER

Warsaw, December 28. In the night of December 27, revolutionaries organized an *armed robbery on the municipal payment center in the district town of Wysokie Mazowieckie*, in the governorate of Łomża. While the deed was carried out, the entire market was occupied by eighty men. The police fled, and the military was not present after the single small unit that comprised the town's garrison were marched out to Riga. Revolutionaries broke up the weak resistance displayed by a few nighttime sentries through the use of armed force. The door of the safe was blown open using nitrocellulose, and *486,000 roubles were stolen*, from which were 20,000 in gold, 300,000 in paper gold, and 160,000 in silver. The perpetrators then fled in five different directions, some by railroad, and some by horse. A *policeman* who followed one of them was *killed*. Telegraph lines had already been cut in advance.

INDIVIDUALS "TAKE ON" THE NEW ELECTORAL LAW

Russian Correspondence received the following telegram in the night of December 27: One of the *most influential leaders of the zemstvos*, Prince Peter *Dolgurokov*, characterized the new electoral law as a *ridiculous attempt* by a government that is forced to give into public opinion nevertheless to maintain the semblance of acting independently. It is born out of the weakness of not having dared to draw the necessary conclusions from the nation's mood. In comparison with the electoral law of August 6, the new law is doubtless much more democratic, but it has been achieved in such a clumsy, roundabout way that the danger of a revolutionary party boycott has in no way been overcome. This situation is made all the more dangerous by the fact *that the revolutionary mood among the people has grown sizably recently*, a fact proven by events in Moscow. Zemstvo representatives and members of the Constitutional Democratic Party will of course enter the new Duma, but only to turn this into the central point of a struggle for political upheaval in the spirit of real freedom and democratization. In society's higher circles, *a very pessimistic atmosphere prevails concerning the events in Moscow*.

This perspective is made all the more important by the fact that Dolgurokov's mirrors the perspectives of a large section of the zemstvo parties.

New Year, New Struggles*

Everything flows and only change endures. What is a year, when seen not through the eyes of an honest petty bourgeois as one chunk of life of their own little "I," but rather as a time measurement in humanity's forward development, [as against] just the development of a single people? A transient wave in the changing tides of unceasing passing impressions. And yet, how many meaningful initiatives and new social formations, how many new vistas over the historical process of becoming, has this disappearing year brought to us.

The year 1904 left us with no major decisions. The political inheritance it handed on to its successor was incomplete and undefined. The battles on the fields of Manchuria still raged, undecided, in the Far East. Although Japan's young military power had succeeded in pushing back the Russian army bit by bit to the north, the result of this wrestling match was still open at the start of 1905. Port Arthur capitulated during the first days of the New Year already, on January 2, and on January 13 the Japanese general Nogi [Maresuke] entered as victor into the city. In March, Mukden,† the old Manchurian imperial city, fell to the Japanese troops after a mighty battle, and on May 28 the Japanese fleet destroyed the replacement naval squadron from the Baltic, under the command of Admiral [Zinovy] Rozhestvensky, in the Korea Strait. The Russian behemoth's defeat was sealed. By the end of August, the tsar felt forced to agree to a peace settlement of historical significance—not just because it broke Russia's position of political power in east Asia, but most of all because it signals the beginning of a new phase in the struggle for the Pacific, which seems destined to play the same role in the economic life of the most civilized peoples as the Mediterranean played in antiquity and the Middle Ages and as the Atlantic Ocean has played since the discovery of the Americas.

Yet the outbreak of revolution in Russia appears to be more meaningful still for the long-term fate of the European peoples, and especially the proletariat. Violence, blown like a forest fire in a storm, spread through one region after the other, from the banks of the Neva to the Caucasus, from Poland to the Urals. When on Bloody Sunday, January 22, Petersburg's striking workers went on pilgrimage to the Winter Palace under the leadership of Priest Gapon to request the tsar's aid in their moment of destitution, the hearts of the proletariat were still filled with a deep trust and a silent reverence for the *"mild and peaceful tsar."* The shooting by the tsar's henchmen into the beseeching crowd, however,

---

* Although no name is printed below this article, it is nevertheless one of the leading articles written by Luxemburg as chief editor of *Vorwärts*, before her departure to Warsaw. It first appeared in *Vorwärts*, No. 305, December 31, 1905, entitled "Neues Jahre, neue Kämpfe. It is translated (by Henry Holland) from Luxemburg's *Gesammelte Werke*, Vol. 6, pp. 865–9.

† Today this is known as Shenyang.

opened the eyes of the masses, who had still hoped that the tsar's intervention could steer political reform onto the right track. The bestial iniquity of the tsar's creatures jolted the people out of its paralyzed trance. Their hearts were seized with wild violence, and their ebullient outrage caused the ice floes to break up with a crack under the Russian palace of ice.

At first it seemed as if the people's passion, whipped up by the atrocity of Bloody Sunday, would break under tsarism's brutal violence, as if the massacre on January 22 would remain no more than a shocking episode in the history of the Romanovs, written in blood. The Russian press rejoiced together with the German papers, their brothers in spirit, and announced that the oppressive lessons taught by live ammunition had forever rid the "inflamed folk" of their desire for freedom and justice. Even those who knew ordinary life in "holy" Russia better—that revolutionary embers hid amid the ashes—did not imagine public fights on the streets and barricades against the tsarist authority, but rather a slower wrestling match lasting for years, the fight flaring up here and being extinguished there. It was common knowledge, wasn't it, that the times of the Great French Revolution with the masses' heroic readiness for sacrifice were done with, [it being] a now-invisible phase of history which people had survived through. The year 1905 showed how wrong this theory was. The kind of heroic courage shown in battles against the troops of a power fitted out with the most modern weapons, played out in Moscow's streets in the final days of the dying year, was *never* to be seen during the French Revolution.

The largest parts of Russia's industrial regions were gripped by the political mass strike only a few weeks after Bloody Sunday. The strike spread like wildfire, so that by the end of March 150 municipalities had caught the strike fever. The executions of Senator Johnson and of Grand Duke [Sergei Alexandrovich] Sergius followed, then the outbreak of disturbances in the Caucasus, peasant revolts in southwest Russian and the Baltic Sea provinces, a new outbreak of disturbances in Baku, the defection of one part of the Black Sea Fleet, Shuvalov's execution, new clashes in the industrial region of the Vistula Land, and the fights on the barricades Łódź.

The sea of blood turned into a huge fire that burned across the economically developed parts of "holy" Russia, until, the fear rising in him, the "tsar of peace" finally felt himself moved to give up a piece of his egoistic magnificence, in order to douse the raging fire. A constitutional convention of August 19 announced the establishment of an Imperial Duma. Too late, however; these weak concessions were unable to pacify the people's whipped-up passions. New political strikes followed, new street fights, and renewed bloodletting organized by the tsarist cabal of courtiers. The railroad workers' general strike, which brought railroad transport to a standstill for more than a week, was swelled enormously when joined by a general strike of the workers in Petersburg, Moscow, Warsaw, Łódź, Kiev, Kharkiv, Samara, and other cities.

Again, Bloody Nicholas sought to calm the raging sea by allowing a constitutional manifesto to be produced on October 30, which promised to *"Russia's loyal sons"* the *"unshakable foundations of civic freedoms,"* and appointed *Count Witte* as prime minister. But, just one day later, the Social Democratic Party of Russia declared that the tsarist manifesto had no authority to order the proletariat's struggle to stand still. Instead of trailing off, the conflicts against the tsarist system have expanded even further in their scope, and the close of the year is lit up by the bloody red of the December Battle of Moscow.

Tsarism has lost its power. It is rotting in a living body. That said, the time is not yet ripe for the establishment of a socialist state in Russia; but equally impossible is the continuation of a rotten absolutist regime. No, the proletariat has learned too much in the fire of the revolution about how to take hold of its power and its interests; the strivings toward a fundamental reformation of property ownership relationships in the rural economy have put down roots too deep. The only possibility is a liberal-democratic regime strongly influenced by social politics.

The year 1905 was a time of struggles not only for the Russian proletariat, however. The Social Democratic workers marched forward in almost all civilized European states toward their goal, capturing new positions, influenced by events in Russia. In Germany, the year 1905 began with a large coal miner's strike in the Ruhr conurbation. A large number of significant strikes soon attached themselves to the coal miners, first in one part of the Empire, then in another, until a big strike broke out in the Berlin electricity industry. The struggle in Italy commenced in February with a general strike by the railroad employees.* This was followed two months later in France by agreement among the French socialists, establishing a position for the united party in the French parliament that it had never occupied during the ministerialist era.† Social Democratic teachings and the politics of workers' autonomy even gained influence in England, as proven by the trade union congress held in September.‡ And in Austria-Hungary, that double state of half-measures, the Social Democratic proletariat strengthened the zeal with which they are fighting for universal and equal suffrage. Parallel to

---

* In February 1905, Italy's railroad employees carried out their work according to a partially obsolete code of railroad regulations in order to prevent a prohibition on the right to strike. Traffic moved very slowly and trade was paralyzed. On March 4, 1905, Prime Minister Giovanni Giolotti resigned for health reasons. The new Prime Minister, Alesandro Fortis, put a bill before parliament, which would give the railroad workers the status of civil servants, thereby removing their right to strike. On April 17, 1905, a railroad strike was declared against the parliamentary bill, in which all railroad workers participated. On April 21, 1905, work began again.

† This refers to the period 1899–1902, when Alexandre Millerand, then a moderate socialist, joined the French government as minister of commerce. His acceptance of a position in a capitalist government proved extremely controversial and was sharply denounced at the time by Luxemburg and other leftist elements in the Second International.

‡ The annual congress of the English and Welsh trade unions met from September 4 to September 8, in Staffordshire.

these major attacks however, an unflagging, smaller battle stretched out through the whole year, a continuous attempt to stand up against the oppressive tendencies of capitalism, to save and pull together whatever could be drawn from culture and humanity in the service of the proletarian classes.

More than any of its predecessors, this dying year deserves the honorable title of a "year of struggle," a year of exhausting work laden with sacrifices; but also a year of progress, of solidarity, and of the most astonishing self-sacrifice. That said, counterstrokes were not lacking either; the enemy [continued its] convulsive efforts to force the forward march of socialism to a halt. Just shortly before the end of the year, Hamburg's plutocracy announced their new disenfranchisement plans.* Yet though some individual plans have gone astray and some quiet hopes have been disappointed, even a fleeting look back at the road the dying year carved for itself will tell us *that the international proletariat's emancipatory struggle has moved a fair way forward*—and faster than most of us had hoped possible before the year's end.

If we are not entirely deceived, then the newly beginning year promises to bring forward the openings that the old year left behind it. The history of humanity [shows] that the contractions of birth produce the greatest fevers; new social formations thrust themselves toward the light. The new wishes to *become*. The year 1906 will not be short of storms and battles demanding utter devotion and taking heavy casualties. We can rely on our hopes that German Social Democracy will know how to fulfill her world-historical duty as the spearhead of these conflicts, and so I say—*to work, onward to new battles!*

---

* Hamburg's city-state parliament, the senate (the German name is *Der Senat der Hamburger Bürgerschaft*), had introduced a proposal to change the voting law on May 4, 1905, so that voters in Hamburg elections would be classified into three groups according to their incomes. This meant the introduction of a three-tier voting system. The justification for the proposal specifically emphasized that this would be a counterweight to the increasing number of Social Democratic votes. Before the decisive parliamentary vote on this proposal at the end of January 1906, on January 17, 80,000 Hamburg workers downed tools, responding to a call by Social Democrats. The altered voting law was passed on January 31, 1906, by a parliamentary majority.

A Year of Struggle*

The year 1905, as it comes to its close, is being immortalized with fiery letters in the history of the world. A year of revolution, a year of struggle for the emancipation of the proletariat from the yoke of barbaric despotism, for the emancipation of all humanity.

From the bloody day of January 22 in Petersburg, through the bloody days in Warsaw, Łódź, Odessa, and Kharkiv, we have now lived up to the bloody week just past in Moscow.

Tsarist rule has celebrated many victories; the revolution has suffered many defeats. The blood of the workers wet the streets, strikes were starved out by hunger and put down with bullet and bayonet, and the mass of the workers were overpowered. Tsarism kept prevailing over the revolution. And the result? Tsarism capitulated in the face of the revolution, essentially admitting its lawlessness. The absolute monarch has surrendered part of his lawmaking power to a parliament. At the same time that it capitulated, tsarism still wanted to deceive the people. Just two months after its capitulation, we see that the very foundations of tsarist rule are shaking. In Moscow, there is the fire of armed insurrection, as well as armed encounters and preparations for battle in many other cities. The army is in part revolutionized. Peasant revolts have spread over huge stretches of Russia. The Urals are engulfed by armed uprisings. In Livonia, [more] battles and confrontations. In Poland, a general strike in spite of martial law, in spite of tsarism's insane efforts to suppress the strike with the force of the bayonet.

The revolution has been "put down" ten times over during this year, and yet on New Year's Eve, the hot breath of the revolution is still filling the air of the tsarist empire. Ten times the revolution has been defeated, and yet here it stands unvanquished, threatening and powerful, triumphant and conquering, at the end of this year of glory.

The revolutionary working class has made countless sacrifices, paying dearly for every advance toward freedom. And yet, in this struggle, among all the sacrifices, it has not been exhausted but has acquired gigantic strength.

How many of us were there under the banner of revolution at the beginning of this year? And how many of us are there today? We were only a small troop, a mere handful, and today we are legions. Every forward thrust brought us new forces; every clash with tsarism increased our ranks tenfold. In a hailstorm of fire and blood the spirit of the proletariat was hardened. During a century of bondage under the terrible weight of the tsarist yoke their souls groaned and their chests

---

* This article first appeared in *Czerwony Sztandar*, No. 33, December 31, 1905, pp. 1–2. Its title in Polish is "Rok walki." It is translated (by George Shriver and Alicja Mann) from the Polish original.

were choked in the ominous stifling silence. And there were moments when more than one of them lost heart—their spirits fell.

Because it seemed as though the voices of those who tried to awaken the proletariat from lethargy had disappeared without leaving an echo behind, the torches in the watchtowers of the revolution were burning out in the darkness. However, from these flickering sparks there burst forth a flame of boundless enthusiasm—the spirit of sacrifice and heroism blazed up in the hearts of tens and hundreds of thousands. Then, the rattle of gunfire dispersed the fog, and here we stand, arm in arm, the great and powerful army of the revolutionary proletariat. That is what this year has given us.

Strong in our belief, confident in our strength and the sanctity of our cause, we march on to a renewed struggle and to new battles.

A year of struggle is behind us; years of struggle lie ahead.

Our accomplishments have been great, because we have won millions of new fighters for the revolution. We forced tsarism to lay bare its weakness, to acknowledge constitutional rights in principle; absolutism collapsed irretrievably under the blows of the working class. We have wrested from tsarism the promise of freedom of association and assembly and the right to strike; we have torn down the prison walls in which we were confined. We have broken free from our chains.

But the enemy is not yet overthrown, we have not yet struck the weapons from his hands, and the fighters for freedom may not yet dream of a respite, because the enemy is making a renewed effort to gather up his remaining strength. Immediately after October 30* the promise-breaking tsar and his ministers began trying to lie their way out of the situation; one decree followed another! Each was more retrograde than the one before, full of falsehood and deceit. With this swindling they wanted to stupefy the masses.

The press decree was one swindle, and the decree [limiting] the right to organize and strike was another. Meanwhile, a bloody offensive against any and all freedoms was being prepared. The trusted representatives of the proletariat were imprisoned.†

The railroad worker comrades were threatened with jail and hard labor. And, finally, things reached the point of brutal provocation, with martial law being imposed on almost the entire territory of the tsarist empire.

This is an attempt to turn back to the rule of the bayonet and bullet. The bloodstained tsar and his bandit government dreamed of suddenly catching the revolutionary proletariat by surprise—a proletariat worn down by the

---

*   The day Nicholas II issued his constitutional manifesto.

†   This is a reference to the arrest of the St. Petersburg Council (Soviet) of Workers' Deputies on December 3, 1905, with approximately 250 persons being detained, many of them being put on trial a year later. See the 1906 speech in defense of the Soviet by its chairman, Leon Trotsky, in his historical account, *1905* (New York: Random House, 1971).

struggle and weakened by hunger—dreamed that it would not offer resistance. These assassins of the people dreamed that they could succeed even if they had renounced absolute power, dreamed that they could offer crumbs to the working people, deceive them, and even put shackles on them.

They were mistaken. In a single moment, the revolutionary proletariat burst forth to fend off the blow, to thwart the plan of counterrevolution.

And now a new battle is underway all over again, a battle in which we must bring all our forces to bear into action because it is not just a question of holding on to what we have already won, but of winning new gains for the cause of freedom.

This onslaught of the counterrevolution should convince every one of us that there is not and cannot be any question of reconciliation between the revolution and the tsarist regime, that only on the ruins of despotism can we begin to build, that not one stone of this fortress can be left lying on top of another, that the serpent of absolutism must be stomped underfoot once and for all.

The year that already lies behind us was [one of] the mobilization of forces of the proletariat, preparing the way for armed revolution. The year that lies before us will lead to the victory of armed revolution.

In the midst of battle, we begin the New Year.

We do not celebrate the New Year with toasts, nor with the veils [szale] of light-minded wishful thinking. We greet it with the cries of battle.

To arms!

Forward into battle!

Long Live the revolution! Death to Tsarism!

A Glossary of Personal Names

Abramov, Vassili Semyonovich (1873–1937), Russian politician; representative from Stavropol at the 1906 Zemstvo Congress.

Adler, Victor (1852–1918), physician and journalist; cofounder and leading member of the Social Democratic Party of Austria; a spokesperson for reformism in the Second International who was often at odds with Luxemburg; elected to the lower Austrian Diet in 1905; during World War I, supported the war; active in the abortive socialist peace conference in Stockholm in 1917.

Akiba, Joseph Ben (50–132 AD), major rabbinical Jewish scholar and theologian, helped compose parts of the *Mishnah* and *Midrash halakha*; often referred to as "chief of the sages." Executed by Roman authorities in the aftermath of the rebellion against their rule by Bar Kokhba.

Alexander II (1818–81), Russian tsar from 1855 to 1881. Though a staunch monarchist, introduced a number of reforms during his reign, foremost among which was the freeing of the serfs in 1861. Brutally suppressed the Polish uprising of 1863 and incorporated Russian-occupied Poland directly into Russia. Assassinated by a member of the People's Will organization in 1881.

Alexander III (1845–94), Russian tsar from 1881 to 1894. An extremely conservative figure who came to power after the assassination (by a revolutionary) of his father Alexander II. He reversed most of Alexander II's reforms and sought to centralize all power within the monarchy. Strongly supported the policies of Great Russian Chauvinism and sought to destroy any autonomous existence for the many subject nationalities of the Empire.

Auer, Ignatz (1846–1907), leading Social Democrat; 1869, joined the SDAP; 1874, secretary of that party's Executive Committee (Parteiausschuss); 1875, at the Gotha (Unity) Congress, elected as one of the secretaries of the SDAP; member of the Reichstag in the years 1877–78, 1880–81, 1884–87, and 1890–1907; in 1890 became secretary of the Executive Committee (Vorstand) of the SPD; an influential reformist from the mid-1890s on.

Axelrod, Pavel B. (1850–1928), in the 1870s, a Narodnik; in 1883, a cofounder of the Emancipation of Labor Group, an early group of Russian Marxists led by Plekhanov; in 1900, an editor of *Iskra*; after 1903, one of the leading Mensheviks. Opposed the Bolshevik seizure of power; lived remaining years in exile.

Balfour, Arthur James (1848–1930), British politician, leading figure in Conservative Party; first elected to Parliament in 1874. Served as chief secretary for Ireland, during which he harshly suppressed an uprising of Irish peasants. Served as prime minister July 1902 to December 1905; led Conservative opposition in Parliament in the years leading up to World War I. Served as foreign secretary in 1916–19. In 1917, authored the famous Balfour Declaration, in the form of a letter, which favored a Jewish "homeland"—but not a state—in Palestine.

Balmashov, Stepan (1882–1902), Russian revolutionary. As student activist at University of Kiev in 1901, participated in a major student strike; in 1902, as a member of the Socialist Revolutionary Party's Combat Organization, assassinated

Russian minister of internal affairs Dmitry Sipyagin. At his trial, he refused to ask for a pardon and was executed at the notorious Shlisselburg Fortress in May 1902.

Bauman, Nikolai (1873–1905), Russian revolutionary. A student activist from 1891 to 1895, became active in the revolutionary underground with both Populist and Marxist groups; 1896–97 active with the St. Petersburg Alliance for the Liberation of the Working Class; arrested in 1897 and incarcerated in Peter and Paul Fortress. Escaped from Siberia in 1899 and worked with Lenin and the RSDRP in Zurich; returned to Russia in 1901 and in 1903 joined the Bolshevik faction of the RSDRP. Arrested in 1904; upon being released by a group of protesters that attacked the prison, he was beaten to death by supporters of the regime. He was long afterwards considered "a martyr of the revolution."

Bebel, Ferdinand August (1840–1913), German Social Democrat. Member of the Reichstag, 1867–81 and 1883–1913; 1869, cofounder of the SDAP; led the legal and illegal struggle of the party during the period of the antisocialist "exceptional" laws in Germany and contributed in a major way to the founding of the party's central organ Der Sozialdemokrat; 1881–90, a member of the regional legislature (*Landtag*) in the state of Saxony. 1892–1913, one of the two co-chairmen of the SPD; from 1889 on, a leading member of the Second International, and from 1900 on, a member of the ISB.

Bernstein, Eduard (1850–1932), German political journalist and Social Democrat. In 1872, joined the SDAP; 1890–1901, lived in emigration in London; 1896–1900, regular contributor to *Neue Zeit*; from 1896 on, one of the main theoreticians of "revisionism," the view that Marxism should be revised and "modernized" along reformist lines. 1901–1905, editor of *Dokumente des Sozialismus. Hefte für Geschichte, Urkunde und Bibliographie der Sozialismus*; member of the Reichstag in 1902–06 and 1912–18. In 1906, became a teacher at the trade union school in Berlin; regular contributor to *Sozialistische Monatshefte*; resigned from the SPD on pacifist grounds after August 4, 1914, when it supported World War I; in 1916, joined the Social Democratic Working Group (*Arbeitsgemeinschaft*); in 1917, became a member of the USPD; in 1919, rejoined the SPD.

Birilev, Alexei Alexeyevich (1844–1915), Russian admiral, State Council member, and minister of the navy. The offspring of a family from the lower nobility who had to work his way through the ranks, he was given command of the Baltic Fleet in 1904 and appointed Military Governor of Kronstadt. In 1905, he was reassigned as the commander of the Pacific Fleet, but declined the commission while traveling to Vladivostok due to the defeat of Russia by the Japanese at the Battle of Tsushima. Between 1905 and 1907, served as Minister of the Navy.

Blanqui, Auguste (1805–81), legendary French revolutionary socialist and insurrectionist, who was imprisoned for thirty-three years. His disciples played an important role in the workers' movement even after his death. Held that the taking of power could be the act only of a small minority and that there could be no socialist transformation of society without a temporary dictatorship that would first disarm the bourgeoisie, confiscate the wealth of the church and large property holders, and put the great industrial and commercial enterprises under state control. Luxemburg often counterpoised her notion of the spontaneous mass strike to Blanquist conceptions.

Block, Hans (1870–1953), German Social Democrat and historian. In 1872 joined the SDAP; from 1873–84, editor of various newspapers associated with the SPD; member of the Reichstag from 1877 to 1918; chairman of the provisional government following the November 1918 Revolution; from 1919 to 1924, member of the regional legislature of the state of Würtemburg.

Bogdanovich, Nicholas (date of birth unknown–1903), Russian politician and government official; served as governor of Ufa; in 1903, he ordered that troops fire on a crowd of workers who were on strike at the Zlatovist works, resulting in sixty-nine deaths; in retaliation, he was assassinated later that year by Grigori Gershuni, a member of the Socialist Revolutionary Combat Organization.

Bogoraz, Vladimir Germanovich (1865–1936), Russian writer, also used pseudonym N. A. Tann. As a student in the 1880s, joined the Populist movement; while in Siberian exile, conducted ethnographic studies of the culture and folklore of indigenous peoples, especially the Chukhi. Following 1917 Revolution, headed the anthropology and ethnology section of the Academy of Sciences; founded the Institute of the Peoples of the North.

Bömelburg, Theodor (1862–1912), German Trade Union leader and Social Democrat. Originally a bricklayer, he was active in several unions connected to the building trades; in 1899, became chairman of the SPD-affiliated Free Trade Unions. A bitter opponent of Luxemburg, he fervently opposed adoption of the mass strike and sought to silence discussion of the issue within the union movement in 1905.

Bourne, Francis Alphonsus (1861–1935), English Catholic prelate. Ordained as priest in 1884; rector of St. John's Seminary in 1896; archbishop of Westminster from 1903 to 1935; elevated to cardinal in 1911. Supported, with some reservations, Pope Pius XI's encyclical which forbade Catholics to become socialists.

Büchner, Friedrich Karl Christian Ludwig (1824–99), German materialist philosopher and physiologist. Early work focused on the operations of the central nervous system; author of *Force and Matter: Empirico-philosophical Studies* (1855) as well as many other works, such as *Progress in Nature and History in Light of the Darwinian Revolution* (1884); his main contribution was to view mental and "spiritual" activity as nothing but a reflection of physical phenomena. His Darwinian positivist-materialism was highly influential in the Free Thinkers movement of the time.

Bülow, Bernhard Heinrich Karl Martin von (1849–1929), German politician. Served as imperial chancellor and Prussian prime minister. During his tenure as chancellor (1900–1909), became notorious for pursuing a highly imperialistic and aggressive foreign policy, which contributed to Imperial Germany's growing diplomatic isolation. Succeeded in concluding the Treaty of Björkö, a mutual defense accord between Germany and Russia, on July 24, 1905; this, however, did not prevent Russia from moving closer to France politically. Domestically, his government rested on the support of the Conservatives, the National Liberals, as well as the centrists. He kept the Social Democrats out of any real power without repressing them as Bismarck did.

Bulygin, Alexander (1851–1919), Russian politician. Governor of Kaluga and Moscow, 1889 to 1902; right-hand man to governor-general of Moscow, 1902 to 1905; minister of the interior from February 1905 to October 1905. Proposed "Bułygin Constitution" of August 1905, which offered a purely advisory Duma (parliament) that excluded most of the populace rather than being a truly representative legislative assembly. Dissatisfaction with his efforts to appease the revolution through such measures led to a series of mass strikes in September and October 1905, whereupon he was fired by the tsar on October 17, 1905. Between 1913 and 1917, again held high-ranking positions within the tsarist regime. Executed by the Bolsheviks in 1919.

Burke, Edmund (1729–97), British political theorist. Considered a pivotal figure in the formation of modern Conservatism, condemned excessive royal and governmental power while opposing the American and French Revolutions; author of *Reflections on the Revolution in France.*

Burrows, Herbert (1845–1922), British socialist and labor activist. Joined the National Secular Society in 1877; helped found the Aristotelian Society in 1880; cofounder of the Social Democratic Federation in 1881 and supported its embrace of socialism in 1884. Helped organize the match-girls strike in 1888 and later helped organize the Union of Women Match-workers; he was a strong supporter of women's suffrage and the rights of women. As the SDF moved to the right and embraced militarism prior to World War I, he left it in 1911.

Burzev, Vladmir Lvovich (1862–1942), Russian revolutionary and historian. As student at St. Petersburg University and Kazan State University in the early and mid-1880s, became active in the revolutionary movement; exiled to Siberia in 1888; escaped and emigrated to Switzerland and London, where he wrote historical works; returned to Russia in 1905 and edited several historical journals. In 1907, he exposed Yevno Azef, leader of the Socialist Revolutionaries, as a tsarist agent. In 1914, supported Russia's entry into World War I and adopted strongly anti-German views. In 1917, sharply opposed Lenin, whom he accused of being a German agent; was arrested on orders of Trotsky in late 1917; released in 1918 and fled Russia. He supported the counterrevolutionary Whites during the Civil War. In the 1930s, authored a work that showed that *The Protocols of the Elders of Zion* was a forgery.

Campbell-Bannerman, Henry (1836–1908), British politician and statesman; leader of the Liberal Party from 1899 to 1908 and prime minister from 1905 to 1908; supporter of free trade, public education, and improvements in social welfare.

Cavaignac, Louis-Eugene (1802–57), French militarist and general. In 1830, supported the revolution that brought Louis-Phillip to power; was stationed in Algeria from 1832–48, where he was instrumental in carrying out the French conquest of the region. Became de facto head of state in June 1848 and moved to violently crush the revolutionary forces on the streets of Paris; during the week of June 23 to 26, 1848, he was responsible for the deaths of thousands. He lost the subsequent presidential election to Louis Napoleon, who had him briefly imprisoned in 1851.

Chamberlain, Joseph Austin (1863–1937), British Conservative politician. Originally associated with the right-of-center Liberal Unionist Party, he later became a leading figure in the Conservative Party; served as chancellor of the exchequer in 1903 and secretary of state for India in 1915; he was the only Conservative leader of the twentieth century who never became prime minister. In the 1930s, he opposed the policies of appeasement followed by his half-brother Neville Chamberlain, and supported Churchill.

Charles I (1600–49), king of England from 1625 to 1649, when he was executed at the end of the English Civil War by the forces allied with Oliver Cromwell.

Chernyshevsky, Nikolai (1828–89), Russian revolutionary and writer; leader of the Russian democratic movement and socialist movement in the 1850s and 1860s and a founding figure of Populism. Inspired by the materialist philosophy of Ludwig Feuerbach, wrote numerous essays on philosophy and politics; arrested and imprisoned in the notorious Peter and Paul Fortress in 1862, where he wrote his famous novel *What Is to Be Done*. Dostoyevsky subjected the book to withering criticism in his *Notes from Underground*.

Chirikov, Evgeny Nikolayevich (1864–1932), Russian novelist and dramatist. As a student at Kazan University, joined an early Marxist group in the mid-1880s; arrested in 1892 for political involvement with the Populists. Met Maxim Gorky in 1886 and shortly afterward befriended Russian critic and writer Nikolai Chernyshevsky; in 1890s moved to Samara, where he wrote realist stories and plays about the lives of peasants and workers. By 1901 drew closer to Lenin and the RSDRP; author of famous play "The Jews" (1903), which while banned by the authorities became acclaimed internationally. Published stories and essays related to the 1905 Revolution, including "The Rebels" (1905). Moved away from revolutionary politics following the defeat of the revolution; left Russia in 1921, died in exile in Prague.

Chukhnin, Grigory Pavlovich (date of birth unknown–1906), Russian admiral who headed the Black Sea Fleet from 1904 to 1906; highly unpopular with sailors because of repressive measures used against them during the 1905 Revolution. He was killed in 1906.

Combes, Émile (1835–1921), French statesman and politician. Entered French politics in the 1880s as part of the secular democratic (but non-socialist) left; minister of public instruction, 1895; prime minister from June 1902 to January 1905, in which he instituted such reforms as the eight-hour day for miners and public assistance for some of the elderly and mentally ill; a strong advocate of the separation of church and state.

Cunow, Heinrich (1862–1936), German economist, historian, sociologist, and ethnographer. One of the leading theoreticians of the Second International, edited the main theoretical journal of German Social Democracy, *Die Neue Zeit*, from 1917–23; a teacher at the SPD party school from 1906, he wrote a number of influential works on the kinship structure of Australian aborigines, the Inca Empire, ancient technology, and the origin of marriage and the family; initially an opponent of Revisionism, in 1914 he supported Germany's entry in World War I and moved to the right; in his last years, argued that socialism could be peacefully introduced through state intervention in the economy.

Custine, Marquis de (1790–1857), French travel writer. Most famous for his 1839 work *Le Russie en 1839*, which was influenced, in part, by the writings of de Tocqueville. His book presented Russia as an extension of "Asiatic despotism," making him one of the foremost exponents of Orientalism.

Daszyński, Ignacy (1866–1936), Polish socialist politician. In 1892 cofounded the Polish Social Democratic Party (PPSD), a forerunner of the PPS; 1892–1919, leading spokesperson for the PPSD and PPS, and a deputy in the Austro-Hungarian Parliament; closely aligned with the positions of Józef Piłsudski, whom he supported throughout his career; elected to the Polish Parliament in 1919 and served in it until 1930.

David, Eduard (1863–1930), German Social Democrat. In 1896, a leading advocate of reformist positions within the SPD; regular contributor to the revisionist organ *Sozialistische Monatshefte*; member of the Reichstag in 1903–18; a fervent supporter of German expansionism and strongly supported Germany's role in World War I.

Davidson, Georg (1872–1942), German Social Democrat and politician. Editor of *Vorwärts* from 1905 to 1910; member of the Reichstag from 1912–18 as representative of SPD; supported the decision of the SPD to approve war credits to the Kaiser in 1914; member of the National Assembly in 1918 and 1919.

Davidson, Randall (1848–1930), English prelate. Leading figure in the Anglican Church in the late 1800s and served as Archbishop of Canterbury from 1903 to 1928, holding the office longer than anyone since the Reformation.

Dmowski, Roman (1864–1939), Polish politician. Co-founded and led the rightwing party National Democracy, which opposed Germany's policies against Poles by allying itself with its main enemy, tsarist Russia. Sought to establish an independent Poland freed from non-Polish and non-Catholic elements; opposed those who sought a multinational Poland, including Piłsudski; in the 1920s became sympathetic to fascism.

Dolgurokov, Prince Pavel Dimitrievich (1866–1927), Russian politician. A product of one of the oldest aristocratic families in Imperial Russia; instrumental in the founding of the liberal Cadet Party in 1905, which he led between 1911 and 1915. Displayed pacifist leanings prior to the outbreak of WWI in 1914, after which he endorsed the war effort. Supported the Whites during the Russian Civil War and was executed by the Communists in 1927.

Dubasov, Fyodor Vasilyevich (1845–1912), governor-general of Moscow from November 24, 1905 to July 5, 1906.

Dunant, Jean Henri/Henry (1828–1910), Swiss humanitarian activist. Established the Red Cross and was subsequently awarded the world's first Nobel Peace Prize. His business dealings led to financial difficulties, which were eventually remedied by generous gifts from Maria Fyodorovna, the widow of Tsar Alexander III.

Durnovo, Pyotr Nikolayevich (1845–1915), Russian politician and bureaucrat. Graduate of the Imperial Naval School; director of police in 1884; assistant minister of interior in charge of post and telegraph, 1900; remained in this position until 1905, when appointed minister of the interior. Opposed closer ties to the United Kingdom and believed that relations with Germany should be a priority. At the outbreak of World War I, advised Nicholas II that its outcome would lead to a socialist revolution in Russia.

Düwell, Wilhelm (1866–1936), German Social Democrat and journalist. Edited various Social Democratic periodicals; often sided with radical tendencies of the

SPD that were opposed to Revisionism; joined the USDP in 1917 and the German Communist Party (KPD) shortly after its founding in 1919.

Dzierżyński, Feliks (pseud.: Józef) (1877–1926), prominent figure in the Polish and Russian workers' movements. In 1895, member of the Lithuanian Social Democracy; from 1897 on, arrested many times, condemned to internal exile, and escaped; in 1900, a cofounder of the SDKPiL; beginning in 1902, lived as an émigré in Berlin and then in Kraków; member of the SDKPiL's Committee Abroad and, beginning in 1905, of the SDKPiL's Chief Executive Committee; in 1906, representative of the SDKPiL on the Central Committee of the RSDLP; after 1908, lived as an émigré, mainly in Kraków; in Warsaw in 1912, arrested and imprisoned in the Citadel and then in Oryol and Moscow, where he was freed by Russia's February Revolution of 1917; upon his release, joined the Bolshevik Party and worked closely with Lenin, rejecting Luxemburg's criticisms of them; after the Bolshevik Revolution, headed the Cheka, the secret police.

Edward VII (1841–1910), king of the United Kingdom and emperor of India from 1901 to 1910; presided over an empire facing increased competition from Germany and the emerging power of the socialist movement.

Einem, Karl von (1853–1934), Prussian militarist and general. Minister of war from 1903 to 1909, during which he oversaw a massive increase in the development of German armaments, especially of heavy artillery. Commanded the German Third Army during its invasion of France in 1914.

Eisner, Kurt (1867–1919), German Social Democrat and political journalist. Editor of *Vorwärts* from 1899 to 1905; Luxemburg succeeded him as editor after a dispute over the mass strike; 1907–10, chief editor of *Fränkische Tagespost* in Nuremburg; a proponent of ethical-socialist views from a reformist perspective. Although he initially supported Germany's entry into World War I, in 1917 became a member of the USPD; in 1918, took part in preparing for and carrying out the November Revolution in Germany; in 1918–19, president of the short-lived Bavarian Socialist Republic; assassinated by counterrevolutionaries on February 21, 1919.

Elm, Adolph von (1857–1916), German Social Democrat; founder of a credit union associated with the German trade unions.

Fyodorovna, Alexandra (1872–1918), empress of Russia. Wife of Tsar Nicholas II; executed along with the tsar and much of his family in 1918.

Fyodorovna, Maria (1847–1928), Dowager empress of Russia. Wife of Tsar Alexander III and mother of Tsar Nicholas II. Often served as political adviser to Nicholas II, especially in the early years of his reign; at her urging Nicholas appointed conservatives to lead the government in 1904. Strongly opposed the influence of Rasputin on the imperial family; fled Russia after the 1917 Revolution and settled in England.

Feinstein-Leder, Władisław (1880–1938), Polish publicist and Social Democrat. In 1904, a leader of the SDKPiL; imprisoned for political reasons in April 1904 and October 1906 to August 1908; after his release immigrated to Berlin, Zurich, and Paris; temporarily withdrew from politics in 1912 due to the split in the SDKPiL between Luxemburg's and Karl Radek's factions. Worked on academic projects in Switzerland between 1915 and 1918; returned to Warsaw 1918 and co-founded the Communist Party of Poland. After being arrested in 1921, fled to Moscow and became an official of the Comintern as well as a Soviet diplomat; in 1929, commissioned by the Comintern to write a booklet on Leo Jogiches, which was rejected and went unpublished until 1976, when Feliks Tych issued it. Arrested in 1937 in Moscow during Stalin's purges and sentenced to eight years in the gulag; died in 1938 on his way to the prison camp.

Fejérváry, Baron Géza Fejérváry de Komlóskeresztes (1833–1914), Hungarian military and political leader. Austro-Hungarian emperor Franz Joseph appointed him as Hungarian prime minister during the tumultuous period of the constitutional crisis, which unfolded between 1903 and 1907. Prime minister in 1905; ran into strong opposition by the majority in the Hungarian parliament, who rejected his government as unconstitutional. He stepped down in 1906, after reaching a compromise with his opponents that led to the formation of the Sándor Wekerle cabinet. After leaving politics, returned to his military career and became commander of the Hungarian Royal Guard.

Filosofov, Dmitri Alexandrovich (1861–1978), Russian politician. In 1905 and 1906, served as the imperial comptroller for Nicholas II.

Franz Joseph I (1830–1916), emperor of Austria-Hungary from 1848 to 1916. Coming to power in the aftermath of the 1848 Revolutions, much of his reign was marked by conservative policies and efforts to resist constitutional reforms. In 1867, granted autonomy to Hungary, creating the "dual monarchy." He was one of the longest serving monarchs in the history of Europe.

Friedeberg, Dr. Raphael (1863–1940), German socialist revolutionary. Trained as a physician, expelled from the University of Königsberg for Social Democratic activities. Wrote for a variety of socialist journals, including *Sozialistischer Akademiker* and *Sozialistische Monatshefte*. Worked to enable workers in Berlin to get health insurance; member of the Berlin City Council. Increasingly ill at ease with opposition to the mass strike within the SPD, left the party in 1907 and worked to develop a synthesis between Marxism and anarchism. Remained in touch with a variety of Marxist and anarchist thinkers, including Trotsky and Lenin; sought to integrate vegetarianism and the therapeutic benefits of fresh air and nature into what he termed "socialist anarchism."

Frohme, Karl Franz Egon (1850–1933), German Social Democrat. Member of the Reichstag, 1881–1924; editor of *Hamburger Echo* and co-editor of *Sozialistische Monatshefte*. A part of the revisionist wing of the SPD, he clashed often with Luxemburg over his rejection of the mass strike and revolutionary action. Supported Germany's entry into World War I and opposed the 1917 Russian Revolution.

Frölich, Paul (1884–1953), German revolutionary. Editor of various Social Democratic periodicals before World War I; closely allied with Luxemburg, first meeting her when he attended the SPD's school in Berlin; opposed World War I, led International Communists of Germany (IKD), which he led into the KPD in 1918; member of the Reichstag as KPD delegate 1921–24; 1923–28, editor of Luxemburg's *Gesammelte Werke* (*Collected Works*), a project that was left unfinished. Expelled from KPD in 1928, joined the KPD-O (KPD Opposition) and later, the Socialist Workers' Party (SAP). In exile, published important biography of Luxemburg, in 1939.

Gapon, Georgi Apollonovich (1870–1906), Russian Orthodox priest and activist. Popular with the working class, led a march in January 1905 to petition the tsar for social reforms, leading to Bloody Sunday when troops fired on the crowd. Although he had earlier worked closely with government-controlled organizations, the revolution and his subsequent exile radicalized him; traveled to West Europe in 1905, where he had lengthy discussions with Social Democrats such as Plekhanov and Lenin; drew close to the Socialist Revolutionary Party; upon his return to Russia at the end of 1905 reportedly entered into discussions with the tsarist government, whereupon he was arrested, tried, and executed by the Socialist Revolutionary Party as a traitor.

Gautsch, Paul von Frankenthurn (1851–1918), Austrian politician. From 1885 to 1893, minister of education of Austro-Hungarian Empire; 1895 to 1897, minister of education in the Cisleithanian government; served several terms as minister of government of Austria.

Gelfand, Israel Lazarevich (pseud.: Parvus) (1867–1924), Russian Social Democrat. In 1890s, active in the German Social Democratic movement; 1895–96, editor of the *Leipziger Volkszeitung*; 1896–98, chief editor of the *Sächsische Arbeiter-Zeitung* in Dresden; in 1902, together with Julian Marchlewski, founded a publishing house in Munich for progressive international literature; 1898–1905, produced a newsletter (*Artikelkorrespondenz*) entitled *Aus der Weltpolitik* (From the World Political Scene); worked closely with Trotsky in formulating theory of permanent revolution, 1904; during the 1905 Revolution in Russia, a member of the St. Petersburg Workers' Council (Soviet); helped produce the newspaper *Nachalo* (The Beginning); 1906–1909, on the editorial staff of the *Arbeiter-Zeitung* in Dortmund. Supported Germany's entry into World War I; in 1915, founded Social Sciences Publishers (*Verlag für Sozialwissenschaft*) and edited the weekly *Die Glocke* (The Bell). After the Bolshevik Revolution in Russia in 1917, offered to assist the Bolsheviks, but Lenin turned him down.

Gerisch, Karl Alwin (1857–1922), German Social Democrat. 1890–92, co-chairman of the SPD; 1894–98, 1903–1906, member of the Reichstag; 1912–17 secretary of the SPD Executive Committee; affiliated with the reformist currents within the SPD.

Gershuni, Grigori Andreyevich (1870–1908), Russian revolutionary. Founding member of the Workers' Party for the Political Liberation of Russia; arrested in 1900; after his release helped form the Socialist Revolutionary Party; founded SR Combat Organization in 1902, committed to carrying out armed attacks on government officials. Helped plan and carry out the assassinations of Minister of the Interior Dmitry Sipyagin in 1902 and the governor of Ufa, N. M. Bogdanovich, in 1903; arrested and sentenced to death in 1904, which was commuted to life imprisonment by Nicholas II; escaped from prison in 1906 and fled to China and then the U.S.; briefly worked with Jane Adams in Chicago; returned to Western Europe, in 1907, where he renewed his work with the Socialist Revolutionary Party in exile.

Gibbon, Edward (1737–94), British historian. Major figure of the European Enlightenment, author of *Decline and Fall of the Roman Empire*. Emphasized the detrimental effect of centralized political power and imperialism while opposing democracy and revolution. He was a sharp critic of the role of Christianity in history.

Goethe, Johann Wolfgang von (1749–1832), German poet, prose writer, dramatist, and naturalist. Renowned for *Faust, Sorrows of Young Werther*, and many other works; the foremost representative of nineteenth-century German classicism and romanticism. Was one of Rosa Luxemburg's favorite writers.

Golde-Stróżecka, Estera (1872–1938), Polish socialist and physician. Leading figure in the PPS; in 1906, split from it to found the PPS-Left, which sought cooperation with the SDKPiL (an offer spurned by Luxemburg); became founding member of Polish Communist Party in 1919; like many Polish Communists, was murdered when Stalin liquidated the bulk of its leadership on the eve of World War II.

Golovin, Fyodor Alexandrovich (1839–1917), Russian landowner. During 1905 Revolution served as chairman of the office of the zemstovs.

Goremykin, Ivan Logginovich (1839–1917), Russian politician. From 1899 to his death, served the tsar as member of the Russian Council of State.

Gorky, Maxim (real name: A.M. Peshkov) (1868–1936), Russian writer. One of the foremost representatives of Russian literary realism, he was also deeply engaged with the radical political currents of his time. Initially close to the Mensheviks, after Russian Revolution of October 1917 supported the Bolsheviks; in his last years, lent his services to Stalin's promotion of "socialist realism."

Goßler, Heinrich von (1851–1927), German militarist and general. Fought in Austro-Prussian War of 1866 and Franco-Prussian War of 1871; 1878, an official in the Department for Army Affairs; became a general in 1895; Prussian war minister from 1896 to 1903; also served as a general of the infantry in 1899.

Grabski, Stanisław (1871–1949), Polish politician and writer. A member of the PPS from 1892 to 1905; by 1905 moved to the right and joined the National Democrats; 1918, elected to the Polish Parliament and served in various ministerial posts under the Piłsudski regime in 1920s; lived in London during World War II, returned to Poland in 1945.

Grillparzer, Franz (1791–1872), Austrian poet and playwright; inspired by Friedrich Schiller, he is widely considered Austria's greatest playwright.

Günzburg, Baron Horace (1833–1909), Russian merchant and philanthropist. In 1863, founder of Society for the Spread of Enlightenment for the Jews of Russia; a fervent supporter of civil rights for Jews, engaged in high-level discussions with government officials on "the Jewish Question"; opposed revolutionary action to improve their conditions; rewarded with the title of baron by Tsar Alexander II.

Guesde, Jules (Mathieu-Basile) (1845–1922), French socialist and journalist. Jailed for opposition to Franco-German War of 1871; originally a follower of Mikhail Bakunin, broke from anarchism and in 1879 became founder of the French Workers' Party; in 1890s, represented the "state-collectivist" tendency in the French working-class movement. Later, evolved into a reformist and supported World War I.

Gurcman, Benedykt (1881–1907), Polish Social Democrat. Taught natural science courses to working-class students; joined SDKPiL but continued to support cooperation with the Polish Socialist Party (PPS). Together with Marcin Kasprzak, was arrested in April 1904, while setting up an underground printing press; in 1905, sentenced to fifteen years in Siberia; died there, in 1907, due to a bowel infection.

Hansemann, Ferdinand von (1861–1900), Prussian politician. From his youth, a member of various right-wing German nationalist organizations; a large landowner in Poznań, he harbored intense hatred of Poles and sought their removal from German-controlled areas; 1894 to 1900, active in German Eastern Marches Society, which advocated the ethnic cleansing of the area of non-Germans. The group proved influential in the later formation of Nazi ideology.

Harden, Maximilian (real name: Maximilian Felix Ernst Witkowski) (1868–1927), writer and journalist. Founder and director of the political weekly *Die Zukunft* (The Future); spokesperson for extreme German nationalism before World War I, he later became a pacifist; most famous for having outed the homosexual relations among Kaiser Wilhelm II's ministers, in what became known as the "Harden-Eulenburg Affair."

Hegel, G. W. F. (1770–1831), German philosopher. Among the foremost philosophers in the Western tradition, his works proved of critical importance in the development of Marx's thought. Much of the socialist movement prior to 1914 tended to treat Hegel as a "dead dog," though subsequent efforts to recovery his thought by Lenin, Lukács, Gramsci, and others proved of critical importance in the development of Western Marxism.

Heine, Wolfgang (1861–1944), German Social Democrat. Active in SPD from 1887; member of Reichstag 1898 to 1918. A leader of the revisionist right-wing of the party, he often clashed with Luxemburg and other leftists; he supported Germany's entry into World War I and strongly opposed the workers' and soldiers' councils that emerged during the German November 1918 Revolution. He served as Prussian minister of justice from late 1918 to March 1919, during which time he helped suppress the Spartakusbund uprising. Fled to Switzerland when the Nazis came to power.

Heyden, Count Pyotr Alexandrovich (1840–1907), Russian politician. A member of the landed aristocracy, served in the ministry of the state in charge of administering the zemstvos; advocated liberal policies before 1905, but soon after swung to the right and supported suppression of the workers' and peasants' movements. Lenin wrote a searing critique of him in an article entitled "In Memory of Count Heyden" in June 1907.

Hué, Otto (1868–1922), German Social Democrat. Born into a working-class family, joined the Social Democratic movement in the later 1880s; worked in various iron and metalworks factories in the Ruhr from 1882 to 1885; over next two decades, edited several Social Democratic periodicals aimed at trade unionists; closely associated with reformist currents in the SPD, though he had relations with some left-wingers. Reichstag deputy 1903 to 1911; opposed agitation to endorse the mass strike and revolutionary action; after the German Revolution served in various government posts within the Weimar Republic.

Hyndman, Henry (1842–1921), English socialist. A supporter of liberalism and utilitarianism in his youth, became a socialist in 1880 under the influence of the work of Ferdinand Lassalle; subsequently made contact with Marx, who did not think highly of him; Marx accused Hyndman of plagiarism in his booklet *England for All*. In 1881, helped found Social Democratic Federation; his authoritarian tendencies led William Morris and Eleanor Marx to leave the party in 1884; 1911, founded British Socialist Party; 1914, formed National Socialist Party after he supported Britain's role in World War I.

Ignatyev, Alexei (1842–1906), Russian general. Actively suppressed strikes and protests during 1905 Revolution; in that year, appointed to a commission by the tsar to secure the "protection of the state system" through military means.

Jaurès, Jean Léon (1859–1914), French socialist and journalist. A leader of the French Socialist Party, the Second International, and the SFIO (French Section of the Second International); his activity in the French workers' movement began in 1892–93; founder of the newspaper *L'Humanité*; helped spearhead the opposition to rising anti-Semitism during the Dreyfus case and called for his vindication; eloquent speaker and writer who often clashed with Luxemburg over his reformist inclinations; one of the most prominent opponents of war, he was assassinated by pro-war chauvinists on July 31, 1914.

Jogiches, Leo (1867–1919), Polish revolutionary. Prominent figure in the Russian, Polish, and German workers' movements; Luxemburg's lover from the early 1890s to 1907. Initially in Vilnius, had connections with *Narodnaya Volya*, but later as an émigré in Switzerland made contacts with the Russian Marxists in the Emancipation of Labor group around Plekhanov; 1893, cofounder of the SDKP (which in 1900 was reconstituted as the SDKPiL) and from 1902 to 1914 served as a member of its central leadership body; 1893, co-editor of *Sprawa Robotnicza*; 1900, moved to Germany; 1916, a co-organizer of the Spartacus Group; 1918, cofounder of the Spartacus League and member of its central leadership body (Zentrale); 1918, member of the Central Committee of the KPD; in March 1919, arrested, then murdered in prison.

John of Kronstadt (1829–1908), Russian Orthodox priest. From 1855, worked at St. Andrew's Cathedral in Kronstadt, the naval base outside the capital; he was a favorite of the royal family because of his alleged healing powers. During 1905 Revolution, formed the Ioannity, an underground religious organization that was strongly anti-Semitic and racist and called for the extermination of leftists and socialists; it sponsored pogroms throughout the empire; considered by many a forerunner of fascism. He was canonized by the Russian Orthodox Church in 1990 and he is celebrated by many in Russia today.

Kachura, Thomas (dates of birth and death unknown), Russian revolutionary. Member of Socialist Revolutionary Combat Organization who tried to assassinate Count van Mikhailovich Obolensky in 1902.

Kalyayev, Ivan (1877–1905), Russian revolutionary and poet. Joined revolutionary movement as a student at St. Petersburg University in 1897; 1901, joined RSDRP but broke with it over what he considered their inaction; 1903, joined the Socialist Revolutionary Party and planned several assassinations of government officials. In February 1905, killed Grand Duke Sergei Alexandrovich; executed by the regime in May 1905. His life is the basis of Albert Camus's play, *Les Justes*.

Kasprzak, Marcin (1860–1905), Polish revolutionary activist. Born into working-class family in the Prussian province of Poznań; moved to Berlin in 1885 and joined SPD; member of the first Polish Socialist party (Proletariat I), as well as the Polish Socialist Party in Prussia (PPS-ZD) and SKDPiL. Returned to Russian-occupied Poland and became active with various socialist groups there, including the PPS. In 1889, helped Luxemburg escape to Switzerland; fled to London in 1891 but returned to Russia in 1893; arrested in 1896 and escaped; returned to Poland in 1904. While resisting a police raid on a socialist underground printing press, was involved in a shoot-out with the police and following arrest and trial was executed by Russian authorities in 1905.

Kautsky, Karl (1854–1938), Social Democratic theoretician. 1882, cofounder of the journal *Die Neue Zeit* and until 1917 its chief editor; influential theoretician of the Second International; a leftist opponent of revisionism and ally of Luxemburg during 1905 Revolution; from 1910 on, when Luxemburg broke from him, he moved closer to reformism with his "strategy of attrition." Declined to condemn the voting of war credits in 1914 that began World War I; 1917, a cofounder of the USPD; after the Bolshevik Revolution of 1917 in Russia, became a fierce critic of Soviet policies; during the November Revolution of 1918–19 in Germany, appointed state secretary in the Foreign Office and chairman of the "Socialization Commission." Returned to SPD in 1920.

Kennemann, Hermann (1815–1910), German politician. Co-founded the German Eastern Marches Society, a far-right and racist organization devoted to the ethnic cleansing of eastern Germany of Poles; ideas proved of importance in later Nazi ideology. He lived and organized in the area around Poznan.

Khilkov, Count Mikhail (dates of birth and death unknown), Russian government official and engineer; supervised construction of hospital trains during Russo-Turkish War of 1887–88 and the building of parts of the Trans-Caspian and Trans-Siberian Railroad in 1890s. Served as minister of transport and communications, 1895–1905; also served as chairman of the Council of Ministers. At the start of the 1905 Revolution, granted concessions to striking railroad workers, only to be rebuffed by the tsar's ministers for doing so; resigned his government posts in November 1905.

Khrustalev-Nosar, Pyotr Alexeyevich (1877–1918), Russian revolutionary. A paralegal, he became the first the president of the St. Petersburg Council of Workers' Deputies, or soviets, during the 1905 Revolution. Leon Trotsky at first served as his deputy until his arrest by the tsarist authorities on November 26, 1905.

Klimov, Vasili Vassilyevich (1869–1937), Russian politician. In 1908, elected as representative to the Duma.

Kokovtsov, Vladimir Nikolayevich (1853–1943), Russian politician. Russian finance minister from February 1904 to October 1905 and from May 1906 to early 1914; after the 1917 Russian Revolution, moved to France.

Korfanty, Wojciech (1873–1939), Polish activist and writer. Studied philosophy from 1895 to 1901; in 1901, editor of Polish-language newspaper, *Górnoślązak* (*The Upper Silesian*), which agitated for national independence; 1903, became member of German Reichstag; 1904, elected to Prussian Landtag, agitating in both for rights of Germany's Polish minority. Opposed socialism from a Christian Democratic perspective. After Poland achieved its independence in 1918, served in various government posts; member of Sejm from 1922 to 1930; an opponent of Piłsudski, he was forced to leave Poland in 1935; returned to Poland 1939, whereupon he was arrested by the Polish government and died in jail.

Krasiński, Zygmunt (1812–59), Polish poet. One of the greatest Romantic poets of Poland, along with Adam Mickiewicz and Juliusz Słowacki; author of *The Un-Divine Comedy*, which prophesized the demise of aristocracy and the triumph of democracy and rule of the masses; also wrote on the crushing of the 1831 insurrection in Poland.

Kunert, Fritz (1850–1931), German Social Democrat. Member of the Reichstag, 1890–1918; 1893–1917, co-editor and member of the editorial board of *Vorwärts*; 1917, joined the USDP, returned to the SPD 1922.

Kutler, Nikolai Nikolayevich (1865–1924), Russian politician. Minister of agriculture during the 1905 Revolution.

Kuzmich, Konstantin Pavlovich (1846–1906), Russian admiral. Naval commander, promoted to rear admiral in 1898, and appointed as chief of staff for the Russian Black Sea Fleet and Black Sea ports. In 1904, promoted to the rank of vice admiral. Assassinated in 1906 while opposing working-class strike action.

Labriola, Antonio (1843–1904), Italian Marxist philosopher. Originally a liberal, became a Marxist in 1889; one of the first post-Marx Marxists to argue for the critical importance of Hegel for Marxist theory; author of *Essays on the Materialist Theory of History*.

Laffan, William MacKay (1848–1909), publisher and editor. Originally from Ireland, moved to the U.S., where he befriended Mark Twain; beginning in 1877, wrote for the *New York Sun*; 1884, publisher of the *Sun*; 1887, founded the *Evening Sun*; in same period, founded Sun News Service, later renamed as Laffan News Agency, which Luxemburg often referred to in her reports on the 1905 Revolution.

Lassalle, Ferdinand (1825–64), German social activist and theorist. Major figure in formation of German socialist movement; participant in 1848–49 revolution; 1849–62, maintained connections with Marx, who ultimately broke from him for being "a future workers' dictator"; in 1863, co-founded the Allgemeine Deutscher Arbeiterverein (General Union of German Workers, or ADAV) which for many years was the largest socialist organization in Germany. Lassalle's followers merged with the "Eisenachers," the purported followers of Marx, in 1875, despite Marx's strong objections, voiced in his *Critique of the Gotha Program*. Lassallean ideas and approaches continued to influence German Social Democracy for decades afterwards.

Lednitzki, Alexander Robertovich (1866–1924), Polish politician. Served as Polish delegate to the Zemstvo Congress of 1905; elected member of the Duma, 1906.

Legien, Karl (1861–1920), German trade unionist and Social Democrat. Originally a wood turner, joined SPD in 1885; 1887 Chairman of the German Association of Turners; 1891–1919, Chairman of the General Commission of German Trade Unions; President of the International Federation of Trade Unions, 1913–19; member of Reichstag, 1893–98 and 1903–20; part of the reformist wing of the SPD, strongly opposed endorsement of the mass strike; enthusiastically supported

Germany's role in World War I; during the war, argued for the expulsion of anti-war opponents from SPD (which he termed the "Jewish gang"). In 1920, mobilized a general strike against the rightist Kapp putsch.

Lenin, Vladimir Ilyich (1870–1924), Russian revolutionary. From 1903, leader of the Bolsheviks; worked closely with Luxemburg, especially during and after 1905 Revolution, though differing with her on many issues, especially on the "national question" and the inseparability of socialism and democracy; after Bolshevik Revolution of 1917, leader of the revolutionary government of Soviet Russia.

Leviné, Eugen (1882–1919), Russian and German revolutionary. After studying at Heidelberg University in Germany, returned to Russia during 1905 Revolution and worked with the Bolsheviks; moved to Germany in 1919 as agent of Communist International, joined KPD; a leader of the Communist-led Second Bavarian Soviet Republic of 1919, formed after the assassination of Kurt Eisner and the collapse of the First Soviet Republic headed by Erich Mühsam and Gustav Landauer. Murdered by the Freikorps when it overthrew the Soviet Republic.

Liebknecht, Wilhelm Philipp Martin Christian Ludwig (1826–1900), German Social Democrat. 1848, participant in the republican uprising in Baden, after that an émigré, at first in Switzerland and then in England; member of the Communist League; 1862, returned to Germany; 1863, became a member of the ADAV and, in 1864, a contributor to *Social-Demokrat*; correspondent for and authorized representative of the International Workingmen's Association (First International) in Germany; 1869, cofounder of the SDAP and editor of *Der Volksstaat*; 1874–1900 (with an interruption in 1887–88), member of the Reichstag; beginning in 1876, editor and, in 1891 and after, chief editor of *Vorwärts*; cofounder of, and leading participant in, the Second International.

Lieven, Prince Anatoly Pavlovich (1872–1937), Russian nobleman. Baltic German prince from the Lieven family who consistently fought against revolution; commanded a counterrevolutionary White movement during the Russian Civil War in Latvia.

Linevich, Nikolai Petrovich (1839–1908), Russian general. A career military officer, general of infantry and adjutant general in the Imperial Russian Army in the Far East during the latter part of the Russo-Japanese War; member of the Council of State under Nicholas II.

Lobko, Pavel (1838–1905), Russian general. Member of the Council of State under Nicholas II.

Lopatin, Hermann (1845–1918), Russian revolutionary and writer. Joined radical movement as student at St. Petersburg University in 1860s; active in Populist movement; studied Marx's work as early as 1868, becoming one of the earliest Russian Marxists; active in First International, a member of its Central Council; became close friend of Marx and worked on a Russian translation of Volume 1 of *Capital*. Arrested and sent to Siberia, escaped to Western Europe in 1873. Remained active in the Populist movement, attempting to steer it toward focusing on the industrial proletariat. Arrested a few years after his return to Russia in 1884, spent 1887 to 1905 in the notorious Shlisselburg Fortress; freed by 1905 Revolution. Supported the February 1917 Revolution but opposed the Bolshevik seizure of power.

Loubet, Émile (1838–1926), French politician. Originally a lawyer, entered French politics in 1870 as member of the Republican Party; enthusiastic champion of French imperial expansion; 1885, minister of public works; president of France, 1899–1906.

Louis XVI (1754–93), king of France from 1774 to 1792; attempted to impose some reforms in the early part of his reign, such as abolishing serfdom, but resisted deeper calls for change and was deposed as a result of the French Revolution of 1789. In 1793, tried and executed by the National Convention for his covert support for the foreign invasion of France.

Manteufel, Baron Otto Karl Gottlieb von (1844–1913), German politician. From 1877–90, member of Reichstag as representative of the Conservative Party; an anti-Semite and extreme German nationalist; from 1896 to 1912, regional director of Brandenburg Province.

Maresuke, Nogi (1849–1912), Japanese general. A commander during the Sino-Japanese War of 1894–95, aided in capturing Port Arthur for Japan; 1904–05 commanded Japanese forces that captured Port Arthur from Russia; committed suicide upon death of the Meiji emperor.

Martov, Julius (1873–1923), Russian Social Democrat. In 1895, took part, with Lenin, in organizing the St. Petersburg League of Struggle for the Emancipation of the Working Class; 1896, arrested and sentenced to three years of internal exile; after that, a member of the editorial board of *Iskra* (The Spark); after 1903, a left-wing leading Menshevik; 1908–11, editor of *Golos Sotsial-Demokrata* (Voice of the Social Democrat); took part in the Zimmerwald Conference in 1915 and the Kienthal Conference in 1916; after the Bolshevik Revolution of 1917, became a sharp critic of the regime; one of the main inspirers of the "second-and-a-half" International of the early 1920s. After the suppression of the left Mensheviks by Lenin, departed Russia for Germany in 1920.

Mehring, Franz (1846–1919), German historian, scholar, and journalist. Published books on Prussian history, the SPD, as well as a biography of Karl Marx; originally a follower of Ferdinand Lassalle, became a Social Democrat and joined SPD in 1891; in 1891–1913, contributed to *Neue Zeit*; 1892–95, headed the association Freie Volksbühne; 1902–07, chief editor of *Leipziger Volkszeitung*; 1906–11, instructor in history at the SPD's Central Party School in Berlin. A leading representative of the German left; in 1913–14, together with Luxemburg and Julian Marchlewski, edited *Sozialdemokratische Korrespondenz*, and also in April 1915, together with Luxemburg, the first issue of the journal *Die Internationale*; he belonged to the International Group (Spartacus Group); and in 1917, a member of the Prussian House of Deputies. A cofounder of the Spartacus League; co-founded KPD.

Mickiewicz, Adam (1795–1853), Polish poet. One of Poland's most eminent poets and dramatists; widely regarded as the chief national poet of Poland; his work was much adored by Luxemburg, despite his advocacy of Polish independence.

Mikhailovich, Grand Duke Alexander (1861–1929), Russian monarchist. Grandson of Tsar Nicholas I, military officer in Russo-Turkish War of 1877–78; 1882, member of Council of Ministers; banished from Russia by Tsar Alexander III for marrying a commoner without permission, spent much of the rest of his life in England;

during Russo-Japanese War, organized a hospital for wounded Russian soldiers, but was never allowed to return to Russia.

Mikhailovsky, Nikolai (1842–1904), Russian sociologist and Populist. Editor of *Otechestvennye Zapiski* (Jottings from Our Native Land), in which he argued that Marx's *Capital* stipulates that countries such as Russia needed to endure an extended period of capitalist development before being ready for socialism—a claim that Marx rejected in a famous (unpublished at the time) letter to the publication. Mikhailovsky rejected the application of Darwinian principles of evolution to society and argued that the social organization of the Russian peasantry was in advance of those of Western Europe.

Milyukov, Pavel N. (1859–1943), Russian politician and historian. A student at Moscow University in 1870s, studied the works of radical thinkers, including Marx; specialized in Russian and Balkan economic history; jailed for his liberal views, after his release, taught and lectured in Bulgaria, the Ottoman Empire, and the U.S.; returned to Russia in 1905 and helped found the Constitutional Democratic Party (the Cadets); also helped form the Union of Unions in 1905; left the Union of Unions at the end of 1905 as it moved toward more radical positions; elected to the Duma in 1907 and 1912; moved to the right in 1914, supporting Russian imperial expansion. Supported the February 1917 Revolution, becoming minister of foreign affairs in the Provisional Government; opposed the Bolshevik Revolution and later supported the counterrevolutionary White armies; died in exile in France.

Minsky, Nikolai Maximovich (1885–1937), Russian poet. Author of *With the Light of Conscience*, a work of poetic mysticism; sympathetic to Marxism, an editor of the Bolshevik publication *Novaya Zhizn* (New Life) in 1905; leading figure in Russian symbolism in the following years; lived in exile in France after defeat of the 1905 Revolution until his death.

Mirbach, Baron Wilhem von (1871–1918), German diplomat. From 1908–11 member of German embassy in St. Petersburg; 1915, German ambassador to Greece; participated in German delegation that negotiated Brest-Litovsk Treaty, 1918; assassinated while in Russia by Yakov Grigorevich Blumkin of the Left Socialist Revolutionary Party.

Molkenbuhr, Brutus (1881–1959), German revolutionary. Member of SPD prior to World War I; after participating in a soldiers' council while in military service during the war, elected to the Executive Council of the Workers' and Soldiers' Council of Greater Berlin; worked with Richard Müller as co-chairman of the council. Opposed Luxemburg's Spartakusbund uprising of January 1919; argued in the ensuing period for the soldiers' councils to be folded into the national army.

Möller-Sakomelski, Alexander Nicolajevitch (1844–1928), Russian general. Commanding officer of Seventh Army Corps of the Russian Imperial Army. During the 1905 Revolution, in charge of putting down the uprising in the Russian Imperial Black Sea Fleet under Pyotr Schmidt in Sevastopol.

Mosse, Rudolf (1842–1920), German publisher. Owner of one of the largest German newspaper groups, including *Berliner Tageblatt*.

Müller, Hermann (1876–1931), German Social Democrat. Joined SPD, 1893; 1899–1906, editor of *Gölitzer Volkswacht*; 1906, member of National Committee of SPD;

after 1905 Revolution adopted reformist views, sharply opposing Luxemburg's advocacy of the mass strike. Supported Germany's entry into World War I; member of Reichstag, 1916–18; German foreign minister, 1919, during which he signed the Versailles Treaty with the Allies. Elected chancellor of Germany, 1920. He was instrumental in suppressing a workers' revolt in the Ruhr in 1920. Leader of SPD parliamentary delegation in 1920s; 1928–30, served as chancellor in a coalition government of the SPD and Centrist parties.

Mühsam, Eric (1878–1934), German poet and revolutionary. In 1900, adopted anarchism and worked with Gustav Landauer; 1904, authored *Die Hochstapler* (The Con Men) and wrote for various far-left-wing publications; 1911, founded anarcho-communist paper *Kain*. Initially supported Germany's entry into World War I but changed his mind and supported workers' strikes against the war in 1917–18. After Kurt Eisner's assassination in 1919, became a leader of the short-lived Bavarian Soviet Republic; fervent opponent of Nazism, arrested soon after Hitler's rise to power and tortured to death.

Muraviev, Count Mikhail Nikolayevich (1845–1900), Russian politician. Official in Ministry of Foreign Affairs, 1864; in 1870s, served in diplomatic posts in France, Germany, and Denmark; 1897–1900, minister of Foreign Affairs; forcefully promoted Russian imperialist intervention in China during Boxer Rebellion.

Napoleon I (1769–1821), emperor of France from 1804 to 1815. Rising through the ranks of the military during the French Revolution, he seized control of France and initiated a series of wars against reactionary European powers known as the Napoleonic Wars. Initiated a series of legal reforms, with the Napoleonic Code, which laid the foundation of modern-day France. Died in exile in St. Helena.

Napoleon III (1808–73), first president of France from 1848 to 1851, and emperor of France from 1851 to 1870; presided over the extension of French control of Algeria, the building of the Suez Canal, and France's seizure of Senegal and parts of Indo-China; decisively defeated in Franco-Prussian War of 1870, he was captured and later retired in England.

Naumann, Pastor Friedrich (1860–1919), German pastor and politician. Supported social reforms and worker's rights but strongly opposed to socialism and communism; befriended Max Weber; 1894, published weekly journal *Die Helfe* (The Help); 1896, co-founded National-Social Association; worked for an accommodation between liberals and Social Democrats; member of Reichstag, 1907. In 1914, defended Germany's entry into World War I and supported imperialism; advocated German territorial expansion in his 1915 book *Mittleeuropa*. In 1919, helped found liberal German Democratic Party and was a principle framer of the Weimar Constitution.

Nevsky, Alexander (1236–52), prince of Novgorod, grand prince of Kiev (1236–52), and grand prince of Vladimir (1252–63). Defeated Teutonic Knights in the famous Battle of the Neva in 1240, while remaining a vassal of the Mongols. Later canonized as a saint by the Russian Orthodox Church.

Nicholas I (1796–1855), emperor of Russia from 1825 until his death. Among Russia's most reactionary rulers, he ruled through brutal autocratic power. Fostered Russian nationalism and repressed the rights of Russia's many national minorities.

His crushing of the Hungarian Revolution of 1848 earned him the enmity of Democrats and Free Thinkers throughout Europe.

Nicholas II (1868–1918), emperor of Russia from 1894 to 1917; forced to abdicate by the February Revolution. Presided over Russia during its defeat of Japan in the Russo-Japanese War of 1904–1905 and the Russian Revolution that followed; led Russia into World War I, in which four million of his countrymen perished. His regime was marked by severe repression and anti-Semitic pogroms as well as political corruption. He was executed by the Bolsheviks during the Civil War.

Obolensky, Ivan Mikhailovich (1853–1910), Russian militarist. Governor-general of Finland in 1904 and 1905; a brutal authoritarian, he worked to crush a general strike called by workers in Finland during the 1905 Revolution; assassinated by revolutionaries.

Oshanina, Mariya Nikolayevna (1853–98), Russian populist and revolutionary. A leading member of Narodnaya Volya, or People's Will organization; member of its executive committee 1879 to 1883; 1882, emigrated to Paris following the government's severe suppression of the group; served as a representative of People's Will Executive from abroad. She was the most outstanding woman theoretician of the Populist movement and engaged in intense debates with figures such as Lopatin, Mikhailovsky, and others.

Parvus, Alexander, see **Gelfand, Israel Lazarevich.**

Peter the Great (1672–1725), tsar of Russia from 1682 until his death. Significantly expanded Russia's territory, both to the east, south, and west, and played an instrumental role in the modernization of Russian society.

Petrov, Grigori Spiridonovich (1866–1925), from 1895 to 1906 a prior at the Church of Mikhailovsky Ordnance Academy. Opposed to the Russian Orthodox Church, he became active in the liberal reformed church movement. Author of many books and pamphlets advocating Christian socialism.

Petrunkevich, Ivan Illyich (1843–1928), Russian politician. Active in the zemstvo movement from the 1870s; 1904, Chairman of the Union of Liberation; leading figure in the liberal Constitutional Democratic Party (Cadets); elected to the Duma in 1906; attended several zemstvo conferences between 1904 and 1906, supporting positions of the left; opposed Bolshevik Revolutions and emigrated to western Europe.

Pfannkuch, Wilhelm (1841–1923), German Social Democrat. 1863, member of the ADAV; member of Reichstag 1884–87, 1898–1906, and 1912–18; 1893, cofounder of the German Woodworkers' Union; 1894, member of the SPD Executive and, in 1917, secretary of the Executive; from 1900, a city councilor in Berlin; supported World War I and German imperialism.

Piłsudski, Józef (1867–1935), Polish politician. Originally active in the People's Will organization, became a Social Democrat in early 1890s and joined PPS, in 1893; 1894, editor of PPS publication *Robotnik*; 1904, headed the PPS Combat Organization which engaged in armed resistance against tsarism. Promoted series of general strikes during the 1905 Revolution and was active in Łódź uprising; advocated boycott of the first Duma; in 1906, split from PPS in arguing that the national struggle should have priority over the fight for socialism; regained control of PPS in 1909; 1918–22, chief of state of independent Poland; returned to power in a 1926 coup and installed himself as dictator of Poland, a position he held until his death.

Plekhanov, Georgi V. (1856–1918), Russian Social Democrat. Initially part of the Populist movement; became a Marxist in early 1880s; author of numerous theoretical and political works; 1880, he left Russia to live in exile in Switzerland; 1883, founded the Emancipation of Labor group; in 1900, the cofounder and coeditor of the newspaper *Iskra* and the journal *Zarya*. He was hostile to Jogiches and Luxemburg from their earliest encounters. After 1903, a Menshevik; did not return to Russia during 1905 Revolution; sharply opposed Luxemburg at the 1907 London Congress of RSDRP; supported World War I; after the February 1917 Revolution, returned to Russia; supporting the Provisional Government, he strongly opposed the Bolshevik Revolution.

Plehve, Vyacheslav Konstantinovich von (1846–1904), Russian politician. In 1876, prosecutor in Warsaw; 1881, head of the dreaded Okhrana, the secret police; worked to destroy the People's Will organization. Interior minister from April 1902; widely regarded as one of the most reactionary and repressive of the tsar's ministers. In August 1902 met with Theodor Herzl concerning his plans for colonization in Palestine; assassinated by Yegor Sassonov of the Socialist Revolutionary Combat Organization.

Pobedonostsev, Konstantin (1827–1907), Russian politician. A political reactionary who was a leading figure of the Russian Orthodox Church, he served as Tsar Alexander III's main adviser. Served as Ober-Procurator of the Holy Synod as a layman overseeing religious policy. A fierce opponent of democracy and social progress, he was a prime architect of the anti-Semitic policies that compelled hundreds of thousands of Jews to flee Russia in last decades of the nineteenth century.

Popiel, Vincent Theophilus Chosciak (date of birth unknown–1912). Polish prelate. Served as archbishop of Warsaw from 1895 to 1912.

Puttkammer, Robert von (1828–1900), German politician. Served as conservative minister of the interior in Germany; enforced Bismarck's antisocialist law and forcibly suppressed strikes during the 1870s and 1880s.

Quelch, Harry (1858–1913), British socialist. Working-class activist who worked in iron, papermaking, and other industries; 1881, joined Social Democratic Federation; formed Socialist League, with William Morris, in 1884; head of London Trades Council in 1890s; 1901, arranged for the publication of Lenin's newspaper *Iskra* in England; attended numerous conferences of Second International and became internationally recognized as a major figure of the socialist left.

Richthofen, Oswald von (1847–1906), German diplomat and politician. Member of Foreign Service, 1875; director of colonial affairs, 1896–98, during which he worked in Namibia at the time that the German military was conducting a genocidal war against its indigenous peoples; secretary of foreign affairs, 1900–1906.

Roberti, E. W. (1843–1902), Russian politician. Delegate to the 1905 Zemstvo Congress.

Romanov, Grand Duke Sergei Alexandrovich (1875–1905), Russian monarchist. The son of Tsar Alexander II and brother of Tsar Alexander III, he exerted great influence over Nicholas II as governor-general of Moscow from 1891 to 1905. A fierce anti-Semite, he was responsible for expelling 20,000 Jews from Moscow and fostering pogroms. He was an extreme reactionary even by the standards of the Russian monarchy of the time; assassinated in February 1905 by a member of the Socialist Revolutionary Party's Combat Organization.

Rosebery, Archibald Philip Primrose (1847–1929), British politician. Leader of Liberal Party from 1894; prime minister, 1894–95; when the Liberals returned to power in 1905, he was not included as part of the government, being considered too rightist.

Rotteck, Karl von (1775–1840), German historian and politician. Initially a supporter of the French Revolution, he adopted liberal positions for most of his career; professor of history at University of Freiburg, 1798–1818; wrote several influential books on natural law theory; member of the regional assembly of Baden from 1818, in which he advocated abolition of serfdom and restrictive anti-labor laws.

Rouvier, Maurice (1842–1911), French politician. In 1871, elected to National Assembly as member of the Republican Party; 1887, minister of finance and premier; 1902, again minister of finance; 1902–1905, premier; during his administration, tensions with Germany escalated over the issue of Morocco.

Rozhestvensky, Zinovy Petrovich (1848–1909), Russian militarist. Admiral in Russian Imperial Navy during Russo-Japanese war, where he was captured by the Japanese; after his release, faced a court-martial in Russia but ended up being pardoned by the tsar.

Ruskin, John (1819–1900), English art critic and social reformer. One of the most influential British writers of the nineteenth century, he was a major figure in promoting free education for workers, pacifism, and respect for the environment; promoted the development of a "social economy" as an alternative to free market capitalism. Many of his later works, especially *Unto This Last*, were influential on the thought of Mohandas Gandhi.

Saveliev, Alexander Alexandrovich (1848–1916), Russian landowner and politician. Member of the Office of the Zemstvos; attended various conferences of the zemstvos during the 1905 Revolution.

Sazonov, Yegor (1879–1904), Russian revolutionary. A member of the Socialist Revolutionary Combat Organization, he assassinated Vyacheslav Plehve in 1904.

Schiemann, Theodor (1847–1921), German historian. Professor of East European history at the University of Berlin from 1906; originally from the Baltic region, he often advised Kaiser Wilhelm II on issues related to Eastern Europe

Schmidt, Pyotr (1867–1906), Russian revolutionary. Joined Imperial Russian Navy, 1883; lieutenant commander of a destroyer during 1905 Revolution; in October 1905 urged the citizens of Odessa to support the revolution; his arrest sparked massive protests, forcing his release; following a mutiny on the cruiser *Ochakov* in November 1905, invited to take command of rebel ships that supported the revolution. Defeated by the Imperial Naval Forces, he was arrested and executed after a brief trial.

Schmidt, Robert (1864–1943), German Social Democrat. Originally a piano builder, joined SPD in early 1890s and served as editor of *Vorwärts* from 1893 to 1902;

1893–98 and 1903–18, member of the Reichstag; 1903–10, head of the Central Executive Committee of Trade Unions. Consistently upheld reformist positions; often at odds with Luxemburg over his opposition to the agitation for a mass strike. Supported Germany's role in World War I and served as minister of food and minister for economic affairs in SPD governments in the 1920s.

Schönstedt, Karl Heinrich von (1883–1924), German politician. From 1894–1905 served as minister of justice for Prussia.

Schwanebach, Pjotr Christianovich (1848–1908), Russian politician. From 1905–1908, a member of the Russian Council of State; a fervent supporter of the monarchy, advocated firm suppression of the 1905 Revolution.

Shipov, Ivan Pavlovich (1865–1919), Russian politician. Served as finance minister during the 1905 Revolution.

Singer, Paul (1844–1911), German Social Democrat. Member of SDAP, 1869; 1883–1911, city councilor in Berlin; 1886, member of the SPD Executive Committee, and in 1890, one of the co-chairmen of the SPD; opposed to aspects of revisionism but far more opposed to the semi-anarchist views of "the Young Ones" (*die Junge*) who were expelled from the SPD in 1895; became a member of the ISB in 1900.

Sipyagin, Dmitry (1853–1902), Russian politician. Governor of Courland, 1888–91; governor of Moscow, 1891–93; minister of the interior, 1899–1902. Assassinated by Stephan Balmashov of the Socialist Revolutionary Combat Organization on April 15, 1902.

Spasowicz, Włodzimierz (1829–1906), Polish lawyer and publicist. Member of Party for Realpolitik (Stronnictwo Polityki Realnej), which advocated accommodation and compromise with tsarist Russia. The social base of this party consisted of large landowners, high-ranking clergy, and arch-conservative elements of the bourgeoisie and intelligentsia.

Stachovitch Mikhail Alexandrovich (1861–1923), Russian nobleman. Representative from the city of Jelatz to the Zemstvo Congress of 1905.

Stadthagen, Arthur (1857–1917), German Social Democrat and lawyer. From 1889–1917, city councilor in Berlin; 1890–1917, member of the Reichstag; 1893–1916, contributor to and editor of *Vorwärts*; before World War I, defended the views of the German left; after 1914, adhered to the centrist forces, and in 1917, became a member of the USPD.

Ströbel, Heinrich (1869–1944), German writer and Social Democrat. From 1893–1900, editor of the *Schleswig-Holsteinische Volkszeitung*, and in 1900–16, of *Vorwärts*; defended the views of the German left for a while, but during World War I moved away from radical left; in 1917, became a member of the USPD; from November 1918 to January 1919, chairman of the cabinet of the Prussian Provisional Government.

Struve, Pyotr (1870–1944), Russian writer and politician. Liberal politician, economist, and publicist, who during the 1890s was a leading representative of the so-called Legal Marxists; 1898, a co-author of the First Manifesto of the RSDRP. Moved to the right and joined the liberal Cadet Party; member of the Second Duma. After the February Revolution of 1917, held leading positions in the state apparatus of the Provisional Government; opposed the October Revolution; after the defeat of the Whites in the Civil War, emmigrated to Czechoslovakia and France.

Stumm-Halberg, Carl Ferdinand Freiherr von (1836–1901), German politician. Member of Reichstag, 1889–1901; promoted conservative policies on economic and foreign policy; an adviser to Kaiser Wilhelm II, he forcefully promoted German imperialist expansion abroad.

Svyatopolk-Mirsky, Pyotr Danilovich (1857–1914), Russian politician. Minister of the interior, 1904, after the assassination of Plehve. Presided over massacre of Bloody Sunday on January 22 1905; denied authorizing shooting of the demonstrators, but was generally blamed for it; retired from political life shortly thereafter.

Świętokowski, Aleksander (1849–1939), Polish writer. Leading figure in the 1870s and 1880s in what is currently known as Warsaw Positivism. During 1905 Revolution, a leading representative of the Democratic Progressive Union (Związek Postępowo-Demokratyczny), which advocated a progressive form of liberalism—such as voting rights for women. He nevertheless opposed the 1905 Revolution. After its defeat, anti-Semitic currents became predominant in the party, and in 1910, it led a campaign against the SDKPiL, in which Luxemburg and Jogiches were singled out for their Jewish origins.

Sytin, Ivan Dmitriyevich (1851–1934), Russian publisher. In the 1880s, became a major publisher of popular literature and texts for children; also published the collected works of Pushkin, Gogol, Tolstoy, and others; after 1917 Revolution, became a consultant to the state publishing house.

Tann, N.A., see Bogoraz, Vladimir Germanovich.

Thielmann, Max Franz Guido Freiherr von (1846–1929), German diplomat. Active in various diplomatic posts in Russia, Denmark, France, the Ottoman Empire, and was the U.S. Secretary of State for the Imperial Treasury from 1897 to 1903.

Thiers, Adolphe (1797–1877), French politician and historian. Served as prime minister of France in 1836, 1840, and 1848. An opponent of Napoleon III, he returned to power in the national elections of February 1871 and sued for peace with the Germans. Forced to flee Paris because of the Paris Commune of 1871, he directed the government forces that broke through the city defenses, resulting in the slaughter of tens of thousands of communards. Following his brutal repression of the Commune, he became president of France, only to be forced from power in 1873 by opposition from the Monarchists.

Tiedemann-Seeheim, Heinrich von (1840–1922), German politician. Cofounder of the German Eastern Marches Society, a racist grouping devoted to securing the ethnic cleansing of Poles and other minorities from the German Empire. Its ideas were influential in the development of Nazi ideology.

Tolstoy, Leo (1828–1910), Russian writer of the realist school. Pacifist and social reformer, influential among generations of Russian writers and activists.

Trepov, Dmitri Fyodorovich (1850–1906), Russian monarchist and policeman. 1896, chief of police of Moscow, used his position to severely repress student protests. Shortly after Bloody Sunday in 1905, appointed governor-general of St. Petersburg with sweeping powers to crush all dissent and opposition; fostered anti-Semitic pogroms and other measures against Jews and other national minorities; June 1905, became minister of the interior, ordering police to "spare no cartridges" in shooting at demonstrators; forced from power as one of the conditions of the October Manifesto of 1905.

Trepov, Fyodor (1809–89), Russian government official and militarist. Part of Russian military suppression of the Polish Uprising in 1830–31; suppressed another uprising in Poland in 1863–64. In 1855 appointed chief of St. Petersburg police and became governor of St. Petersburg in 1873. In 1878 shot and wounded by Vera Zasulich in response to his mistreatment of political prisoners; shortly thereafter he retired from the military.

Trotsky, Leon (1879–1940), Russian revolutionary. Joined socialist movement, 1897; initially a supporter of the Mensheviks following 1903 split in the RSDRP; led St. Petersburg Soviet during the 1905 Revolution, the most important one in the empire; published *Nachalo*, an influential paper in the 1905 Revolution; moved closer to Bolsheviks during the February 1917 Revolution, joining them later in 1917 and becoming people's commissar of foreign affairs, 1917–18, and then head of the Red Army; leader of Left Opposition to Stalin, 1923; expelled from USSR, 1927; founded Fourth International, 1938; murdered while in exile in Mexico by agents of Stalin.

Trubetzkoi, Prince Pyotr Nikolaiyevich (1858–1911), Russian politician. From 1908 to 1911, a member of the Russian Council of State; supported the conservative policies of Nicholas II as the regime sought to roll back the gains of the 1905 Revolution.

Tyszkiewicz, Count Wladyslaw (1865–1935), Polish politician. An extreme conservative, he became a leading figure among National Democrats, a right-wing nationalist party that sharply opposed the PPS and SDKPiL; it kept its distance from the 1905 Revolution, largely due to its lack of confidence or interest in the Russian working class. Headed a delegation to St. Petersburg in May 1905 asking for the reintroduction of Polish-language schooling in Russian-occupied Poland.

Umbreit, Paul (1868–1932), German Social Democrat. Active in the SPD-affiliated Free Trade Unions from 1889; headed General Commission of German Trade Unions, 1900; opposed Luxemburg's agitation for the mass strike and generally sided with the reformist elements within the SPD. Strongly supported Germany's role in World War I and wanted leftist critics of the war to be expelled from the SPD; 1918, active in the Socialization Commission; major representative of rightest tendencies in German Social Democracy.

Vandervelde, Émile (1866–1938), Belgian socialist. Originally a liberal, joined the Social Democratic movement in 1885; 1886, helped form the Belgian Workers' Party; initially strongly influenced by Jules Guesde; 1894, member of Belgian parliament; supported World War I in 1914; 1918–21, president of the International Socialist Bureau; 1925–27, minister of foreign affairs.

Vasilyev, Nikita Vasilyevich (1855–date of death unknown), Russian police official. Colonel in the tsarist secret police, the gendarmerie, and a supporter of "police socialism." He severely repressed workers' strikes and public protests before and during the 1905 Revolution.

Vogt, Karl (1817–95), German scientist and politician. Professor of zoology at the University of Giessen, 1847; worked closely with Louis Agassiz, supporting theory of polygenist evolution—the notion that the various races of humanity descended from distinct species; held extremely racist views toward Blacks and Jews. Active in the 1848 Revolutions, but soon moved to the right; Marx replied to his slanderous attacks on him in the booklet *Herr Vogt*, which showed that Vogt had secretly been in the pay of Louis Napoleon. Darwin mentions him critically in *The Descent of Man*.

Volkonski, Sergei (1880–1937), Russian theatrical worker. From 1899–1902, director of the Imperial Theatre; after 1917 Revolution, taught acting in Moscow; arrested by the Cheka, Lenin's secret police, in 1919; lived in Paris from 1926, became known as one of the foremost directors in Western Europe; moved to the U.S. shortly before his death.

Voß, Christian Friedrich (1724–95), German publisher. Issued the *Vossische Zeitung*, a daily liberal-bourgeois paper.

Warski, Adolf Jerzy (1868–1937), Polish revolutionary. Member of first Proletariat Party; cofounder of the Union of Polish Workers and the SDKPiL; 1892–96, lived as an émigré in France; 1896–1904, in Germany; in 1890–96, worked on *Sprawa Robotnicza*; in 1902–13, on editorial board of *Czerwony Sztandar*; 1901–1904 as well as 1908–10, on board of *Przegląd Socjaldemokratyczny*; 1906–12, representative of the SDKPiL in the Central Committee of the RSDRP; took part in the Zimmerwald Conference in 1915 and the Kienthal Conference in 1916; 1918, cofounder of the Communist Workers Party of Poland. Opposed to Stalin, he was arrested by agents of Stalin's government and executed, along with innumerable other Polish communists, in 1937.

Webb, Sidney James (1859–1947), English economic theorist and politician; leading Fabian and reformist socialist; in the 1930s strongly supported Stalin's regime in the USSR.

Wielopolski, Aleksander (1803–77), Polish aristocrat. In 1846, wrote pamphlet arguing that Poland should abandon hopes for independence and submit to Russian rule; the tsarist regime in response offered him modest posts in the government, in which he sought, largely without success, to ameliorate the conditions of peasants and Jews. Fiercely opposed the 1863 Polish national uprising.

Wilhelm II (1859–1941), German emperor (Kaiser) and King of Prussia from 1888 to 1918. Forced from power by German Revolution of November 1918, died in exile in the Netherlands.

Witte, Count Sergei Yulyevich (1849–1915), Russian politician. Highly influential prime minister in Imperial Russia; attracted foreign capital to boost Russia's industrialization; served under the last two emperors of Russia, Alexander III and Nicholas II. Framed the October Manifesto of 1905, convinced it would solve the problems with the tsarist autocracy; October 20, 1905 became first chairman of the Russian Council of Ministers (prime minister); assisted by his Council, he designed Russia's first constitution; within a few months he fell in disgrace as a reformer. He resigned before the First Duma assembled.

Williams, John (1854–1917), Irish socialist. In the 1870s, active in the Irish nationalist movement; by 1880 became a Marxist and helped found Social Democratic Federation in the early 1880s; supported Hyndman in disputes within the organization; active in organizing unemployed workers.

Zasulich, Vera (1849–1919), Russian revolutionary. Initially a supporter of revolutionary terror, seriously wounded Colonel Fyodor Trepov, governor of St. Petersburg, in an assassination attempt, in 1878; she was acquitted in a famous trial and went into exile in Switzerland. A convert to Marxism, she worked closely with Plekhanov and the Emancipation of Labor group; wrote famous letter to Marx in 1881 asking if Russia was destined to endure a stage of capitalism before being able to reach socialism; became leading figure of Menshevism after split in the RSDRP in 1903; moved to the right, supported World War I, and opposed the Bolshevik seizure of power in 1917.

Zetkin, Clara Josephine (1857–1933), teacher and Social Democrat. From 1892–1917, chief editor of the Social Democratic women's publication *Die Gleichheit*; 1895–1917, member of the Control Commission of the SPD and from 1906 to 1917, member of the SPD's Education Committee; in 1907, secretary of the International Women's Secretariat; 1910, an initiator of the practice of holding an annual International Women's Day as a day of struggle for equal rights, peace, and socialism. A leading representative of the German left, she was a contributor to *Die Internationale* and a cofounder of the International Group (Spartacus Group); June 1917 to April 1919, chief editor of the newly founded women's supplement to the newspaper *Leipziger Volkszeitung*; from 1919 until her death, a leading member of the KPD.

Zinoviev, Grigori (1883–1936), Russian revolutionary. Joined RSDRP, 1901; member of Bolsheviks, from 1903; member of RSDRP Central Committee, 1907; chairman of St. Petersburg Soviet during 1917 Revolution; one of Lenin's closest followers, led Comintern from 1919–26; after initially supporting Stalin, broke with him in 1925 and led United Opposition within the Bolshevik Party from 1926 to 1927; after breaking from Trotsky and adhering to Stalin, was arrested by Stalin in 1934 and executed.

Zubatóv, Sergei (1864–1917), Russian police official. Joined the revolutionary movement as a youth, but soon abandoned the cause and became an informant for the tsarist regime; starting in 1896, headed Moscow office of the Okhrana, the secret police; fostered the promotion of pro-government trade unions, known as *zuvbatovshchina*, to control the workers' movement. Forced from his position as police chief in 1903 by Plehve in response to his failure to curb massive workers' strikes; committed suicide in 1917 upon hearing of Nicholas II's abdication.

Index